IN   OUT

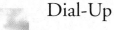

IN	OUT
Wireless	Dial-Up
28-Page Chapters	40-Page Chapters
TiVo	VCRs
www.ichapters.com	$100 Textbooks
Energy Drinks	Snapple
Podcasts	Written Review Sheets
Grey's Anatomy	*Dr. Quinn, Medicine Woman*
One-Stop Election 2008 News and Chapter-Links	Time-Consuming Searches
Wii	SuperNintendo
Learning YOUR Way	Learnin
99¢ Audio Downloads	$20 CD
AAO	Wordy Textbooks

D1532914

AAO:
POLITICS
TO GO

ARE YOU IN?

WADSWORTH
CENGAGE Learning

America at Odds, Alternate Edition
Sixth Edition
Edward Sidlow and Beth Henschen

Publisher: Clark Baxter

Executive Editor: Carolyn Merrill

Senior Development Editor: Stacey Sims

Editorial Assistant: Katheryn Hayes

Senior Marketing Manager: Trent Whatcott

Marketing Communications Manager: Heather Baxley

Technology Project Manager: Lee McCracken

Senior Content Project Manager: Ann Borman

Manufacturing Manager: Marcia Locke

Photo Account Manager: Anne Sheroff

Copy Editor: Pat Lewis

Proofreader: Judy Kiviat, Martha Ghent

Indexer: Bob Marsh

Compositor: Parkwood Composition Service

Art Director: Linda Helcher

Interior Design: Ke Design

Cover Design: Didona Design

Cover Image: Radius Images/© Photo Library

For product information and technology assistance, contact us at **Cengage Learning Academic Resource Center, 1-800-423-0563**

For permission to use material from this text or product, submit all requests online at **www.cengage.com/permissions**
Further permission questions can be emailed to **permissionrequest@cengage.com**

Library of Congress Control Number: 2007941597

Student Edition ISBN-13: 978-0-495-50370-5
Student Edition ISBN-10: 0–495–50370-3

Instructor's Edition ISBN-13: 978-0-495-56542-0
Instructor's Edition ISBN-10: 0–495–56542-3

Wadsworth
10 Davis Drive
Belmont, CA 94002-3098
USA

Cengage Learning products are represented in Canada by Nelson Education, Ltd.

For your course and learning solutions, visit **academic.cengage.com**
Purchase any of our products at your local college store or at our preferred online store **www.ichapters.com**

Chapter Opener photo credits: Ch 1 Wes Thompson/Corbis; Ch 2 Photo Disc/ Getty Images; Ch 3 redjar/Creative Commons; Ch 4 Scott Barrow/ Corbis; Ch 5 AP Photo/Wisconsin State Journal, Craig Schreiner; Ch 6 Roberto Schmidt/AFP/Getty Images; Ch 7 AP Photo/Charles Neibergall; Ch 8 AP Photo/Carlos Osorio; Ch 9 AP Photo/Charles Neibergall; Ch 10 Yuri Gripas/Reuters/Corbis; Ch 11 Dennis Flaherty; Ch 12 Philip Coblentz/Brand X/Corbis; Ch 13 Atlantide Phototravel/Corbis; Ch 14 Rudy Sulgan/Corbis

Printed in the United States of America
1 2 3 4 5 6 7 11 10 09 08 07

To Maureen (Mo-Jo) Isaac,
who has the biggest heart of anyone we know

Brief Contents

Contents

redjar/Creative Commons

CHAPTER 3
FEDERALISM   47

Part Two   Our Liberties and Rights

Scott Barrow/Corbis

Craig Schreiner/Wisconsin State Journal

CHAPTER 4
CIVIL LIBERTIES   70

CHAPTER 5
CIVIL RIGHTS   97

Part Three   The Politics of Democracy

Roberto Schmidt/AFP/Getty Images

CHAPTER 6
INTEREST GROUPS   125

AP Photo/Charles Neibergall

CHAPTER 7
POLITICAL PARTIES   147

AP Photo/Carlos Osorio

AP Photo/Charles Neibergall

Yuri Gripas/Reuters/Corbis

CHAPTER 10
POLITICS AND THE MEDIA 216

Part Four   Institutions

Dennis Flaherty

CHAPTER 11
CONGRESS   237

Philip Coblentz/Brand X/Corbis

CHAPTER 12
THE PRESIDENCY   262

Atlantide Phototravel/Corbis

CHAPTER 13
THE BUREAUCRACY   289

Rudy Sulgan/Corbis

CHAPTER 14
THE JUDICIARY   313

AMERICA AT ODDS

ALTERNATE EDITION

Preface

It does not take long for a student of American government to get the message: Americans are at odds over numerous political issues. In response to the terrorist attacks of September 11, 2001, the Bush administration launched a "war on terrorism" that had serious consequences for Americans' civil rights and liberties. To counter the terrorist threat, President George W. Bush also expanded the powers of the presidency to a degree that, in the eyes of some Americans, threatened the constitutional underpinnings of our nation. Americans were also bitterly divided about the war in Iraq. Many believed that it was a mistake to have invaded Iraq in 2003, and by late 2007, nearly 80 percent of Americans wanted the war to be brought to an end. Indeed, widespread opposition to the war was the driving force behind the election of a majority of Democrats to Congress in the 2006 midterm elections.

Although Americans have faced a host of challenges since 9/11, this did not mean that our country was falling apart at the seams. Indeed, political conflict and divergence of opinion have always characterized our political traditions and way of governing. Nonetheless, our democracy continues to endure, and the U.S. Constitution continues to serve as a model for new democracies around the world.

America at Odds, Sixth Edition, looks at government and politics in this country as a series of conflicts that have led to compromises. Along the way, your students will sometimes encounter a bit of irreverence—none of us should take ourselves too seriously all of the time.

This text was written with today's generation of students in mind. As such, it does the following:

- Provides the historical context for today's most significant political controversies.

- Forthrightly presents different perspectives on key issues currently being debated, including how to ensure our nation's security against terrorism while protecting our civil liberties.

- Helps your students test their beliefs and assumptions, and determine their positions on major political issues.

- Assists your students in the process of acquiring informed political values and opinions.

- Fully explains the major problems facing the American political system.

- Looks at the global connections that exist between the American political system and the systems of other countries around the world.

A GROUNDBREAKING NEW SIXTH EDITION FORMAT

America at Odds's daring new format has been designed to engage even the most apathetic American government student with its glossy, magazine-style format and dynamic visual appeal. Streamlined, portable, and complete with study resources, the new edition does more than ever before to accommodate the way students actually use their textbooks, while at the same time maintaining the "debate-the-issues" approach that so effectively involves them in discussing and debating concepts of American government. New *Politics to Go tear-out review cards* at the end of the book provide learning objectives with summaries of key concepts, visuals, and key terms for each chapter—making it easier for students to prepare for class and for exams. And because today's students are technologically savvy, we now provide **portable study resources in multiple formats** via The *America at Odds* Resource Center at **www.americaatodds.com**. Resources there include flashcards, podcasts, chapter reviews, quizzes, and more that students can download to use whichever way they prefer (cell phone, computer download, MP3 files, etc.) in order to study more efficiently. Access to the site is available at no additional cost when packaged with each student text.

FEATURES THAT TEACH

As exciting as the innovative new Sixth Edition format may be, we have not lost sight of the essential goals and challenges of teaching American government. Any American government text must present the basics of the American political process and its institutions, and it

xvii

must excite and draw the student into the *subject*. That is exactly what we do in *America at Odds*, Sixth Edition. Among other things, the Sixth Edition of *America at Odds* deals with current issues and events—such as the political tug-of-war between the president and Congress and the campaigns for the 2008 presidential elections—that are familiar to students.

Additionally, we present many of today's controversial political issues in special features. Each of the nearly one hundred newly written features contained in the Sixth Edition covers a topic of high interest to students. Feature topics range from global warming to whether Google and Yahoo should support China's program of Internet censorship to the National Popular Vote movement. *America at Odds*, Sixth Edition, includes the following different types of features:

- *Learning Objectives*—Every chapter-opening page includes a list of four or more Learning Objectives that let students know what concepts will be covered in the chapter. Each Learning Objective has an identifying number (such as LO¹ or LO²). The same number also precedes the major heading of the chapter section in which that topic is presented. This allows students to quickly locate where in the chapter a particular topic is discussed.

- *America at Odds*—This chapter-opening feature examines a major controversy over which the public is divided and has strong views. Each of these features concludes with a section entitled "Where Do You Stand?" These sections, which consist of two questions, invite the student to form or express his or her own opinions on the arguments presented in the feature.

  Students can explore the issue further by accessing the Web site links provided in the "Explore This Issue Online" section. These links were chosen either to represent the opposing viewpoints posed in the feature or to provide a resource for further research.

- *Join the Debate*—The theme of controversy continues in these shorter features that are integrated within the text of every chapter. Each *Join the Debate* feature briefly introduces students in a concise, yet thought-provoking manner to an issue that divides Americans. These features will keep your students thinking and questioning their own political attitudes and values.

- *The Politics of National Security*—These features are designed to focus on the political implications of the effort to defend the nation against terrorist attacks. These features have a broad scope—some deal with actions taken to secure the homeland and others with national security issues relating to foreign policy

and American military engagements abroad. Each of these features ends with a section entitled "You Be the Judge." This section recaps the opposing positions on the issue discussed in the feature and then asks the student where she or he stands on the issue.

- *Perception versus Reality*—Perhaps nowhere in our media-generated view of the world are there more misconceptions than in the area of American government and politics. This feature tries to help your students understand the difference between the public's general perception of a particular political event or issue and the reality of the situation. The perception is often gleaned from responses to public opinion surveys. The reality usually is presented in the form of objective data that show that the world is not quite what the public often thinks it is. At the end of each of these features is a section entitled "Blog On." Here, we provide URLs for relevant blog sites that the student can access to read others' opinions on the issue under discussion or to share his or her own opinion with others.

- *The Rest of the World*—One of the best ways to understand the American political system is by comparing it with other political systems. Students need to know that in much of the world, the political process is different. By understanding this, they can better understand and appreciate what goes on in this country, both in Washington, D.C., and in state capitals. Nearly every chapter has one of these features. At the end of each of these features, the student is asked to further examine some aspect of the topic under discussion in a question "For Critical Analysis."

- Chapter-ending *America at Odds:* feature—New to the Sixth Edition of *America at Odds*, this feature (for example, "America at Odds: The Contours of American Democracy") often opens with a general discussion of the historical evolution of the aspect of government addressed in the chapter. When relevant, the founders' views and expectations relating to the topic are set forth and then compared to the actual workings of our political system in that area today. This part of the feature is designed to indicate how American politics and government currently measure up to the expectations of the founders or to those of today's Americans. Following this discussion, we present two questions for debate and discussion. Each question briefly outlines two sides of a current political controversy and then asks the student to identify her or his position on the issue. The feature closes with a "Take Action" section that offers tips to students on what they can do to make a difference in an area of interest to them.

Every chapter ends with the following sections:

- *Politics on the Web*—This section gives selected Web sites that students can access for more information on issues discussed in the chapter.

- *Online Resources for This Chapter*—This section directs students to the text's Companion Web site, where students can find additional resources for the chapter.

THE SUPPLEMENTS

Both instructors and students today expect, and indeed require, a variety of accompanying supplements to teach and learn about American government. *America at Odds,* Sixth Edition, takes the lead in providing the most comprehensive and user-friendly supplements package on the market today. These supplements include those listed below.

Supplements for Instructors

- **PowerLecture with JoinIn™ for** *America at Odds* includes virtually all the instructor materials specific to the book in a single resource on CD-ROM. Contents include:
  - **Interactive PowerPoint® Lectures** This one-stop lecture and class preparation tool makes it easy for you to assemble, edit, publish, and present custom lectures for your course, using Microsoft® PowerPoint. The interactive PowerPoint lectures bring together text-specific outlines; audio and video clips from historic to current-day events; animated learning modules illustrating key concepts; tables, statistical charts and graphs, and photos from the book, as well as outside sources. In addition, you can add your own materials—culminating in a powerful, personalized, media-enhanced presentation.
  - *Test Bank* **in Microsoft Word and ExamView® computerized testing** Instructors will find a large array of well-crafted multiple-choice questions, along with their answers. There are also short-answer and essay questions for each chapter.
  - *Instructor's Manual* This includes Learning Objectives; Chapter Outlines; discussion questions; suggestions for stimulating class activities and projects; tips on integrating media into your class, including step-by-step instructions on how to create your own podcasts; suggested readings and Web resources; and a section specially designed to help teaching assistants and adjunct instructors.
  - *Resource Integration Guide* This guide outlines the rich collection of resources available to instructors and students within the chapter-by-chapter framework of the book, suggesting how and when each supplement can be used to optimize learning.
  - *JoinIn* Book-specific "clicker" questions test and track student comprehension of key concepts. Political Polling questions simulate voting, engage the classroom, foster dialogue on group behaviors and values, and add personal relevance. Results can be compared to national data, leading to lively discussions. Visual Literacy questions tied to images from the book add useful pedagogical tools and high-interest feedback during your lecture. Save the data from your students' responses all semester—track their progress and show them how political science works by incorporating this exciting new tool into your classroom. *Contact your Wadsworth/Cengage Learning representative for more information about JoinIn on TurningPoint and our exclusive infrared or radio frequency hardware solutions.*

- **The** *America at Odds* **Resource Center** The *America at Odds* Resource Center offers a variety of rich learning resources designed to enhance the student experience. These resources include podcasts, quizzes, simulations, animated learning modules, self-assessments, video, and links to Election 2008 information and analysis. All resources are correlated with key chapter learning concepts, and users can browse or search for content in a variety of ways. More than a collection of ancillary learning materials, The *America at Odds* Resource Center also features important content and community tools that extend the education experience, including tools for instructors to author their own content, content-sharing features, blogs (online journals) available for each registered user, and a built-in messaging center for class communications. Contact your Wadsworth/Cengage Learning representative for access to The *America at Odds* Resource Center.

- **WebTutor™ for WebCT™ and Blackboard®** Leverage the power of the Internet and bring your course to life with this course management program. You or your students can use this wealth of interactive resources with those on the text's Companion Web site to supplement the classroom experience and ensure students leave with the resources to succeed in today's business world. You can even use this effective resource as an integrated solution for distance learning or a Web-enhanced course.

- **Political Theatre DVD** Video and audio clips drawn from key political events from the last seventy-five years: presidential speeches, campaign ads, debates, news reports, national convention coverage, demonstrations, speeches by civil rights leaders, and more.

■ **JoinIn on TurningPoint for Political Theatre** For even more interaction, combine **Political Theatre** with the innovative teaching tool of a classroom response system through JoinIn. Poll your students with questions we have created for you or create your own. Built within the Microsoft PowerPoint software, it's easy to integrate into your current lectures, in conjunction with the "clicker" hardware of your choice.

■ **ABC News Videos for American Government** A collection of three- to six-minute video clips on relevant political issues. They serve as great lecture or discussion launchers. Available on VHS or DVD.

■ **Video Case Studies for American Government** Free to adopters, this award-winning video contains twelve case studies on recent policy issues, such as affirmative action. Each case ends with questions designed to spark classroom discussion.

■ **Turnitin®** This proven online plagiarism-prevention software promotes fairness in the classroom by helping students learn to correctly cite sources and allowing instructors to check for originality before reading and grading papers. Turnitin quickly checks student papers against billions of pages of Internet content, millions of published works, and millions of student papers. Within seconds, it generates a comprehensive originality report. A booklet, *How to Avoid Plagiarism Using Turnitin,* is also available; ask your Cengage Learning representative for details.

■ **Building Democracy: Readings in American Government** This extraordinary collection provides access to more than five hundred historical documents and scholarly readings to create the ideal supplement for any American government course. Cengage Learning Custom Solutions' intuitive **TextChoice** Web site at **www.textchoice.com/democracy** allows you to quickly browse the collection, preview selections, arrange your table of contents, and create a custom cover that will include your own course information. Or, if you prefer, your local Cengage Learning representative will be happy to guide you through the process.

Consider for Students— Available Packaged with the Book

■ The *America at Odds* **Resource Center** offers a variety of rich learning resources designed to enhance the student experience. These resources include podcasts, quizzes, simulations, animated learning modules, self-assessments, video, and links to Election 2008 information and analysis. All resources are correlated with key chapter learning concepts, and users can browse or search for content in a variety of ways. More than a collection of ancillary learning materials, The *America at Odds* Resource Center also features important content and community tools that extend the education experience, including blogs (online journals) available for each registered user and a built-in messaging center for class communications. The printed access card bundled with your book contains a passcode and instructions on how to access The *America at Odds* Resource Center at **www.academic.cengage.com/login**. If your book didn't include an access card, visit **ichapters.com** to purchase access.

■ **The Companion Web site for** *America at Odds,* at **www.americaatodds.com**, offers students free and open access to Learning Objectives, Quizzes, Chapter Glossaries, Flashcards, Crossword Puzzles, and Internet Activities.

WHAT'S NEW IN THE SIXTH EDITION?

We thought that those of you who have used the Fifth Edition of *America at Odds* would like to know what changes have been made for the Sixth Edition. Generally, all of the text, tables, figures, and features in this book have been rewritten or updated as necessary to reflect the most recent developments in American government and politics. The Sixth Edition incorporates the results of the most recent presidential and congressional elections throughout the text as they relate to chapter topics. This edition also presents an up-to-date discussion of the war on terrorism and the war in Iraq. Other key changes and additions for the Sixth Edition include those described below.

Significant Changes to the Chapters

As already indicated, each chapter in *America at Odds,* Sixth Edition, has been updated and revised in order to reflect the most current developments in American politics and government. New features have been added to every chapter, and references to new laws and court decisions have been included. Throughout the text, we have incorporated references to the 2004 and 2006 elections and the 2008 elections as appropriate. Here, we list some other significant changes made to selected chapters.

■ Chapter 1 (The Contours of American Democracy)— The section discussing political ideology has been rewritten. All of the six features in the chapter are newly written and address such topics as the spending trade-offs we are making to fight the war in Iraq and Estonia's recent experience with cyber warfare.

Chapter 2 (The Constitution)—New features address a variety of topics, including whether the president has become too powerful, Russia's short-lived flirtation with true democracy, whether presidential signing statements are destroying the balance of powers, and government counterterrorist legislation and other actions that have imposed restraints on our civil liberties.

Chapter 3 (Federalism)—New subsections focus on the politics of federalism, federalism and the Bush administration, and federalism and the war on terrorism. A number of new features deal with current conflicts between the states and the federal government over such issues as the Real ID Act of 2005, the proposed interstate compact to elect the president by popular vote, and the No Child Left Behind Act.

Chapter 4 (Civil Liberties)—The section discussing freedom of religion has been revised to update the discussion of religion in the schools, and a new subsection on evolution versus intelligent design has been added. A new subsection on free speech for students has also been added. References to the Supreme Court's 2007 decisions on free speech for high school students and on partial-birth abortions have also been included. The section on privacy rights has been significantly expanded. New features look at the expansion of government DNA databases, techniques used in Saudi Arabia to combat terrorism, whether the Bible should be taught in public schools, restraints on expression in the military, and whether the death penalty should be abolished.

Chapter 5 (Civil Rights)—A new subsection looks at the continuing struggle of African Americans to reach income and educational parity with whites. The section discussing political participation by Hispanics has been revised, and a new subsection on gays and lesbians in the military has been added. The discussion of affirmative action has been rewritten to address recent developments, including the Supreme Court's 2007 decision on public school policies that take race into account. The chapter-opening *America at Odds* feature looks at the immigration issue. Other features examine racial profiling in the war on terrorism, the gender gap in wages, discriminatory Internet ads for roommates, and affirmative action in India.

Chapter 6 (Interest Groups)—An explanation of the distinction between private goods and public goods adds clarity to the free rider problem, and the meaning of the term *public-interest group* is now examined more closely. New subsections on recent lobbying scandals and Congress's lobbying reform efforts in 2007 have been added. New features address current debates over gun control, issue ads, the "revolving door" between Congress and the lobbying establishment, and lobbying scandals.

Chapter 7 (Political Parties)—The chapter now reflects the status and concerns of the two major parties today and presents (in Table 7–1) the current agendas of the Republican and Democratic parties. Also included is a new subsection on the changing American electorate. Features focus on difficulties facing the Republican Party today, the consequences for Democratic ambitions of having only a slim majority in Congress, political parties in Iraq, the neoconservative response to 9/11, Unity08's attempt to create a bipartisan presidential ticket, and whether the two-party system is destroying America.

Chapter 8 (Public Opinion and Voting)—Several new subsections discussing voting turnout and attempts to improve voting procedures have been added. New features address the issues of online polling, whether colleges should train better citizens, whether a military draft would have kept us out of Iraq, the accuracy of public opinion polls, voter fraud, and electronic voting in the recent French presidential elections.

Chapter 9 (Campaigns and Elections)—The section discussing the presidential primaries was updated to reflect developments in the "rush to be first" and the new Mega-Tuesday of February 5. A discussion of the recent Supreme Court decision on issue ads has also been added. A *Join the Debate* feature looks at the pros and cons of New Hampshire's determination to hold the first primary, no matter what. Other features focus on such topics as the 2008 presidential campaigns and the war in Iraq, and whether congressional campaigns should be publicly financed.

Chapter 10 (Politics and the Media)—The sections on negative advertising, media bias, and political news and campaigns on the Web have been rewritten to reflect new developments and new scholarship in these areas. A subsection looks at blogs, the emergence of citizen journalism, and the impact of the blogosphere on our news culture. New features examine the problem of inaccuracy regarding information available on the Web, the near disappearance of an independent media in Russia, whether the media should be prohibited from publishing secret government information, and the U.S. government's attempts to counter anti-American bias in the Arab media.

Chapter 11 (Congress)—New features cover a number of current issues, including what would happen if terrorists attacked Congress, whether Congress should spend time on "symbolic votes," and whether "earmarks" should be banned.

■ Chapter 12 (The Presidency)—This chapter has been revised and rewritten as necessary to reflect the expansion of presidential powers under President George W. Bush. A new subsection deals with President Bush's unprecedented use of signing statements. The chapter-opening *America at Odds* feature raises the question of how George W. Bush will be ranked by historians in the future, while other features examine such topics as the president's power to persuade, whether a president's moral convictions should play a role in policymaking, and the secrecy of the Bush administration.

■ Chapter 13 (The Bureaucracy)—A new subsection discusses the changes in the bureaucracy made during the Bush administration. New features focus on a number of issues concerning the bureaucracy, including whether the Food and Drug Administration should be more vigilant, whether all the "red tape" is worth the cost, wages of government workers versus workers in the private sector, the pros and cons of outsourcing war-related work, and the spending binges of federal agencies in the last quarter of the fiscal year.

■ Chapter 14 (The Judiciary)—New sections examine the legal tug-of-war between the Bush administration and the federal courts during the war on terrorism and the ideology of the Roberts Court, and the section discussing the justices' approach to legal interpretation has been revised. The chapter-opening *America at Odds* feature looks at the controversy caused by the Justice Department's firing of several U.S. attorneys for allegedly political reasons and the subsequent congressional investigation into this matter. Other features examine the importance of the right to *habeas corpus* in the American legal tradition, whether partisan ideology matters in Supreme

Court appointments, and judicial review in other nations.

■ Chapter 15 (Domestic Policy)—The chapter has been updated to reflect recent data on the topics covered. New features discuss whether ethanol is the solution to solving our energy problems, how much we are getting in return for homeland security spending, whether we should be all that concerned about global warming, whether senior citizens are reaping too many government benefits relative to those received by children and other groups in America, the effect of tax cuts on the rich versus other groups, and the growing popularity of the flat tax in other countries.

■ Chapter 16 (Foreign Policy)—The section discussing the war on terrorism has been rewritten and expanded to place it in today's perspective and to indicate the problems facing the nation's policymakers with respect to the Iraq war. New text has also been added to update the sections on the threat of nuclear proliferation and to discuss the Bush administration's response to nuclear developments in North Korea and Iran. New features address such questions as whether the isolation of oppressive regimes from the international community is an effective policy, whether nuclear weapons should be abolished, the relative powers of the European Union and the nations included in that union, and whether private entities should be allowed to run for government office—to improve efficiency and lessen corruption in developing countries.

■ Chapter 17 (State and Local Politics)—The chapter has been updated to include new data as necessary. New features focus on whether campaign contributions affect judicial neutrality, whether certain states in the South are too hospitable to business, and the growing lack of candidates in some communities for the position of city manager.

ACKNOWLEDGMENTS

A number of political scientists reviewed the previous editions of *America at Odds*. We remain indebted to the following scholars for their thoughtful suggestions on how to create a text that best suits the needs of today's students and faculty:

David Gray Adler
Idaho State University

Weston H. Agor
University of Texas, El Paso

Ross Baker
Highland Park, New Jersey

Glenn Beamer
University of Virginia

Carol Sears Botsch
University of South Carolina, Aiken

Henry Bowers
Henry Ford Community College, Michigan

Lynn Brink
Northlake College, Texas

John Francis Burke
University of Houston

Luther F. Carter
Francis Marion University, South Carolina

Rebecca Cartwright
Montgomery College

Brian Cherry
Northern Michigan University

Richard G. Chesteen
University of Tennessee at Martin

Richard Christofferson
University of Wisconsin,
Stevens Point

M. Jeffrey Colbert
University of North Carolina,
Greensboro

Lane Crothers
Illinois State University

Cecile D. Durish
Austin Community College, Texas

Larry Elowitz
Georgia College and State
University

Craig Emmert
Texas Tech University

Terri Fine
University of Central Florida

Paul D. Foote
Abraham Baldwin Agricultural
College, Georgia

Scott R. Furlong
University of Wisconsin, Green Bay

Gail E. Garbrandt
University of Akron, Ohio

John Geer
Vanderbilt University

Christian Goergen
College of DuPage, Illinois

Paul Goren
Southern Illinois University

J. Tobin Grant
Southern Illinois University

Jim Graves
Kentucky State University

Joanne Green
Texas Christian University

Richard Himelfarb
Hofstra University, New York

Glen D. Hunt
Austin Community College, Texas

Marianne Ide
Monterey Peninsula College,
California

William E. Kelly
Auburn University, Alabama

Matt Kerbel
Villanova University,
Pennsylvania

Brian Kessel
Columbia College, Maryland

James D. King
University of Wyoming

Melvin C. Laracey
University of Texas at
San Antonio

John D. Lees
Oakland University, Michigan

Steven A. Light
University of North Dakota

James J. Lopach
University of Montana

Mark D. Maironis
Eastern Michigan University

Sam W. Mckinstry
East Tennessee State University

William McLauchlan
Purdue University, Indiana

Paz Pena
Austin Community College

Anthony Perry
Henry Ford Community College,
Michigan

Paul Savoie
Long Beach City College, California

Wendy E. Scattergood
University of Wisconsin, Green Bay

Linda J. Simmons
Northern Virginia Community
College

Ruth Ann Strickland
Appalachian State University,
North Carolina

Larry Taylor
Georgia Southern University

Gabriel Ume
Palo Alto College, Texas

Sharon G. Whitney
Tennessee Technological University

Bruce M. Wilson
University of Central Florida

J. David Woodard
Clemson University, South Carolina

Michele Zebich-Knos
Kennesaw State University, Georgia

In preparing the Sixth Edition of *America at Odds,* we benefited from the criticism
and comments of a number of users and reviewers of the Fifth Edition. We thank
the following reviewers for their conscientious work:

Yan Bai
Grand Rapids Community College

J. St. Lawrence Brown
Spokane Community College

Michael Kanner
University of Colorado

Christine Kelleher
University of Michigan

John Kerr
University of Arkansas

Amy Miller
Western Kentucky University

Jalal Nejad
Northwest Vista College

Robert Sullivan
Dallas Baptist University

Don K. Williams
Western New England College,
Massachusetts

Mary Young
Southwestern Michigan College

Our styles of teaching and mentoring students were shaped in important ways by our graduate faculty at Ohio State University. We thank Lawrence Baum, Herbert Asher, Elliot Slotnick, and Randall Ripley for lessons well taught. The students we have had the privilege of working with at many fine universities during our careers have also taught us a great deal. We trust that some of what appears on these pages reflects their insights, and we hope that what we have written will capture the interest of current and future students. Of course, we owe an immeasurable debt to our families, whose divergent views on political issues reflect an America at odds.

We thank Sean Wakely, president of Wadsworth Publishing Company, for all of his encouragement and support throughout our work on this project. We were also fortunate to have the editorial advice of Clark Baxter, publisher, and Carolyn Merrill, executive editor, and the assistance of Stacey Sims, senior developmental editor, who supervised all aspects of the supplements and the text. We thank Rebecca Green, assistant editor, for her handling of the supplements and related items. We also thank Lavina Leed Miller for her tremendous help in coordinating the project and for her research,

copyediting, and proofreading assistance. We received additional copyediting and proofreading assistance from Pat Lewis, Judy Kiviat, and Martha Ghent. We are also grateful to Sue Jasin of K&M Consulting, Vickie Reierson, and Roxie Lee. We are especially indebted to the staff at Parkwood Composition. Their ability to generate the pages for this text quickly and accurately made it possible for us to meet our ambitious schedule. We appreciate the enthusiasm of Janise Fry, our hard-working marketing manager, Trent Whatcott, her successor, and the cheerful support of Ann Borman, our project editor, at Wadsworth Publishing Company. We would also like to acknowledge Bill Stryker, our production manager, for producing the most attractive and user-friendly American government text on the market today.

If you or your students have ideas or suggestions, you can write us directly or send us information through Wadsworth Publishing Company.

E.I.S.
B.M.H.

CHAPTER **1**

THE CONTOURS OF AMERICAN DEMOCRACY

LEARNING OBJECTIVES

LO¹ Explain what is meant by the terms *politics* and *government*.

LO² Identify the various types of government systems.

LO³ Summarize some of the basic principles of American democracy and the basic American political values.

LO⁴ Describe how the various topics discussed in this text relate to the "big picture" of American politics and government.

AMERICA AT ODDS

Do We Really Have a Representative Democracy?

Some people say that we have the best democracy that money can buy. Others like things just the way they are—the system has worked for more than two hundred years, so what is the problem? Perhaps the real debate is over whether we still have a representative democracy. As you will find out later in this chapter, in this type of political system the public elects representatives, who then carry out the public's will by passing legislation. In a nation of more than 300 million people, though, even the most astute elected representative finds it impossible to determine "the public's will." This is because the public often has conflicting opinions on any given issue. Therefore, even under the best of circumstances, our representative democracy will not create a nation in which everyone is happy with what the government does.

A Representative Democracy? Nothing Could Be Further from the Truth

We elect members of Congress. They are supposed to serve their *constituents* (the people who live in their state if the members are senators and those who live in their district if they are representatives). Members of Congress who don't serve the interests of their constituents should at least act in the best interests of the nation. The reality, though, is something else entirely.

Congress has been sold to the highest bidder. The main job of a member of Congress is to be reelected. The best way to be reelected is to amass bigger and bigger reelection campaign war chests. Members do this by giving in to the pressures brought by certain industries or groups, which in turn help fund reelection campaigns. Consider just one example: when a new bill was passed to fund prescription drugs in 2003, representatives of the pharmaceutical industry virtually wrote the bill themselves. In 2007, the Senate considered a bill that would allow the federal government to negotiate drug prices with large pharmaceutical companies. The bill failed to pass. Why? The pharmaceutical industry spent hundreds of thousands of dollars lobbying against the legislation. Such "congressional vote buying" goes on all the time.

Moreover, how representative is the presidency in our democracy? President George W. Bush had some of the lowest job-approval ratings of any president in the history of this nation. Talk about ignoring public opinion. The president refused to budge on his basic views about the war in Iraq, even though the majority of Americans wanted to bring the war to an end. He did not listen to anyone—including members of Congress, military and other experts, and a large majority of Americans—if their

views differed from his own. Americans may vote for their elected officials, but those officials do not seem to represent the American people.

WE ARE THE ENVY OF THE WORLD, SO WHAT IS THE PROBLEM?

Those who claim that we do not really have a representative democracy also point to the relatively low voter turnout in local, state, and federal elections. Others, however, assert that low voter turnout is a good sign. It means that most people are satisfied with how America is being governed. When Americans become dissatisfied with their government, voter turnout increases.

After all, when the government ignores the wishes of the electorate for too long, citizens do have recourse: they can simply refuse to reelect their representatives in the next congressional elections. They may even decide not to elect members of the same political party. In 1994, the so-called Republican Revolution occurred just two years after a Democrat, Bill Clinton, was elected president. Voters gave control over both chambers of Congress to the Republicans. And so we entered an era of divided government, in which one party held the presidency and the other party controlled the Congress.

When Americans became increasingly dissatisfied with President George W. Bush's policies, particularly his insistence on continuing the war in Iraq, they punished him. In the 2006 midterm elections, the voters gave the Democrats control over both chambers of Congress. Voters seemed also to be disgusted with the ethics scandals that had plagued the Republican-led Congress. So, how much more representative do you want our democracy to be?

Where do you stand?

1. How important do you think it is for elected government officials to represent their constituents' interests? What if the national interest is different?
2. Do you think that low voter turnout means that people are satisfied with our government or are simply "turned off" by government? Why?

Explore this issue online

- Students interested in curbing the impact of wealthy special interests on politics can visit Democracy Matters at **www.democracymatters.org**. NBA basketball star Adonal Foyle founded this activist group.
- For a series of arguments on why campaign finance reform is dangerous, check out the writings of the Cato Institute, a conservative/libertarian think tank at **www.cato.org/research/crg/finance.html**.

INTRODUCTION

Regardless of how Americans feel about government, one thing is certain: they can't live without it. James Madison (1751–1836) once said, "If men were angels, no government would be necessary." Today, his statement still holds true. People are not perfect. People need an organized form of government and a set of rules by which to live.

Note, though, that even if people were perfect, they would still need to establish rules to guide their behavior. They would somehow have to agree on how to divide up a society's resources, such as its land, among themselves and how to balance individual needs and wants against those of society generally. These perfect people would also have to decide *how* to make these decisions. They would need to create a process for making rules and a form of government to enforce those rules. It is thus not difficult to understand why government is one of humanity's oldest and most universal institutions. No society has existed without some form of government. The need for authority and organization will never disappear.

As you will read in this chapter, a number of different systems of government exist in the world today. In the United States, we have a democracy in which decisions about pressing issues ultimately are made by the people's representatives in government. Because

> "**Let us never forget** that government is ourselves and not an alien power over us. The ultimate rulers of our democracy are not a President and senators and congressmen and government officials, but the **voters** of this country."
>
> FRANKLIN D. ROOSEVELT,
> THIRTY-SECOND PRESIDENT OF THE UNITED STATES
> 1933–1945

people rarely have identical thoughts and feelings about issues, it is not surprising that in any democracy citizens are often at odds with one another. Certainly, Americans are at odds over many political and social issues, including the issue discussed in the chapter-opening feature. Throughout this book, you will read about contemporary issues that have brought various groups of Americans into conflict with one another.

Realize, though, that the aim of this book is not to depict a nation that is falling apart at the seams. Rather, it is to place the conflicting views currently being expressed by Americans in a historical perspective. Having citizens at odds with one another is nothing new in this country. Indeed, throughout this nation's history, Americans have had strikingly different ideas about what decisions should be made, and by whom. Differences in opinion are part and parcel of a democratic government. Ultimately, these differences are resolved, one way or another, through the American political process and our government **institutions.**

With more than 300 million people living in the United States, there are bound to be conflicts. Here, Americans demonstrate in front of the United States Supreme Court building in Washington, D.C. Is such conflict necessarily bad for America?

dbking/Creative Commons

institution An ongoing organization that performs certain functions for society.

LO¹ WHAT ARE POLITICS AND GOVERNMENT?

Politics means many things to many people. To some, politics is an expensive and extravagant game played in Washington, D.C., in state capitols, and in city halls, particularly during election time. To others, politics involves all of the tactics and maneuvers carried out by the president and Congress. Most formal definitions of politics, however, begin with the assumption that **social conflict**—disagreements among people in a society over what the society's priorities should be—is inevitable. Conflicts will naturally arise over how the society should use its scarce resources and who should receive various benefits, such as wealth, status, health care, and higher education. (See, for example, the conflict discussed in this chapter's *The Politics of National Security* feature.) Resolving such conflicts is the essence of **politics.** Political scientist Harold Lasswell perhaps said it best when he defined politics as the process of determining "who gets what, when, and how" in a society.[1]

There are also many different notions about the meaning of government. From the perspective of political science, though, **government** can best be defined as the individuals and institutions that make society's rules and that also possess the *power* and *authority* to enforce those rules. Although this definition of government sounds remote and abstract, what the government does is very real indeed. As one scholar put it, "Make no mistake. What Congress does directly and powerfully affects our daily lives."[2] The same can be said for decisions made by state legislators and local government officials, as well as for decisions rendered by the courts—the judicial branch of government. Of course, a key question remains: How do specific individuals obtain the power and authority to govern? As you will read shortly, the answer to this question varies from one type of political system to another.

To understand what government is, you need to understand what it actually does for people and society. Generally, in any country government serves at least three essential purposes: (1) it resolves conflicts; (2) it provides public services; and (3) it defends the nation and its culture against attacks by other nations.

Resolving Conflicts

Even though people have lived together in groups since the beginning of time, none of these groups has been free of social conflict. As mentioned, disputes over how to distribute a society's valued resources inevitably arise because valued resources, such as property, are limited, while people's wants are unlimited. To resolve such disputes, people need ways to determine who wins and who loses, and how to get the losers to accept those decisions. Who has the legitimate power and authority to make such decisions? This is where government steps in.

Governments decide how conflicts will be resolved so that public order can be maintained. Governments have **power**—the ability to influence the behavior of others. Power is getting someone to do something that he or she would not otherwise do. Power may involve the use of force (often called coercion), persuasion, or rewards. Governments also have **authority,** which they can exercise only if their power is legitimate. As used here, the term *legitimate power* means power that is collectively recognized and accepted by society as legally and morally correct. Power and authority are central to a government's ability to resolve conflicts by making and enforcing laws, placing limits on what people can do, and developing court systems to make final decisions.

For example, the judicial branch of government—specifically, the United States Supreme Court—resolved the conflict over whether the votes in certain Florida counties could be recounted after the 2000 presidential elections. Because of the Court's stature and authority as a government body, there was little resistance to its

> "Politics is the process of determining who gets what, when, and how."
>
> HAROLD LASSWELL, POLITICAL SCIENTIST 1902–1978

social conflict Disagreements among people in a society over what the society's priorities should be with respect to the use of scarce resources.

politics The process of resolving conflicts over how society should use its scarce resources and who should receive various benefits, such as public health care and public higher education. According to Harold Lasswell, politics is the process of determining "who gets what, when, and how" in a society.

government The individuals and institutions that make society's rules and that also possess the power and authority to enforce those rules.

power The ability to influence the behavior of others, usually through the use of force, persuasion, or rewards.

authority The ability to exercise power, such as the power to make and enforce laws, legitimately.

WHAT ARE WE GIVING UP TO FIGHT THE WAR IN IRAQ?

Virtually all policymaking decisions involve trade-offs. In the real world of scarce resources, no spending decision by any government—federal, state, or local—can be undertaken without a trade-off and therefore a cost. What the government spends, the rest of the economy cannot spend. Within government, spending on one program means less spending on another.

FINANCING THE WAR IN IRAQ

The initial cost of the war in Iraq was, by war-spending standards, relatively small—not even $100 billion. By the end of 2008, however, more than $700 billion will have been spent in Iraq, for the war, the ongoing "occupation," and the relatively unsuccessful rebuilding efforts. By 2007, U.S. citizens were paying for the care, feeding, and protection of more than 150,000 U.S. troops (and it was impossible to put a dollar sign on the more than 3,500 U.S. soldiers killed in Iraq and the more than 25,000 who had been seriously wounded). There were also more than 85,000 private contractors in Iraq, most of whom had been hired by the U.S. government and were paid with taxpayer dollars.

THE U.S. EMBASSY IN BAGHDAD— NOTHING BUT THE BEST

The Bush administration told the U.S. Congress that the new embassy in Baghdad would cost about $600 million. When the embassy is finished, it will be the largest in world history. Its twenty-one buildings with offices for eight thousand U.S. staff workers will sit on 104 acres, the size of eighty football fields. The embassy will have its own water-treatment plant and power-generating system—and the largest swimming pool in all of Iraq. Presumably, a significant percentage of the $600 million spent on this embassy should be included in the cost of the war in Iraq.

SOME ACTUAL TRADE-OFFS

Although no exact trade-offs can be calculated for war spending, the National Priorities Project has come up with some startling estimates. Based on $500 billion of spending as of the beginning of 2008, any of the following programs could have been funded with the funds spent on the war:

- The federal government could have offered more than 20 million students four-year scholarships at public universities.
- The federal government could have subsidized about 4 million additional public housing units.
- The federal government could have paid for more than 50 million children to attend a year of the Head Start preschool program.

YOU BE THE JUDGE

Some concerned citizens believe that the hundreds of billions of dollars spent on the war on Iraq (to say nothing of the lost lives and wounded soldiers) cannot be justified by government claims that establishing a democracy in the Middle East is critical for long-term American security. Others are convinced that if we walk away from the war in Iraq, we will end up paying more for a secure America in the future. Where do you stand on this issue?

---

decision *not* to allow the recounting—although the decision was strongly criticized by many because it virtually handed the presidency to George W. Bush.

Providing Public Services

Another important purpose of government is to provide **public services**—essential services that many individuals cannot provide for themselves. Governments undertake projects that individuals usually would not or could not do on their own, such as building and maintaining roads, providing welfare programs, operating public schools, and preserving national parks. Governments also provide such services as law enforcement, fire protection, and public health and safety programs. As Abraham Lincoln once stated:

The legitimate object of government is to do for

> **public services** Essential services that individuals cannot provide for themselves, such as building and maintaining roads, providing welfare programs, operating public schools, and preserving national parks.

a community of people whatever they need to have done but cannot do at all, or cannot so well do for themselves in their separate and individual capacities. But in all that people can individually do for themselves, government ought not to interfere.[3]

Some public services are provided equally to all citizens of the United States. For example, government services such as national defense and domestic law enforcement allow all citizens, at least in theory, to feel that their lives and property are safe. Laws governing clean air and safe drinking water benefit all Americans. Other services are provided only to citizens who are in need at a particular time, even though they are paid for by all citizens through taxes. Examples of such services include health and welfare benefits, and public housing. Laws such as the Americans with Disabilities Act explicitly protect the rights of people with disabilities, although all Americans pay for such protections whether they have disabilities or not.

Defending the Nation and Its Culture

Historically, matters of national security and defense have been given high priority by governments and have demanded considerable time, effort, and expense. The U.S. government provides for the common defense and national security with its Army, Navy, Marines, Air

> "IN ALL THAT PEOPLE CAN INDIVIDUALLY DO FOR THEMSELVES, GOVERNMENT OUGHT NOT TO INTERFERE."
>
> ABRAHAM LINCOLN,
> SIXTEENTH PRESIDENT OF THE UNITED STATES
> 1861–1865

Force, and Coast Guard. The State Department, Defense Department, Homeland Security Department, Central Intelligence Agency, National Security Agency, and other agencies also contribute to this defense network. As part of an ongoing policy of national security, many departments and agencies in the federal government are constantly dealing with other nations. The Constitution gives our national government exclusive power over relations with foreign nations. No individual state can negotiate a treaty with a foreign nation.

Of course, in defending the nation against attacks by other nations, a government helps to preserve the nation's culture, as well as its integrity as an independent unit. Failure to defend successfully against foreign attacks may have significant consequences for a nation's culture. For example, consider what happened in Tibet in the 1950s. When the former government of that country was unable to defend itself against the People's Republic of China, the conquering (mainland) Chinese set out on a systematic program to destroy Tibet's culture.

Since the terrorist attacks on the World Trade Center and the Pentagon in 2001, defending the homeland against future terrorist attacks has become a priority of our government. Primarily, the government's focus has been on physical terrorism (attacks using bombs and other explosive devices). Yet terrorism can also take place in cyberspace—see this chapter's *The Rest of the World* feature for a recent example of cyberattacks against a government's communications systems.

LO² DIFFERENT SYSTEMS OF GOVERNMENT

Through the centuries, the functions of government just discussed have been performed by many different types of government structures. A government's structure is influenced by a number of factors, such as history, customs, values, geography, climate, resources, and human experiences and needs. No two nations have exactly the same form of government. Over time, however, political analysts have developed various ways of classifying different systems of government. One of the most meaningful ways of classifying governments is according to *who* governs. Who has the power to make the rules and laws that all must obey?

These Tibetan children sit in a classroom dominated by pictures of dictators, including Vladimir Lenin (1870–1924) of the former Soviet Union, and Chairman Mao (1893–1976), who ruled China with an iron fist from 1945 to 1976.

Nancy Jo Johnson/Creative Commons

THE REST OF
THE WORLD

Cyber Warfare against Estonia

The Internet has been a wonderful invention. It has changed the lives of many people around the world, and it has transformed the way we do business and run governments. With all good things, though, come some bad. The possibility of cyber warfare and cyberterrorism became a real concern in the 1990s.

Cyberterrorists are those who exploit computers to cause serious harm to businesses or governments. Just as "real" terrorists destroyed the World Trade Center towers and a portion of the Pentagon in September 2001, cyberterrorists might explode "logic bombs" to shut down central computers. Such activities can pose a danger to national security in any country. Indeed, some say that the emphasis since 9/11 on "real" terrorism of the physical kind has left the American government (as well as governments in other countries) vulnerable to cyberattacks. What happened in Estonia in 2007 served as a grim reminder of this vulnerability.

LITTLE ESTONIA— FULLY WIRED AND UNDER ATTACK

At the end of April 2007, Estonia, purportedly Europe's most wired nation, suffered a series of cyberattacks that crippled its Web sites. Estonian Defense Minister Jaak Aaviksoo announced that more than a million computers worldwide were engaged in attacking Estonia during a two-week period. Most of these attacks were aimed at government Web sites, but some corporate Web sites were attacked, too. The defense minister claimed that the initial attacks came from Russian government offices.

Russia and Estonia generally have not gotten along very well since the latter broke away from the now-defunct Soviet Union in 1991, after more than

Peter Van den Bossche/
Creative Commons

five decades of Soviet occupation. Estonians believe that Russia was angered by Estonia's decision to move a statue from a downtown square in the capital city of Tallinn to a cemetery outside the town. The statue, known as the Bronze Soldier, commemorates Soviet army troops who were killed fighting the Nazis during World War II. According to the Estonians, immediately after the statue was moved, instructions in Russian appeared all over the Internet explaining how to jam Estonian sites with so-called denial-of-service attacks. These attacks allow hackers to overload a single network by directing massive amounts of Internet traffic to the site.

IT'S HARD TO KEEP AHEAD OF CYBERTERRORISTS

Denial-of-service attacks have been used in the United States and elsewhere by hackers wishing to show how clever they are. The cyberattacks against the Estonian government, however, constitute the first organized cyberterrorism event ever recorded. Rarely are cyberterrorists caught. Nonetheless, the U.S. government has taken the Estonian cyberattack seriously and has increased its attempts to prepare for such attacks. The National Infrastructure Advisory Council is developing a national strategy, but many computer experts are not sure how useful it will be in the event of a true cyberterrorist attack on this country.

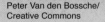

For Critical Analysis

How would you distinguish between simple "hacking," which usually involves an attempt to bring down computers via viruses, and true cyberterrorism?

Rule by One: Autocracy

In an **autocracy,** the power and authority of the government are in the hands of a single person. At one time, autocracy was a common form of government, and it still exists in some parts of the world. Autocrats usually obtain their power either by inheriting it or by force.

MONARCHY One form of autocracy, known as a **monarchy,** is government by a king, queen, emperor, empress, tsar, or tsarina. In a monarchy, the monarch,

who usually acquires power through inheritance, is the highest authority in the government.

Historically, many monarchies were *absolute monarchies,* in which the ruler held complete and unlimited power as a matter of divine right. Prior to the eighteenth century, the theory of divine right was

> **autocracy** A form of government in which the power and authority of the government are in the hands of a single person.
>
> **monarchy** A form of autocracy in which a king, queen, emperor, empress, tsar, or tsarina is the highest authority in the government; monarchs usually obtain their power through inheritance.

widely accepted in Europe. The **divine right theory,** variations of which had existed since ancient times, held that God gave those of royal birth the unlimited right to govern other men and women. In other words, those of royal birth had a "divine right" to rule. According to this theory, only God could judge those of royal birth. Thus, all citizens were bound to obey their monarchs, no matter how unfair or unjust they seemed to be. Challenging this power was regarded not only as treason against the government but also as a sin against God.

Most modern monarchies, however, are *constitutional monarchies,* in which the monarch shares governmental power with elected lawmakers. The monarch's power is limited, or checked, by other government leaders and perhaps by a constitution or a bill of rights. These constitutional monarchs serve mainly as *ceremonial* leaders of their governments, as in Great Britain, Denmark, and Sweden.

Farrell Grehan/Photo Researchers

This New Hampshire town meeting is an example of direct democracy.

tion come before the needs of individuals, and all citizens must work for the common goals established by the government. Examples of this form of government include Adolf Hitler's government in Nazi Germany from 1933 to 1945, Benito Mussolini's rule in Italy from 1923 to 1943, and Joseph Stalin's rule in the Soviet Union from 1929 to 1953. More contemporary examples of totalitarian dictators include Fidel Castro in Cuba, Kim Jong Il in North Korea, and, until his government was dismantled in 2003, Saddam Hussein in Iraq.

Rule by Many: Democracy

The most familiar form of government to Americans is **democracy,** in which the supreme political authority rests with the people. The word *democracy* comes from the Greek *demos,* meaning "the people," and *kratia,* meaning "rule." The main idea of democracy is that government exists only by the consent of the people and reflects the will of the majority.

THE ATHENIAN MODEL OF DIRECT DEMOCRACY

Democracy as a form of government began long ago. **Direct democracy** exists when the people participate directly in government decision making. In its purest form, direct democracy was practiced in Athens and other ancient Greek city-states about 2,500 years ago. Every Athenian citizen participated in the governing assembly and voted on all major issues. Although some consider the Athenian form of direct democracy ideal because it demanded a high degree of citizen participation, others point out that most residents in the Athenian city-state (women, foreigners, and slaves) were not deemed to be citizens and thus were not allowed to participate in government.

Clearly, direct democracy is possible only in small communities in which citizens can meet in a chosen place and decide key issues and policies. Nowhere in the world does pure direct democracy exist today. Some New England town meetings, though, and a few of the smaller political subunits, or cantons, of Switzerland still use a modified form of direct democracy.

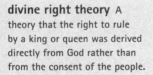

divine right theory A theory that the right to rule by a king or queen was derived directly from God rather than from the consent of the people.

dictatorship A form of government in which absolute power is exercised by a single person who usually has obtained his or her power by the use of force.

democracy A system of government in which the people have ultimate political authority. The word is derived from the Greek *demos* (people) and *kratia* (rule).

direct democracy A system of government in which political decisions are made by the people themselves rather than by elected representatives. This form of government was practiced in some areas of ancient Greece.

DICTATORSHIP Another form of autocracy is a **dictatorship,** in which a single leader rules, although not through inheritance. Dictators often gain supreme power by using force, either through a military victory or by overthrowing another dictator or leader. Dictators hold absolute power and are not accountable to anyone else.

A dictatorship can also be *totalitarian,* which means that the leader (or group of leaders) seeks to control almost all aspects of social and economic life. The needs of the na-

REPRESENTATIVE DEMOCRACY Although the founders of the United States were aware of the Athenian model and agreed that government should be based on the consent of the governed, many feared that a pure, direct democracy would deteriorate into mob rule. They believed that large groups of people meeting together would ignore the rights and opinions of people in the minority and would make decisions without careful thought. They concluded that a representative democracy would be the better choice because it would enable public decisions to be made in a calmer and more deliberate manner.

> "PEOPLE OFTEN SAY THAT, IN A **DEMOCRACY**, DECISIONS ARE MADE BY A MAJORITY OF THE PEOPLE. OF COURSE, THAT IS NOT TRUE. DECISIONS ARE MADE BY A MAJORITY OF THOSE WHO MAKE THEMSELVES HEARD AND WHO **VOTE**— A VERY DIFFERENT THING."
> — WALTER H. JUDD, U.S. REPRESENTATIVE FROM MINNESOTA 1943–1963

In a **representative democracy,** the will of the majority is expressed through a smaller group of individuals elected by the people to act as their representatives. These representatives are responsible to the people for their conduct and can be voted out of office. Our founders preferred to use the term **republic,** which means essentially a representative democracy—with one difference. A republic, by definition, has no king or queen; rather, the people are sovereign. In contrast, a representative democracy may be headed by a monarch. For example, as Britain evolved into a representative democracy, it retained its monarch as the head of state.

In the modern world, there are basically two forms of representative democracy: presidential and parliamentary. In a *presidential democracy,* the lawmaking and law-enforcing branches of government are separate but equal. For example, in the United States, Congress is charged with the power to make laws, and the president is charged with the power to carry them out. In a *parliamentary democracy,* the lawmaking and law-enforcing branches of government overlap. In Great Britain, for example, the prime minister and the cabinet are members of the legislature, called Parliament. Parliament thus both enacts the laws and carries them out.

Other Forms of Government

Autocracy and democracy are but two of many forms of government. Traditionally, other types of government have included those that are ruled "by the few." For exam-ple, an aristocracy (from the Greek word *aristos*) is a government in which the "best," or a small privileged class, rule. A *plutocracy* is a government in which the wealthy (*ploutos* in Greek means "wealth") exercise ruling power. A *meritocracy* is a government in which the rulers have earned, or merited, the right to govern because of their special skills or talents.

A difficult form of government for Americans to understand is a *theocracy*— a term derived from the Greek words meaning "rule by the deity" or "rule by God." In a theocracy, there is no separation of church and state. Rather, the government rules according to religious precepts. Indeed, in most Muslim (Islamic) countries, government and religion are intertwined to a degree that is quite startling to both Europeans and Americans. In Iran, for example, the Koran (or Qur'an), not the national constitution, serves as the basis for the law. The Koran consists of sacred writings that Muslims (those of the Islamic faith) believe were revealed to the prophet Muhammad by Allah through the angel Gabriel. In Iran, the Council of Guardians, an unelected group of clerics (religious leaders), ensures that laws and lawmakers conform to the teachings of Islam.

LO³ AMERICAN DEMOCRACY

This country, with all its institutions, belongs to the people who inhabit it. Whenever they shall grow weary of the existing government, they can exercise their constitutional right to amend it, or their revolutionary right to dismember or overthrow it.[4]

With these words, Abraham Lincoln underscored the most fundamental concept of American government: that the people, not the government, are ultimately in control.

representative democracy A form of democracy in which the will of the majority is expressed through smaller groups of individuals elected by the people to act as their representatives.

republic Essentially, a term referring to a representative democracy—in which there is no king or queen and the people are sovereign. The people elect smaller groups of individuals to act as the people's representatives.

The British Legacy

In writing the U.S. Constitution, the framers incorporated two basic principles of government that had evolved in England: *limited government* and *representative government.* In a sense, then, the beginnings of our form of government are linked to events that occurred centuries earlier in England. They are also linked to the writings of European philosophers, particularly the English political philosopher John Locke. From these writings, the founders of our nation derived ideas to justify their rebellion against Britain and the establishment of a "government by the people."

National Archives

The Magna Carta.

LIMITED GOVERNMENT   At one time, the English monarch had virtually unrestricted powers. This changed in 1215, when King John was forced by his nobles to accept the Magna Carta, or Great Charter. This monumental document provided for a trial by a jury of one's peers (equals). It prohibited the taking of a person's life, liberty, or property except by the lawful judgment of that person's peers. The Magna Carta also forced the king to obtain the nobles' approval of any taxes he imposed on his subjects. Government thus became a contract between the king and his subjects.

The importance of the Magna Carta to England cannot be overemphasized, because it clearly established the principle of **limited government**— a government on which strict limits are placed, usually by a constitution. Hence, the Magna Carta signaled the end of the monarch's absolute power. Although the rights provided under the Magna Carta originally applied only to the nobility, the document formed the basis of the future constitutional government for all individuals in England and eventually in the United States.

The principle of limited government was expanded four hundred years later, in 1628, when King Charles I signed the Petition of Rights. Among other things, this petition prohibited the monarch from imprisoning political critics without a jury trial. Perhaps more important, the petition declared that even the king or queen had to obey the law of the land.

In 1689, the English Parliament (described shortly) passed the English Bill of Rights, which further extended the concept of limited government. This document included several important ideas:

- The king or queen could not interfere with parliamentary elections.

- The king or queen had to have Parliament's approval to levy (collect) taxes or to maintain an army.

- The king or queen had to rule with the consent of the people's representatives in Parliament.

- The people could not be subjected to cruel or unusual punishment or to excessive fines.

The English colonists in North America were also English citizens, and thus the English Bill of Rights of 1689 applied to them as well. As a result, virtually all of the major concepts in the English Bill of Rights became part of the American system of government.

REPRESENTATIVE GOVERNMENT   In a representative government, the people, by whatever means, elect individuals to make governmental decisions for all of the citizens. Usually, these representatives of the people are elected to their offices for specific periods of time. This group of representatives is often referred to as a **parliament,** which is a **bicameral** (two-house) **legislature.** The English Parliament consists of the House of Lords (upper chamber) and the House of Commons (lower chamber). The English form of government provided a model for Americans to follow. Many of the American colonies had bicameral legislatures—as did, eventually, the U.S. Congress that was established by the Constitution.

limited government
A form of government based on the principle that the powers of government should be clearly limited either through a written document or through wide public understanding; characterized by institutional checks to ensure that government serves public rather than private interests.

parliament The name of the national legislative body in countries governed by a parliamentary system, as in Great Britain and Canada.

bicameral legislature
A legislature made up of two chambers, or parts. The United States has a bicameral legislature, composed of the House of Representatives and the Senate.

POLITICAL PHILOSOPHY—SOCIAL CONTRACTS AND NATURAL RIGHTS   Our democracy resulted from what can be viewed as a type of **social contract** among early Americans to create and abide by a set of governing rules. Social-contract theory was developed in the seventeenth and eighteenth centuries by philosophers, such as John Locke (1632–1704) and Thomas Hobbes (1588–1679) in England and Jean-Jacques Rousseau (1712–1778) in France. According to this theory, individuals voluntarily agree with one another, in a "social contract," to give up some of their freedoms to obtain the benefits of orderly government; the government is given adequate power to secure the mutual protection and welfare of all individuals. Generally, social-contract theory, in one form or another, provides the theoretical underpinnings of most modern democracies, including that of the United States.

Although Hobbes and Rousseau also posited social contracts as the bases of governments, neither theorist was as influential in America as John Locke was. Locke argued that people are born with **natural rights** to life, liberty, and property. He theorized that the purpose of government was to protect those rights; if it did not, it would lose its legitimacy and need not be obeyed. Locke's assumption that people, by nature, are rational and are endowed with certain rights is an essential component of his theory that people can govern themselves. As you will read in Chapter 2, when the American colonists rebelled against British rule, such concepts as "natural rights" and a government based on a "social contract" became important theoretical tools in justifying the rebellion.

Principles of American Democracy

American democracy is based on five fundamental principles:

- *Equality in voting.* Citizens need equal opportunities to express their preferences about policies or leaders.

Digital Vision/Getty Images

- *Individual freedom.* All individuals must have the greatest amount of freedom possible without interfering with the rights of others.
- *Equal protection of the law.* The law must entitle all persons to equal protection of the law.
- *Majority rule and minority rights.* The majority should rule, while guaranteeing the rights of minorities so that the latter may sometimes become majorities through fair and lawful means.
- *Voluntary consent to be governed.* The people who make up a democracy must agree voluntarily to be governed by the rules laid down by their representatives.

These principles frame many of the political issues that you will read about in this book. They also frequently lie at the heart of America's political conflicts. Does the principle of minority rights mean that minorities should receive preferential treatment in hiring and firing decisions? Does the principle of individual freedom mean that individuals can express whatever they want on the Internet, including hateful, racist comments? Such conflicts over individual rights and freedoms and over society's priorities are natural and inevitable. Resolving these conflicts is what politics is all about. What is important is that Americans are able to reach acceptable compromises—because of their common political heritage.

American Political Values

Historically, as the nations of the world emerged, the boundaries of each nation normally coincided with boundaries of a population that shared a common ethnic heritage, language,

social contract A voluntary agreement among individuals to create a government and to give that government adequate power to secure the mutual protection and welfare of all individuals.

natural rights Rights that are not bestowed by governments but are inherent within every man, woman, and child by virtue of the fact that he or she is a human being.

and culture. From its beginnings as a nation, however, America has been defined less by the culture shared by its diverse population than by a set of ideas, or its political culture. A **political culture** can be defined as a patterned set of ideas, values, and ways of thinking about government and politics.

The ideals and standards that constitute American political culture are embodied in the Declaration of Independence, one of the founding documents of this nation, which will be discussed further in Chapter 2 and presented in its entirety in Appendix A. The political values outlined in the Declaration of Independence include natural rights (to life, liberty, and the pursuit of happiness), equality under the law, government by the consent of the governed, and limited government powers. In some ways, the Declaration of Independence defines Americans' sense of right and wrong. It presents a challenge to anyone who might wish to overthrow our democratic processes or deny our citizens their natural rights.

Fundamental political values shared by most Americans include liberty, equality, and property. These values provide a basic framework for American political discourse and debate because they are shared by most Americans, yet individual Americans often interpret their meanings quite differently.

LIBERTY   The term **liberty** refers to a state of being free from external controls or restrictions. In the United States, the Constitution sets forth our *civil liberties* (see Chapter 4), including the freedom to practice whatever religion we choose and to be free from any state-imposed religion. Our liberties also include the freedom to speak freely on any topics and issues. Because people cannot govern themselves unless they are free to voice their opinions, freedom of speech is a basic requirement in a true democracy.

Clearly, though, if we are to live together with others, there have to be some restrictions on individual liberties. If people were allowed to do whatever they wished, without regard for the rights or liberties of others, pandemonium would result. Hence, a more accurate definition of liberty would be as follows: *liberty is the freedom of individuals to believe, act, and express themselves freely so long as doing so does not infringe on the rights of other individuals in the society.*

political culture The set of ideas, values, and attitudes about government and the political process held by a community or a nation.

liberty The freedom of individuals to believe, act, and express themselves freely so long as doing so does not infringe on the rights of other individuals in the society.

JOIN THE DEBATE

Should Google and Yahoo Be Helping China's Repressive Government?

China represents potentially the largest market for online businesses in the world. Both Google and Yahoo know that fact and are actively pushing their respective Chinese search engines and other online offerings. To market "Google China," though, Google had to tailor its search engine to meet the Chinese government's censorship requirements. In China, almost all Web sites that criticize the government or provide information on sensitive topics are censored—that is, Web users in China cannot access them. Government agencies enforce the censorship and encourage citizens to inform on one another. Both Google and Yahoo (and Microsoft as well) share information, when requested, with the Chinese government. Yahoo China, for example, shared information about a journalist who wrote in support of prodemocratic protests. The Chinese government used the evidence obtained by that information-sharing process to convict the journalist of "leaking state secrets." She is now serving a ten-year prison sentence.

Google's code of conduct opens with the company's informal motto: "Don't be evil." Is Google really following this motto? Human rights groups do not think so. They maintain that the company is earning profits by assisting the Chinese Communist Party in suppress-

Chinese students navigate to underground Internet cafés despite the 2006 ban on such businesses by the Communist government.

ing free speech. During a congressional hearing on the issue, Congressman Tom Lantos (D., Calif.) said that the "sickening collaboration" with the Chinese government was "decapitating the voice of dissidence" in that nation.

Google and the others defend their actions. Google points out, for example, that its Chinese search engine at least lets users know which sites are being censored. Google claims that its approach is essentially the "lesser of two evils": if U.S. companies do not cooperate with the Chinese government, Chinese residents will have less user-friendly Internet access. Supporters of Google and Yahoo maintain, in addition, that even censored Internet access is a step toward more open access in the future because technology is, in itself, a revolutionary force.

EQUALITY The goal of **equality** has always been a central part of American political culture. Many of the first settlers came to this country to be free of unequal treatment and persecution. They sought the freedom to live and worship as they wanted. They believed that anyone who worked hard could succeed, and America became known as the "land of opportunity." The Declaration of Independence confirmed the importance of equality to early Americans by stating, "We hold these Truths to be self-evident, that all Men are created equal." Because of the goal of equality, the Constitution prohibited the government from granting titles of nobility. Article I, Section 9, of the Constitution states, "No Title of Nobility shall be granted by the United States." (The Constitution did not prohibit slavery, however—see Chapter 2.)

But what, exactly, does equality mean? Does it mean simply political equality—the right to vote and run for political office? Does it mean that individuals should have equal opportunities to develop their talents and skills? What about those who are poor, suffer from disabilities, or are otherwise at a competitive disadvantage? Should it be the government's responsibility to ensure that these groups also have equal opportunities? Although most Americans believe that all persons should have the opportunity to fulfill their potential, few contend that it is the government's responsibility to totally eliminate the economic and social differences that lead to unequal opportunities. Indeed, some contend that efforts to achieve equality, in the sense of equal justice for all, are misguided attempts to create an ideal society that can never exist.

> "The thing about **democracy**, beloveds, is that it is not neat, orderly, or quiet. It requires a certain relish for **confusion.**"
> — MOLLY IVINS, AMERICAN JOURNALIST 1944–2007

PROPERTY As noted earlier, the English philosopher John Locke asserted that people are born with "natural" rights and that among these rights are life, liberty, and *property*. The Declaration of Independence makes a similar assertion: people are born with certain "unalienable" rights, including the right to life, liberty, and the *pursuit of happiness*. For Americans, property and the pursuit of happiness are closely related. Americans place a great value on land ownership, on material possessions, and on the monetary value of their jobs. Property gives its owners political power and the liberty to do whatever they want—within limits.

An important limitation on the private ownership of land is set forth in the "takings clause" of the Fifth Amendment to the U.S. Constitution. That clause states that the government may take private property for *public use*, but on one condition: the government must pay the property owner "just compensation." This power of the government to take private property for public use is known as *eminent domain*.

Political Values in a Multicultural Society

From the earliest English and European settlers to the numerous cultural groups who today call America their home, American society has always been a multicultural society. Until recently, most Americans viewed the United States as the world's melting pot. They accepted that American society included numerous ethnic and cultural groups, but they expected that the members of these groups would abandon their cultural distinctions and assimilate the language and customs of Americans. One of the outgrowths of the civil rights movement of the 1960s, however, was an emphasis on

equality A concept that holds, at a minimum, that all people are entitled to equal protection under the law.

FIGURE 1-1

DISTRIBUTION OF THE U.S. POPULATION BY RACE AND HISPANIC ORIGIN, 1980 TO 2075

By about 2060, minorities will constitute a majority of the U.S. population.

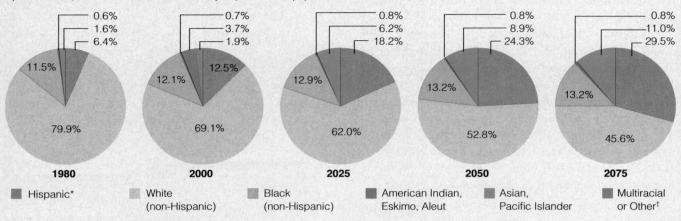

| Hispanic* | White (non-Hispanic) | Black (non-Hispanic) | American Indian, Eskimo, Aleut | Asian, Pacific Islander | Multiracial or Other† |

Data for 2025, 2050, and 2075 are projections.

*Persons of Hispanic origin can be of any race.
†The "multiracial or other" category in 2000 is not an official census category but represents all non-Hispanics who chose either "some other race" or two or more races in the 2000 census. This category has no official projections beyond 2000.
Source: U.S. Bureau of the Census.

multiculturalism, the belief that the many cultures that make up American society should remain distinct and be protected—and even encouraged—by our laws.

The ethnic makeup of the United States has changed dramatically in the last two decades, however, and will continue to change (see Figure 1–1). Already, whites are a minority in California. For the nation as a whole, non-Hispanic whites will be in the minority by the year 2060 or shortly thereafter. Some Americans fear that rising numbers of immigrants will threaten traditional American political values and culture.

Artistic Expression versus Equality

There are many competing political values in our society. Liberty, for one, involves freedom of expression and certainly freedom of artistic expression. Another value—equality—has resulted in a variety of laws prohibiting discrimination even when the parties involved are private individuals acting in their private capacities. There is constant tension between these two basic American political values that sometimes erupts into conflicts involving race, color, or national origin. An interesting debate arose in 2007 when PBS announced a seven-part series directed and produced by Ken Burns, the documentary filmmaker who brought us *The Civil War, Baseball,* and *Jazz.* His latest series, titled *The War,* tells a story of World War II as revealed by the personal accounts of a handful of women and men from four typical American towns.

How could freedom of expression run up against the political value of equality in this context? The answer lies in the lack of representation of minority groups in the documentary. Specifically, the Congressional Hispanic Caucus, the American GI Forum, and other Latino organizations attempted to get Burns to reedit his film. The documentary, according to them, "slights Hispanics' contributions to the war effort." Representative Joe Baca (D., Calif.) stated, "We will not settle for separate but equal treatment in this documentary."

Part of the funding for the documentary came from the federal government through the Corporation for Public Broadcasting via PBS. Nonetheless, neither PBS nor Ken Burns agreed to reedit the film. Burns pointed out that he was "looking for universal human experience of battle." He said that he "left out lots of people in many different kinds of groups, because we weren't looking at it in that way." As for PBS, it pointed out that the Public Broadcasting Act of 1967 guarantees the editorial independence of publicly funded national media.

Unemployed Americans wait in a "soup line" to obtain government aid during the Great Depression.

American Political Ideology

In a general sense, **ideology** refers to a system of political ideas. These ideas typically are rooted in religious or philosophical beliefs concerning human nature, society, and government. Generally, assumptions as to what the government's role should be with respect to basic values, such as liberty or equality, are important determinants of one's political ideology.

With respect to political ideology, Americans tend to fall into two broad political camps: liberals and conservatives. Originally, the term *liberal* was used to refer to someone who advocated change, new philosophies, and new ideas. The term *conservative* described a person who valued past customs and traditions that had proved their value over time. In today's American political arena, however, the terms *liberalism* and *conservatism* have both taken on additional meanings.

LIBERALISM   Modern **liberalism** in the United States traces its roots to the administration of Franklin D. Roosevelt (1933–1945). Roosevelt's New Deal programs, launched to counter the effects of the Great Depression, involved the government in the American economic sphere to an extent hitherto unknown. Thereafter, the word *liberalism* became associated with the concept of "big government" and government

intervention to aid economically disadvantaged groups and to promote equality.

Today's liberals continue to believe that the government has a responsibility to undertake social-welfare programs, at the taxpayers' expense, to assist the poor and the disadvantaged. Further, today's liberals believe that the national government should take steps to ensure that our civil rights and liberties are protected and that the government must look out for the interests of the individual against the majority. Liberals typically believe in the separation of church and state, and generally think that the government should not involve itself in the moral or religious life of the nation.

CONSERVATISM   Modern **conservatism** in this country can also trace its roots to the Roosevelt administration. Conservatives before that era, now generally referred to as the "old right," were primarily concerned with free competition in the marketplace and maintaining the freedom of corporations to do as they wished without government interference. They also opposed U.S. intervention in foreign affairs and resisted immigration. The Roosevelt administration, however, gave conservatives a

President Franklin D. Roosevelt signs legislation to expand federal government activities. The Roosevelt administration embodied modern liberalism and served as an example of what conservatives do not want— big government.

ideology Generally, a system of political ideas that are rooted in religious or philosophical beliefs concerning human nature, society, and government.

liberalism A set of political beliefs that includes the advocacy of active government, including government intervention to improve the welfare of individuals and to protect civil rights.

conservatism A set of beliefs that includes a limited role for the national government in helping individuals and in the economic affairs of the nation, support for traditional values and lifestyles, and a cautious response to change.

common cause: opposition to the New Deal and to big government. As one scholar noted, "No factor did more to stimulate the growth of modern conservatism than the election of Franklin Roosevelt. . . . He is the man conservatives most dislike, for he embodies the big-government ideology they most fear."[5]

As conservative ideology evolved in the latter half of the twentieth century, it incorporated a number of other elements in addition to the emphasis on free enterprise and antipathy toward big government. By the time of Ronald Reagan (1981–1989), conservatives came to be described as those who placed a high value on the principles of community, continuity, law and order, states' rights, family values, and individual initiative. Today's conservatives tend to fall into two basic categories: *economic conservatives* (those who seek to minimize government spending and intervention in the economy) and *social conservatives* (those, such as Christian evangelicals, who seek to incorporate religious and family values into politics and government).

The Traditional Political Spectrum

Traditionally, liberalism and conservatism have been regarded as falling within a political spectrum that ranges from the far left (extremely liberal) to the far right (extremely conservative). As Figure 1–2 illustrates, there is a close relationship between those holding liberal views and those identifying themselves politically as Democrats. Similarly, in terms of party affiliation and voting, conservatives tend to identify with the Republican Party.

MODERATES People whose views fall in the middle of the political spectrum are generally called **moderates**. Moderates rarely classify themselves as either liberal or conservative, and they

moderate A person whose views fall in the middle of the political spectrum.

radical left Persons on the extreme left side of the political spectrum who would like to significantly change the political order, usually to promote egalitarianism (human equality).

radical right Persons on the extreme right side of the political spectrum. The radical right includes reactionaries (who would like to return to the values and social systems of some previous era) and libertarians (who believe in no regulation of the economy or individual behavior, except for defense and law enforcement).

may vote for either Republicans or Democrats. Many moderates do not belong to either major political party and often describe themselves as *independent* (see Chapter 7).

THE EXTREME LEFT AND RIGHT On both ends of the political spectrum are those who espouse radical views. The **radical left** consists of those who would like significant changes to the political order, usually to promote egalitarianism (human equality). Often, members of the radical left do not wish to work within the established political processes to reach their goals. They may even accept or advocate using violence or overthrowing the government in order to obtain those goals. Socialists believe in equality and, usually, active government involvement in the economy to bring about this goal. Communists believe in total equality and base their beliefs on the political philosophy of Karl Marx (1818–1883).

Karl Marx.

The **radical right** includes reactionaries, those who wish to turn the clock back to some previous era when there weren't, for example, so many civil rights for the nation's minorities and women. Reactionaries strongly oppose liberal and progressive politics and resist political and social change. Like those on the radical left, members of the radical right may even advocate the use of violence to achieve their goals. A less extreme right-wing ideology is libertarianism. Libertarians believe in virtually total political and economic liberty for individuals and no government regulation of the economy or individual behavior (except for defense and law enforcement).

FIGURE 1–2
THE POLITICAL SPECTRUM

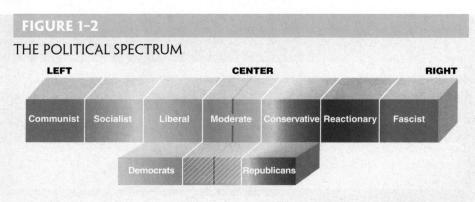

Politicians and political candidates represent numerous variations in the political spectrum. Hillary Clinton, a Democrat, has many different views than Rudy Giuliani, a Republican, although they share some positions, too.

Ideology and Today's Electorate

Those who hold strongly to political ideologies that are well thought out and internally coherent and consistent are called **ideologues.** Ideologues usually fit easily on one side or the other of the political spectrum. Most Americans, though, do not adhere firmly to a particular political ideology. They generally are not interested in all political issues and have a mixed set of opinions that do not neatly fit under a liberal or conservative label.

Keep in mind also that not all Democrats share all of the liberal views discussed earlier. A Democrat may be fiscally conservative (that is, against increased gov-ernment spending and involvement in the nation's economic affairs) on the one hand, but socially liberal on the other—or vice versa. Such a person may identify with the Democrats simply because, on the whole, the Democratic Party's positions on issues are more acceptable to him or her than those of the Republican Party. Republicans also do not constitute a cohesive group that is consistently in favor of a fixed array of political, social, and economic policy prescriptions. In sum, millions of Americans do not fit neatly into the liberal-conservative spectrum. Indeed, it is difficult to completely capture the diversity of combinations that exist in the American electorate with respect to political views and ideology.

ideologue An individual who holds very strong political opinions.

LO⁴ AMERICAN DEMOCRACY AT WORK

By now, you may have decided that Americans are at odds over every possible issue. But even the most divisive issues can be and are resolved through the political process. How does this process work? Who are the key players? These questions will be answered in the remaining chapters of this book. In the meantime, though, it is helpful to have some kind

One political institution created by the Constitution was the U.S. Senate, shown here. Today, one hundred senators debate on a regular basis in this room.

of a "road map" to guide you through these chapters so that you can see how each topic covered in the text relates to the big picture.

The Big Picture

The U.S. Constitution is the supreme law of the land. It sets forth basic governing rules by which Americans, when they ratified the Constitution, agreed to abide. It is appropriate, then, that we begin this text, following this introductory chapter, with a discussion of how and why the Constitution was created, the type of governing structure it established, and the rights and liberties it guarantees for all Americans. These topics, covered in Chapters 2 through 5, are necessarily the point of departure for any discussion of our system of government. As you will see, some of the most significant political controversies today have to do with how various provisions in this founding document should be applied, over two hundred years later, to modern-day events and issues.

Who Governs?

Who acquires the power and authority to govern, and how do they obtain that power and authority? Generally, of course, the "winners" in our political system are the successful candidates in elections. But the electoral process is influenced by more than just the issue positions taken by the candidates. As you read Chapters 6 through 10, keep the following questions in mind: How do interest groups influence elections? How essential are political parties to the electoral process? To

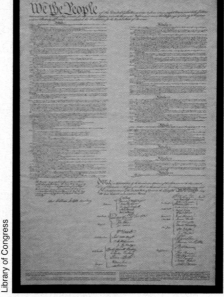

The Constitution.

Library of Congress

PhotoDisc

what extent do public opinion and voting behavior play a role in determining who the winners and losers will be? Why are political campaigns so expensive, and what are the implications of high campaign costs for our democracy? Finally, what role do the media, including the Internet, play in fashioning the outcomes of campaigns?

Once a winning candidate assumes a political office, that candidate becomes a part of one of the institutions of government. In Chapter 11 and the remaining chapters of this text, we examine these institutions and the process of government decision making. You will learn how those who govern the nation make laws and policies to decide "who gets what, when, and how" in our society. Of course, the topics treated in these chapters are not isolated from the materials covered earlier in the text. For example, when formulating and implementing federal policies, as well as state and local policies, the wishes of interest groups cannot be ignored, particularly those of wealthy groups that can help to fund policymakers' reelections. And public opinion and the media not only affect election outcomes but also influence which issues will be included on the policymaking agenda.

The political system established by the founders of this nation has endured for more than two hundred years. The challenge facing Americans now is how to make sure that it will continue to endure.

AMERICA AT ODDS:
The Contours of American Democracy

As you learned in this chapter, American citizens do not participate directly in making government decisions, as in a *direct democracy*. Rather, the people elect representatives to make such decisions. In Chapter 2, you will read about the founders' distaste for direct democracy. They feared that if "the masses" were directly involved in government decision making, the result would be instability, if not chaos. Indeed, the Constitution as originally written allowed citizens to vote only for members of the House of Representatives, not for members of the Senate. Senators were initially elected by their respective state legislatures. (The Seventeenth Amendment to the Constitution, which was adopted in 1913, changed this procedure, and Americans now vote directly for members of the Senate as well.) Even today, the president is not elected directly by the people, but by the electoral college, as will be explained in Chapter 9.

It is useful to compare the founders' intentions with today's practices because doing so helps us to assess whether and in what ways we have strayed from the founders' intentions. The final feature in each chapter of this text will look at the chapter topic in this light, in order to provide a better understanding of the current status of our democracy. In this first chapter-ending feature, we return to the important question raised in the opening *America at Odds* feature: Do we really have a representative democracy? Certainly, the founders could not have envisioned a Congress so strongly influenced by monied interests and party politics. Nor, in all likelihood, could they have foreseen the failure of so many of today's Americans to participate in our democracy. On average, only about half of the voting-age population actually turns out to vote. The conclusion is obvious: if Americans truly want a representative democracy, their participation in the political process is crucial. Our elected leaders cannot represent the people if the people do not let their opinions be known.

As you read through the pages of this book, you will see that Americans are at odds over numerous issues concerning this country's performance and leadership, including the issues presented next. You will also learn about how you can take part in political debate and action, and let your voice be heard. As President Dwight D. Eisenhower (1953–1961) once said, "politics ought to be the part-time profession of every citizen who would protect the rights and privileges of free people and who would preserve what is good and fruitful in our national heritage."

Issues for Debate & Discussion

1. Young Americans have the lowest voter-turnout rate in the country. Some maintain that this is because it is too difficult to vote—you have to register, get to the polling place, and then try to decipher the ballot. In contrast, to vote for the next American Idol, all you have to do is pick up the phone and dial a number. Some believe that if voting were made simpler, young Americans would turn out in greater numbers. Others believe America's youth stay away from the polls because they are disinterested in politics, if not alienated by the political system. What is your position on this issue?

2. Suppose that you are a representative in Congress. Public opinion polls show that nearly 70 percent of the voters in your district support a proposal to go to war with a Middle Eastern nation that harbors terrorists. You believe that such a war would be disastrous for the United States. In this situation, some would claim that because you were elected to represent your constituents' interests, you should vote for the war. Others would argue that you should vote as your conscience dictates, even if that is contrary to the wishes of your constituents or even the majority of Americans—and even if it means that you will not be reelected to Congress. What position do you take on this issue?

Take Action

From the time you are born until you reach your final resting place, government affects your everyday life. It affects your ability to express yourself freely, to join others to share like interests or to advocate a position on an issue that is important to you, to practice the religion of your choice (or not to practice any religion), and to exercise important rights if you are accused of a crime. Government decision making also affects the health and safety of our population, as well as the health of our environment.

Because our democracy is now more than two hundred years old, it is easy to assume that it will last forever. It is also easy to forget that the reason we still enjoy these rights and benefits is that whenever they have been threatened in the past, people have spoken out—they have taken action to remove the threat. Americans can take advantage of numerous methods to influence their society and their government. In the remaining chapters of this book, this *Take Action* section will give examples of how you can take action to make a difference when you are at odds with government policymakers on important issues.

POLITICS ON THE WEB

Each chapter of *America at Odds,* Sixth Edition, concludes with a list of Internet resources and addresses. Once you are on the Internet, you can use the addresses, or uniform resource locators (URLs), listed in the *Politics on the Web* sections in this book to access the ever-growing number of resources available on the Internet relating to American politics and government.

Internet sites tend to come and go, and there is no guarantee that a site included in a *Politics on the Web* feature will be there by the time this book is in print. We have tried, though, to include sites that have so far proved to be fairly stable. If you do have difficulty reaching a site, do not immediately assume that the site does not exist. First, recheck the URL shown in your browser. Remember, you have to type the URL exactly as written: upper case and lower case are important. If the URL appears to be keyed in correctly, then try the following technique: delete all of the information after the forward slash mark that is farthest to the right in the address, and press "enter." Sometimes, this will allow you to reach a home page from which you can link to the topic at issue.

A seemingly infinite number of sites on the Web offer information on American government and politics. A list of even the best sites would fill pages. For reasons of space, in this chapter and in those that follow, the *Politics on the Web* sections will include references to only a few selected sites. Following the links provided by these sites will take you to a host of others. The Web sites listed below all provide excellent points of departure for those who wish to learn more about American government and politics today.

- The U.S. government's "official" Web site offers extensive information on the national government and the services it provides for citizens. To access this site, go to **www.usa.gov**.

- This Nation is a nonpartisan site dealing with current political questions. To access this site, go to **www.thisnation.com**.

- To find news on the Web, you can go to the site of any major news organization or even your local newspaper. Links to online newspapers, both within the United States and in other countries, are available at **www.newspapers.com**.

- Additionally, CNN's Politics Web site offers a wealth of news, news analysis, polling data, and news articles dating back to 1996. Go to **www.cnn.com/POLITICS**.

- To learn how new computer and communications technologies are affecting the constitutional rights and liberties of Americans, go to the Web site of the Center for Democracy and Technology at **www.cdt.org**.

- The Pew Research Center for the People and the Press offers survey data online on a number of topics relating to American politics and government. The URL for the center's site is **people–press.org**.

- Yale University Library, one of the great research institutions, has an excellent collection of sources relating to American politics and government. Go to **www.library.yale.edu/socsci**.

ONLINE RESOURCES FOR THIS CHAPTER

This text's Companion Web site, at **www.americaatodds. com,** offers links to numerous resources that you can utilize to learn more about the topics covered in this chapter.

PODCASTS FLASHCARDS INTERACTIVE QUIZZES ONLINE POLLING VIDEO SIMULATOINS ANIMATED LEARNING

DO YOU WANT POLITICS TO GO?

AAO: POLITICS TO GO

Buy Now!

AAO: POLITICS TO GO

Turn to the back of the book to find your Politics to Go review card for this chapter

CHAPTER 2
THE CONSTITUTION

LEARNING OBJECTIVES

LO¹ Point out some of the influences on the American political tradition in the colonial years.

LO² Explain why the American colonies rebelled against Great Britain.

LO³ Describe the structure of government established by the Articles of Confederation and some of the strengths and weaknesses of the Articles.

LO⁴ List some of the major compromises made by the delegates at the Constitutional Convention, and discuss the Federalist and Anti-Federalist positions with respect to ratifying the Constitution.

LO⁵ Summarize the Constitution's major principles of government and how the Constitution can be amended.

AMERICA AT ODDS

Has the President Become Too Powerful?

Most of the founders did not want the new country to become another England with all of the power placed in a king. To prevent this, they came up with the ingenious political system that we have today. As you will read later in this chapter, this system divides the government's powers among three branches—the executive, legislative, and judicial branches of government. The founders also built into the Constitution a series of checks and balances, by which each branch of government could check the actions of the other two branches. Today, though, some people contend that the "imperial presidency" of George W. Bush made a mockery of our system of checks and balances. Those critical of Bush are convinced that he usurped too many powers for the presidency. Others are not so sure.

Under Bush, There Seem to Have Been No Limits

Georgetown University Law Center professor David Cole contends that, during the Bush administration, the constitutional principle most under attack was the separation of powers.[1] In the name of the war on terrorism, President Bush expanded the powers of the president at the expense of the other two branches of the federal government. In part, this expansion was due to the lack of any oversight or objections by the Republican-controlled Congress prior to 2007. Additionally, Bush extensively used *executive orders* (to be discussed in Chapter 12), which do not require congressional approval. He used such orders to extend his authority over much of what the executive branch of the government does. For example, a Bush executive order required that a Regulatory Policy Office be established in every federal agency. A political appointee headed this new office in each agency. Thus, all federal agencies had a "big brother" making sure that their rules and actions were consistent with the Bush administration's policies.

Consider also that Bush's executive branch attempted to "hijack" the Justice Department by firing U.S. attorneys for political reasons. Furthermore, Bush threatened our civil liberties, whittling away at our privacy rights and other constitutional liberties by monitoring phone and Internet use, collecting personal banking and other information, and conducting other data-mining operations involving personal information—and often exceeding the boundaries

of constitutional law while doing so. Of course, Bush justified many of his power-grabbing actions as necessary for the ongoing war on terrorism. In fact, most of our resources were going to fight the war in Iraq rather than the war on terrorism.

PRESIDENT BUSH WAS JUST DOING HIS JOB TO PROTECT AMERICANS

President Bush liked to call himself a "wartime president." And we continue to be in wartime—it's a war against those who would destroy America's way of life. Throughout history, all presidents in time of war have assumed extra powers. As the commander in chief, the president needs to be able to act swiftly and decisively. He has the inherent constitutional authority to do so.

According to some constitutional scholars, the president enjoys complete discretion in the exercise of his authority as commander in chief in conducting operations against hostile forces. Just as Congress cannot interfere with strategic and tactical decisions on the battlefield, it cannot interfere with the way the president is fighting the war on terrorism. In addition, what's wrong with an executive order establishing a Regulatory Policy Office in every federal agency? All presidents before Bush attempted to streamline the bureaucracy. Bush was just following in this long line of efforts to improve the government's functioning. Indeed, as of late 2007, there had been no serious terrorist actions on U.S. soil since September 11, 2001. What Bush was doing must have been working.

Where do you stand?

1. Typically, the expanded wartime powers of past presidents have ended with the termination of the military conflict. Do you think expanded presidential powers are justified in the war on terrorism that will never really have a definite termination date? Why or why not?
2. The president is the only nationally elected government official. How might this fact be used to justify an expansion of presidential power?

Explore this issue online

- President Richard Nixon (1969–1974) had strong beliefs in favor of expansive presidential powers. He was also forced to resign on threat of impeachment and conviction as a result of his actions while in office. You can read Nixon's justifications for broad presidential powers at **www.landmarkcases.org/nixon/nixonview.html**.
- For an extended argument against President George W. Bush's attempts to extend the powers of the president, see Elizabeth Drew's article in the *New York Review of Books* at **www.nybooks.com/articles/19092**.

AP Photo/Jacqueline Larma

Since September 11, 2001, there have been numerous changes to the way flights are handled, especially if they are foreign carriers coming from other countries. Many foreign airlines, at least for a while, had to have at least one armed law enforcement officer on board if they planned to land anywhere in the United States. The Department of Homeland Security has issued other directives, too.

INTRODUCTION

Whether President George W. Bush was exceeding his constitutional authority is just one of many debates concerning the government established by the U.S. Constitution. The Constitution, which was written more than two hundred years ago, continues to be the supreme law of the land. Time and again, its provisions have been adapted to the changing needs and conditions of society. The challenge before today's citizens and political leaders is to find a way to apply those provisions to an information age and to terrorist movements that could not possibly have been anticipated by the founders. Will the Constitution survive these challenges? Most Americans assume that it will—and with good reason: no other written constitution in the world today is as old as the U.S. Constitution. To understand why, you have to go back to the beginnings of our nation's history.

LO¹ THE BEGINNINGS OF AMERICAN GOVERNMENT

When the framers of the Constitution met in Philadelphia in 1787, they brought with them some valuable political assets. One asset was their English political heritage (see Chapter 1). Another was the hands-on political experience they had acquired during the colonial era. Their political knowledge and experience enabled them to establish a constitution that could meet not only the needs of their own time but also the needs of generations to come.

The American colonies were settled by individuals from many nations, including England, France, Holland, Norway, Spain, and Sweden. The majority of the colonists, though, came from England. The British colonies in North America were established by private individuals and private trading companies and were under the rule of the British Crown. The British colonies, which were located primarily along the Atlantic seaboard of today's United States, eventually numbered thirteen.

Although American politics owes much to the English political tradition, the colonists actually derived most of their understanding of social compacts, the rights of the people, limited government, and representative government from their own experiences. Years before Parliament adopted the English Bill of Rights or John Locke wrote his *Two Treatises on Government* (1690), the American colonists were putting the ideas expressed in those documents into practice.

John Locke (1632–1704), an English philosopher. Locke argued that human beings were equal and endowed by nature with certain rights, such as the right to life, liberty, and property. The purpose of government, according to Locke, was to protect those rights. Locke's theory of natural rights and his contention that government stemmed from a social contract among society's members were an important part of the political heritage brought to this country by the English colonists.

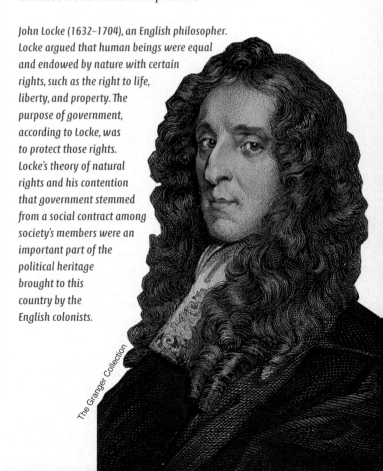

The Granger Collection

Library of Congress

This painting illustrates the Pilgrims aboard the Mayflower *signing the Mayflower Compact on November 11, 1620.*

The First British Settlements

In the 1580s, Sir Walter Raleigh convinced England's queen, Elizabeth I, to allow him to establish the first English outpost in North America on Roanoke Island, off the coast of what is now North Carolina. The attempted settlement was unsuccessful, however. The first permanent English settlement in North America was Jamestown, in what is now Virginia.[2] Jamestown was established in 1607 as a trading post of the Virginia Company of London.[3]

The first New England colony was founded by the Plymouth Company in 1620 at Plymouth, Massachusetts. The settlers at Plymouth, who called themselves Pilgrims, were a group of English Protestants who came to the New World on the ship *Mayflower*. Even before the Pilgrims went ashore, they drew up the **Mayflower Compact,** in which they set up a government and promised to obey its laws. The reason for the compact was that the group was outside the jurisdiction of the Virginia Company, which had arranged for them to settle in Virginia, not Massachusetts. Fearing that some of the passengers might decide that they were no longer subject to any rules of civil order, the leaders on board the *Mayflower* agreed that some form of governmental authority was necessary. The Mayflower Compact, which was essentially a social contract, has historical significance because it was the first of a series of similar contracts among the colonists to establish fundamental rules of government.[4]

Mayflower Compact A document drawn up by pilgrim leaders in 1620 on the ship *Mayflower*. The document stated that laws were to be made for the general good of the people.

Bill of Rights The first ten amendments to the U.S. Constitution. They list the freedoms—such as the freedoms of speech, press, and religion—that a citizen enjoys and that cannot be infringed on by the government.

The Massachusetts Bay Colony was established as another trading outpost in New England in 1630. In 1639, some of the Pilgrims at Plymouth, who felt that they were being persecuted by the Massachusetts Bay Colony, left Plymouth and settled in what is now Connecticut. They developed America's first written constitution, which was called the Fundamental Orders of Connecticut. This document called for the laws to be made by an assembly of elected representatives from each town. The document also provided for the popular election of a governor and judges. Other colonies, in turn, established fundamental governing rules. The Massachusetts Body of Liberties protected individual rights. The Pennsylvania Frame of Government, passed in 1682, and the Pennsylvania Charter of Privileges of 1701 established principles that were later expressed in the U.S. Constitution and **Bill of Rights** (the first ten amendments to the Constitution). By 1732, all thirteen colonies had been established, each with its own political documents and a constitution (see Figure 2–1).

Colonial Legislatures

As mentioned, the British colonies in America were all under the rule of the British monarchy. Britain, however, was thousands of miles away (it took two months to sail across the Atlantic). Thus, to a significant extent, colonial legislatures carried on the "nuts and bolts" of colonial government. These legislatures, or *representative assemblies,* consisted of representatives elected by

FIGURE 2-1

THE THIRTEEN COLONIES

Georgia, the last of the thirteen colonies, was established in 1732. By this time, each of the thirteen colonies had developed its own political system, complete with necessary political documents and a constitution.

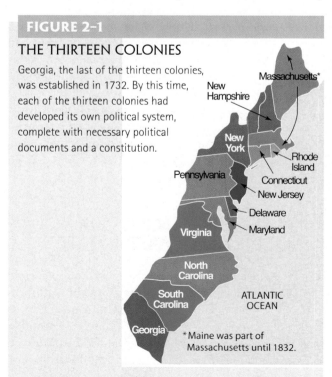

New Hampshire
Massachusetts*
New York
Rhode Island
Pennsylvania
Connecticut
New Jersey
Delaware
Maryland
Virginia
North Carolina
South Carolina
Georgia
ATLANTIC OCEAN

*Maine was part of Massachusetts until 1832.

the colonists. The earliest colonial legislature was the Virginia House of Burgesses, established in 1619. By the time of the American Revolution, all of the colonies had representative assemblies, many of which had been in existence for more than a hundred years.

Through their participation in colonial governments, the colonists gained crucial political experience. Colonial leaders became familiar with the practical problems of governing. They learned how to build coalitions among groups with diverse interests and how to make compromises. Indeed, according to Yale University professor Jon Butler, by the time of the American Revolution in 1776 Americans had formed a complex, sophisticated political system. They had also created a wholly new type of society characterized by, among other things, ethnic and religious diversity.[5] Because of their political experiences, the colonists were quickly able to set up their own constitutions and state systems of government—and eventually a new national government—after they declared their independence from Great Britain in 1776.

LO² THE REBELLION OF THE COLONISTS

Scholars of the American Revolution point out that, by and large, the American colonists did not want to become independent of Great Britain. For the majority of the colonists, Britain was the homeland, and ties of loyalty to the British monarch were strong. Why, then, did the colonists revolt against Britain and declare their independence? What happened to sever the political, economic, and emotional bonds that tied the colonists to Britain? The answers to these questions lie in a series of events in the mid-1700s that culminated in a change in British policy with respect to the colonies. Table 2–1 shows the chronology of the major political events in early U.S. political history.

One of these events was the Seven Years' War (1756–1763) between Britain and France, which Americans often refer to as the French and Indian War. The British victory in the Seven Years' War permanently altered the relationship between Britain and its American colonies. After successfully ousting the French from North America, the British expanded their authority over the colonies. To pay its war debts and to finance the defense of its expanded North American empire, Britain needed revenues. The British government decided to obtain some of these revenues by imposing taxes on the American colonists and exercising more direct control over colonial trade. At the same time, Americans

TABLE 2-1

SIGNIFICANT EVENTS IN EARLY U.S. POLITICAL HISTORY

1585	English outpost set up in Roanoke.
1607	Jamestown established; Virginia Company lands settlers.
1620	Mayflower Compact signed.
1630	Massachusetts Bay Colony set up.
1639	Fundamental Orders of Connecticut adopted.
1641	Massachusetts Body of Liberties adopted.
1682	Pennsylvania Frame of Government passed.
1701	Pennsylvania Charter of Privileges written.
1732	Last of thirteen colonies established.
1756	French and Indian War declared.
1765	Stamp Act; Stamp Act Congress meets.
1773	Boston Tea Party.
1774	First Continental Congress.
1775	Second Continental Congress; Revolutionary War begins.
1776	Declaration of Independence signed.
1777	Articles of Confederation drafted.
1781	Last state signs Articles of Confederation.
1783	"Critical period" in U.S. history begins; weak national government until 1789.
1786	Shays' Rebellion.
1787	Constitutional Convention.
1788	Ratification of Constitution.
1791	Ratification of Bill of Rights.

were beginning to distrust the expanding British presence in the colonies. Additionally, having fought alongside British forces, Americans thought that they deserved more credit for the victory. The British, however, attributed the victory solely to their own war effort.

Furthermore, the colonists began to develop a sense of identity separate from the British. Americans were shocked at the behavior of some of the British soldiers and the cruel punishments meted out to enforce discipline among the British troops. The British, in turn, had little good to say about the colonists with whom they had fought, considering them brutish, uncivilized, and undisciplined. It was during this time that the colonists began to use the word *American* to describe themselves.

"Taxation without Representation"

In 1764, in an effort to obtain needed revenues, the British Parliament passed the Sugar Act, which imposed a tax on all sugar imported into the American colonies. Some colonists, particularly in Massachusetts, vigorously opposed this tax and proposed a boycott of certain British imports. This boycott launched a "nonimportation" movement that soon spread to other colonies.

THE STAMP ACT OF 1765 The following year, Parliament passed the Stamp Act, which imposed the first direct tax on the colonists. Under the act, all legal documents, newspapers, and other items, including playing cards and dice, had to use specially embossed (stamped) paper that was purchased from the government.

The Stamp Act generated even stronger resentment among the colonists than the Sugar Act had aroused. James Otis, Jr., a Massachusetts attorney, declared that there could be "no taxation without representation." The American colonists could not vote in British elections and therefore were not represented in the British Parliament. They viewed Parliament's attempts to tax them as contrary to the principle of representative government. The British saw the matter differently. From the British perspective, it was only fair that the colonists pay taxes to help support the costs incurred by the British government in defending its American territories and maintaining the troops that were permanently stationed in the colonies following the Seven Years' War.

In October 1765, nine of the thirteen colonies sent delegates to the Stamp Act Congress in New York City. The delegates prepared a declaration of rights and grievances, which they sent to King George III. This action marked the first time that a majority of the colonies had joined together to oppose British rule. The British Parliament repealed the Stamp Act.

FURTHER TAXES AND THE COERCIVE ACTS Soon, however, Parliament passed new laws designed to bind the colonies more tightly to the central government in London. Laws that imposed taxes on glass, paint, lead, and many other items were passed in 1767. The colonists protested by boycotting all British goods. In 1773, anger over taxation reached a powerful climax at the Boston Tea Party, in which colonists dressed as Mohawk Indians dumped almost 350 chests of British tea into Boston Harbor as a gesture of tax protest.

The British Parliament was quick to respond to the Tea Party. In 1774, Parliament passed the Coercive Acts (sometimes called the "Intolerable Acts"), which closed the harbor and placed the government of Massachusetts under direct British control.

The Continental Congresses

In response to the "Intolerable Acts," Rhode Island, Pennsylvania, and New York proposed a colonial congress. The Massachusetts House of Representatives requested that all colonies select delegates to send to Philadelphia for such a congress.

First Continental Congress The first gathering of delegates from twelve of the thirteen colonies, held in 1774.

During the so-called Boston Tea Party in 1773, the colonists dumped chests of British tea into Boston Harbor as a gesture of tax protest.

THE FIRST CONTINENTAL CONGRESS The **First Continental Congress** met on September 5, 1774, at Carpenter's Hall in Philadelphia. Of the thirteen colonies, only Georgia did not participate. The First Continental Congress decided that the colonies should send a petition to King George III to explain their grievances, which they did. The congress also passed other resolutions continuing the boycott of British goods and requiring each colony to establish an army.

To enforce the boycott and other trading sanctions against Britain, the delegates to the First Continental Congress urged that "a committee be chosen in every county, city and town, by those who are qualified to vote for representatives in the legislature, whose business it shall be attentively to observe the conduct of all persons." Over the next several months, all colonial legislators supported this action. The committees of "safety" or "observation," as they were called, organized militias, held special courts, and suppressed the opinions of those who remained loyal to the British Crown. Committee members spied on neighbors' activities and reported to the press the names of those who violated the trading sanctions against Britain. The names were then printed in the local papers, and the transgressors were harassed and ridiculed in their communities.

THE SECOND CONTINENTAL CONGRESS Almost immediately after receiving the petition, the British government condemned the actions of the First Continental Congress as open acts of rebellion. Britain responded with even stricter and more repressive measures. On April 19, 1775, British soldiers (Redcoats) fought with colonial citizen soldiers (Minutemen) in the towns of Lexington and Concord in Massachusetts, the first battles of the American Revolution. The battle at Concord was memorialized by the poet Ralph Waldo Emerson as the "shot

Patrick Henry addressing the Virginia Assembly in the spring of 1775. His passionate speech in favor of independence concluded with the words, "Give me liberty or give me death!"—which became the battle cry of the Revolution.

heard round the world." Less than a month later, delegates from all thirteen colonies gathered in Pennsylvania for the **Second Continental Congress,** which immediately assumed the powers of a central government. The Second Continental Congress declared that the militiamen who had gathered around Boston were now a full army. It also named George Washington, a delegate to the Second Continental Congress who had some military experience, as its commander in chief.

The delegates to the Second Continental Congress still intended to reach a peaceful settlement with the British Parliament. One declaration stated specifically that "we [the congress] have not raised armies with ambitious designs of separating from Great Britain, and establishing independent States." The continued attempts to effect a reconciliation with Britain, even after the outbreak of fighting, underscore the colonists' reluctance to sever their relationship with the home country. As one scholar put it, "Of all the world's colonial peoples, none became rebels more reluctantly than did Anglo-Americans in 1776."[6]

Breaking the Ties: Independence

Public debate about the problems with Great Britain continued to rage, but the stage had been set for declaring independence. One of the most rousing arguments in favor of independence was presented by Thomas Paine, a former English schoolmaster and corset maker,[7] who wrote a pamphlet called *Common Sense.* In that pamphlet, which was published in Philadelphia in January 1776, Paine addressed the crisis using "simple fact, plain argument, and common sense." He mocked King George III and attacked every argument that favored loyalty to the king. He called the king a "royal

brute" and a "hardened, sullen-tempered Pharaoh [Egyptian king in ancient times]."[8]

Paine's writing went beyond a personal attack on the king. He contended that America could survive economically on its own and no longer needed its British connection. He wanted the developing colonies to become a model nation for democracy in a world in which other nations were oppressed by strong central governments.

None of Paine's arguments was new; in fact, most of them were commonly heard in tavern debates throughout the land. Instead, it was the pungency and eloquence of Paine's words that made *Common Sense* so effective:

> A government of our own is our natural right: and when a man seriously reflects on the precariousness of human affairs, he will become convinced, that it is infinitely wiser and safer, to form a constitution of our own in a cool and deliberate manner, while we have it in our power, than to trust such an interesting event to time and chance.[9]

Many historians regard Paine's *Common Sense* as the single most important publication of the American Revolution. The pamphlet became a best seller; more than 100,000 copies were sold within a few months after its publication.[10] It put independence squarely on the agenda. Above all, *Common Sense* severed the remaining ties of loyalty to the British monarch, thus

Second Continental Congress The congress of the colonies that met in 1775 to assume the powers of a central government and to establish an army.

Thomas Paine (1737–1809). In addition to his successful pamphlet Common Sense, *Paine also wrote a series of sixteen pamphlets, under the title* The Crisis, *during the American Revolution. He returned to England and, in 1791 and 1792, wrote* The Rights of Man, *in which he defended the French Revolution. Paine returned to the United States in 1802.*

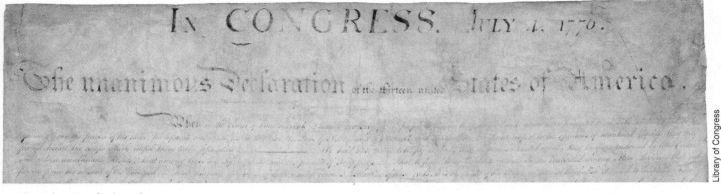

The Declaration of Independence.

removing the final psychological barrier to independence. Indeed, later John Adams would ask,

> What do we mean by the Revolution? The War? That was no part of the Revolution. It was only an effect and consequence of it. The Revolution was in the minds of the people, and this was effected, from 1760 to 1775, in the course of fifteen years before a drop of blood was drawn at Lexington.[11]

INDEPENDENCE FROM BRITAIN—THE FIRST STEP

By June 1776, the Second Continental Congress had voted for free trade at all American ports for all countries except Britain. The congress had also suggested that all colonies establish state governments separate from Britain. The colonists realized that a formal separation from Great Britain was necessary if the new nation was to obtain supplies for its armies and commitments of military aid from foreign governments. On June 7, 1776, the first formal step toward independence was taken when Richard Henry Lee of Virginia placed the following resolution before the congress:

> RESOLVED, That these United Colonies are, and of right ought to be, free and independent States, that they are absolved from allegiance to the British Crown, and that all political connection between them and the state of Great Britain is, and ought to be, totally dissolved.

The congress postponed consideration of Lee's resolution until a formal statement of independence could be drafted. On June 11, a "Committee of Five" was appointed to draft a declaration that would present to the world the colonies' case for independence.

THE DECLARATION OF INDEPENDENCE

A member of the Committee of Five, Thomas Jefferson drafted the declaration in just under three weeks. After two other committee members, Benjamin Franklin and John Adams, had made some changes to the document, it was submitted to the congress for consideration on July 2. On that day, the congress adopted Lee's resolution of independence and immediately began consid-

ering the draft of the Declaration of Independence. Further alterations were made to the document, and it was formally adopted on the afternoon of July 4, 1776.

THE SIGNIFICANCE OF THE DECLARATION OF INDEPENDENCE

The Declaration of Independence is one of the world's most famous documents. Like Paine, Thomas Jefferson, who wrote most of the document, elevated the dispute between Britain and the American colonies to a universal level. Jefferson opened the second paragraph of the declaration with the following words, which have since been memorized by countless American schoolchildren and admired the world over:

> We hold these Truths to be self-evident, that all Men are created equal, that they are endowed by their Creator with certain unalienable Rights, that among these are Life, Liberty, and the Pursuit of Happiness—That to secure these Rights, Governments are instituted among Men, deriving their just Powers from the Consent of the Governed, that whenever any Form of Government becomes destructive of these Ends, it is the Right of the People to alter or to abolish it, and to institute new Government.

The concepts expressed in the Declaration of Independence clearly reflect Jefferson's familiarity with

The committee chosen to draft a declaration of independence is shown at work in this nineteenth-century engraving. They are, from the left, Benjamin Franklin, Thomas Jefferson, John Adams, Philip Livingston, and Roger Sherman.

European political philosophy, particularly the works of John Locke.[12] Locke's philosophy, though it did not cause the American Revolution, provided the philosophical underpinnings by which it could be justified.

FROM COLONIES TO STATES Even before the Declaration of Independence, some of the colonies had transformed themselves into sovereign states with their own permanent governments. In May 1776, the Second Continental Congress had directed each of the colonies to form "such government as shall . . . best be conducive to the happiness and safety of their constituents [those represented by the government]." Before long, all thirteen colonies had created constitutions. Eleven of the colonies had completely new constitutions; the other two colonies, Rhode Island and Connecticut, made minor modifications to old royal charters. Seven of the new constitutions contained bills of rights that defined the personal liberties of all state citizens. All constitutions called for limited governments.

Many citizens were fearful of a strong central government because of their recent experiences under the British Crown. They opposed any form of government that resembled monarchy in any way. Consequently, wherever such antiroyalist sentiment was strong, the legislature—composed of elected representatives—itself became all-powerful. In Pennsylvania and Georgia, for example, **unicameral** (one-chamber) **legislatures** were unchecked by any executive authority. Indeed, antiroyalist sentiment was so strong that the executive branch was extremely weak in all thirteen states. This situation would continue until the ratification of the U.S. Constitution.

LO³ THE CONFEDERATION OF STATES

Antiroyalist sentiments also influenced the thinking of the delegates to the Second Continental Congress, who formed a committee to draft a plan of confederation. A **confederation** is a voluntary association of *independent* states (see Chapter 3). The member states agree to let the central government undertake a limited number of activities, such as forming

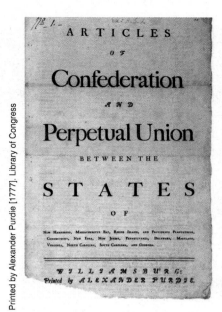

Printed by Alexander Purdie [1777]. Library of Congress

The Articles of Confederation, signed by all thirteen colonies on March 1, 1781, was America's first national constitution.

an army, but the states do not allow the central government to place many restrictions on the states' own actions. The member states typically can still govern most state affairs as they see fit.

On November 15, 1777, the Second Continental Congress agreed on a draft of the plan, which was finally signed by all thirteen colonies on March 1, 1781. The **Articles of Confederation,** the result of this plan, served as this nation's first national constitution and represented an important step in the creation of our governmental system.[13]

The Articles of Confederation established the Congress of the Confederation as the central governing body. This congress was a unicameral assembly of representatives, or ambassadors, as they were called, from the various states. Although each state could send anywhere from two to seven representatives to the congress, each state, no matter what its size, had only one vote. The issue of sovereignty was an important part of the Articles of Confederation:

> Each State retains its sovereignty, freedom, and independence, and every power, jurisdiction, and right, which is not by this Confederation expressly delegated to the United States in Congress assembled.

The structure of government under the Articles of Confederation is shown in Figure 2–2 on the next page.

Powers of the Government of the Confederation

Congress had several powers under the Articles of Confederation, and these enabled the new nation to achieve a number of accomplishments. The Northwest Ordinance settled states' claims to western lands and established a basic pattern for the government of new territories. Also, the 1783 peace treaty negotiated with Great Britain granted to the United States all

unicameral legislature
A legislature with only one chamber.

confederation A league of independent states that are united only for the purpose of achieving common goals.

Articles of Confederation
The nation's first national constitution, which established a national form of government following the American Revolution. The Articles provided for a confederal form of government in which the central government had few powers.

FIGURE 2-2

AMERICAN GOVERNMENT UNDER THE ARTICLES OF CONFEDERATION

STATES

★ Retained their independent political authority.
★ Held every power not expressly delegated to Congress.

Each state sent two to seven representatives.

PRESIDENT

★ Appointed by Congress to preside over meetings.
★ Had no real executive authority.

CONGRESS

★ One-house assembly of state representatives, in which each state possessed one vote.
★ Needed the approval of at least nine states to exercise most powers.
★ Needed the consent of all states to amend the Articles.

COMMITTEE OF STATES

★ Consisted of one delegate from each state, appointed by Congress.
★ Authorized to act according to the wishes of Congress while Congress was in recess.

CIVIL COMMITTEES AND CIVIL OFFICERS

★ Appointed by Congress to manage general affairs under the direction of Congress.

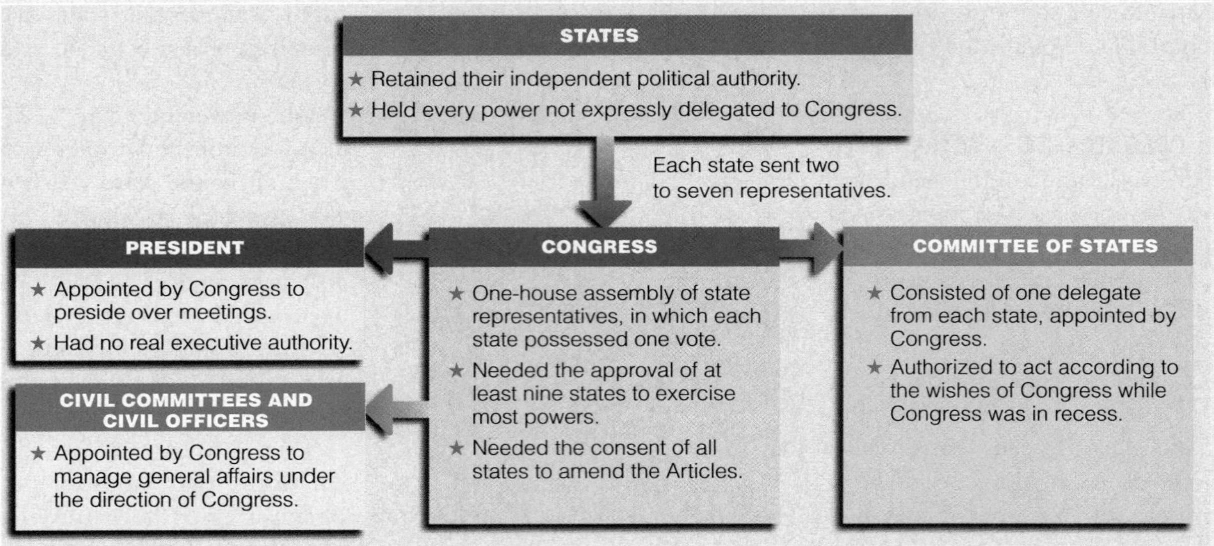

FIGURE 2-3

POWERS OF THE CENTRAL GOVERNMENT UNDER THE ARTICLES OF CONFEDERATION

Although the Articles of Confederation were later scrapped, they did allow the early government of the United States to achieve several important goals, including winning the Revolutionary War.

WHAT THE CONGRESS COULD DO	ACCOMPLISHMENT
Congress could establish and control the armed forces, declare war, and make peace.	The United States won the Revolutionary War.
Congress could enter into treaties and alliances.	Congress negotiated a peace treaty with Great Britain.
Congress could settle disputes among the states under certain circumstances.	Congress passed the Northwest Ordinance, which settled certain states' land claims.
Congress could regulate coinage (but not paper money) and set standards for weights and measures.	Congress carried out these functions, but the inability to regulate paper money proved a major weakness.
Congress could borrow money from the people.	Congress did borrow money, but without the power to tax, it had trouble repaying the loans or obtaining new ones.
Congress could create a postal system, courts to address issues related to ships at sea, and government departments.	Congress created a postal system and departments of foreign affairs, finance, and war.

of the territory from the Atlantic Ocean to the Mississippi River and from the Great Lakes and Canada to what is now northern Florida (see Figure 2–3).

In spite of these accomplishments, the central government created by the Articles of Confederation was, in fact, quite weak. The Congress of the Confederation had no power to raise revenues for the militia or to force the states to meet military quotas. Essentially, this meant that the new government did not have the power to enforce its laws. Even passing laws was difficult because the Articles of Confederation provided that nine states had to approve any law before it was enacted.[14] Figure 2–4 lists these and other powers that the central government lacked under the Articles of Confederation.

Nonetheless, the Articles of Confederation proved to be a good "first draft" for the Constitution, and at least half of the text of the Articles would later appear in the Constitution. The Articles were an unplanned experiment that tested some of the principles of government that had been set forth earlier in the Declaration of Independence. Some argue that without the experience of government under the Articles of Confederation, it would have been difficult, if not impossible, to arrive at the compromises that were necessary to create the Constitution several years later.

A Time of Crisis— The 1780s

The Revolutionary War ended on October 18, 1781. The Treaty of Paris, which confirmed the colonies' independence from Britain, was signed in 1783. Peace with the British may have been won, but peace within the new nation was hard to find. The states bickered among themselves and refused to support the new central government in almost every way. As George Washington stated, "We are one nation today and thirteen tomorrow. Who will treat us on such terms?"

The states also increasingly taxed each other's imports and at times even prevented trade altogether. By 1784, the new nation was suffering from a serious economic depression. States started printing their own money at dizzying rates, which led to inflation. Banks were calling in old loans and refusing to issue new ones. Individuals who could not pay their debts were often thrown into prison.

FIGURE 2-4

POWERS THAT THE CENTRAL GOVERNMENT LACKED UNDER THE ARTICLES OF CONFEDERATION

The government's lack of certain powers under the Articles of Confederation taught the framers of the Constitution several important lessons, which helped them create a more effective government under that new document.

WHAT THE CONGRESS COULD NOT DO	RESULT
Congress could not force the states to meet military quotas.	The central government could not draft soldiers to form a standing army.
Congress could not regulate commerce between the states or with other nations.	Each state was free to set up its own system of taxes on goods imported from other states. Economic quarrels among the states broke out. There was difficulty in trading with other nations.
Congress could enter into treaties but could not enforce its power or control foreign relations.	The states were not forced to respect treaties. Many states entered into treaties independent of Congress.
Congress could not directly tax the people.	The central government had to rely on the states to collect and forward taxes, which the states were reluctant to do. The central government was always short of money.
Congress had no power to enforce its laws.	The central government depended on the states to enforce its laws, which they rarely did.
Nine states had to approve any law before it was enacted.	Most laws were difficult, if not impossible, to enact.
Any amendment to the Articles required all thirteen states to consent.	In practice, the powers of the central government could not be changed.
There was no national judicial system.	Most disputes among the states could not be settled by the central government.
There was no executive branch.	Coordinating the work of the central government was almost impossible.

SHAYS' REBELLION The tempers of angry farmers in western Massachusetts reached the boiling point in August 1786. Former Revolutionary War captain Daniel Shays, along with approximately two thousand armed farmers, seized county courthouses and disrupted the debtors' trials. Shays and his men then launched an attack on the national government's arsenal in Springfield. **Shays' Rebellion** continued to grow in intensity and lasted into the winter, when it was finally stopped by the Massachusetts volunteer army, paid by private funds.[15]

Similar disruptions occurred throughout most of the New England states and in some other areas as well. The upheavals, and particularly Shays' Rebellion, were an important catalyst for change. The revolts scared American political and business leaders and caused more and more Americans to realize that a *true* national government had to be created.

Shays' Rebellion A rebellion of angry farmers in western Massachusetts in 1786, led by former Revolutionary War captain Daniel Shays. This rebellion and other similar uprisings in the New England states emphasized the need for a true national government.

THE ANNAPOLIS MEETING The Virginia legislature called for a meeting of representatives from all of the states at Annapolis, Maryland, on September 11, 1786, to address the problems facing the nation. Five of the thirteen states sent delegates, two of whom were Alexander Hamilton of New York and James Madison of Virginia. Both of these men favored a strong central government.[16] They persuaded the other delegates to issue a report calling on the states to hold a convention in Philadelphia in May of the following year.

The Congress of the Confederation at first was reluctant to give its approval to the Philadelphia convention. By mid-February 1787, however, seven of the states had named delegates to the Philadelphia meeting. Finally, on February 21, the congress

Constitutional Convention The convention (meeting) of delegates from the states that was held in Philadelphia in 1787 for the purpose of amending the Articles of Confederation. In fact, the delegates wrote a new constitution (the U.S. Constitution) that established a federal form of government to replace the governmental system that had been created by the Articles of Confederation.

Library of Congress

The signing of the Constitution.

called on the states to send delegates to Philadelphia "for the sole and express purpose of revising the Articles of Confederation." That Philadelphia meeting became the **Constitutional Convention.**

LO⁴ DRAFTING AND RATIFYING THE CONSTITUTION

Although the convention was supposed to start on May 14, 1787, few of the delegates had actually arrived in Philadelphia on that date. The convention formally opened in the East Room of the Pennsylvania State House on May 25, after fifty-five of the seventy-four delegates had arrived.[17] Only Rhode Island, where feelings were strong against creating a more powerful central government, did not send any delegates.

Who Were the Delegates?

Among the delegates to the Constitutional Convention were some of the nation's best-known leaders. George Washington was present, as were Alexander Hamilton, James Madison, George Mason, Robert Morris, and Benjamin Franklin (then eighty-one years old), who had to be carried to the convention on a portable chair. Some notable leaders were absent, including Thomas Jefferson and John Adams, who were serving as ambassadors in Europe, and Patrick Henry, who did not attend because he "smelt a rat." (Henry favored local government and was wary that the convention might favor a stronger central government.)

For the most part, the delegates were from the best-educated and wealthiest classes. Thirty-three delegates were lawyers, nearly half of the delegates were college graduates, three were physicians, seven were former chief executives of their respective states, six owned large

James Madison (1751–1836). Madison's contributions at the Constitutional Convention in 1787 earned him the title "Master Builder of the Constitution." As a member of Congress from Virginia, he advocated the Bill of Rights. He was secretary of state under Thomas Jefferson (1801–1809) and became our fourth president in 1809.

Library of Congress

plantations, at least nineteen owned slaves, eight were important business owners, and twenty-one had fought in the Revolutionary War. In other words, the delegates to the convention constituted an elite assembly. No ordinary farmers or merchants were present. Indeed, in his classic work on the Constitution, Charles Beard maintained that the Constitution was produced primarily by wealthy property owners who wanted a stronger government that could protect their property rights.[18]

The Virginia Plan

James Madison had spent months reviewing European political theory before he went to the Philadelphia convention. His Virginia delegation arrived before anybody else, and he immediately put its members to work. On the first day of the convention, Governor Edmund Randolph of Virginia was able to present fifteen resolutions outlining what was to become known as the *Virginia Plan*. This was a masterful political stroke on the part of the Virginia delegation. Its proposals immediately set the agenda for the remainder of the convention.

The fifteen resolutions contained in the Virginia Plan proposed an entirely new national government under a constitution. The plan, which favored large states such as Virginia, called for the following:

- A bicameral legislature. The lower house was to be chosen by the people. The smaller upper house was to be chosen by the elected members of the lower house. The number of representatives would be in proportion to each state's population (the larger states would have more representatives). The legislature could void any state laws.
- A national executive branch, elected by the legislature.
- A national court system, created by the legislature.

The smaller states immediately complained because they would have fewer representatives in the legislature. After two weeks of debate, they offered their own plan—the *New Jersey Plan*.

The New Jersey Plan

William Paterson of New Jersey presented an alternative plan favorable to the smaller states. He argued that because each state had an equal vote under the Articles of Confederation, the convention had no power to change this arrangement. The New Jersey Plan proposed the following:

- Congress would be able to regulate trade and impose taxes.
- Each state would have only one vote.
- Acts of Congress would be the supreme law of the land.
- An executive office of more than one person would be elected by Congress.
- The executive office would appoint a national supreme court.

"WE THE PEOPLE OF THE UNITED STATES . . . DO ORDAIN AND ESTABLISH THIS CONSTITUTION FOR THE UNITED STATES OF AMERICA."

FROM THE PREAMBLE TO THE U.S. CONSTITUTION

The Compromises

Most delegates were unwilling to consider the New Jersey Plan. When the Virginia Plan was brought up again, delegates from the smaller states threatened to leave, and the convention was in danger of dissolving. On July 16, Roger Sherman of Connecticut broke the deadlock by proposing a compromise plan. Compromises on other disputed issues followed.

THE GREAT COMPROMISE Roger Sherman's plan, which has become known as the **Great Compromise** (or the Connecticut Compromise), called for a legislature with two houses:

- A lower house (the House of Representatives), in which the number of representatives from each state would be determined by the number of people in that state.
- An upper house (the Senate), which would have two members from each state; the members would be elected by the state legislatures.

The Great Compromise gave something to both sides: the large states would have more representatives in the House of Representatives than the small states, yet each state would be granted equality in the Senate—because each state, regardless of size, would have two senators. The Great Compromise thus resolved the small-state/large-state controversy.

Great Compromise A plan for a bicameral legislature in which one chamber would be based on population and the other chamber would represent each state equally. The plan, also known as the Connecticut Compromise, resolved the small-state/large-state controversy.

THE THREE-FIFTHS COMPROMISE   A second compromise had to do with how many representatives each state would have in the House of Representatives. Although slavery was legal in parts of the North, most slaves and slave owners lived in the South. Indeed, in the southern states, slaves constituted about 40 percent of the population. Counting the slaves as part of the population would thus greatly increase the number of southern representatives in the House. The delegates from the southern states wanted the slaves to be counted as persons; the delegates from the northern states disagreed. Eventually, the **three-fifths compromise** settled this deadlock: each slave would count as three-fifths of a person in determining representation in Congress. (The three-fifths compromise was eventually overturned in 1868 by the Fourteenth Amendment, Section 2.)

SLAVE IMPORTATION   The three-fifths compromise did not satisfy everyone at the Constitutional Convention. Many delegates wanted slavery to be banned completely in the United States. The delegates compromised on this question by agreeing that Congress could not prohibit the importation of slaves into the country until the year 1808. The issue of slavery itself, however, was never really addressed by the delegates to the Constitutional Convention. As a result, the South won twenty years of unrestricted slave trade and a requirement that escaped slaves who had fled to the northern states be returned to their owners. Domestic slave trading was untouched.

BANNING EXPORT TAXES   The South's economic health depended in large part on its exports of agricultural products. The South feared that the northern majority in Congress might pass taxes on these exports. This fear led to yet another compromise: the South agreed to let Congress have the power to regulate **interstate commerce** as well as commerce with other nations; in exchange, the Constitution guaranteed that no export taxes would ever be imposed on products exported by the states. Today, the United States is one of the few countries that does not tax its exports.

three-fifths compromise
A compromise reached during the Constitutional Convention by which it was agreed that three-fifths of all slaves were to be counted for purposes of representation in the House of Representatives.

interstate commerce   Trade that involves more than one state.

The Final Draft Is Approved

The Great Compromise was reached by mid-July. Still to be determined was the makeup of the executive branch and

The Granger Collection

This woodcut of slaves before the Civil War shows the slave overseer with a whip in his hand. During the fifteenth and sixteenth centuries, the British, French, Dutch, Spanish, and Portuguese engaged in a brutal slave trade along the African coast. Slaves were first brought to Virginia in 1619. Britain outlawed the slave trade in 1807 and abolished slavery in the entire British Empire in 1833.

the judiciary. A five-man Committee of Detail undertook the remainder of this work and on August 6 presented a rough draft to the convention. On September 8, a committee was named to "revise the stile [style] of, and arrange the Articles which had been agreed to" by the convention. The Committee of Stile was headed by Gouverneur Morris of Pennsylvania.[19] On September 17, 1787, the final draft of the Constitution was approved by thirty-nine of the remaining forty-two delegates.

Looking back on the drafting of the Constitution, an obvious question emerges: Why didn't the founders ban slavery outright? Certainly, as already mentioned, many of the delegates thought that slavery was morally wrong and that the Constitution should ban it entirely. Many Americans have since regarded the framers' failure to deal with the slavery issue as a betrayal of the Declaration of Independence, which proclaimed that "all Men are created equal." Others have pointed out how contradictory it was that the framers of the Constitution complained about being "enslaved" by the British yet ignored the problem of slavery in this country.

A common argument supporting the framers' action (or lack of it) with respect to slavery is that they had no alternative but to ignore the issue. If they had taken a stand on slavery, the Constitution certainly would not have been ratified. Indeed, if the antislavery delegates

PERCEPTION VERSUS REALITY
The Slavery Issue

Thomas Jefferson, a slave owner, pronounced, "all Men are created equal," as he wrote the Declaration of Independence. Jefferson considered slavery a "hideous blot" on America. George Washington, also a slave owner, regarded the institution of slavery as "repugnant." Patrick Henry, another southerner, also publicly deplored slavery. Given such views among the leading figures of the era, why didn't the founders stay true to the Declaration of Independence and free the slaves?

The Perception

Most Americans assume that southern economic interests and racism alone led the founders to abandon the principles of equality expressed in the Declaration of Independence. African slaves were the backbone of American agriculture, particularly for tobacco, the most profitable export. Without their slaves, southern plantation owners would not have been able to earn such high profits. Presumably, southerners would not have ratified the Constitution unless it protected the institution of slavery.

The Reality

The third chief justice of the United States Supreme Court, Oliver Ellsworth, declared that "as population increases, poor laborers will be so plenty as to render slaves useless. Slavery in time will not be a speck in our country."[20] He was wrong, of course. But according to Pulitzer Prize–winning historian Gordon S. Wood, Ellsworth's sentiments mirrored those of most prominent leaders in the United States in the years leading up to the creation of our Constitution. Indeed, great thinkers of the time firmly believed that the liberal principles of the Revolution would destroy the institution of slavery.

At the time of the Constitutional Convention, slavery was disappearing in the northern states (it would be eliminated there by 1804). The founders thought the same thing would happen in the southern states. After all, there were more antislavery societies in the South than in the North. The founders also thought that the ending of the international slave trade in 1808 would eventually end slavery in the United States. Consequently, the issue of slavery was taken off the table when the Constitution was created simply because the founders had a mistaken belief about the longevity of the institution. They could not have predicted at the time that the slave states, particularly Virginia, could produce slaves for the expanding areas of the Deep South and the Southwest.[21]

BLOG ON

Slavery and the Constitution is just one of many subjects that you can read about in the Legal History Blog at **legalhistoryblog.blogspot.com**. If you type "slavery" into the Search Blog box and hit Enter, you will see the full list of postings on this topic.

had insisted on banning slavery, the delegates from the southern states might have walked out of the convention—and there would have been no Constitution to ratify. For another look at this issue, however, see this chapter's *Perception versus Reality* feature.

The Debate over Ratification

The ratification of the Constitution set off a national debate of unprecedented proportions. The battle was fought chiefly by two opposing groups—the **Federalists** (those who favored a strong central government and the new Constitution) and the **Anti-Federalists** (those who opposed a strong central government and the new Constitution).

In the debate over ratification, the Federalists had several advantages. They assumed a positive name, leaving their opposition with a negative label. The Federalists also had attended the Constitutional Convention and thus were familiar with the arguments both in favor of and against various constitutional provisions. The Anti-Federalists, in contrast, had no actual knowledge of those discussions because they had not attended the convention. The Federalists also had time, money, and prestige on their side. Their impressive list of political thinkers and writers included Alexander Hamilton, John Jay, and James Madison. The Federalists could communicate with each other more readily because they were mostly bankers, lawyers, and merchants who lived in urban areas, where

> **Federalists** A political group, led by Alexander Hamilton and John Adams, that supported the adoption of the Constitution and the creation of a federal form of government.
>
> **Anti-Federalists** A political group that opposed the adoption of the Constitution because of the document's centralist tendencies and because it did not include a bill of rights.

IN THE READING-ROOM.

The fate of the proposed Constitution was decided in the state-ratifying conventions (nine states had to ratify for the Constitution to take effect), but it was the subject of intense debates everywhere—in homes, taverns, coffeehouses, and newspapers. By the time New Hampshire became the ninth state to ratify the Constitution in June 1788, it had become clear that the people of the United States demanded a bill of rights.

communication was easier. The Federalists organized a quick and effective ratification campaign to elect themselves as delegates to each state's ratifying convention.

THE FEDERALISTS ARGUE FOR RATIFICATION Alexander Hamilton, a leading Federalist, started answering the Constitution's critics in New York by writing newspaper columns under the pseudonym "Caesar." The Caesar letters appeared to have little effect, so Hamilton switched his pseudonym to "Publius" and enlisted John Jay and James Madison to help him write the papers. In a period of less than a year, these three men wrote a series of eighty-five essays in defense of the Constitution. These essays, which were printed not only in New York newspapers but also in other papers throughout the states, are collectively known as the *Federalist Papers.*

Generally, the papers attempted to allay the fears expressed by the Constitution's critics. One fear was that the rights of minority groups would not be protected. Another was that a minority might block the passage of measures that the majority felt were in the national interest. Many critics also feared that a republican form of government would not work in a nation the size of the United

faction A group of persons forming a cohesive minority.

tyranny The arbitrary or unrestrained exercise of power by an oppressive individual or government.

States. Various groups, or **factions,** would struggle for power, and chaos would result. Madison responded to the latter argument in *Federalist Paper* No. 10 (see Appendix F), which is considered a classic in political theory. Among other things, Madison argued that the nation's size was actually an advantage in controlling factions: in a large nation, there would be so many diverse interests and factions that no one faction would be able to gain control of the government.[22]

THE ANTI-FEDERALISTS' RESPONSE
Perhaps the greatest advantage of the Anti-Federalists was that they stood for the status quo. Usually, it is more difficult to institute changes than it is to stay with what is already known, experienced, and understood. Among the Anti-Federalists were such patriots as Patrick Henry and Samuel Adams. Patrick Henry said of the proposed Constitution: "I look upon that paper as the most fatal plan that could possibly be conceived to enslave a free people."

In response to the *Federalist Papers,* the Anti-Federalists published their own essays, using such pseudonyms as "Montezuma" and "Philadelphiensis." They also wrote brilliantly, attacking nearly every clause of the new document. Many Anti-Federalists contended that the Constitution had been written by aristocrats and would lead the nation to aristocratic **tyranny** (the exercise of absolute, unlimited power). Other Anti-Federalists feared that the Constitution would lead to an overly powerful central government that would limit personal freedom.[23]

The Anti-Federalists strongly argued that the Constitution needed a bill of rights. They warned that without a bill of rights, a strong national government might take away the political rights won during the American Revolution. They demanded that the new Constitution clearly guarantee personal freedoms. The Federalists generally did not think that a bill of rights was all that important. Nevertheless, to gain the necessary support, the Federalists finally promised to add a bill of rights to the Constitution as the first order of business under the new government. This promise turned the tide in favor of the Constitution.

Ratification

The contest for ratification was close in several states, but the Federalists finally won in all of the state conventions. In 1787, Delaware, Pennsylvania, and New Jersey voted to ratify the Constitution, followed by Georgia and Connecticut early in the following year. Even though the Anti-Federalists were perhaps the majority in Massachusetts, a successful political campaign by the Federalists led to ratification by that state on February 6, 1788.

Following Maryland and South Carolina, New Hampshire became the ninth state to ratify the Constitution on June 21, 1788, thus formally putting the Constitution into effect. New York and Virginia had not yet ratified, however, and without them the Constitution would have no true power. Those worries were dispelled in the summer of 1788, when both Virginia and New York ratified the new Constitution. North Carolina waited until November 21 of the following year to ratify the Constitution, and Rhode Island did not ratify until May 29, 1790.

LO⁵ THE CONSTITUTION'S MAJOR PRINCIPLES OF GOVERNMENT

The framers of the Constitution were fearful of the powerful British monarchy, against which they had so recently rebelled. At the same time, they wanted a central government strong enough to prevent the kinds of crises that had occurred under the weak central authority of the Articles of Confederation. The principles of government expressed in the Constitution reflect both of these concerns.

> **"THE LIBERTIES** OF A PEOPLE NEVER WERE, NOR EVER WILL BE, SECURE, WHEN THE TRANSACTIONS OF THEIR RULERS MAY BE **CONCEALED** FROM THEM."
>
> PATRICK HENRY, AMERICAN PATRIOT 1736–1799

JOIN THE DEBATE

Should Knowledge of the Constitution Be Required of All Citizens?

What do you know about this nation's Constitution? If you are a typical American, not very much. According to the National Constitution Center, only 20 percent of Americans know how many senators serve in the U.S. Senate (one hundred). If you know that James Madison is considered the father of the U.S. Constitution, then you are among the minuscule 2 percent who do. Can you name one right guaranteed by the First Amendment? If you can't, you have lots of company—75 percent of Americans can't do this either. The National Constitution Center also discovered that one in six Americans believes that the Constitution establishes this country as a Christian nation.

So, there is no question that most Americans are quite ignorant on the supreme law of the land. Perhaps all citizens should be required to have some understanding of the Constitution. If people do not understand what their constitutional rights and liberties are, how can they know when those rights are being violated? We require immigrants to pass a test to become citizens. That test requires immigrants to show that they have a basic knowledge of our Constitution. They have to know how many senators are in Congress. They have to be able to name one right guaranteed by the First Amendment. In view of the results of the National Constitution Center's survey, most Americans would fail the citizenship test. Because of the chipping away of our constitutional rights and liberties through various government actions since the terrorist attacks of September 11, 2001, Americans now, more than ever, need to be familiar with what those rights and liberties are. As Martin Luther King, Jr., once said, "Our lives begin to end when we become silent about things that matter."

Not everyone is so worried about Americans' lack of knowledge of the Constitution. Indeed, ignorance of the Constitution is no greater today than it was a century ago. Our nation and way of life have survived more than two hundred years with most people knowing little about the Constitution's details. Besides, most people have some practical constitutional knowledge. With so many popular TV shows about crime, almost everyone has a passing

Russia's Short-Lived Flirtation with True Democracy

From the Russian Revolution in 1917 to the end of the Soviet Union in 1991, Russians lived under a Communist dictatorship. For centuries prior to 1917, they had lived under an autocracy headed by tsars. In short, Russians had no experience with democracy before the fall of the Soviet Union.

A DEMOCRACY AT LAST . . .

On December 25, 1993, the Russian Federation (its formal name) saw its first constitution. If you read a translation of that constitution, you would conclude that modern Russia is now a democracy. That conclusion seemed to be true for a number of years because Russians freely voted for members of the Duma (the Russian counterpart of our Congress). They voted overwhelmingly in favor of President Vladimir Putin, too. Western commentators did express some concern that Putin was formerly the head of that country's brutal secret service. Nevertheless, after meeting Putin, President George W. Bush said, "I looked him in the eyes, and I know I can work with this man."

. . . OR NOT

Perhaps Putin showed his true colors when he referred to the collapse of the Soviet Union as "the greatest geopolitical catastrophe of the twentieth century." Under Putin's presidency, freedom of the press has all but disappeared—the state has simultaneously shut down independent sources of information and expanded government ownership of the media. A formerly promising independent court system has all but vanished. Since 2006, Putin's administration has instituted electoral reforms so that his political party, United Russia, is guaranteed control of the Duma and the presidency. Today, Putin's government has the right to exclude candidates from party slates and to bar parties from running altogether. The Duma has sixty legal reasons to eliminate an unwanted candidate from the electoral list.

Increasingly, Russian authorities are arresting and detaining public activists. In the economy, the Russian government has gradually taken control of all oil, natural gas, and other natural resources. Anyone who has not gone along with Putin has ended up in prison.

THE RUSSIAN PUBLIC'S REACTION

Are Russian citizens worried about this reversion to an undemocratic state? Apparently not, for public opinion polls in Russia show that more than 70 percent of the Russian people approve of Putin's "strong leadership." Under the Russian Constitution, the presidential term is four years, and no president can serve more than two terms. Putin's second term will end in March 2008. Thus, by the time you read this, Russia should have a new president—or maybe not.

For Critical Analysis

Why do you think so many Russians are unconcerned about the erosion of democracy in their country?

---

familiarity with the rights of the accused. Most people also know that they have rights if they face unequal treatment, such as racial discrimination, in the workplace. Furthermore, with the Internet, information about the Constitution is no more than a few keystrokes away.

Limited Government and Popular Sovereignty

The Constitution incorporated the principle of limited government, which means that government can do only what the people allow it to do through exercise of a duly developed system of laws. This principle can be found in many parts of the Constitution. For example, while Articles I, II, and III indicate exactly what the national government *can* do, the first nine amendments to the Constitution list the ways in which the government *cannot* limit certain individual freedoms.

Implicitly, the principle of limited government rests on the concept of popular sovereignty. Remember the phrases that frame the Preamble to the Constitution: "We the People of the United States . . . do ordain and establish this Constitution for the United States of America." In other words, it is the people who form the government and decide on the powers that the government can exercise. If the government exercises powers beyond those granted to it by the Constitution, it is acting illegally. The idea that no one is above the law, including government officers, is often called the **rule of law.**

Ultimately, the viability of a democracy rests on the willingness of the people and their leaders to adhere to the rule of law. A nation's written constitution, such as that of Iraq under the dictator Saddam Hussein, may guarantee numerous rights and liberties for its citizens. Yet, unless the government of that nation enforces those rights and liberties, the law does not rule the nation. Rather, the government decides what the rules will be. Consider the situation in Russia today. After the collapse of the Soviet Union, Russia established a federal republic. By all appearances, though, President Vladimir Putin is not constrained by the principles set forth in Russia's constitution—see this chapter's *The Rest of the World* feature for details.

The Principle of Federalism

The Constitution also incorporated the principle of federalism. In a **federal system** of government, the central (national) government shares sovereign powers with the various state governments. Federalism was the solution to the debate over whether the national government or the states should have ultimate sovereignty.

The Constitution gave the national government significant powers—powers that it had not had under the Articles of Confederation. For example, the Constitution expressly states that the president is the nation's chief executive as well as the commander in chief of the armed forces. The Constitution also declares that the Constitution and the laws created by the national government are supreme—that is, they take precedence over conflicting state laws. Other powers given to the national government include the power to coin money, to levy and collect taxes, and to regulate interstate commerce, granted by the **commerce clause.** Finally, the national government was authorized to undertake all laws that are "necessary and proper" to carrying out its expressly delegated powers.

Because the states feared too much centralized control, the Constitution also allowed for numerous states' rights. These rights include the power to regulate commerce within state borders and generally the authority to exercise any powers that are not delegated by the Constitution to the central government. (See Chapter 3 for a detailed discussion of federalism.)

Separation of Powers

As James Madison once said, after you have given the government the ability to control its citizens, you have to "oblige it to control itself." To force the government to "control itself" and to prevent the rise of tyranny,

Madison devised a scheme, the **Madisonian Model,** in which the powers of the national government were separated into different branches: the legislative, executive, and judicial.[24] The legislative branch (Congress) passes laws; the executive branch (the president) administers and enforces the laws; and the judicial branch (the courts) interprets the laws. By separating the powers of government, no one branch would have enough power to dominate the others. This principle of **separation of powers** is laid out in Articles I, II, and III of the Constitution.

Checks and Balances

A system of **checks and balances** was also devised to ensure that no one group or branch of government can exercise exclusive control. Even though each branch of government is independent of the others, it can also check the actions of the others. Look at Figure 2–5 on page 40, and you can see how this is done. As the figure shows, the president checks Congress by holding a **veto power,** which is the ability to return bills to Congress for reconsideration. Congress, in turn, controls taxes and spending, and the Senate must approve presidential appointments. The judicial branch of government can also act as a check on the other branches of government through its power of *judicial review*—the power to rule congressional or presidential actions unconstitutional.[25] In turn, the president and the Senate exercise some control over the judiciary through the president's

---

rule of law A basic principle of government that requires both those who govern and those who are governed to act in accordance with established law.

federal system A form of government that provides for a division of powers between a central government and several regional governments. In the United States, the division of powers between the national government and the fifty states is established by the Constitution.

commerce clause The clause in Article I, Section 8, of the Constitution that gives Congress the power to regulate interstate commerce (commerce involving more than one state).

Madisonian Model The model of government devised by James Madison in which the powers of the government are separated into three branches: executive, legislative, and judicial.

separation of powers The principle of dividing governmental powers among the executive, the legislative, and the judicial branches of government.

checks and balances A major principle of American government in which each of the three branches is given the means to check (to restrain or balance) the actions of the others.

veto power A constitutional power that enables the chief executive (president or governor) to reject legislation and return it to the legislature with reasons for the rejection. This prevents or at least delays the bill from becoming law.

FIGURE 2-5

CHECKS AND BALANCES AMONG THE BRANCHES OF GOVERNMENT

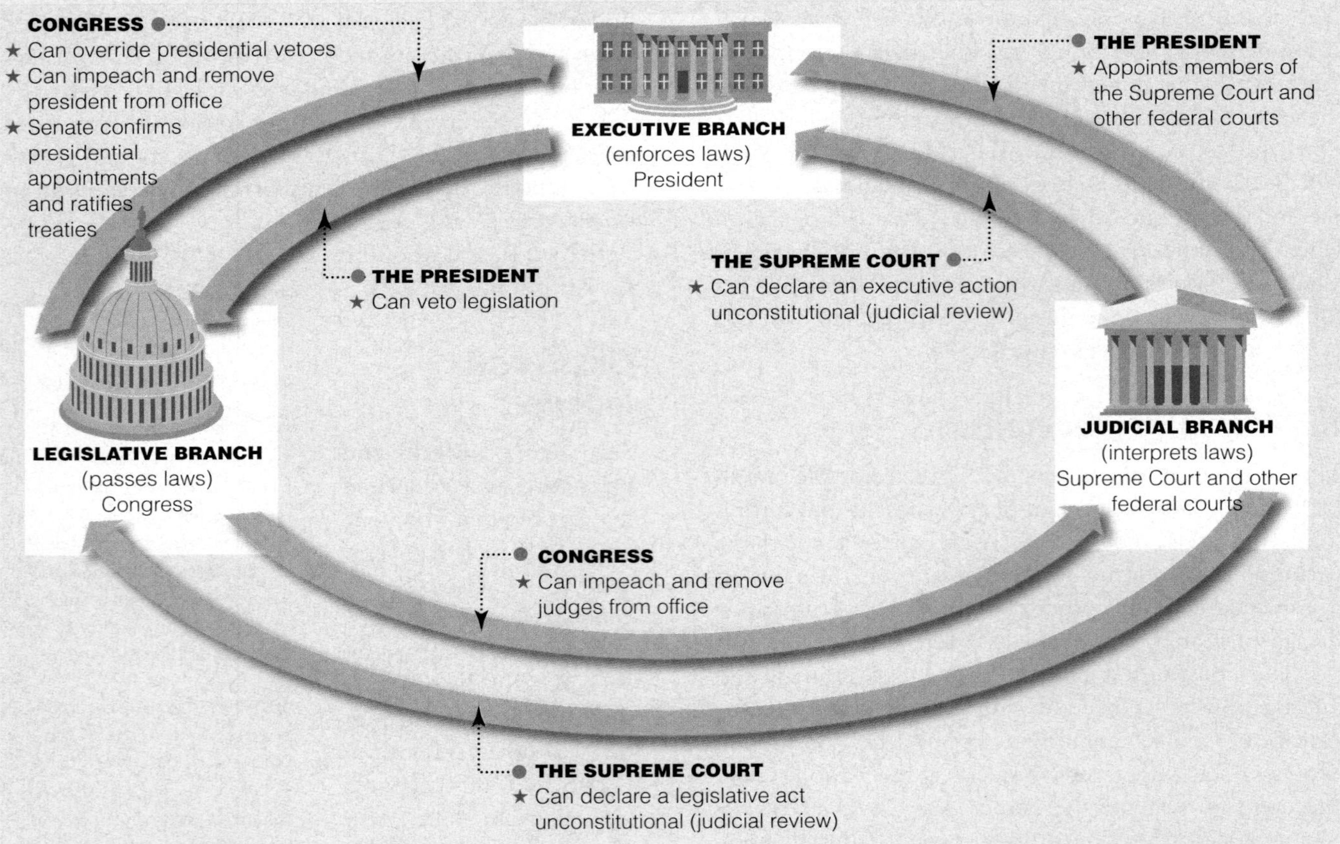

CONGRESS
★ Can override presidential vetoes
★ Can impeach and remove president from office
★ Senate confirms presidential appointments and ratifies treaties

THE PRESIDENT
★ Appoints members of the Supreme Court and other federal courts

EXECUTIVE BRANCH
(enforces laws)
President

THE PRESIDENT
★ Can veto legislation

THE SUPREME COURT
★ Can declare an executive action unconstitutional (judicial review)

LEGISLATIVE BRANCH
(passes laws)
Congress

JUDICIAL BRANCH
(interprets laws)
Supreme Court and other federal courts

CONGRESS
★ Can impeach and remove judges from office

THE SUPREME COURT
★ Can declare a legislative act unconstitutional (judicial review)

power to appoint federal judges and the Senate's role in confirming presidential appointments.

Among the other checks and balances built into the American system of government are staggered terms of office. Members of the House of Representatives serve for two years, members of the Senate for six, and the president for four. Federal court judges are appointed for life but may be impeached and removed from office by Congress for misconduct. Staggered terms and changing government personnel make it difficult for individuals within the government to form controlling factions. The American system of government also includes numerous other checks and balances, many of which you will read about in later chapters of this book. We look next at another obvious check on the powers of government: the Bill of Rights.

JOIN THE DEBATE

Are Presidential Signing Statements Destroying the Balance of Powers?

What do presidents Jackson, Tyler, Lincoln, Wilson, Franklin D. Roosevelt, Clinton, and G. W. Bush have in common? They all used "signing statements"—statements made while signing legislation indicating that there may be constitutional problems with the bill or clarifying how the legislation should be applied. This practice may sound strange, but the Supreme Court has upheld it. Although, as noted, several earlier presidents issued such statements, George W. Bush made the signing statement into an art form.

During his first term alone, Bush used signing statements 435 times—more than all of the previous presidents combined. There is a corollary to this fact: during the same period, Bush never once vetoed a bill. He will go down in history as one of the presidents with the fewest vetoes, but in effect, he has vetoed certain aspects of hundreds of laws. For example, when Bush signed a new law restricting the use of torture when interrogating detainees, he added a signing statement asserting that the president's power as commander in chief gave him the authority to bypass the very law he had just signed. Those who were outraged at Bush's use of signing statements claimed that he couldn't sign a bill and then state that parts of it were not binding on the executive branch, no matter what the reason. If any part of a bill was unconstitutional, then he had a duty to veto it. By his use of signing statements, Bush skewed the balance of powers within our federal government way too far in his favor.

> "**I believe** there are more instances of the **abridgement** of freedom of the people by gradual and silent encroachments by those in power than by violent and sudden usurpations."
>
> JAMES MADISON,
> FOURTH PRESIDENT OF THE UNITED STATES
> 1809–1817

Not everybody is so concerned about the shifting balance of powers within the federal government. They note that Congress still has the ability to deny funds for executive branch activities. They also point out that the president may have a duty to interpret laws, just as the Supreme Court does. Indeed, all three branches of the federal government have this power and this duty. The president's oath of office requires her or him to preserve, protect, and defend the Constitution. What better way to protect it than by making sure that an unconstitutional aspect of congressional legislation is not carried out by the executive branch?

The Bill of Rights

To secure the ratification of the Constitution in several important states, the Federalists had to provide assurances that amendments would be passed to protect individual liberties against violations by the national government. At the state ratifying conventions, delegates set forth specific rights that should be protected.

James Madison considered these recommendations as he labored to draft what became the Bill of Rights.

After sorting through more than two hundred state recommendations, Madison came up with sixteen amendments. Congress tightened the language somewhat and eliminated four of the amendments. Of the remaining twelve, two—one dealing with the apportionment of representatives and the other with the compensation of the members of Congress—were not ratified by the states during the ratification process.[26] By 1791, all of the states had ratified the ten amendments that now constitute our Bill of Rights. Table 2–2 on the next page presents the text of the first ten amendments to the Constitution, along with explanatory comments. (Note that neither a constitution nor a bill of rights, in itself, is any guarantee that civil liberties will be enforced. See, for example, this chapter's *The Politics of National Security* feature on page 43 for a discussion of how the government has curtailed some of our civil liberties during the so-called war on terrorism.)

The Constitution Compared to the Articles of Confederation

As mentioned earlier, the experiences under the government of the Confederation, particularly the weakness of the central government, strongly influenced the writing of the U.S. Constitution. The Constitution shifted many powers from the states to the central government (the Constitution's division of powers between the states and the national government will be discussed at length in Chapter 3).

One of the weaknesses of the Confederation had been the lack of an independent executive authority. The Constitution remedied this problem by creating an independent executive—the president—and by making the president commander in chief of the army and navy and of the state militias when called into national service. The president was also given extensive appointment powers, although Senate approval was required for certain appointments.

Another problem under the Confederation was the lack of a judiciary that was independent of the state courts. The Constitution established the United States

TABLE 2-2

THE BILL OF RIGHTS

Amendment I.
Religion, Speech, Press, Assembly, and Petition

Congress shall make no law respecting an establishment of religion, or prohibiting the free exercise thereof; or abridging the freedom of speech, or of the press; or the right of the people peaceably to assemble, and to petition the Government for a redress of grievances.

Congress may not create an official church or enact laws limiting the freedom of religion, speech, the press, assembly, and petition. These guarantees, like the others in the Bill of Rights (the first ten amendments), are not absolute—each may be exercised only with regard to the rights of other persons.

Amendment II.
Militia and the Right to Bear Arms

A well regulated Militia, being necessary to the security of a free State, the right of the people to keep and bear Arms, shall not be infringed.

To protect itself, each state has the right to maintain a volunteer armed force. States and the federal government regulate the possession and use of firearms by individuals.

Amendment III.
The Quartering of Soldiers

No Soldier shall, in time of peace be quartered in any house, without the consent of the Owner, nor in time of war, but in a manner to be prescribed by law.

Before the Revolutionary War, it had been common British practice to quarter soldiers in colonists' homes. Military troops do not have the power to take over private houses during peacetime.

Amendment IV.
Searches and Seizures

The right of the people to be secure in their persons, houses, papers, and effects, against unreasonable searches and seizures, shall not be violated, and no Warrants shall issue, but upon probable cause, supported by Oath or affirmation, and particularly describing the place to be searched, and the persons or things to be seized.

Here, the word warrant *means "justification" and refers to a document issued by a magistrate or judge indicating the name, address, and possible offense committed. Anyone asking for the warrant, such as a police officer, must be able to convince the magistrate or judge that an offense probably has been committed.*

Amendment V.
Grand Juries, Self-Incrimination, Double Jeopardy, Due Process, and Eminent Domain

No person shall be held to answer for a capital, or otherwise infamous crime, unless on a presentment or indictment of a Grand Jury, except in cases arising in the land or naval forces, or in the Militia, when in actual service in time of War or public danger; nor shall any person be subject for the same offense to be twice put in jeopardy of life or limb; nor shall be compelled in any criminal case to be a witness against himself, nor be deprived of life, liberty, or property, without due process of law; nor shall private property be taken for public use, without just compensation.

There are two types of juries. A grand jury considers physical evidence and the testimony of witnesses and decides whether there is sufficient reason to bring a case to trial. A petit jury hears the case at trial and decides it. "For the same offense to be twice put in jeopardy of life or limb"

means to be tried twice for the same crime. A person may not be tried for the same crime twice or forced to give evidence against herself or himself. No person's right to life, liberty, or property may be taken away except by lawful means, called the due process of law. Private property taken for public purposes must be paid for by the government.

Amendment VI.
Criminal Court Procedures

In all criminal prosecutions, the accused shall enjoy the right to a speedy and public trial, by an impartial jury of the State and district wherein the crime shall have been committed, which district shall have been previously ascertained by law, and to be informed of the nature and cause of the accusation; to be confronted with the witnesses against him; to have compulsory process for obtaining witnesses in his favor, and to have the Assistance of Counsel for his defence.

Any person accused of a crime has the right to a fair and public trial by a jury in the state in which the crime took place. The charges against that person must be so indicated. Any accused person has the right to a lawyer to defend him or her and to question those who testify against him or her, as well as the right to call people to speak in his or her favor at trial.

Amendment VII.
Trial by Jury in Civil Cases

In Suits at common law, where the value in controversy shall exceed twenty dollars, the right of trial by jury shall be preserved, and no fact tried by a jury, shall be otherwise re-examined in any Court of the United States, than according to the rules of the common law.

A jury trial may be requested by either party in a dispute in any case involving more than $20. If both parties agree to a trial by a judge without a jury, the right to a jury trial may be put aside.

Amendment VIII.
Bail, Cruel and Unusual Punishment

Excessive bail shall not be required, nor excessive fines imposed, nor cruel and unusual punishments inflicted.

Bail is that amount of money that a person accused of a crime may be required to deposit with the court as a guarantee that she or he will appear in court when requested. The amount of bail required or the fine imposed as punishment for a crime must be reasonable compared with the seriousness of the crime involved. Any punishment judged to be too harsh or too severe for a crime shall be prohibited.

Amendment IX.
The Rights Retained by the People

The enumeration in the Constitution, of certain rights, shall not be construed to deny or disparage others retained by the people.

Many civil rights that are not explicitly enumerated in the Constitution are still held by the people.

Amendment X.
Reserved Powers of the States

The powers not delegated to the United States by the Constitution, nor prohibited by it to the States, are reserved to the States respectively, or to the people.

Those powers not delegated by the Constitution to the federal government or expressly denied to the states belong to the states and to the people. This clause in essence allows the states to pass laws under their "police powers."

THE POLITICS OF NATIONAL SECURITY

CIVIL LIBERTIES UNDER FIRE

In the wake of the terrorist attacks of September 11, 2001, the federal government has sought to strengthen national security, sometimes at the expense of our civil liberties. It is true that the attacks on the World Trade Center towers and the Pentagon revealed serious flaws in the government's ability to protect the American homeland. The government has taken several steps since then to combat terrorism, including the establishment of a new cabinet department—the Department of Homeland Security. Americans are at odds about certain other actions taken by the government to counter terrorism, however, especially when they restrain our civil liberties.

SURVEILLANCE WITHOUT WARRANTS

Soon after 9/11, President George W. Bush issued an executive order authorizing the National Security Agency (NSA) to conduct surveillance of certain domestic phone calls without first obtaining a warrant. A number of noted constitutional scholars stated that this program was illegal. After all, the Fourth Amendment requires that a search warrant be obtained from a court before conducting such surveillance. Not surprisingly, when the public learned about the program in 2005, there was an outcry of astonishment. The Bush administration eventually announced that it would obtain warrants before conducting such surveillance in the future.

THE PATRIOT ACT AND ITS ABUSES

Shortly after 9/11, the administration drafted the USA Patriot Act and pushed it through Congress. This act increased the government's access to individuals' personal information and severely restricted the legal rights of suspected terrorists. It also granted the federal government great latitude by allowing government officials to investigate persons who are only vaguely associated with terrorists. The act even allows government agents to conduct searches and seize evidence without probable cause. This means that the government can find out what periodicals you read, where you travel, and how you spend your income. And, for the first time in this nation's history, the government has the legal right to read your mail before you receive it.

The Patriot Act also expanded the use of the "national security letter"— a type of administrative subpoena (a legal demand for evidence). The Federal Bureau of Investigation (FBI) has sent letters to various entities, such as banks and telephone companies, to obtain personal data on persons suspected of having links to terrorist organizations. From 2004 to 2007, the FBI used these letters on nearly 150,000 occasions to obtain personal information. The FBI systematically underreported the use of these letters, however. Moreover, the letters were used in some circumstances that were not even authorized by the overly generous Patriot Act.

YOU BE THE JUDGE

1. Because we are not at war, there is no justification for the federal government's curtailment of our civil liberties, which are guaranteed by the Bill of Rights. Do you agree or disagree with this statement? Explain your reasons.
2. Most Americans have nothing to hide and therefore have no reason to fear government snooping. Is this a valid argument? Why or why not?

Supreme Court and authorized Congress to establish other "inferior" federal courts.

To protect against possible wrongdoing, the Constitution also provided for a way to remove federal officials from office—through the impeachment process. The Constitution provides that a federal official who commits "Treason, Bribery, or other high Crimes and Misdemeanors" may be impeached (accused, or charged with wrongdoing) by the House of Representatives and tried by the Senate. If found guilty of the charges by a two-thirds vote in the Senate, the official can be removed from office and prevented from ever assuming another federal government post. The official may also face judicial proceedings for the alleged wrongdoing after removal from office.

Under the Articles of Confederation, amendments to the Articles required the unanimous consent of the states. As a result, it was virtually impossible to amend the Articles. As you will read shortly, the framers of the Constitution provided for an amendment process that requires the approval of only three-fourths of the states. Although the process is still extraordinarily cumbersome, it is easier to amend the Constitution than it was to change the Articles of Confederation.

Amending the Constitution

Since the Constitution was written, more than eleven thousand amendments have been introduced in Congress. Nonetheless, in the years since the ratification of the Bill of Rights, the first ten amendments to the Constitution, only seventeen proposed amendments have actually survived the amendment process and become a part of our Constitution. It is often contended that members of Congress use the amendment process simply as a political ploy. By proposing an amendment, a member of Congress can show her or his position on an issue, knowing that the odds *against* the amendment's being adopted are high.

One of the reasons there are so few amendments is that the framers, in Article V, made the formal amendment process extremely difficult—although it was much easier than it had been under the Articles of Confederation, as just discussed. There are two ways to propose an amendment and two ways to ratify one. As a result, there are only four possible ways for an amendment to be added to the Constitution.

METHODS OF PROPOSING AN AMENDMENT The two methods of proposing an amendment are as follows:

1. A two-thirds vote in the Senate and in the House of Representatives is required. All of the twenty-seven existing amendments have been proposed in this way.

2. If two-thirds of the state legislatures request that Congress call a national amendment convention, then Congress could call one. The convention could propose amendments to the states for ratification. There has yet to be a successful amendment proposal using this method.

The notion of a national amendment convention is exciting to many people. Many national political and judicial leaders, however, are uneasy about the prospect of convening a body that conceivably could do what the Constitutional Convention did—create a new form of government.

In two separate instances, the call for a national amendment convention almost became reality. Between 1963 and 1969, thirty-three state legislatures (out of the necessary thirty-four) attempted to call a convention to amend the Constitution to eliminate the Supreme Court's "one person, one vote" decisions (see Chapter 11). Since 1975, thirty-two states have asked for a national convention to propose an amendment requiring that the federal government balance its budget. Generally, the major national convention campaigns have reflected dissatisfaction, on the part of certain conservative and rural groups, with the national government's social and economic policies.

METHODS OF RATIFYING AN AMENDMENT There are two methods of ratifying a proposed amendment:

1. Three-fourths of the state legislatures can vote in favor of the proposed amendment. This method is considered the "traditional" ratification method and has been used twenty-six times.

2. The states can call special conventions to ratify the proposed amendment. If three-fourths of the states approve, the amendment is ratified. This method has been used only once—to ratify the Twenty-first Amendment.

You can see the four methods for proposing and ratifying amendments in Figure 2–6. As you can imagine, to meet the requirements for proposal and ratification, any amendment must have wide popular support in all regions of the country.

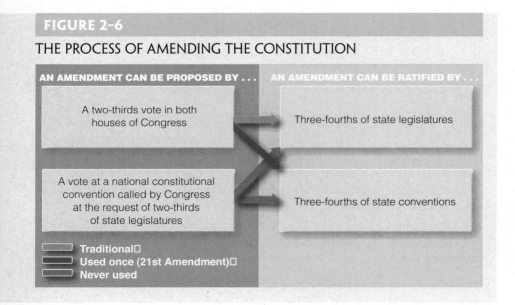

FIGURE 2-6

THE PROCESS OF AMENDING THE CONSTITUTION

AN AMENDMENT CAN BE PROPOSED BY . . .

A two-thirds vote in both houses of Congress

A vote at a national constitutional convention called by Congress at the request of two-thirds of state legislatures

AN AMENDMENT CAN BE RATIFIED BY . . .

Three-fourths of state legislatures

Three-fourths of state conventions

Traditional
Used once (21st Amendment)
Never used

AMERICA AT ODDS:
The Constitution

At the time the Constitution was created, there was a great deal of doubt about whether the arrangement would actually work. James Madison, among others, hoped that the framers had created a government "for the ages." Indeed, Madison's vision has been realized, in large part because of the division of governmental powers and the various checks and balances that were incorporated into the Constitution. These constitutional provisions have safeguarded the nation against tyranny—one of the greatest fears of the founders.

Yet, when drafting the Constitution, the framers left many issues unresolved. For example, Americans fighting the Revolutionary War agreed that they were fighting for liberty and equality. Once the war was over, however, there was little consensus on the meaning of these terms, and Americans have been at odds over how they should be interpreted for the last two hundred years or more. Additionally, as you read in this chapter, the founders left the issue of slavery to be debated by future generations—leading ultimately to the bloodbath of the Civil War and to problems that continue to challenge Americans even today. The fundamental disagreement between the Federalists and Anti-Federalists over how powerful the central government should be relative to the states is another conflict that has surfaced again and again. Finally, one of the most rigorous debates today concerning the Constitution is whether President George W. Bush's expansion of presidential powers relative to Congress and the judiciary destroyed the balance of powers envisioned by the framers.

Issues for Debate & Discussion

1. Some Americans believe that too many significant issues involving our constitutional rights and liberties are ultimately decided not by our elected representatives, but by the nine unelected justices on the Supreme Court. These Americans would like to see the constitutional amendment process be made simpler so that when disputes arise over the meaning of certain constitutional terms or concepts, such as whether the right to privacy includes the right to have an abortion, the Constitution could be amended to resolve the issue. Others believe that the framers made the amendment process difficult precisely so that the Constitution wouldn't be amended every time opinions on a certain issue changed. What is your position on this issue?

2. A question that has come to the fore in recent years is whether the United States should be in the business of "exporting liberty" to other countries, such as Iraq. Some Americans believe that the United States has a moral obligation to assist in establishing democracies in other nations. Others contend that the United States should stay out of other countries' affairs. Moreover, this group argues that it is impossible to expect nations with economies, cultures, religions, and customs different from our own to create and sustain an American-style democracy. Where do you stand on this issue?

Take Action

As you have read, the founders envisioned that the Constitution, to remain relevant, would need to be changed over time. It has been amended twenty-seven times, but many more amendments have been proposed. You can take action in a debate over the Constitution by supporting or opposing a proposed amendment, such as the flag-burning amendment. In 1989, the Supreme Court ruled that state laws prohibiting the burning of the American flag as part of a peaceful protest violate the freedom of expression protected by the First Amendment. Until the Constitution is amended to allow flag-burning to be prohibited, the Supreme Court's ruling remains the law of the land. Congress has introduced resolutions on several occasions in the past, and again in January 2007, Congress introduced a resolution to propose a constitutional amendment giving Congress the power "to prohibit the physical desecration of the flag of the United States." If you strongly support or oppose this amendment, you can take action by writing your representatives and senators in Congress or by forming protest groups to voice your concerns.

Samuel Peebles/El Dorado News-Times/AP

Amendments that would prohibit the burning of the American flag have been proposed in the past, but one has never been ratified and become a part of the U.S. Constitution.

- The World Wide Web version of the Constitution provides hypertext links to amendments and other changes. Go to **www. law.cornell.edu/constitution/constitution.overview.html**.

- The National Constitution Center in Philadelphia has a Web page at **www.constitutioncenter.org**. The site offers an online version of the *Federalist Papers,* a Constitution quiz, basic facts about the Constitution, and other information.

- James Madison's notes are one of our most important sources for the debates and exchanges that took place during the Constitutional Convention. These notes are now online at **www.thisnation.com/library/madison/index.html**.

- An online version of the Anti-Federalist Papers is available at the Web site of the West El Paso Information Network (WEPIN). Go to **wepin.com/articles/afp/index.htm**.

- For information on the effect of new computer and communications technologies on the constitutional rights and liberties of Americans, go to the Center for Democracy and Technology at **www.cdt.org**.

- The Cyberspace Law Institute (CLI) also focuses on law and communications technology. Go to **www.cli.org/papers.html**.

- The constitutions of almost all of the states are now online. You can find them at **www.findlaw.com/11stategov**.

- To find historical documents from the founding period, including the charter to Sir Walter Raleigh in 1584, the Royal Proclamation of 1763, and writings by Thomas Paine, go to **www.yale.edu/lawweb/avalon/alfalist.htm**.

- You can find constitutions for other countries at **www.servat.unibe.ch/law/icl/index.html**.

ONLINE RESOURCES FOR THIS CHAPTER

This text's Companion Web site, at **www.americaatodds. com**, offers links to numerous resources that you can utilize to learn more about the topics covered in this chapter.

Turn to the back of the book to find your Politics to Go review card for this chapter

CHAPTER 3
FEDERALISM

LEARNING OBJECTIVES

LO¹ Explain what federalism means, how federalism differs from other systems of government, and why it exists in the United States.

LO² Indicate how the Constitution divides governing powers in our federal system.

LO³ Summarize the evolution of federal-state relationships in the United States over time.

LO⁴ Describe developments in federalism under the Bush administration.

LO⁵ Explain what is meant by the term *fiscal federalism.*

The Real ID Act—Can the States Afford It?

In 2005, Congress passed the Real ID Act. This legislation established national standards for state-issued driver's licenses as well as other state-issued identification cards. The federal government has never been involved in this process before. Under our federal system, the states regulate who can legally obtain a driver's license. Consequently, the various states have developed different procedures and standards for issuing driver's licenses, including requirements relating to proof of residency and identity.

The Real ID Act changes all of that because it requires that every applicant for a driver's license (or other state-issued identification card) provide documentation verifying her or his name, residence, and place and date of birth, plus some form of photo ID to prove that whoever is applying for the license is actually that person. When the law was passed, Congress estimated that the states would have to spend only about $100 million to implement it. According to the National Governors Association, however, implementing the Real ID Act's requirements will cost the states more than $11 billion over a five-year period. Part of these expenditures will go toward the creation of a nationwide database containing all information about issued driver's licenses.

An Expensive Idea Whose Time Has Not Come

Senator Patrick J. Leahy (D., Vt.) predicts that state motor vehicle departments will not be able to implement the Real ID Act because of the costs involved in verifying all documents presented by applicants. Indeed, most of the states see the act as yet another unfunded federal mandate that they can ill afford to put into practice. The states also believe that creating a nationwide network of all such information will increase the possibility of identity theft. In 2007, Idaho passed a law stating that zero expenditures would be made during 2008 for implementation of the act. Other states, including Arkansas, Arizona, Colorado, Hawaii, Michigan, North Dakota, and Utah, have also passed resolutions opposing the Real ID Act.

UNIFORM DRIVER'S LICENSES ARE IMPORTANT FOR OUR SECURITY

Those in favor of the Real ID Act point to what happened before September 11, 2001. Ziad Jarrah, one of the hijackers of United Flight 93, which crashed in Pennsylvania, was stopped for speeding two days before the 9/11 tragedy. He gave the police one of his two Florida driver's licenses. With a system of uniform driver's licenses, which would prevent a person from having more than one license, the authorities might have apprehended him.

Furthermore, Americans will be insisting that the states comply with the Real ID Act, whether they want to or not. The act provides that no one will be allowed to board an airplane or enter a federal building unless he or she has a driver's license from a state that is in full compliance or another approved identification such as a passport. Thus, if a state does not comply, its citizens' lives will be significantly restricted.

It is not really a question of whether the states can afford to implement the Real ID Act; they will be forced to comply. True, the cost of compliance will be relatively high in the next few years. Nevertheless, once most states' residents have furnished proper identification to obtain a driver's license or other state-issued ID, they will not have to do so for renewals. Then, the states' costs will drop dramatically.

Where do you stand?

1. Some argue that even though the states will be issuing the uniform driver's licenses, the licenses will in essence be national identity cards. Is this a correct analysis? Why or why not?
2. Illegal immigrants will be unable to obtain driver's licenses after the Real ID Act is fully implemented. Is this good or bad? Why?

Explore this issue online

- It will come as no surprise to anyone familiar with the American Civil Liberties Union (ACLU) that this long-established rights organization opposes the Real ID Act. Indeed, the ACLU has created a Web site specifically dedicated to combating the act. You can find this site at **www.realnightmare.org**.
- The Department of Homeland Security has proposed a set of rules for implementing the Real ID Act. You can find these rules at **www.dhs.gov/xprevprot/laws**. Does the widespread hostility to the act appear to have had any impact on the proposed rules?

Electronic identification systems are tested regularly. Will the United States end up with such a system nationally?

INTRODUCTION

The controversy over the Real ID Act is just one example of how different levels of government in our federal system can be at odds with one another. Let's face it—those who work for the national government based in Washington, D.C., would like the states to fully cooperate with the national government in the implementation of national policies. At the same time, those who work in state government don't like to be told what to do by the national government, especially when the implementation of a national policy is costly for the states. Finally, those who work in local governments would like to run their affairs with the least amount of interference from both their state governments and the national government.

Such conflicts arise because our government is based on the principle of **federalism,** which means that government powers are shared by the national government and the states. When the founders of this nation opted for federalism, they created a practical and flexible form of government capable of enduring for centuries. At the same time, however, they planted the seeds for future conflict between the states and the national government over how government powers should be shared. As you will read in this chapter—and throughout this book—many of today's most pressing issues have to do with which level of government should exercise certain powers, such as the power to control education policy.

The relationship between the national government and the governments at the state and local levels has never been free of conflict. Indeed, even before the Constitution was adopted, the Federalists and Anti-Federalists engaged in a heated debate over the issue of national versus state powers. As you learned in Chapter 2, the Federalists won the day by convincing Americans to adopt the Constitution. The Anti-Federalists' concern for states' rights, however, has surfaced again and again in the course of American history.

LO¹ FEDERALISM AND ITS ALTERNATIVES

There are various ways of ordering relations between central governments and local units. Federalism is one of these ways. Learning about federalism and how it differs from other forms of government is important to understanding the American political system.

What Is Federalism?

Nowhere in the Constitution does the word *federalism* appear. This is understandable, given that the concept of federalism was an invention of the founders. Since the Federalists and the Anti-Federalists argued more than two hundred years ago about what form of government we should have, hundreds of definitions of federalism have been offered. Basically, though, as mentioned in Chapter 2, in a *federal system,* government powers are divided between a central government and regional, or subdivisional, governments.

Although this definition seems straightforward, its application certainly is not. After all, virtually all nations—even the most repressive totalitarian regimes—have some kind of subnational governmental units. Thus, the existence of national and subnational governmental units by itself does not make a system federal. *For a system to be truly federal, the powers of both the national units and the subnational units must be specified in a constitution.* Under true federalism, individuals are governed by two separate governmental authorities (national and state authorities) whose expressly designated constitutional powers cannot be altered without rewriting or altering (by amendment, for example) the constitution. Table 3–1 on the next page lists some of the countries that the Central Intelligence Agency has classified as having a federal system of government.¹

Federalism in theory is one thing; federalism in practice is another. As you will read shortly, the Constitution sets forth specific powers that can be exercised by the national

federalism A system of shared sovereignty between two levels of government—one national and one subnational—occupying the same geographic region.

government and provides that the national government has the implied power to undertake actions necessary to carry out its expressly designated powers. All other powers are "reserved" to the states. The broad language of the Constitution, though, has left much room for debate over the specific nature and scope of certain powers, such as the national government's implied powers and the powers reserved to the states. Thus, the actual workings of our federal form of government have depended, to a great extent, on the historical application of the broad principles outlined in the Constitution.

To further complicate matters, the term *federal government,* as it is used today, refers to the national, or central, government. When individuals talk of the federal government, they mean the national government; they are not referring to the federal *system* of government, which is made up of both the national government and the state governments.

Alternatives to Federalism

Perhaps an easier way to define federalism is to discuss what it is *not.* Most of the nations in the world today have a **unitary system** of government. In such a system, the constitution vests all powers in the national government. If the national government so chooses, it can delegate certain activities to subnational units. The reverse is also true: the national government can take away, at will, powers delegated to subnational governmental units. In a unitary system, any subnational government is a "creature of the national government." The governments of Britain, France, Israel, Japan, and the Philippines are examples of unitary systems. In the United States, because the Constitution does not mention local governments (cities and counties), we say that city and county governmental units are "creatures of state government." That means that state governments can—and do—both give powers to and take powers from local govern-

unitary system A centralized governmental system in which local or subdivisional governments exercise only those powers given to them by the central government.

confederal system A league of independent sovereign states, joined together by a central government that has only limited powers over them.

TABLE 3-1

COUNTRIES THAT HAVE A FEDERAL SYSTEM TODAY

Country	Population (in Millions)
Argentina	40.3
Australia	20.4
Austria	8.2
Brazil	190.0
Canada	33.4
Ethiopia	76.5
Germany	82.4
India	1,129.9
Malaysia	24.8
Mexico	108.7
Nigeria	135.0
Pakistan	164.7
Switzerland	7.6
United States	301.1
Venezuela	26.0

Source: Central Intelligence Agency, *The World Fact Book,* 2007 (Washington, D.C.: U.S. Government Printing Office, 2007).

ments. (For further discussion of how unitary systems differ from federal systems, see this chapter's *The Rest of the World* feature.)

The Articles of Confederation created a confederal system (see Chapter 2). In a **confederal system,** the national government exists and operates only at the direction of the subnational governments. During the Civil War, eleven southern states formed the Confederate States of America, or the Confederacy. Invoking the ideology of the Anti-Federalists, the members of the Confederacy desired an expansion of states' rights and greater autonomy. These states resented the authority of a strong national government, especially on the issue of slavery, so they decided to leave the Union. (For a further discussion of the Civil War era and secession, see page 58 in this chapter.) Few true confederal systems are in existence today.

Federalism—An Optimal Choice for the United States?

The Articles of Confederation failed because they did not allow for a sufficiently strong central government. The framers of the Constitution, however, were fearful of tyranny and a too-powerful central government. The natural outcome had to be a compromise—a federal system.

The appeal of federalism was that it retained state powers and local traditions while establishing a strong national government capable of handling common problems, such as national defense. A federal form of government also furthered the goal of creating a division of powers (to be discussed shortly). There are other reasons why the founders opted for a federal system, and a federal structure of government continues to offer many advantages (as well as some disadvantages) for U.S. citizens.

ADVANTAGES OF FEDERALISM   One of the reasons a federal form of government is well suited to the United States is its large size compared to many other countries. Even in the days when the United States consisted of only thirteen states, its geographic area was larger than that of France or England. In those days, travel was slow and communication was difficult, so people in outlying

THE REST OF THE WORLD

Life in a Unitary System

Jiji Press/AFP/Getty Images

Japan has a unitary system of government. Its parliament, shown here vociferously debating a proposal to reform the nation's pension system, wields extensive power over the entire nation.

Even in a country with a unitary system, the central government must delegate some power to regional or local administrative units. No matter how small the country, it usually doesn't make sense for the central government to decide such things as the speed limit on every city street. Note, though, that under a unitary system, once the decision about speed limits is made on the local level, the central government can override that decision if it chooses. Local governments in a unitary system have only as much or as little power as the central government decides they should have, and the central government can give or take away that power at its discretion.

AN EXAMPLE—JAPAN'S POSTWAR CONSTITUTION

Japan contains forty-seven prefectures—subdivisional units that manage local affairs—but the central government maintains a large amount of control over them. Japan's present constitution was written in 1946 when the country was under U.S. occupation following World War II. The United States, therefore, greatly influenced Japan's postwar constitution. Despite the U.S. preference for a federal system, however, the tradition of strong central power in Japan prevailed. The Japanese islands were unified 1,500 years ago and were ruled by an emperor, considered divine by the Japanese people. After World War II, the emperor renounced his divinity and today serves only as a political figurehead, but centuries of centralized government left their mark on Japan.

The 1946 constitution created a representative democracy in which the National Diet, elected by the people, wields legislative power. A prime minister and cabinet are chosen by the Diet from its own members. As is typical in a unitary system, the central government in Japan controls local taxation, collecting nearly two-thirds of the nation's taxes and sending half back to local governments. These transferred revenues are targeted for specific programs that reflect national policies, not local initiatives.

EVEN UNITARY SYSTEMS ARE DECENTRALIZING

In spite of Japan's unitary system, its prefectures collect one-third of the taxes for local use, and the constitution does prescribe certain autonomous functions for local government. Such decentralization is also occurring in other countries with unitary systems, such as France and Great Britain. France has recently decreased the degree of its government centralization, and Britain has allowed a degree of regional autonomy in Northern Ireland, Scotland, and Wales.

The key difference between a federal and a unitary system, then, is that the central government in a unitary system has the power to grant, and to take away, local autonomy.

For Critical Analysis

Why might the central government in a unitary system relinquish some of its power over regional governments? Conversely, why might the central government take power away from regional governments?

---

areas were isolated. The news of any particular political decision could take several weeks to reach everyone. Therefore, even if the framers of the Constitution had wanted a more centralized system (which most of them did not), such a system would have been unworkable.

Look at Figure 3–1 on the following page. As you can see, to a great extent the practical business of governing this country takes place in state and local governmental units. Federalism, by providing a multitude of arenas for decision making, keeps government closer to the people and helps make democracy possible.

The existence of numerous government subunits in the United States also makes it possible to experiment with innovative policies and programs

FIGURE 3-1

GOVERNMENTAL UNITS IN THE UNITED STATES TODAY

The most common type of governmental unit in the United States is the special district, which is generally concerned with issues such as solid waste disposal, mass transportation, fire protection, or similar matters. Often, the jurisdiction of special districts crosses the boundaries of other governmental units, such as cities or counties. They also tend to have fewer restrictions than other local governments as to how much debt they can incur and so are created to finance large building projects.

THE NUMBER OF GOVERNMENTS IN THE UNITED STATES TODAY

Government	Number
Federal government	1
State governments	50
Local governments	
Counties	3,034
Municipalities (mainly cities or towns)	19,431
Townships (less extensive powers)	16,506
Special districts (water, sewer, and so on)	35,356
School districts	13,522
Subtotal local governments	87,849
Total	**87,900**

PERCENTAGE OF ALL GOVERNMENTS IN THE UNITED STATES TODAY

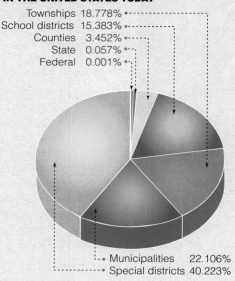

Townships 18.778%
School districts 15.383%
Counties 3.452%
State 0.057%
Federal 0.001%

Municipalities 22.106%
Special districts 40.223%

Source: U.S. Census Bureau, *Preliminary Report, 2006 Census of Governments.*

at the state or local level. Many observers, including Supreme Court Justice Louis Brandeis, have emphasized that in a federal system, state governments can act as "laboratories" for public-policy experimentation. When a state adopts a program that fails, any negative effects are relatively limited. A program that succeeds can be copied by other states. For example, several states today are experimenting with new health-care programs. Depending on the outcome of a specific experiment, other states may (or may not) implement similar programs. State innovations can also serve as models for federal programs. For example, California was a pioneer in air-pollution control. Many of that state's regulations were later adapted by the federal government to federal regulatory programs.

We have always been a nation of different political subcultures. The Pilgrims who founded New England were different from the settlers who established the agricultural society of the South. Both of these groups were different from those who populated the Middle Atlantic states. The groups who founded New England were religiously oriented, while those who populated the Middle Atlantic states were more business oriented. Those who settled in the South were more individualistic than the other groups; that is, they were less inclined to act as a unit and more inclined to act independently of each other. A federal system of government allows the political and cultural interests of regional groups to be reflected in the laws governing those groups.

SOME DRAWBACKS TO FEDERALISM Federalism offers many advantages, but it also has some drawbacks. For example, although federalism in many ways promotes greater self-rule, or democracy, some scholars point out that local self-rule may not always be in society's best interests. These observers argue that the smaller the political unit, the higher the probability that it will be dominated by a single political group, which may or may not be concerned with the welfare of the majority of the local unit's citizens. For example, entrenched segregationist politicians in southern states denied African Americans their civil rights and voting rights for decades, as you will learn in Chapter 5.

Federalism also poses the danger that national powers will be expanded at the expense of the states. President Ronald Reagan (1981–1989) once said, "The Founding Fathers saw the federalist system as constructed something like a masonry wall. The States are the bricks, the national government is the mortar. . . . Unfortunately, over the years, many people have increasingly come to believe that Washington is the whole wall."[2]

At the same time, powerful state and local interests can block progress and impede national plans. State and local interests often diverge from those of the national government. For example, as you will read later in this chapter, several of the states have recently been at odds with the national government over how to address the problem of global warming. Finding acceptable solutions to such conflicts has not always been easy. Indeed, as will be discussed shortly, in the 1860s, war—not politics—decided the outcome of a struggle over states' rights.

Federalism has other drawbacks as well. One of them is the lack of uniformity of state laws, which can complicate business transactions that cross state borders. Another problem is the difficulty of coordinating government policies at the national, state, and local levels. Additionally, the simultaneous regulation of business by all levels of government creates considerable red tape that imposes substantial costs on the business community.

LO² THE CONSTITUTIONAL DIVISION OF POWERS

The founders created a federal form of government by dividing sovereign powers into powers that could be exercised by the national government and powers that were to be reserved to the states. Although there is no systematic explanation of this **division of powers** between the national and state governments, the original Constitution, along with its amendments, sets forth what the national and state governments can (and cannot) do.

The Powers of the National Government

The Constitution delegates certain powers to the national government. It also prohibits the national government from exercising certain powers.

POWERS DELEGATED TO THE NATIONAL GOVERNMENT The Constitution grants three types of powers to the national government: expressed powers, implied powers, and inherent powers. Article I, Section 8, of the Constitution expressly enumerates twenty-seven powers that Congress may exercise. Two of these **expressed powers** are the power to coin money and the power to regulate interstate commerce. Constitutional amendments have provided for other expressed powers. For example, the Sixteenth Amendment, added in 1913, gives Congress the power to impose a federal income tax. Article II, Section 2, of the Constitution expressly delegates certain powers to the president. These powers include making treaties and appointing certain federal officeholders.

The constitutional basis for the **implied powers** of the national government is found in Article I, Section 8, Clause 18, often called the **necessary and proper clause.** This clause states that Congress has the power to make "all Laws which shall be necessary and proper for carrying into Execution the foregoing [expressed] Powers, and all other Powers vested by this Constitution in the Government of the United States, or in any Department or Officer thereof." The necessary and proper clause is often referred to as the *elastic clause,* because it gives elasticity to our constitutional system.

The national government also enjoys certain **inherent powers**—powers that governments have simply to ensure the nation's integrity and survival as a political unit. For example, any national government must have the inherent ability to make treaties, regulate immigration, acquire territory, wage war, and make peace. Although the national government's inherent powers are few, they are important.

POWERS PROHIBITED TO THE NATIONAL GOVERNMENT The Constitution expressly prohibits the national government from undertaking certain actions, such as imposing taxes on exports, and from passing laws

One of the expressed powers of Congress is the power to coin money. On April 2, 1792, Congress established the Mint of the United States in Philadelphia. Congress subsequently established mints in Denver and San Francisco.

AP Photo/Dan Loh

division of powers
A basic principle of federalism established by the U.S. Constitution. In a federal system, powers are divided between units of government (such as the federal and state governments).

expressed powers
Constitutional or statutory powers that are expressly provided for by the Constitution or by congressional laws.

implied powers The powers of the federal government that are implied by the expressed powers in the Constitution, particularly in Article I, Section 8.

necessary and proper clause Article I, Section 8, Clause 18, of the Constitution, which gives Congress the power to make all laws "necessary and proper" for the federal government to carry out its responsibilities; also called the *elastic clause.*

inherent powers The powers of the national government that, although not always expressly granted by the Constitution, are necessary to ensure the nation's integrity and survival as a political unit. Inherent powers include the power to make treaties and the power to wage war or make peace.

"The **States** can best govern our home concerns and the general government our foreign ones. I wish therefore . . . never to see all offices transferred to Washington, where, further withdrawn from the eyes of the people, they may more secretly be bought and sold at market."

THOMAS JEFFERSON,
THIRD PRESIDENT OF THE UNITED STATES
1801–1809

restraining certain liberties, such as the freedom of speech or religion. Most of these prohibited powers are listed in Article I, Section 9, and in the first eight amendments to the Constitution. Additionally, the national government is prohibited from exercising powers, such as the power to create a national public school system, that are not included among its expressed and implied powers.

The Powers of the States

The Tenth Amendment to the Constitution states that powers that are not delegated to the national government by the Constitution, nor prohibited to the states, "are reserved to the States respectively, or to the people."

POLICE POWERS   The Tenth Amendment thus gives numerous powers to the states, including the power to regulate commerce within their borders and the power to maintain a state militia. In principle, each state has the ability to regulate its internal affairs and to enact whatever laws are necessary to protect the health, morals, safety, and welfare of its people. These powers of the states are called **police powers.** The establishment of public schools and the regulation of marriage and divorce are uniquely within the purview of state and local governments.

police powers The powers of a government body that enable it to create laws for the protection of the health, morals, safety, and welfare of the people. In the United States, most police powers are reserved to the states.

Because the Tenth Amendment does not specify what powers are reserved to the states, these powers have been defined differently at different times in our history. In periods of widespread support for increased regulation by the national government, the Tenth Amendment tends to recede into the background of political discourse. When the tide turns the other way, the Tenth Amendment is resurrected to justify arguments supporting increased states' rights (see, for example, the discussion of the new federalism later in this chapter). Because the United States Supreme Court is the ultimate arbiter of the Constitution, the outcome of disputes over the extent of state powers often rests with the Court.

POWERS PROHIBITED TO THE STATES   Article I, Section 10, denies certain powers to state governments, such as the power to tax goods that are transported across state lines. States are also prohibited from entering into treaties with other countries. In addition, the Thirteenth, Fourteenth, Fifteenth, Nineteenth, Twenty-fourth, and Twenty-sixth Amendments also prohibit certain state actions. (The complete text of these amendments is included in Appendix B.)

Interstate Relations

The Constitution also contains provisions relating to interstate relations. The states have constant commercial and social interactions among themselves, and these interactions often do not directly involve the national government. The relationships among the states in our federal system of government are sometimes referred to as *horizontal federalism.*

The Constitution outlines a number of rules for interstate relations. For example, the Constitution's full

States have the power to protect the health, morals, safety, and welfare of their citizens.

Myrleen Ferguson Cate/PhotoEdit

faith and credit clause requires each state to honor every other state's public acts, records, and judicial proceedings. The issue of gay marriage, however, has made this constitutional mandate difficult to follow. If a gay couple legally married in Massachusetts moves to a state that bans same-sex marriage, which state's law takes priority? The United States Supreme Court may ultimately have to decide this issue.

Horizontal federalism may also include agreements, known as *interstate compacts,* among two or more states to regulate the use or protection of certain resources, such as water or oil and gas. California and Nevada, for example, have formed an interstate compact to regulate the use and protection of Lake Tahoe, part of which lies within each of those states. We look next at a recently proposed interstate compact that has garnered much attention.

JOIN THE DEBATE

The Stealth Interstate Compact for a National Popular Vote

As you will read in Chapter 9, Americans don't vote directly for their president. Rather, they vote indirectly through the electoral college. Under this system, a candidate who wins a plurality (more votes than any other candidate) of a state's popular votes receives *all* of that state's electoral votes. Consequently, it is possible for a candidate to win the electoral votes of enough states to become president even though he or she did not win the national popular vote.

Any attempt to abolish the electoral college would require the difficult process of amending the Constitution. As an alternative, an interstate compact, known as the National Popular Vote (NPV) plan, has been proposed. If all states agree to the compact, then each state's electoral votes will go to the candidate who wins the national popular vote. In essence, the proposed compact would do an end run around the electoral college system. If such a compact had been in effect in 2000, for example, Al Gore (who received the most popular votes) would have become president, rather than George W. Bush.

Many Americans support the NPV movement because it is one way to elect the president by popular vote without having to amend the Constitution, which is a near impossibility. Indeed, the electoral college has been the subject of more proposed amendments than any other part of the Constitution. Nevertheless, the NPV plan does not make everybody jump for joy. Critics of the plan point out that the founders created the electoral college system because they did *not* want the president to be elected by popular vote. The electoral college has lent stability to our democracy over time. Although the NPV compact might not violate the letter of the Constitution, skirting the electoral college procedure in such a way would go against the spirit of the Constitution.

Concurrent Powers

Concurrent powers can be exercised by both the state governments and the federal government. Generally, a state's concurrent powers apply only within the geographic area of the state and do not include functions that the Constitution delegates exclusively to the national government, such as the coinage of money and the negotiation of treaties. An example of a concurrent power is the power to tax. Both the states and the national government have the power to impose income taxes—and a variety of other taxes. States, however, are prohibited from imposing tariffs (taxes on imported goods), and the federal government may not tax articles exported by any state. Figure 3–2 on the next page, which summarizes the powers granted and denied by the Constitution, lists other concurrent powers.

The Supremacy Clause

The Constitution makes it clear that the federal government holds ultimate power. The **supremacy clause** in Article VI, Clause 2, states that the U.S. Constitution and the laws of the federal government "shall be the supreme Law of the Land." In other words, states cannot use their reserved or concurrent powers to counter national policies. Whenever state or local officers, such as judges or sheriffs, take

concurrent powers Powers held by both the federal and the state governments in a federal system.

supremacy clause Article VI, Clause 2, of the Constitution, which makes the Constitution and federal laws superior to all conflicting state and local laws.

FIGURE 3-2

THE CONSTITUTIONAL DIVISION OF POWERS

As illustrated here, the Constitution grants certain powers to the national government and to the state governments, while denying them other powers. Some powers, called *concurrent powers,* can be exercised at either the national or the state level, but generally the states can exercise these powers only within their own borders.

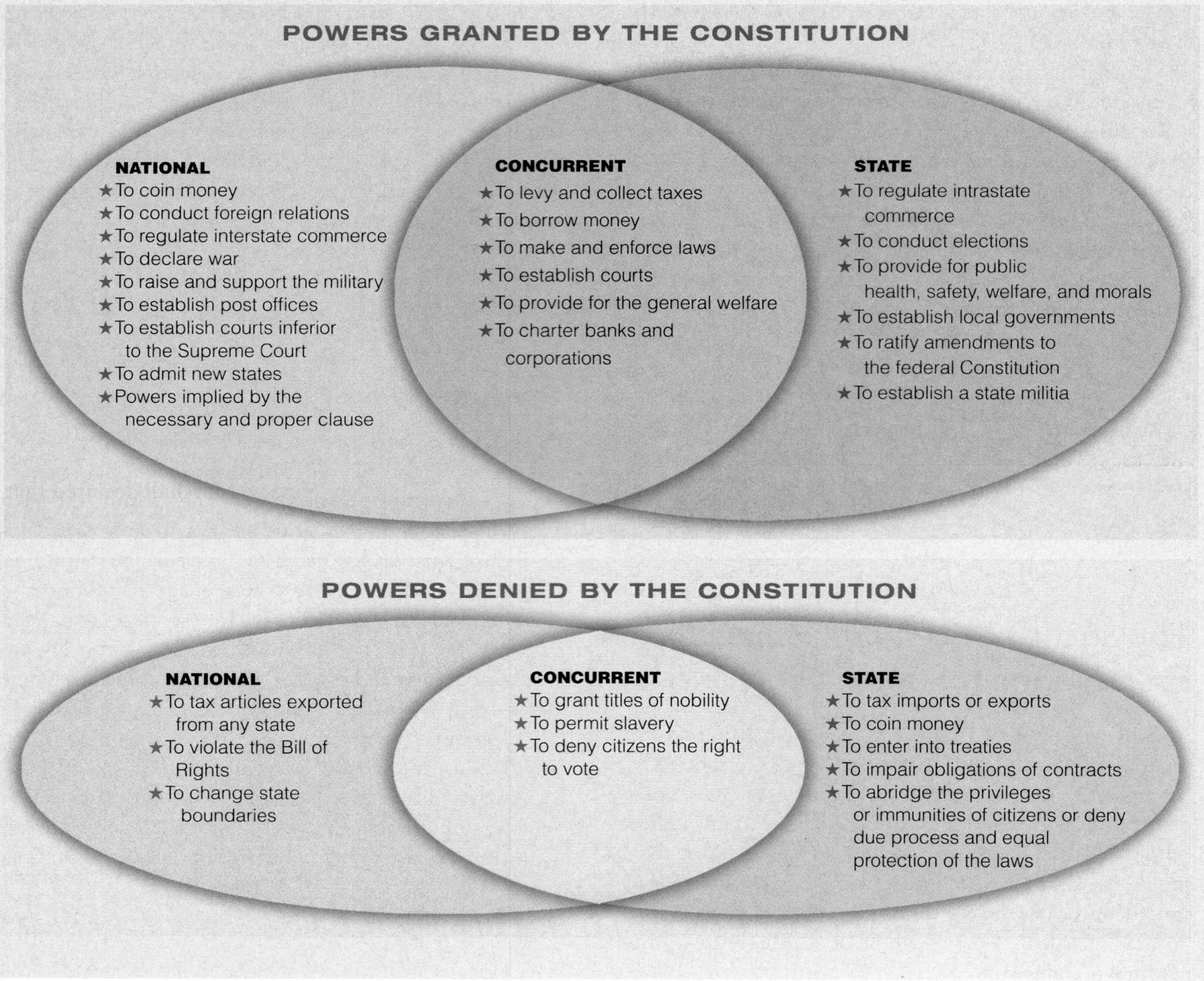

POWERS GRANTED BY THE CONSTITUTION

NATIONAL
★ To coin money
★ To conduct foreign relations
★ To regulate interstate commerce
★ To declare war
★ To raise and support the military
★ To establish post offices
★ To establish courts inferior to the Supreme Court
★ To admit new states
★ Powers implied by the necessary and proper clause

CONCURRENT
★ To levy and collect taxes
★ To borrow money
★ To make and enforce laws
★ To establish courts
★ To provide for the general welfare
★ To charter banks and corporations

STATE
★ To regulate intrastate commerce
★ To conduct elections
★ To provide for public health, safety, welfare, and morals
★ To establish local governments
★ To ratify amendments to the federal Constitution
★ To establish a state militia

POWERS DENIED BY THE CONSTITUTION

NATIONAL
★ To tax articles exported from any state
★ To violate the Bill of Rights
★ To change state boundaries

CONCURRENT
★ To grant titles of nobility
★ To permit slavery
★ To deny citizens the right to vote

STATE
★ To tax imports or exports
★ To coin money
★ To enter into treaties
★ To impair obligations of contracts
★ To abridge the privileges or immunities of citizens or deny due process and equal protection of the laws

office, they become bound by an oath to support the U.S. Constitution. National government power always takes precedence over any conflicting state action.[3]

LO³ THE STRUGGLE FOR SUPREMACY

Much of the political and legal history of the United States has involved conflicts between the supremacy of the national government and the desires of the states to remain independent. The most extreme example of this conflict was the Civil War in the 1860s. Through the years, because of the Civil War and several key Supreme Court decisions, the national government has increased its power.

Early U.S. Supreme Court Decisions

Two Supreme Court cases, both of which were decided in the early 1800s, played a key role in establishing the constitutional foundations for the supremacy of the national government. Both decisions were issued while John Marshall was chief justice of the Supreme Court. In his thirty-four years as chief justice (1801–1835), Marshall did much to establish the prestige and the independence of the Court. In *Marbury v. Madison*,[4] he clearly enunciated the principle of judicial review, which has since become an important part of the checks and balances in the American system of government. Under his leadership, the Supreme Court also established, through the following cases, the superiority of federal authority under the Constitution.

McCULLOCH v. MARYLAND (1819) The issue in *McCulloch v. Maryland*,[5] a case decided in 1819, involved both the necessary and proper clause and the supremacy clause. When the state of Maryland imposed a tax on the Baltimore branch of the Second Bank of the United States, the branch's chief cashier, James McCulloch, decided not to pay the tax. The state court ruled that McCulloch had to pay it, and the national government appealed to the United States Supreme Court. The case involved much more than a question of taxes. At issue was whether Congress had the authority under the Constitution's necessary and proper clause to charter and contribute capital to the Second Bank of the United States. A second constitutional issue was also involved: If the bank was constitutional, could a state tax it? In other words, was a state action that conflicted with a national government action invalid under the supremacy clause?

John Marshall, chief justice of the United States Supreme Court from 1801 to 1835, was instrumental in establishing the supremacy of the national government.

"A legislative act contrary to the Constitution is not law."
JOHN MARSHALL,
CHIEF JUSTICE OF THE U.S. SUPREME COURT
1801–1835

Chief Justice Marshall pointed out that no provision in the Constitution grants the national government the *expressed* power to form a national bank. Nevertheless, if establishing such a bank helps the national government exercise its expressed powers, then the authority to do so could be implied. Marshall also said that the necessary and proper clause included "all means that are appropriate" to carry out "the legitimate ends" of the Constitution.

Having established this doctrine of implied powers, Marshall then answered the other important constitutional question before the Court and established the doctrine of national supremacy. Marshall declared that no state could use its taxing power to tax an arm of the national government. If it could, the Constitution's declaration that the Constitution "shall be the supreme Law of the Land" would be empty rhetoric without meaning. From that day on, Marshall's decision became the basis for strengthening the national government's power.

GIBBONS v. OGDEN (1824) As you learned in Chapter 2, Article I, Section 8, gives Congress the power to regulate commerce "among the several States." But the framers of the Constitution did not define the word *commerce*. At issue in *Gibbons v. Ogden*[6] was how the *commerce clause* should be defined and whether the national government had the exclusive power to regulate commerce involving more than one state. The New York legislature had given Robert Livingston and Robert Fulton the exclusive right to operate steamboats in New York waters, and they licensed Aaron Ogden to operate a ferry between New York and New Jersey. Thomas Gibbons, who had a license from the U.S. government to operate boats in interstate waters, decided to compete with Ogden, but he did so without New York's permission. Ogden sued Gibbons in the New York state courts and won. Gibbons appealed.

Chief Justice Marshall defined *commerce* as including all business dealings, including steamboat travel. Marshall also stated that the power to regulate interstate commerce was an *exclusive* national power and had no limitations other than those specifically found in the Constitution. Since this 1824 decision, the national government has used the commerce clause numerous times to justify its regulation of virtually all areas of economic activity.

The Civil War— The Ultimate Supremacy Battle

The great issue that provoked the Civil War (1861–1865) was the future of slavery. Because people in different sections of the country had radically different beliefs about slavery, the slavery issue took the form of a dispute over states' rights versus national supremacy. The war brought to a bloody climax the ideological debate that had been outlined by the Federalist and Anti-Federalist factions even before the Constitution was ratified.

As just discussed, the Supreme Court headed by John Marshall interpreted the commerce clause in such a way as to increase the power of the national government at the expense of state powers. By the late 1820s, however, a shift back to states' rights began, and the question of the regulation of commerce became one of the major issues in federal-state relations. When the national government, in 1823 and again in 1830, passed laws imposing tariffs (taxes) on goods imported into the United States, the southern states objected, believing that such taxes were against their best interests.

One southern state, South Carolina, attempted to *nullify* the tariffs, or to make them void. South Carolina claimed that in conflicts between state governments and the national government, the states should have

> "This nation, **under God**, shall have a new **birth of freedom**— and that government of the people, by the people, for the people, shall not perish from the earth."
>
> ABRAHAM LINCOLN, GETTYSBURG ADDRESS 1863

the ultimate authority to determine the welfare of their citizens. Additionally, some southerners believed that democratic decisions could be made only when all the segments of society affected by those decisions were in agreement. Without such agreement, a decision should not be binding on those whose interests it violates. This view was used to justify the **secession**—withdrawal— of the southern states from the Union.

When the South was defeated in the war, the idea that a state has a right to secede from the Union was defeated also. Although the Civil War occurred because of the South's desire for increased states' rights, the result was just the opposite—an increase in the political power of the national government.

Dual Federalism— From the Civil War to the 1930s

Scholars have devised various models to describe the relationship between the states and the national government at

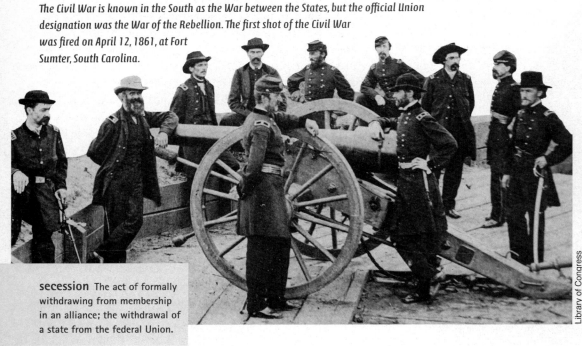

The Civil War is known in the South as the War between the States, but the official Union designation was the War of the Rebellion. The first shot of the Civil War was fired on April 12, 1861, at Fort Sumter, South Carolina.

Library of Congress

secession The act of formally withdrawing from membership in an alliance; the withdrawal of a state from the federal Union.

different times in our history. These models are useful in describing the evolution of federalism after the Civil War. The model of **dual federalism** assumes that the states and the national government are more or less equals, with each level of government having separate and distinct functions and responsibilities. The states exercise sovereign powers over certain matters, and the national government exercises sovereign powers over others.

For much of our nation's history, this model of federalism prevailed. Certainly, after the Civil War the courts tended to support the states' rights to exercise their police powers and concurrent powers to regulate intrastate activities. In 1918, for example, the Supreme Court ruled unconstitutional a 1916 federal law excluding from interstate commerce the products created through the use of child labor. The law was held unconstitutional because it attempted to regulate a local problem.[7] The era of dual federalism came to an end in the 1930s, when the United States was in the depths of the greatest economic depression it had ever experienced.

Cooperative Federalism and the Growth of the National Government

The model of **cooperative federalism,** as the term implies, involves cooperation by all branches of government. This model views the national and state governments as complementary parts of a single governmental mechanism, the purpose of which is to solve the problems facing the entire United States. For example, federal law enforcement agencies, such as the Federal Bureau of Investigation, lend technical expertise to solve local crimes, and local officials cooperate with federal agencies.

Cooperative federalism grew out of the need to solve the pressing national problems caused by the Great Depression, which began in 1929. In 1933, to help bring the United States out of the depression, President Franklin D. Roosevelt (1933–1945) launched his **New Deal,** which involved many government spending and public-assistance programs. Roosevelt's New Deal legislation not only ushered in an era of cooperative federalism, which has more or less continued until the present day, but also marked the real beginning of an era of national supremacy.

WAS THE EXPANSION OF NATIONAL POWERS INEVITABLE? Some scholars argue that even if the Great Depression had not occurred, we probably would still have witnessed a growth in the powers of the national government. As the country became increasingly populated, industrialized, and interdependent with other nations, problems and situations that once were treated locally began to have a profound impact on Americans hundreds or even thousands of miles away. Environmental pollution does not respect state borders, nor do poverty, crime, and violence. National defense, space exploration, and an increasingly global economy also call for national—not state—action. Thus, the ascendancy of national supremacy in the twentieth century had a logical set of causes.

COOPERATIVE FEDERALISM AND THE WELFARE STATE Certainly, the 1960s and 1970s saw an even greater expansion of the national government's role in domestic policy. The Great Society legislation of President Lyndon Johnson's administration (1963–1969) created Medicaid, Medicare, the Job Corps, Operation Head Start, and other programs. The Civil Rights Act of 1964 prohibited discrimination in public accommodations, employment, and other areas on the basis of race, color, national origin, religion, or gender. In the 1970s, national laws protecting consumers, employees, and

dual federalism A system of government in which both the federal and the state governments maintain diverse but sovereign powers.

cooperative federalism The theory that the states and the federal government should cooperate in solving problems.

New Deal A program ushered in by the Roosevelt administration in 1933 to bring the United States out of the Great Depression. The New Deal included many government spending and public-assistance programs, in addition to thousands of regulations governing economic activity.

In a 1938 radio broadcast, President Franklin D. Roosevelt called upon the nation's voters to elect New Deal candidates. The Roosevelt administration's New Deal programs played a role in lifting the country out of the Great Depression of the 1930s and ushered in an era of national supremacy as well as cooperative federalism.

During the 1960s and 1970s, the federal government created numerous nationwide programs, such as Head Start, which promotes school readiness for low-income children. Nonetheless, state and local governments were called upon to organize and administer them, as well as add funding. Here, a teacher in a Head Start program in Hillsboro, Oregon, works with preschoolers on an outdoor art project.

the environment imposed further regulations on the economy. Today, few activities are beyond the reach of the regulatory arm of the national government.

Nonetheless, the massive social programs undertaken in the 1960s and 1970s also precipitated greater involvement by state and local governments. The national government simply could not implement those programs alone. For example, Head Start, a program that provides preschool services to children of low-income families, is administered by local nonprofit organizations and school systems, although it is funded by federal grants. The model in which every level of government is involved in implementing a policy is sometimes referred to as **picket-fence federalism.** In this model, the policy area is the vertical picket on the fence, while the levels of government are the horizontal support boards. America's welfare system has relied on this model of federalism, although, as you will read, relatively recent reforms have attempted to give more power to the state and local levels.

picket-fence federalism
A model of federalism in which specific policies and programs are administered by all levels of government—national, state, and local.

preemption A doctrine rooted in the supremacy clause of the Constitution that provides that national laws or regulations governing a certain area take precedence over conflicting state laws or regulations governing that same area.

U.S. SUPREME COURT DECISIONS AND COOPERATIVE FEDERALISM   The two U.S. Supreme Court decisions discussed earlier (*McCulloch v. Maryland*

and *Gibbons v. Ogden*) became the constitutional cornerstone of the regulatory powers that the national government enjoys today. From the 1930s to the mid-1990s, the Supreme Court consistently upheld Congress's power to regulate domestic policy under the commerce clause. Even activities that occur entirely within a state were rarely considered outside the regulatory power of the national government. For example, in 1942 the Supreme Court held that wheat production by an individual farmer intended wholly for consumption on his own farm was subject to federal regulation because the home consumption of wheat reduced the demand for wheat and thus could have a substantial effect on interstate commerce.[8]

By 1980, the Supreme Court acknowledged that the commerce clause had "long been interpreted to extend beyond activities actually in interstate commerce to reach other activities, while wholly local in nature, which nevertheless substantially affect interstate commerce."[9] Today, Congress can regulate almost any kind of economic activity, no matter where it occurs. Increasingly, though, as you will read shortly, the Supreme Court is curbing Congress's regulatory powers under the commerce clause.

John Marshall's validation of the supremacy clause of the Constitution has also had significant consequences for federalism. One important effect of the supremacy clause today is that the clause allows for federal **preemption** of certain areas in which the national government and the states have concurrent powers. When Congress chooses to act exclusively in an area in which the states and the national government have concurrent powers, Congress is said to have *preempted* the area. When Congress preempts an area, such as aviation, the courts have held that a valid federal law or regulation takes precedence over a conflicting state or local law or regulation covering the same general activity. As noted earlier, national regulations affect virtually all areas of today's economic and social landscape. It is thus not surprising that many Americans tend to associate the very term *regulation* with national regulation—see this chapter's *Perception versus Reality* feature for a further discussion of this topic.

LO⁴ FEDERALISM TODAY

By the 1970s, some Americans began to question whether the national government had acquired too many powers. Had the national government gotten too big? Was it too deeply in debt as a result of annual budget deficits that created a national debt running into the trillions? Should steps be taken to reduce the regulatory power and scope of the national gov-

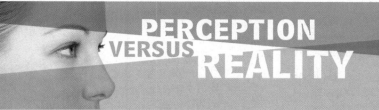

PERCEPTION VERSUS REALITY

The Federal Government Regulates Everything

In our federal system, the national (federal) government is not supposed to be "superior" to the state governments. Nonetheless, in the area of social and economic regulation, when the federal government expresses its intention to exclusively regulate some activity, the states cannot override federal law. In other words, federal government regulation can preempt, or take priority over, state regulation because, under the supremacy clause of the Constitution, the Constitution and federal laws are the "supreme Law of the Land." Because of the supremacy of federal laws over state laws, many believe that the federal government, in essence, regulates everything.

The Perception

If you glance at the hundreds of thousands of pages in the *Code of Federal Regulations*, you have to be impressed. The federal government has done an extensive job of regulating, particularly since the 1970s. Federal government regulations set out rules on workplace safety. Others establish standards for health and food. Reams of regulations govern the drug-approval process. In the environmental area, the federal government regulates how cleanly car engines must burn and how much soot factories can emit, among many other things. It is no wonder that most Americans look to the federal government to solve current problems in areas in which regulation or lawmaking has not been very strong, such as immigration and global warming. It is also not surprising that to many Americans, the phrase *government regulation* means regulation by the federal government.

The Reality

When a problem exists and the federal government does nothing about it, the states don't just stand still. After all, the states also have regulatory powers. States can use their *police powers* or their *concurrent powers* to pass laws to protect the health and welfare of their citizens. For example, before Congress increased the minimum wage in 2007, it had remained at the same level for many years. During that time, a lot of the states concluded that the federal minimum wage was not keeping up with inflation. Rather than waiting for the federal government to take action, a number of states (and some cities) increased the minimum wage in their jurisdictions, sometimes to as high as $10 per hour for certain public jobs. In the area of environmental regulation, California has led the way, often with the stated goal of fighting perceived global warming. In September 2006, Governor Arnold Schwarzenegger signed a law that commits that state to cut all carbon emissions by 25 percent by 2020.

In the area of health-care insurance, Massachusetts passed a law creating a scheme for universal insurance. Those individuals who do not have health insurance must pay an income tax penalty. Uninsured moderate-income families receive a subsidy. Any employer with ten or more workers can be assessed a fine of almost $300 per worker for not offering health-care insurance.

The states have also passed laws and regulations against illegal immigration, against invasions of privacy, and in favor of discount programs for prescription drugs. The states are where the action is.

BLOG ON

The site **www.stateline.org** is a great place to find out what state governments are doing. Also check out **jerrybrown.typepad.com**. Jerry Brown is the attorney general of California and was the governor of that state from 1975 to 1983. He is not shy about promoting California solutions to national issues, and his blog has many vocal readers.

ernment? Since that time, the model of federalism has evolved in ways that reflect these and other concerns.

The New Federalism— More Power to the States

During the 1970s and 1980s, several administrations attempted to revitalize the doctrine of dual federalism, which they renamed the "new federalism." The **new federalism** involved a shift from *nation-centered* federalism to *state-centered* federalism. One of the major goals of the new federalism was to return to the states certain powers that had been exercised by the national government since the 1930s. The term **devolution**—the transfer of powers to political subunits—is often used to describe this process. Although a product of

new federalism A plan to limit the federal government's role in regulating state governments and to give the states increased power to decide how they should spend government revenues.

devolution The surrender or transfer of powers to local authorities by a central government.

conservative thought and initiated by Republicans, the devolutionary goals of the new federalism were also espoused by the Clinton administration (1993–2001).

An example of the new federalism is the welfare reform legislation passed by Congress in 1996, which gave the states more authority over welfare programs. In the late 1990s, Congress also managed to balance its budget for the first time in decades, but deficits returned in the 2000s. As you will read in Chapter 13, reducing the size of the national government has proved difficult, as have attempts to reduce government spending.

The Supreme Court and the New Federalism

During and since the 1990s, the Supreme Court has played a significant role in furthering the cause of states' rights. In a landmark 1995 decision, *United States v. Lopez,*[10] the Supreme Court held, for the first time in sixty years, that Congress had exceeded its constitutional authority under the commerce clause. The Court concluded that the Gun-Free School Zones Act of 1990, which banned the possession of guns within one thousand feet of any school, was unconstitutional because it attempted to regulate an area that had "nothing to do with commerce." In a significant 1997 decision, the Court struck down portions of the Brady Handgun Violence Prevention Act of 1993, which obligated state and local law enforcement officers to do background checks on prospective handgun buyers until a national instant check system could be implemented. The Court stated that Congress lacked the power to "dragoon" state employees into federal service through an unfunded **federal mandate** of this kind.[11]

Since then, the Court has continued to limit the national government's regulatory powers. In 2000, for example, the Court invalidated a key provision of the federal Violence Against Women Act of 1994, which allowed women to sue in federal court when they were victims of gender-motivated violence, such as rape. The Court upheld a federal appellate court's ruling that the commerce clause did not justify national regulation of noneconomic, criminal conduct.[12]

Today, the U.S. Supreme Court is less noticeably guided by an ideology of states' rights, but some of its decisions have had the effect of enhancing the power of the states. For example, in one case, *Massachusetts v. Environmental Protection*

federal mandate
A requirement in federal legislation that forces states and municipalities to comply with certain rules. If the federal government does not provide funds to the states to cover the costs of compliance, the mandate is referred to as an *unfunded* mandate.

Smog often obscures visibility in New York City. One of the causes is automobile exhaust. The city government has suggested an "entry" tax for motorists entering congested areas of the city.

Agency,[13] Massachusetts and some other states sued the Environmental Protection Agency (EPA) for failing to regulate greenhouse-gas emissions. The states asserted that the agency was required to do so by the Clean Air Act of 1990. The EPA argued that it lacked the authority under the Clean Air Act to regulate greenhouse-gas emissions. The Court ruled for the states, holding that the EPA did have the authority to regulate such emissions and should take steps to do so.

The Shifting Boundary between Federal and State Authority

Clearly, the boundary between federal and state authority is shifting. Notably, issues relating to the federal structure of our government, which in the past several decades have not been at the forefront of the political arena, are now the subject of heated debate among Americans and their leaders. The federal government and the states seem to be in a constant tug-of-war over federal regulation, federal programs, and federal demands on the states.

THE POLITICS OF FEDERALISM   The Republican Party is often viewed as the champion of states' rights. Certainly, the party has claimed such a role. For example, when the Republicans took control of both chambers of Congress in 1995, they promised devolution, which, as already noted, refers to a shifting of power from the national level to the individual states. Smaller central government and a state-centered federalism have long been regarded as the twin pillars of Republican ideology. In contrast, Democrats usually have sought greater centralization of power in Washington, D.C.

Since the Clinton administration, however, the party tables seem to have been turned. As mentioned earlier, it was under Clinton that welfare reform legislation giving more responsibility to the states—a goal that had been endorsed by the Republicans for some time—became a reality. Also, although traditionally the Republicans have been more concerned than the Democrats about a balanced federal budget, it was the Clinton administration that accomplished this. Under George W. Bush, in contrast, deficit spending—and government spending generally—reached unprecedented heights.

FEDERALISM AND THE BUSH ADMINISTRATION   At the beginning of George W. Bush's administration, the new president announced the creation of a task force on federalism that would consult with governors on federal rulemaking and draft an executive order on federalism requiring federal departments and agencies to "respect the rights of our states and territories."[14] The executive order was never issued. Instead of supporting the rights of the states, the Bush administration and its supporters abandoned the states' rights camp on numerous occasions. Indeed, after decades of championing states' rights, today's Republicans seem to be redefining their party's approach to federalism.

For example, marriage and family law has traditionally been under the purview of state governments. Yet

the Bush administration backed the Federal Marriage Amendment (FMA) to the U.S. Constitution. That proposed amendment defined marriage as being between one man and one woman. The FMA, had it been adopted, would have subverted state court decisions in favor of civil unions and marriage rights for same-sex couples. Additionally, Bush's first attorney general, John Ashcroft, made numerous attempts to block California's medical-marijuana initiative and Oregon's physician-assisted suicide law. As another example, consider educational assessment, which has long been regarded as a prerogative of state governments. Nonetheless, in 2002 President Bush signed the No Child Left Behind Act into law, forcing schools to meet national testing benchmarks to receive federal funding.

JOIN THE DEBATE

Is Federal Interference in Education a Good Idea?

Some things have always been done by the states, and providing for education is one of them. Indeed, most funding for public schooling from kindergarten through twelfth grade comes from local governments by way of property taxes. In the last few decades, though, the state governments have been funding part of public education. Then, under the administration of George W. Bush, the federal government entered the education arena in a direct way. In 2002, President Bush signed a sweeping education bill called the No Child Left Behind (NCLB) Act. This act significantly expanded the federal government's role in education. The act requires public schools to provide choice for students attending failing schools; to issue annual report cards; and to implement annual, standards-based assessment tests. It also sets strict timelines for the states to show improvement in poorly performing schools.

A teacher in North Port, Florida, works with elementary students. Under the federal No Child Left Behind Act, schools whose student test scores are too low face sanctions. Consequently, teachers are starting to "teach to the test" to ensure passing grades by most students.

AP Photo/Chris O'Meara

Supporters of the federal government's incursion into public education believe that accountability to national educational standards with an emphasis on test results will improve the quality of public education throughout the United States. The NCLB Act requires each state to report to parents about the standards that are measured so that they can assess their children's achievements as well as the effectiveness of the public schools. The NCLB Act requires schools to focus on those students who are underserved. The idea is that, by doing so, eventually unequal opportunities in the schools will be reduced.

Critics of the NCLB Act argue that the federal government has no right to get involved in public education. If a particular public educational system is bad, people can vote with their feet by moving to other districts or states. Opponents also argue that the NCLB Act forces schools that want to receive federal funds under the act to forfeit programs that at times can be very effective. Others claim that the act imposes a hardship on states that cannot afford to provide the additional funds necessary to meet all of the act's requirements. Furthermore, critics of the NCLB Act point out that when testing becomes one of the primary tools for assessing student achievement, teachers simply start "teaching to the test." As a result of such teaching, students may leave public schools with a better set of narrow test-taking skills, but they will have a test-limited knowledge base.

FEDERALISM AND THE "WAR ON TERRORISM"   The U.S. Constitution gives Congress the power and authority to provide for the common defense. Nevertheless, most of the burden of homeland defense falls on state and local governments. These governments are the "first responders" to crises, including terrorist attacks. Additionally, state and local governments are responsible for detecting, preparing for, preventing, and recovering from terrorist attacks.

After the terrorist attacks of September 11, 2001, the Bush administration increased demands on state and local governments to participate in homeland security. As with the implementation of any national policy, the requirements

imposed on the states with respect to homeland security were costly. Firefighting departments needed more equipment and training. Emergency communications equipment had to be purchased. State and local governments were required to secure ports, ensure water safety and airport security, install new bomb-detecting equipment, and take a multitude of other steps. Although the federal government provided funds to the states to cover some of these expenses, much of the cost of homeland security was borne by the states.

The war in Iraq also depleted the ranks of state and local police, firefighters, and other emergency personnel. Many individuals working in these areas were also in the National Guard and called up to active duty. Some of the ramifications of the use of the National Guard to help fight the war in Iraq are discussed in this chapter's *The Politics of National Security* feature.

LO⁵ THE FISCAL SIDE OF FEDERALISM

As everybody knows, big government is costly. But how can government spending be reduced without sacrificing government programs that many feel are essential? This question, which to a significant extent frames the debate over federalism today, requires an understanding of the fiscal side of federalism.

Since the advent of cooperative federalism in the 1930s, the national government and the states have worked hand in hand to implement programs mandated by the national government. Whenever Congress passes a law that preempts a certain area, the states are, of course, obligated to comply with the requirements of

U.S. soldiers brandish their M4 firearms with M203 grenade launchers in a show of increased security during President George W. Bush's inauguration ceremony in January 2005. In post-September 11, 2001, America, the Bush administration focused on the need to combat terrorism and provide for homeland security at both the federal and state levels.

Jason Reed/Reuters/Landov

THE STATES HAVE LOST CONTROL OVER THE NATIONAL GUARD

State militias have a long history. Our nation's founders believed that the United States should have a small standing army complemented by citizen-soldiers. Accordingly, the U.S. Constitution, in Article I, Section 8, gives Congress the power to use the militia to suppress insurrections and repel invasions. The Militia Act of 1903 organized the militias into the present National Guard system.

Today, control over the National Guard has become a source of tension between the states and the federal government. Many state governors feel that they have lost control over their own National Guard units.

A LONG HISTORY OF THE NATIONAL GUARD FIGHTING ABROAD

In World War I, the National Guard made up about 35 percent of our country's combat divisions in France. In World War II, that percentage was smaller, but still significant. Members of the National Guard were used during the Korean War (1950–1953) and Vietnam War (1964–1975), as well as during the first war in Iraq in 1991. Members of the Guard have been sent on U.S. peacekeeping operations in Bosnia, Haiti, Kosovo, Kuwait, Saudi Arabia, and Somalia. In other words, sending members of the National Guard outside the United States to fight the current war in Iraq and to assist in the peacekeeping efforts in Afghanistan is not unprecedented.

THE STATES ARE LEFT IN THE LURCH

Since 2001, 80 percent of the men and women in the National Guard have been sent overseas in the largest deployment since World War II. Under the Constitution, the governor of each state controls his or her National Guard units—in times of peace. Otherwise, the president can call them up for federal duty, as has been done for the conflicts in Afghanistan and Iraq. With so many members of the Guard going abroad, however, only a few are available to deal with state emergencies, such as hurricanes and tornadoes. Much of the Guard's equipment has been shipped to Afghanistan and Iraq, too, leaving many states not only without members of the Guard but also without their equipment in case of emergency. In the spring of 2007, Kansas governor Kathleen Sebelius claimed that her state could no longer respond properly to even small tornadoes. Around the same time, Maryland governor Martin O'Malley said that Maryland's National Guard has insufficient personnel even to secure a local military base. (This state had to hire private security guards.)

INCREASED FEDERALIZATION OF THE NATIONAL GUARD

In 2007, the John Warner National Defense Authorization Act changed federal law so that the state governors are no longer the sole commanders in chief of the National Guard during emergencies within the states. Now, the president of the United States is legally able to take control of a state's National Guard without the governor's consent. Not surprisingly, all fifty governors signed a letter to Congress opposing this increase in presidential power.

YOU BE THE JUDGE

Some Americans believe that when confronted with a national security problem, the president should be able to use all of America's armed forces in any way he or she chooses. Others argue that the Constitution clearly gives the states independent control over their National Guard units, except during wartime, and we are not technically at war at this time. Where do you stand on this issue?

that law. As already noted, a requirement that a state provide a service or undertake some activity to meet standards specified by a federal law is called a *federal mandate*. Many federal mandates concern civil rights or environmental protection. Recent federal mandates require the states to provide persons with disabilities with access to public buildings, sidewalks, and other areas; to establish minimum water-purity and air-purity standards for specific localities; and to extend Medicaid coverage to all poor children.

To help the states pay for some of the costs associated with implementing national policies, the national government gives back some of the tax dollars it collects to the states—in the form of grants. As you will see, the states have come to depend on grants as an important source of revenue.

Federal Grants

Even before the Constitution was adopted, the national government granted lands to the states to finance education. Using the proceeds from the sale of these lands, the states were able to establish elementary schools and later, *land-grant colleges*. Cash grants started in 1808, when Congress gave money to the states to pay for the state militias. Federal grants were also made available for other purposes, such as building roads and railroads.

Only in the twentieth century, though, did federal grants become an important source of funds to the states. The major growth began in the 1960s, when the dollar amount of grants quadrupled to help pay for the Great Society programs of the Johnson administration. Grants became available for education, pollution control, conservation, recreation, highway construction and maintenance, and other purposes.

There are two basic types of federal grants: categorical grants and block grants. A **categorical grant** is targeted for a specific purpose as defined by federal law—the federal government defines hundreds of categories of state and local spending. Categorical grants give the national government control over how states use the money by imposing certain conditions. For example, a categorical grant may require that the funds not be used for purposes that discriminate against any group or for construction projects that pay below the local union wage. Depending on the project, the government might require that an environmental impact statement be prepared.

In contrast, a **block grant** is given for a broad area, such as criminal justice or mental-health programs. First started in 1966, block grants now constitute a growing percentage of all federal aid programs. A block grant gives the states more discretion over how the funds will be spent. Nonetheless, the federal government can exercise control over state decision making through these grants by using *cross-cutting requirements*. Title VI of the 1964 Civil Rights Act, for example, bars discrimination in the use of all federal funds, regardless of their sources.

Bridging the Tenth Amendment—Fiscal Federalism

Grants of funds to the states from the national government are one way that the Tenth Amendment to the U.S. Constitution can be bridged. Remember that the Tenth Amendment reserves all powers not delegated to the national government to the states and to the people. You might well wonder, then, how the federal government has been able to exercise control over matters that traditionally have been under the control of state governments, such as the minimum drinking age. The answer involves the giving or withholding of federal grant dollars. The power of the national government to influence state policies through grants is often referred to as **fiscal federalism.**

For example, during President Ronald Reagan's administration (1981–1989), the national government wanted the states to raise the minimum drinking age to twenty-one years. States that refused to do so were threatened with the loss of federal highway construction funds. The threat worked—it was not long before all states had changed their minimum-drinking-age laws accordingly.[15] In the 1990s, Congress used this same threat to encourage the states to lower their blood-alcohol limits for drunk driving to .08 percent by 2004. Those states that failed to comply with the .08 percent limit would face reductions in federal highway funds.

The education reforms embodied in the No Child Left Behind (NCLB) Act rely on fiscal federalism for their implementation. The states receive block grants for educational purposes and, in return, must meet federally imposed standards relating to testing and accountability. A common complaint, however, is that the existing NCLB Act is an underfunded federal mandate. Critics

categorical grant A federal grant targeted for a specific purpose as defined by federal law.

block grant A federal grant given to a state for a broad area, such as criminal justice or mental-health programs.

fiscal federalism The power of the national government to influence state policies through grants.

The states still have extensive police powers that they exercise at their discretion. For example, Northern California has implemented the AVOID campaign against drunk driving. Here, a police officer administers a Breathalyzer test at a sobriety checkpoint.

Justin Sullivan/Getty Images

argue that the national government does not provide sufficient funds to implement it.

The Cost of Federal Mandates

As mentioned, when the national government passes a law preempting an area in which the states and the national government have concurrent powers, the states must comply with that law in accordance with the supremacy clause of the Constitution. Thus, when such laws require the states to implement certain programs, the states must comply—but compliance with federal mandates can be costly.

One way that competitive federalism works is by states offering lower taxes to manufacturing firms that agree to locate in their states. This was one of the reasons Toyota started a plant in Huntsville, Alabama.

For example, the estimated total cost of complying with federal mandates concerning water purity, over just a four-year period, is in the vicinity of $29 billion. In all, the estimated cost of federal mandates to the states in the 2000s has exceeded $70 billion annually. Although Congress passed legislation in 1995 to curb the use of "unfunded" federal mandates (that is, mandates that are not funded by the federal government), the legislation was more rhetoric than reality.

Competitive Federalism

The debate over federalism is sometimes reduced to a debate over taxes. Which level of government will raise taxes to pay for government programs, and which will cut services to avoid raising taxes?

How states answer that question gives citizens an option: they can move to a state with fewer services and lower taxes, or to a state with more services but higher taxes. Political scientist Thomas R. Dye calls this model of federalism **competitive federalism.** State and local governments compete for business and citizens. If the state of Ohio offers tax advantages for locating a factory there, for example, a business may be more likely to do so, providing more jobs for Ohio residents. If Ohio has very strict environmental regulations, however, that same business may choose not to build its factory there, no matter how beneficial the tax advantages, because complying with the regulations will be costly. Although Ohio citizens lose the

opportunity for more jobs, they may enjoy better air and water quality than citizens of the state where the new factory is ultimately built.

Some observers consider the competitive nature of federalism an advantage: Americans have several variables to consider when they choose a state in which to live. Others consider it a disadvantage: a state that offers more social services or lower taxes may suddenly experience an increase in population as people "vote with their feet" to take advantage of that state's laws. This population increase can overwhelm the state's resources and force it to cut social services or raise taxes.

It appears likely, then, that the debate over how our federal system functions, as well as the battle for control between the states and the federal government, will continue. The Supreme Court, which has played umpire in this battle, will also likely continue to issue rulings that influence the balance of power.

competitive federalism
A model of federalism devised by Thomas R. Dye in which state and local governments compete for businesses and citizens, who in effect "vote with their feet" by moving to jurisdictions that offer a competitive advantage.

AMERICA AT ODDS:
Federalism

The federal form of government established by our nation's founders was, in essence, an experiment, a governmental system that was new to the annals of history. Indeed, federalism has been an ongoing experiment throughout our nation's life. More than once in our history, the line dividing state and national powers has shifted, sometimes giving the states more prominence and at other times giving the national government a more dominant role. Today, more than two hundred years later, we can say that the framers' choice of a federal form of government was a wise one. On the whole, with the one exception of the Civil War in the 1860s, the federal structure has allowed this country to thrive and prosper—and to offer a variety of living environments for its citizens.

The fact that we have a federal form of government allows the fifty states to have significant influence over such matters as the level of taxation, the regulation of business, and the creation and enforcement of criminal laws. For example, in Nevada you can purchase alcoholic beverages 24 hours a day, 365 days a year. In the neighboring state of Utah, the purchase of alcoholic beverages is severely restricted. Whether you can legally carry a concealed gun is a function of the state where you live. In some states, concealed firearms are allowed; in others, they are strictly forbidden. The funding and quality of education also vary from state to state. In sum, our federal arrangement gives you a choice that you would not have in a country with a unitary system of government, such as France. In the United States, you can pick up and move to another state in search of a more appealing business, work, or moral and social environment than the one offered by your state.

Issues for Debate & Discussion

- A few years ago, decisions in the state courts of Florida allowed the husband of Terri Schiavo, who had been in a persistent vegetative state for many years, to have her feeding tube removed. Claiming that they were promoting "a culture of life," members of Congress enacted a law, which President George W. Bush supported, allowing Schiavo's case to be heard by a federal court. (As you will read in Chapter 14, federal court jurisdiction—the authority to hear and decide cases—is limited to cases involving a treaty, the Constitution, or a federal law, for example, or to cases involving citizens from different states.) Bush's collaboration with Congress in the Schiavo matter won strong approval from many Christians and pro-life Americans, who applauded his moral leadership. Others claimed that the federal government's involvement in the Schiavo matter blatantly violated the constitutionally established division of powers in our federal system. What is your position on this issue?
- The Clean Air Act of 1990 gave California the right to establish its own environmental standards if the state first obtains a waiver from the federal Environmental Protection Agency (EPA). (This exception was made because California faces unique problems, including a high concentration of emissions due to the number of cars.) In an attempt to curb global warming, California recently passed a law calling for strict emissions standards for automobiles, trucks, and sport utility vehicles. The EPA has yet to provide the waiver that will allow California to implement this legislation. To prevent such delays, some contend that the states should have more authority to regulate environmental pollutants and greenhouse gases. Others argue that air pollution is a national problem and thus should be regulated by the national government, not by the individual states. What is your position on this issue? What arguments can you think of to support either side of this debate?

Take Action

In this chapter's *Perception versus Reality* feature on page 61, we discussed how Americans often think that all regulation comes from the national government. Similarly, individuals who want to take action to improve our society and government sometimes think that improvements must be made at the national level. If we are to reduce poverty or homelessness, improve health care, protect the environment, or create a safer and healthier world for children, the national government will have to take the lead. In fact, though, because of our federal structure, if you want to make a difference in these or other areas, you can do so by "thinking locally." By volunteering your services to a cause that concerns you, such as improving the environment or helping the poor, you can make a big difference in the lives that you touch.

Arthur Blaustein, who teaches community development at the University of California at Berkeley, has volunteered his services to a variety of causes over the past thirty years. For Blaustein, community service is both personally gratifying and energizing. It involves more than just giving; it is also about receiving and is "very much a two-way street." He suggests that if you want to volunteer, you will be more likely to stick with your decision if you choose an activity that suits your individual talents and interests. It is also important to make a definite time commitment, whether it be a few hours each week or even just a few hours each month. To find information on volunteering, you can use VolunteerMatch. Enter your ZIP code on its Web site (**www.volunteermatch.org**) to find volunteer opportunities in your community. Other organizations that work to meet critical needs in education, health, and the environment include AmeriCorps (**www.americorps.org**) and the Corporation for National and Community Service (**www.cns.gov**).

- You can access the *Federalist Papers,* as well as state constitutions, information on the role of the courts in resolving issues relating to federalism, and information on international federations, at the following site: **www.constitution.org/cs_feder.htm**.

- You can find information on state governments, state laws and pending legislation, and state issues and initiatives at **www.statescape.com**.

- Supreme Court opinions, including those discussed in this chapter, can be found at the Court's official Web site. Go to **www.supremecourtus.gov**.

- A good source for information on state governments and issues concerning federalism is the Web site of the Council of State Governments. Go to **www.statenews.org**.

- The Electronic Policy Network offers "timely information and leading ideas about federal policy and politics." It also has links to dozens of sites providing materials on federalism and public policy. Go to **www.movingideas.org**.

- The Brookings Institution, the nation's oldest think tank, is a good source for information on emerging policy challenges, including federal-state issues, and for practical recommendations for dealing with those challenges. To access the institution's home page, go to **www.brook.edu**.

- If you are interested in a libertarian perspective on issues such as federalism, the Cato Institute has a Web page at **www.cato.org**.

- The Web site of the National Governors Association offers information on many issues affecting the nation, ranging from health-care reform to education to new and innovative state programs. You can access information on these issues, as well as many key issues relating to federalism, at **www.nga.org**.

- *Governing* magazine, an excellent source for state and local news, can be found online at **www.governing.com**.

ONLINE RESOURCES FOR THIS CHAPTER

This text's Companion Web site, at **www.americaatodds. com**, offers links to numerous resources that you can utilize to learn more about the topics covered in this chapter.

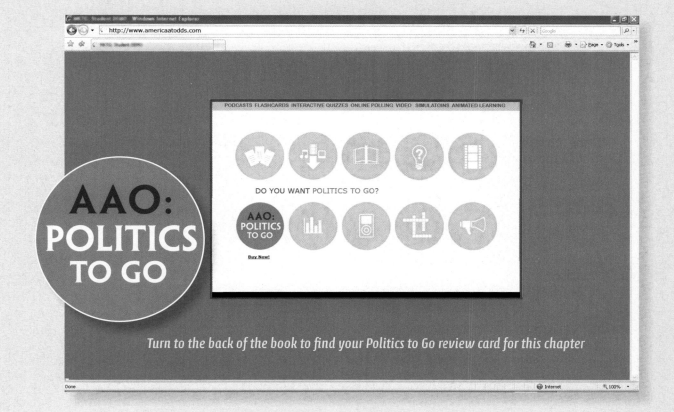

Turn to the back of the book to find your Politics to Go review card for this chapter

CHAPTER 4
CIVIL LIBERTIES

LEARNING OBJECTIVES

LO¹ Define the term *civil liberties,* explain how civil liberties differ from civil rights, and state the constitutional basis for our civil liberties.

LO² List and describe the freedoms guaranteed by the First Amendment and explain how the courts have interpreted and applied these freedoms.

LO³ Discuss why Americans are increasingly concerned about privacy rights.

LO⁴ Summarize how the Constitution and the Bill of Rights protect the rights of accused persons.

Should the Government Expand DNA Databases?

According to Christopher Dunn of the New York Civil Liberties Union, "Because DNA, unlike fingerprints, provides an enormous amount of personal information, burgeoning government DNA databases pose serious threats to privacy." While the U.S. Constitution does not specifically guarantee our right to privacy, the United States Supreme Court has held that such a right is implied by other constitutional rights that are specifically outlined in the Bill of Rights (the first ten amendments to the Constitution). In addition, both Congress and state legislatures have passed laws to protect individuals' privacy rights. But those rights can be threatened by DNA sampling. After all, if someone samples your DNA (usually by passing a cotton swab inside your mouth), you have just provided a sample of your genetic code. Americans are at odds about whether the direct invasion of privacy caused by DNA sampling is worth the benefits it provides for law enforcement.

DNA Sampling Has a Double Benefit—It Helps Us Catch the Criminals and Exonerate the Innocent

James Curtis Giles of Dallas spent ten years in prison for a crime that he did not commit. He is a free man today because DNA evidence exonerated him. Giles is only one of several hundred accused and convicted criminals who are free today because of DNA evidence. Because of such benefits, New York governor Eliot Spitzer wants to expand that state's DNA database to include samples from anyone found guilty of almost any misdemeanor. (Those convicted of more serious crimes are already in the DNA database.) Spitzer wants DNA samples to be obtained from defendants and prisoners by court order and then included in the state's database. Once DNA is in the database, law enforcement officials can run a sample of DNA found at a crime scene against the database and possibly identify the perpetrator. Police officials and prosecutors throughout the country agree that an expanded DNA database is one of the most effective tools in law enforcement.

EXPANDED DNA SAMPLING WILL RESULT IN PRIVACY RIGHTS BEING THROWN OUT THE WINDOW

Many civil liberties groups are firmly against expanded DNA sampling. At the least, they want strict protections to ensure that DNA samples can be used only for legitimate law enforcement purposes. After all, DNA profiles can reveal individuals' mental disorders and physical diseases. If the samples are not properly handled, insurance companies could use them to deny policy applications. Eventually, DNA samples could even be used in child-custody battles. One parent might be able to "prove" that the other has a genetic tendency toward inappropriate behavior. Consider also that an amendment to the federal Violence Against Women Act requires DNA sampling of anyone who is merely arrested. This is a clear violation of privacy rights. After all, many people who are arrested are never formally charged and are released.

In addition, where will the DNA sampling stop? At first, DNA was collected just from those who had committed sexual assaults and other serious crimes. Now authorities want to obtain DNA even from those convicted of minor misdemeanors. Soon, everyone entering college might be required to provide a sample, and then everyone else. Before you know it, Big Brother will have genetic information on all of us.

Where do you stand?

1. Several hundred prisoners have been exonerated by DNA evidence. Does this benefit outweigh the cost—the invasion of privacy caused by expanded DNA sampling? Why or why not?
2. From the biological point of view, nothing is more private than one's DNA. In your view, is our right to privacy threatened by increased DNA sampling? If so, in what way?

Explore this issue online

- The Rape, Abuse and Incest National Network strongly believes in the value of a DNA database—see **www.rainn.org/public-policy/issues/dna-evidence**.
- Harvard professor David Lazer worries that inclusion in the database effectively means that your close relatives are in the database as well. See **www.ksg.Harvard.edu/ksgnews/KSGInsight/lazer.html**.

CIVIL LIBERTIES ARE LEGAL AND CONSTITUTIONAL RIGHTS THAT PROTECT CITIZENS FROM GOVERNMENT ACTIONS.

INTRODUCTION

The debate over DNA sampling, which we looked at in the chapter-opening *America at Odds* feature, is but one of many controversies concerning our civil liberties. **Civil liberties** are legal and constitutional rights that protect citizens from government actions. For example, the First Amendment to the U.S. Constitution prohibits Congress from making any law that abridges the right to free speech. The First Amendment also guarantees freedom of religion, freedom of the press, and freedom to assemble (to gather together for a common purpose, such as to launch a protest against a government policy or action). These and other freedoms and guarantees set forth in the Constitution and the Bill of Rights are essentially *limits* on government action.

Perhaps the best way to understand what civil liberties are and why they are important to Americans is to look at what might happen if we did not have them. If you were a student in China, for example, you would have to exercise some care in what you say and do. That country prohibits speech that is contrary to the socialist ideology or the cultural aims of the nation. If you criticized the government in e-mail messages to your friends

civil liberties Individual rights protected by the Constitution against the powers of the government.

writ of *habeas corpus* An order that requires an official to bring a specified prisoner into court and explain to the judge why the person is being held in prison.

bill of attainder A legislative act that inflicts punishment on particular persons or groups without granting them the right to a trial.

or on your Web site, you could end up in court on charges that you had violated the law—and perhaps even go to prison.

Note that some Americans confuse *civil liberties* (discussed in this chapter) with *civil rights* (discussed in the next chapter) and use the terms interchangeably. Nonetheless, scholars make a distinction between the two. They point out that whereas civil liberties are limitations on government action, setting forth what the government *cannot do*, civil rights specify what the government *must* do—to ensure equal protection under the law for all Americans, for example.

LO¹ THE CONSTITUTIONAL BASIS FOR OUR CIVIL LIBERTIES

The founders believed that the constitutions of the individual states contained ample provisions to protect citizens from government actions. Therefore, the founders did not include many references to individual civil liberties in the original version of the Constitution. These references were added by the Bill of Rights, ratified in 1791. Nonetheless, the original Constitution did include some safeguards to protect citizens against an overly powerful government.

Safeguards in the Original Constitution

Article I, Section 9, of the Constitution provides that the writ of *habeas corpus* (a Latin phrase that roughly means "produce the body") will be available to all citizens except in times of rebellion or national invasion. A **writ of *habeas corpus*** is an order requiring that an official bring a specified prisoner into court and show the judge why the prisoner is being kept in jail. If the court finds that the imprisonment is unlawful, it orders the prisoner to be released. If our country did not have such a constitutional provision, political leaders could jail their opponents without giving them the opportunity to plead their cases before a judge. Without this opportunity, many opponents might conveniently disappear or be left to rot away in prison.

The Constitution also prohibits Congress and the state legislatures from passing bills of attainder. A **bill of attainder** is a legislative act that directly punishes a specifically named individual (or a group or class of individuals) without a trial. For example, no legislature can pass a law that punishes a named Hollywood celebrity for unpatriotic statements.

The Constitution also prohibits Congress from passing *ex post facto* laws. The Latin term *ex post facto* roughly means "after the fact." An **ex post facto law** punishes individuals for committing an act that was legal when it was committed but that has since become a crime.

The Bill of Rights

As you read in Chapter 2, one of the contentious issues in the debate over ratification of the Constitution was the lack of protections for citizens from government actions. Although many state constitutions provided such protections, the Anti-Federalists wanted more. The promise of the addition of a bill of rights to the Constitution ensured its ratification.

The Bill of Rights was ratified by the states and became part of the Constitution on December 15, 1791. Look at the text of the Bill of Rights on page 42 in Chapter 2. As you can see, the first eight amendments grant the people specific rights and liberties. The remaining two amendments reserve certain rights and powers to the people and to the states.

Basically, in a democracy, government policy tends to reflect the view of the majority. A key function of the Bill of Rights, therefore, is to protect the rights of minority groups against the will of the majority. When there is disagreement over how to interpret the Bill of Rights, the courts step in. The United States Supreme Court, as our nation's highest court, has the final say on how the Constitution, including the Bill of Rights, should be interpreted. The civil liberties that you will read about in this chapter have all been shaped over time by Supreme Court decisions. For example, it is the Supreme Court that determines where the freedom of speech ends and the right of society to be protected from certain

These visitors wait in line in front of the United States Supreme Court building. The nine Supreme Court justices make decisions that affect our individual liberties.

AP Photo/Joe Marquette

forms of speech begins. Because of its pivotal role in our government, the Supreme Court has often been called the guardian of our liberties (but see this chapter's *Perception versus Reality* feature on the following page for a closer look at today's Supreme Court with respect to this tradition).

Ultimately, the responsibility for protecting minority rights lies with the American people. Each generation has to learn anew how it can uphold its rights by voting, expressing opinions to elected representatives, and bringing cases to the attention of the courts when constitutional rights are threatened.

The Incorporation Issue

For many years, the courts assumed that the Bill of Rights limited only the actions of the national government, not the actions of state or local governments. In other words, if a state or local law was contrary to a basic freedom, such as the freedom of speech, the federal Bill of Rights did not come into play. The founders believed that the states, being closer to the people, would be less likely to violate their own citizens' liberties. Moreover, state constitutions, most of which contain bills of rights, protect citizens against state government actions. The United States Supreme Court upheld this view when it decided, in *Barron v. Baltimore* (1833), that the Bill of Rights did not apply to state laws.[1]

Eventually, however, the courts—and notably, the Supreme Court—began to take a different view. Because the Fourteenth Amendment played a key role in this development, we look next at the provisions of that amendment.

ex post facto law
A criminal law that punishes individuals for committing an act that was legal when the act was committed but that has since become a crime.

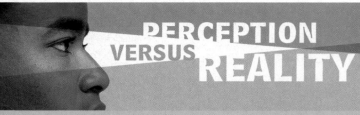

PERCEPTION VERSUS REALITY

The Supreme Court— Guardian of Our Liberties?

In the United States, the Supreme Court is considered the final arbiter of the Constitution, and, as such, it defines the extent of our civil liberties. If our civil liberties have been trampled upon, we expect the Supreme Court to right the situation. We expect our nation's highest court to make sure our liberties are always protected.

The Perception

Repeatedly, the Supreme Court has come to the aid of the individual who is in conflict with society or with government. The Supreme Court has taken a stand against many reprehensible restrictions on rights and liberties in our society. Indeed, during the 1950s and 1960s, the Supreme Court took the lead in desegregating our schools, as well as in expanding the civil rights of minorities and the liberties of all Americans.

The Reality

In 1896, it was the United States Supreme Court that provided a constitutional basis for existing segregation laws in the South. The Court held that such laws did not violate the equal protection clause of the Constitution because *separate facilities for blacks were equal to those for whites*. As a result, this nation was saddled for decades with government-approved "separate-but-equal" facilities for African Americans in transportation and elsewhere.

In addition, we must face the reality that the current Supreme Court may not turn out to be a champion of our civil rights and liberties. In a 2006 opinion, the Roberts Court held that evidence is admissible in court even though the police personnel who obtained it didn't knock to announce their presence before forcefully entering a home. Consequently, the previous knock-and-announce rule is no more.

Finally, consider the constitutionality of the Military Commissions Act of 2006. This act removed noncitizens' challenges to their detention as enemy combatants from the jurisdiction of the federal courts. All such challenges have to be reviewed by a military commission. When the act was challenged as unconstitutional, a federal court of appeals held that it did not violate the Constitution. The Supreme Court refused to review the case, thus letting the lower court's decision stand. Because the lower court had held that the 2006 act was constitutional, that meant that many prisoners designated as enemy combatants continued to be held at the Guantánamo Bay Naval Base in Cuba for years, without an opportunity to be heard in court. Thus, these prisoners were effectively denied their right to *habeas corpus*.[2] (In June 2007, the Bush administration announced that it planned to close the base, but it did not say what would happen to the prisoners if the prison closed. Also, the Supreme Court agreed to review a case involving the rights of prisoners at Guantánamo in its 2007–2008 term.)

BLOG ON

The American Constitution Society at **www.acsblog.org** takes a strong position in favor of civil liberties and watches the Supreme Court closely. The trade-off between civil liberties and security is only one of the many issues tackled at the Becker-Posner Blog at **www.becker-posner-blog.com**. It is hosted by University of Chicago economics professor Gary Becker and U.S. circuit court judge Richard Posner.

---

due process clause The constitutional guarantee, set out in the Fifth and Fourteenth Amendments, that the government will not illegally or arbitrarily deprive a person of life, liberty, or property.

due process of law The requirement that the government use fair, reasonable, and standard procedures whenever it takes any legal action against an individual; required by the Fifth and Fourteenth Amendments.

THE RIGHT TO DUE PROCESS

In 1868, three years after the end of the Civil War, the Fourteenth Amendment was added to the Constitution. The **due process clause** of this amendment ensures that state governments will protect their citizens' rights. The due process clause reads, in part, as follows:

No State shall . . . deprive any person of life, liberty, or property, without due process of law.

The right to **due process of law** is simply the right to be treated fairly under the legal system. That system and its officers must follow "rules of fair play" in making decisions, in determining guilt or innocence, and in punishing those who have been found guilty.

Procedural Due Process. *Procedural* due process requires that any governmental decision to take life, liberty, or property be made equitably. For example, the government must use fair procedures in determining whether

TABLE 4-1

INCORPORATING THE BILL OF RIGHTS INTO THE 14TH AMENDMENT

Year	Issue	Amendment Involved	Court Case
1925	Freedom of speech	I	*Gitlow v. New York*, 268 U.S. 652.
1931	Freedom of the press	I	*Near v. Minnesota*, 283 U.S. 697.
1932	Right to a lawyer in capital punishment cases	VI	*Powell v. Alabama*, 287 U.S. 45.
1937	Freedom of assembly and right to petition	I	*De Jonge v. Oregon*, 299 U.S. 353.
1940	Freedom of religion	I	*Cantwell v. Connecticut*, 310 U.S. 296.
1947	Separation of church and state	I	*Everson v. Board of Education*, 330 U.S. 1.
1948	Right to a public trial	VI	*In re Oliver*, 333 U.S. 257.
1949	No unreasonable searches and seizures	IV	*Wolf v. Colorado*, 338 U.S. 25.
1961	Exclusionary rule	IV	*Mapp v. Ohio*, 367 U.S. 643.
1962	No cruel and unusual punishments	VIII	*Robinson v. California*, 370 U.S. 660.
1963	Right to a lawyer in all criminal felony cases	VI	*Gideon v. Wainwright*, 372 U.S. 335.
1964	No compulsory self-incrimination	V	*Malloy v. Hogan*, 378 U.S. 1.
1965	Right to privacy	Various	*Griswold v. Connecticut*, 381 U.S. 479.
1966	Right to an impartial jury	VI	*Parker v. Gladden*, 385 U.S. 363.
1967	Right to a speedy trial	VI	*Klopfer v. North Carolina*, 386 U.S. 213.
1969	No double jeopardy	V	*Benton v. Maryland*, 395 U.S. 784.

Starting in 1925, however, the Supreme Court gradually began using the due process clause to say that states could not abridge a civil liberty that the national government could not abridge. In other words, the Court *incorporated* the protections guaranteed by the national Bill of Rights into the liberties protected under the Fourteenth Amendment. As you can see in Table 4–1, the Supreme Court was particularly active during the 1960s in broadening its interpretation of the due process clause to ensure that states and localities cannot infringe on civil liberties protected by the Bill of Rights. Today, the liberties still not incorporated include the right to bear arms, the right to refuse to quarter soldiers, and the right to a grand jury hearing.

a person will be subjected to punishment or have some burden imposed on him or her. Fair procedure has been interpreted as requiring that the person have at least an opportunity to object to a proposed action before an impartial, neutral decision maker (which need not be a judge).

Substantive Due Process. *Substantive* due process focuses on the content, or substance, of legislation. If a law or other governmental action limits a *fundamental right*, it will be held to violate substantive due process, unless it promotes a *compelling or overriding state interest*. All First Amendment rights plus the rights to interstate travel, privacy, and voting are considered fundamental. Compelling state interests could include, for example, the public's safety.

OTHER LIBERTIES INCORPORATED The Fourteenth Amendment also states that no state "shall make or enforce any law which shall abridge the privileges or immunities of citizens of the United States." For some time, the Supreme Court considered the "privileges and immunities" referred to in the amendment to be those conferred by state laws or constitutions, not the federal Bill of Rights.

LO² PROTECTIONS UNDER THE FIRST AMENDMENT

As mentioned earlier, the First Amendment sets forth some of our most important civil liberties. Specifically, the First Amendment guarantees the freedoms of religion, speech, the press, and assembly, and the right to petition the government. In

The right to bear arms is included in the Second Amendment to the U.S. Constitution, yet the Supreme Court has not incorporated this right into the liberties protected under the Fourteenth Amendment.

AP Photo/*Salt Lake Tribune*/Al Hartmann

the pages that follow, we look closely at each of these freedoms and discuss how, over time, Supreme Court decisions have defined their meaning and determined their limits.

Freedom of Religion

The First Amendment prohibits Congress from passing laws "respecting an establishment of religion, or prohibiting the free exercise thereof." The first part of this amendment is known as the **establishment clause.** The second part is called the **free exercise clause.**

That the freedom of religion was the first freedom mentioned in the Bill of Rights is not surprising. After all, many colonists came to America to escape religious persecution. Nonetheless, these same colonists showed little tolerance for religious freedom within the communities they established. For example, in 1610 the Jamestown colony enacted a law requiring attendance at religious services on Sunday "both in the morning and the afternoon." Repeat offenders were subjected to particularly harsh punishments. For those who twice violated the law, for example, the punishment was a public whipping. For third-time offenders, the punishment was death. The Maryland Toleration Act of 1649 declared that anyone who cursed God or denied that Jesus Christ was the son of God was to be punished by death. In all, nine of the thirteen colonies had established official religions by the time of the American Revolution.

This context is helpful in understanding why, in 1802, President Thomas Jefferson, a great proponent of religious freedom and tolerance, wanted the establishment clause to be "a wall of separation

The **First Amendment** to the Constitution mandates separation of church and state. Nonetheless, references to God are common in public life, as the phrase, **"In God We Trust"** on this coin demonstrates.

between church and state." The context also helps to explain why even state leaders who supported state religions might have favored the establishment clause—to keep the national government from interfering in such state matters. After all, the First Amendment says only that *Congress* can make no law respecting an establishment of religion; it says nothing about whether the *states* could make such laws. And, as noted earlier, the protections in the Bill of Rights initially applied only to actions taken by the national government, not the state governments.

THE ESTABLISHMENT CLAUSE The establishment clause forbids the government to establish an official religion. This makes the United States different from countries that are ruled by religious governments, such as the Islamic government of Iran. It also makes us different from nations that have in the past strongly discouraged the practice of any religion at all, such as the People's Republic of China.

What does this separation of church and state mean in practice? For one thing, religion and government, though constitutionally separated in the United States, have never been enemies or strangers. The establishment clause does not prohibit government from supporting religion in *general*; it remains a part of public life. (See this chapter's *The Rest of the World* feature for a discussion of how another country, Saudi Arabia, approaches the question of religion in public life.) Most government officials take an oath of office in the name of God, and our coins and paper currency carry the motto "In God We Trust." Clergy of different religions serve with each branch of the armed forces. Public meetings and even sessions of Congress open with prayers. Indeed, the establishment clause often masks the fact that Americans are, by and large, religious and would like their political leaders to be people of faith.

The "wall of separation" that Thomas Jefferson referred to, however, does exist and has been upheld by the Supreme Court on many occasions. An important rul-

establishment clause The section of the First Amendment that prohibits Congress from passing laws "respecting an establishment of religion." Issues concerning the establishment clause often center on prayer in public schools, the teaching of fundamentalist theories of creation, and government aid to parochial schools.

free exercise clause The provision of the First Amendment stating that the government cannot pass laws "prohibiting the free exercise" of religion. Free exercise issues often concern religious practices that conflict with established laws.

THE REST OF THE WORLD

Saudi Arabia's Novel Approach to Fighting Terrorism

In the United States, the Constitution prohibits the government from establishing an official religion. Hence, church and state are separate entities. In Saudi Arabia and Iran, there is no such separation. Indeed, in most Muslim countries, government and religion are intertwined to a degree that is quite startling to Americans. With this background, you can better understand the role of Muslim clerics (religious leaders) in helping the Saudis fight terrorism.

TERRORISM HITS HOME IN SAUDI ARABIA

For several years in the early 2000s, the port city of Jeddah, in Saudi Arabia, saw increasingly violent terrorist attacks not only on tourists and the U.S. consulate but also on the Saudi government. In a two-year period, there were twenty-two terrorist attacks, killing almost one hundred civilians and wounding many more. Then, in 2005, there were no attacks. In 2006 and 2007, there was only one. What caused this change of heart in the Saudi domestic terrorist community? Some attribute it to a crackdown by the Saudi government, but others maintain that a unique Saudi amnesty program was primarily responsible for the near elimination of terrorist attacks in that country.

REHABILITATING AL QAEDA TERRORISTS

At the end of 2004, the Saudi government offered amnesty to terrorists who turned themselves in. More than sixty terrorists immediately took advantage of the offer. The Saudi government put them through psychological, religious, and even family counseling. Each of these programs carried the euphemistic name of "advisory committee." Many of the younger former terrorists went through the programs and were allowed to return to their families and finish their education. (The alternative was indefinite prison terms.) Some of the advisory committees included Muslim clerics who argued against the use of violence in heated discussions with the terrorists.

The results have been promising. About 1,500 Saudis have entered the amnesty program since it began. The government claims that more than 500 have been rehabilitated and "brought back" from al Qaeda.

For Critical Analysis

Could such a program work in an isolated environment such as Guantánamo Bay, where hundreds of accused terrorists are being kept by the United States? Why or why not?

Bilal Qabalan/AFP/Getty Images

A Saudi government official announces on television the beginning of an amnesty program aimed at al Qaeda terrorists, offering them rehabilitation through so-called advisory committees.

---

ing by the Supreme Court on the establishment clause came in 1947 in *Everson v. Board of Education.*[3] The case involved a New Jersey law that allowed the state to pay for bus transportation of students who attended parochial schools (schools run by churches or other religious groups). The Court stated as follows: "No tax in any amount, large or small, can be levied to support any religious activities or institutions." The Court upheld the New Jersey law, however, because it did not aid the church *directly* but provided for the safety and benefit of the students. The ruling both affirmed the importance of separating church and state and set the precedent that not *all* forms of state and federal aid to church-related schools are forbidden under the Constitution.

A full discussion of the various church-state issues that have arisen in American politics would fill volumes. Here we examine three of these issues: prayer in the schools, evolution versus creationism, and government aid to parochial schools.

Prayer in the Schools. On occasion, some schools have promoted a general sense of religion without

A teacher leads her students in a prayer. While many Americans contend that prayer should be allowed in public schools, the United States Supreme Court has held that school-sponsored prayer is constitutionally impermissible.

Karim Shambi-Basha/Corbis Sygma

proclaiming allegiance to any particular church or sect. Whether the states have a right to allow this was the main question presented in 1962 in *Engel v. Vitale,*[4] also known as the "Regents' Prayer case." The State Board of Regents in New York had composed a nondenominational prayer (a prayer not associated with any particular religion) and urged school districts to use it in classrooms at the start of each day. The prayer read as follows:

> Almighty God, we acknowledge our dependence upon Thee, and we beg Thy blessings upon us, our parents, our teachers, and our Country.

Some parents objected to the prayer, contending that it violated the establishment clause. The Supreme Court agreed and ruled that the Regents' Prayer was unconstitutional. Speaking for the majority, Justice Hugo Black wrote that the First Amendment must at least mean "that in this country it is no part of the business of government to compose official prayers for any group of the American people to recite as a part of a religious program carried on by government."

Prayer in the Schools–The Debate Continues.
Since the *Engel v. Vitale* ruling, the Supreme Court has continued to shore up the wall of separation between church and state in a number of decisions. Generally, the Court has had to walk a fine line between the wishes of those who believe that religion should have a more prominent place in our public institutions and those who do not. For example, in a 1980 case, *Stone v. Graham,*[5] the Supreme Court ruled that a Kentucky law requiring that the Ten Commandments be posted in all public schools

violated the establishment clause. Many groups around the country opposed this ruling. Currently, a number of states have passed or proposed laws permitting (but not *requiring,* as the Kentucky law did) the display of the Ten Commandments on public property, including public schools. Supporters of such displays contend that they will help reinforce the fundamental religious values that are a part of the American heritage. Opponents claim that the displays blatantly violate the establishment clause.

Another controversial issue is whether "moments of silence" in the schools are constitutional. In 1985, the Supreme Court ruled that an Alabama law authorizing a daily one-minute period of silence for meditation and voluntary prayer was unconstitutional. Because the law specifically endorsed prayer, it appeared to support religion.[6] Since then, the lower courts have generally held that a school may require a moment of silence but only if it serves a clearly secular purpose (such as to meditate on the day's activities).[7] Yet another issue concerns prayers said before public school sporting events, such as football games. In 2000, the Supreme Court held that student-led pregame prayer using the school's public-address system was unconstitutional.[8]

In sum, the Supreme Court has ruled that the public schools, which are agencies of government, cannot sponsor religious activities. It has *not,* however, held that individuals cannot pray, when and as they choose, in schools or in any other place. Nor has it held that the Bible cannot be studied as a form of literature in the schools.

When an Oklahoma school attempted to bar a young Muslim girl from wearing a head scarf to school, President George W. Bush intervened. Why would the U.S. government protect the right to wear religious symbols in public schools? What other civil liberties ensured by the U.S. Constitution might protect the right to wear religious dress in public schools?

AP Photo/Amy DeMoss/Muskogee Daily Phoenix

JOIN THE DEBATE

Teaching the Bible in Public Schools

The Constitution's First Amendment prohibits the government from passing any law "respecting an establishment of religion." Not surprisingly, many Americans found it quite shocking when, in 2006, Georgia became the first state to offer funds for a high school elective course covering the Old and New Testaments of the Christian Bible. The textbook used was the Bible, of course. As noted, the Supreme Court has never interpreted the First Amendment to mean that a public school may not teach *about* religion. In other words, teaching about the Bible is presumably no more unconstitutional than teaching about the works of Shakespeare (which contain more than one thousand references to Scripture).

Those in favor of teaching about the Bible in public schools argue that it is, after all, one of the most influential books ever created. Most Americans, even evangelical Christians, are woefully ignorant of its contents. Many cannot even name the Bible's first book (Genesis). If we want our young people to grow up understanding literature, movies, history, and world politics, we should provide them with a minimum knowledge of the contents of the Bible.

Modern-day American school secularists point out that there is a fine line between teaching what is in the Bible and teaching religion. In any event, non-Christian or atheist families who have children in public schools find it offensive that public taxpayers' dollars are used to teach the Bible. The most they are willing to accept is a course on comparative religion that would examine many major religions, including Buddhism, Hinduism, Judaism, Islam, and Christianity. They argue that it would be too easy for a teacher to go from teaching about the Bible to teaching that the Bible imparts some sort of "truth."

Evolution versus Creationism. Certain religious groups, particularly in the southern states, have long opposed the teaching of evolution in the schools. These groups contend that evolutionary theory, a scientific theory with overwhelming support, directly coun-

The theory of evolution implies that human beings descended from apes. Those with certain religious beliefs, in contrast, support the view that human beings were created fully formed. The public schools often must deal with this controversy over human origins.

ters their religious belief that human beings did not evolve but were created fully formed, as described in the biblical story of the creation. The Supreme Court, however, has held unconstitutional state laws that forbid the teaching of evolution in the schools.

For example, in *Epperson v. Arkansas,*[9] a case decided in 1968, the Supreme Court held that an Arkansas law prohibiting the teaching of evolution violated the establishment clause because it imposed religious beliefs on students. In 1987, the Supreme Court also held unconstitutional a Louisiana law requiring that the biblical story of the creation be taught along with evolution. The Court deemed the law unconstitutional, in part because it had as its primary purpose the promotion of a particular religious belief.[10]

Nevertheless, some state and local groups continue their efforts against the teaching of evolution. Recently, for example, Alabama approved a disclaimer to be inserted in biology textbooks, stating that evolution is "a controversial theory some scientists present as a scientific explanation for the origin of living things." Such laws and policies are also being challenged on constitutional grounds, however. For example, in Cobb County, Georgia, stickers were inserted into science textbooks stating that "evolution is a theory, not a fact," and that "the theory should be approached with an open mind, studied carefully, and critically considered." When Cobb County's actions were challenged in court as unconstitutional, a federal judge held that the stickers conveyed a "message of endorsement of religion," thus violating the First Amendment.

A volunteer petitions people outside a polling place at which voters are deciding whether to allow the teaching of intelligent design as an alternative to the theory of evolution.

Evolution versus Intelligent Design.

Some schools have adopted the concept of "intelligent design" as an alternative to the teaching of evolution. Advocates of intelligent design believe that an intelligent cause, and not an undirected process such as natural selection, lies behind the creation and development of the universe and living things. Proponents of intelligent design claim that it is a scientific theory and thus that its teaching should not violate the establishment clause in any way. Opponents of intelligent design theory claim that it is pseudoscience at best and that, in fact, the so-called theory masks its supporters' belief that God is the "intelligent cause."

Intelligent design does not have widespread public support. According to a recent Harris poll, only 10 percent of Americans endorse this view of creation. Although Kansas decided in 2005 to teach intelligent design in all Kansas public schools, in 2007 a new board of directors overruled that decision before the policy was implemented.

Lemon test A three-part test enunciated by the Supreme Court in the 1971 case of *Lemon v. Kurtzman* to determine whether government aid to parochial schools is constitutional. To be constitutional, the aid must (1) be for a clearly secular purpose; (2) in its primary effect, neither advance nor inhibit religion; and (3) avoid an "excessive government entanglement with religion." The *Lemon* test has also been used in other types of cases involving the establishment clause.

school voucher An educational certificate, provided by the government, that allows a student to use public funds to pay for a private or a public school chosen by the student or his or her parents.

Aid to Parochial Schools.

Americans have long been at odds over whether public tax dollars should be used to fund activities in parochial schools—private schools that have religious affiliations. Over the years, the courts have often had to decide whether specific types of aid do or do not violate the establishment clause. Aid to church-related schools in the form of transportation, equipment, or special educational services for disadvantaged students has been held permissible. Other forms of aid, such as funding teachers' salaries and paying for field trips, have been held unconstitutional.

Since 1971, the Supreme Court has held that, to be constitutional, a state's school aid must meet three requirements: (1) the purpose of the financial aid must be clearly secular (not religious); (2) its primary effect must neither advance nor inhibit religion; and (3) it must avoid an "excessive government entanglement with religion." The Court first used this three-part test in *Lemon v. Kurtzman*,[11] and hence it is often referred to as the **Lemon test**. In the *Lemon* case, the Court denied public aid to private and parochial schools for the salaries of teachers of secular courses and for textbooks and instructional materials in certain secular subjects. The Court held that the establishment clause is designed to prevent three main evils: "sponsorship, financial support, and active involvement of the sovereign [the government] in religious activity."

In 2000, the Supreme Court applied the *Lemon* test to a federal law that gives public school districts federal funds for special services and instructional equipment. The law requires that the funds be shared with all private schools in the district. A central issue in the case was whether using the funds to supply computers to parochial schools had a clearly secular purpose. Some groups claimed that it did not, because students in parochial schools could use the computers to access religious materials online. Others, including the Clinton administration (1993–2001), argued that giving high-tech assistance to parochial schools did have a secular purpose and was a religiously neutral policy. The Supreme Court sided with the latter argument and held that the law did not violate the establishment clause.[12]

School Voucher Programs.

Another contentious issue has to do with the use of **school vouchers**—educational certificates provided by state governments that students can use at any school, public or private. In an effort to improve their educational systems, several school districts have been experimenting with voucher systems. President George W. Bush also proposed vouchers as part of his plan to reform education. A dozen or so states and the District of Columbia now have voucher programs under which schoolchildren may attend private elementary or high schools using vouchers paid for by taxpayers' dollars. In 2007, Utah became the first state to pass a law creating a comprehensive, statewide school choice program. By 2020, the program will allow all children in the state to use vouchers to fund their education at private schools if they wish to transfer out of public schools.

In 2002, the United States Supreme Court ruled that a voucher program in Cleveland, Ohio, was constitutional. Under the program, the state provided up to $2,250 to low-income families, who could use the funds to send their children to either public or private schools. The Court concluded that the taxpayer-paid voucher program did not unconstitutionally entangle church and state because the funds went to parents, not to schools. The parents theoretically could use the vouchers to send their children to secular private academies or charter schools, even though 95 percent used the vouchers at religious schools.[13]

Despite the Supreme Court ruling, several constitutional questions surrounding school vouchers remain unresolved. For example, some state constitutions are more explicit than the federal Constitution in denying the use of public funds for religious education. Even after the Supreme Court ruling in the Ohio case, a Florida court ruled in 2002 that a voucher program in that state violated Florida's constitution.[14]

THE FREE EXERCISE CLAUSE   As mentioned, the second part of the First Amendment's statement on religion consists of the free exercise clause, which forbids the passage of laws "prohibiting the free exercise of religion." This clause protects a person's right to worship or believe as he or she wishes without government interference. No law or act of government may violate this constitutional right.

Belief and Practice Are Distinct.   The free exercise clause does not necessarily mean that individuals can act in any way they want on the basis of their religious beliefs. There is an important distinction between belief and practice. The Supreme Court has ruled consistently that the right to hold any *belief* is absolute. The government has no authority to compel you to accept or

This proponent of a school voucher program in Cleveland, Ohio, believes that only the students of rich parents have much school choice. In other words, her implicit argument is that school vouchers will give the same school choice to children who are poor as to those who are rich.

reject any particular religious belief. The right to *practice* one's beliefs, however, may have some limits. As the Court itself once asked, "Suppose one believed that human sacrifice were a necessary part of religious worship?"

The Supreme Court first dealt with the issue of belief versus practice in 1878 in *Reynolds v. United States*.[15] Reynolds was a Mormon who had two wives. Polygamy, or the practice of having more than one spouse at a time, was encouraged by the customs and teachings of his religion. Polygamy was also prohibited by federal law. Reynolds was convicted and appealed the case, arguing that the law violated his constitutional right to freely exercise his religious beliefs. The Court did not agree. It said that to allow Reynolds to practice polygamy would make the doctrines of religious beliefs superior to the law.

THE FREE EXERCISE CLAUSE PROTECTS A PERSON'S RIGHT TO WORSHIP OR BELIEVE AS HE OR SHE WISHES WITHOUT GOVERNMENT INTERFERENCE.

Religious Practices and the Workplace.   The free exercise of religion in the workplace was bolstered by Title VII of the Civil Rights Act of 1964, which requires employers to accommodate their employees' religious practices unless such accommodation causes an employer to suffer an "undue hardship." Thus, if an employee claims that his or her religious beliefs prevent him or her from working on a particular day of the week, such as Saturday or Sunday, the employer must attempt to accommodate the employee's needs.

Several cases have come before lower federal courts concerning employer dress codes that contradict the religious customs of employees. For example, in 1999 the Third Circuit Court of Appeals ruled in favor of two Muslim police officers in Newark, New Jersey, who claimed that they were required by their faith to wear beards and would not shave them to comply with the police department's grooming policy. A similar case was brought in 2001 by Washington, D.C., firefighters who were suspended for violating their department's safety regulations regarding long hair and beards. Muslims, Rastafarians, and others refused to change the grooming habits required by their religions and were successful in court.[16]

> "If there is any principle of the Constitution that more imperatively calls for attachment than any other, it is the principle of **free thought,** not free thought for those who agree with us but freedom for the thought that we hate."
>
> OLIVER WENDELL HOLMES,
> ASSOCIATE JUSTICE OF THE U.S. SUPREME COURT
> 1903–1933

Freedom of Expression

No one in this country seems to have a problem protecting the free speech of those with whom they agree. The real challenge is protecting unpopular ideas. The protection needed is, in Justice Oliver Wendell Holmes's words, "not free thought for those who agree with us but freedom for the thought that we hate." The First Amendment is designed to protect the freedom to express *all* ideas, including those that may be unpopular or different.

The First Amendment has been interpreted to protect more than merely spoken words; it also pro-

tects **symbolic speech**—speech involving actions and other nonverbal expressions. Some common examples include picketing in a labor dispute or wearing a black armband in protest of a government policy. Even burning the American flag as a gesture of protest has been held to be protected by the First Amendment.

THE RIGHT TO FREE SPEECH IS NOT ABSOLUTE

Although Americans have the right to free speech, not *all* speech is protected under the First Amendment. Our constitutional rights and liberties are not absolute. Rather, they are what the Supreme Court—the ultimate interpreter of the Constitution—says they are. Although the Court has zealously safeguarded the right to free speech, at times it has imposed limits on speech in the interests of protecting other rights of Americans. These rights include security against harm to one's person or reputation, the need for public order, and the need to preserve the government.

Generally, throughout our history, the Supreme Court has attempted to balance our rights to free speech against these other needs of society. As Justice Holmes once said, even "the most stringent protection of free speech would not protect a man in falsely shouting fire in a theatre and causing a panic."[17] We look next at some of the ways that the Court has limited the right to free speech.

EARLY RESTRICTIONS ON EXPRESSION At times in our nation's history, various individuals have not supported our form of democratic government. Our government, however, has drawn a fine line between legitimate criticism and the expression of ideas that may seriously harm society. Clearly, the government may pass laws against violence, espionage, sabotage, and treason. **Espionage** is the practice of spying for a foreign power. **Sabotage** involves actions normally intended to hinder or damage the nation's defense or war effort. **Treason** is specifically defined in the Constitution as levying war against the United States or adhering (remaining loyal) to its enemies (Article III, Section 3). But what about **seditious speech,** which urges resistance to lawful authority or advocates overthrowing the government?

---

symbolic speech The expression of beliefs, opinions, or ideas through forms other than speech or print; speech involving actions and other nonverbal expressions.

espionage The practice of spying on behalf of a foreign power to obtain information about government plans and activities.

sabotage A destructive act intended to hinder a nation's defense efforts.

treason As enunciated in Article III, Section 3, of the Constitution, the act of levying war against the United States or adhering (remaining loyal) to its enemies.

seditious speech Speech that urges resistance to lawful authority or that advocates the overthrowing of a government.

As early as 1798, Congress took steps to curb seditious speech when it passed the Alien and Sedition Acts, which made it a crime to utter "any false, scandalous, and malicious" criticism against the government. The acts were considered unconstitutional by many but were never tested in the courts. Several dozen individuals were prosecuted under the acts, and some were actually convicted. In 1801, President Thomas Jefferson pardoned those sentenced under the acts, and Congress soon repealed them. During World War I, Congress passed the Espionage Act of 1917 and the Sedition Act of 1918. The 1917 act prohibited attempts to interfere with the operation of the military forces, the war effort, or the process of recruitment. The 1918 act made it a crime to "willfully utter, print, write, or publish any disloyal, profane, scurrilous [insulting], or abusive language" about the government. More than two thousand persons were tried and convicted under this act, which was repealed at the end of World War I.

In 1940, Congress passed the Smith Act, which forbade people from advocating the violent overthrow of the U.S. government. The Supreme Court first upheld the constitutionality of the Smith Act in *Dennis v. United States,*[18] which involved eleven top leaders of the Communist Party who had been convicted of violating the act. The Court found that their activities went beyond the permissible peaceful advocacy of change. According to the Smith Act, these activities threatened society's right to national security. Subsequently, however, the Court modified its position. Since the 1960s, the Court has defined seditious speech to mean only the advocacy of imminent and concrete acts of violence against the government.[19]

LIMITED PROTECTION FOR COMMERCIAL SPEECH

Advertising, or **commercial speech,** is also protected by the First Amendment, but not as fully as regular speech. Generally, the Supreme Court has considered a restriction on commercial speech to be valid as long as the restriction "(1) seeks to implement a substantial government interest, (2) directly advances that interest, and (3) goes no further than necessary to accomplish its objective." Problems arise, though, when restrictions on commercial advertising achieve one substantial government interest yet are contrary to the interest in protecting free speech and the right of consumers to be informed. In such cases, the courts have to decide which interest takes priority.

Liquor advertising is a good example of this kind of conflict. For example, in one case, Rhode Island argued that its law banning the advertising of liquor prices served the state's goal of discouraging liquor consumption (because the ban discouraged bargain hunting and thus kept

More than 450 conscientious objectors were imprisoned as a result of the Espionage Act of 1917, including Rose Pastor Stokes who was sentenced to ten years in prison for saying, in a letter to the *Kansas City Star,* that "no government which is for the profiteers can also be for the people, and I am for the people while the government is for the profiteers."

liquor prices high). The Supreme Court, however, held that the ban was an unconstitutional restraint on commercial speech. The Court stated that the First Amendment "directs us to be especially skeptical of regulations that seek to keep people in the dark for what the government perceives to be their own good."[20] In contrast, restrictions on tobacco advertising are the result of a policy choice that free speech can be restrained in the interests of protecting the health of society, particularly the health of young Americans.

UNPROTECTED SPEECH
Certain types of speech receive no protection under the First Amendment. These types of speech include libel and slander, "fighting words," and obscenity.

Libel and Slander.
No person has the right to libel or slander another. **Libel** is a published report of a falsehood that tends to injure a person's reputation or character. **Slander** is the public utterance (speaking)

commercial speech
Advertising statements that describe products. Commercial speech receives less protection under the First Amendment than ordinary speech.

libel A published report of a falsehood that tends to injure a person's reputation or character.

slander The public utterance (speaking) of a statement that holds a person up for contempt, ridicule, or hatred.

At times, books by Mark Twain and James Joyce have been banned in the United States. These posters provided by the American Civil Liberties Union show that a lot more American authors' books have been banned at various times in this country. Their "sin" was obscenity.

of a statement that holds a person up for contempt, ridicule, or hatred. To prove libel and slander, however, certain criteria must be met. The statements made must be untrue, must stem from an intent to do harm, and must result in actual harm.

The Supreme Court has ruled that public figures (public officials and others in the public limelight) cannot collect damages for remarks made against them unless they can prove the remarks were made with "reckless" disregard for accuracy. Generally, it is believed that because public figures have greater access to the media than ordinary persons do, they are in a better position to defend themselves against libelous or slanderous statements.

"Fighting Words." Another form of speech that is not protected by the First Amendment is what the Supreme Court has called **"fighting words."** This is speech that is so inflammatory that it will provoke the average listener to violence. The Court has ruled that "fighting words" must go beyond merely insulting or controversial language. The words must be a clear invitation to immediate violence or breach of

"fighting words" Words that, when uttered by a public speaker, are so inflammatory that they could provoke the average listener to violence.

obscenity Indecency or offensiveness in speech, expression, behavior, or appearance. Whether specific expressions or acts constitute obscenity normally is determined by community standards.

the peace. Sometimes, however, determining when hateful speech becomes an actual threat against a person or an invitation to start a riot can be difficult. For example, an individual was arrested for allegedly praising the World Trade Center terrorist attacks to a crowd in Times Square just a few days after September 11, 2001. His arrest was upheld in court by a judge who noted that his words "were plainly intended to incite the crowd to violence, and not simply to express a point of view." Nonetheless, some legal experts argue that upholding this arrest on the "fighting words" doctrine is untenable because the defendant was expressing political speech.[21]

Obscenity. Obscene speech is another form of speech that is not protected under the First Amendment. Although the dictionary defines **obscenity** as that which is offensive and indecent, the courts have had difficulty defining the term with any precision. Supreme Court Justice Potter Stewart's famous statement, "I know it when I see it," certainly gave little guidance on the issue.

One problem in defining obscenity is that what is obscene to one person is not necessarily obscene to another; what one reader considers indecent, another reader might see as "colorful." Another problem is that society's views on obscenity change over time. Major literary works of such great writers as D. H. Lawrence (1885–1930), Mark Twain (1835–1910), and James Joyce (1882–1941), for example, were once considered obscene in most of the United States.

After many unsuccessful attempts to define obscenity, in 1973 the Supreme Court came up with a three-part test in *Miller v. California*.[22] The Court decided that a book, film, or other piece of material is legally obscene if it meets the following criteria:

1. The average person applying contemporary [present-day] standards finds that the work taken as a whole appeals to the prurient interest—that is, tends to excite unwholesome sexual desire.

2. The work depicts or describes, in a patently [obviously] offensive way, a form of sexual conduct specifically prohibited by an antiobscenity law.

3. The work taken as a whole lacks serious literary, artistic, political, or scientific value.

The very fact that the Supreme Court has had to set up such a complicated test shows how difficult defining obscenity is. The Court went on to state that, in effect, local communities should be allowed to set their own standards for what is obscene. What is obscene to many people in one area of the country might be perfectly acceptable to those in another area.

Obscenity in Cyberspace. One of the most controversial issues in regard to free speech in cyberspace concerns obscene and pornographic materials. Such materials can be easily accessed by anyone of any age anywhere in the world at numerous Web sites. Many people strongly believe that the government should step in to prevent obscenity on the Internet. Others believe, just as strongly, that speech on the Internet should not be regulated.

The issue came to a head in 1996, when Congress passed the Communications Decency Act (CDA). The law made it a crime to transmit "indecent" or "patently offensive" speech or images to minors (those under the age of eighteen) or to make such speech or images available online to minors. Violators of the act could be fined up to $250,000 or imprisoned for up to two years. In 1997, the Supreme Court held that the law's sections on indecent speech were unconstitutional. According to the Court, those sections of the CDA were too broad in their scope and significantly restrained the constitution-

> "BE NOT INTIMIDATED . . . NOR SUFFER YOURSELVES TO BE **WHEEDLED OUT OF YOUR LIBERTIES** BY ANY PRETENSE OF POLITENESS, DELICACY, OR **DECENCY.**"
>
> JOHN ADAMS, SECOND PRESIDENT OF THE UNITED STATES 1797–1801

ally protected free speech of adults.[23] Congress made a further attempt to regulate Internet speech in 1998 with the Child Online Protection Act. The act imposed criminal penalties on those who distribute material that is "harmful to minors" without using some kind of age-verification system to separate adult and minor Web users. Ultimately, the Supreme Court barred enforcement of the act, ruling that the act likely violated constitutionally protected free speech, and sent the case back to the district court for a trial.[24]

Having failed twice in its attempt to regulate online obscenity, Congress decided to try a different approach. In late 2000, it passed the Children's Internet Protection Act (CIPA). This act requires schools and libraries to use Internet filtering software to protect children from pornography or risk losing federal funds for technology upgrades. The CIPA was also challenged on constitutional grounds, but in 2003 the Supreme Court held that the act did not violate the First Amendment. The Court concluded that because libraries can disable the filters for any patrons who ask, the system was reasonably flexible and did not burden free speech to an unconstitutional extent.[25]

In 1996, with the Child Pornography Prevention Act, Congress also attempted to prevent the distribution and possession of "virtual" child pornography—computer-generated images of children engaged in lewd and lascivious behavior. These images, when digitally rendered, are amazingly real, even though they are created entirely on a computer, with no child actors involved. In 2002, the Supreme Court reviewed the 1996 act and found it unconstitutional. The Court ruled that the act did not establish the necessary link between "its prohibitions and the affront to community standards prohibited by the obscenity definition."[26]

FREE SPEECH FOR STUDENTS? America's schools and college campuses experience an ongoing tension between the guarantee of free speech and the desire to restrain speech that is offensive to others. Typically, cases involving free speech in the schools raise the following question: Where should the line between unacceptable speech and merely offensive speech be drawn? Schools at all levels—elementary schools, high schools, and colleges and universities—have grappled with this issue. Generally, the courts allow elementary schools a wide latitude in terms of what students may and may not say to other students. Offensive speech must rise to a serious level before a parent may bring a suit against an elementary school district for violating federal laws prohibiting discrimination. For example, in a 1999 case in which a parent alleged that her daughter had been sexually harassed at elementary school, the Supreme Court held that speech is harassing, as opposed to being merely offensive, if it is "so severe, pervasive, and objectively offensive that it effectively bars the victim's access to an educational opportunity or benefit."[27]

At the high school level, the Supreme Court has allowed some restraints to be placed on the freedom of expression. For example, as you will read shortly, in the discussion of freedom of the press, the Court does allow school officials to exercise some censorship over high school publications. And, in a controversial 2007 case, the Court upheld a school principal's decision to suspend a high school student who unfurled a banner reading "Bong Hits 4 Jesus" at an event off the school premises. The Court sided with the school officials, who maintained that the banner appeared to advocate illegal drug use in violation of school policy. Many legal commentators and scholars strongly criticized this decision.[28]

A difficult question faced by many universities today is whether the right to free speech includes the right to make hateful remarks about others based on their race, gender, or sexual orientation. Some claim that allowing people with extremist views to voice their opinions can lead to violence. In response to this question, several universities have gone so far as to institute speech codes to minimize the disturbances that hate speech might cause. Although these speech codes have often been ruled unconstitutional on the ground that

they restrict freedom of speech,[29] such codes continue to exist on many college campuses. For example, the student assembly at Wesleyan University passed a resolution in 2002 stating that the "right to speech comes with implicit responsibilities to respect community standards."[30] Campus rules governing speech and expression, however, can foster the idea that "good" speech should be protected, but "bad" speech should not. Furthermore, who should decide what is considered "hate speech"?

Freedom of the Press

The framers of the Constitution believed that the press should be free to publish a wide range of opinions and information, and generally the free speech rights just discussed also apply to the press. The courts have placed certain restrictions on the freedom of the press, however. Over the years, the Supreme Court has developed various guidelines and doctrines to use in deciding whether freedom of speech and the press can be restrained.

CLEAR AND PRESENT DANGER

One guideline the Court has used resulted from a case in 1919, *Schenck v. United States.*[31] Charles T. Schenck was convicted of printing and distributing leaflets urging men to resist the draft during World War I. The government claimed that his actions violated the Espionage Act of 1917, which made it a crime to encourage disloyalty to the government or resistance to the draft. The Supreme Court upheld both the law and the convictions. Justice Holmes, speaking for the Court, stated as follows:

> The question in every case is whether the words used are used in such circumstances and are of such a nature as to create a *clear and present danger* that they will bring about the substantive evils that Congress has a right to prevent. It is a question of proximity [closeness] and degree. [Emphasis added.]

AP Photo/Nick Ut

These students at Claremont McKenna College in California demonstrate against a series of hate crimes in the area.

Thus, according to the *clear and present danger test,* government should be allowed to restrain speech only when that speech clearly presents an immediate threat to public order. It is often hard to say when speech crosses the line between being merely controversial and being a "clear and present danger," but the principle has been used in many cases since *Schenck.*

The clear and present danger principle seemed too permissive to some Supreme Court justices. Several years after the *Schenck* ruling, in the case of *Gitlow v. New York,*[32] the Court held that speech could be curtailed even if it had only a *tendency* to lead to illegal action. Since the 1920s, however, this guideline, known as the *bad-tendency test,* generally has not been supported by the Supreme Court.

THE PREFERRED-POSITION DOCTRINE Another guideline, called the *preferred-position doctrine,* states that certain freedoms are so essential to a democracy that they hold a preferred position. According to this doctrine, any law that limits these freedoms should be presumed unconstitutional unless the government can show that the law is absolutely necessary. Thus, freedom of speech and the press should rarely, if ever, be diminished, because spoken and printed words are the prime tools of the democratic process.

PRIOR RESTRAINT Stopping an activity before it actually happens is known as *prior restraint.* With respect to freedom of the press, prior restraint involves *censorship,* which occurs when an official removes objectionable materials from an item before it is published or broadcast. An example of censorship and prior restraint would be a court's ruling that two paragraphs in an upcoming article in the local newspaper had to be removed before the article could be published. The Supreme Court has generally ruled against prior restraint, arguing that the government cannot curb ideas *before* they are expressed. (Should the military be al-

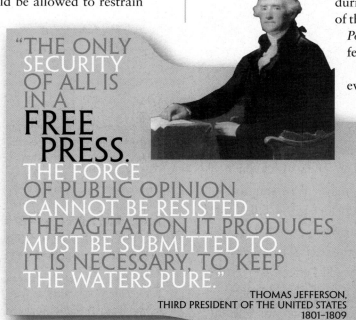

"THE ONLY SECURITY OF ALL IS IN A **FREE PRESS.** THE FORCE OF PUBLIC OPINION CANNOT BE RESISTED . . . THE AGITATION IT PRODUCES MUST BE SUBMITTED TO. IT IS NECESSARY, TO KEEP THE WATERS PURE."

THOMAS JEFFERSON,
THIRD PRESIDENT OF THE UNITED STATES
1801–1809

lowed to censor news reporting during wartime? For a discussion of this issue, see this chapter's *The Politics of National Security* feature on the next page.)

On some occasions, however, the Court has allowed prior restraint. For example, in a 1988 case, *Hazelwood School District v. Kuhlmeier,*[33] a high school principal deleted two pages from the school newspaper just before it was printed. The pages contained stories on students' experiences with pregnancy and discussed the impact of divorce on students at the school. The Supreme Court, noting that students in school do not have exactly the same rights as adults in other settings, ruled that high school administrators *can* censor school publications. The Court said that school newspapers are part of the school curriculum, not a public forum. Therefore, administrators have the right to censor speech that promotes conduct inconsistent with the "shared values of a civilized social order."

Freedom of Assembly

The First Amendment also protects the right of the people "peaceably to assemble" and communicate their ideas on public issues to government officials, as well as to other individuals. Parades, marches, protests, and other demonstrations are daily events in this country and allow groups to express and publicize their ideas. The Supreme Court has often put this freedom of assembly, or association, on a par with freedom of speech and freedom of the press. In the interests of public order, however, the Court has allowed municipalities to require permits for parades, sound trucks, and demonstrations.

Like unpopular speech, unpopular assemblies or protests often generate controversy. One controversial case arose in 1977, when the American Nazi Party decided to march through the largely Jewish suburb of Skokie, Illinois. The city of Skokie enacted three ordinances

THE POLITICS OF NATIONAL SECURITY

FREEDOM OF EXPRESSION— UNLESS YOU ARE IN THE MILITARY

Governments the world over have always tried to manage war news. The United States is no exception. During the first Gulf War in 1991, the Pentagon expertly managed the war news by controlling when journalists could report. So-called pools of reporters were created; those who were not in a pool were not allowed to report on events as they happened. The pool-reporting concept was most effective in restricting the imagery available to television cameras. Many Americans believe, however, that censoring war news in any way is wrong.

IMAGES OF MILITARY COFFINS CENSORED

Any war has military casualties. At various times in our history, though, the Pentagon has barred reporters from witnessing the transportation of soldiers' coffins. Indeed, from the first Gulf War through 2005, the media showed virtually no pictures of military coffins. In 2004,

an employee of a defense contractor in Kuwait photographed a plane filled with coffins. After the *Seattle Times* ran the photo, the worker was fired. Not everyone is against such heavy-handed censorship, though. The National Military Family Association officially supports a ban on such photos: "Some families tell us they find the pictures 'disturbing.'"

ALL AMERICANS CAN ACCESS YOU-TUBE AND MYSPACE, UNLESS THEY ARE IN THE MILITARY ABROAD

One Bush administration attempt at managing the news coming from Afghanistan and Iraq involved such popular Web sites as YouTube and MySpace. In the spring of 2007, the Pentagon shut off overseas soldiers' access to these popular Web sites, as well as to eleven others. Why? The reason was that soldiers had been posting personal photos and videos on these sites to keep in touch with their loved ones stateside. Rather than explicitly censor such activities, the Pentagon simply asserted that soldiers overseas were taking up too much Internet bandwidth by watching online videos. This reaction to YouTube struck some as strange, given that the military had already launched its own channel providing a "boots on the ground" perspective of combat scenes.

YOU BE THE JUDGE

Just as it has done in the past, the U.S. government today is attempting to put a less gruesome face on U.S. military actions abroad. Some argue that such censorship attempts are at odds with the Constitution's guarantees of freedom of expression and freedom of the press. Others believe that allowing the military to control media coverage of the war is important to national security. Where do you stand on this issue?

designed to prohibit the types of demonstrations that the Nazis planned to undertake. The American Civil Liberties Union (ACLU) sued the city on behalf of the Nazis, defending their right to march (in spite of the ACLU's opposition to the Nazi philosophy). A federal district court agreed with the ACLU and held that the city of Skokie had violated the Nazis' First Amendment guarantees by denying them a permit to march. The appellate court affirmed that decision. The Supreme Court refused to review the case, thus letting the lower court's decision stand.[34]

What about laws that prevent gang members from assembling on city streets? Do such laws violate the

gang members' First Amendment rights or other constitutional guarantees? Courts have answered this question differently, depending in part on the nature of the laws in question.

In some cases, for example, "antiloitering" laws have been upheld by the courts. In others, they have not. In 1999, the Supreme Court held that Chicago's antiloitering ordinance violated the right to due process because, among other things, it left too much "lawmaking" power in the hands of the police, who had to decide what constitutes "loitering."[35] How a particular court balances gang members' right of assembly against the

All groups—even the racially intolerant Ku Klux Klan—are guaranteed the freedom of assembly under the First Amendment.

rights of society may also come into play. In 1997, for example, the California Supreme Court had to decide whether court injunctions barring gang members from appearing in public together in certain areas of San Jose, California, were constitutional. The court upheld the injunctions, declaring that society's rights to peace and quiet and to be free from harm outweighed the gang members' First Amendment rights to gather together in public.[36]

The Right to Petition the Government

The First Amendment also guarantees the right of the people "to petition the government for a redress of grievances." This important right sometimes gets lost among the other, more well-known First Amendment guarantees, such as the freedoms of religion, speech, and the press. Nonetheless, the right to petition the government is as important and fundamental to our democracy as the other First Amendment rights.

The right to petition the government allows citizens to lobby members of Congress and other government officials, to sue the government, and to submit petitions to the government. A petitioner may be an individual

The right to **privacy** is "the most comprehensive of rights and the right most valued by **civilized** men."

LOUIS BRANDEIS,
ASSOCIATE JUSTICE OF THE U.S. SUPREME COURT
1916-1939

or a long list of signatures. In the past, Americans have petitioned the government to ban alcohol, give the vote to women, and abolish slavery. They have petitioned the government to improve roads and obtain economic relief. Whenever someone writes to her or his congressional representative for help with a problem, such as not receiving a Social Security payment, that person is petitioning the government.

LO³ THE RIGHT TO PRIVACY

Supreme Court Justice Louis Brandeis stated in 1928 that the right to privacy is "the most comprehensive of rights and the right most valued by civilized men."[37] The majority of the justices on the Supreme Court at that time did not agree. In 1965, however, in the landmark case of *Griswold v. Connecticut*,[38] the justices on the Supreme Court held that a right to privacy is implied by other constitutional rights guaranteed in the First, Third, Fourth, Fifth, and Ninth Amendments. For example, consider the words of the Ninth Amendment: "The enumeration in the Constitution, of certain rights, shall not be construed to deny or disparage others retained by the people." In other words, just because the Constitution, including its amendments, does not specifically mention the right to privacy does not mean that this right is denied to the people.

Since then, the government has also passed laws ensuring the privacy rights of individuals. For example, in 1966 Congress passed the Freedom of Information Act, which, among other things, allows any person to request copies of any information about her or him contained in government files. In 1974, Congress passed the Privacy Act, which restricts government disclosure of data to third parties. In 1994, Congress passed the Driver's Privacy Protection Act, which

Abortion continues to be extremely controversial in the United States. Pro-choice supporters demonstrate their desire that abortion remain legal. In stark contrast, on the right, an antiabortion protester stands in front of the United States Supreme Court building in Washington, D.C. Before the Roe v. Wade decision in 1973, whether abortion was legal depended on state legislation.

prevents states from disclosing or selling a driver's personal information without the driver's consent.[39] In late 2000, the federal Department of Health and Human Services issued a regulation ensuring the privacy of a person's medical information. Health-care providers and insurance companies are restricted from sharing confidential information about their patients.

Although Congress and the courts have acknowledged a constitutional right to privacy, the nature and scope of this right are not always clear. For example, Americans continue to debate whether the right to privacy includes the right to have an abortion or the right of terminally ill persons to commit physician-assisted suicide. Americans are also at odds over how to deal with what is perhaps one of the most difficult challenges of our time—how to protect privacy rights in cyberspace. Since the terrorist attacks of September 11, 2001, another pressing privacy issue has been how to monitor potential terrorists to prevent another attack without violating the privacy rights of all Americans.

The Abortion Controversy

One of the most divisive and emotionally charged issues being debated today is whether the right to privacy means that women can choose to have abortions.

ABORTION AND PRIVACY   In 1973, in the landmark case of *Roe v. Wade*,[40] the Supreme Court, using the *Griswold* case as a precedent, held that the "right of privacy . . . is broad enough to encompass a woman's decision whether or not to terminate her pregnancy." The right is not absolute throughout pregnancy, however. The

Court also said that any state could impose certain regulations to safeguard the health of the mother after the first three months of pregnancy and, in the final stages of pregnancy, could act to protect potential life.

Since the *Roe v. Wade* decision, the Supreme Court has adopted a more conservative approach and has upheld restrictive state laws requiring counseling, waiting periods, notification of parents, and other actions prior to abortions.[41] Yet the Court has never overturned the *Roe* decision. In fact, in 1997 and again in 2000, the Supreme Court upheld laws requiring "buffer zones" around abortion clinics to protect those entering the clinics from unwanted counseling or harassment by antiabortion groups.[42] In 2000, the Supreme Court invalidated a Nebraska statute banning "partial-birth" abortions, a procedure used during the second trimester of pregnancy.[43] Undeterred by the fate of the Nebraska law, President George W. Bush signed the Partial Birth Abortion Ban Act in 2003. In a close (five-to-four) and controversial 2007 decision, the Supreme Court upheld the constitutionality of the 2003 act.[44]

Many were surprised at the Court's decision on partial-birth abortion, given that the federal act banning this practice was quite similar to the Nebraska law that had been struck down by the Court in 2000, just seven years earlier. Since that decision was rendered, however, the Court has generally become more conservative with the appointment of two new justices. Dissenting from the majority opinion in the case, Justice Ruth Bader Ginsburg said that the ruling was an "alarming" departure from three decades of Supreme Court decisions on abortion. Although the *Roe* decision remains intact, some commentators contend that the current Supreme Court is pursuing a policy of "chipping away" at abortion rights, little by little.

ABORTION AND POLITICS American opinion on the abortion issue has become more nuanced than the labels "pro-life" and "pro-choice" would indicate. For example, a 2007 Gallup poll found that 45 percent of the respondents considered themselves pro-choice and 45 percent called themselves pro-life. Yet when respondents were asked whether abortion should be legal or illegal, public opinion is more conservative than the attachments to these labels would suggest. About 58 percent thought that abortion should either be limited to only a few circumstances or be illegal in all circumstances; 41 percent thought that it should be legal in all or most circumstances.

Some contend that President George W. Bush's appointment of more than 250 federal judges is causing a rightward shift in the judiciary and that this shift will result in more conservative abortion rulings in the future. Certainly, the Supreme Court headed by Bush appointee John Roberts seems to be leaning in a rightward direction on the issue.

Do We Have the "Right to Die"?

Whether it is called euthanasia (mercy killing), assisted suicide, or a dignified way to leave this world, it all comes down to one basic question: Do terminally ill persons have, as part of their civil liberties, a right to die and to be assisted in the process by physicians or others? Phrased another way, are state laws banning physician-assisted suicide in such circumstances unconstitutional?

In 1997, the issue came before the Supreme Court, which characterized the question as follows: Does the liberty protected by the Constitution include a right to commit suicide, which itself includes a right to assistance in doing so? The Court's clear and categorical answer to this question was no. To hold otherwise, said the Court, would be "to reverse centuries of legal doctrine and practice, and strike down the considered policy choice of almost every state."[45] (Suicide, including attempts to aid or promote suicide, is defined as a crime in most, if not all, states.) Although the Court upheld the states' rights to ban such a practice, the Court did not hold that state laws *permitting* assisted suicide were unconstitutional. In

AP Photo/Charles Dharapak

To fill the vacancy created by the death of Supreme Court chief justice William Rehnquist, President George W. Bush nominated John Roberts (left). The U.S. Senate confirmed Roberts's nomination and he became the current chief justice. He supports a conservative political ideology. Many believe that the Roberts Court will gradually become more conservative than the Rehnquist Court. In what areas might the Roberts Court show that it is more conservative?

1997, Oregon became the first state—and so far, the only one—to implement such a law. Oregon's law was upheld by the Supreme Court in 2006.[46]

The Supreme Court's enunciation of its opinion on this topic has not ended the debate, though, just as the debate over abortion did not stop after the 1973 *Roe v. Wade* decision legalizing abortion. And Americans continue to be at odds over this issue.

Personal Privacy and National Security

Since the terrorist attacks of September 11, 2001, one of the most common debates in the news media and on Capitol Hill has been how the United States can address the urgent need to strengthen national security while still protecting civil liberties, particularly the right to privacy. As you will read throughout this book, various programs have been proposed or attempted, and some have already been dismantled after public outcry. For example, the Homeland Security Act passed in late 2002 included language explicitly prohibiting a controversial program called Operation TIPS (Terrorism Information and Prevention System). Operation TIPS was proposed to create a national reporting program for "citizen volunteers" who regularly work in neighborhoods and communities, such as postal carriers and meter readers, to

Robert Mueller, the director of the Federal Bureau of Investigation, discusses National Security Letters, which have been used to obtain personal, individual information about U.S. citizens from private companies, such as banks. When these letters have been used, the individuals being scrutinized have not known about this activity.

report suspicious activity to the government. The public backlash against the program was quick and resolute—neighbors would not spy on neighbors.

Other laws and programs that infringe on Americans' privacy rights were also created in the wake of 9/11 in the interests of protecting the nation's security. As you read in *The Politics of National Security* feature in Chapter 2, the USA Patriot Act of 2001 gave the government broad latitude to investigate people who are only vaguely associated with terrorists. Under this law, the government can access personal information on American citizens to an extent heretofore never allowed by law. The Federal Bureau of Investigation was also authorized to use "National Security Letters" to demand personal information about individuals from private companies (such as banks and phone companies). In one of the most controversial programs, the National Security Agency (NSA) was authorized to monitor certain domestic phone calls without first obtaining a warrant. When Americans learned of the NSA's actions in 2005, the ensuing public furor forced the Bush administration to agree to henceforth obtain warrants for such monitoring activities.

Some Americans, including many civil libertarians, are so concerned about the erosion of privacy rights that they wonder why the public outcry has not been even more vehement. They point out that trading off even a few civil liberties, including

probable cause Cause for believing that there is a substantial likelihood that a person has committed or is about to commit a crime.

our privacy rights, for national security is senseless. After all, these liberties are at the heart of what this country stands for. When we abandon any of our civil liberties, we weaken our country rather than defend it. Essentially, say some members of this group, the Bush administration is doing what the terrorists have been unable to accomplish—destroying our country. Other Americans believe that we have little to worry about. Those who have nothing to hide should not be concerned about government surveillance or other privacy intrusions undertaken by the government to make our nation more secure against terrorist attacks.

LO⁴ THE RIGHTS OF THE ACCUSED

The United States has one of the highest murder rates in the industrialized world. It is therefore not surprising that many Americans have extremely strong opinions about the rights of persons accused of criminal offenses. Indeed, some Americans complain that criminal defendants have too many rights.

Why do criminal suspects have rights? The answer is that all persons are entitled to the protections afforded by the Bill of Rights. If criminal suspects were deprived of their basic constitutional liberties, all people would suffer the consequences. In fact, these liberties take on added significance in the context of criminal law. After all, in a criminal case, a state official (such as the district attorney, or D.A.) prosecutes the defendant, and the state has immense resources that it can bring to bear against the accused person. By protecting the rights of accused persons, the Constitution helps to prevent the arbitrary use of power on the part of the government.

The Rights of Criminal Defendants

The basic rights, or constitutional safeguards, provided for criminal defendants are set forth in the Bill of Rights. These safeguards include the following:

■ The Fourth Amendment protection from unreasonable searches and seizures.

■ The Fourth Amendment requirement that no warrant for a search or an arrest be issued without **probable cause** (cause for believing that there is a substantial likelihood that a person has committed or is about to commit a crime).

■ The Fifth Amendment requirement that no one be deprived of "life, liberty, or property, without due process of law." (As discussed earlier in this chapter, this

double jeopardy To prosecute a person twice for the same criminal offense; prohibited by the Fifth Amendment in all but a few circumstances.

self-incrimination Providing damaging information or testimony against oneself in court.

requirement is also included in the Fourteenth Amendment, which protects persons against actions by state governments.)

■ The Fifth Amendment prohibition against **double jeopardy** (being tried twice for the same criminal offense).

■ The Fifth Amendment provision that no person can be required to be a witness against (incriminate) himself or herself. (This is often referred to as the constitutional protection against **self-incrimination.** It is the basis for a criminal suspect's "right to remain silent" in criminal proceedings.)

■ The Sixth Amendment guarantees of a speedy trial, a trial by jury, a public trial, and the right to confront witnesses.

■ The Sixth Amendment guarantee of the right to counsel at various stages in some criminal proceedings. (The right to counsel was established in 1963 in *Gideon v. Wainwright*.[47] The Supreme Court held that if a person is accused of a felony and cannot afford an attorney, an attorney must be made available to the accused person at the government's expense.)

■ The Eighth Amendment prohibitions against excessive bail and fines and against cruel and unusual punishments.

JOIN THE DEBATE

Should the Death Penalty Be Abolished?

An ongoing debate among Americans has to do with whether the death penalty violates the Eighth Amendment's prohibition against "cruel and unusual punishments." Although an overwhelming majority of Americans continue to support the death penalty, as they have in the past, the debate over this issue remains forceful.

The United States Supreme Court has held that the question of whether an execution is "cruel and unusual" is determined by the "changing norms and standards of society." What are those norms and standards today? That is at the heart of the issue. Back in 1972, the Supreme Court invalidated all existing death sentence laws as being impermissibly arbitrary. Since then, all of the states that have death penalties have changed their laws to satisfy Supreme Court guidelines.

Those in favor of the death penalty argue that some crimes are so horrible that executing the person responsible is the only fitting response. Murder is not the same kind of act as robbery, and thus its perpetrators should be treated much more harshly. Furthermore, what about the victims? The Victims' Rights Movement is premised on the idea that society owes more than a seat at the alleged perpetrator's trial to those who have experienced the trauma of a murdered family member. Victims' families often speak of a sense of "closure" or "justice" that a murderer's execution brings. After all, a murderer eliminates his or her victim's civil liberties completely and forever. Why should the murderer expect to enjoy any of the rights and liberties that he or she has denied to another?

Despite such arguments, in 2007 twelve out of thirteen members of New Jersey's Death Penalty Study Commission recommended that the state replace the death penalty with life imprisonment without parole. Juries increasingly seem to agree: whereas 277 death sentences were meted out in 1999, barely over 100 were pronounced in 2006. Opponents of the death penalty argue that poor defendants who cannot afford to hire an attorney are more likely to be found guilty. Race also appears to play a role in determining whether the death penalty will be imposed. African Americans constitute only 12 percent of the general population but make up 42 percent of those on death row. The United States stands alone among all Western nations as the only country with the death penalty. Finally, if a defendant is actually put to death after conviction, there is no going back if we later discover that she or he was innocent.

UPI Photo/Roger L. Wollenberg/Landov

The Exclusionary Rule

Any evidence obtained in violation of the constitutional rights spelled out in the Fourth Amendment normally is not admissible at trial. This rule, which has been applied in the federal courts since at least 1914, is known as the **exclusionary rule.** The rule was extended to state court proceedings in 1961.[48] The reasoning behind the exclusionary rule is that it forces law enforcement personnel to gather evidence properly. If they do not, they will be unable to introduce the evidence at trial to convince the jury that the defendant is guilty.

The *Miranda* Warnings

In the 1950s and 1960s, one of the questions facing the courts was not whether suspects had constitutional rights—that was not in doubt—but how and when those rights could be exercised. For example, could the right to remain silent (under the Fifth Amendment's prohibition against self-incrimination) be exercised during pretrial interrogation proceedings or only during the trial? Were confessions obtained from suspects admissible in court if the suspects had not been advised of their right to remain silent and other constitutional rights? To clarify these issues, in 1966 the Supreme Court issued a landmark decision in *Miranda v. Arizona.*[49] In that case, the Court enunciated the **Miranda warnings** that are now familiar to virtually all Americans:

> Prior to any questioning, the person must be warned that he has a right to remain silent, that any statement he does make may be used against him, and that he has a right to the presence of an attorney, either retained or appointed.

The Erosion of *Miranda*

As part of a continuing attempt to balance the rights of accused persons against the rights of society, the Supreme Court has made a number of exceptions to the *Miranda* ruling. In 1986, for example, the Court held that a confession need not be excluded even though the police failed to inform a suspect in custody that his attorney had tried to reach him by telephone.[50] In an important 1991 decision, the Court stated that a suspect's conviction will not be automatically overturned if the suspect was coerced into making

exclusionary rule A criminal procedural rule requiring that any illegally obtained evidence not be admissible in court.

Miranda warnings A series of statements informing criminal suspects, on their arrest, of their constitutional rights, such as the right to remain silent and the right to counsel; required by the Supreme Court's 1966 decision in *Miranda v. Arizona.*

This police officer is reading the accused his *Miranda* warnings. Since the 1966 *Miranda* decision, the Supreme Court has relaxed its requirements in some situations, such as when a criminal suspect who is not under arrest enters a police station voluntarily.

a confession. If the other evidence admitted at trial was strong enough to justify the conviction without the confession, then the fact that the confession was obtained illegally can be, in effect, ignored.[51] In yet another case, in 1994 the Supreme Court ruled that a suspect must unequivocally and assertively state his right to counsel in order to stop police questioning. Saying, "Maybe I should talk to a lawyer" during an interrogation after being taken into custody is not enough. The Court held that police officers are not required to decipher the suspect's intentions in such situations.[52]

Miranda may eventually find itself obsolete regardless of any decisions made in the courts. A relatively new trend in law enforcement has been for agencies to record interrogations and confessions either on videotape or digitally. Thomas P. Sullivan, a former U.S. attorney in Chicago, and his staff interviewed personnel in more than 230 law enforcement agencies in thirty-eight states that record custodial interviews of suspects. Sullivan found that nearly all police officers said the procedure saved time and money, created valuable evidence to use in court, and made it more difficult for defense attorneys to claim that their clients were illegally coerced.[53] Some scholars have suggested that recording all custodial interrogations would satisfy the Fifth Amendment's prohibition against coercion and in the process render the *Miranda* warnings unnecessary.

AMERICA AT ODDS:
Civil Liberties

For more than two hundred years, Americans have been among the freest people in the world. This is largely because our courts have upheld, time and again, the liberties set forth in the Bill of Rights and because the government has enforced the courts' decisions. Every generation of Americans has given strength to the Bill of Rights by bringing pressure to bear on the government when these liberties have been violated. If either the courts or the government fails to enforce these liberties, then the Bill of Rights itself becomes irrelevant—a useless piece of paper. Many nations with written constitutions that set forth liberal rights and liberties for their citizens nonetheless are ruled by oppressive dictatorships. The constitution of Saddam Hussein's Iraq, for example, specified numerous rights and liberties, but they remained largely fictional.

At times in our nation's history, the government has placed restraints on certain rights and liberties, typically in wartime. You read about one example in this chapter—the Alien and Sedition Acts of 1798, which criminalized speech critical of government. Another example is the "internment" of Japanese Americans in the 1940s during World War II, which stemmed from a fear that this group of Americans could aid one of our enemies in that war—Japan. Today, many argue that more of our civil liberties have been sacrificed than ever before to protect against a "war on terrorism" that is not even a war in any traditional sense. Are such sacrifices necessary? Some Americans, including President George W. Bush and his supporters, believed they were. Others, including many members of Congress, did not agree. Generally, Americans remain divided on this important issue.

Issues for Debate & Discussion

- Since 9/11, cities across America have become much more vigilant in monitoring people's activities on the streets and at bridges, tunnels, airports, and subways. Since 2003, the New York City Police Department has gone even further. It has been videotaping political assemblies and other public events, including a march in Harlem and a demonstration by homeless people before the mayor's home, even without any evidence showing that these gatherings would be anything but peaceful. The New York police have also used undercover police officers to infiltrate political gatherings. Some believe that such monitoring activities are justified because of the threat of terrorism. Others claim that they go too far in intruding on our right to privacy. What is your position on this issue?

- Look at the arguments for and against teaching the Bible in public schools in this chapter's *Join the Debate* feature on page 79. In your opinion, does teaching the Bible violate the establishment clause in any way? Generally, what is your position on this issue?

Take Action

If you are ever concerned that your civil liberties are being threatened by a government action, you can exercise one of your liberties—the right to petition the govern-ment—to object to the action. Often, those who want to take action feel that they are alone in their struggles until they begin discussing their views with others. Brenda Koehler, a writing student attending college in Kutztown, Pennsylvania, relates how one of her friends, "Charyn," took action in response to the USA Patriot Act of 2001. Concerned about the extent to which this act infringed on Americans' civil liberties, she began e-mailing her friends and others about the issue. Eventually, a petition against the enforcement of the act in her town was circulated, and the city council agreed to consider the petition. Koehler did not expect anything to come from the review and assumed that the council would dismiss the petition without even reading the three-hundred-page Patriot Act. On the day of the hearing, the council chambers were packed with town citizens who shared Koehler's and her friends' concerns. The council adjourned the meeting for a week so that it could review the act, and when it met the next week, the resolution to oppose enforcing the act was adopted. Although one person's efforts are not always so successful, there will certainly be no successes at all if no one takes action.[54]

The American Civil Liberties Union has a Web site that tracks all kinds of issues pertaining to the protection of civil liberties. To see what your fellow citizens are doing to protect civil liberties, go to **www.aclu.org**.

- Almost three dozen First Amendment groups have launched the Free Expression Network Clearinghouse, which is a Web site designed to feature legislation updates, legal briefings, and news on cases of censorship in local communities. Go to **www.FREEExpression.org**.

- The leading civil liberties organization, the American Civil Liberties Union (ACLU), can be found at **www.aclu.org**.

- A group named the Liberty Counsel calls itself "a nonprofit religious civil liberties education and legal defense organization established to preserve religious freedom." You can access this organization's home page at **www.lc.org**.

- For information on the effect of new computer and communications technologies on the constitutional rights and liberties of Americans, go to the Center for Democracy and Technology at **www.cdt.org**.

- For information on privacy issues relating to the Internet, go to the Electronic Privacy Information Center's Web site at **www.epic.org/privacy**.

- To access United States Supreme Court decisions on civil liberties, go to the Court's official Web site at **www. supremecourtus.gov**.

ONLINE RESOURCES FOR THIS CHAPTER

This text's Companion Web site, at **www.americaatodds. com,** offers links to numerous resources that you can utilize to learn more about the topics covered in this chapter.

¡NINGÚN SER
HUMANO ES
ILEGAL!

لا يوجد إنسان
غير قانوني!

NO HUMAN BEIN
IS ILLEGAL!

CHAPTER **5**

CIVIL RIGHTS

LEARNING OBJECTIVES

LO¹ Explain the constitutional basis for our civil rights and for laws prohibiting discrimination.

LO² Discuss the reasons for the civil rights movement and the changes it effected in American politics and government.

LO³ Describe the political and economic achievements of women in this country over time and identify some obstacles to equality that they continue to face.

LO⁴ Summarize the struggles for equality faced by other groups in America.

LO⁵ Explain what affirmative action is and why it has been so controversial in this country.

IMMIGRANTS

AMERICA AT ODDS

More Immigration—Good or Bad for America?

Immigration remains one of the most divisive issues facing Americans and their elected representatives today. During the congressional elections in 2006, candidates' stands on immigration often determined whether they were elected (or reelected).

There are really two issues with respect to immigration—what to do about current illegal immigrants and what to do about encouraging (or discouraging) more legal immigrants. Today, there are at least twelve million illegal immigrants living and working in the United States. Most of them are Hispanics.

Congress has reacted in various ways to the illegal immigration issue. At times, it has established an amnesty program to allow illegal immigrants who have been working in the United States for five years to obtain legal residency. More recently, it has voted in favor of a large, secure fence on the U.S.-Mexican border. Federal legislation proposed in 2007 included a complicated system that would allow current illegal immigrants to become legal. Among other things, an illegal immigrant would have to pay back taxes, in addition to a fee of around $5,000. Under existing law, priority for legal admission to the United States is given to immigrants who are family members of someone already in this country. Under the proposed legislation, future priority would be given to those who possess needed skills rather than to family members.

Immigration—Too Much of a Good Thing

While agreeing that immigration has been beneficial to the United States in the past, some people insist that times have changed. If we grant amnesty to the existing twelve million illegal immigrants, we will encourage even more individuals to cross our borders illegally.

Moreover, most immigrants today have few job skills. Immigrants without a high school degree now head about a third of immigrant households. Researcher Robert E. Rector has estimated that each of these households costs U.S. taxpayers almost $20,000 per year, for a total net cost of $90 billion per year.

While it may be true that high-skilled immigrants are needed in the current economy, low-skilled workers simply take jobs away from Americans. There is also the issue of security. We have to protect our borders better if we are to prevent terrorists from entering the United States.

In any event, an additional amnesty program in the United States will unleash a flow of additional illegal immigrants. Why? Because they will believe that eventually, they, too, will become "legals" under yet a new amnesty program that Congress will pass in the future.

WE ARE A NATION OF IMMIGRANTS AND ALWAYS WILL BE

Others take a different view of the immigration issue. They point out that unless your ancestors are Native Americans, you are either an immigrant or a descendant of an immigrant. It seems disingenuous, then, for any American to be against immigration. Indeed, the "close the door after me" mentality seems to be quite un-American.

Why worry about the net taxpayer cost per immigrant, when the vast majority of immigrants are not eligible to receive any welfare benefits? In any event, immigrants come here to work, not to receive government handouts.

If immigration (legal and illegal) is so bad for the United States, why is the unemployment rate so low? Standards of living in the United States have been improving for decades, not in spite of immigration but because of it.

Under current immigration laws, most of the foreigners who are educated in our universities, particularly at the Ph.D. level, cannot stay to work in the United States after graduation. This seems counterproductive, given that American corporations are clamoring for more high-skilled workers. Immigrants are the bedrock of this country. Now is not the time to keep them out.

Where do you stand?

1. No matter how Congress tackles the issue of illegal immigration, it will have to deal with the twelve million illegal immigrants already here. What do you think should be done?
2. Until the early 1900s, almost no restrictions were placed on who or how many immigrants could come to live and work in the United States. Would you be in favor of a similar program today? Why or why not?

Explore this issue online

- For a Web site strongly sympathetic to immigrants, including illegal immigrants, go to **www.justiceforimmigrants.org**, which is sponsored by the Catholic Campaign for Immigration Reform. Are the proposals advocated by this group realistic?
- There is no shortage of anti-immigration commentary on the Web. Some of it, however, is generated by radicals who can be accused of promoting ethnic hostility. For vehement opposition to immigration that avoids this difficulty, check out CNN commentator Lou Dobbs at **www.loudobbs.com**.

INTRODUCTION

As noted in Chapter 4, people sometimes confuse civil rights with civil liberties. Generally, though, the term **civil rights** refers to the rights of all Americans to equal treatment under the law, as provided for by the Fourteenth Amendment. One of the functions of our government is to ensure—through legislation or other actions—that this constitutional mandate is upheld.

Although the democratic ideal is for all people to have equal rights and equal treatment under the law, and although the Constitution guarantees those rights, this ideal has often remained just that—an ideal. It is people who put ideals into practice, and as James Madison (1751–1836) once pointed out (and as we all know), people are not angels. As you will read in this chapter, the struggle of various groups in American society to obtain equal treatment has been a long one, and it still continues. Today, some twelve million illegal immigrants, primarily from Mexico, are struggling to obtain legal status in this nation, a topic discussed in this chapter's opening *America at Odds* feature.

In a sense, the history of civil rights in the United States is a history of discrimination against various groups. Discrimination against women, African Americans, and Native Americans dates back to the early years of this nation, when the framers of the Constitution refused to grant these groups rights that were granted to others (that is, to white, property-owning males). During our subsequent history, as peoples from around the globe immigrated to this country at various times and for various reasons, each of these immigrant groups has faced discrimination in one form or another. More recently, other groups, including older Americans, persons suffering from disabilities, and gay men and lesbians, have struggled for equal treatment under the law.

Central to any discussion of civil rights is the interpretation of the equal protection clause of the Fourteenth Amendment to the Constitution. For that reason, we look first at that clause and how the courts, particularly the United States Supreme Court, have interpreted it and applied it to civil rights issues.

> CIVIL RIGHTS REFERS TO THE RIGHTS OF ALL AMERICANS TO EQUAL TREATMENT UNDER THE LAW, AS PROVIDED FOR BY THE FOURTEENTH AMENDMENT.

LO¹ THE EQUAL PROTECTION CLAUSE

Equal in importance to the due process clause of the Fourteenth Amendment is the **equal protection clause** in Section 1 of that amendment, which reads as follows: "No State shall . . . deny to any person within its jurisdiction the equal protection of the laws." Section 5 of the amendment provides a legal basis for federal civil rights legislation: "The Congress shall have power to enforce, by appropriate legislation, the provisions of this article."

The equal protection clause has been interpreted by the courts, and especially the Supreme Court, to mean that states must treat all persons in an equal manner and may not discriminate *unreasonably* against a particular group or class of individuals unless there is a sufficient reason to do so. The task of distinguishing between reasonable discrimination and unreasonable discrimination is difficult. Generally, in deciding this question, the Supreme Court balances the constitutional rights of individuals to equal protection against government interests in protecting the safety and welfare of citizens. Over time, the Court has developed various tests, or standards, for determining whether the equal protection clause has been violated.

Strict Scrutiny

If the law or action prevents some group of persons from exercising a **fundamental right** (such as all First Amendment rights), the law or action will be subject to the "strict-scrutiny" standard. Under this standard, the law or action must be necessary to promote a *compelling state*

---

civil rights The rights of all Americans to equal treatment under the law, as provided for by the Fourteenth Amendment to the Constitution.

equal protection clause Section 1 of the Fourteenth Amendment, which states that no state shall "deny to any person within its jurisdiction the equal protection of the laws."

fundamental right A basic right of all Americans, such as all First Amendment rights. Any law or action that prevents some group of persons from exercising a fundamental right will be subject to the "strict-scrutiny" standard, under which the law or action must be necessary to promote a compelling state interest and must be narrowly tailored to meet that interest.

interest and must be narrowly tailored to meet that interest. A law based on a **suspect classification,** such as race, is also subject to strict scrutiny by the courts, meaning that the law must be justified by a compelling state interest.

Intermediate Scrutiny

Because the Supreme Court had difficulty deciding how to judge cases in which men and women were treated differently, another test was developed—the "intermediate-scrutiny" standard. Under this standard, laws based on gender classifications are permissible if they are "substantially related to the achievement of an important governmental objective." For example, a law punishing males but not females for statutory rape is valid because of the important governmental interest in preventing teenage pregnancy in those circumstances and because virtually all of the harmful and identifiable consequences of teenage pregnancies fall on young females.[1] A law prohibiting the sale of beer to males under twenty-one years of age and to females under eighteen years would not be valid, however.[2]

Generally, since the 1970s, the Supreme Court has scrutinized gender classifications closely and has declared many gender-based laws unconstitutional. In 1979, the Court held that a state law allowing wives to obtain alimony judgments against husbands but preventing husbands from receiving alimony from wives violated the equal protection clause.[3] In 1982, the Court declared that Mississippi's policy of excluding males from the School of Nursing at Mississippi University for Women was unconstitutional.[4] In a controversial 1996 case, *United States v. Virginia,*[5] the Court held that Virginia Military Institute, a state-financed institution, violated the equal protection clause by refusing to accept female applicants. The Court said that the state of Virginia had failed to provide a sufficient justification for

For many years, the Virginia Military Institute did not allow female students. That changed in 1996 when the U.S. Supreme Court ruled that this state-financed institution violated the equal protection clause.

its gender-based classification. Nonetheless, the goal of equal treatment for women, which dates back to the Constitution, has yet to be fully achieved.

The Rational Basis Test (Ordinary Scrutiny)

A third test used to decide whether a discriminatory law violates the equal protection clause is the **rational basis test.** When applying this test to a law that classifies or treats people or groups differently, the justices ask whether the discrimination is rational. In other words, is it a reasonable way to achieve a legitimate government objective? Few laws tested under the rational basis test—or the "ordinary-scrutiny" standard, as it is also called—are found invalid, because few laws are truly unreasonable. A municipal ordinance that prohibits certain vendors from selling their wares in a particular area of the city, for example, will be upheld if the city can meet this rational basis test. The rational basis for the ordinance might be the city's legitimate government interest in reducing traffic congestion in that particular area.

LO² AFRICAN AMERICANS

The equal protection clause was originally intended to protect the newly freed slaves after the Civil War (1861–1865). In the early years after the war, the U.S. government made an effort to protect the rights of blacks living in the former states of the Confederacy. The Thirteenth Amendment (which

---

suspect classification
A classification, such as race, that provides the basis for a discriminatory law. Any law based on a suspect classification is subject to strict scrutiny by the courts—meaning that the law must be justified by a compelling state interest.

rational basis test A test (also known as the "ordinary-scrutiny" standard) used by the Supreme Court to decide whether a discriminatory law violates the equal protection clause of the Constitution. Few laws evaluated under this test are found invalid.

granted freedom to the slaves), the Fourteenth Amendment (which guaranteed equal protection under the law), and the Fifteenth Amendment (which stated that voting rights could not be abridged on account of race) were part of that effort. By the late 1880s, however, southern legislatures began to pass a series of segregation laws—laws that separated the white community from the black community. Such laws were commonly called "Jim Crow" laws (from a song that was popular in black minstrel shows). Some of the most common Jim Crow laws called for racial segregation in the use of public facilities, such as schools, railroads, and, later, buses. These laws were also applied to housing, restaurants, hotels, and many other facilities.

Homer Plessy.

Separate but Equal

In 1892, a group of Louisiana citizens decided to challenge a state law that required railroads to provide separate railway cars for African Americans. A man named Homer Plessy, who was seven-eighths Caucasian and one-eighth African, boarded a train in New Orleans and sat in the railway car reserved for whites. When Plessy refused to move at the request of the conductor, he was arrested for breaking the law.

Four years later, in 1896, the Supreme Court provided a constitutional basis for these segregation laws. In *Plessy v. Ferguson,*[6] the Court held that the law did not violate the equal protection clause because *separate* facilities for blacks were *equal* to those

Signs such as the one shown here next to drinking fountains were commonplace in the South from the 1870s to the 1960s. The "separate-but-equal" doctrine, enunciated by the Supreme Court in 1896, justified Jim Crow laws that permitted racial segregation.

for whites. The lone dissenter, Justice John Marshall Harlan, disagreed: "Our Constitution is colorblind, and neither knows nor tolerates classes among citizens." The majority opinion, however, established the **separate-but-equal doctrine,** which was used to justify segregation in many areas of American life for nearly sixty years.

In the late 1930s and 1940s, the United States Supreme Court gradually moved away from this doctrine. The major breakthrough, however, did not come until 1954, in a case involving an African American girl who lived in Topeka, Kansas.

The *Brown* Decisions and School Integration

In the 1950s, Topeka's schools, like those in many cities, were segregated. Mr. and Mrs. Oliver Brown wanted their daughter, Linda Carol Brown, to attend a white school a few blocks from their home instead of an all-black school that was twenty-one blocks away. With the help of lawyers from the National Association for the Advancement of Colored People (NAACP), Linda's parents sued the board of education to allow their daughter to attend the nearby school.

In *Brown v. Board of Education of Topeka,*[7] the Supreme Court reversed *Plessy v. Ferguson.* The Court unanimously held that segregation by race in public education was unconstitutional. Chief Justice Earl Warren wrote as follows:

> Does segregation of children in public schools solely on the basis of race, even though the physical facilities and other "tangible" factors may be equal, deprive the children of the minority group of equal educational opportunities? We believe that it does. . . . [Segregation generates in children] a feeling of inferiority as to their status in the community that may affect their hearts and minds in a way unlikely ever to be undone. . . . We conclude that in the field of public education the doctrine of "separate but equal" has no place. Separate educational facilities are inherently unequal.

The following year, in 1955, in *Brown v. Board of Education*[8] (sometimes called *Brown II*), the Supreme Court ordered

separate-but-equal doctrine A Supreme Court doctrine holding that the equal protection clause of the Fourteenth Amendment did not forbid racial segregation as long as the facilities for blacks were equal to those provided for whites. The doctrine was overturned in the *Brown v. Board of Education of Topeka* decision of 1954.

On the left, U.S. troops attempt to prevent violence at Central High School in Little Rock, Arkansas in 1957. Above, the nine black students (known as the "Little Rock Nine") who entered that all-white school under armed escort are shown forty years later. Standing behind them is then president Bill Clinton, Arkansas governor Mike Huckabee, and Little Rock mayor Jim Dailey.

desegregation to begin "with all deliberate speed," an ambiguous phrase that could be (and was) interpreted in a variety of ways.

REACTIONS TO SCHOOL INTEGRATION The Supreme Court ruling did not go unchallenged. Bureaucratic loopholes were used to delay desegregation. Another reaction was "white flight." As white parents sent their children to newly established private schools, some formerly white-only public schools became 100 percent black. In Arkansas, Governor Orval Faubus used the state's National Guard to block the integration of Central High School in Little Rock in 1957, which led to increasing violence in the area. The federal court demanded that the troops be withdrawn. Only after President Dwight D. Eisenhower federalized the Arkansas National Guard and sent in troops to help quell the violence did Central High finally become integrated.

By 1970, school systems with **de jure segregation** —segregation that is legally sanctioned—had been abolished. But that meant only that no public school could legally identify itself as being reserved for all whites or all blacks. It did not mean that **de facto segregation** (actual segregation that is not required by law but is produced by circumstances, such as the existence of neighborhoods or communities populated primarily by African Americans) was eliminated. Attempts to overcome *de facto* segregation have included redrawing school district lines, reassigning pupils, and busing.

BUSING Busing is the transporting of students by bus to schools physically outside their neighborhoods in an effort to achieve racially desegregated schools. The Supreme Court first sanctioned busing in 1971 in a case involving the school system in Charlotte, North Carolina.[9] Following this decision, the Court upheld busing in several northern cities, as well as in Denver, Colorado.[10] Proponents believe that busing improves the educational and career opportunities of minority children and also enhances the ability of children from different ethnic groups to get along with each other.

Nevertheless, busing was unpopular with many groups from its inception. Parents and children complained that they lost the convenience of neighborhood schools. Local governments and school boards resented having the courts tell them what to do. Some black parents argued that busing exposed their children to the hostility of white students in the schools to which they

de jure segregation Racial segregation that is legally sanctioned—that is, segregation that occurs because of laws or decisions by government agencies.

de facto segregation Racial segregation that occurs not as a result of deliberate intentions but because of past social and economic conditions and residential patterns.

busing The transportation of public school students by bus to schools physically outside their neighborhoods to eliminate school segregation based on residential patterns.

Library of Congress

On February 2, 1960, a group of black college students in Greensboro, North Carolina, staged a sit-in because they were refused service at a lunch counter reserved for whites.

Dr. Martin Luther King, Jr. During the protest period, he was jailed and his house was bombed. Despite the hostility and the overwhelming odds, the protesters were triumphant.

In 1956, a federal court prohibited the segregation of buses in Montgomery, and the era of the **civil rights movement**—the movement by minorities and concerned whites to end racial segregation—had begun. The movement was led by a number of diverse groups and individuals, including Dr. Martin Luther King and his Southern Christian Leadership Conference (SCLC). Other groups, such as the Congress of Racial Equality (CORE), the NAACP, and the Student Nonviolent Coordinating Committee (SNCC), also sought to secure equal rights for African Americans.

were bused. Some blacks also resented the implication that minority children can learn only if they sit next to white children. Opposition to busing was so pronounced in some areas that bused students had to be escorted by police to prevent potential violence.

By the mid-1970s, the courts had begun to retreat from their former support for busing. In 1974, the Supreme Court rejected the idea of busing children across school district lines.[11] In 1986, the Court refused to review a lower court decision to end a desegregation plan in Norfolk, Virginia.[12] By the 1990s, some large-scale busing programs were either being cut back or terminated. In *Missouri v. Jenkins*[13] in 1995, the Supreme Court ruled that the state of Missouri could stop spending money to attract a multiracial student body through major educational improvements, called magnet schools. Today, busing orders to end *de facto* segregation are not upheld in court. Indeed, *de facto* segregation in America's schools is still widespread.

The Civil Rights Movement

In 1955, one year after the first *Brown* decision, an African American woman named Rosa Parks, a long-time activist in the NAACP, boarded a public bus in Montgomery, Alabama. When it became crowded, she refused to move to the "colored section" at the rear of the bus. She was arrested and fined for violating local segregation laws. Her refusal and arrest spurred the local African American community to organize a year-long boycott of the entire Montgomery bus system. The protest was led by a twenty-seven-year-old Baptist minister,

NONVIOLENCE AS A TACTIC Civil rights protesters in the 1960s began to apply the tactic of nonviolent **civil disobedience**—the deliberate and public refusal to obey laws considered unjust—in civil rights actions throughout the South. For example, in 1960, in Greensboro, North Carolina, four African American students sat at the "whites only" lunch counter at Woolworth's and ordered food. The waitress refused to serve them and the store closed early, but more students returned the next day to sit at the counter, with supporters picketing outside. **Sit-ins** spread to other lunch counters across the South. In some instances, students were heckled or even dragged from the store by angry whites. But the protesters never reacted with violence. They simply returned to their seats at the counter, day after day. Within months of the first sit-in, lunch counters began to reverse their policies of segregation.

Civil rights activists were trained in the tools of nonviolence—how to use nonthreatening body language, how to go limp when dragged or assaulted, and how to protect themselves from clubs or police dogs. As the civil rights movement gained momentum, the media images of nonviolent protesters being

civil rights movement
The movement in the 1950s and 1960s, by minorities and concerned whites, to end racial segregation.

civil disobedience The deliberate and public act of refusing to obey laws thought to be unjust.

sit-in A tactic of nonviolent civil disobedience. Demonstrators enter a business, college building, or other public place and remain seated until they are forcibly removed or until their demands are met. The tactic was used successfully in the civil rights movement and in other protest movements in the United States.

attacked by police, sprayed with fire hoses, and attacked by dogs shocked and angered Americans across the country. This public backlash led to nationwide demands for reform. The March on Washington for Jobs and Freedom, led by Martin Luther King, Jr., in 1963, aimed in part to demonstrate the widespread public support for legislation to ban discrimination in all aspects of public life.

CIVIL RIGHTS LEGISLATION IN THE 1960S As the civil rights movement demonstrated its strength, Congress began to pass civil rights laws. It became clear that while the Fourteenth Amendment prevented the *government* from discriminating against individuals or groups, the private sector—businesses, restaurants, and so on—could still freely refuse to employ and serve nonwhites.

The Civil Rights Act of 1964 was the first and most comprehensive civil rights law. It forbade discrimination on the basis of race, color, religion, gender, and national origin. The major provisions of the act were as follows:

- It outlawed discrimination in public places of accommodation, such as hotels, restaurants, snack bars, movie theaters, and public transportation.

- It provided that federal funds could be withheld from any federal or state government project or facility that practiced any form of discrimination.

- It banned discrimination in employment.

- It outlawed arbitrary discrimination in voter registration.

- It authorized the federal government to sue to desegregate public schools and facilities.

Other significant laws passed by Congress during the 1960s included the Voting Rights Act of 1965, which made it illegal to interfere with anyone's right to vote in any election held in this country (see Chapter 8 for a discussion of the historical restrictions on voting that African Americans faced), and the Civil Rights Act of 1968, which prohibited discrimination in housing.

JOIN THE DEBATE

Martin Luther King, Jr., shakes hands with President Lyndon B. Johnson just after Johnson had signed the Civil Rights Act of 1964. At the signing, Johnson asked all Americans to join in the effort "to bring justice and hope to all our people and to bring peace to our land."

FP/AFP/Getty Images

Should Fair Housing Rules Apply to Internet Ads for Roommates?

Gone are the days when, if you were looking for a college roommate, you would tack up little paper notices throughout your college community. The Internet has changed the housing market forever. Today, if you are seeking a roommate, you can post your request on a large number of Internet sites. Your search for a roommate, though, may put you in violation of fair housing rules. After all, federal and state laws prevent sellers and renters of housing from discriminating against anyone based on a variety of criteria, such as race, sexual orientation, and religion. Should these same laws apply to you when you have already rented a place but need a roommate?

Any discrimination is wrong, no matter for what purpose, say many Americans. Consider also that minority Americans scouring the roommate section of any housing Web site might be emotionally distressed at the tenor of some of the roommate-wanted ads. Imagine reading the following ad, which Gene Kavenoki placed on the popular Roommates.com site: "I am *not* looking for freaks, geeks, prostitutes, druggies, pet cobras, black Muslims, or mortgage brokers." That ad resulted in a lawsuit against Roommates.com by a fair housing group in California.

Some people contend, though, that there's a distinction between finding a roommate for a place you have already rented and owning a lodging that you wish to rent out. Typically, roommates share common facilities, such as bathrooms and kitchens. Clearly, a person seeking a roommate must have the right to determine who is, and who is not, going to share his or her bathroom and kitchen. If you are allergic to tobacco smoke, you should be able to specify a nonsmoker, even if that is discrimination. If you are a female, surely you should be able to specify that only females may apply, even if that constitutes discrimination against males.

THE BLACK POWER MOVEMENT Not all African Americans embraced nonviolence. Several outspoken leaders in the mid-1960s were outraged at the slow pace of change in the social and economic status of blacks. Malcolm X, a speaker and organizer for the Nation of Islam (also called the Black Muslims), rejected the goals of integration and racial equality espoused by the civil rights movement. He called instead for black separatism and black pride. Although he later moderated some of his views, his rhetorical style and powerful message influenced many African American young people. Among them was Stokely Carmichael. Carmichael had been a leader in the civil rights movement, a freedom rider, and later chairman of the SNCC, but by 1966 he had become frustrated with the tactic of nonviolence. He began to exhort civil rights activists to defend themselves, to demand political and economic power, and to demonstrate racial pride.

By the late 1960s, with the assassinations of Malcolm X in 1965 and Martin Luther King, Jr., in 1968, the era of mass acts of civil disobedience in the name of civil rights came to an end. Some civil rights leaders ceased to believe that further change was possible. Some left the United States alto-gether. Stokely Carmichael emigrated to Guinea in West Africa. Others entered politics and worked to advance the cause of civil rights from within the system.

Political Participation

As you will read in Chapter 8, African Americans were restricted from voting for many years after the Civil War, despite the Fifteenth Amendment (1870). These discriminatory practices persisted in the twentieth century. In the early 1960s, only 22 percent of African Americans of voting age in the South were registered to vote, compared with 63 percent of voting-age whites. In Mississippi, the most extreme example, only 6 percent of voting-age African Americans were registered to vote. Such disparities led to the enactment of the Voting Rights Act of 1965, which ended discriminatory voter-registration tests and gave federal voter registrars the power to prevent racial discrimination in voting.

Today, the percentages of voting-age blacks and whites registered to vote are nearly equal. As a result of this dramatic change, political participation by African Americans has increased, as has the number of African American elected officials. Today, more than nine thousand African Americans serve in elective office in the United States. At least one congressional seat in each southern state is held by an African American, as are more than 15 percent of the state legislative seats in the South. A number of African Americans have achieved high political office, including Colin Powell, who served as President George W. Bush's

Black Muslim leader Malcolm X speaks to an audience at a Harlem rally in 1963. His talk, in which he restated the Black Muslim theme of complete separation of whites and African Americans, outdrew a nearby rally sponsored by a civil rights group by ten to one.

Library of Congress

first secretary of state, and Condoleezza Rice, his second secretary of state. Barack Obama, a U.S. senator from Illinois, was a leading contender to be the Democratic Party's candidate in the 2008 presidential races. Indeed, in contrast to public opinion fifty years ago, when only 38 percent of Americans said that they would be willing to vote for an African American as president, today this number has risen to more than 90 percent.

Nonetheless, only two African Americans have been elected to a state governorship, and only a handful of African Americans have been elected to the U.S. Senate since 1900. The 110th Congress includes one African American in the Senate (Democratic senator Barack Obama from Illinois) and forty African Americans in the House. In all, only about 8 percent of the members of Congress are African American. The increase in political participation by African Americans is thus somewhat more illusory than the numbers suggest. Although several African Americans have aspired to the presidency, to date none has won the nomination of either major party, though, as mentioned, Senator Obama was a strong candidate for the Democratic nomination in 2008.

Continuing Challenges

Although African Americans no longer face *de jure* segregation, they continue to struggle for income and educational parity with whites. Recent census data show that incomes in white households are two-thirds higher than those in black households. And the poverty rate for blacks is roughly three times that for whites.

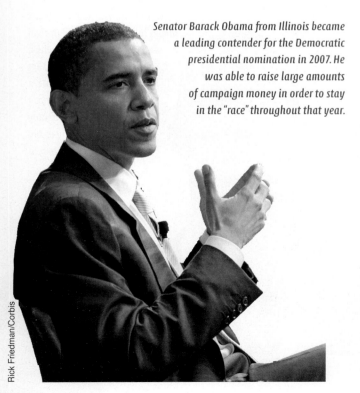

Senator Barack Obama from Illinois became a leading contender for the Democratic presidential nomination in 2007. He was able to raise large amounts of campaign money in order to stay in the "race" throughout that year.

Rick Friedman/Corbis

The education gap between blacks and whites also persists despite continuing efforts by educators—and by government, through the federal No Child Left Behind Act, for example—to reduce it. Recent studies show that, on average, African American students in high school can read and do math at only the average level of whites in junior high school. While black adults have narrowed the gap with white adults in earning high school diplomas, the disparity has widened for college degrees.

These problems tend to feed on each other. Schools in poorer neighborhoods generally have fewer educational resources available, resulting in lower achievement levels for their students. Thus, some educational experts suggest that it all comes down to money. Many parents of minority students in struggling school districts push less for integration and more for funds for their children's schools. A number of these parents have initiated lawsuits against their state governments, demanding that the states give poor districts more resources. According to Ted Shaw, president of the NAACP's Legal Defense and Educational Fund, many black Americans say, "Give us the resources, give us the money, we're tired of chasing white folks, and we don't need integrated schools to have a good education." It could be, says Shaw, that this attitude is born of weariness and cynicism after years of struggling to obtain racially integrated schools.[14] In any event, experts from all political persuasions agree that the educational achievement disparity between white and black Americans is the biggest problem in American education today.

LO³ WOMEN

The failure of the framers of the Constitution to give women political rights was viewed by many early Americans as an act of betrayal. Not only did the Constitution betray the Declaration of Independence's promise of equality, but it also betrayed the women who had contributed to the making of that independence during the Revolutionary War. Nonetheless, not until the 1840s did women's rights groups begin to form.

The Struggle for Voting Rights

In 1848, Lucretia Mott and Elizabeth Cady Stanton organized the first "woman's rights" convention in Seneca Falls, New York. The three hundred people who attended approved a Declaration of Sentiments: "We hold these truths to be self-evident: that all men *and women* are created equal." In the following years, other women's groups held conventions in various cities in the Midwest and the East. With the outbreak of the Civil War, though, women's rights advocates devoted their energies to the war effort.

The movement for political rights again gained momentum in 1869, when Susan B. Anthony and Elizabeth Cady Stanton formed the National Woman Suffrage Association. **Suffrage**—the right to vote—became their goal. For members of the National Woman Suffrage Association, suffrage was only one step on the road toward greater social and political rights for women. Lucy Stone and other women, who had founded the American Woman Suffrage Association, thought that the right to vote should be the only goal. By 1890, the two organizations had joined forces, and the resulting National American Woman Suffrage Association had indeed only one goal—the enfranchisement of women. When little progress was made, small, radical splinter groups took to the streets. Parades, hunger strikes, arrests, and jailings soon followed.

World War I (1914–1918) marked a turning point in the battle for women's rights. The war offered many opportunities for women. Thousands of women served as volunteers, and about a million women joined the workforce, holding jobs vacated by men who entered military service. After the war, President Woodrow Wilson wrote to Carrie Chapman Catt, one of the leaders of the women's movement, "It is high time that [that] part of our debt should be acknowledged." Two years later, in 1920, seventy-two years after the Seneca Falls convention, the Nineteenth Amendment to the Constitution was ratified: "The right of citizens of the United States to vote shall not be denied or abridged by the United States or by any State on account of sex." Although the United States may have

"THE RIGHT OF CITIZENS OF THE UNITED STATES TO VOTE SHALL NOT BE DENIED OR ABRIDGED BY THE UNITED STATES OR BY ANY STATE ON ACCOUNT OF SEX."

THE NINETEENTH AMENDMENT OF THE U.S. CONSTITUTION, 1920

Library of Congress

seemed slow in giving women the right to vote, it was really not far behind the rest of the world (see Table 5–1).

Women in American Politics Today

More than ten thousand members have served in the U.S. House of Representatives. Only 1 percent of them have been women. Women continue to face a "men's club" atmosphere in Congress, although in 2002, for the first time, a woman, Nancy Pelosi (D., Calif.), was elected minority leader of the House of Representatives. Pelosi again made history when, after the Democratic victories in the 2006 elections, she was elected as Speaker of the House of Representatives, the first woman ever to hold that position. In the 110th Congress, 16 percent of the 435 members of the House of Representatives and 16 percent of the 100 members of the Senate are women. Considering that eligible female voters outnumber eligible male voters, women are vastly underrepresented in the U.S. Congress.

FEDERAL OFFICES The same can be said for the number of women receiving presidential appointments to federal offices. Franklin Roosevelt (1933–1945) appointed the first woman to a cabinet post—Frances Perkins, who was secretary of labor from 1933 to 1945. In recent administrations, several women have held cabinet posts. In addition, Ronald Reagan (1981–1989) appointed the first woman ever to sit on the Supreme Court, Sandra Day O'Connor. Bill Clinton (1993–2001) appointed Ruth Bader Ginsburg to the Supreme Court, and, in his second term, he appointed Madeleine Albright as secretary of state, the first woman to hold that position. President George W. Bush appointed Condoleezza Rice first as his national

TABLE 5–1
YEARS, BY COUNTRY, IN WHICH WOMEN GAINED THE RIGHT TO VOTE
1893: New Zealand
1902: Australia
1913: Norway
1918: Britain
1918: Canada
1919: Germany
1920: United States
1930: South Africa
1932: Brazil
1944: France
1945: Italy
1945: Japan
1947: Argentina
1950: India
1952: Greece
1953: Mexico
1956: Egypt
1963: Kenya
1971: Switzerland
1984: Yemen

suffrage The right to vote; the franchise.

Nancy Pelosi (D., Calif.) became the first female Speaker of the House of Representatives after the 2006 elections.

President George W. Bush appointed Elaine Chao as the secretary of labor.

Condoleezza Rice was the second female secretary of state in our nation's history.

security adviser and then to the position of secretary of state. Other Bush cabinet members included Secretary of Labor Elaine Chao, Secretary of Transportation Mary Peters, and Secretary of Education Margaret Spellings. Bush also appointed a number of other women to significant offices in his administration.

STATE POLITICS Women have made greater progress at the state level, and the percentage of women in state legislatures has been rising steadily. Women now constitute nearly one-fourth of state legislators. Notably, in 1998, women won races for each of the top five offices in Arizona, the first such occurrence in U.S. history. Generally, women have been more successful politically in the western states than elsewhere. In Washington, more than one-third of the state's legislative seats are now held by women. At the other end of the spectrum, though, are states such as Alabama. In that state, less than 10 percent of the lawmakers are women.

Today, various women's organizations are attempting to increase the number of women in government. These organizations include the National Council of Women's Organizations, the National Women's Political Caucus, Black Women Organized for

Political Action, and the Feminist Majority Foundation. Additionally, women have formed *political action committees* (PACs—see Chapter 6) to support female candidates for political office. One of the largest PACs is EMILY's List, which promotes and supports Democratic women candidates running for seats in Congress and state governorships. (EMILY stands for "Early Money Is Like Yeast—It Makes the Dough Rise.")

Women in the Workplace

An ongoing challenge for American women is to obtain equal pay and equal opportunity in the workplace. In spite of federal legislation and programs to promote equal treatment of women in the workplace, women continue to face various forms of discrimination.

WAGE DISCRIMINATION In 1963, Congress passed the Equal Pay Act. The act requires employers to pay an equal wage for substantially equal work—males cannot be paid more than females who perform essentially the same job. The following year, Congress passed the Civil Rights Act of 1964, Title VII of which prohibits employment discrimination on the basis of race, color,

"I feel like a man trapped in a woman's salary."

PERCEPTION VERSUS REALITY

The Gender Gap in Wages

A woman's place is no longer in the home, and it has not been for decades. Indeed, as the labor force participation rate of men has fallen, that of women has actually risen. Back in the early 1960s, women earned about 58 cents for every dollar earned by men. Today, that figure stands at just over 76 cents.

The Perception

It is true that over the last three decades, women's wages, relative to men's, have risen, if ever so slowly. Because of this gradual increase in women's pay relative to men's, most Americans have assumed that the slow but steady trend will continue. Eventually, women will achieve pay parity with men.

The Reality

The gender gap in pay has been stuck since the mid-1990s. Indeed, for college-educated women, the gender gap has become wider.

The more a woman earns, the larger the gap becomes. In other words, the closer to the top of the corporate ladder a woman gets, the further behind she is relative to her male counterparts with respect to pay—not only within the same corporation but also when compared to other corporations.

The current United States Supreme Court also appears unlikely to play a leading role in reducing the gender gap. In a decision in 2007, the Supreme Court limited workers' abilities to sue for pay discrimination.[15] The Court ruled that employees have to file pay-discrimination complaints within 180 days of the "alleged unlawful employment practice." This time limit applies even if an employee didn't learn about the pay discrimination until after that period had lapsed. For Lilly Ledbetter, a supervisor at Goodyear Tire Company, the ruling meant that she was unable to sue her employer for the multi-thousand-dollar difference between her salary and those of male employees who held positions with exactly the same job description as her position.

BLOG ON

You will find plenty of detailed information on the gender wage gap and other workplace issues at **lawprofessors.typepad.com/laborprof_blog,** one of a family of law professor blogs sponsored by West Group. Penelope Trunk's Brazen Careerist at **blog.penelopetrunk.com** offers heated discussions about issues facing women who are working in the corporate world.

---

national origin, gender, and religion. Women, however, continue to face wage discrimination.

It is estimated that for every dollar earned by men, women earn about 76 cents. Although the wage gap has narrowed significantly since 1963, when the Equal Pay Act was enacted (at that time women earned 58 cents for every dollar earned by men), it still remains. This is particularly true for women in management positions and older women. Female managers now earn, on average, only 70 percent of what male managers earn. And women between the ages of forty-five and fifty-four make, on average, only 73 percent of what men in that age group earn. Also, when a large number of women are in a particular occupation, the wages that are paid in that occupation continue to be relatively low.

Additionally, even though an increasing number of women now hold business and professional jobs once held by men, relatively few of these women are able to rise to the top of the career ladder in their firms due to the lingering bias against women in the workplace.

This bias has created the so-called **glass ceiling**—the often subtle obstacles to advancement that professional women encounter on the job. Today, less than one-sixth of the top executive positions in the largest American corporations are held by women. (For a further discussion of the gender gap in wages, see this chapter's *Perception versus Reality* feature.)

SEXUAL HARASSMENT

Title VII's prohibition of gender discrimination has also been extended to prohibit sexual harassment. **Sexual harassment** occurs when job opportunities, promotions, salary increases, or even the ability to retain one's job depend on whether an employee

glass ceiling The often subtle obstacles to advancement faced by professional women in the workplace.

sexual harassment Unwanted physical contact, verbal conduct, or abuse of a sexual nature that interferes with a recipient's job performance, creates a hostile environment, or carries with it an implicit or explicit threat of adverse employment consequences.

complies with demands for sex- ual favors. A special form of sexual harassment, called hostile- environment harassment, occurs when an employee is subjected to sexual conduct or comments in the workplace that interfere with the employee's job performance or that create an intimidating, hostile, or offensive environment.

The Supreme Court has up- held the right of persons to be free from sexual harassment on the job on a number of occasions. In 1986, the Court indicated that creating a hostile environment by sexual harassment violates Title VII, even when job status is not af- fected, and in 1993 the Court held that to win damages in a suit for sexual harassment, a victim does not need to prove that the harassment caused psychological harm.[16] In 1998, the Court made it clear that sexual harassment includes harassment, by members of the same sex.[17] In the same year, the Court held that employers are liable for the harassment of em- ployees by supervisors in their workplaces unless the employers can show that (1) they exercised reasonable care in preventing such problems (by implementing antiharassment policies and procedures, for example) and (2) the employees failed to take advantage of any corrective opportunities provided by the employers.[18] Additionally, the Civil Rights Act of 1991 greatly ex- panded the remedies available for victims of sexual ha- rassment. Under the act, victims can seek damages as well as back pay, job reinstatement, and other compen- sation previously unavailable.

LO⁴ SECURING RIGHTS FOR OTHER GROUPS

I n addition to African Americans and women, a number of other groups in U.S. society have faced discriminatory treatment. To discuss all of these groups would require volumes.

Here, we look first at three significant ethnic groups that have all had to struggle for equal treatment— Hispanics, Asian Americans, and Native Americans— and also consider the rights of immigrants generally. Then we examine the struggles of other groups of Americans—elderly people, persons with disabilities, and gay men and lesbians.

HISPANICS LIVING IN THE UNITED STATES BY PLACE OF ORIGIN

As you can see in this chart, most Hispanics (just over two-thirds) are from Mexico.

Mexican 66.9%

Central and South American 14.3%

Puerto Rican 8.6%

Cuban 3.7%

Other Hispanic 6.5%

Source: U.S. Bureau of the Census.

Hispanics

Hispanics, or Latinos, as they are often called, constitute the larg- est ethnic minority in the United States. Whereas African Americans represent about 13 percent of the U.S. population, Hispanics now constitute about 15 percent of the population. Each year, the Hispanic population grows by nearly one million people, one-third of whom are newly arrived legal immigrants. By 2050, Hispanics are expected to constitute about one-fourth of the U.S. population.

Hispanics can be of any race, and to classify them as a single minority group is misleading. Spanish-speaking individuals tend to identify themselves by their country of origin, rather than as Hispanics. As you can see in Figure 5–1, the largest Hispanic group consists of Mexican Americans, who constitute more than 66 percent of the Hispanic population living in the United States. Close to 9 percent of Hispanics are Puerto Ricans, and approximately 4 percent are Cuban Americans. A significant number of the remaining Hispanics are from Latin American countries.

Economically, Hispanic households seem to have become entrenched as this country's working poor. About 22 percent of Hispanic families now live below the poverty line, compared with 8 percent of white fam- ilies. Researchers have found it difficult to pinpoint any reasons for such extensive poverty among Hispanics. Hispanic leaders, however, tend to attribute the low in- come levels to language problems, lack of job training, and continuing immigration. (Immigration disguises statistical progress because language problems and lack of job training are usually more notable among new immigrants than among those who have lived in the United States for several years.)

PARTY IDENTIFICATION AND ELECTORAL SIGNIFICANCE

In their party identification, Hispanics tend to follow some fairly well-established patterns. Traditionally, Mexican Americans and Puerto Ricans have tended to identify with the Democratic Party, which has favored more government assistance and support programs for disadvantaged groups. Cubans, in contrast, tend to identify with the Republican Party. This is largely be- cause of a different history. Cuban émigrés fled from that country during and after the Communist revolu-

Bill Richardson typifies a modern politically successful Hispanic American. Now governor of New Mexico, he previously served as a U.S. representative, ambassador to the United Nations, and as the U.S. secretary of energy.

tion led by Fidel Castro. The strong anti-Communist sentiments of the Cubans propelled them toward the more conservative party—the Republicans. Today, relations with Communist Cuba continue to be the dominant political issue for Cuban Americans.

Given their increasing numbers, the electoral importance of Hispanics cannot be denied. Significantly, Latinos tend to be located in some of the most populous states, including California, Florida, Illinois, New York, and Texas. In the 2004 elections, these states accounted for 168 electoral college votes. Understandably, in the 2008 presidential races candidates from both parties tried to woo Hispanic voters.

The debate over immigration reform has had a significant impact on Hispanic voters, especially in California. Exit polls conducted during the 2006 midterm elections showed that for 69 percent of Hispanic voters, immigration was their number-one priority. Before the 2006 midterm elections, to appeal to the party base, Republican ads attacked proposed legislation that would have made it possible for illegal immigrants to obtain legal status. According to some observers, many Hispanics perceived the ads as attacking all Hispanics and were motivated to vote against Republicans in the 2006 elections. Certainly, Hispanic turnout in the 2006 elections increased—it was 37 percent higher than it had been in the previous midterm elections (in 2002), even though there was an 8.5 percent decrease in voter turnout nationwide. Of those Hispanics who voted, only 29 percent voted for Republican candidates, which stands in sharp contrast to the 44 percent of the Hispanic vote garnered by George W. Bush in the 2004 presidential elections.

POLITICAL PARTICIPATION Generally, Hispanics in the United States have a comparatively low level of political participation. This is understandable, given that one-third of Hispanics are below voting age, and another one-fourth are not citizens and thus cannot vote. Voter turnout among Hispanics is generally low compared to the population at large. Yet the Hispanic voting rate is rising as more immigrants become citizens and as more Hispanics reach voting age. Notably, when comparing citizens of equal incomes and educational backgrounds, Hispanic citizens' participation rate is higher than average. Even poor Hispanics are more likely to vote than poor whites.

Increasingly, Hispanics are holding political offices, particularly in those states with large Hispanic populations. Today, more than 5 percent of the state legislators in Arizona, California, Colorado, Florida, New Mexico, and Texas are of Hispanic ancestry. Cuban Americans have been notably successful in gaining local political power, particularly in Dade County, Florida.

President George W. Bush has appointed a number of Hispanics to federal offices, including some cabinet positions. In his second administration, for example, he nominated Alberto Gonzales (since resigned) to head the Justice Department and Carlos Gutierrez as secretary of commerce. Hispanics are also increasing their presence in Congress, albeit slowly. Following the 2006 elections, there were twenty-three Hispanics in the House

Delores C. Huerta is the co-founder and first vice president emeritus of the United Farm Workers of America. Here, she is shown encouraging young girls to vote when they turn eighteen.

of Representatives and three Hispanics in the Senate. In all, though, Hispanics constitute only about 5 percent of the members of the 110th Congress. As with African Americans and women, Hispanic representation in Congress is notably disproportionate to the size of the Hispanic population in the United States.

Asian Americans

Asian Americans have also suffered, at times severely, from discriminatory treatment. The Chinese Exclusion Act of 1882 prevented persons from China and Japan from coming to the United States to prospect for gold or to work on the railroads or in factories in the West. After 1900, immigration continued to be restricted—only limited numbers of persons from China and Japan were allowed to enter the United States. Those who were allowed into the country faced racial prejudice by Americans who had little respect for their customs and culture. In 1906, after the San Francisco earthquake, Japanese American students were segregated into special schools so that white children could use their buildings.

The Japanese bombing of Pearl Harbor in 1941, which launched the entry of the United States into World War II (1939–1945), intensified Americans' fear of the Japanese. Actions taken under an executive order issued by President Franklin D. Roosevelt in 1942 subjected many Japanese Americans to curfews, excluded them from certain "military areas," and evacuated them to internment camps (also called "relocation centers").[19] In 1988, Congress provided funds to compensate former camp inhabitants—$1.25 billion for approximately 60,000 people.

Today, Japanese Americans and Chinese Americans lead other ethnic groups in median income and median education. Indeed, Asians who have immigrated to the United States since 1965 represent the most highly skilled immigrant group in American history. Nearly 40 percent of Asian Americans over the age of twenty-five have college degrees.

More recently, immigrants from Asia, particularly from Southeast Asia, have faced discrimination. More than a million Indochinese war refugees, most from Vietnam, have immigrated to the United States since the 1970s.

Library of Congress

In what many consider to be one of America's low points, 120,000 Japanese Americans were moved to "internment camps" during World War II. Shown here is the Manzanar Camp in California.

Like their predecessors, the newer immigrants quickly increased their median income. Most came with relatives and were sponsored by American families or organizations. Thus, they had good support systems to help them get started.

Immigrants' Rights

Hispanic Americans and Asian Americans are joined every day by a steady stream of immigrants to the United States, some also from Latin America and Asia and others from the Middle East, Africa, and Europe. Approximately one million immigrants enter the United States each year. Thirty-three million people born outside the United States currently live here, the highest percentage of foreign-born residents since 1930. The percentage of immigrants who eventually become citizens has been on the rise in recent years. Today, naturalized citizens account for approximately 6 percent of eligible voters. This trend has focused more political attention on the rights of immigrants. Issues such as access to public services, health care, and education have dominated the debate.

The terrorist attacks of September 11, 2001, centered particular attention on U.S. immigration policy and the rights of immigrants. Several of the hijackers were here legally on student visas. In the weeks following the attacks, the federal government detained nearly 1,500 immigrants of Middle Eastern descent. Although many civil rights advocates decry the treatment of Arab Americans and immigrants, the response of the nation as a whole has been muted because the fear of future terrorist attacks is so great.

Racial profiling, a form of discrimination that occurs when, for example, a police officer pulls a driver

racial profiling A form of discrimination in which law enforcement assumes that people of a certain race are more likely to commit crimes. Racial profiling has been linked to more frequent traffic stops of African Americans by police and increased security checks of Arab Americans in airports.

over for no reason other than the driver's skin color, has received attention mainly in how it has been applied to African Americans. The practice has also been used in the prosecution of the war on terrorism. Civil rights groups claim that immigrants from the Middle East, North Africa, India, Indonesia, the Philippines, and Pakistan have been singled out by airport security workers, border guards, and immigration officials for searches and detention. Airlines have removed passengers from flights solely because they were of Middle Eastern or Asian appearance. We examine the issue of racial profiling and the war on terrorism further in this chapter's *The Politics of National Security* feature on the next page.

Native Americans

During the last few centuries, the populations of most groups in America—including African Americans—increased rapidly. In contrast, the Native American population in the United States was cut in half. That population dropped from about one million in 1600 to half a million in 1925, the demographic low point.

Today, more than two million people in the United States identify themselves as Native Americans. Most Native Americans live in Arizona, California, New Mexico, and Oklahoma, about half of them on reservations. Of all of the groups that have suffered discriminatory treatment in the United States, Native Americans stand out because of the unique nature of their treatment.

In 1789, Congress designated the Native American tribes as foreign nations so that the government could sign land and boundary treaties with them. As members of foreign nations, Native Americans had no civil rights under U.S. laws. This situation continued until 1924, when citizenship rights were extended to all persons born in the United States.

EARLY POLICIES TOWARD NATIVE AMERICANS   The Northwest Ordinance, passed by the Congress of the Confederation in 1787, stated that "the utmost good faith shall always be observed towards the Indians; their lands and property shall never be taken from them without their consent; and in their property, rights, and liberty, they shall never be invaded or disturbed, unless in just and lawful wars authorized by Congress." Over the next hundred years, many agreements were made with the Indian tribes; many were also broken by Congress, as well as by individuals who wanted Indian lands for settlement or exploration.

Young men from a variety of tribes pose for a photograph in 1872 on their arrival at a Virginia boarding school for Native Americans. Later, they donned school uniforms, and another photo was taken (to be used for "before and after" comparisons). This was a typical practice at Native American boarding schools.

In the early 1830s, the government followed a policy of separation. To prevent conflicts, boundaries were established between lands occupied by Native Americans and those occupied by white settlers. In 1830, Congress instructed the Bureau of Indian Affairs (BIA), which Congress had established in 1824 as part of the War Department, to remove all tribes to lands (reservations) west of the Mississippi River in order to free land east of the Mississippi for white settlement.

In the late 1880s, the U.S. government changed its policy. The goal became the "assimilation" of Native Americans into American society. Each family was given a parcel of land within the reservation to farm. The remaining acreage was sold to whites, thus reducing the number of acres in reservation status from 140 million to about 47 million acres. Tribes that would not cooperate with this plan lost their reservations altogether. To further the goal of cultural assimilation, agents from the BIA, which runs the Indian reservation system with the tribes, set up Native American boarding schools for the children to remove them from their parents' influence. In these schools, Native American children were taught to speak English, to practice Christianity, and to dress like white Americans.

NATIVE AMERICANS TODAY   Native Americans have always found it difficult to obtain political power. In part, this is because the tribes are small and scattered, making organized political movements difficult. Today,

RACIAL PROFILING IN THE WAR ON TERRORISM

acial profiling by police has been a controversial practice for some time. Former president Bill Clinton called racial profiling, as it has been applied to African Americans and Hispanics, a "morally indefensible, deeply corrosive practice." Since September 11, 2001, Arab Americans have also become victims of this practice, but with little public outcry. Private citizens and public officials alike have "profiled" people of Middle Eastern appearance as potential terrorists.

RACIAL PROFILING AT AIRPORTS

As might be expected, several instances of racial profiling of Arab Americans have taken place at airports. Not only have Arab Americans been targeted, but so have many individuals of Middle Eastern appearance. For example, on December 31, 2001, three men were removed from a Continental Airlines flight after a passenger told the captain that "those brown-skinned men are behaving suspiciously." In fact, none of the men was an Arab: one was Filipino, one was Sri Lankan, and one was Latino.

In November 2006, four Islamic religious leaders boarded a flight in Minneapolis. A passenger on board informed a flight attendant that she had overheard the men making anti-American statements. The men were taken off the airplane, handcuffed, and questioned; eventually, they were released. Of the many passengers removed from airplanes since 9/11, none has been charged with a crime or found to have terrorist connections.

RACIAL PROFILING BY THE FEDERAL GOVERNMENT

One of the most disturbing legal trends in this country has been the growing discrimination by the government against Muslims, Arabs, and South Asians, all in the name of national security. For example, shortly after 9/11, then Attorney General John Ashcroft arrested and put in prison more than a thousand Muslim and Arab men, charging that they had violated immigration laws. But the Justice Department refused to disclose the identities of these men, permit them to have lawyers, or even allow them to contact their families. According to Georgetown University law professor David Cole, "Thousands were detained in this blind search for terrorists without any real evidence of terrorism, and ultimately without netting virtually any terrorists of any kind."

In December 2002, the government began implementing the National Security Entry-Exit Registration System, which requires foreign visitors from specific countries, most of them in the Middle East, to report to a U.S. Citizenship and Immigration Services office to register. Registrants are fingerprinted and photographed, and some are forced to answer questions under oath about their religious beliefs and political affiliations. In one year alone, the government registered more than 80,000 foreign nationals and instituted deportation proceedings against more than 13,500 of them.

Martin Luther King, Jr., once said, "Injustice anywhere is a threat to justice everywhere." Ironically, although the Bush administration's focus has been on "spreading democracy," and its attendant civil rights and liberties, to other nations, the U.S. government has been more successful at curbing the civil liberties and rights of Americans. Although no bill has as yet been introduced in Congress to ban racial profiling, some Democratic leaders have stated that they intend to pursue such legislation during the 110th Congress.

YOU BE THE JUDGE

Some claim that racial profiling is an effective practice in preventing future acts of terrorism. Others argue that racial profiling violates the civil rights of the victims of this practice. Where do you stand on this issue?

Native Americans remain a fragmented political group because large numbers of their population live off the reservations. Nonetheless, by the 1960s, some Native Americans succeeded in forming organizations to strike back at the U.S. government and to reclaim their heritage, including their lands.

The first militant organization was called the National Indian Youth Council. In the late 1960s, a small group of persons identifying themselves as Indians occupied Alcatraz Island, claiming that the island was part of their ancestral lands. Other militant actions followed. For example, in 1973, supporters of the American Indian Movement took over Wounded Knee, South Dakota, where about 150 Sioux Indians had been killed by the U.S. Army in 1890.[20] The occupation was undertaken to protest the government's policy toward Native Americans and to call attention to the injustices they had suffered.

COMPENSATION FOR PAST INJUSTICES

As more Americans became aware of the concerns of Native Americans, Congress started to compensate them for past injustices. In 1990, Congress passed the Native American Languages Act, which declared that Native American languages are unique and serve an important role in maintaining Indian culture and continuity. Under the act, the government and the Indian community share responsibility for the survival of native languages and native cultures. Courts, too, have shown a greater willingness to recognize Native American treaty rights. For example, in 1985, the Supreme Court ruled that three tribes of Oneida Indians could claim damages for the use of tribal land that had been unlawfully transferred in 1795.[21]

The Indian Gaming Regulatory Act of 1988 allows Native Americans to have gambling operations on their reservations. Although the profits from casino gambling operations have helped to improve the economic and social status of many Native Americans, some Native Americans feel that the casino industry has irreparably hurt their traditional culture. Poverty and unemployment remain widespread on the reservations.

Protecting Older Americans

Today, about 38 million Americans (nearly 13 percent of the population) are aged sixty-five or over. By the year 2040, it is estimated that this figure will almost double. Clearly, as the American population grows older, the problems of aging and retirement will become increasingly important national issues. Because many older people rely on income from Social Security, the funding of Social Security benefits continues to be a major issue on the national political agenda.

Many older people who would like to work find it difficult because of age discrimination. Some companies have unwritten policies against hiring, retaining, or promoting people they feel are "too old," making it impossible for some older workers to find work or to continue with their careers. At times, older workers have fallen

Miguel Gandert/Corbis

A Native American dealer works behind a blackjack table at Casino Hollywood on New Mexico's Pueblo San Felipe. Today, many Native American tribes run lucrative gambling operations. Some critics argue that the casinos are wrongfully transforming the traditional Native American way of life.

victim to cost-cutting efforts by employers. To reduce operational expenses, companies may replace older, higher-salaried employees with younger workers who are willing to work for less pay. As part of an effort to protect the rights of older Americans, Congress passed the Age Discrimination in Employment Act (ADEA) in 1967. This act prohibits employers, employment agencies, and labor organizations from discriminating against individuals over the age of forty on the basis of age.

In 2000, the Supreme Court limited the applicability of the ADEA somewhat when it held that lawsuits under this act could not be brought against a state government employer.[22] Essentially, this means that this act does not protect state employees against age-based discrimination by their state employers. (Note, though, that most states also have laws prohibiting age-based discrimination, and state employees can sue in state courts under those laws.)

Obtaining Rights for Persons with Disabilities

Like age discrimination, discrimination based on disability crosses the boundaries of race, ethnicity, gender, and religion. Persons with disabilities, especially physical deformities or severe mental impairments, have to face social bias against them because they are "different." Although attitudes toward persons with disabilities have changed considerably in the last several decades, persons with disabilities continue to suffer from discrimination in all its forms.

Persons with disabilities first became a political force in this country in the 1970s, and in 1973, Congress passed the first legislation protecting this group of persons—the Rehabilitation Act. This act prohibited discrimination against persons with disabilities in programs receiving federal aid. The Individuals with Disabilities Education Act (formerly called the Education for All Handicapped Children Act of 1975) requires public schools to provide children with disabilities with free, appropriate, and individualized education in the least restrictive environment appropriate to their needs. Further legislation in 1978 led to regulations for ramps, elevators, and the like in all federal buildings. The Americans with Disabilities Act (ADA) of 1990, however, is by far the most significant legislation protecting the rights of this group of Americans.

The ADA requires that all public buildings and public services be accessible to persons with disabilities. The act also mandates that employers "reasonably accommodate" the needs of workers or job applicants with disabilities who are otherwise qualified for particular jobs unless to do so would cause the employer to suffer an "undue hardship." The ADA defines persons with disabilities as persons who have physical or mental impairments that "substantially limit" their everyday activities. Health conditions that have been considered disabilities under federal law include blindness, alcoholism, heart disease, cancer, muscular dystrophy, cerebral palsy, paraplegia, diabetes, and acquired immune deficiency syndrome (AIDS). The ADA, however, does not require employers to hire or retain workers who, because of their disabilities, pose a "direct threat to the health or safety" of their co-workers.

In 2001, the Supreme Court reviewed a case raising the question of whether suits under the ADA could be brought against state employers. The Court concluded, as it did with respect to the ADEA, that states are immune from lawsuits brought to enforce rights under this federal law.[23]

Gay Men and Lesbians

Until the late 1960s and early 1970s, gay men and lesbians tended to keep quiet about their sexual preferences because to expose them usually meant facing harsh consequences. This attitude began to change after a 1969 incident in New York City, however. When the police raided the Stonewall Inn—a bar popular with gay men and lesbians—on June 27 of that year, the bar's patrons responded by throwing beer cans and bottles at the police. The riot continued for two days. The Stonewall Inn incident launched the gay power movement. By the end of the year, gay men and lesbians had formed fifty organizations, including the Gay Activist Alliance and the Gay Liberation Front.

A CHANGING LEGAL LANDSCAPE The number of gay and lesbian organizations has grown from fifty in 1969 to several thousand today. These groups have exerted significant political pressure on legislatures, the media, schools, and churches. In the decades following the Stonewall incident, more than half of the forty-nine states that had sodomy laws—laws prohibiting homosexual conduct—repealed them. In seven other states, the courts invalidated such laws. Then, in 2003, the United States Supreme Court issued a ruling that effectively invalidated all remaining sodomy laws in the country. In *Lawrence v. Texas,*[24] the Court ruled that sodomy laws violated the Fourteenth Amendment's due process clause. According to the Court, "The liberty protected by the Constitution allows homosexual persons the right to choose

Americans with disabilities demonstrate in Washington, D.C., in support of the Americans with Disabilities Act (ADA), which was signed into law by President George H. W. Bush in 1990.

Terry Ashe/Getty News Images

to enter upon relationships in the confines of their homes and their own private lives and still retain their dignity as free persons."

Today, twelve states and more than 230 cities and counties in the United States have laws prohibiting discrimination against homosexuals in housing, education, banking, employment, and public accommodations. In a landmark case in 1996, *Romer v. Evans*,[25] the Supreme Court held that a Colorado amendment that would have invalidated all state and local laws protecting homosexuals from discrimination violated the equal protection clause of the Constitution. The Court stated that the amendment would have denied to homosexuals in Colorado—but to no other Colorado residents— "the right to seek specific protection from the law."

CHANGING ATTITUDES Laws and court decisions protecting the rights of gay men and lesbians reflect social attitudes that are much changed from the days of the Stonewall incident. Liberal political leaders have been supporting gay rights for at least two decades. In 1984, presidential candidate Walter Mondale openly sought the gay vote, as did Jesse Jackson in his 1988 presidential campaign. Former president Bill Clinton strongly supported gay rights.

Even some conservative politicians have softened their stance on the issue. For example, during his 2000 presidential campaign, George W. Bush met with representatives of gay groups to discuss issues important to them. Although Bush stated that he was opposed to the idea of gay marriage, he promised that he would not

Same-sex marriages continue to illicit controversy throughout the United States. These demonstrators celebrate a Massachusetts law allowing same-sex marriages.

> "The **Liberty** protected by the Constitution allows homosexual persons the right to choose to enter upon relationships in the confines of their homes and their own private lives and still retain their **dignity** as free persons."
>
> UNITED STATES SUPREME COURT,
> *LAWRENCE V. TEXAS*
> 2003

disqualify anyone from serving in his administration on the basis of sexual orientation.

According to Gallup's 2007 Values and Beliefs survey, public tolerance for gay and lesbian rights has reached its highest level ever in Gallup's annual survey of attitudes over the past three decades. The survey showed that nearly 60 percent of Americans believe that homosexuality should be sanctioned as an acceptable alternative lifestyle, up from just over 30 percent in 1982. Although most Americans (about 90 percent) believe that gay men and lesbians should have equal job opportunities, the public is strongly divided on the issue of same-sex marriage. Whereas 46 percent of Americans believe that same-sex marriages should be recognized as valid, 53 percent oppose such marriages.

SAME-SEX MARRIAGE To date, only one state—Massachusetts—allows same-sex marriages. Although opponents of the Massachusetts law pushed for a state constitutional amendment to define marriage as between a man and a woman, the proposed amendment failed to garner enough votes to be placed on the ballot as a referendum in the 2008 elections. Connecticut, New Jersey, New Hampshire, and Vermont now permit

AP Photo/Rich Pedroncelli

Proponents of a constitutional amendment that defines marriage as between one man and one woman demonstrate their support for this concept. So far, they have not been successful.

civil unions that give same-sex partners many of the legal benefits of married partners. Some other states, including California and Maine, have legalized similar arrangements known as domestic partnerships. Nineteen states have adopted constitutional amendments explicitly banning same-sex marriages, and all but four of the remaining states have statutes banning such marriages.

GAYS AND LESBIANS IN THE MILITARY For gay men and lesbians who wish to join the military, one of the battlefields they face is the "Don't ask, don't tell" policy. This policy, which bans openly gay or lesbian persons from the military, was implemented in 1993 by President Bill Clinton when it became clear that any other alternative would not be accepted. Generally, attitudes toward accepting gay men and lesbians in the military divide along party lines—with the Democrats approving such a policy and the Republicans opposing it.

What do soldiers themselves think about serving alongside gay men and lesbians? According to a 2007 Zogby poll of service members returning from Afghanistan and Iraq, three-quarters of those polled said that they would have no problem serving with gay men or lesbians.

equal employment opportunity A goal of the 1964 Civil Rights Act to end employment discrimination based on race, color, religion, gender, or national origin and to promote equal job opportunities for all individuals.

affirmative action A policy calling for the establishment of programs that give special consideration, in jobs and college admissions, to members of groups that have been discriminated against in the past.

Although Congress is planning to introduce legislation to repeal the "Don't ask, don't tell" policy, whether it will gain enough support to override a potential presidential veto remains to be seen.

LO⁵ BEYOND EQUAL PROTECTION— AFFIRMATIVE ACTION

One provision of the Civil Rights Act of 1964 called for prohibiting discrimination in employment. Soon after the act was passed, the federal government began to legislate programs of **equal employment opportunity.** Such programs require that employers' hiring and promotion practices guarantee the same opportunities to all individuals. Experience soon showed that minorities often had fewer opportunities to obtain education and relevant work experience than did whites. Because of this, they were still excluded from many jobs. Even though discriminatory practices were made illegal, the change in the law did not make up for the results of years of discrimination. Consequently, under President Lyndon B. Johnson (1963–1969), a new policy was developed.

Called **affirmative action,** this policy requires employers to take positive steps to remedy *past* discrimination. Affirmative action programs involve giving special consideration, in jobs and college admissions, to members of groups that have been discriminated against in the past. Until recently, all public and private employers who received federal funds were required to adopt and implement these programs. Thus, the policy of affirmative action has been applied to all agencies of the federal, state, and local governments and to all private employers who sell goods to or perform services for any agency of the federal government. In short, it has covered nearly all of the nation's major employers and many of its smaller ones.

Affirmative Action Tested

The Supreme Court first addressed the issue of affirmative action in 1978 in *Regents of the University of California v. Bakke.*[26] Allan Bakke, a white male, had been denied admission to the University of California's medical school at Davis. The school had set aside sixteen of the one hundred seats in each year's entering class for applicants who wished to be considered as members of designated minority groups. Many of the students

THE REST OF THE WORLD

India Faces an Affirmative Action Nightmare

Affirmative action programs in the United States have involved relatively few targeted minorities. India has a much more complicated situation. For centuries, there have been more than six thousand castes and subcastes. The lowest of the castes, the so-called untouchables, or Dalits, officially was abolished in 1950, but "untouchability" has remained, nonetheless. The government has designated this caste as "Backward."

AFFIRMATIVE ACTION FOR SCHEDULED CASTES

India's lowest castes and subcastes are part of the so-called Scheduled Castes, which represent 25 percent of the population. Affirmative action programs were put into place to bring more of those in the Scheduled Castes into universities and government jobs. This affirmative action program has been in effect for more than sixty years. It is a quota system for members of what the government labels Backward Castes (mainly untouchables) and Other Backward Castes. When the Indian government expanded its affirmative action program for university applicants, a nationwide furor resulted. Nonetheless, today 49.5 percent of places at major universities are reserved for Backward and Other Backward Castes.

SOME SHEPHERDS AND FARMERS WANT THEIR CASTE STATUS TO BE OFFICIALLY DOWNGRADED

At the beginning of 2007, tens of thousands of protesters blocked the roads out of an Indian farming region. Their goal was to have their Scheduled Caste category downgraded to the lowest of the low (untouchable). Why? They realized that if they became part of the government's official Backward Caste (untouchables), as opposed to being just part of Other Backward Castes, they would benefit from more affirmative action programs. They also realized that they would be eligible for more government welfare. They were demanding that their status be lowered even though, as new members of the untouchable caste, they might be prevented from using the same water pumps that others in the rest of their villages use.

For Critical Analysis

An Indian sociologist, Dipankar Gupta, commented, "If you play the caste game, you will end up with caste war." What did he mean?

---

admitted through this special program had lower test scores than Bakke. Bakke sued the university, claiming that he was a victim of **reverse discrimination**—discrimination against whites. Bakke argued that the use of a **quota system,** in which a specific number of seats were reserved for minority applicants only, violated the equal protection clause.

The Supreme Court was strongly divided on the issue. Some justices believed that Bakke had been denied equal protection and should be admitted. A majority on the Court, however, concluded that both the Constitution and the Civil Rights Act of 1964 allow race to be used as a factor in making admissions decisions, although race could not be the *sole* factor. Because the university's quota system was based solely on race, it was unconstitutional. For more affirmative action problems elsewhere, see *The Rest of the World* feature.

Strict Scrutiny Applied

In 1995, the Supreme Court issued a landmark decision in *Adarand Constructors, Inc. v. Peña*.[27] The Court held that any federal, state, or local affirmative action program that uses racial classifications as the basis for making decisions is subject to "strict scrutiny" by the courts. As discussed earlier in this chapter, this means that, to be constitutional, a discriminatory law or action must be narrowly tailored to meet a *compelling* government interest. In effect, the *Adarand* decision narrowed the application of

reverse discrimination The assertion that affirmative action programs that require special consideration for minorities discriminate against those who have no minority status.

quota system A policy under which a specific number of jobs, promotions, or other types of placements, such as university admissions, must be given to members of selected groups.

"Larry is a white male, but he hasn't been able to do much with it."

affirmative action programs. An affirmative action program can no longer make use of quotas or preferences and cannot be maintained simply to remedy past discrimination by society in general. It must be narrowly tailored to remedy actual discrimination that has occurred, and once the program has succeeded, it must be changed or dropped.

The Diversity Issue

Following the *Adarand* decision, several lower courts faced cases raising the question of whether affirmative action programs designed to achieve diversity on college campuses were constitutional. For example, in a 1996 case, *Hopwood v. State of Texas*,[28] two white law school applicants sued the University of Texas School of Law in Austin, claiming that they had been denied admission because of the school's affirmative action program. The program allowed admissions officials to take racial and other factors into consideration when determining which students would be admitted. A federal appellate court held that the program violated the equal protection clause because it discriminated in favor of minority applicants. In its decision, the court directly challenged the *Bakke* decision by stating that the use of race even as a means of achieving diversity on college campuses "undercuts the Fourteenth Amendment." In other words, race could never be a factor, even though it was not the sole factor, in such decisions.

In 2003, the United States Supreme Court reviewed two cases involving issues similar to that in

the *Hopwood* case. Both cases involved admissions programs at the University of Michigan. In *Gratz v. Bollinger*,[29] two white applicants who were denied undergraduate admission to the university alleged reverse discrimination. The school's policy gave each applicant a score based on a number of factors, including grade point average, standardized test scores, and personal achievements. The system *automatically* awarded every "underrepresented" minority (African American, Hispanic, and Native American) applicant twenty points—one-fifth of the points needed to guarantee admission. The Court held that this policy violated the equal protection clause.

In contrast, in *Grutter v. Bollinger*,[30] the Court held that the University of Michigan Law School's admissions policy was constitutional. In that case, the Court concluded that "[u]niversities can, however, consider race or ethnicity more flexibly as a 'plus' factor in the context of individualized consideration of each and every applicant." The significant difference between the two admissions policies, in the Court's view, was that the law school's approach did not apply a mechanical formula giving "diversity bonuses" based on race or ethnicity. In short, the Court concluded that diversity on college campuses was a legitimate goal and that limited affirmative action programs could be used to attain this goal.

The Supreme Court Revisits the Issue

The Michigan cases were decided in 2003. By 2007, when another case involving affirmative action came before the Court, the Court had a new chief justice, John G. Roberts, Jr., who replaced the late Chief Justice William Rehnquist, and a new associate justice, Samuel Alito, Jr., who took Sandra Day O'Connor's place on the Court after she retired. Both men were appointed by President George W. Bush, and the conservative views of both justices have moved the Court significantly to the right. Justice O'Connor had often been the "swing" vote on the Court, sometimes voting with the more liberal justices and sometimes joining the conservative bloc. Hers was the deciding vote in the five-to-four decision upholding the University of Michigan Law School's affirmative action program.

Some claim that the more conservative composition of today's Court strongly influenced the outcome in a case that came before the court in 2007: *Parents Involved in Community Schools v. Seattle School District No. 1*.[31] The case concerned the policies of two school districts, one in Louisville, Kentucky, and

Public education issues continue to spark demonstrations throughout the United States. GoodSchools.org is the Web site of the Massachusetts Teachers Association. Some of its members and supporters are seen here in front of the United State Supreme Court building in Washington, D.C.

one in Seattle, Washington. Both schools were trying to achieve a more diversified student body by giving preference to minority students if space in the schools was limited and a choice among applicants had to be made. Parents of white children who were turned away from schools in these districts because of these policies sued the school districts, claiming that the policies violated the equal protection clause. Ultimately, the case reached the Supreme Court, and the Court, in a close (five-to-four) vote, held in favor of the parents, ruling that the policies violated the equal protection clause. The Court's decision did not overrule the 2003 case, involving the University of Michigan Law School, however, for the Court did not say that race could not be used as a factor in university admissions policies. Nonetheless, some claim that the decision represents a significant change on the Court with respect to affirmative action policies.

State Actions

Beginning in the mid-1990s, some states have taken actions to ban affirmative action programs or replace them with alternative policies. For example, in 1996, by a ballot initiative, California amended its state constitution to prohibit any "preferential treatment to any individual or group on the basis of race, sex, color, ethnicity, or national origin in the operation of public employment, public education, or public contracting."

Two years later, voters in the state of Washington approved a ballot measure ending all state-sponsored affirmative action in that state. Florida has also ended affirmative action, and in 2006 a ballot initiative in Michigan, just three years after the Supreme Court decisions discussed above, banned affirmative action in that state. In 2007, Ward Connerly, an opponent of affirmative action who spearheaded the initiatives banning affirmative action in California and Michigan, stated that he was attempting to gather support in nine other states to put similar initiatives on the ballots for the 2008 elections.

In the meantime, many public universities are trying to find "race-blind" ways to attract more minority students to their campuses. For example, Wayne State University Law School in Detroit implemented a new admissions policy that doesn't mention race but allows admissions officials to consider such factors as living on an Indian reservation or in mostly black areas of Detroit. Ohio State University founded a magnet school to help prepare potential applicants to the university. Some universities send recruiters into poor and low-performing schools to try to interest students in coming to their campuses.

JOIN THE DEBATE

Affirmative Action on College Campuses—Is It Time for a Change in Thinking?

Affirmative action policies on college campuses are generally translated into preferential admission treatment for disadvantaged minorities. These policies have been around for decades. They have also been challenged in the courts, as you have just read. Some states have also seen voter initiatives designed to reduce, if not eliminate, such preferential treatment in college admissions. The debate is not about to end, but is it time to change the way we think about this subject?

For some Americans, the arguments in favor of preferential college admissions for disadvantaged minorities remain convincing. Those on this side of the debate contend that this country will never fully compensate minorities for the decades, if not centuries, of oppression. Affirmative action is just a small step in the right direction. In any event, young people today who are starting out at a disadvantage need extra help getting into colleges. Affirmative action helps level the playing field for these individuals when they apply to college. Affirmative action is needed to give disadvantaged minorities the opportunity to show that they are

just as capable as other students. Finally, ethnic and racial diversity on college campuses is desirable in and of itself, and it won't occur if left to chance.

Those on the other side of this debate believe that times have changed and our thinking should change, too. By eliminating affirmative action programs of all types, we will get closer to a color-blind society in which people are judged only on their achievements. Moreover, minorities today do not need affirmative action to succeed—they can do it on their own. It is demeaning to admit minorities to college because of preferential treatment rather than because of their own abilities and hard work. Finally, affirmative action results in a lowering of the standards of accountability that are required to motivate students to perform better.

Students are of a mixed mind with respect to affirmative action programs on America's college campuses. The students on the left are against affirmative action programs that use race as a criterion for admission. They are in favor of a "color blind" admissions policy.

AP Photo/Danny Moloshok

AMERICA AT ODDS:
Civil Rights

As noted in Chapter 4, our civil liberties are guaranteed in the Bill of Rights. Our civil rights, however, have evolved only slowly over time, as various groups pressured the public and Congress to make the Constitution's equal protection clause a reality. Today, we tend to take our civil rights for granted. But consider that even as late as 1950, which is relatively recent in the long span of our nation's history, few of the rights discussed in this chapter existed. In 1950, the prevailing view was that "a woman's place is in the home," and there was no such thing as a lawsuit for gender discrimination or sexual harassment. In 1950, racial segregation was pervasive—and legal. At that time, there were no legal protections for older Americans who were fired from their jobs because of their age; nor were there any laws protecting persons with disabilities and gay men and lesbi-ans from discrimination. Equal employment opportunity was not required by law, and few civil and political rights were guaranteed for minority groups.

Clearly, our nation has come a long way since the time when only white males enjoyed the right to vote and to fully participate in American political life. This is not to say that there isn't a long way still to go. As you read in this chapter, minorities in this country continue to struggle for equal rights and opportunities, and women continue to face gender discrimination in the workplace, in politics, and in nearly every arena. How to ensure equal treatment for all Americans continues to be a major challenge facing the nation's lawmakers—and *all* Americans.

Issues for Debate & Discussion

- Some claim that racial or ethnic profiling can sometimes be jus-tified. For example, if Arab truck drivers hauling loads of hazard-ous materials are ten times as likely to be terrorists as non-Arab truck drivers hauling such loads, then it makes sense to stop the drivers and interrogate them simply because of their ethnicity. Others argue that racial or ethnic profiling cannot be justified in any circumstances. What is your position on this issue?
- Native American casinos first appeared on the American scene in the 1980s. Proponents of these casinos argue that these lucrative gambling establishments are an economic necessity for tribal groups and that the income generated by the casinos has helped Native Americans gain self-respect and economic self-sufficiency. Opponents of Native American casinos contend that gambling leads to increased crime, alcoholism, drug addiction, and corruption. These critics also maintain that Native Ameri-cans should not be permitted to hold exclusive rights to operate casinos in states that otherwise restrict gambling. What is your position on this issue?

Take Action

As mentioned in the introduction to this feature, despite the progress that has been made toward attaining equal treatment for all groups of Americans, much remains to be done. Countless activist groups continue to pursue the goal of equality for all Americans. If you wish to contribute your time and effort toward this goal, there are literally hundreds of ways to go about it. You can easily find activist opportunities just by going to the Web sites of the groups listed in this chapter's *Politics on the Web* section on the next page. There, you will find links to groups that seek to protect and enhance the rights of African Americans, Latinos, women, the elderly, persons with disabilities, and others. At the Justice for Immigrants Web site given in this chapter's opening *America at Odds* feature, you can sign up to receive e-mails from the Immigrant Justice Action Network. If there are any gatherings or events planned for your neighborhood, such as a demonstration for immigrants' rights, you can participate in them—or volunteer to help organize them. Finally, you can search the Web for blogs on a civil rights issue that particularly interests you, read about what others on that site are saying, and "tell the world" your opinion on the issue.

- Stanford University's Web site contains primary documents written by Martin Luther King, Jr., as well as secondary documents written about King. The URL for the "Martin Luther King Directory" is **www.stanford.edu/group/King**.

- If you are interested in learning more about the Equal Employment Opportunity Commission (EEOC), the laws it enforces, and how to file a charge with the EEOC, go to **www.eeoc.gov**.

- The home page for the National Association for the Advancement of Colored People (NAACP), which contains extensive information about African American civil rights issues, is **www.naacp.org**.

- For information on Hispanics in the United States, Latino Link is a good source. You can find it at **www.latinolink.org**.

- The most visible and successful advocacy group for older Americans is AARP (formerly known as the American Association of Retired Persons). Its home page contains helpful links and much information. Go to **www.aarp.org**.

- The home page of the National Organization for Women (NOW) has links to numerous resources containing information on the rights and status of women both in the United States and around the world. You can find NOW's home page at **www.now.org**.

- You can access the Web site of the Feminist Majority Foundation, which focuses on equality for women, at **www.feminist.org**.

- For information on the Americans with Disabilities Act (ADA), including the text of the act, go to **www.jan.wvu.edu/portals/dbtac.htm**.

- The Gay and Lesbian Alliance against Defamation has an online News Bureau. To find this organization's home page, go to **www.glaad.org**.

ONLINE RESOURCES FOR THIS CHAPTER

This text's Companion Web site, at **www.americaatodds. com,** offers links to numerous resources that you can utilize to learn more about the topics covered in this chapter.

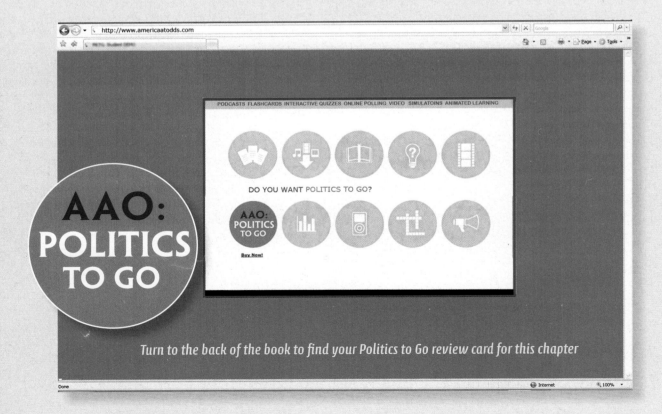

Turn to the back of the book to find your Politics to Go review card for this chapter

CHAPTER 6
INTEREST GROUPS

LEARNING OBJECTIVES

LO¹ Explain what an interest group is, how interest groups form, and how interest groups function in American politics.

LO² Indicate how interest groups differ from political parties.

LO³ Identify the various types of interest groups.

LO⁴ Discuss how the activities of interest groups help to shape government policymaking.

LO⁵ Describe how interest groups are regulated by government.

AMERICA AT ODDS

Has the Time Come for Stricter Gun Control Laws?

One of the most successful interest groups in American history has been the National Rifle Association (NRA). Partly because of the Second Amendment to the U.S. Constitution, which guarantees the right to bear arms, and partly because of the effectiveness of the NRA's lobbying, the United States has the laxest gun control laws in the developed world.

To some extent, the public is at odds with the very effective lobbying results of the NRA. Every day, about thirty people are murdered by firearms in the United States. When one person murdered more than thirty people in one day—as happened at Virginia Tech University in the spring of 2007—the gun control debate heated up again. Nonetheless, recent polls show that the Virginia Tech shootings did not sway many people's views. A survey conducted just after the Virginia Tech massacre found that about 59 percent of Americans polled believed that stricter gun controls might help prevent such tragedies. But only 30 percent truly believed that gun control would make a difference in the future. Figure into this equation that almost one-third of Americans own a gun of some kind.

It's an Aberration for Americans to Own So Many Guns So Easily

Gun control advocates point out the obvious—guns cause many deaths in America. Specifically, firearms are responsible for about 14,000 murders each year. In addition, about 16,000 suicides are carried out with firearms. Finally, there are 650 fatal firearm accidents. Since the last time a president was killed (John F. Kennedy, in 1963), more Americans have died by gunfire in the United States than died in foreign battlefields throughout the entire twentieth century.

Supporters of stricter gun control criticized the Bush administration for allowing the assault-weapons ban to lapse in 2004. What civilian needs an AK-47 automatic rifle? Are we expecting a foreign invasion?

At a minimum, all guns should have childproof locks. And what about a more complete registration system for guns and gun owners? Only criminals would worry about that. The massive amount of firepower that criminals have in the United States is a direct result of our lax gun control laws. Even just keeping guns in the home, presumably for protection, is dangerous. A gun in the home is many times more likely to kill a family member than to stop a criminal.

WE HAVE A CONSTITUTIONAL RIGHT TO BEAR ARMS

Those who oppose gun control laws point out that the Second Amendment gives every American the right to bear arms. Unless the Constitution is amended to change this provision, no law can deprive Americans of this right. Today, forty states with two-thirds of the nation's population allow their residents to carry a concealed weapon if they can show that they are law-abiding citizens and have obtained a permit. Very few concealed-weapons permits have been revoked. Only in rare instances have those with concealed-weapons permits used them unlawfully.

Even though Virginia has a concealed-weapons law, the campus at Virginia Tech was designated by its administration as a gun-free zone. Consequently, when a deranged student started firing at students and faculty, no one was able to stop him. In contrast, on other campuses, similarly deranged killers have been stopped by faculty or bystanders who had legally concealed weapons and knew how to use them. Indeed, some evidence shows that law-abiding citizens are safer in jurisdictions that have concealed-weapons laws. Why? The reason is simply that would-be criminals are not sure who has a weapon and therefore are less likely to randomly use guns to commit their crimes.

Ultimately, more restrictions on gun ownership would not lead to a decrease in crime, and such restrictions might even cause an increase in crime. Criminals, by definition, do not obey the law. Convicted felons are already prohibited by law from possessing firearms, so even if we had more extensive registration requirements, felons would not register their firearms.

Where do you stand?

1. "The 'gun culture' has created an environment in which violent crime, particularly crime committed with firearms, makes most Americans feel unsafe on the streets and in their homes." Do you believe this statement to be true? Why or why not?
2. "If guns are outlawed, we will be less safe because only criminals will have guns." Do you accept this reasoning? Explain.

Explore this issue online

- The News Batch Web site provides relatively evenhanded coverage of many important topics. See **www.newsbatch.com/guncontrol.htm** for background information on and links to other sites concerning gun control.
- A mandatory stop when researching this issue is the NRA's Web site at **www.nra.org**. Another site that opposes gun control is **www.saf.org**, the Web site of the Second Amendment Foundation, which sponsors lawsuits on behalf of gun owners' rights. Million Mom March, at **www.millionmommarch.org**, is a major group advocating gun control.

INTRODUCTION

The groups supporting and opposing gun control provide but one example of how Americans form groups to pursue or protect their interests. All of us have interests that we would like to have represented in government: farmers want higher prices for their products, young people want good educational opportunities, environmentalists want clean air and water, and the homeless want programs that provide food and shelter.

The old adage that there is strength in numbers is certainly true in American politics. As discussed in Chapter 4, the right to organize groups is protected by the Constitution, which guarantees people the right "peaceably to assemble, and to petition the Government for a redress of grievances." The United States Supreme Court has defended this important right over the years.

Special interests significantly influence American government and politics. Indeed, some Americans think that this influence is so great that it jeopardizes representative democracy. Others maintain that interest groups are a natural consequence of democracy. After all, throughout our nation's history, people have organized into groups to protect special interests. Because of the important role played by interest groups in the American system of government, in this chapter we focus solely on such groups. We look at what they are, why they are formed, and how they influence policymaking.

LO¹ INTEREST GROUPS AND AMERICAN GOVERNMENT

An **interest group** is an organization of people sharing common objectives who actively attempt to influence government policymakers through direct and indirect methods. Whatever their goals—more or fewer social services, higher or lower prices—interest groups pursue these goals on every level and in every branch of government.

On any given day in Washington, D.C., you can see national interest groups in action. If you eat breakfast in the Senate dining room, you might see congressional committee staffers reviewing testimony with representatives from women's groups. Later that morning, you might visit the Supreme Court and watch a civil rights lawyer arguing on behalf of a client in a discrimination suit. Lunch in a popular Washington restaurant might find you listening in on a conversation between an agricultural lobbyist and a congressional representative.

That afternoon you might visit an executive department, such as the Department of Labor, and watch bureaucrats working out rules and regulations with representatives from a business interest group. Then you might stroll past the headquarters of the National Rifle Association (NRA), AARP (formerly the American Association of Retired Persons), or the National Wildlife Federation.

> **interest group** An organized group of individuals sharing common objectives who actively attempt to influence policymakers in all three branches of the government and at all levels.

How Interest Groups Form

Interest groups form in response to change: a political or economic change, a dramatic shift in population or technology that affects how people live or work, or a change in social values or cultural norms. Some groups form to support the change or even speed it along, while others form to fight change. For example, during the economic boom of the 1990s, interest groups formed to support easing immigration restrictions on highly skilled workers who were in great demand in technology industries. After the terrorist attacks of September 11, 2001, however, other groups formed to support more restrictions on immigration.

As you will read shortly, there are many different types of interest groups—some represent the interests of a particular industry, while others lobby on behalf of employees. Some interest groups promote policies to protect the environment, and others seek to protect

These visitors at a National Rifle Association (NRA) convention are able to examine the "latest and greatest" firearms. The NRA is one of the nation's most successful interest groups.

AP Photo/Keith Srakocic

patron An individual or organization that provides financial backing to an interest group.

consumers. These types of groups may be interested in a broad array of issues. A consumer group may want to protect consumers from dangerous products as well as high prices. Other groups form in response to a single issue, such as a potential highway project. These groups are sometimes more successful than multi-issue groups.

FINANCING   To have much success in gaining members and influencing policy, an interest group must have **patrons**—people or organizations willing to finance the group. Although groups usually collect fees or donations from their members, few can survive without large grants or donations. The level of financing required to form and expand an interest group successfully depends on the issues involved and the amount of lobbying the group needs to do. A group that pays professional lobbyists to meet with lawmakers in Washington, D.C., will require more funding than a group that operates with leaflets printed out from a Web site and distributed by volunteers.

As you can see in Figure 6–1, the budgets of different interest groups can vary widely. AARP has a budget of about $925 million, while the League of Women Voters operates with only about $5.1 million. Some in-

Alexis de Tocqueville (1805–1859) was a well-known French political historian. He lived during a time of political upheaval in France and took a keen interest in the young democracy in America. He toured the United States and Canada as a young man and collected his observations in Democracy in America, which was published in 1835.

The Granger Collection

> "If men are to remain **civilized** or to become civilized, the art of association must develop and improve among them at the same speed as **equality** of conditions spread."
>
> ALEXIS DE TOCQUEVILLE, *DEMOCRACY IN AMERICA* (VOL. 2, PART II, CHAPTER 5, 1835)

terest groups can become very powerful very quickly if they have wealthy patrons. Other groups can raise money in a hurry if a particular event galvanizes public attention on an issue. For example, the devastating Indian Ocean tsunami brought in millions of dollars for international relief groups, such as the American Red Cross, in 2004 and 2005.

INCENTIVES TO JOIN A GROUP   The French political observer and traveler Alexis de Tocqueville wrote in 1835 that Americans have a tendency to form "associations" and have perfected "the art of pursuing in common the object of their common desires." "In no other country of the world," said Tocqueville, "has the principle of association been more successfully used or applied to a greater multitude of objectives than in America."[1] Of course, Tocqueville could not foresee the thousands of associations that now exist in this country. Surveys show that more than 85 percent of Americans belong to at least one group. Table 6–1 on page 130 shows the percentage of Americans who belong to various types of groups today.

This penchant for joining groups is just part of the story, however. Americans have other incentives for joining interest groups. Some people enjoy the camaraderie and sense of belonging that comes from associating with other people who share their interests and goals. Some groups offer their members material incentives for joining, such as discounts on products, subscriptions, or group insurance programs. But sometimes these incentives are not enough to persuade people to join.

THE FREE RIDER PROBLEM   This world in which we live is one of scarce resources. As a consequence, there are *private goods* and *public goods*. Most of the goods

FIGURE 6-1

PROFILES OF SELECTED INTEREST GROUPS

Name: AARP
Founded: 1958
Membership: 38 million working or retired persons 50 years of age or older.
Description: AARP strives to better the lives of older people, especially in the areas of health care, worker equity, and minority affairs. AARP sponsors community crime prevention programs, research on the problems of aging, and a mail-order pharmacy.
Budget: $925,000,000
Address: 601 E St. N.W., Washington, DC 20049
Phone: (888) 687-2277   **Web site:** www.aarp.org

Name: League of Women Voters of the United States (LWVUS)
Founded: 1920
Membership: 150,000 members and supporters.
Description: The LWVUS promotes active and informed political participation. It distributes candidate information, encourages voter registration and voting, and takes action on issues of public policy. The group's national interests include international relations, natural resources, and social policy.
Budget: $5,073,000
Address: 1730 M St. N.W., Suite 1000 Washington, DC 20036
Phone: (202) 429-1965   **Web site:** www.lwv.org

Name: National Education Association (NEA)
Founded: 1857
Membership: 3.2 million elementary and secondary school teachers, college and university professors, academic administrators, and others.
Description: The NEA's committees investigate and take action in the areas of benefits, civil rights, educational support, personnel, higher education, human relations, legislation, minority affairs, and women's concerns. Many NEA locals function as labor unions.
Budget: $307,000,000
Address: 1201 16th St. N.W., Washington, DC 20036
Phone: (202) 833-4000   **Web site:** www.nea.org

Name: National Rifle Association (NRA)
Founded: 1871
Membership: 4.3 million members
Description: The NRA promotes rifle, pistol, and shotgun shooting, as well as hunting, gun collecting, and home firearm safety. It educates police firearm instructors and sponsors teams to participate in international competitions.
Budget: $200,000,000
Address: 11250 Waples Mill Road, Fairfax, VA 22030
Phone: (800) NRA-3888   **Web site:** www.nra.org

Name: The Sierra Club (SC)
Founded: 1892
Membership: 750,000 persons concerned with the interrelationship between nature and humankind.
Description: The Sierra Club protects and conserves natural resources, saves endangered areas, and resolves problems associated with wilderness, clean air, energy conservation, and land use. Its committees are concerned with agriculture, economics, environmental education, hazardous materials, the international environment, Native American sites, political education, and water resources.
Budget: $92,000,000
Address: 85 2d St., 2d Floor, San Francisco, CA 94105
Phone: (415) 977-5500 **Web site:** www.sierraclub.org

and services that you use are private goods. If you consume them, no one else can consume them at the same time. For example, when you are using your computer, no one else can sit in front of it and type at the same time. With the other class of goods, called public goods, however, your use of a good does not diminish its use by someone else. National defense is a good example. If this country is protected through its national defense system, your protection from enemy invasion does not reduce anybody else's protection.

TABLE 6-1

PERCENTAGE OF AMERICANS BELONGING TO VARIOUS GROUPS

Health organizations	16%
Social clubs	17
Neighborhood groups	18
Hobby, garden, and computer clubs	19
PTA and school groups	21
Professional and trade associations	27
Health, sport, and country clubs	30
Religious groups	61

Source: AARP.

People cannot be excluded from enjoying a public good, such as national defense, just because they did not pay for it. If an interest group is successful in lobbying for laws that will improve air quality, for example, everyone who breathes that air will benefit, whether they paid for the lobbying effort or not. This is called the **free rider problem.** In some instances, the free rider problem can be overcome. For example, social pressure may persuade some people to join or donate to a group for fear of being ostracized. The government can also step in to ensure that the burden of lobbying for the public good is shared by all. When the government classifies interest groups as nonprofit organizations, it confers on them tax-exempt status. The groups' operating costs are reduced because they do not have to pay taxes, and the impact of the government's lost revenue is absorbed by all taxpayers.

How Interest Groups Function in American Politics

Despite the bad press that interest groups tend to get in the United States, they do serve several purposes in American politics:

- Interest groups help bridge the gap between citizens and government and enable citizens to explain their views on policies to public officials.

- Interest groups help raise public awareness and inspire action on various issues.

- Interest groups often provide public officials with specialized and detailed information that might be difficult to obtain otherwise. This information may be useful in making policy choices.

free rider problem The difficulty faced by interest groups that lobby for a public good. Individuals can enjoy the outcome of the group's efforts without having to contribute, such as by becoming members of the group.

pluralist theory A theory that views politics as a contest among various interest groups—at all levels of government—to gain benefits for their members.

- Interest groups serve as another check on public officials to make sure that they are carrying out their duties responsibly.

ACCESS TO GOVERNMENT In a sense, the American system of government invites the participation of interest groups by offering many points of access for groups wishing to influence policy. Consider the possibilities at just the federal level. An interest group can lobby members of Congress to act in the interests of the group. If the Senate passes a bill opposed by the group, the group's lobbying efforts can shift to the House of Representatives. If the House passes the bill, the group can try to influence the new law's application by lobbying the executive agency that is responsible for implementing the law. The group might even challenge the law in court, directly (by filing a lawsuit) or indirectly (by filing a brief as an *amicus curiae*,[2] or "friend of the court").

PLURALIST THEORY The **pluralist theory** of American democracy focuses on the participation of groups

Volunteers of the Vermont Public Interest Research Group are filling ten thousand cups of water at the statehouse's steps. This interest group wants Vermont legislators to pass clean water legislation.

AP Photo/Toby Talbot

in a decentralized structure of government that offers many points of access to policymakers. According to the pluralist theory, politics is a contest among various interest groups. These groups vie with each other—at all levels of government—to gain benefits for their members. Pluralists maintain that the influence of interest groups on government is not undemocratic because individual interests are indirectly represented in the policymaking process through these groups. Although not every American belongs to an interest group, inevitably some group will represent each individual's interests. Each interest is satisfied to some extent through the compromises made in settling conflicts among competing interest groups.

Pluralists also contend that because of the extensive number of interest groups vying for political benefits, no one group can dominate the political process. Additionally, because most people have more than one interest, conflicts among groups do not divide the nation into hostile camps. Not all scholars agree that this is how interest groups function, however.

There are thousands of interest groups in this country, including this one that is looking out for the health and welfare of children. This toy safety group encourages Congress to pass stricter legislation protecting children.

LO² HOW DO INTEREST GROUPS DIFFER FROM POLITICAL PARTIES?

Although interest groups and political parties are both groups of people joined together for political purposes, they differ in several important ways. As you will read in Chapter 7, a political party is a group of individuals outside government who organize to win elections, operate the government, and determine policy. Interest groups, in contrast, do not seek to win elections or operate the government. Clearly, though, they do seek to influence policy. Interest groups also differ from political parties in other ways, including the following:

■ Interest groups are often policy *specialists,* whereas political parties are policy *generalists.* Political parties are broad-based organizations that must attract the support of many opposing groups and consider a large number of issues. Interest groups, in contrast, have only a handful of key policies to push. An environmental group will not be as concerned about the economic status of Hispanics as it is about polluters. A manufacturing group is more involved with pushing for fewer regulations than it is with inner-city poverty.

■ Interest groups are usually more tightly organized than political parties. They are often financed through contributions or dues-paying memberships. Organizers of interest groups communicate with members and potential members through conferences, mailings, newsletters, and electronic formats, such as e-mail.

■ A political party's main sphere of influence is the electoral system; parties run candidates for political office. Interest groups try to influence the outcome of elections, but unlike parties, they do not compete for public office. Although a candidate for office may be sympathetic to—or even be a member of—a certain group, he or she does not run for election as a candidate of that group.

LO³ DIFFERENT TYPES OF INTEREST GROUPS

American democracy embraces almost every conceivable type of interest group, and the number is increasing rapidly. No one has ever compiled a *Who's Who* of interest groups, but you can get an idea of the number and variety by looking through the annually published *Encyclopedia of Associations.* Look again at Figure 6–1 on page 129 to see profiles of some selected important interest groups.

Some interest groups have large memberships. AARP, for example, has about 38 million members. Others, such as the Tulip Growers Association, have as few as fourteen members. Some, such as the NRA, are household names and have been in existence for many years, while others crop up overnight. Some are highly

These members of AARP attend a rally in Richmond, Virginia, in 2007. They were demonstrating in favor of long-term health care services.

structured and are run by professional, full-time staffs, while others are loosely structured and informal.

The most common interest groups are those that promote private interests. These groups seek public policies that benefit the economic interests of their members and work against policies that threaten those interests. Other groups, sometimes called **public-interest groups,** are formed with the broader goal of working for the "public good"; the American Civil Liberties Union and Common Cause are examples. Let there be no mistake, though, about the name *public interest.* There is no such thing as a clear public interest in a nation of more than 300 million diverse people. The two so-called public-interest groups just mentioned do not represent the American people but only a relatively small part of the American population. In reality, all lobbying groups, organizations, and other political entities always represent special interests.

public-interest group An interest group formed for the purpose of working for the "public good." Examples of public-interest groups are the American Civil Liberties Union and Common Cause.

trade organization An association formed by members of a particular industry, such as the oil industry or the trucking industry, to develop common standards and goals for the industry. Trade organizations, as interest groups, lobby government for legislation or regulations that specifically benefit their groups.

Business Interest Groups

Business has long been well organized for effective action. Hundreds of business groups are now operating in Washington, D.C., in the fifty state capitals, and at the local level across the coun-

try. Two umbrella organizations that include small and large corporations and businesses are the U.S. Chamber of Commerce and the National Association of Manufacturers (NAM). In addition to representing about three million individual businesses, the Chamber has more than three thousand local, state, and regional affiliates. It has become a major voice for millions of small businesses.

The hundreds of **trade organizations** are far less visible than the Chamber of Commerce and the NAM, but they are also important in seeking policy goals for their members. Trade organizations usually support policies that benefit specific industries. For example, people in the oil industry work for policies that favor the development of oil as an energy resource. Other business groups have worked for policies that favor the development of coal, solar power, and nuclear power. Trucking companies would work for policies that would result in more highways being built. Railroad companies would, of course, not want more highways built because that would hurt their business.

Traditionally, business interest groups have been viewed as staunch supporters of the Republican Party. This is because Republicans are more likely to promote a "hands-off" government policy toward business. Over the last decade, however, donations from corporations to the Democratic National Committee more than doubled. Why would business groups make contributions to the Democratic National Committee? Fred McChesney, a professor of law and business, offers an interesting answer to this question. He argues that campaign contributions are often made not for political favors but rather to avoid political disfavor. Just as government officials can take away wealth from citizens (in the form of taxes, for example), politicians can extort from private parties payments *not* to expropriate private wealth.[3] (For an example of the power of business interests, see this chapter's *The Politics of National Security* feature on page 134.)

Labor Interest Groups

Interest groups representing labor have been some of the most influential groups in our country's history. They date back to at least 1886, when the American Federation of Labor (AFL) was formed. The largest and most powerful labor interest group today is the AFL-CIO (the American Federation of Labor–Congress of Industrial Organizations), a confederation of fifty-four national and international labor unions representing nearly ten million workers. Several million additional workers are members of other unions (not affiliated with the AFL-CIO), such as the United Electrical Workers.

Like labor unions everywhere, American labor unions press for policies to improve working conditions and ensure better pay for their members. On some issues, however, unions may take opposing sides. For example, separate unions of bricklayers and carpenters may try to change building codes to benefit their own members even though the changes may hurt other unions. Unions may also compete for new members. In many states, the National Education Association and the AFL-CIO's American Federation of Teachers compete fiercely for members.

Although unions were highly influential in the late 1800s and the early 1900s, their strength and political power have waned in the last several decades, as you can see in Figure 6–2. Today, organized labor represents only 12 percent of the **labor force**—defined as all of the people over the age of sixteen who are working or actively looking for a job. While labor groups have generally experienced a decline in lobbying power, public employee unions have grown in both numbers and political clout in recent years. Public employees enjoy some of the nation's best health-care and retirement benefits because of the efforts of their labor groups.

Agricultural Interest Groups

Many groups work for general agricultural interests at all levels of government. Three broad-based agricultural

These picketers belong to the United Auto Workers (UAW). The union called a strike, and union members and supporters demonstrated outside the General Motors plant in Warren, Michigan, in the fall of 2007. (The strike was short-lived, though, as the UAW and General Motors reached an agreement, mainly on which entity would be responsible for health care costs in the future).

groups represent millions of American farmers, from peanut farmers to dairy producers to tobacco growers. They are the American Farm Bureau Federation (Farm Bureau), the National Grange, and the National Farmers Union. The Farm Bureau, with more than 6.1 million members, is the largest and generally the most effective of the three. Founded in 1919, the Farm Bureau achieved one of its greatest early successes when it helped to obtain government guarantees of "fair" prices during the Great Depression of the 1930s.[4] The Grange, founded in 1867, is the oldest group. It has units in 3,600 communities in thirty-seven states, with a total membership of about 300,000 rural families. The National Farmers Union comprises approximately 250,000 farm and ranch families.

Like special interest labor groups, producers of various specific farm commodities, such as dairy products, soybeans, grain, fruit, corn, cotton, beef, and sugar beets, have formed their own organizations. These specialized groups,

labor force All of the people over the age of sixteen who are working or actively looking for jobs.

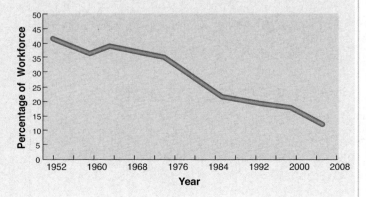

FIGURE 6–2

UNION MEMBERSHIP, 1952 TO PRESENT

This figure shows the percentage of the workforce represented by unions from 1952 to the present. As you can see, union membership has declined significantly over the past several decades.

Percentage of Workforce (y-axis: 0 to 50)
Year (x-axis: 1952, 1960, 1968, 1976, 1984, 1992, 2000, 2008)

THE POLITICS OF NATIONAL SECURITY

THE MILITARY-INDUSTRIAL COMPLEX

Given the lack of a military draft at the present time and the shortage of volunteers, the U.S. Army has been spread thin while fighting the war on terrorism. Needing more personnel, especially in Iraq, the George W. Bush administration turned to private contractors.

Although there is nothing new about private contractors playing a role in American war efforts, they were used in Iraq on an unprecedented scale. As you will read in *The Politics of National Security* feature in Chapter 13, where we discuss the extent of the "outsourcing" involved in the Iraq war in some detail, about $450 billion per year was being spent for war-related work performed by private contractors. In this feature, we focus on the implications of the interrelationship between the government and private contractors for our democracy.

PRIVATE CONTRACTORS AND SPECIAL INTERESTS

The intertwining of the special interests of defense contractors with the war effort in Iraq has produced some possibly unsettling results. For example, Texas oil services giant Halliburton Corporation was awarded multibillion-dollar contracts for handling fuel-related and infrastructure work in Iraq during the occupation and rebuilding process. Vice President Dick Cheney once headed Halliburton, and the company still pays him nearly $1 million annually as part of a severance contract.

Bechtel Corporation, a California-based firm, won a contract to improve Iraq's infrastructure. At that time, an employee of Bechtel was also a member of the Defense Policy Board, which was then advising the secretary of defense. Additionally, the contract bidding was open only to six select companies, which had contributed a total of $3.6 million to reelect Republican politicians over the previous three years.

United Nations (UN) auditors questioned the U.S. decision to award more than $1 billion in reconstruction contracts to American companies without any competitive bidding whatsoever. UN auditors also complained that they could not determine how private contractors used government funds. The Bush administration was not cooperative in providing access to accounting records for the U.S. government's Development Fund for Iraq.

EISENHOWER'S WARNING

President Dwight D. Eisenhower, during his 1961 farewell address, puzzled many Americans by warning that "we must guard against the acquisition of unwarranted influence, whether sought or unsought, by the military-industrial complex." Eisenhower was referring to the increasingly close relationship among the federal government, the U.S. military, and private defense contractors.

Eisenhower, who had been a general during World War II (1939–1945) and who served as president during the last year of the Korean War (1950–1953), had firsthand knowledge of the joining of interests that he called the military-industrial complex. According to Eisenhower, "The potential for the disastrous rise of misplaced power exists and will persist." With the growing reliance on private contractors, some contend that the United States may be drifting toward the "unwarranted influence" and "misplaced power" against which Eisenhower cautioned.

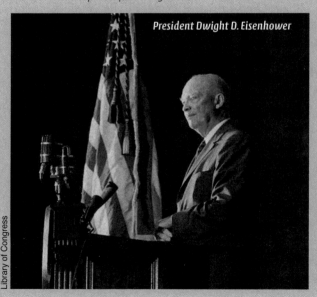

President Dwight D. Eisenhower

Library of Congress

YOU BE THE JUDGE

Some contend that all government contracts should be awarded through a bidding process from which companies with any connections to government decision makers are excluded. Before bidding would begin, all potential bidders would be investigated to ensure that none had government connections. Others argue that such an investigative process would bring government contracting to a standstill and that the system is fine as it is. Where do you stand on this issue?

AP Photo/Michael Conroy

A number of national interest groups protect the interests of farmers. Through their lobbying efforts and campaign contributions, these groups have wielded significant influence on congressional policymaking with respect to agricultural subsidies and other forms of assistance. Many political analysts contend that such subsidies harm the poor in developing countries. Why?

such as the Associated Milk Producers, Inc., also have a strong influence on farm legislation. Like business and labor groups, farm organizations sometimes find themselves in competition. In some western states, for example, barley farmers, cattle ranchers, and orchard owners may compete to influence laws governing water rights. Different groups also often disagree over the extent to which the government should regulate farmers.

Consumer Interest Groups

Groups organized for the protection of consumer rights were very active in the 1960s and 1970s. Some are still active today. The best known and perhaps the most effective are the public-interest consumer groups organized under the leadership of consumer activist Ralph Nader. Another well-known consumer group is Consumers Union, a nonprofit organization started in 1936. In addition to publishing *Consumer Reports,* Consumers Union has been influential in pushing for the removal of phosphates from detergents, lead from gasoline, and pesticides from food. Consumers Union strongly criticizes government agencies when they act against consumer interests.

Consumer groups have been organized in every city. They deal with such problems as poor housing, discrimination against minorities and women, discrimination in the granting of credit, and business inaction on consumer complaints.

Senior Citizen Interest Groups

While the population of the nation as a whole has tripled since 1900, the number of elderly has increased eightfold. Persons over the age of sixty-five now account for 13 percent of the population, and many of these people have united to call attention to their special needs and concerns. Senior citizens have a great deal at stake in the current debate over certain programs, such as Social Security. Interest groups formed to promote the interests of the elderly have been very outspoken and persuasive. As pointed out before, AARP has about 38 million members and is a potent political force.

Environmental Interest Groups

With the current concern for the environment, the membership of established environmental groups has blossomed, and many new groups have formed. They are becoming some of the most powerful interest groups in Washington, D.C. The National Wildlife Federation has about four million members. Table 6–2 lists some of the major environmental groups and the number of members in each group.

Environmental groups have organized to support pollution controls, wilderness protection, and clean-air legislation. They have opposed strip-mining, nuclear power plants, logging activities, chemical waste dumps, and many other potential environmental hazards.

Professional Interest Groups

Most professions that require advanced education or specialized training have organizations to protect and promote

TABLE 6–2
SELECTED ENVIRONMENTAL INTEREST GROUPS

Name of Group	Year Founded	Number of U.S. Members
Environmental Defense Fund	1967	500,000
Greenpeace USA	1971	250,000
Izaak Walton League of America	1922	40,000
League of Conservation Voters	1970	40,000
National Audubon Society	1905	500,000
National Wildlife Federation	1936	4,000,000
The Nature Conservancy	1951	1,000,000
The Sierra Club	1892	750,000
The Wilderness Society	1935	300,000
The World Wildlife Fund	1948	1,200,000

Sources: Foundation for Public Affairs, 1996; and authors' updates.

AP Photo/Troy Maben

Most of these demonstrators in front of the capitol building in Boise, Idaho, are members of the National Education Association and their families. They were protesting proposed cuts in that state's education budget.

their interests. These groups are concerned mainly with the standards of their professions, but they also work to influence government policy. Some also function as labor unions. Four major professional groups are the American Medical Association, representing physicians; the American Bar Association, representing lawyers; and the National Education Association and the American Federation of Teachers, both representing teachers. In addition, there are dozens of less well known and less politically active professional groups, such as the Screen Actors Guild, the National Association of Social Workers, and the American Political Science Association.

Single-Issue Interest Groups

Numerous interest groups focus on a single issue. For example, Mothers Against Drunk Driving (MADD) lobbies for stiffer penalties for drunk-driving convictions. Formed in 1980, MADD now boasts more than three million members and supporters. The abortion debate has created various single-issue groups, such as the Right to Life organization (which opposes abortion) and NARAL Pro-Choice America (which supports it). Other examples of single-issue groups are the NRA and the American Israel Public Affairs Committee (a pro-Israel group).

Government Interest Groups

Efforts by state and local governments to lobby the federal government have escalated in recent years. When states experience budget shortfalls, these governments often lobby in Washington, D.C., for additional federal funds. The federal government has sometimes lobbied in individual states, too. During the 2004 elections, for example, the U.S. Attorney General's office lobbied against medical marijuana in states that were considering ballot measures on the issue.

LO⁴ HOW INTEREST GROUPS SHAPE POLICY

Interest groups operate at all levels of government and use a variety of strategies to steer policies in ways beneficial to their interests. Sometimes, they attempt to influence policymakers directly, but at other times they try to exert indirect influence on policymakers by shaping public opinion. The extent and nature of the groups' activities depend on their goals and their resources.

Direct Techniques

Lobbying and providing election support are two important **direct techniques** used by interest groups to influence government policy.

LOBBYING   Today, **lobbying** refers to all of the attempts by organizations or individuals to influence the passage, defeat, or contents of legislation or to influence the administrative decisions of government. (The term *lobbying* arose because, traditionally, individuals and groups interested in influencing government policy would gather in the foyer, or lobby, of the legislature to corner legislators and express their concerns.) A **lobbyist** is an individual who handles a particular interest group's lobbying efforts. Most of the larger interest groups have lobbyists in Washington, D.C. These lobbyists often include former members of Congress or former employees of executive bureaucracies who are experienced in the methods of political influence and who "know people." Many lobbyists also work at state and local levels. In

direct technique Any method used by an interest group to interact with government officials directly to further the group's goals.

lobbying All of the attempts by organizations or by individuals to influence the passage, defeat, or contents of legislation or to influence the administrative decisions of government.

lobbyist An individual who handles a particular interest group's lobbying efforts.

fact, lobbying at the state level has increased in recent years as states have begun to play a more significant role in policymaking. Table 6–3 summarizes some of the basic methods by which lobbyists directly influence legislators and government officials.

THE EFFECTIVENESS OF LOBBYING Lobbying is one of the most widely used and effective ways to influence legislative activity. For example, Mothers Against Drunk Driving has had many lobbying successes at both the state and the federal levels. The NRA has successfully blocked most proposed gun control laws, even though a majority of Americans are in favor of such laws. An NRA brochure describes its lobbying operation as "the strongest, most formidable grassroots lobby in the nation." Nevertheless, the NRA has occasionally been defeated in its lobbying efforts by interest groups that support gun control.

Lobbying can be directed at the legislative branch of government, at administrative agencies, and even at the courts. For example, pharmaceutical companies routinely lobby the Food and Drug Administration to convince the agency to approve new prescription drugs. Lobbying can also be directed at changing international policies. For example, after political changes had opened up Eastern Europe to business in the late 1980s and early 1990s, intense lobbying by Western business groups helped persuade the United States and other industrial powers to reduce controls on the sale of high-technology products, such as personal computers, to Eastern European countries.

PROVIDING ELECTION SUPPORT Interest groups often become directly involved in the election process. Many interest group members join and work with political parties to influence party platforms and the nomination of candidates. Interest groups provide campaign support for legislators who favor their policies and sometimes urge their own members to try to win posts in party organizations. Most important, interest groups urge their members to vote for candidates who support the views of the group. They can also threaten legislators with the withdrawal of votes. No candidate can expect to have support from *all* interest groups, but if the candidate is to win, she or he must have support (or little opposition) from the most powerful ones.

TABLE 6–3

DIRECT LOBBYING TECHNIQUES

Technique	Description
Making Personal Contacts with Key Legislators	A lobbyist's personal contacts with key legislators or other government officials—in their offices, in the halls of Congress, or on social occasions, such as dinners, boating expeditions, and the like—are one of the most effective direct lobbying techniques. The lobbyist provides the legislators with information on a particular issue in an attempt to convince them to support the interest group's goals.
Providing Expertise and Research Results for Legislators	Lobbyists often have knowledge and expertise that are useful in drafting legislation, and this expertise can be a major strength for an interest group. Because many harried members of Congress cannot possibly be experts on everything they vote on and therefore eagerly seek information to help them make up their minds, some lobbying groups conduct research and present their findings to those legislators.
Offering "Expert" Testimony before Congressional Committees	Lobbyists often provide "expert" testimony before congressional committees for or against proposed legislation. A bill to regulate firearms, for example, might concern several interest groups. The NRA would probably oppose the bill, and representatives from the interest group might be asked to testify. Groups that would probably support the bill, such as law enforcement personnel or wildlife conservationists, might also be asked to testify. Each side would offer as much evidence as possible to support its position.
Providing Legal Advice to Legislators	Many lobbyists assist legislators in drafting legislation or prospective regulations. Lobbyists are a source of ideas and sometimes offer legal advice on specific details.
Following Up on Legislation	Because executive agencies responsible for carrying out legislation can often increase or decrease the power of the new law, lobbyists may also try to influence the bureaucrats who implement the policy. For example, beginning in the early 1960s, regulations outlawing gender discrimination were broadly outlined by Congress. Both women's rights groups favoring the regulations and interest groups opposing the regulations lobbied for years to influence how those regulations were carried out.

Paul Conklin/PhotoEdit

Lobbyists often line up in the lobbies, or halls, of Congress while awaiting their turn to consult with members of Congress.

One of the main goals of the liberal interest group America Coming Together is to "get out the vote." Here, volunteers in Springfield, Pennsylvania, are doing just that.

Since the 1970s, federal laws governing campaign financing have allowed corporations, labor unions, and special interest groups to raise funds and make camp-aign contributions through **political action committees (PACs).** Both the number of PACs and the amount of money they spend on elections have grown astronomically in recent years. There were about 1,000 PACs in 1976; today, there are more than 4,500 PACs. In 1973, total spending by PACs amounted to $19 million; in the last presidential election cycle, total spending by PACs exceeded $900 million. We will discuss PACs in more detail in Chapter 9.

Although campaign contributions do not guarantee that officials will vote the way the groups wish, contributions usu-

political action committee (PAC) A committee that is established by a corporation, labor union, or special interest group to raise funds and make contributions on the establishing organization's behalf.

indirect technique Any method used by interest groups to influence government officials through third parties, such as voters.

rating system A system by which a particular interest group evaluates (rates) the performance of legislators based on how often the legislators have voted with the group's position on particular issues.

ally do ensure that the groups will have the ear of the public officials they have helped to elect. PACs have also succeeded in bypassing campaign-contribution limits, thereby obtaining the same type of "vote-buying" privileges that wealthy individual contributors enjoyed in the past.

Indirect Techniques

Interest groups also try to influence public policy indirectly through third parties or the general public. Such **indirect techniques** may appear to be spontaneous, but they are generally as well planned as the direct lobbying techniques just discussed. Indirect techniques can be particularly effective because public officials are often more impressed by contacts from voters than from lobbyists.

SHAPING PUBLIC OPINION Public opinion weighs significantly in the policymaking process, so interest groups cultivate their public images carefully. If public opinion favors a certain group's interests, then public officials will be more ready to listen and more willing to pass legislation favoring that group. To cultivate public opinion, an interest group's efforts may include television publicity, newspaper and magazine advertisements, mass mailings, and the use of public relations techniques to improve the group's public image.

For example, environmental groups run television ads to dramatize threats to the environment. Oil companies respond to criticism about increased gasoline prices with advertising showing their concern for the public welfare. The goal of all these activities is to influence public opinion and bring grassroots pressure to bear on officials.

Some interest groups also try to influence legislators through **rating systems.** A group selects legislative issues that it feels are important to its goals and rates legislators according to the percentage of times they vote favorably on that legislation. For example, a score of 90 percent on the Americans for Democratic Action (ADA) rating scale means that the legislator supported that group's position to a high degree. Other groups tag members of Congress who support (or fail to support) their interests to a significant extent with telling labels. For instance, the Communications Workers of America refers to policymakers who take a position consistent with its members' own views as "Heroes" and those who take the opposite position as "Zeroes." Needless to say, such tactics can be an effective form of indirect lobbying, particularly with legislators who do not want to earn a low ADA score or be placed on the "Zeroes" list.

ISSUE ADS AND "527s"   One of the most powerful indirect techniques used by interest groups is the "issue ad"—a television or radio ad supporting or opposing a particular issue. The Supreme Court has made it clear that the First Amendment's guarantee of free speech protects interest groups' rights to set forth their positions on issues. Nevertheless, issue advocacy is controversial because the funds spent to air issue ads have had a clear effect on the outcome of elections.

Both parties have benefited from such interest group spending. As you will read in Chapter 9, the Bipartisan Campaign Reform Act of 2002 attempted to address the power of these ads by banning unlimited donations to campaigns and political parties, called *soft money*. The reform would have severely curbed the use of issue ads, but partisan groups called "527s" (after the provision in the tax code that covers them) discovered a loophole in the law. Soft money could still be collected so long as 527s did not officially work with campaigns or candidates. Wealthy individuals were quick to donate large sums to 527s. In the 2004 presidential elections, such 527 organizations as MoveOn.org, America Coming Together, and Swift Boat Veterans for Truth (now known as Swift Vets and POWs for Truth) played an influential role.

JOIN THE DEBATE

Should Issue Ad Spending Be Limited?

Make no mistake, spending on issue ads is big business. By November 2008, Bill Gates and another multibillionaire, Eli Broad, will have spent more than $60 million to push education onto the agenda of the 2008 presidential race. This project is the most expensive single-issue initiative ever in a presidential race. Before that, the most ever spent on single-issue ads was $22 million. The Swift Vets and POWs for Truth, earlier known as Swift Boat Veterans for Truth, spent that amount to defeat Senator John Kerry in the 2004 presidential elections.

Some concerned Americans believe that spending on issue ads should be limited. When nonprofit organizations pay for issue ads, these ads legally cannot support a specific candidate. Let's be realistic, though. If a nonprofit organization pays for issue ads supporting, say, gun control and only one candidate is also in favor of gun control, is anybody fooled? Moreover, consider the education issue ads paid for by Gates and Broad. Education is important, but is it really more important than terrorism, the war in Iraq, and health care? What about child well-being? Isn't that important, too? The 2007 UNICEF Report scored overall child well-being in the United States as one of the lowest in the Western world.

On the other side of the debate, many point out that our Constitution allows for freedom of speech and expression. In 1976, the Supreme Court confirmed that anybody could spend as much as he or she wants on advocacy of a political cause. That means that any person or group that wants to spend $60 million promoting education reform can do so. Moreover, the more issue ads there are in the political marketplace, the better. Most Americans are unaware of many of the problems facing this country. Thus, we should actually encourage issue ads to help the public become better informed.

MOBILIZING CONSTITUENTS   Interest groups sometimes urge members and other constituents to contact government officials—by letter, e-mail, or telephone—to show their support for or opposition to a certain policy. Large interest groups can generate hundreds of thousands of letters, e-mail messages, and phone calls. Interest groups often provide form letters or postcards

Many new groups use issue ads as an indirect way to support specific candidates. The group MoveOn.org effectively used this technique to help the Democrats win control of Congress in the 2006 midterm elections.

AP Photo/Chuck Burton

AP Photo/Noah Berger

Protests, marches, and rallies are often used to support or oppose a particular issue. In 2007, supporters of our troops in Iraq attended a rally in Lafayette, California.

AP Photo/George Ruhe

The majority of Americans polled in 2007 seemed to want U.S. troops withdrawn from Iraq. One organized group, Military Families Speak Out, which consists of families that have relatives in Iraq, showed their strength at a rally in downtown Hartford, Connecticut.

for constituents to fill out and mail. The NRA has successfully used this tactic to fight strict federal gun control legislation by delivering half a million letters to Congress within a few weeks. Policymakers recognize that the letters were initiated by an interest group, but they are still made aware that an issue is important to that group.

GOING TO COURT   The legal system offers another avenue for interest groups to influence the political process. Civil rights groups paved the way for interest group litigation in the 1950s and 1960s with major victories in cases concerning equal housing, school desegregation, and employment discrimination. Environmental groups, such as the Sierra Club, have also successfully used litigation to protect their interests. For example, an environmental group might challenge in court an activity that threatens to pollute the environment or that will destroy the natural habitat of an endangered species. The legal challenge forces those engaging in the activity to bear the costs of defending themselves and possibly delays their project. In fact, much of the success of environmental groups has been linked to their use of lawsuits.

Interest groups can also influence the outcome of litigation without being a party to a lawsuit. Frequently, interest groups file *amicus curiae* ("friend of the court") briefs in appellate (reviewing) courts. These briefs state the group's legal argument in support of their desired outcome in a case. For example, in the case *Metro-Goldwyn-Mayer Studios, Inc. v. Grokster, Ltd.*[5]—involving the legality of file-sharing software—hundreds of *amicus* briefs were filed by various groups on behalf of the petitioners. Groups filing *amicus* briefs for the case, which was heard by the Supreme Court in 2005, included the National Basketball Association, the National Football League, the National Association of Broadcasters, the Association of American Publishers, and numerous state

governments. Often, interest groups have statistics and research that support their position on a certain issue, and this research can have considerable influence on the justices deciding the case. Also, filing a brief in a case gives the group publicity, which aids in promoting its causes.

DEMONSTRATION TECHNIQUES   Some interest groups stage protests to make a statement in a dramatic way. The Boston Tea Party of 1773, in which American colonists dressed as Native Americans and threw tea into Boston Harbor to protest British taxes, is testimony to how long this tactic has been around. Over the years, many groups have organized protest marches and rallies to support or oppose such issues as legalized abortion, busing, gay and lesbian rights, government assistance to farmers, the treatment of Native Americans, restrictions on the use of federally owned lands in the West, trade relations with China, and the activities of global organizations, such as the World Trade Organization. Not all demonstration techniques are peaceful. Some environmental groups, for example, have used such tactics as spiking trees and setting traps on logging roads that puncture truck tires. Pro-life groups have bombed abortion clinics, and members of People for the Ethical Treatment of Animals (PETA) have broken into laboratories and freed animals being used for experimentation.

LO[5] TODAY'S LOBBYING ESTABLISHMENT

Without a doubt, interest groups and their lobbyists have become a permanent feature in the landscape of American government. The major interest groups all have headquarters in Washington, D.C., close to the center of government. Professional lobbyists and staff members of various interest groups move freely between their groups' headquarters and congressional offices and committee rooms. Interest group representatives are routinely consulted when Congress drafts new legislation. As already mentioned, interest group representatives are frequently asked to testify before congressional committees or subcommittees on the effect or potential effect of particular legislation or regulations. In sum, interest groups have become an integral part of the American government system.

As interest groups have become a permanent feature of American government, lobbying has developed into a profession. A professional lobbyist—one who has mastered the techniques of lobbying discussed earlier in this chapter—is a valuable ally to any interest group seeking to influence government. Professional lobbyists can and often do move from one interest group to another.

In recent years, it has become increasingly common for those who leave positions with the federal government to become lobbyists or consultants for the private-interest groups they helped to regulate. In spite of legislation and regulations that have been created in an attempt to reduce this "revolving door" syndrome, it is still functioning quite well.

> "NEVER DOUBT THAT A SMALL GROUP OF THOUGHTFUL, COMMITTED **CITIZENS** CAN CHANGE THE WORLD; INDEED, IT'S THE **ONLY** THING THAT EVER HAS."
>
> MARGARET MEAD,
> AMERICAN ANTHROPOLOGIST
> 1901–1978

group's or corporation's legislative efforts. More important, these former officials normally have an established network of personal contacts, which is an extremely beneficial political asset in the world of lobbying. Should this "revolving door" between former government officials and the lobbying establishment be shut?

Yes, say many opponents of the revolving door. These critics point out that, over the past few years, more than 40 percent of the former members of Congress have become lobbyists. The current one-year "cooling-off" period that prevents former officials from making lobbying contacts should be extended indefinitely—former officials should never be allowed to lobby. Sometimes, the revolving door is blatantly obvious. After the one-thousand-page prescription drug bill was passed a few years ago, all of the main actors who helped pass it went to work for the pharmaceutical industry. This has to stop.

On the other side of the debate are those who find positive benefits in the revolving door. There is nothing wrong or illegal about working as a paid lobbyist—it is a job like any other. Lobbying forms the backbone of our democratic process. Without lobbying, members of Congress would have little information about the most important topics on the political agenda. Special interest groups and large corporations have a right to hire the best lobbyists possible to represent their interests. Those

JOIN THE DEBATE

Should the "Revolving Door" Be Closed?

Former government officials, particularly those who held key positions in Congress or in the executive branch, have little difficulty finding work as lobbyists. They often have inside information that can help an interest

"The whole time I served in the U.S. Congress, I dreamed of exactly this: being a wealthy lobbyist sitting here with you."

persons who have the most current contacts with members of Congress are clearly valuable as lobbyists. Don't forget that special interests compete among themselves. The keener the competition, the better the outcome will be for the American public.

Why Do Interest Groups Get Bad Press?

Despite their importance to democratic government, interest groups, like political parties, are sometimes criticized by both the public and the press. Our image of interest groups and their special interests is not very favorable. You may have run across political cartoons depicting lobbyists standing in the hallways of Congress with briefcases stuffed with money, waiting to lure representatives into a waiting limousine.

These cartoons are not entirely factual, but they are not entirely fictitious either. President Richard Nixon (1969–1974) was revealed to have yielded to the campaign contributions of milk producers by later authorizing a windfall increase in milk subsidies. In 1977, "Koreagate," a scandal in which a South Korean businessman was accused of offering lavish "gifts" to several members of Congress, added to the view that politicians were too easily susceptible to the snares of special interests. In the early 1990s, it was revealed that a number of senators who received generous contributions from one particular savings and loan association subsequently supported a "hands-off" policy by savings and loan regulators. The savings and loan association in question later got into financial trouble, costing the taxpayers billions of dollars. But, see the *Perception v. Reality* feature for another view of this issue.

As you will read shortly, Congress has tried to impose stricter regulations on lobbyists. The most important legislation regulating lobbyists was passed in 1946 and revised in 1995 and again in 2007. The problem with stricter regulation is that it could abridge First Amendment rights.

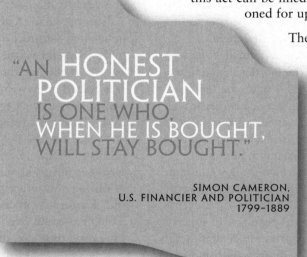

"AN HONEST POLITICIAN IS ONE WHO, WHEN HE IS BOUGHT, WILL STAY BOUGHT."

SIMON CAMERON,
U.S. FINANCIER AND POLITICIAN
1799–1889

The Regulation of Interest Groups

In an attempt to control lobbying, Congress passed the Federal Regulation of Lobbying Act in 1946. The major provisions of the act are as follows:

■ Any person or organization that receives money to be used principally to influence legislation before Congress must register with the clerk of the House and the secretary of the Senate.

■ Any group or persons registering must identify their employer, salary, amount and purpose of expenses, and duration of employment.

■ Every registered lobbyist must give quarterly reports on his or her activities, which are to be published in the *Congressional Quarterly*.

■ Anyone failing to satisfy the specific provisions of this act can be fined up to $10,000 and be imprisoned for up to five years.

The act was very limited and did not succeed in regulating lobbying to any great degree for several reasons. First, the Supreme Court restricted the application of the law only to those lobbyists who seek to influence federal legislation directly.[6] Any lobbyist seeking to influence legislation indirectly through public opinion did not fall within the scope of the law. Second, only persons or organizations whose principal purpose was to influence legislation were required to register. Many groups avoided registration by claiming that their principal function was something else. Third, the act did not cover lobbying directed at agencies in the executive branch or lobbyists who testified before congressional committees. Fourth, the public was almost totally unaware of the information in the quarterly reports, and Congress created no agency to oversee interest group activities. Not until 1995 did Congress finally address these loopholes by enacting new legislation.

The Lobbying Disclosure Act of 1995

In 1995, Congress passed new lobbying legislation—the Lobbying Disclosure Act—that reformed the 1946 act in the following ways:

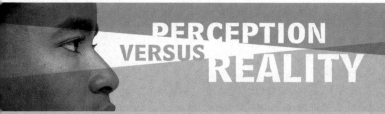

PERCEPTION VERSUS REALITY

Do Lobbyists Deserve All the Blame?

Just mention the word *lobbyist,* and the red flags pop up. Most Americans have a negative opinion about those in the lobbying industry. Not surprisingly, when a congressional scandal involving kickbacks and bribery surfaces, cries for lobbying reforms are heard around the country. The last set of lobbying reforms, in 2007, occurred after a scandal involving Jack Abramoff, a lobbyist who is now in prison.

The Perception

By definition, a lobbyist is hired by a special interest group or a corporation to influence government policies. Lobbyists are professionals, and as such, they are paid by special interests and corporations to ply their skills. They are not paid to act in the national interest. Rather, a lobbyist's job is to convince government officials to undertake actions that are beneficial to the single industry or group that the lobbyist represents. To do so effectively, a lobbyist needs access to members of Congress and other government officials. A common perception is that lobbyists are somewhat "shady" operatives who wheel and deal with government officials to get the best possible outcome for the groups that pay them. Typically, whenever lobbyists become involved in unethical or even illegal dealings in Washington, D.C., the public tends to blame the lobbyists rather than members of Congress.

The Reality

It takes two to tango. Lobbyists don't just walk into the offices of members of Congress with sacks of cash (although this has occasionally happened, to be sure). First and foremost, the job of the lobbyist is to inform members of Congress about the effects of proposed legislation on the interest group the lobbyist represents—or even to suggest legislation. After all, members of Congress cannot be "on top" of every problem that faces America. More important, members of Congress, especially in the House of Representatives, spend a lot of their time making sure that they are reelected. Consequently, members of Congress require large sums for their reelection campaigns. On many occasions, members of Congress have either implicitly or explicitly "shaken down" lobbyists for campaign contributions. In this sense, lobbyists are victims as much as they are perpetrators. Political researcher Norman Ornstein discovered that former majority leader of the House of Representatives Tom DeLay (R., Tex.) ran a type of "Tammany Hall operation" that ensured that only Republicans were hired for big lobbying jobs and that they were paid well. Once hired, everyone was expected to contribute some of his or her income to Republican campaign chests.

BLOG ON

Most conservative blogs argue that restrictions on campaign contributions place unacceptable limits on the freedom of speech. The Liberty Papers at **www.thelibertypapers.org** is one such blog. In contrast, Common Cause at **www.commonblog.com** advocates strong measures to limit the political influence of well-funded groups.

- Strict definitions now apply to determine who must register with the clerk of the House and the secretary of the Senate as a lobbyist. A lobbyist is anyone who either spends at least 20 percent of his or her time lobbying members of Congress, their staffs, or executive-branch officials, or is paid more than $5,000 in a six-month period for such work. Any organization that spends more than $20,000 in a six-month period conducting such lobbying activity must also register. These amounts have since been raised to $6,000 and $24,500, respectively.

- Lobbyists must report their clients, the issues on which they lobbied, and the agency or chamber of Congress they contacted, although they do not need to disclose the names of those they contacted.

Tax-exempt organizations, such as religious groups, were exempted from these provisions, as were organizations that engage in grassroots lobbying, such as a media campaign that asks people to write or call their congressional representative. Nonetheless, the number of registered lobbyists nearly doubled in the first few years of the new legislation.

Lobbying Scandals in the Early 2000s

In 2005, a number of lobbying scandals in Washington, D.C., came to light. A major figure in the scandals was

Jack Abramoff, an influential lobbyist who had ties to many Republican legislators (and a few Democrats) in Congress and to various officials in the Bush administration. Abramoff gained access to the power brokers in the capital by giving them campaign contributions, expensive gifts, and exotic trips.

Eventually, Abramoff pled guilty to charges of fraud, tax evasion, and conspiracy to bribe public officials, in return for agreeing to cooperate with federal officials in their investigation into the wide-reaching scandal. In 2006, Abramoff was sentenced to five years and ten months in prison. In early 2007, Congressman Robert Ney

AP Photo/U.S. District Court

This photo was used in a trial as an exhibit to show the collaboration of lobbyist Jack Abramoff and government officials. Abramoff is shown on the left. Representative Bob Ney (R., Ohio) is shown on the far right. Next to Ney is then chief of staff of the General Services Administration David Safavian, who was accused of e-mailing confidential information to Abramoff. The latter then helped his clients obtain a redevelopment project. Within two weeks of illegally providing this information, Abramoff provided Safavian with a trip to the famed St. Andrews Golf Course in Scotland (shown here) and to London.

(R., Ohio) was sentenced to thirty months in prison for conspiracy and making false statements to investigators. In June 2007, a former Bush administration official, Steven Griles, who had served as deputy secretary of the interior, was sentenced to ten months in prison for obstructing the investigation by making false statements and withholding information. The investigation into the Abramoff scandal, which is ongoing, led to renewed interest in lobbying reform.

Lobbying Reform Efforts in 2007

Following the midterm elections of 2006, the new Democratic majority in the Senate and House of Representatives undertook a lobbying reform effort. The goal of the reforms was to force lobbyists to disclose their expenditures on House and Senate election campaigns above and beyond straight campaign contributions.

Bundled campaign contributions, in which a lobbyist arranges for contributions from a variety of sources, would have to be reported. Expenditures on the sometimes lavish parties to benefit candidates would have to be reported as well. (Of course, partygoers were expected to pay for their food and drink with a check written out to the candidate.) The new rules covered PACs as well as registered lobbyists, which led one lobbyist to observe sourly that this wasn't lobbying reform but campaign-finance reform.

By mid-2007, both the House and the Senate had passed bills containing the changes, but the Senate had failed to send its bill to the conference committee to iron out the differences between the House and Senate versions. The fate of the legislation therefore remains uncertain.

AMERICA AT ODDS:
Interest Groups

Interest groups were a cause of concern even before the Constitution was written. Recall from Chapter 2 that those opposed to the Constitution (the Anti-Federalists) claimed that a republican form of government could not work in a country this size because so many factions—interest groups—would be contending for power. The result would be anarchy and chaos. James Madison attempted to allay these fears (in *Federalist Papers* No. 10—see Appendix F) by arguing that the "mischiefs of factions" could be controlled. The large size of the United States would mean that so many diverse interests and factions would be contending for power that no one faction would be able to gain control of the government.

What Madison did not foresee was the extent to which money has become intertwined with lawmaking in this country. Wealthy pharmaceutical companies, insurance companies, financial firms, and other entities have often been far too influential in Congress and in the executive branch. On some occasions, they have virtually written the bills enacted by Congress. The challenge for our political leaders today is to somehow distance political decisions from the influence of wealthy, elite groups. As you will read in Chapter 9, Congress has tried on several occasions to regulate campaign spending and contributions to address this problem. The problem is, some of the very people addressing the issue—members of Congress—benefit from the status quo, which hampers the prospect of any aggressive campaign-finance reform.

Issues for Debate & Discussion

- One of the most controversial issues of our time with respect to interest groups has to do with issue advocacy. Issue ads paid for by certain groups, such as a pro-life organization or an antiwar group, can often be clearly in support of or against a specific candidate, even though the candidate's name is not mentioned. Yet, as you will read in Chapter 9, the funds used to pay for this type of campaign advertising are not regulated by the government. Some believe that there should be a cap on the amount of funds that any one group can spend for issue ads. Others assert that such a limit would violate the constitutional guarantee of freedom of expression, and free political speech is a core requirement of any true democracy. What is your position on this issue?
- Some claim that companies that bid for government contracts (or that are awarded such contracts without a bidding procedure) are often well-established, wealthy firms. Such firms can use campaign contributions to government leaders to pressure those leaders to go to war so that the companies can receive profitable contracts for war-related work. Others claim that political leaders would never undertake (or continue) a war simply to get reelected and stay in power. What is your position on this issue?

Take Action

An obvious way to get involved in politics is to join an interest group whose goals you endorse, including one of the organizations on your campus. You can find lists of interest groups operating at the local, state, and national levels by simply going to a search engine online, such as Google, and keying in the words "interest groups." If you have a particular interest or goal that you would like to promote, consider forming your own group, as a group of Iowa students did when they formed a group called Students Toward Environmental Protection. In the photo below, a student at Grinnell College in Iowa holds a protest sign during a rally. The students wanted Iowa's lawmakers to issue tougher regulations governing factory farms and to expand the state's bottle deposit requirements.

AP Photo/Charlie Neibergall

POLITICS ON THE WEB

- To find particular interest groups online, a good point of departure is the Internet Public Library Association, which provides links to hundreds of professional and trade associations. Go to **www.ipl.org/ref/AON**.

- The Institute for Global Communications offers a host of lobbying and public-interest activities. Its home page can be accessed at **www.igc.apc.org**.

- You can access the National Rifle Association online at **www.nra.org**.

- AARP's Web site can be found at **www.aarp.org**.

- To learn about the activities of the National Education Association, go to **www.nea.org**.

- You can find information on environmental issues and the activities of the National Resources Defense Council at **www.nrdc.org**.

ONLINE RESOURCES FOR THIS CHAPTER

This text's Companion Web site, at **www.americaatodds. com,** offers links to numerous resources that you can utilize to learn more about the topics covered in this chapter.

PODCASTS FLASHCARDS INTERACTIVE QUIZZES ONLINE POLLING VIDEO SIMULATOINS ANIMATED LEARNING

DO YOU WANT POLITICS TO GO?

AAO: POLITICS TO GO

Buy Now!

Turn to the back of the book to find your Politics to Go review card for this chapter

CHAPTER 7
POLITICAL PARTIES

LEARNING OBJECTIVES

LO¹ Summarize the origins and development of the two-party system in the United States.

LO² Provide some of the reasons why the two-party system has endured.

LO³ Explain how political parties function in our democratic system.

LO⁴ Describe the different types of third parties and how they function in the American political system.

LO⁵ Discuss the structure of American political parties.

AMERICA AT ODDS

Is the (Republican) Party Over?

The Republican Party was formed by antislavery activists. Its first elected president was Abraham Lincoln in 1860. The modern Republican Party emerged in the 1960s and has been associated with conservatism, which you learned about in Chapter 1. The GOP (Grand Old Party), as the Republican Party is often called, perhaps reached its heyday of conservatism under President Ronald Reagan (1981–1989). Reagan Republicanism stood for a strong military, small government, states' rights, and core American values, including family values. Some believe that the coalition of interests that held the Republican Party together for the last several decades is now irreparably broken. Others are not so sure.

The Republican Tide (and with It, the Republican Party) Has Shifted Out to Sea

Some Americans have concluded that the Republican Party that came to dominate American politics during the Reagan era is now out to sea. The coalition of evangelical groups (social conservatives) and economic conservatives that formed the basis of the party has fallen apart during the presidency of George W. Bush. The religious right became dissatisfied with the Republicanism of the Bush years because a number of the programs important to that group were not taken seriously by the Bush administration and the Republican-led Congress. Economic conservatives also became disenchanted with the party because of the excessive spending that has characterized the Bush administration.

Bush and today's Republicans are a new breed of conservatives. They share few of the core values of Reagan-era conservatism. This seems to be true of rank-and-file Republicans as well. In midsummer 2007, 65 percent of those who identified with the Republican Party continued to support Bush and his policies (although this marked a decline from the 75 percent who did so during the early months of 2007). Notably, as the 2008 presidential race got under way in 2007, the views expressed by the Republican candidates were also very similar to the Bush brand of conservatism. This support for Bush and his policies shows how far today's Republican Party has moved from its traditional moorings.

Among the general public, though, there is decreasing support for the ideology of today's Republican Party. In recent polls, about half of the respondents either identify with, or lean toward, the Democratic Party. In contrast, only 35 percent of the respondents identify with, or lean toward, the Republican Party. The key trends that nurtured the Republican "Revolution" of 1994 and kept Republicans in control of Congress through 2006 are now becoming less predominant, according to the Pew Research Center for the People and the Press. For example, the proportion of Americans who support traditional social values has trended downward since 1994. The Republican Party's party may be over.

REPORTS OF THE GOP'S DEATH ARE PREMATURE

The party of Abraham Lincoln has existed for 150 years. It has faced difficult times in the past and surmounted them. Some of the basic core values of Republicans, such as the importance of religion, remain alive and well today. America remains a religious nation, and some Americans will always support a party that endorses Christian values. Just because the evangelical wing of the Republican Party is losing some of its influence does not mean that the Republican Party as a whole will fade away.

Today, more than ever before, we need a strong military defense against terrorism. The Republican Party has historically been the party that voters look to for national security and defense, and it will continue to hold that banner high.

Finally, in our two-party system the Republican Party will continue to be the only realistic alternative to the Democratic Party. No third party has the slightest chance of replacing it. As you will read later in this chapter, our political system is stacked in favor of perpetuating the two-party system. This fact alone will ensure the continuation of the GOP.

Where do you stand?

1. Does it really matter that the Republican Party of today does not resemble the Republican Party of twenty years ago? Why or why not?
2. Current polls show an increase in the percentage of Americans who think that the government should help the needy even if doing so increases the public debt. Does this trend mean that the traditional conservative Republican value of small government will never return? Why or why not?

Explore this issue online

- You can find information and debate on all things Republican at **www.instapundit.com**, one of the most conservative blogs on the Internet. It is produced by Glenn Reynolds, a law professor at the University of Tennessee.
- For a more official Republican source, consider the College Republican National Committee at **www.crnc.org**. This is a key site for Republican student organizers.

INTRODUCTION

Political ideology and party affiliation can spark heated debates between Americans, as you read in the chapter-opening *America at Odds* feature. A **political party** can be defined as a group of individuals who organize to win elections, operate the government, and determine policy. Political parties serve as major vehicles for citizen participation in our political system. It is hard to imagine democracy without political parties. Political parties provide a way for the public to choose who will serve in government and which policies will be carried out. Even citizens who do not identify with any political party or who choose not to participate in elections are affected by party activities and influence on government.

Political parties were an unforeseen development in American political history. The founders defined many other important institutions, such as the presidency and Congress, and described their functions in the Constitution. Political parties, however, are not even mentioned in the Constitution. In fact, the founders decried factions and parties. Thomas Jefferson probably best expressed the founders' antiparty sentiments when he declared, "If I could not go to heaven but with a party, I would not go there at all."[1]

If the founders did not want political parties, who was supposed to organize political campaigns and mobilize supporters of political candidates? Clearly, there was a practical need for some kind of organizing group to form a link between citizens and their government. Even our early national leaders, for all their antiparty feelings, realized this; several of them were active in establishing or organizing the first political parties.

LO[1] A SHORT HISTORY OF AMERICAN POLITICAL PARTIES

Political parties have been a part of American politics since the early years of our nation. Throughout the course of our history, several parties have formed, and some have disappeared. Even today, although we have only two major political parties, numerous other parties are also contending for power, as will be discussed later in this chapter.

The First Political Parties

The founders reacted negatively to the idea of political parties because they thought the power struggles that would occur between small economic and political groups would eventually topple the balanced democracy they wanted to create. Nonetheless, two major

> " **BOTH OF OUR POLITICAL PARTIES, AT LEAST THE HONEST PORTION OF THEM, AGREE CONSCIENTIOUSLY IN THE SAME OBJECT: THE PUBLIC GOOD; BUT THEY DIFFER ESSENTIALLY IN WHAT THEY DEEM THE MEANS OF PROMOTING THAT GOOD.** "
>
> THOMAS JEFFERSON TO ABIGAIL ADAMS, 1804

political factions—the Federalists and Anti-Federalists—were formed even before the Constitution was ratified. Remember from Chapter 2 that the Federalists pushed for the ratification of the Constitution because they wanted a stronger national government than the one that had existed under the Articles of Confederation. The Anti-Federalists argued against ratification. They supported states' rights and feared a too-powerful central government.

These two national factions continued, in somewhat altered form, after the Constitution was ratified. Alexander Hamilton, the first secretary of the Treasury, became the leader of the Federalist Party, which supported a strong central government that would encourage the development of commerce and manufacturing. The Federalists generally thought that a democracy should be ruled by its wealthiest and best-educated citizens. Opponents of the Federalists and Hamilton's policies referred to themselves not as Anti-Federalists, but as Republicans. Today, they are often referred to as Democratic Republicans, or Jeffersonian Republicans, to distinguish this group from the later Republican Party. The Democratic Republicans were more sympathetic to the "common man" and favored a more limited role for government. They believed that the nation's welfare would be best served if the states had more power than the central government. In their view, Congress should dominate the government, and government policies should help the nation's shopkeepers, farmers, and laborers.

political party A group of individuals who organize to win elections, operate the government, and determine policy.

This woodcut shows John Adams, who was the Federalists' candidate to succeed George Washington. Adams defeated Thomas Jefferson, but Jefferson became the vice president—a rare example of individuals from different political parties serving at the same time in these two positions.

Thomas Jefferson was a Democratic Republican (not related to today's Republican Party), who became our third president and served two terms. The Democratic Republicans dominated American politics for more than two decades.

From 1796 to 1860

The nation's first two parties clashed openly in the elections of 1796, in which John Adams, the Federalists' candidate to succeed George Washington as president, defeated Thomas Jefferson. Over the next four years, Jefferson and James Madison worked to extend the influence of the Democratic Republican Party. In the presidential elections of 1800 and 1804, Jefferson won the presidency under the Democratic Republican banner. His party also won control of Congress. The Federalists never returned to power and thus became the first (but not the last) American party to go out of existence. (See the time line of American political parties in Figure 7–1.)

The Democratic Republicans dominated American politics for the next twenty years. Jefferson was succeeded in the White House by two other Democratic Republicans—James Madison and James Monroe. In the mid-1820s, however, the Democratic Republicans split into two groups. Andrew Jackson, who was elected president in 1828, aligned himself with the group that called themselves the Democrats. The Democrats were mostly small farmers and debtors. The other group, the National Republicans (later the Whig Party), was led by the well-known John Quincy Adams and Henry Clay, and the great orator Daniel Webster. It was a coalition of bankers, business owners, and southern planters.

As the Whigs and Democrats competed for the White House throughout the 1840s and 1850s, the two-party system as we know it today emerged. Both parties were large, with well-known leaders and supporters across the nation. They both had grassroots organizations of party workers committed to winning as many political offices (at all levels of government) for the party as possible. Both the Whigs and the Democrats remained vague on the issue of slavery, and the Democrats were divided into northern and southern camps. By the mid-1850s, the Whig coalition fell apart, and most Whigs were absorbed into the new Republican Party, which opposed the extension of slavery into new territories. Campaigning on this platform, the Republicans succeeded in electing Abraham Lincoln as the first Republican president in 1860.

From the Civil War to the Great Depression

By the end of the Civil War in 1865, the Republicans and the Democrats were the most prominent political parties. From the elec-

Andrew Jackson (1767–1845) was part of the newly named party of Democrats. At that time, Democrats were mainly small farmers and debtors. Jackson won the presidential election in 1828, defeating the candidate for the National Republicans.

FIGURE 7–1

A TIME LINE OF U.S. POLITICAL PARTIES

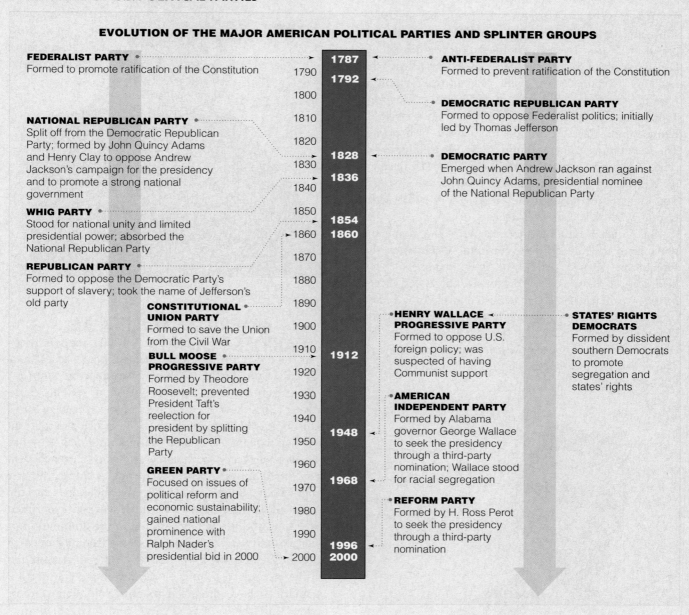

EVOLUTION OF THE MAJOR AMERICAN POLITICAL PARTIES AND SPLINTER GROUPS

FEDERALIST PARTY
Formed to promote ratification of the Constitution

ANTI-FEDERALIST PARTY
Formed to prevent ratification of the Constitution

DEMOCRATIC REPUBLICAN PARTY
Formed to oppose Federalist politics; initially led by Thomas Jefferson

NATIONAL REPUBLICAN PARTY
Split off from the Democratic Republican Party; formed by John Quincy Adams and Henry Clay to oppose Andrew Jackson's campaign for the presidency and to promote a strong national government

DEMOCRATIC PARTY
Emerged when Andrew Jackson ran against John Quincy Adams, presidential nominee of the National Republican Party

WHIG PARTY
Stood for national unity and limited presidential power; absorbed the National Republican Party

REPUBLICAN PARTY
Formed to oppose the Democratic Party's support of slavery; took the name of Jefferson's old party

CONSTITUTIONAL UNION PARTY
Formed to save the Union from the Civil War

BULL MOOSE PROGRESSIVE PARTY
Formed by Theodore Roosevelt; prevented President Taft's reelection for president by splitting the Republican Party

GREEN PARTY
Focused on issues of political reform and economic sustainability; gained national prominence with Ralph Nader's presidential bid in 2000

HENRY WALLACE PROGRESSIVE PARTY
Formed to oppose U.S. foreign policy; was suspected of having Communist support

STATES' RIGHTS DEMOCRATS
Formed by dissident southern Democrats to promote segregation and states' rights

AMERICAN INDEPENDENT PARTY
Formed by Alabama governor George Wallace to seek the presidency through a third-party nomination; Wallace stood for racial segregation

REFORM PARTY
Formed by H. Ross Perot to seek the presidency through a third-party nomination

Timeline years: 1787, 1790, 1792, 1800, 1810, 1820, 1828, 1830, 1836, 1840, 1850, 1854, 1860, 1870, 1880, 1890, 1900, 1910, 1912, 1920, 1930, 1940, 1948, 1950, 1960, 1968, 1970, 1980, 1990, 1996, 2000

---

tion of Abraham Lincoln in 1860 until the election of Franklin Delano Roosevelt in 1932, the Republican Party remained the majority party in national politics, winning all but four presidential elections.

After the Great Depression

The social and economic impact of the Great Depression of the 1930s destroyed the majority support that the Republicans had enjoyed for so long and contributed to a realignment in the two-party system. In a **realigning election,** the popular support for and relative strength of the parties shift. As a result, the minority (opposition) party may emerge as the majority party. (A realigning election can also reestablish the majority party in power, albeit with a different coalition of supporters.) The landmark realigning election of 1932 brought Franklin

realigning election An election in which the popular support for and relative strength of the parties shift as the parties are reestablished with different coalitions of supporters.

D. Roosevelt to the presidency and the Democrats back to power at the national level. Realigning elections also occurred in 1860, 1896, and, arguably, 1968.

Roosevelt was reelected to the presidency in 1936, 1940, and 1944. When he died in office in 1945, his vice president, Harry Truman, assumed the presidential office. Truman ran for the presidency in 1948 and won the election. A Republican candidate, Dwight D. Eisenhower, won the presidential elections of 1952 and 1956. From 1960 through 1968, the Democrats, led first by John F. Kennedy and then by Lyndon B. Johnson, held power. The Republicans came back into power in 1968 and, except for Jimmy Carter's one term (1977–1981), retained the presidency until Bill Clinton was elected in 1992. The Republicans regained the presidency in 2001, when George W. Bush became president.

In Congress, the Democrats were the dominant party from the Great Depression until 1994, when the Republicans gained control of both chambers. They held control of Congress from then until 2006, except for two years when the Democrats controlled the Senate by one vote. Following the 2006 midterm elections, the Democrats again had a majority in Congress. (See this chapter's *Perception versus Reality* feature for a discussion of the "Democratic Revolution" brought about by the 2006 elections.)

The realigning election of 1932 brought Franklin Delano Roosevelt to the presidency and the Democrats back to power at the national level.

Library of Congress

From the election of Abraham Lincoln (shown here) in 1860 until the election of Franklin Delano Roosevelt in 1932, the Republican Party remained the majority party in national politics.

Library of Congress

LO² AMERICA'S POLITICAL PARTIES TODAY

In the United States, we have a **two-party system.** (For an example of a multiparty system, see this chapter's *The Rest of the World* feature on page 154.) This means that two major parties—the Democrats and the Republicans—dominate national politics. Why has the two-party system become so firmly entrenched in the United States? According to some scholars, the first major political division between the Federalists and the Anti-Federalists established a precedent that continued over time and ultimately resulted in the domination of the two-party system. Today, both the Republican Party and the Democratic Party tend to be moderate, middle-of-the-road parties built on compromise. The parties' similarities have often led to criticism; their sternest critics call them "Tweedledee" and "Tweedledum."[2] (We will discuss the policy positions of the two parties in more detail later in this chapter.)

According to most polls, a sizable number of Americans (about 40 percent) do not affiliate with either of the major political parties. For these individuals, known broadly as *independents,* neither of the major parties addresses issues that are important to them or represents their views. Nonetheless, the two-party system continues to thrive. A number of factors help to explain this phenomenon.

two-party system A political system in which two strong and established parties compete for political offices.

PERCEPTION VERSUS REALITY

The Democratic Revolution of 2006

The American public was fed up—fed up with Republican scandals in Congress and fed up with the war in Iraq. When the voters spoke in November 2006, they ushered in a Democratic Congress. Before the elections, Democrats had promised, at a minimum, "six for 2006," which included negotiating lower prescription drug prices for government contracts, reducing university costs, and approving government funding for stem-cell research. They also were obligated to address the voters' desire to bring the war in Iraq to an end.

The Perception

After the Democrats took control of both chambers of Congress, voters assumed that the "new kids on the block" would fulfill their campaign promises, the most important of which was to end the war in Iraq. The public believed that Congress, which holds the power of the purse, would force a withdrawal of our troops from Iraq. The public also assumed that congressional Democrats would keep their promises to "get to the bottom" of what the White House knew before invading Iraq.

The Reality

We are still in Iraq. The Democrats did succeed in passing legislation that conditioned the passage of emergency war funding on a timetable for withdrawal as well as redeployment of the troops in Iraq. President Bush, however, vetoed the bill, and the Democrats did not have the necessary votes (two-thirds of each chamber) to override his veto. With respect to the "six for 2006" major policy promises, almost nothing was achieved in 2007. True, an increased federal minimum wage was attached to a war-funding bill signed into law by President Bush in May 2007. But little else was accomplished in terms of legislation on important issues. Six months after the Democrats took control, the approval rating for Congress dropped to 39 percent (only 6 percentage points above Bush's rating).

Actually, no one should be surprised at the reality of the "Democratic Revolution." There was a similar "Republican Revolution" in 1994 when the Republicans took control of both chambers of Congress for the first time since 1954. At that time, a Democratic president (Clinton) was still in power and remained there through 2000, just as a Republican will be in power until 2009. Then, as now, the revolution petered out quickly. Then, as now, the reformers' zeal disappeared once they arrived in Congress. Members of both chambers have settled down to playing the political game—using federal funds to influence future votes in order to hold onto power in any way possible.

BLOG ON

Democratic activists flock to the Daily Kos at **www.dailykos.com**, a blog founded by Markos Moulitsas Zúniga. The Daily Kos is not only the most famous and most popular liberal blog but one of the most visited destinations in the entire blogosphere, with about 600,000 hits each day. Comments have been posted by visitors ranging from Senator Ted Kennedy and President Jimmy Carter to elementary school students. Another important Democratic Party-oriented blog is Talking Points Memo at **www.talkingpointsmemo.com**. You can post comments at **www.tpmcafe.com**.

The Self-Perpetuation of the Two-Party System

One of the major reasons for the perpetuation of the two-party system is simply that there is no alternative. Minor parties, called *third parties,*[3] traditionally have found it extremely difficult to compete with the major parties for votes. There are many reasons for this, including election laws and institutional barriers.

ELECTION LAWS FAVORING TWO PARTIES American election laws tend to favor the major parties. In many states, for example, the established major parties need relatively few signatures to place their candidates on the ballot, whereas a third party must get many more signatures. The criterion is often based on the total party vote in the last election, which penalizes a new party competing for the first time.

The rules governing campaign financing also favor the major parties. As you will read in Chapter 9, both major parties receive federal funds for campaign expenses and for their national conventions. Third parties, in contrast, receive federal funds only if they garner 5 percent of the vote, and they receive the funds only *after* the election.

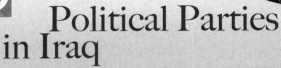

THE REST OF THE WORLD

Political Parties in Iraq

U.S. Marine Corps/Sgt. David J. Murphy

In the United States, we have a two-party system. Many—if not most—other countries have multiparty systems. The 2005 Iraqi Constitution created such a system. That country is a federal republic—at least on paper. It has the equivalent of a parliament, called the Council of Representatives, which creates legislation. The parliament also elects a president, who then selects a prime minister from the majority coalition. The parliament ratifies treaties and approves the nominations of government officials.

REGISTERED POLITICAL ENTITIES—THE MORE THE MERRIER

During the first parliamentary elections in Iraq, more than three hundred political entities were registered. In addition, there

were nineteen coalitions, each of which included several parties. The most successful group is the Shiite coalition, called the United Iraqi Alliance, which holds 128 of the 235 seats in the parliament. Next is the Kurdistan Alliance, which holds 53 seats.

Even with three hundred plus political entities in existence, political parties continue to form. For example, some two hundred Sunni sheiks created a new party in western Iraq as a way to oppose al Qaeda terrorist groups.

MANY PARLIAMENTARIANS, BUT FEW PARLIAMENTARY ACTIONS

There were high hopes for the first democratically elected parliament in Iraq. Most of those hopes have been dashed by the reality that only rarely are enough members of parliament present to conduct actual lawmaking. Each representative earns about $10,000 a month in salary and benefits, including money for bodyguards. Nonetheless, the majority of the members do not show up for work, often because of the risky security situation. Those representatives who live far away have to stay at a hotel that is barely safe and serves mediocre food. For most elected representatives, parliament is a hardship post.

For Critical Analysis

Why wouldn't a two-party system work in Iraq?

INSTITUTIONAL BARRIERS TO A MULTIPARTY SYSTEM The structure of our institutions—from single-member congressional districts to the winner-take-all electoral system—prevents third parties from enjoying electoral success. One of the major institutional barriers is the winner-take-all feature of the electoral college system for electing the president (discussed in more detail in Chapter 9). In a winner-take-all system, which applies in all but two of the states (Maine and Nebraska), the winner of a state's popular vote gets all of that state's electoral votes. Thus, third-party candidates have little incentive to run for president because they are unlikely to get enough popular votes to receive any state's electoral votes.

Another institutional barrier to a multiparty system is the single-member district. Today, all federal and most state legislative districts are single-member districts—that is, voters elect one member from their district to the House of Representatives and to their state legislature.[4] In most European countries, by contrast, districts are drawn as multimember districts and are represented by multiple elected officials from different parties, according to the proportion of the vote their party received.

Finally, third parties find it difficult to break through in an electoral system that perpetuates their own failure. Because third parties normally do not win elections, Americans tend not to vote for them or to contribute to

The electorate   The party organization   The party in government

Peter Beavis/Stone/Getty

Center: AP Photo/Ron Edmonds
Right: Carol T. Powers/Bloomberg News

their campaigns, so they do not win elections. As long as Americans hold to the perception that third parties can never win big in an election, the current two-party system is likely to persist.

Components of the Two Major American Parties

The two major American political parties are sometimes described as three-dimensional entities. This is because each party consists of three components: (1) the party in the electorate, (2) the party organization, and (3) the party in government.

THE PARTY IN THE ELECTORATE The party in the **electorate** is the largest component, consisting of all of those people who describe themselves as Democrats or Republicans. There are no dues, no membership cards, and no obligatory duties. Members of the party in the electorate never need to work on a campaign or attend a party meeting. In most states, they may register as Democrats or Republicans, but registration is not legally binding and can be changed at will.

THE PARTY ORGANIZATION Each major party has a national organization with national, state, and local offices. As will be discussed later in this chapter, the party organizations include several levels of people who maintain the party's strength between elections, make its rules, raise money, organize conventions, help with elections, and recruit candidates.

THE PARTY IN GOVERNMENT The party in government consists of all of the candidates who have won elections and now hold public office. Even though members of Congress, state legislators, presidents, and all other office-holders almost always run for office as either Democrats

> "I AM NOT A MEMBER OF ANY ORGANIZED POLITICAL PARTY. I AM A DEMOCRAT."
>
> WILL ROGERS,
> AMERICAN HUMORIST
> 1879–1935

or Republicans, the individual candidates do not always agree on government policy. The party in government helps to organize the government's agenda by coaxing and convincing its own party members to vote for its policies. If the party is to translate its promises into public policies, the job must be done by the party in government.

Where the Parties Stand on the Issues

Each of the two major political parties, as well as most of the minor parties, develops a **party platform,** or declaration of beliefs. The platform represents the official party position on various issues, although neither all party members nor all candidates running on the party's ticket share these positions exactly. The major parties usually revise their platforms every four years at the party's national convention, which is held to nominate a presidential and a vice presidential candidate. A new party agenda is also usually announced every two years as a new session of Congress gets under way. The party agendas of the Democrats and Republicans for the 110th Congress are shown in Table 7–1 on the next page.

Party platforms do not necessarily tell you what candidates are going to do when they take office, however. For example, although the Democratic Party is generally known as the party of the "little people" and generally favors social legislation to help the underclass in society, it was a Democratic president, Bill Clinton, who signed a major welfare reform bill in 1996, forcing many welfare recipients off the welfare rolls. The Democrats are also known to side with labor unions, yet President Clinton approved the North American Free Trade Agreement, despite bitter public denunciations by most of the

electorate All of the citizens eligible to vote in a given election.

party platform The document drawn up by each party at its national convention that outlines the policies and positions of the party.

TABLE 7-1

AGENDAS OF THE DEMOCRATIC AND REPUBLICAN PARTIES FOR THE 110TH CONGRESS

DEMOCRATIC AGENDA

Honest Leadership and Open Government—We will end the Republican culture of corruption and restore a government as good as the people it serves, starting with real ethics reform.

Real Security—We will protect Americans at home and lead the world by telling the truth to our troops, our citizens, and our allies. We believe in a strong national defense that is both tough and smart, recognizing that homeland security begins with hometown security.

Energy Independence—We will create a cleaner, greener, and stronger America by reducing our dependence on foreign oil. We will eliminate billions in subsidies for oil and gas companies and use the savings to provide consumer relief and develop energy alternatives. We will also invest in energy-independent technology.

Economic Prosperity and Educational Excellence—We will create jobs that stay in America and restore opportunity for all Americans, starting with raising the minimum wage, expanding Pell grants, and making college tuition tax deductible. We also believe in budget discipline that reduces our deficit.

A Health-Care System That Works for Everyone—We will join thirty-six other industrialized nations in making sure everyone has access to affordable health care, starting by fixing the prescription drug program and investing in stem-cell and other medical research.

Secure Retirement—We will ensure that retirement with dignity is the right and expectation of every single American, starting with pension reform, expanding saving incentives, and preventing the privatization of Social Security.

REPUBLICAN AGENDA

Education—We will develop a lifelong approach to education, training, and research that prepares all Americans for jobs of the future, promotes access to college, and ensures accountability of federal dollars.

Energy—We will support innovating new technologies to develop America's energy resources that create jobs and reduce our dependence on foreign oil and gas while preserving the environment.

Global War on Terrorism—We will strengthen our ports and borders, complete the mission in Iraq, and hunt down radical Islamic terrorists around the world.

Health Care—We will ensure that patients have access to quality and more affordable health care while lowering the cost of health insurance, offering more choices for services, and increasing coverage for the uninsured.

Immigration/Border Security—[left blank in publicized agenda]

Jobs and the Economy—We will create an environment to grow jobs by less taxation and litigation, sensible regulation, greater research and development, quality education, and strong infrastructure.

Judicial Nominations—We will confirm judges who will follow the law—not make the law—by ensuring timely up-or-down votes for all nominees on the Senate floor.

Tax Relief—We will create simpler, fairer, and lower taxes to promote job creation.

---

nation's unions. Additionally, the Democrats have traditionally been associated with "big government" and deficit spending, but under President Bill Clinton there was a budget surplus.

Similarly, although the Republican Party has long advocated "small government" and states' rights, federal government spending has been taken to new heights during the Bush administration, and budget surpluses haven't been seen since the Clinton years. Generally, as mentioned in the chapter-opening *America at Odds* feature, the Republicanism of the Bush administration and its support-

> **"LET US NOT SEEK THE REPUBLICAN ANSWER OR THE DEMOCRATIC ANSWER, BUT THE RIGHT ANSWER. LET US NOT SEEK TO FIX THE BLAME FOR THE PAST. LET US ACCEPT OUR OWN RESPONSIBILITY FOR THE FUTURE."**
>
> JOHN FITZGERALD KENNEDY,
> THIRTY-FIFTH PRESIDENT OF THE UNITED STATES
> 1961–1963

ers has little in common with the Republicanism of the Ronald Reagan era (1981–1989). Reagan politics reflected a coalition of interests that fell under the umbrella of the Republican Party: economic conservatism (the attempt to minimize government interference in the business affairs of the nation) and social conservatism. Today, these "bases" of the Republican Party are both skeptical of the Republicanism endorsed by Bush and the Republican leadership in Congress.

Many have commented in recent years that candidates for office from both major parties seem to be less concerned with party agendas than with being elected or reelected. To gain or remain in power, they will try to please the majority of voters, even if that means adopting a plank from the other party's platform.

JOIN THE DEBATE

Is the Two-Party System Ruining American Politics?

Some believe that our two-party system is slowly but surely destroying the fabric of our political system. This group claims that today's political candidates are more concerned with winning votes than with demonstrating leadership qualities or taking positions on issues that are important to the nation. Instead, candidates plan their campaigns around their perceptions of what the voters want to hear, based on polling data. Campaign messages are adjusted accordingly in order to appeal to more voters. The candidates from each party look for decisive "wedge" issues on which to base a highly negative political campaign. "Dirty tricks" and "little lies" about opposing candidates are fed to the media, and by the time these tricks and lies are exposed for what they are, the damage is done. Because only two parties dominate the American political arena, and campaigns are designed to divide rather than unite Americans, the electorate in general does not have a voice. After all, most Americans hold moderate political views—that is, they are in the middle of the political spectrum.

Critics of the two-party system contend that the parties' energies are devoted solely to gaining and maintaining power, not to providing needed leadership concerning challenges facing the nation. Consider that the Republicans have been attempting to obtain one-party rule since as early as the 1960s. They achieved it in the 2000 elections only to see it disappear after the 2006 elections. The voters spoke loudly and clearly, yet some Republicans still hold out hope that their losses in the latest midterm elections were just a temporary setback and that they will succeed again in the future.

Not everyone agrees with these criticisms. If the two-party system is so bad, why has it endured for centuries? Why should we be so alarmed if it hasn't yet destroyed the country? True, the parties aren't what they used to be, at least in terms of their traditional philosophical underpinnings. Nonetheless, the two parties still represent the basic division of opinion that was present even before the states ratified the Constitution. This division pits those who desire a small national government that remains in the background of everyday life against those who want a strong national government that is willing to interfere in the nation's affairs to protect the poor and other disadvantaged groups. At any rate, when a political party no longer reflects its constituents' wishes, the party has to change its views and policies. In the past, when one party was totally out of touch with reality, it was replaced. This occurred in the mid-1800s when the Whig Party disintegrated. The Republican Party replaced it.

Party Affiliation

What does it mean to belong to a political party? In many European countries, being a party member means that you actually join a political party. You get a membership card to carry around in your wallet, you pay dues, and you vote to select your local and national party leaders. In the United States, becoming a member of a political party is far less involved. To be a member of a political party, an American citizen has only to think of herself or himself as a Democrat or a Republican (or a member of a third party, such as the Green Party, the Libertarian Party, or the American Independent Party). Members of parties do not have to pay dues, work for the party, or attend party meetings. Nor must they support the party platform.[5]

Generally, the party in the electorate consists of **party identifiers** (those who identify themselves as being members of a particular party) and the **party elite**—active party members who choose to work for the party and even become candidates for office. Political parties need year-round support from the latter group to survive. During election campaigns in particular, candidates depend on active party members or volunteers to mail literature, answer phones, conduct door-to-door canvasses, organize speeches and appearances, and, of course, donate money. Between elections, parties also need active members to plan the

party identifier A person who identifies himself or herself as being a member of a particular political party.

party elite A loose-knit group of party activists who organize and oversee party functions and planning during and between campaigns.

upcoming elections, orga-
nize fund-raisers, and stay
in touch with party lead-
ers in other communities
to keep the party strong.
Generally, the major functions of American politi-
cal parties are carried out
by the party elite.

WHY PEOPLE JOIN POLITICAL PARTIES

Generally, in the United
States people belong to
a political party because
they agree with many of
its main ideas and support
some of its candidates. In
a few countries, such as
the People's Republic of
China, people belong to
a political party because
they are required to do so
to get ahead in life, regardless of whether they agree with
the party's ideas and candidates.

Most colleges and universities have mascots that represent their athletic teams. So, too, do the two major political parties. On the left, you see the donkey that became the Democratic Party mascot. On the right, you see the elephant that became the Republican Party mascot. Whatever might have been the symbolism behind these cartoon figures when they were created, the two mascots for the major parties in the United States have no particular meaning today. Americans simply know that a caricature of a donkey is the symbol of the Democratic Party, and a caricature of an elephant is the symbol of the Republican Party.

People join political parties for a multitude of reasons. One reason is that people wish to express their
solidarity, or mutual agreement, with the views of
friends, loved ones, and other like-minded people.
People also join parties because they enjoy the excitement of politics. In addition, many believe they will
benefit materially from joining a party through better
employment or personal career advancement. The traditional institution of **patronage**—rewarding the party
faithful with government jobs or contracts—lives on,
even though it has been limited to prevent abuses.[6]
Finally, some join political parties because they wish to
actively promote a set of ideals and principles that they
feel are important to American politics and society.

As a rule, people join political parties because of
their overall agreement with what a particular party
stands for. Thus, when interviewed, people may make
the following remarks when asked why they support
the Democratic Party: "It seems that the economy
is better when the Democrats are in control." "The
Democrats are for the working people." People
might say about the Republican Party: "The
Republicans help small businesses more than the
Democrats." "The Republicans deal better with foreign
policy and defense issues."

DEMOGRAPHIC FACTORS AND PARTY IDENTIFICATION

Regardless of how accurate or inaccurate these stereo-
types are, individuals with similar characteristics do
tend to align themselves more often with one or the
other major party. Such factors as race, age, income,
education, marital status, and geography all influence
party identification.

Normally, slightly more men than women identify
with the Republican Party, and more women than men
identify themselves as Democrats. While slightly more
whites identify with the Republican Party, people in the
other categories (nonwhite, black, and Hispanic) overwhelmingly classify themselves as Democrats. As to age,
the most notable differences in party preferences are
found in those between the ages of eighteen and twenty-
four, and in those over the age of fifty-five. A significantly
larger number of people in these groups identify themselves as Democrats than as Republicans. As mentioned,
other factors, such as income, religion, marital status,
and geography, also seem to influence party preference.

Although there is clearly a link between these factors and party preference, each party encompasses
diverse interests and activities. Both political parties
welcome various groups and strive to attract as many
members as possible.

solidarity Mutual agreement with others in a particular
group.

patronage A system of
rewarding the party faithful and
workers with government jobs or
contracts.

RED VERSUS BLUE AMERICA   As just mentioned, geography is one of the factors that can determine party identification. Yet geographic maps after a presidential election, showing the state-by-state distribution of the candidates' electoral votes, can be deceiving. Consider the electoral map drawn up by news organizations following the 2004 presidential elections (top right). The map depicted states won by Democratic Party candidate John Kerry in blue, while the states won by Republican candidate President George W. Bush were in red. The visual evidence provided by these maps showed clusters of "blue states" on the West Coast, the upper Midwest, and the Northeast, while vast tracts in the southern and middle United States were bathed in red.

The sheer amount of land covered by "red states" on the electoral map was visually impressive. Many Americans looked at the map and assumed that Bush had won a stunning majority. The 2004 presidential election results were far from a landslide, however, regardless of the visual impression given by the electoral map. President Bush won the elections by less than a 3 percent margin in the popular vote. Similarly, the electoral college count was one of the closest in American history (Bush won by a mere thirty-five electoral votes), with ultimate victory hinging on a narrow win in Ohio for Bush. Indeed, Bush's victory was far from lopsided.

The electoral map also overstated the perceived geographic divide plaguing the United States. Simply looking at red and blue states on a map fails to recognize that citizens within those states did not necessarily vote overwhelmingly in favor of one candidate or the other. In 2004, Bush won a greater percentage of the votes in fifteen of the twenty states that he had lost in the 2000 elections. In fact, only in twelve states did either candidate garner more than 60 percent of the vote. Furthermore, Bush or Kerry won every county of a state in only seven states. Broken down to the county and local levels, the states show patches of both red and blue.

A CHANGING ELECTORATE?   For over a decade, polls on party identification have shown a rough parity in terms of support for each major political party. About a third of the voters identified themselves as Democrats, a third as Republicans, and a third as independents. Recently, though, pollsters have been noting a dramatic shift in party identification. As noted in this chapter's opening *America at Odds* feature, support for the Republican Party is clearly waning. A poll taken by the Pew Research Center for People and the Press in March 2007 found that about half of those surveyed identified with, or leaned toward, the Democratic Party, and only 35 percent identified with, or

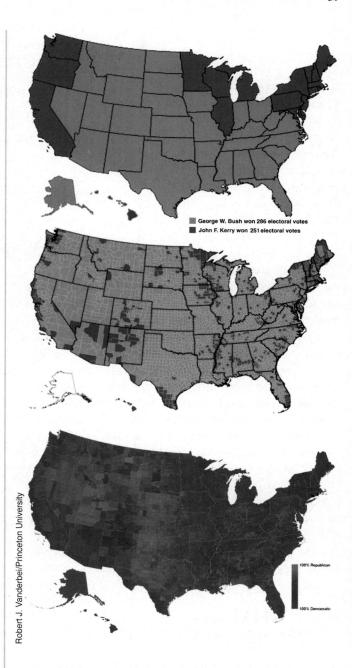

The top U.S. map shows the 2004 presidential election results by electoral votes, with Democrats in blue and Republicans in red. The middle map shows the results by county. The bottom map shows the results by percentage of the popular vote.

leaned toward, the Republican Party. The survey also found that public attitudes are drifting more toward Democratic values, as reflected in increased support for government aid to the disadvantaged and more skepticism about the use of military force. Support for traditional family values, which helped to fuel Republican dominance for over a decade, has decreased.

Today, more voters identify themselves as independents (about 40 percent) than consider themselves either Democrats or Republicans. Yet a *Washington Post*/CBS News poll taken just before the November 2006 elections showed that voters who characterize themselves as independents tend to favor the Democrats over the Republicans almost two to one—59 percent to 31 percent, respectively. In the past, in contrast, typically one-third of the independents would vote Republican, one-third would vote Democratic, and one-third were undecided until the last minute—and thus the targets of much campaign advertising.

Democrats are making headway even in areas, such as national security, in which Republicans have long held the advantage. According to a May 2007 Gallup poll, Americans also have more confidence in Democrats than Republicans to "do the right thing" for the economy— the first time in seven years that Democrats ranked higher than Republicans on this issue. A June 2007 Gallup poll reported that voters place more trust in Democrats to handle "all the issues you care about."

The question, of course, is whether these changes in public attitudes are significant. Are they indicative of a long-term trend? Or do they just reflect the public's general dissatisfaction with today's Republican leadership and the Bush administration's policies, particularly on the Iraq war?

LO³ WHAT DO POLITICAL PARTIES DO?

As noted earlier, the Constitution does not mention political parties. Historically, though, political parties have played a vital role in our democratic system. Their main function has been to link the people's policy preferences to actual government policies. Political parties also perform many other functions.

Selecting Candidates

One of the most important functions of the two political parties is to recruit and nominate candidates for political office. This function simplifies voting choices for the electorate. Political parties take the

primary A preliminary election held for the purpose of choosing a party's final candidate.

> "**Democracy** is the recurrent suspicion that more than half of the people are right more than half of the time."
>
> E. B. WHITE,
> AMERICAN AUTHOR
> 1900–1965

large number of people who want to run for office and narrow the field to one candidate. They accomplish this by the use of the **primary,** which is a preliminary election to choose a party's final candidate. This candidate then runs against the opposing party's candidate in the general election.

Informing the Public

Political parties help educate the public about important current political issues. In recent years, these issues have included defense and environmental policies, health insurance, our tax system, welfare reform, crime, education, and Social Security. Each party presents its view of these issues through television announcements, newspaper articles or ads, Web site materials, campaign speeches, rallies, debates, and pamphlets. These activities help citizens learn about the issues, consider proposed solutions, and form opinions.

Through these activities, political parties also help to stimulate citizens' interest and participation in public

One of the major activities of political party workers is to "man the phones." Here, you see campaign workers at a typical party phone bank.

AP Photo/Al Goldis

Ed Kashi/Corbis

Volunteer campaign workers prepare to distribute voter information literature to support their party's candidates and issues. What motivates individuals to become campaign volunteers?

affairs. They seek people to work at party headquarters or to help with door-to-door canvasses, which involve distributing campaign literature and asking people to vote for the party's candidate. Political parties also ask volunteers to work at polling places where people cast their votes during elections and to drive voters to the polling places. Through such pursuits, citizens can participate in the political process.

Coordinating Policymaking

In our complex government, parties are essential for coordinating policy among the various branches of the government. The political party is usually the major institution through which the executive and legislative branches cooperate with each other. Each president, cabinet head, and member of Congress is normally a member of the Democratic or the Republican Party. The party with fewer members in the legislature is the **minority party.** The party with the most members is the **majority party.** The president works through party leaders in Congress to promote the administration's legislative program. Ideally, the parties work together to fashion compromises—legislation that is acceptable to both parties and that serves the national interest. In recent years, however, particularly with the unified Republican government during the first six years of the Bush administration, there has been little bipartisanship in Congress. A notable exception was right after the terrorist attacks of September 11, 2001, when the president, the Congress, and indeed the entire nation were united. What happened to this unity of interests? For a discus-

sion of that question, see this chapter's *The Politics of National Security* feature on page 162. Parties also act as the glue of our federal structure by connecting the various levels of government with a common bond. (For a more detailed discussion of the role played by political parties in Congress, see Chapter 11.)

Checking the Power of the Party in Government

The party that does not control Congress or a state legislature, or the presidency or a state governorship, also plays a vital function in American politics. The "out party" does what it can to influence the "in party" and its policies, and to check the actions of the party in power. For example, depending on how evenly Congress is divided, the out party (minority party) may be able to attract to its side some of the members of the majority party to pass or defeat certain legislation. The out party will also work to inform the voters of the shortcomings of the in party's agenda and plan strategies for winning the next election.

Balancing Competing Interests

Political parties are often described as vast umbrellas under which Americans with diverse interests can gather. Political parties are essentially **coalitions**—individuals and groups with a variety of interests and opinions who join together to support the party's platform, or parts of it.

The Republican Party, for example, includes a number of groups with many different views on the issue of abortion. The role of party leaders in this situation is to adopt a broad enough view on the issue so that the various groups will not be alienated. In this way, different groups can hold their individual views and still come together under the umbrella of the Republican Party. Leaders of both the Democratic Party and the Republican Party modify contending views and arrange compromises

minority party The political party that has fewer members in the legislature than the opposing party.

majority party The political party that has more members in the legislature than the opposing party.

coalition An alliance of individuals or groups with a variety of interests and opinions who join together to support all or part of a political party's platform.

THE POLITICS OF NATIONAL SECURITY

FROM 9/11 TO TODAY— BIPARTISANSHIP TO PARTISANSHIP

When terrorists brought down the World Trade Center towers and crashed a plane into the Pentagon on September 11, 2001, the phrase "We are all Americans" was heard day after day. The country was united behind its president and commander in chief. Congress put partisanship aside. It immediately passed a joint resolution authorizing the president "to use all necessary and appropriate force against those nations, organizations, or persons he determines planned, authorized, committed, or aided the terrorist attacks" or "harbored such persons or organizations." Not too long after 9/11, the U.S. military ousted the Taliban government in Afghanistan because it had supported and harbored al Qaeda terrorists. Today, that bipartisanship in fighting the war on terrorism has disappeared. What happened?

President Bush addresses the United Nations in September 2002, making his case for military action against Iraq.

AP Photo/Doug Mills

A DEFENSE POLICY PROMOTED BY NEOCONSERVATIVES

The terrorists' attacks on 9/11 provided a perfect springboard for the implementation of the neoconservatives' foreign policy goals. *Neoconservatives,* sometimes called neocons, believe that America should not rely on multilateral institutions, such as the United Nations, to create peace in the world. They believe that the U.S. military should be used to attack and "rebuild" (establish democratic governments in) nations that may pose future threats to the United States, particularly nations in the Middle East. As far back as 1998, for example, the Project for the New American Century, a neocon

think tank, urged President Clinton to undertake military action to eliminate "the possibility that Iraq will be able to use or threaten to use weapons of mass destruction."

9/11—ANOTHER PEARL HARBOR?

On 9/11, President Bush wrote in his diary, "The Pearl Harbor of the 21st Century took place today." Neoconservatives could not have said it better. One of them, then secretary of defense Donald Rumsfeld, said in a *New York Times* interview that 9/11 had created "the kind of opportunity that World War II offered, to refashion the world." It did not take long for many neoconservatives to prod the Bush administration into action. The concept of "preventive war" became part of the so-called Bush doctrine on national defense. *Preemptive* war occurs when a country attacks another nation after learning that an attack from that other nation is imminent. But this concept was not sufficient to justify attacking Iraq, for there was no evidence that Iraq was about to attack the United States. Military action against Iraq was, in effect, a *preventive* war—that is, it was aimed at preventing a future attack that was not imminent and not even threatened. Preventive war is not sanctioned by international law.

INVADING IRAQ— PARTISANSHIP IS BACK

Not too many months after the war began, partisanship was evident again. Critics of the war claimed that Bush had fabricated the evidence that dictator Saddam Hussein was developing nuclear weapons. Others found evidence that there were no serious links between al Qaeda and Saddam Hussein. The post-9/11 congressional unity ended up as a pro-war, anti-war division. The divisiveness became bitter. The Bush administration and others in favor of the war called those against it "traitors" or "unpatriotic." By 2006, the voters had had enough. Control of Congress went back to the Democrats.

YOU BE THE JUDGE

Some Americans—an increasingly small percentage—believe that our military intrusions into Afghanistan and Iraq were necessary to eliminate state-supported terrorism and the possibility that weapons of mass destruction would be developed and perhaps used against us. Others contend that the invasion of Iraq was based on faulty information and that, besides, America has no right to engage in preventive war, which is in violation of international law. Where do you stand on this issue?

among different groups. In so doing, the parties help to unify, rather than divide, their members.

Running Campaigns

Through their national, state, and local organizations, parties coordinate campaigns. Political parties take care of a large number of small and routine tasks that are essential to the smooth functioning of the electoral process. For example, they work at getting party members registered and at conducting drives for new voters. Sometimes, party volunteers staff the polling places.

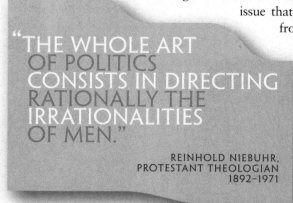

"THE WHOLE ART OF POLITICS CONSISTS IN DIRECTING RATIONALLY THE IRRATIONALITIES OF MEN."

REINHOLD NIEBUHR, PROTESTANT THEOLOGIAN 1892–1971

LO⁴ THIRD PARTIES AND AMERICAN POLITICS

Throughout American history, smaller minor parties, or **third parties,** have competed for power in the nation's two-party system. Indeed, as mentioned earlier, third parties have been represented in most of our national elections. Although third parties have found it difficult—if not impossible—to gain credibility within the two-party American system, they play an important role in our political life.

The Many Kinds of Third Parties

Third parties are as varied as the causes they represent, but all of these parties have one thing in common: their members and leaders want to challenge the major parties because they believe that certain needs and values are not being properly addressed. Third parties name candidates who propose to remedy the situation.

Some third parties have tried to appeal to the entire nation; others have focused on particular regions of the country, states, or local areas. Most third parties have been short lived. A few, however, including the Socialist Labor Party (founded in 1891) and the Socialist Party (founded in 1901), lasted for a long time. The number and variety of third parties make them difficult to classify, but most fall into one of the general categories discussed in the following subsections.

ISSUE-ORIENTED PARTIES An issue-oriented third party is formed to promote a particular cause or timely issue. For example, the Free Soil Party was organized in 1848 to op-

pose the expansion of slavery into the western territories. The Prohibition Party was formed in 1869 to advocate prohibiting the use and manufacture of alcoholic beverages. Most issue-oriented parties fade into history as the issue that brought them into existence fades from public attention, is taken up by a major party, or is resolved.

Some issue-oriented parties endure, however, when they expand their focus beyond a single area of concern. For example, the Green Party USA (the Green Party) was founded in 1972 to raise awareness of environmental issues, but it is no longer a single-issue party. Ralph Nader, the presidential candidate for the Green Party in 2000, campaigned against alleged corporate greed and the major parties' ostensible indifference to a number of issues, including universal health insurance, child poverty, the excesses of globalism, and the failure of the drug war.

IDEOLOGICAL PARTIES As discussed in Chapter 1, an *ideology* is a system of political ideas rooted in beliefs about human nature, society, and government. An ideological party supports a particular political doctrine or a set of beliefs. For example, a party such as the Socialist Workers Party may believe that our free enterprise system should be replaced by one in which government or workers own all of the factories in the economy. The party's members may believe that competition should be replaced by cooperation and social responsibility so as to achieve an equitable distribution of income. In contrast, an ideological party such as the Libertarian Party may oppose virtually all forms of government interference with personal liberties and private enterprise.

SPLINTER OR PERSONALITY PARTIES A splinter party develops out of a split within a major party. Often, this split involves the formation of a party to elect a specific person. For example, when Theodore Roosevelt did not receive the Republican Party's nomination for president in 1912, he created the Bull Moose Party (also called the Progressive Party) to promote his platform. From the Democrats have come Henry Wallace's Progressive Party and the States' Rights (Dixiecrat) Party, both formed in 1948. In 1968, the American Independent Party was formed to support George Wallace's campaign for president.

third party In the United States, any party other than one of the two major parties (Republican and Democratic).

Theodore Roosevelt and his Progressive (Bull Moose) Party changed the outcome of the 1912 election.

Bettmann/Corbis

Doug Duran/MCT/Landov

Third parties may not be able to win elections, but they can continue to influence election outcomes. For example, Ralph Nader was a presidential candidate for the Green Party in the 2000 elections. He garnered several percentage points of the popular vote. Some argue that had he not run, his supporters would have mostly voted for Democratic presidential candidate Al Gore, thus depriving Republican presidential candidate George W. Bush of his election victory.

Most splinter parties have been formed around a leader with a strong personality, which is why they are sometimes called personality parties. When that person steps aside, the party usually collapses. An example of a personality party is the Reform Party, which was formed in 1996 mainly to provide a campaign vehicle for H. Ross Perot.

The Effect of Third Parties on American Politics

Although most Americans do not support third parties or vote for their candidates, third parties have influenced American politics in several ways, some of which we examine here.

THIRD PARTIES BRING ISSUES TO THE PUBLIC'S ATTENTION

Third parties have brought many political issues to the public's attention. They have exposed and focused on unpopular or highly debated issues that major parties have preferred to ignore. Third parties are in a position to take bold stands on issues that are avoided by major parties because third parties are not trying to be all things to all people. Progressive social reforms such as the minimum wage, women's right to vote, railroad and banking legislation, and old-age pensions were first proposed by third parties. The Free Soilers of the 1850s, for example, were the first true an-

Bettmann/Corbis

This 1912 cartoon shows both major political parties trying to get the attention of the Bull Moose (Theodore Roosevelt's third party).

tislavery party, and the Populists and Progressives put many social reforms on the political agenda.

Some people have argued that third parties are often the unsung heroes of American politics, bringing new issues to the forefront of public debate. Some of the ideas proposed by third parties were never accepted, while others were taken up by the major parties as these ideas became increasingly popular.

THIRD PARTIES CAN AFFECT THE VOTE

Third parties can influence not only voter turnout but also election outcomes. Third parties have occasionally taken victory from one major party and given it to another, thus playing the "spoiler" role.

For example, in 1912, when the Progressive Party split off from the Republican Party, the result was three major contenders for the presidency: Woodrow Wilson, the Democratic candidate; William Howard Taft, the regular Republican candidate; and Theodore Roosevelt, the Progressive candidate. The presence of the Progressive Party "spoiled" the Republicans' chances for victory and gave the election to Wilson, the Democrat.

Without Roosevelt's third party, Taft might have won. Similarly, many commentators contended that Ralph Nader "spoiled" the chances of Democratic candidate Al Gore in the 2000 elections, because many of those who voted for Nader would have voted Democratic had Nader not been a candidate. In fact, to minimize Nader's impact on the vote for Gore, some "vote swapping" was done via the Internet. Voters in states that were solidly in the Gore camp reportedly agreed to vote for Nader, and, in exchange, Nader supporters in closely contested states agreed to cast their votes for Gore.

A significant showing by a minor party also reduces an incumbent party's chances of winning the election, as you can see in Figure 7–2. In 1992, for example, third-party candidate H. Ross Perot captured about 19 percent of the vote. Had those votes been distributed between the candidates of the major parties, incumbent George H. W. Bush and candidate Bill Clinton, the outcome of the election might have been different.

THIRD PARTIES PROVIDE A VOICE FOR DISSATIS-FIED AMERICANS Third parties also provide a voice for voters who are frustrated with and alienated from the Republican and Democratic parties. Americans who are unhappy with the two major political parties can still participate in American politics through third parties that reflect their opinions on political issues. Indeed, young Minnesota voters turned out in record numbers during the 1998 elections to vote for Jesse Ventura, a Reform Party candidate for governor in that state. Similarly, Ralph Nader was able to engage young Americans who might never have gone to the polls in 2000 if he had not been a candidate.

Today, voter dissatisfaction with the state of the nation—and with both political parties—is at a record high. Put another way, national satisfaction is at a record low. According to a May 2007 Gallup poll, the level of national satisfaction has dropped to 25 percent—the lowest rating since 1979. Factors contributing to this

FIGURE 7–2

THE EFFECT OF THIRD PARTIES ON VOTE DISTRIBUTION, 1848–1992

In eight presidential elections, a third party's candidate received more than 10 percent of the popular vote—in six of those elections, the incumbent party lost. As shown here, only in 1856 and 1924 did the incumbent party manage to hold on to the White House in the face of a significant third-party showing.

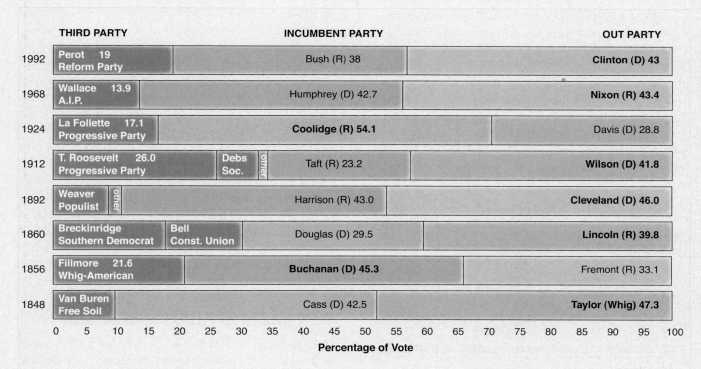

	THIRD PARTY		INCUMBENT PARTY	OUT PARTY
1992	Perot 19 Reform Party		Bush (R) 38	Clinton (D) 43
1968	Wallace 13.9 A.I.P.		Humphrey (D) 42.7	Nixon (R) 43.4
1924	La Follette 17.1 Progressive Party		Coolidge (R) 54.1	Davis (D) 28.8
1912	T. Roosevelt 26.0 Progressive Party	Debs Soc. / other	Taft (R) 23.2	Wilson (D) 41.8
1892	Weaver Populist	other	Harrison (R) 43.0	Cleveland (D) 46.0
1860	Breckinridge Southern Democrat	Bell Const. Union	Douglas (D) 29.5	Lincoln (R) 39.8
1856	Fillmore 21.6 Whig-American		Buchanan (D) 45.3	Fremont (R) 33.1
1848	Van Buren Free Soil		Cass (D) 42.5	Taylor (Whig) 47.3

0 5 10 15 20 25 30 35 40 45 50 55 60 65 70 75 80 85 90 95 100

Percentage of Vote

Source: *Congressional Quarterly Weekly Report*, June 13, 1992, p. 1729.

dissatisfaction include the Iraq war, health-care problems, high gasoline prices, and the frequent gridlock between the Democratic Congress and President Bush.

JOIN THE DEBATE

Is a Bipartisan Presidential Ticket Possible?

Americans appear to be dissatisfied with both parties. Older citizens, who remember the parties in the past, find today's two major political parties unrecognizable. Additionally, the ferociously negative nature of recent campaigns has turned off many Americans to politics. Finally, any person wishing to become a Republican or Democratic candidate for president constantly has to modify what he or she "stands for" in order to win votes and gain the support of interest groups that will finance his or her campaign. Enter Unity08, a third party that wants to run a bipartisan presidential ticket.

The founders of Unity08—a Web-based party—firmly believe that a Republican/Democratic presidential slate is just the ticket for disillusioned voters. Actor Sam Waterston is one of Unity08's leaders, as is former Maine governor Angus King. These and other proponents of Unity08 point out that billionaire H. Ross Perot received 19 percent of the vote in 1992 even though he ran as a third-party candidate and started his real campaign very late in the election cycle. Another reason that Unity08 might eventually succeed is that it is truly different from other third-party movements. It isn't putting forward its own candidates. Rather, it is using the Internet to determine who will be on Unity08's bipartisan ticket.

There are, of course, a lot of reasons why a third party, even with a bipartisan ticket, won't succeed. As one consultant, Lance Tarrance, said, "Third parties are like organ transplants—they're not tolerated well and are often rejected." Politics today are more ideological and more partisan than ever before, so why would Americans latch on to a bipartisan presidential ticket? Then there is the problem of money: the two main parties will spend billions, whereas Unity08 will have only millions to spend. Even if the bipartisan ticket is a good idea, the money spent by the major parties on media advertising will undoubtedly pay off. At best, Unity08 may force the major parties to be less divisive in their campaigns, but even that is not a certainty.

LO⁵ HOW AMERICAN POLITICAL PARTIES ARE STRUCTURED

In theory, each of the major American political parties has a standard, pyramid-shaped organization (see Figure 7–3). This theoretical structure is much like that of a large company, in which the bosses are at the top and the employees are at various lower levels.

Actually, neither major party is a closely knit or highly organized structure. Both parties are fragmented and *decentralized,* which means there is no central power with a direct chain of command. If there were, the national chairperson of the party, along with the national committee, could simply dictate how the organization would be run, just as if it were Microsoft or General Electric. In reality, state party organizations are all very different and are only loosely tied to the party's national structure. Local party organizations are often quite independent from the state organization. There is no single individual or group who gives orders to all party members. Instead, a number of personalities, frequently at odds with one another, form loosely identifiable leadership groups.

State and Local Party Organizations

In both the Democratic and Republican parties, state and local party organizations are separate from the national party organizations. Most state and local parties work closely with their national organizations only during major elections.

STATE ORGANIZATIONS The powers and duties of state party organizations differ from state to state. In general, the state party organization is built around a central committee and a chairperson. The committee works to raise funds, recruit new party members, maintain a strong party organization, and help members running for state offices.

The state chairperson is usually a powerful party member chosen by the committee. In some cases, however, the chairperson is selected by the governor or a senator from that state.

LOCAL ORGANIZATIONS Local party organizations differ greatly, but generally there is a party unit for each district in which elective offices are to be filled. These districts include congressional and legislative districts, counties, cities and towns, wards, and precincts.

A **ward** is a political division or district within a city. A **precinct** can be either a political district within a city, such as a block or a neighborhood, or a portion of a rural county. The local, grassroots foundations of politics are formed within voting precincts. Polling places are located within the precincts. Political parties elect or appoint precinct captains or chairpersons who organize the precinct, assist new members, register voters, and take care of party business.

The National Party Organization

On the national level, the party's presidential candidate is considered to be the leader of the party. In some cases, well-known members of Congress are viewed as national party leaders. In addition to the party leaders, the structure of each party includes four major elements: the national convention, the national committee, the national chairperson, and the congressional campaign committee.

THE NATIONAL CONVENTION Most of the public attention that the party receives comes at the **national convention,** which is held every four years during the summer before the presidential election. The news media always cover these conventions, and as a result, they have become quite extravagant. They are often described as the party's national voice and are usually held in major cities.

The national conventions are attended by delegates chosen by the states in various ways. The delegates' most important job is to choose the party's presidential and vice-presidential candidates, who together make up the **party ticket.** The delegates also write the party platform, which, as mentioned, sets forth the party's positions on national issues. Essentially, through its platform, the party promises to initiate certain policies

FIGURE 7-3

THE THEORETICAL STRUCTURE OF THE AMERICAN POLITICAL PARTY

The relationship between state and local parties varies from state to state. Further, some state parties resist national party policies.

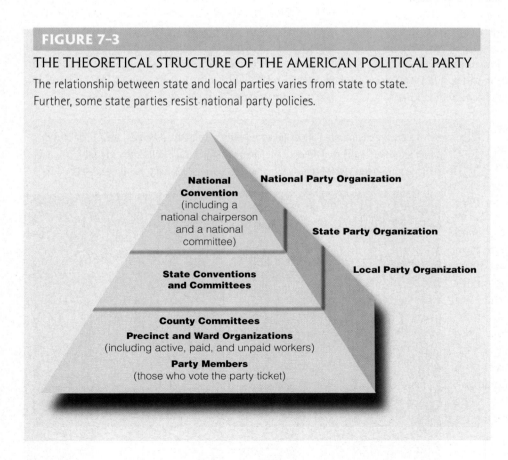

ward A local unit of a political party's organization, consisting of a division or district within a city.

precinct A political district within a city (such as a block or a neighborhood) or a portion of a rural county; the smallest voting district at the local level.

national convention The meeting held by each major party every four years to select presidential and vice-presidential candidates, write a party platform, and conduct other party business.

party ticket A list of a political party's candidates for various offices.

Cheering delegates at the 2004 Democratic National Convention in Boston listened to top party leaders, such as former presidents Bill Clinton and Jimmy Carter, who outlined the themes of the presidential election. Delegates selected Senator John Kerry of Massachusetts as their presidential candidate.

Delegates hold "W" signs at the 2004 Republican National Convention, which was held in New York City. The delegates were showing their support for George W. Bush, who won the party's nomination as its presidential candidate.

if it wins the presidency. Despite the widespread perception that, once in office, candidates can and do ignore these promises, in fact, many of them become law.[7]

THE NATIONAL COMMITTEE   Each state elects a number of delegates to the **national party committee.** The Republican National Committee and the Democratic National Committee direct the business of their respective parties during the four years between national conventions. The committees' most important duties, however, are to organize the next national convention and to plan how to obtain a party victory in the next presidential elections.

THE NATIONAL CHAIRPERSON   Each party's national committee elects a **national party chairperson** to serve as administrative head of the national party. The main duty of the national chairperson is to direct the work of the national committee from party headquarters in Washington, D.C. The chairperson

is involved in raising funds, providing for publicity, promoting party unity, recruiting new voters, and other activities. In presidential election years, the chairperson's attention is focused on the national convention and the presidential campaign.

THE CONGRESSIONAL CAMPAIGN COMMITTEES   Each party has a campaign committee, made up of senators and representatives, in each chamber of Congress. Members are chosen by their colleagues and serve for two-year terms. The committees work to help reelect party members to Congress.

national party committee
The political party leaders who direct party business during the four years between the national party conventions, organize the next national convention, and plan how to obtain a party victory in the next presidential elections.

national party chairperson
An individual who serves as a political party's administrative head at the national level and directs the work of the party's national committee.

On the left, the chairman of the Democratic National Committee, Howard Dean, speaks at the Communication Workers of America Conference in March 2006. Mike Duncan (right), a banker from Kentucky, was elected chairman of the Republican National Committee in 2007.

AMERICA AT ODDS:
Political Parties

As noted in this chapter, nowhere in the Constitution are political parties even mentioned. Yet, since the beginning of this nation, they have been at the heart of our political landscape. An early division of political attitudes among Americans was clearly reflected in the debate between the Federalists and the Anti-Federalists over the ratification of the Constitution. Today, Americans continue to be divided in their opinions as to what the government should—or should not—do. Generally, the two major political parties—the Republicans and the Democrats—represent, at least in part, this division of political attitudes.

How does our country measure up in terms of the two-party system? Has it been good or bad for this country? Some say simply that the two-party system has provided—and continues to provide—effective and stable leadership. After all, "the proof is in the pudding"—the "pudding" being the nation's ability to endure for more than two hundred years. Others are very dissatisfied with the parties today, as indicated earlier in this chapter. Much of this dissatisfaction has to do with the serious problems that have no easy solution, including the war in Iraq and the health-care challenge. Finding solutions to these problems will be difficult for whichever party wins the presidency in 2008 and controls Congress thereafter. Until those solutions are found and implemented, it is unlikely that either political party will receive high marks from the American electorate.

Issues for Debate & Discussion

1. At the national level, divided government exists when the president is from one political party and Congress is controlled by the other party. Some believe that divided government is better for the country because Congress can better exercise "checks" on the presidential administration. This group asserts that such checks are necessary to prevent Congress from endorsing the president's agenda, regardless of its merits, out of party loyalty. Others claim that unified government (which exists when the president and congressional control are in the hands of one party's members) is better because it allows the government to implement its policies more quickly and effectively. What is your position on this issue?

2. An ongoing controversy among Americans has to do with whether third-party presidential candidates should be allowed to participate in televised debates. Under the rules of the Commission for Presidential Debates (CPD) that were applied to the 2004 presidential elections, only candidates who had a level of support of at least 15 percent of the national electorate could participate. Critics of this rule point out that free elections mean little if minor-party candidates do not have realistic access to public forums, such as televised debates. Supporters of the CPD's position argue that opening up the presidential debates to third-party candidates, even to those with virtually no electoral support, would lead to chaos and that some standards for deciding who can and cannot participate in the debates are necessary. What is your position on this issue?

Take Action

Getting involved in political parties is as simple as going to the polls and casting your vote for the candidate of one of the major parties—or of a third party. If you want to go a step further, you can attend a speech given by a political candidate or even volunteer to assist a political party or specific candidates' campaign activities.

Eliot J. Schechter/Bloomberg News/Landov

From left to right: Senator Barack Obama of Illinois, Senator Hillary Clinton of New York, former senator Mike Gravel of Alaska, former senator John Edwards of North Carolina, Representative Dennis Kucinich of Ohio, Senator Chris Dodd of Connecticut, and Governor Bill Richardson of New Mexico debate during the Destino 2008 Democratic Candidate Forum at the University of Miami Bank Atlantic Center in Coral Gables, Florida, in 2007.

- For a list of political Web sites available on the Internet, sorted by country and with links to parties, organizations, and governments throughout the world, go to **www.politicalresources.net**.
- The Democratic Party is online at **www.democrats.org**.
- The Republican National Committee is online at **www.rnc.org**.
- The Libertarian Party has a Web site at **www.lp.org**.
- The Socialist Party's Web site can be accessed at **sp-usa.org**.
- The Green Party's Web site can be accessed by going to **www.greenparty.org**.
- For information on the Reform Party, go to its Web site at **www.reformparty.org**.

ONLINE RESOURCES FOR THIS CHAPTER

This text's Companion Web site, at **www.americaatodds.com**, offers links to numerous resources that you can utilize to learn more about the topics covered in this chapter.

CHAPTER 8

PUBLIC OPINION AND VOTING

LEARNING OBJECTIVES

LO¹ Explain what public opinion is and how it is measured.

LO² Describe the political socialization process.

LO³ Summarize the history of polling in the United States, and explain how polls are conducted and how they are used in the political process.

LO⁴ Indicate some of the factors that affect voter turnout, and discuss what has been done to improve voter turnout and voting procedures.

LO⁵ Discuss the different factors that affect voter choices.

Online Polling—The Wave of the Future?

Opinion polling has been used in politics for decades. The news media have often used poll results to sell newspapers and later to generate interest in radio programs and television news shows. Political candidates like to conduct polls to determine which issues are most important during a campaign. These same candidates use polls to find out if they are going to win or lose in the next elections. Polling techniques have become more scientific as polling organizations have improved the process of random sampling. Indeed, no traditional pollster would even consider using a survey that did not reflect the general population. After all, the concept behind small-sample polling is to come up with polling results that reflect what the American public truly believes.

Enter a new type of polling organization—no more ringing doorbells, interviewing on the street, or calling phone numbers. Instead, go to the Internet because that is where the action is. Internet-based polling companies believe that they can find out about consumer preferences and even predict election outcomes by using a panel of online respondents who answer questions through an online survey. The panelists are recruited from different subsections of the population, such as the elderly, the young, low-income groups, high-income groups, those who have a college education, those who have only a high school education, and the like. One such company, YouGov, promised in 2007 to have a full-on Internet polling system in place for the presidential elections in 2008.

Online Polling Is Here to Stay, and That's for the Better

YouGov started in 2001 in Britain. It claims that its online polling results have reflected actual votes better than traditional polling methods have. The *Daily Telegraph,* one of London's largest newspapers, uses YouGov to poll its online panelists twice a month. The *Daily Telegraph* is satisfied with the results. The key, of course, is creating a *balanced* panel of regular online respondents. The panelists, who are paid for their participation, have to come from all sectors of the population, but that is not so hard to do when working on the Internet.

In any event, traditional polling organizations that rely on telephone surveys are encountering problems. As more and more people use cell phones instead of fixed landline phones, it has become increasingly difficult to track down people at their homes. With Internet polling, you can pinpoint a narrow group of people almost immediately and find out what they think about a particular topic.

INTERNET POLLING'S TIME IS NOT YET READY FOR THE BIG LEAGUE

Skeptics of online polling point out that there are large groups of individuals who are still not connected to the Internet. Older voters, lower-income voters, and rural voters tend to be underrepresented in the online world. Consequently, no Internet polling system can truly be representative of the entire population. As Joel Benenson, who worked on the presidential campaign of Senator Barack Obama (D., Ill.), said, "There are some uses for online polling, but it still misses out on too much of the population for us."

The variances are too great to judge the views of the general population from the results of an online poll. Some argue that Internet polling is like the Wild West—no sheriff, no reference points, and no rules. Even those who believe that some online polling is useful are unwilling to use it to make decisions about important public-policy issues of the day.

Where do you stand?

1. What percentage of the U.S. population needs to be connected to the Internet in order for online polling to become accurate? Explain.
2. Does it matter what type of polling technique is used as long as it results in relatively accurate forecasts? Explain your answer.

Explore this issue online

- The National Council on Public Polls, an association of almost all of the famous polling organizations, has strong opinions about what makes a poll valid. It describes Internet polls as "completely unreliable." See the council's advice on how to read polls at **www.ncpp.org**.
- Internet polling is a major topic at **www.fantasypoliticsusa.com**, a political blog with a presidential fantasy game patterned on *American Idol.*

INTRODUCTION

Many Americans are concerned about the low number of citizens who have turned out to vote during some recent elections. After all, if people do not vote, how can their opinions affect public policy? In a democracy, at a minimum, members of the public must form opinions and openly express them to their elected public officials. Only when the opinions of Americans are communicated effectively to elected representatives can those opinions form the basis of government action. As President Franklin D. Roosevelt once said, "A government can be no better than the public opinion that sustains it."

What exactly is *public opinion*? How do we form our opinions on political issues? How can public opinion be measured accurately? And, as asked in this chapter's opening *America at Odds* feature, will Internet polling be the wave of the future? Finally, what factors affect voter participation?

Researchers and scholars have addressed these questions time and again. They are important questions because the backbone of our democracy has always been civic participation—taking part in the political life of the country. Civic participation means many things, but perhaps the most important way that Americans participate in their democracy is through voting—expressing their opinions in the polling places.

"A GOVERNMENT CAN BE NO BETTER THAN THE PUBLIC OPINION THAT SUSTAINS IT."

FRANKLIN DELANO ROOSEVELT,
THIRTY-SECOND PRESIDENT OF THE UNITED STATES
1933–1945

ticle stating that "a significant number of Americans" feel a certain way about an issue, you are probably hearing that a particular opinion is held by a large enough number of people to make government officials turn their heads and listen. For example, public opinion surveys in 2006 and 2007 showed that the majority of Americans opposed the Iraq war. When the Democrats took control of Congress in 2007, they responded to public opinion by doing what they could to oppose President George W. Bush's "stay the course" policy. Additionally, as the 2008 presidential primary races got under way, one of the leading issues addressed by all candidates was the war in Iraq.

LO¹ WHAT IS PUBLIC OPINION?

People hold opinions—sometimes very strong ones—about a variety of issues, ranging from the ethics of capital punishment to the latest trends in fashion. In this chapter, however, we are concerned with only a portion of those opinions. For our purposes here, we define **public opinion** as the views of the citizenry on a particular issue. Public opinion is the sum total of a complex collection of opinions held by many people on issues in the public arena, such as taxes, health care, Social Security, clean-air legislation, and unemployment.

When you hear a news report or read a magazine ar-

An NBC pollster conducts an interview. Public opinion polls allow us to measure public opinion on a given issue at a given point in time.

Billy E. Barnes/PhotoEdit

public opinion The views of the citizenry about politics, public issues, and public policies; a complex collection of opinions held by many people on issues in the public arena.

LO² HOW DO PEOPLE FORM POLITICAL OPINIONS?

When asked, most Americans are willing to express an opinion on political issues. Not one of us, however, was born with such opinions. Most people acquire their political attitudes, opinions, beliefs, and knowledge through a complex learning process called **political socialization.** This process begins early in childhood and continues throughout the person's life.

Most political socialization is informal, and it usually begins during early childhood, when the dominant influence on a child is the family. Although parents normally do not sit down and say to their children, "Let us explain to you the virtues of becoming a Democrat," their children nevertheless come to know the parents' feelings, beliefs, and attitudes. The strong early influence of the family later gives way to the multiple influences of school, peers, television, co-workers, and other groups. People and institutions that influence the political views of others are called **agents of political socialization.**

The Importance of Family

As just suggested, most parents or guardians do not deliberately set out to form their children's political ideas and beliefs. They are usually more concerned with the moral, religious, and ethical values of their offspring. Yet a child first sees the political world through the eyes of his or her family, which is perhaps the most important force in political socialization. Children do not "learn" political attitudes the same way they learn to master in-line skating. Rather, they learn by hearing their parents' everyday conversations and stories about politicians and issues and by observing their parents' actions. They also learn from watching and listening to their siblings,

as well as from the kinds of situations in which their parents place them.

The family's influence is strongest when children clearly perceive their parents' attitudes. For example, in one study, more high school students could identify their parents' political party affiliation than their parents' other attitudes or beliefs. In many situations, the political party of the parents becomes the political party of the children, particularly if both parents belong to the same party.

The Schools and Educational Attainment

Education also strongly influences an individual's political attitudes. From their earliest days in school, children learn about the American political system. They say the Pledge of Allegiance and sing patriotic songs. They celebrate national holidays, such as Presidents' Day and Veterans' Day, and learn about the history and symbols associated with them. In the upper grades, young people acquire more knowledge about government and democratic procedures through civics classes and through student government and various clubs. They also learn citizenship skills through school rules and regulations. Generally, those with more education have more knowledge about politics and policy than those with less education. The level of education also influences a person's political values, as will be discussed later in this chapter.

Political socialization starts at a very young age, usually within the family unit. Children also learn about politics and government through such activities as reciting the Pledge of Allegiance in school and participating in Fourth of July celebrations.

Mary Kate Denny/PhotoEdit

political socialization
A learning process through which most people acquire their political attitudes, opinions, beliefs, and knowledge.

agents of political socialization People and institutions that influence the political views of others.

Michael Newman/PhotoEdit

Students learn about the political process early on when they participate in class elections.

dents know less about American civics at the end of their college careers than when they started.

Clearly, there is a failure of civics instruction at the college level. Many believe that if America's young people know little or nothing about the nation's history and institutions, they will be unable to fulfill their obligations and duties as citizens in our democracy. Today's students are, after all, tomorrow's leaders. How can they possibly make decisions consistent with our founding documents and traditions? Colleges should require students to take courses in political science and American government in order to graduate. Colleges should also require all students to pass a comprehensive examination on this nation's political institutions.

Not everyone is so worried. Some people do not believe that institutions of higher education should be in the business of training better citizens. Knowledge of our political process and government should already have been instilled during the elementary, junior high, and high school years. We should focus on teaching civics to students from kindergarten through twelfth grade, not on teaching civics in college. Young adults should spend their time in colleges and universities learning how to make a good living so that they can contribute to the productivity and economic growth of this nation.

Although the schools have always been important agents of political socialization, many Americans today believe that our schools are not fulfilling this mission. Too many students are graduating from high school—and even college—with too little knowledge of the American system of government.

JOIN THE DEBATE

Should Colleges Be Training Grounds for Better Citizens?

As you discovered in the *Join the Debate* feature for Chapter 2 on page 37, the majority of Americans cannot name even one of their First Amendment rights. The National Assessment of Educational Progress in 2007 showed that only about one-fourth of twelfth graders had a proficient knowledge of civics. Even though many assume that college graduates know more about civics than high school seniors do, in fact they do not. The Intercollegiate Studies Institute sponsored a sample of more than 14,000 college freshmen and seniors across the country. The conclusion? Even the nation's most prestigious colleges and universities do not increase students' knowledge about America's history and institutions. Moreover, many stu-

The Media

The **media**—newspapers, magazines, television, radio, and the Internet—also have an impact on political socialization. The most influential of these media is, of course, television. Television does not necessarily decrease the level of information about politics. On the contrary, it continues to be the leading source of political and public affairs information for most people.

Some contend that the media's role in shaping public opinion is increasing to the point at which the media are as influential as the family, particularly among high school students. For example, in her analysis of the media's role in American

media Newspapers, magazines, television, radio, the Internet, and any other printed or electronic means of communication.

politics, media scholar Doris A. Graber points out that high school students, when asked where they obtain the information on which they base their attitudes, mention the mass media far more than their families, friends, and teachers.[1] Graber's conclusion takes on added significance in view of a 2006 Gallup poll showing that only about half of the parents polled were concerned about their children's TV-viewing habits, even when their children watched TV "a great deal" or a "fair amount" of time. Also, only about half of the respondents were aware that their television sets were equipped with parental controls, and most within that group rarely if ever used those functions.

Other studies have shown that the media's influence on people's opinions may not be as great as was once thought. Generally, people watch television, read articles, or access online sites with preconceived ideas about the issues. These preconceived ideas act as a kind of perceptual screen that blocks out information that is not consistent with those ideas. For example, if you are already firmly convinced that daily meditation is beneficial for your health, you probably will not change your mind if you watch a TV show that asserts that those who meditate live no longer on aver-

> "I have experienced many instances of being obliged... to change opinions, even on **important subjects,** which I once thought right but found to be otherwise."
>
> BENJAMIN FRANKLIN,
> AMERICAN STATESMAN
> 1706–1790

age than people who do not. Generally, the media tend to wield the most influence over the views of persons who have not yet formed opinions about certain issues or political candidates. (See Chapter 10 for a more detailed discussion of the media's role in American politics.)

Opinion Leaders

Every state or community has well-known citizens who are able to influence the opinions of their fellow citizens. These people may be public officials, religious leaders, teachers, or celebrities. They are the people to whom others listen and from whom others draw ideas and convictions about various issues of public concern. These opinion leaders play a significant role in the formation of public opinion. Al Gore, for example, has long been a powerful and outspoken opinion leader for environmental concerns.

Opinion leaders often include politicians or former politicians, such as Al Gore, as just mentioned. Certainly, Americans' attitudes are influenced by the public statements of important government leaders such as the president or secretary of state. Sometimes, however, opinion leaders can fall from grace when they express views radically different from what most Americans believe. This was true for President George W. Bush. His insistence on continuing the widely unpopular war in Iraq was a major factor in causing his approval ratings to dip to historically low levels.

Major Life Events

Often, the political attitudes of an entire generation of Americans are influenced by a major event. For example, the Great Depression (1929–1939), the most severe economic depression in modern U.S. history, persuaded many Americans who lived through it that the federal government should step in when the economy is in decline. Many observers then felt that increased federal spending and explicit job-creation programs contributed to the economic recovery. The generation that lived through World War II (1939–

Opinion leaders, such as former vice president Al Gore (shown here), help in forming public opinion. Gore produced a documentary on climate change and then went around the world speaking about his environmental concerns.

AP Photo

WITH A MILITARY DRAFT, WOULD WE STILL BE IN IRAQ?

uring the 1960s and early 1970s, there were street protests year after year against the Vietnam War (1964–1975). In a sentence, the Vietnam War was intensely unpopular. At the time, polls showed that more than 70 percent of Americans wanted the war to end. Flash forward about three decades to the war in Iraq. It, too, is an extremely unpopular war. But there are almost no street demonstrations against it. Some say that this is because the number of U.S. soldiers killed in Iraq is much smaller than the number who died during the Vietnam War. Others point to another possible explanation—there is no military draft today as there was during the Vietnam War.

Anti-war march on the Pentagon in 1967.

AP Photo

SHOULD WE BRING BACK THE DRAFT?

Through much of our nation's history, we had a military draft, but it often was not popular. Riots over the military draft occurred as early as the Civil War in New York City. One constant aspect of the military draft was that draftees were not paid very much. Consequently, during any war, much of the financial burden of the war fell on them, not on the average taxpayer. The low-pay issue notwithstanding, some argue that we should reinstitute the draft. Those in favor of bringing back the draft, such as Representative Charles Rangel (D., N.Y.) and John Roper of Emory & Henry College, believe that citizen soldiers accomplished their mission in every war from 1775 to 1973, when the draft was eliminated and the all-volunteer army that we still have today was instituted.

WITH A UNIVERSAL DRAFT, WOULD WE HAVE INVADED IRAQ?

Representative Rangel claims that President Bush never would have invaded Iraq had there been a universal military draft in place. Even those who do not agree with him believe that the pressure to withdraw earlier from Iraq would have been greater if young men (and women) were being drafted, including sons and daughters of lawmakers. Violent opposition to the war would probably have been far greater if those killed or seriously wounded had been draftees.

YOU BE THE JUDGE

Some Americans, including Representative Rangel, believe that we should bring back the draft so that the physical risks of sacrificing life and limb are spread more equally throughout society. Others maintain that an all-volunteer army leads to better military performance. Where do you stand on this issue?

1945) tends to believe that American intervention in foreign affairs is good. In contrast, the generation that came of age during the Vietnam War (1964–1975) is more skeptical of American interventionism. A national tragedy, such as the terrorist attacks of September 11, 2001, is also likely to influence the political attitudes of a generation of Americans, though in what way is as yet difficult to predict. Certainly, the U.S. government's

response to that event, and particularly the war in Iraq, has elicited deep concern on the part of Americans. Notably, however, opposition to the war has not led to the widespread antiwar demonstrations that took place during another unpopular war—in Vietnam—years ago. This chapter's *The Politics of National Security* feature offers a possible explanation for the absence of such protests against the Iraq war.

These Tulane University students are working on a clean-up project after Hurricane Katrina devastated parts of New Orleans. The social views of these students are heavily influenced by the attitudes and beliefs of their peers. To some extent, the same is true with respect to their political views.

Peer Groups

Once children enter school, the views of friends begin to influence their attitudes and beliefs. From junior high school on, the **peer group**—friends, classmates, co-workers, club members, or religious group members—becomes a significant factor in the political socialization process. Most of this socialization occurs when the peer group is intimately involved in political activities. For example, your political beliefs might be influenced by a peer group with which you are working on a common political cause, such as preventing the clear-cutting of old-growth forests or saving an endangered species. Your political beliefs probably would not be as strongly influenced by peers with whom you snowboard regularly or attend concerts.

Some Americans worry that peer influence, particularly at the high school level, may be a negative agent in the political socialization process because of the increasing hostility among teens to traditional American values and political culture. For example, one poll indicated that about one-third of teens believe that they are under a "great deal" or "some" pressure from their peers to "break the rules." Additionally, about half of the teens surveyed said that

peer group Associates, often those close in age to oneself; may include friends, classmates, co-workers, club members, or religious group members. Peer group influence is a significant factor in the political socialization process.

public opinion poll A numerical survey of the public's opinion on a particular topic at a particular moment.

they "like to live dangerously" and to "shock people." Polls also indicate that a significant number of high school students blame peer influence for the "bad things" that are happening in America, such as school killings.

For whatever reason, there is a wide perception among Americans that there has been a notable decline in our moral values. According to a Gallup poll released in May 2007, 83 percent of those polled rated the state of moral values in this country as "only fair" or "poor," and 82 percent thought that the situation was getting worse.

Economic Status and Occupation

A person's economic status may influence her or his political views. For example, poorer people are more likely to favor government assistance programs. On an issue such as abortion, lower-income people are more likely to be conservative—that is, to be against abortion—than are higher-income groups (of course, there are many exceptions).

Where a person works will also affect her or his opinion. Individuals who spend a great deal of time working together tend to be influenced by their co-workers. For example, labor union members working together for a company will tend to have similar political opinions, at least on the issue of government involvement in labor. Individuals working for a nonprofit agency that depends on government funds will tend to support government spending in that area. Business managers are more likely to favor tax laws helpful to businesses than are factory workers.

LO³ MEASURING PUBLIC OPINION

If public opinion is to affect public policy, then public officials must be made aware of it. They must know which issues are of current concern to Americans and how strongly people feel about those issues. They must also know when public opinion changes. Of course, public officials most commonly learn about public opinion through election results, personal contacts, interest groups, and media reports. The only relatively precise way to measure public opinion, however, is through the use of public opinion polls.

A **public opinion poll** is a numerical survey of the public's opinion on a particular topic at a particular moment.

The results of opinion polls are most often cast in terms of percentages: 62 percent feel this way, 27 percent do not, and 11 percent have no opinion. Of course, a poll cannot survey the entire U.S. population. Therefore, public opinion pollsters have devised scientific polling techniques for measuring public opinion through the use of **samples**—groups of people who are typical of the general population.

Early Polling Efforts

Since the 1800s, magazines and newspapers have often spiced up their articles by conducting **straw polls,** or mail surveys, of readers' opinions. Straw polls try to read the public's collective mind by simply asking a large number of people the same question. Today, many newspapers and magazines still run "mail-in" polls. Increasingly, though, straw polls make use of telephone technology—encouraging people to call "900" numbers, for example—or the Internet. Visitors to a Web page can instantly register their opinion on an issue with the click of a mouse. The problem with straw polls is that the opinions expressed usually represent only a small subgroup of the population, or a **biased sample.** A survey of those who read the *Wall Street Journal* will most likely produce different results than a survey of those who read the *Reader's Digest.*

The most famous of all straw-polling errors was committed by the *Literary Digest* in 1936 when it tried to predict the presidential election's outcome. The *Digest* had accurately predicted the winning candidates in several earlier presidential elections, but in 1936 the *Digest* predicted that Alfred Landon would easily defeat incumbent Franklin D. Roosevelt. Instead, Roosevelt won by a landslide. The editors of the *Digest* had sent mail-in cards to citizens whose names appeared in telephone directories, to its own subscribers, and to automobile owners—in all, to a staggering 2,376,000 people. In the mid-Depression year of 1936, however, people who owned a car or a telephone or who subscribed to the *Digest* were certainly not representative of the majority of Americans. The vast majority of Americans were on the opposite end of the socioeconomic ladder. Despite the enormous number of people surveyed, the sample was unrepresentative and consequently inaccurate.

Several newcomers to the public opinion poll industry, however, did predict Roosevelt's landslide victory. Two of these organizations are still at the forefront of the polling industry today: the Gallup Organization, started by George Gallup; and Roper Associates, founded by Elmo Roper and now known as the Roper Center.

Polling Today

As you read in the chapter-opening *America at Odds* feature, polling is used extensively by political candidates and policymakers today. Politicians and the news media generally place a great deal of faith in the accuracy of poll results. Polls can be remarkably accurate when they are conducted properly. In the last fourteen presidential elections, Gallup polls conducted early in September predicted the eventual winners in eleven of the fourteen races. Even polls taken several months in advance have been able to predict the eventual winner quite well. This success is largely the result of careful sampling techniques.

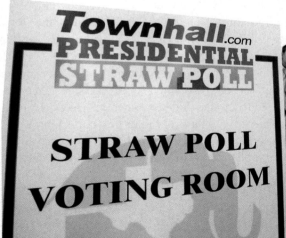

Straw polls started in the 1800s to increase newspaper and magazine sales. Today, they are still used. This straw poll, taken in September 2007, asked Texas residents whom they would vote for in the 2008 presidential elections.

Tom Pennington/MCT/Landov

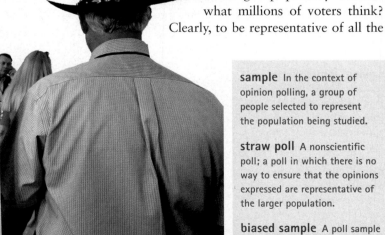

SAMPLING Today, most Gallup polls sample between 1,500 and 2,000 people. How can interviewing such a small group possibly indicate what millions of voters think? Clearly, to be representative of all the

sample In the context of opinion polling, a group of people selected to represent the population being studied.

straw poll A nonscientific poll; a poll in which there is no way to ensure that the opinions expressed are representative of the larger population.

biased sample A poll sample that does not accurately represent the population.

voters in the population, a sample must consist of a group of people who are typical of the general population. If the sample is properly selected, the opinions of those in the sample will be representative of the opinions held by the population as a whole. If the sample is not properly chosen, then the results of the poll may not reflect the ideas of the general population.

The most important principle in sampling is randomness. A **random sample** means that each person within the entire population being polled has an equal chance of being chosen. For example, if a poll is trying to measure how women feel about an issue, the sample should include respondents from all groups within the female population in proportion to their percentage of the entire population. A properly drawn random sample, therefore, would include appropriate numbers of women in terms of age, racial and ethnic characteristics, occupation, geography, household income level, and religious affiliation.

BIAS   In addition to trying to secure a random sample, poll takers also want to ensure that there is no bias in their polling questions. How a question is phrased can significantly affect how people answer it. Consider a question about whether high-speed connections to the Internet should be added to the school library's computer center. One way to survey opinions on this issue is simply to ask, "Do you believe that the school district should provide high-speed connections to the Internet?" Another way to ask the same question is, "Are you willing to pay higher property taxes so that the school district can have high-speed connections to the Internet?" Undoubtedly, the poll results will differ depending on how the question is phrased.

Polling questions also sometimes reduce complex issues to questions that simply call for "yes" or "no" answers.

> "A **POPULAR** GOVERNMENT WITHOUT POPULAR INFORMATION, OR THE MEANS OF ACQUIRING IT, IS BUT A PROLOGUE TO A FARCE OR A **TRAGEDY**, OR PERHAPS BOTH."
>
> JAMES MADISON,
> FOURTH PRESIDENT OF THE UNITED STATES
> 1809–1817

For example, a survey question might ask respondents whether they favor giving aid to foreign countries. A respondent's opinion on the issue might vary, depending on the recipient country or the purpose and type of the aid. The poll would nonetheless force the respondent to give a "yes" or "no" answer that does not necessarily reflect his or her true opinion.

Respondents to such questions sometimes answer "I don't know" or "I don't have enough information to answer," even when the poll does not offer such answers. Interestingly, a study of how polling is conducted on the complex issue of school vouchers (school vouchers were discussed in Chapter 4) found that about 4 percent volunteered the answer "I don't know" when asked if they favored or opposed vouchers. When respondents were offered the option of answering "I haven't heard or read enough to answer," however, the proportion choosing that answer jumped to 33 percent.[2]

RELIABILITY OF POLLS   In addition to potential bias, poll takers must also be concerned about the general reliability of their polls. Those interviewed may be influenced by the interviewer's personality or tone of voice. They may answer without having any information on the issue, or they may give the answer that they think will please the interviewer. Additionally, any opinion poll contains a **sampling error,** which is the difference between what the sample results show and what the true results would have been had everybody in the relevant population been interviewed. (For a further look at how polling can lead to misleading results, see this chapter's *Perception versus Reality* feature.)

Opinion polls of voter preferences cannot reflect rapid shifts in public opinion unless they are taken frequently. During the 2004 presidential elections, polls showed George W. Bush ahead at times and John Kerry ahead at other times. The media reported extensively on the many polls conducted, with seemingly wild discrepancies. In the weeks prior to Election Day, a poll from Gallup, *USA Today,* and CNN showed Bush leading Kerry by a margin of eight points. Meanwhile, a poll by ABC News and the *Washington Post* showed Bush leading by a three-point margin. Yet another poll by the *New York Times* and CBS News showed the race as a tie.

random sample In the context of opinion polling, a sample in which each person within the entire population being polled has an equal chance of being chosen.

sampling error In the context of opinion polling, the difference between what the sample results show and what the true results would have been had everybody in the relevant population been interviewed.

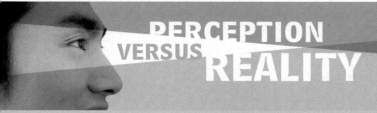

PERCEPTION VERSUS REALITY

The Accuracy of Public Opinion Polls

Today, more than ever before, Americans are bombarded with the results of public opinion polls. If you can think of a political candidate, topic, issue, or concept, chances are one or more public polling organizations can tell you what "Americans really think" about that candidate or topic. Polling organizations increasingly use telephone interviews and the Internet to conduct their polls. Because these polls are much cheaper to conduct than "feet on the street" polling, it is not surprising that more poll results are available literally every day. If you subscribe to the online services of the Gallup poll, for example, at least once a week Gallup will send you about a dozen topics on which that organization has obtained information about Americans' opinions.

The Perception

Those Americans who hear or read about public opinion polls naturally assume that polling organizations undertook them in a scientific way and presented accurate results. Those who know a little bit about polling also assume that the small numbers of people polled are from a random sample.

The Reality

Many polls are not based on a random sample. Consider a recent poll published by the American Medical Association that claimed to have found that college women were engaging in an "alarming rate" of unprotected sex during spring break. That "random" sample included only women who voluntarily answered ten questions. Of the group volunteering, only 25 percent had actually ever taken a spring-break trip. Yet those who read about the poll in the *New York Times* would naturally assume that the pollsters had used scientific polling techniques, including a random sampling, when conducting the poll.

Think also about how respondents answer interviewers' questions. Consider one *New York Times*/CBS News poll in which voters were asked if they had voted in a presidential election. Seventy-three percent said yes, although the U.S. Census Bureau later determined that only 64 percent of eligible voters had actually voted in that election. Analysts concluded that those who had been interviewed wanted to appear to be "good citizens," so not all of them told the truth.

Do not forget about sampling error. Assume that two candidates for president are neck and neck in the opinion polls, but that the sampling error is 4 percent. That means that one candidate could actually be ahead by 54 percent to 46 percent, or vice versa.

BLOG ON

- You'll find a poll-lover's dream at Mark Blumenthal's **www.pollster.com/blogs**, where readers debate about all the recent polls. Pollster.com's main page, **www.pollster.com**, is also a trove of information about polls. Blumenthal previously managed the Mystery Pollster blog at **www.mysterypollster.com**, which is now an archive.
- America Online (AOL) is one of the largest sites around, and it offers blogs on almost every topic. You can join AOL's discussion of polls at **news.aol.com/elections-blog/category/polls**.

EXIT POLLS The reliability of polls was also called into question by the use of exit polls in the 2000 presidential elections. The Voter News Service (VNS)—a consortium of news networks—conducted polls of people exiting polling places on Election Day. These exit polls were used by the news networks to predict the winner of the Florida race—and they were wrong, not just once, but twice. First, they claimed that the Florida vote had gone to Al Gore. Then, a few hours later, they said it had gone to George W. Bush. Finally, they said the Florida race was too close to call.

These miscalls of the election outcome in Florida caused substantial confusion—and frustration—for the candidates as well as for the voters. They also led to a significant debate over exit polls: Should exit polls be banned, even though they provide valuable information on voter behavior and preferences?

One noticeable difference in the media coverage of the 2002 congressional elections was the lack of exit polls. On Election Day in 2002, the VNS announced that it would not release exit poll data, stating that it was "not satisfied with the accuracy" of its exit polls. Media outlets were forced to rely more heavily on returns from state election officials, and many close elections were not called until very late that night. In January 2003, the VNS went out of business.

Exit polls were also employed during the 2004 presidential elections. Again the results were disastrous.

During the early hours of the elections, exit polls caused the media to conclude that Democratic candidate John Kerry was leading in the race. Preliminary results of exit polls were leaked to the Internet by midafternoon. The word went out worldwide that Kerry was ahead of Bush and by a relatively large margin. After the votes were tallied, however, the exit poll results were shown to have inflated Kerry's support by 6.5 percent—the largest margin of error in decades.

MISUSE OF POLLS   Today, a frequently heard complaint is that, instead of measuring public opinion, polls can end up creating it. For example, to gain popularity, a candidate might claim that all the polls show that he is ahead in the race. People who want to support the winning candidate (rather than the candidate of their choice) may support this candidate despite their true feelings. This is often called the "bandwagon" effect. Presidential approval ratings lend themselves to the bandwagon effect.

The media also sometimes misuse polls. Many journalists take the easy route during campaigns and base their political coverage almost exclusively on poll findings, with no mention of the chance for bias or the margin of error in the poll. A useful checklist for evaluating the quality of opinion polls is presented in Table 8–1. An increasingly common misuse of polls by politicians is the *push poll*, discussed next.

DEFINING A PUSH POLL   A relatively recent tactic in political campaigns is to use **push polls,** which ask "fake" polling questions that are actually designed to "push" voters toward one candidate or another. The use of push polls has become so prevalent today that many states are taking steps to ban them. The problem with trying to ban push polls, or even to report accurately on which candidates are using them, is that defining a push poll can be difficult.

The National Council on Public Polls describes push polls as outright political manipulation, the spreading of rumors and lies by one candidate about another. For example, a push poll might ask, "Do you believe the rumor that Candidate A misused campaign funds to pay for a family vacation to Hawaii?" Push pollsters usually do not give their

push poll A campaign tactic used to feed false or misleading information to potential voters, under the guise of taking an opinion poll, with the intent to "push" voters away from one candidate and toward another.

TABLE 8-1

CHECKLIST FOR EVALUATING PUBLIC OPINION POLLS

Because public opinion polls are so widely used by the media and policymakers, and their reliability is so often called into question, several organizations have issued guidelines for evaluating polls. Below is a list of questions that you can ask to evaluate the quality and reliability of a poll. You can find the answers to many, if not all, of these questions in the polling organization's report accompanying the poll results.

1. Who conducted the poll, and who sponsored or paid for it?
2. How many people were interviewed for the survey, and what part of the population did they represent (for example, registered voters, likely voters, persons over age eighteen)?
3. How were these people chosen, and how random was the sample?
4. How were respondents contacted and interviewed (by telephone, by mail-in survey)?
5. Who should have been interviewed but was not (what was the "non-response" rate—people who should have been part of the random sample but who refused to be interviewed, do not have telephones, or do not have listed telephone numbers, for example)?
6. What is the margin of error for the poll? (The acceptable margin of error for national polls is usually plus or minus 4 percent.)
7. What questions did the poll ask?
8. In what order were the questions asked?
9. When was the poll conducted?
10. What other polls were conducted on this topic, and do they report similar findings?

name or identify the poll's sponsor. The interviews last less than a minute, whereas legitimate pollsters typically interview a respondent for five to thirty minutes. Based on these characteristics, it can sometimes be easy to distinguish a push poll from a legitimate poll conducted by a respected research organization. The checklist in Table 8–1 can also help you distinguish between a legitimate poll and a push poll.

Some researchers argue that identifying a push poll is not that easy, however. Political analyst Charlie Cook points out that "there are legitimate polls that can ask push questions, which test potential arguments against a rival to ascertain how effective those arguments might be in future advertising. . . . These are not only legitimate tools of survey research, but any political pollster who did not use them would be doing his or her clients a real disservice."[3] Distinguishing between push polls and push questions, then, is sometimes difficult—which is usually the intent of the push pollsters. A candidate does not want to be accused of conducting push polls because the public considers them a "dirty trick" and

FIGURE 8–1

VOTER TURNOUT SINCE 1964

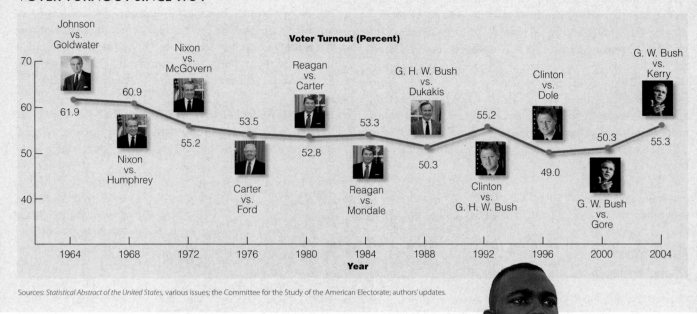

Voter Turnout (Percent)

Johnson vs. Goldwater — 61.9

60.9 — Nixon vs. Humphrey — 55.2

Nixon vs. McGovern

53.5 — Carter vs. Ford

Reagan vs. Carter — 52.8

53.3 — Reagan vs. Mondale — 50.3

G. H. W. Bush vs. Dukakis

55.2 — Clinton vs. G. H. W. Bush

Clinton vs. Dole — 49.0

50.3 — G. W. Bush vs. Gore

G. W. Bush vs. Kerry — 55.3

Year
1964   1968   1972   1976   1980   1984   1988   1992   1996   2000   2004

Sources: *Statistical Abstract of the United States,* various issues; the Committee for the Study of the American Electorate; authors' updates.

may turn against the candidate who uses them. In several recent campaigns, candidates have accused each other of conducting push polls—accusations that could not always be proved or disproved. The result has been an increase in public cynicism about opinion polls and the political process in general.

LO⁴ VOTING AND VOTER TURNOUT

Voting is arguably the most important way in which citizens participate in the political process. Because we do not live in a direct democracy, Americans use the vote to elect politicians to represent their interests, values, and opinions in government. In many states, public-policy decisions—such as access to medical marijuana—are decided by voters. Americans' right to vote also helps keep elected officials accountable to campaign promises because they must face reelection.

Factors Affecting Voter Turnout

If voting is so important, then why do so many Americans fail to exercise their right to vote? Why is voter turnout—the percentage of the voting-age population that actually turns out to vote—so relatively low? As you will read shortly, in the past, legal restrictions based on income, gender, race, and other factors kept a number of people from voting. Today, those restrictions have

An African American does his part to "get out the vote" before an election. African Americans faced significant restrictions on voting until the 1950s and 1960s, when new laws and policies helped to end both formal and informal barriers to voting for this group. Today, although voter turnout among African Americans is increasing, they remain underrepresented at the polls.

virtually disappeared, yet voter turnout in presidential elections has hovered around the 50 to 55 percent level for the past four decades, as you can see in Figure 8–1.

Bob Daemmrich/Sygma/Corbis

According to a Pew Research Center survey of voter turnout, one of the reasons for low voter turnout is that a significant number of nonvoters (close to 40 percent) do not feel that they have a duty to vote. The survey also found that nearly 70 percent of nonvoters said that they did not vote because they lacked information about the candidates.[4] And many observers cite the increasing public cynicism about the political process, particularly among younger Americans, as an important factor in voter turnout. Finally, some people believe that their vote will not make any difference, so they do not bother to become informed on the candidates or issues and go to the polls.

The Legal Right to Vote

In the United States today, all citizens who are at least eighteen years of age have the right to vote. This was not always true,

however. Recall from Chapter 5 that restrictions on *suffrage*, the legal right to vote, have existed since the founding of our nation. Expanding the right to vote has been an important part of the gradual democratization of the American electoral process. Table 8–2 summarizes the major amendments, Supreme Court decisions, and laws that extended the right to vote to various American groups.

HISTORICAL RESTRICTIONS ON VOTING   Those who drafted the Constitution left the power to set suffrage qualifications to the individual states. Most states limited suffrage to adult white males who owned property, but these restrictions were challenged early on in the history of the republic. By 1810, religious restrictions on the right to vote were abolished in all states, and property ownership and tax-payment

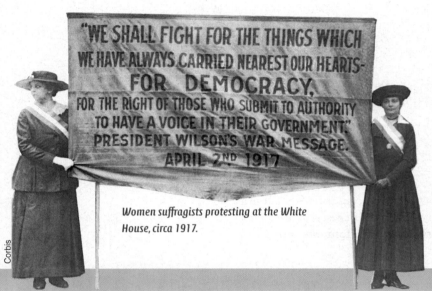

Women suffragists protesting at the White House, circa 1917.

Corbis

TABLE 8–2

EXTENSION OF THE RIGHT TO VOTE

Year	Action	Impact
1870	Fifteenth Amendment	Discrimination based on race outlawed.
1920	Nineteenth Amendment	Discrimination based on gender outlawed.
1924	Congressional act	All Native Americans given citizenship.
1944	*Smith v. Allwright*	Supreme Court prohibits white primary.
1957	Civil Rights Act of 1957	Justice Department can sue to protect voting rights in various states.
1960	Civil Rights Act of 1960	Courts authorized to appoint referees to assist voter-registration procedures.
1961	Twenty-third Amendment	Residents of District of Columbia given right to vote for president and vice president.
1964	Twenty-fourth Amendment	Poll tax in national elections outlawed.
1965	Voting Rights Act of 1965	Literacy tests prohibited; federal voter registrars authorized in seven southern states.
1970	Voting Rights Act Amendments of 1970	Voting age for federal elections reduced to eighteen years; maximum thirty-day residency requirement for presidential elections; state literacy tests abolished.
1971	Twenty-sixth Amendment	Minimum voting age reduced to eighteen for all elections.
1975	Voting Rights Act Amendments of 1975	Federal voter registrars authorized in ten more states; bilingual ballots to be used in certain circumstances.
1982	Voting Rights Act Amendments of 1982	Extended provisions of Voting Rights Act amendments of 1970 and 1975; private parties allowed to sue for violations.

Civil rights protesters, led by Martin Luther King, Jr., march on the road from Selma to Montgomery, Alabama, in March 1965. During the five-day, fifty-mile march, federal troops were stationed every one hundred yards along the route to protect the marchers from violent attacks by segregationists.

discussed in Chapter 5. Furthermore, the Nineteenth Amendment gave women the right to vote in 1920. In 1971, the Twenty-sixth Amendment reduced the voting age to eighteen.

Some restrictions on voting rights still exist. Every state except North Dakota requires voters to register with the appropriate state or local officials before voting. Residency requirements are also usually imposed for voting. Since 1970, no state can impose a residency requirement of more than thirty days. Twenty-five states require that length of time, while the other twenty-five states require fewer or no days. Another voting requirement is citizenship. Aliens may not vote in any public election held anywhere in the United States. Most states also do not permit prison inmates, mentally ill people, convicted felons, or election-law violators to vote.

requirements gradually began to disappear as well. By 1850, all white males were allowed to vote. Restrictions based on race and gender continued, however.

The Fifteenth Amendment, ratified in 1870, guaranteed suffrage to African American males. Yet, for many decades, African Americans were effectively denied the ability to exercise their voting rights. Using methods ranging from mob violence to economic restrictions, groups of white southerners kept black Americans from voting. Some states required those who wished to vote to pass **literacy tests** and to answer complicated questions about government and history before they could register to vote. These tests, however, were not evenly applied to whites and African Americans. The **poll tax,** a fee of several dollars, was another device used to prevent African Americans from voting. At the time, this tax was a sizable burden, not only for most blacks but also for immigrants, small farmers, and the poor generally. Another popular restriction was the **grandfather clause,** which restricted the franchise (voting rights) to those whose grandfathers had voted.

Still another voting barrier was the **white primary**— African Americans were prohibited from voting in the primary elections. The United States Supreme Court initially upheld this practice, concluding that the political parties were private entities, not public, and thus could do as they wished. Eventually, in 1944, the Court banned the use of white primaries.[5]

VOTING RIGHTS TODAY Today, these devices for restricting voting rights are explicitly outlawed by constitutional amendments and by the Voting Rights Act of 1965, as

Attempts to Improve Voter Turnout

Some voters have said that various voting requirements and restrictions keep them from voting on Election Day. Attempts to improve voter turnout typically involve a partisan dimension. This is because many unregistered voters are African Americans and immigrants, and affiliate with the Democratic Party rather than with the Republican Party. For example, Republicans generally opposed the passage of the National Voter Registration Act (the "Motor Voter Law") of 1993, which simplified the voter-registration process. The act requires states to provide all eligible citizens with the opportunity to register to vote when they apply for or renew a driver's license. The law also requires that states allow

literacy test A test given to voters to ensure that they could read and write and thus evaluate political information; a technique used in many southern states to restrict African American participation in elections.

poll tax A fee of several dollars that had to be paid before a person could vote; a device used in some southern states to prevent African Americans from voting.

grandfather clause A clause in a state law that restricted the franchise (voting rights) to those whose grandfathers had voted; one of the techniques used in the South to prevent African Americans from exercising their right to vote.

white primary A primary election in which African Americans were prohibited from voting. The practice was banned by the Supreme Court in 1944.

A worker moves bundled, vote-by-mail ballots in Portland, Oregon. Oregon, which is the only state in the country to conduct all elections exclusively by mail, now ranks among the top three states with the highest voter participation. Many credit the vote-by-mail system as the main reason for this ranking.

mail-in registration, with forms given at certain public-assistance agencies. Since the law took effect on January 1, 1995, it has facilitated millions of registrations.

In 1998, Oregon voters approved a ballot initiative that allowed voting by mail in all elections in that state, including presidential elections. As a result, voter turnout in that state increased dramatically. In the 2004 presidential elections, 84 percent of registered Oregon voters voted. Some argue that if mail-in voting were allowed nationwide, voter turnout would increase significantly. Others believe that voting by mail has a number of disadvantages, including greater possibilities for voter fraud.

JOIN THE DEBATE

Voter Fraud—A Real Problem or Much Ado about Nothing?

Cries of voter fraud came from the Democrats in 2000 and again in 2004. (As of 2007, ninety thousand ballots cast in Ohio in the 2004 elections remained un-counted. Prosecutors obtained two felony convictions in Cleveland related to a "rigged" recount there.) Flash forward to the 2006 midterm elections in which the Republicans took a shellacking. Guess who then claimed voter fraud? In at least five states (Missouri, Nevada, New Mexico, Washington, and Wisconsin), Republicans were involved in highly contested elections. Not surprisingly, the Republican administration pushed U.S. attorneys to prosecute voter claims of alleged fraud, particularly in those five states.

When the Democrats claimed voter fraud, the victorious Republicans attributed the claims to "sour grapes." When the Republicans asserted voter fraud, the Democrats reacted similarly. According to political analyst Harold Meyerson of the *Washington Post*, "Voter fraud is a myth—not an urban or a real myth, as such, but a Republican one." The Justice Department's Ballot Access and Voting Integrity Initiative resulted in only 120 federal prosecutions with 86 convictions after a five-year period. Most of those charged were Democrats who mistakenly filled out registration forms or misunderstood eligibility rules. Many Americans contend that voter fraud will always exist on a small scale, but it's not a serious problem today. Rather, the Republicans have trumped up charges of voter fraud in order to pass state laws, such as laws requiring photo IDs and special documents, that make it harder for poorer and disadvantaged groups (mostly Democrats) to vote.

Other Americans believe that voter fraud is a significant problem. The Election Assistance Commission issued a report indicating that the pervasiveness of voter fraud is still open to debate. Lapses in enforcing voting and registration rules continue to occur. Thousands upon thousands of ineligible voters are allowed to vote. Numerous convicted felons—who are not allowed to vote in some states—end up voting anyway. The only effective method of reducing voter fraud is to require photo IDs at polling places. Voter fraud is not a myth created by the Republicans for partisan reasons.

Attempts to Improve Voting Procedures

Because of serious problems in achieving accurate vote counts in recent elections, particularly in the 2000 presidential elections, steps have been taken to attempt to ensure more accuracy in the voting process. In 2002, Congress passed the Help America Vote Act, which, among other things, provided funds to the states to

THE REST OF
THE WORLD

French Voters Go Electronic

Electronic voting in the United States has come under scrutiny because of alleged imperfections in the software. E-voting machines have been condemned by several university studies as well as by the federal Government Accountability Office. New electronic machines created a major fiasco in Cleveland, Ohio, in that state's 2006 primary elections.

Nonetheless, the French government used similar machines in its hotly contested 2007 presidential elections. Out of 37.4 million people who voted in May of that year, about 1.5 million voted electronically in eighty municipalities.

MANY GROUPS WERE AGAINST E-VOTING

Virtually all of the presidential candidates, except the one who won (Nicolas Sarkozy), tried to stop the use of electronic voting. Actually, e-voting had already occurred in European and regional elections for three years prior to the latest presidential elections. The French government had reported no serious problems with them. Nonetheless, a number of cities chose to exclude e-voting as a possibility in 2007.

Throwing caution to the wind, Reims (the capital of the Champagne district) signed on for electronic voting. The city anticipated

AP Photo/Claude Paris

French voters waited in long lines in Paris during the 2007 presidential elections.

that about one hundred thousand registered voters would try the system, but relatively few voters showed up. Those who did were allowed to vote electronically for the kind of tree that would be planted on one of the city's main avenues.

LONG DELAYS WERE THE NORM

Electronic voting is supposed to be quick, easy, and understandable. But only one voting machine was available per polling station in most municipalities in France. Consequently, voters waited in long lines while those ahead of them figured out how to use the new machines. In particular, older individuals often forgot to validate their choices before leaving the voting booth. They had to go back, thereby causing additional delays. Not surprisingly, when Sarkozy won, supporters of the losing candidates complained about "dubious" vote counts and various discrepancies that always favored Sarkozy.

For Critical Analysis

Is there ever going to be a truly foolproof method of voting? Why or why not?

---

help them purchase new electronic voting equipment. Concerns about the possibility of fraudulent manipulation of electronic voting machines then replaced the worries over inaccurate vote counts caused by the previous equipment. (There were also worries about electronic voting in the 2007 French presidential elections—see this chapter's *The Rest of the World* feature for details.)

In the 2006 elections, the new electronic voting systems functioned fairly smoothly on the whole, but about half of the states using them did report problems. Several electronic systems repeatedly crashed or refused to start, and some even "flipped" votes from the selected candidate to the opposing candidate. In one Florida county, an estimated eighteen thousand votes appar-

ently went unrecorded by electronic voting equipment. Because of these and other problems with electronic voting, some states are considering going back to paper ballots. Indeed, Florida recently announced that it would do so. Congress has also called for the states to create a "paper trail" of voting choices to ensure greater accuracy in vote counting.

Who Actually Votes

Just because an individual is eligible to vote does not necessarily mean that the person will actually go to the polls on Election Day and vote. Why do some eligible voters go to the polls while others do not? Although nobody can answer this question with absolute conviction, certain factors, including those discussed next, appear to affect voter turnout.

EDUCATIONAL ATTAINMENT   Among the factors affecting voter turnout, education appears to be the most important. The more education a person has, the more likely it is that she or he will be a regular voter. People who graduated from high school vote more regularly than those who dropped out, and college graduates vote more often than high school graduates.

INCOME LEVEL AND AGE   Differences in income also lead to differences in voter turnout. Wealthy people tend to be overrepresented among regular voters. Generally, older voters turn out to vote more regularly than younger voters do, although participation tends to decline among the very elderly. Participation likely increases with age because older people tend to be more settled, are already registered, and have had more experience with voting.

MINORITY STATUS   Racial and ethnic minorities traditionally have been underrepresented among the ranks of voters. In several recent elections, however, participation by these groups, particularly African Americans and Hispanics, has increased.

Turnout among both African Americans and Hispanics rose significantly in the 1996 elections, but it did not show a further increase in 2000 or 2004. African American turnout in 2004 held steady at around 10 percent of overall turnout, which mirrors the 1996 percentage. Turnout among Hispanics, who constituted 6 percent of the voting electorate in 1996, even decreased somewhat in the 2004 elections—to roughly 4 percent. Of course, in absolute terms, the number of Hispanics in the United States has increased. In the years between 1996 and 2004, the majority of newly naturalized citizens in the United States were of Hispanic origin. In addition, as noted in Chapter 5, voter turnout among Hispanics during the 2006 midterm elections increased significantly (by 37 percentage points) over what

it had been during the previous midterm elections, in 2002.

LO⁵ WHY PEOPLE VOTE AS THEY DO

What prompts some citizens to vote Republican and others to vote Democratic? What persuades voters to choose certain kinds of candidates? Obviously, more is involved than measuring one's own position against the candidates' positions and then voting accordingly. Voters choose candidates for many reasons, some of which are explored here. These questions cannot be answered with absolute certainty, but because of the technology of opinion polling, researchers have collected more information on voting than on any other form of political participation in the United States. These data shed some light on why people decide to vote for particular candidates.

Party Identification

Many voters have a standing allegiance to a political party, or a party identification, although the proportion of the population that does so is shrinking. For established voters, party identification is one of the most important and lasting predictors of how a person will vote. Party identification is an emotional attachment to a party that is influenced by family, age, peer groups,

Older Americans generally turn out to vote in greater numbers than do younger Americans, in part because older people tend to be more settled, are already registered, and have had more experience with voting.

AP Photo/Charles Krupa

and other factors that play a role in the political socialization process discussed earlier.

Increasingly, there are indications that party identification has lost some of its impact. A growing number of voters now call themselves independents. Despite this label, many independents actually do support one or the other of the two major parties quite regularly. Figure 8–2 shows how those who identified themselves as Democrats, Republicans, and independents voted in the 2004 presidential elections.

Perception of the Candidates

Voters' choices also depend on their image of the candidates. Voters often base their decisions more on their *impressions* of the candidates than on the candidates' *actual* qualifications.

To some extent, voter attitudes toward candidates are based on emotions rather than on any judgment about experience or policy. In 2004, for example, voters' decisions in the presidential elections were largely guided by their perceptions of which candidate they could trust on matters of national security. President George W. Bush was more successful than his opponent, John Kerry, in convincing Americans that he had a plan for the war on terrorism—both at home and abroad. Bush pointed to his experience and leadership in the difficult years following the September 11 attacks. At the same time, many portrayed Kerry as indecisive and lacking a clear plan for the war on terrorism. Kerry failed to capitalize on the fact that he had been a decorated officer in Vietnam, while Bush had never served on active duty in the armed forces.

Policy Choices

When people vote for candidates who share their positions on particular issues, they are engaging in policy voting. If a candidate for senator in your state opposes gun control laws, for example, and you decide to vote for her for that reason, you have engaged in policy voting.

Historically, economic issues have had the strongest influence on voters' choices. When the economy is doing well, it is very difficult for a challenger, particularly at the presidential level, to defeat the incumbent. In con-

trast, when the country is experiencing inflation, rising unemployment, or high interest rates, the incumbent will likely be at a disadvantage. War, however, usually takes priority over economic issues in shaping voters' attitudes. The war in Iraq was certainly the single issue that dominated the 2006 elections, and it was one of the primary issues in the 2008 presidential elections as well.

Some of the most heated debates in American political campaigns have involved social issues, such as abortion, gay and lesbian rights, the death penalty, and religion in the schools. In general, presidential candidates prefer to avoid taking a definite stand on these types of issues, because voters who have strong opinions about such issues are likely to be offended if a candidate does not share their views.

Socioeconomic Factors

Some factors that influence how people vote can be described as socioeconomic. These factors include a person's educational attainment, income level, age, gender, religion, and geographic location. Some of these factors have to do with the circumstances into which individuals are born; others have to do with personal choices. Figure 8–3 on the next page shows how various groups voted in the 2004 presidential elections.

EDUCATIONAL ATTAINMENT As a general rule, people with more education are more likely to vote Republican, although at the upper levels of educational attainment this pattern breaks down. Typically,

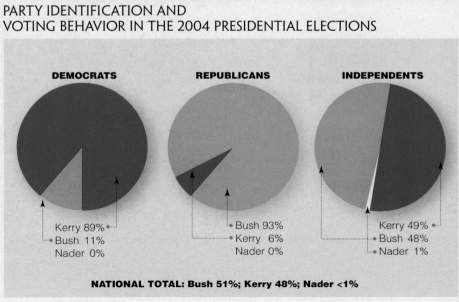

FIGURE 8-2

PARTY IDENTIFICATION AND
VOTING BEHAVIOR IN THE 2004 PRESIDENTIAL ELECTIONS

DEMOCRATS

REPUBLICANS

INDEPENDENTS

Kerry 89%
Bush 11%
Nader 0%

Bush 93%
Kerry 6%
Nader 0%

Kerry 49%
Bush 48%
Nader 1%

NATIONAL TOTAL: Bush 51%; Kerry 48%; Nader <1%

Source: CNN.com.

FIGURE 8-3

VOTING BY GROUPS IN THE 2004 PRESIDENTIAL ELECTIONS

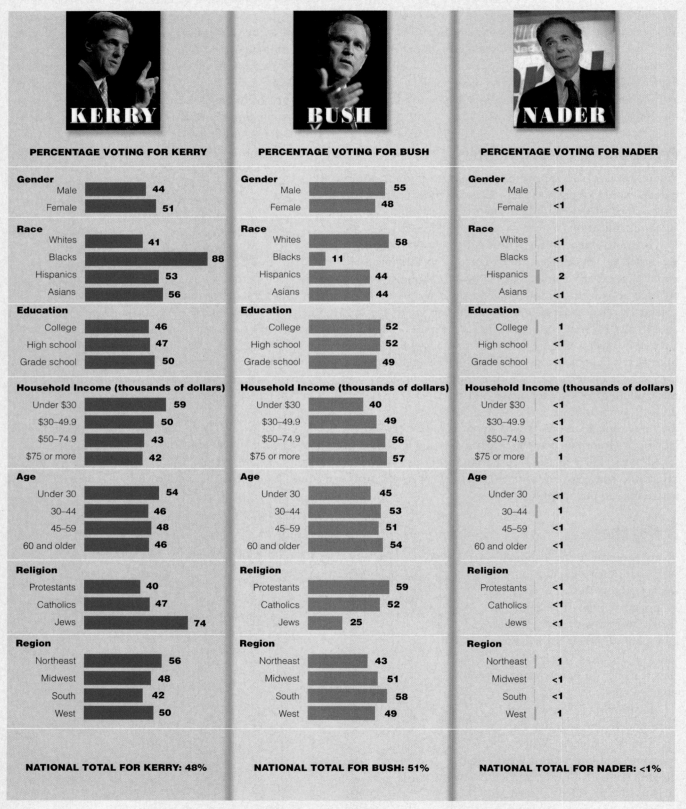

	PERCENTAGE VOTING FOR KERRY	PERCENTAGE VOTING FOR BUSH	PERCENTAGE VOTING FOR NADER
Gender			
Male	44	55	<1
Female	51	48	<1
Race			
Whites	41	58	<1
Blacks	88	11	<1
Hispanics	53	44	2
Asians	56	44	<1
Education			
College	46	52	1
High school	47	52	<1
Grade school	50	49	<1
Household Income (thousands of dollars)			
Under $30	59	40	<1
$30–49.9	50	49	<1
$50–74.9	43	56	<1
$75 or more	42	57	1
Age			
Under 30	54	45	<1
30–44	46	53	1
45–59	48	51	<1
60 and older	46	54	<1
Religion			
Protestants	40	59	<1
Catholics	47	52	<1
Jews	74	25	<1
Region			
Northeast	56	43	1
Midwest	48	51	<1
South	42	58	<1
West	50	49	1

NATIONAL TOTAL FOR KERRY: 48%   **NATIONAL TOTAL FOR BUSH: 51%**   **NATIONAL TOTAL FOR NADER: <1%**

Source: CNN.com.

those with less education are more inclined to vote for the Democratic nominee. Educational attainment as a factor in voting can be linked to income level. One in seventeen Americans from families with a household income of $30,000 or less finishes college, while one in two of those from families making $80,000 or more completes a four-year degree.

OCCUPATION AND INCOME LEVEL Professionals and businesspersons tend to vote Republican, although this pattern is changing. Manual laborers, factory workers, and especially union members are more likely to vote Democratic. In the past, the higher the income, the more likely it was that a person would vote Republican. Conversely, a much larger percentage of low-income individuals voted Democratic. But this pattern is also breaking down, and there are no hard-and-fast rules. Some very poor individuals are devoted Republicans, just as some extremely wealthy persons are supporters of the Democratic Party.

> "Whenever a fellow tells me he is **bipartisan**, I know he is going to vote **against** me."
>
> HARRY TRUMAN,
> THIRTY-THIRD PRESIDENT
> OF THE UNITED STATES
> 1945–1953

AGE Although one might think that a person's chronological age would determine political preferences, apparently age does not matter very much. Some differences can be identified, however: young adults tend to be more liberal than older Americans on most issues, and young adults tend to hold more progressive views than older persons on such issues as racial and gender equality.

Although older Americans tend to be somewhat more conservative than younger groups, their greater conservatism may be explained simply by the fact that individuals maintain the values they learned when they first became politically aware. Forty years later, those values may be considered relatively conservative. Additionally, people's attitudes are sometimes shaped by the events that unfolded as they grew up. Individuals who grew up during an era of Democratic Party dominance will likely remain Democrats throughout their lives. The same will hold true for those who grew up during an era of Republican Party dominance.

In elections from 1952 through 1980, voters under the age of thirty clearly favored the Democratic presidential candidates. This trend reversed itself in 1984 when voters under age thirty voted heavily for

Ronald Reagan. George H. W. Bush maintained that support in 1988. In 1992, however, Bill Clinton won back the young voters by 10 percentage points, a margin that expanded to 20 percentage points in 1996. In 2004, Democrat John Kerry won the youth vote over Republican George W. Bush by 9 percentage points.

GENDER Until relatively recently, there seemed to be no fixed pattern of voter preferences by gender in presidential elections. One year, more women than men would vote for the Democratic candidate; another year, more men than women would do so. Some political analysts believe that a **gender gap** became a major determinant of voter decision making in the 1980 presidential elections, however. In that year, Ronald Reagan outdrew Jimmy Carter by 16 percentage points among male voters, whereas women gave about an equal number of votes to each candidate. Although the gender gap has varied since 1980, it reappeared in force in 1996, when President Clinton received 54 percent of women's votes and only 43 percent of men's votes. The gender gap was also significant in 2000, with more women (54 percent) than men (42 percent) voting for Gore, and more men (53 percent) than women (43 percent) voting for Bush. The gender gap partially contracted in 2004, as John Kerry won only 51 percent of the female vote, compared to George W. Bush's 48 percent. The male vote remained strongly Republican, however, as Bush beat Kerry by 11 percentage points among men.

RELIGION AND ETHNIC BACKGROUND Traditionally, the majority of Protestants have voted Republican, while Catholics and Jews have tended to be Democrats. Voters of Italian, Irish, Polish, Eastern European, and Slavic descent have generally supported Democrats, while those of British, Scandinavian, and French descent have voted Republican.

African Americans vote principally for Democrats. They have given the Democratic presidential candidate a clear majority of their votes in every election since 1952, although this majority weakened

gender gap A term used to describe the difference between the percentage of votes cast for a particular candidate by women and the percentage of votes cast for the same candidate by men.

in the 1980s. Democratic presidential candidates have received, on average, more than 80 percent of the African American vote since 1956. In 2004, the percentage reached 88 percent.

GEOGRAPHIC REGION Where a voter lives also influences his or her preferences. For more than one hundred years after the Civil War, most white southerners, regardless of background or socioeconomic status, were Democrats. In large part, this is because the Republicans were in power when the Civil War broke out, and many southerners thus blamed the Republicans for that conflict and its results for the South. Known as the **Solid South,** this strong coalition has recently crumbled in the presidential elections, although the rural vote in parts of the South still tends to be Democratic.

Although the Solid South is no more, it appears that something like a Solid Northeast may be emerging, with a strong Democratic majority. Republicans continue to draw much of their strength from the mountain and plains states in the West and from rural areas throughout the country (except in the South).

IDEOLOGY AS AN INDICATOR OF VOTING BEHAVIOR A significant percentage of Americans today identify themselves as moderates. Recent polls indicate that 45 percent of Americans consider themselves to be moderates, 21 percent consider themselves liberals, and 35 percent identify themselves as conservatives. Additionally—and somewhat surprisingly—most Americans do not see a relationship between today's issues and political ideology. For example,

African Americans have voted primarily for Democrats since 1952. Here, Democratic presidential candidate Hillary Clinton is shown mingling with audience members at the Black Congressional Caucus conference in 2007.

AP Photo/Gerald Herbert

"IN POLITICS, AN ORGANIZED MINORITY IS A POLITICAL MAJORITY."
JESSE JACKSON, CIVIL RIGHTS ACTIVIST 1941–PRESENT

polling data show that only a small fraction—about 2 percent—of Americans identify either side of the abortion debate with conservatism or liberalism.

For some Americans, then, where they fall in the political spectrum is a strong indicator of how they will vote: liberals vote for Democrats, Greens, or other liberal candidates, and conservatives vote for Republicans, Libertarians, or other conservative candidates. The large numbers of Americans who fall in the political center do not adhere strictly to an ideology. In most elections, the candidates compete aggressively for these voters because they know their "base"—on the left or right—is secure.

In 1949, historian Arthur Schlesinger, Jr., described the position between the political extremes as the **vital center.** The center is vital because, without it, reaching the compromises that are necessary to a political system's continuity may be difficult, if not impossible. Voter apathy and low voter turnout are found most commonly among those in the center. That means that the most motivated voters are the "ideologically zealous."[6]

Solid South A term used to describe the tendency of the southern states to vote Democratic after the Civil War.

vital center The center of the political spectrum, or those who hold moderate political views. The center is vital because without it, it may be difficult, if not impossible, to reach the compromises that are necessary to a political system's continuity.

AMERICA AT ODDS:
Public Opinion and Voting

At the time the Constitution was drafted, the phrase *public opinion* meant something quite different from what it means today. At that time, the "public" referred to a narrow sphere of elite, educated gentlemen. According to John Randolph in a 1774 political pamphlet, "When I mention the public, I mean to include only the rational part of it. The ignorant vulgar are as unfit to judge of the modes, as they are unable to manage the reins of government."[7] During the 1800s, this elitist view gave way to one that included all Americans in the "public," and public opinion came to be regarded as "the vital principle underlying American government, society, and culture."[8] Today, public opinion remains a "vital principle" throughout the political sphere.

The framers of the U.S. Constitution left the power to establish voting qualifications to the individual states. Under that arrange-ment, initially only property-owning white males were able to vote. As discussed in this chapter, over time the franchise was extended to other groups, and now all Americans over the age of eighteen—with certain exceptions, such as prisoners—have the right to vote. Typically, however, only around one-half of voting-age Americans actually do vote. The fact that voter turnout among older Americans is higher than among younger Americans clearly has an effect on the policies adopted by our government, as does the relatively low turnout among poorer and disadvantaged groups of Americans. Because the views of the latter groups tend to be more liberal than conservative, liberal Democrats have been in the forefront of efforts to increase voter turnout among these groups.

Issues for Debate & Discussion

1. Some Americans argue that all states should implement vote-by-mail systems for all elections. Vote-by-mail systems would increase voter participation; allow voters more time for deliberation; avoid the problems caused by voting equipment, including the new electronic voting systems; and provide for accurate vote counting. Additionally, the blitz of last-minute, largely negative advertising before elections would likely be reduced because many mail-in voters would have already sent in their ballots two or three weeks before the election. Opponents of mail-in voting contend that going to the polling place on Election Day generates political energy and facilitates personal contact with other concerned citizens. These critics also point out that mail-in voting would allow voters to be strongly influenced by their families or friends. Finally, this group believes that voting by mail would almost certainly increase fraudulent voting during elections. Where do you stand on this issue?

2. Many Americans believe that our government representatives, when creating policies, should be guided by the public's views on the issues at hand. After all, in a democracy, the elected leaders should ensure that their decisions are consistent with the will of the citizenry. Others contend that elected officials should not be led by public opinion but by their own expertise and convictions in a given policy area. Consider that racial segregation was at one time supported by a majority of Americans. Was segregation therefore a reasonable policy? Where do you stand on this issue?

Take Action

"Citizens at the polls are the most powerful agents of change." Thus say political analysts Thomas Mann and Norman Ornstein.[9] But if citizens are not informed on the political issues of the day or about the candidates' qualifications, there is little sense in going to the polls. Indeed, as mentioned in this chapter, one of the reasons for the relatively low voter turnout in this country is a sense on the part of some citizens that they lack information. As also noted, peer groups are important in the political socialization process. But just as you might be influenced by your peers, you can also influence them.

If you would like to take action to increase interest in our political life, one thing you might do is host a political salon. This would be a gathering, either in your home or at some other place, that would focus on learning about political issues and opinions. You can invite friends, other students, co-workers, or other persons who might be interested to attend the salon, which could be held weekly, monthly, or at some other interval. At the first meeting, you can set the "rules" for the salon. What topics do you want to discuss? How much time do you want to devote to each topic? What reading or research, if any, should be undertaken before the meetings? Depending on the views and energies of those who attend the salon, you might also devise an activist agenda to increase voter turnout. For example, you could plan a get-out-the-vote drive for the next election.

- Recent polls conducted and analyzed by the Roper Center for Public Opinion Research can be found at **www.ropercenter.uconn.edu**.

- According to its home page, the mission of the American National Election Studies (ANES) "is to produce high-quality data on voting, public opinion, and political participation that serves the research needs of social scientists, teachers, students, and policymakers concerned with understanding the theoretical and empirical foundations of mass politics in a democratic society." The ANES is a good source of information on public opinion. To reach this site, go to **www.electionstudies.org**.

- At the Gallup Organization's Web site, you can find the results of recent polls as well as an archive of past polls and information on how polls are conducted. Go to **www.gallup.com**.

- You can find further links to poll data and other sources on public opinion at the following site: **www.publicagenda.org**.

- The Polling Report Web site provides polling results on a number of issues, organized by topics. The site is easy to use and up to date. Go to **www.pollingreport.com**.

- PBS features a section on its Web site titled "PBS by the People," which provides some good tips on how to analyze a poll. Go to **www.pbs.org/elections/savvyanalyze.html**.

ONLINE RESOURCES FOR THIS CHAPTER

This text's Companion Web site, at **www.americaatodds.com,** offers links to numerous resources that you can utilize to learn more about the topics covered in this chapter.

Turn to the back of the book to find your Politics to Go review card for this chapter

9
CAMPAIGNS AND ELECTIONS

LEARNING OBJECTIVES

LO¹ Discuss how candidates are nominated.

LO² Indicate what is involved in launching a political campaign today and describe the structure and functions of a campaign organization.

LO³ Summarize the laws that regulate campaign financing and the role of money in modern political campaigns.

LO⁴ Explain how elections are held and how the electoral college functions in presidential elections.

AMERICA AT ODDS

ON PODCAST

Should We Elect the President by Popular Vote?

When Americans go to the polls every four years to cast their ballots for president, many do not realize that they are not, in fact, voting directly for the candidates. Rather, they are voting for *electors*—individuals chosen in each state by political parties to cast the state's electoral votes for the candidate who wins that state's popular vote. The system by which electors cast their votes for president is known as the *electoral college*.

Each state is assigned electoral votes based on its number of members in Congress. Although each state has the same number of senators in the U.S. Senate (two), the number of representatives a state has in the U.S. House of Representatives is determined by the size of its population. That means that, in all, there are currently 538 electoral votes.[1]

To become president, a candidate must win 270 of these 538 electoral votes. Most states have a "winner-take-all" system in which the candidate who receives a plurality of the popular votes (more than any other candidate) in a state receives all of that state's electoral votes, even if the margin of victory is very slight. The winner-take-all system means that a candidate who wins the popular vote nationally may yet lose in the electoral college—and vice versa. Many Americans believe that we should let the popular vote, not the electoral college, decide who becomes president.[2] Others are not so sure.

Let the People Elect Our President

In 2000, Democratic candidate Al Gore won the popular vote yet narrowly lost to Republican George W. Bush in the electoral college. Many Americans questioned the legitimacy of Bush's election. They also decried the electoral college as an outdated invention of the late 1700s. To be sure, among the reasons for the system's original design was to ensure that the interests of smaller states were not totally over-shadowed by their more populous neighbors. Yet the electoral college gives the smaller states a disproportionate amount of clout. Consider, for example, that one electoral vote in California now corresponds to roughly 615,848 people, while an electoral vote in more sparsely settled Wyoming represents only 164,594 individuals. Clearly, the votes of Americans are not weighted equally, and this voting inequality is contrary to the "one person, one vote" principle of our democracy.

According to its critics, the electoral college also provides imaginary majorities. Under the system, it is possible for a candidate to win narrow majorities in numerous states (and thus all of the electoral votes in those states), lose significantly in other states, and yet still emerge with an overwhelming majority of electoral votes. For example, Bill Clinton garnered only 43 percent of the popular vote in 1992 but won by a landslide in the electoral college (370 votes, compared to 168 for George H. W. Bush).

THE ELECTORAL COLLEGE PROTECTS THE SMALL STATES AND ENSURES STABILITY

Supporters of the electoral college argue that if the system were abolished, small states would suffer. Because each state has as many electors as its total number of members in Congress, the electoral college helps to protect the small states from being over-whelmed by the large states.

The electoral college also helps to maintain a relatively stable and coherent party system. If the president were elected by popular vote, we would have countless parties vying for the nation's highest office—as occurs in such nations as France, Italy, and Germany. Moreover, the system provides another benefit: it helps to prevent single-issue or regional candidates—candidates who are not focused on the interests of the nation as a whole—from being elected to the presidency. To prevail in the electoral college, a candidate must build a national coalition, campaign in Santa Fe as well as New York City, and propose policies that unite, rather than divide, the nation.

Finally, the electoral college vote has diverged from the popular vote in only three elections during our nation's history—in 1876, 1888, and 2000. These exceptions do not justify abolishing the system.

Where do you stand?

1. Do you believe that a candidate elected by the popular vote would be more representative of the entire nation than a candidate elected by the electoral college? Why or why not?
2. Suppose that instead of using the "winner-take-all" system, all states awarded their electoral votes according to the proportion of the popular vote each candidate received. How would this affect the final outcome in the electoral college?

Explore this issue online

- For critical views of the electoral college, go to the Web site of The Center for Voting and Democracy at **www.fairvote.org** and click on "Presidential Elections Reform Program."
- For an article making a case for the electoral college, go to the Web site of Accuracy in Media (a media watchdog group) at **www.aim.org**. Select "Briefings" from the menu on the left and then click on "December 2004."

INTRODUCTION

During elections, candidates vie to become representatives of the people—in both national and state offices. The population of the United States is now more than 300 million. Clearly, all voting-age citizens cannot gather in one place to make laws and run the government. We have to choose representatives to govern the nation and to act on behalf of our interests. We accomplish this through popular elections.

Campaigning for election has become an arduous task for every politician. As you will see in this chapter, American campaigns are long, complicated, and very expensive undertakings. They can also be wearing on the citizens who are not running for office. Yet they are an important component of our political process because it is through campaigns that citizens learn about the candidates and decide how they will cast their votes. As you read in the chapter-opening *America at Odds* feature, Americans are divided as to whether the president should be elected by direct popular vote instead of by the electoral college.

LO¹ HOW WE NOMINATE CANDIDATES

The first step on the long road to winning an election is the nomination process. Nominations narrow the field of possible candidates and limit each political party's choice to one person. In the past, self-nomination was the most common way to become a candidate, and this method is still used in small towns and rural sections of the country. A self-proclaimed candidate usually files a petition to be listed on the ballot. Each state has laws that specify how many signatures a candidate must obtain to show that he or she has some public support. An alternative is to be a write-in candidate—voters write the candidate's name on the ballot on Election Day.

Serious candidates for most offices are rarely nominated in these ways, however. As you read in Chapter 7, most candidates for high office are nominated by a political party and receive considerable support from party activists throughout their campaigns.

Party Control over Nominations

George Washington was essentially unopposed in the first U.S. elections in 1789—no other candidate was seriously considered in any state. By the end of Washington's eight years in office, however, political

divisions among the nation's leaders had solidified into political parties, the Federalists and the Democratic Republicans (see Chapter 7). Party leaders recognized that the ability to choose nominees was essential to their political power. Beginning in 1797, they began to hold congressional conferences, later called **caucuses,**[3] to nominate candidates in secret. The voters at large played no part in choosing nominees.

By the presidential race of 1824, the caucus method of nomination had become a controversial issue. Andrew Jackson and other presidential candidates who felt that the caucus was undemocratic derisively referred to the system as "King Caucus." Faced with rising opposition, party leaders were forced to find other methods of nominating candidates. As the caucus system faded away in presidential politics, its use diminished at the state and local levels as well. Today, only a few states continue to use caucuses in their electoral politics.

The Party Nominating Convention

As the use of the caucus method diminished around the country, it was replaced in many states by party conventions. A **nominating convention** is an official meeting of a political party to choose its candidates and to select **delegates**—persons sent to a higher-level party convention to represent the people of one geographic area. For example, delegates at a local

caucus A meeting held by party leaders to choose political candidates. The caucus system of nominating candidates was eventually replaced by nominating conventions and, later, by direct primaries.

nominating convention An official meeting of a political party to choose its candidates. Nominating conventions at the state and local levels also select delegates to represent the citizens of their geographic areas at a higher-level party convention.

delegate A person selected to represent the people of one geographic area at a party convention.

party convention would nominate candidates for local office and would also choose delegates to represent the party at the state convention. By 1840, the convention system had become the most common way of nominating candidates for government offices at every level.

Little by little, criticism of corruption in nominating conventions at the state level caused state legislatures to disband most of them. They are still used in some states, including Connecticut, Delaware, Michigan, and Utah, to nominate candidates for some state offices. At the national level, the convention is still used to select presidential and vice-presidential candidates.

The Direct Primary and Loss of Party Control

In most states, direct primaries gradually replaced nominating conventions. A **direct primary** is an election held within each of the two major parties—Democratic and Republican—to pick its candidates for the general election. This is the method most commonly used today to nominate candidates for office.

Most states require the major parties to use a primary to choose their candidates for the U.S. Senate and the House of Representatives, for the governorship and all other state offices, and for most local offices as well. A few states, however, use different combinations of nominating conventions and primaries to pick candidates for the top offices. Although the primaries are *party* nominating elections, they are closely regulated by the states. The states set the dates and conduct the primaries. The states also provide polling places, election officials, registration lists, and ballots, in addition to counting the votes.

The advent of the direct primary has meant some loss

direct primary An election held within each of the two major parties—Democratic and Republican—to choose the party's candidates for the general election.

closed primary A primary in which only party members can vote to choose that party's candidates.

of party control over the nominating process. As you will read shortly, state laws have created different types of primaries across the country, though they generally fall into two broad categories: *closed primaries* and *open primaries*. Open primaries allow voters to vote for a party's candidates even if they do not belong to that party. As open primaries have become more common, the nominating process has become less party centered and more candidate centered. Louisiana is unique in that all candidates run in the same, nonpartisan primary election. Figure 9–1 shows which states have closed (or semiclosed), open (or semiopen), or nonpartisan primaries.

CLOSED PRIMARIES   In a **closed primary,** only party members can vote to choose that party's candidates, and they may vote only in the primary of their own party. Thus, only registered Democrats can vote in the Democratic primary to select candidates of the Democratic Party. Only registered Republicans can vote for the Republican candidates. A person usually establishes party membership when she or he registers to vote. Some states have a *semiclosed* primary, which allows voters to register with a party or change their party affiliations on Election Day. Regular party workers favor the closed primary because it promotes party loyalty. Independent voters oppose it because it excludes them from the nominating process.

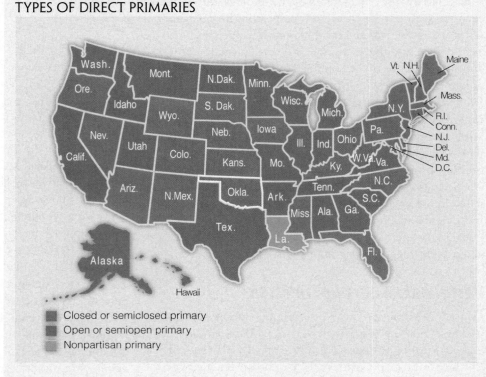

FIGURE 9–1

TYPES OF DIRECT PRIMARIES

■ Closed or semiclosed primary
■ Open or semiopen primary
■ Nonpartisan primary

During the run-up to the primary season in 2008, John Edwards (left), Hillary Clinton (center), and Barack Obama (right) were considered the Democratic presidential front runners.

At one point in the run-up to the 2008 primaries, the presidential front runners for the Republicans were Mitt Romney (left), Rudy Giuliani (center), and John McCain (right).

OPEN PRIMARIES   An **open primary** is a direct primary in which voters can vote for a party's candidates regardless of whether they belong to the party. In most open primaries, all voters receive both a Republican ballot and a Democratic ballot. Voters then choose either the Democratic or the Republican ballot in the privacy of the voting booth. In a *semiopen* primary, voters request the ballot for the party of their choice.

Nominating Presidential Candidates

In some respects, being nominated for president is more difficult than being elected. The nominating process narrows a very large number of hopefuls down to a single candidate from each party. Choosing a presidential candidate is unlike nominating candidates for any other office. One reason for this is that the nomination process combines several different methods.

PRESIDENTIAL PRIMARIES   The majority of the states hold presidential primaries, beginning early in the election year. For a candidate, a good showing in the early primaries results in plenty of media attention as television networks and newspaper reporters play up the results. Subsequent state primaries tend to serve as contests to eliminate unlikely candidates. Sometimes, the political parties have tried to manipulate primary dates to maximize their candidates' media attention. The order and timing of primary dates also influence the candidates' fund-raising.

State legislatures and state parties make the laws that determine how the primaries are set up, who may enter them, and who may vote in them. Several different methods of voting are used in presidential primaries. In some states, for example, primary voters only

select delegates to a party's national convention and do not know which candidates the delegates intend to vote for at the convention. In other states, the voters cast ballots for candidates, and the delegates must vote for the winning candidate at the national convention.

In some states, delegates to the national convention are chosen through caucuses or conventions instead of through presidential primaries. Iowa, for example, holds caucuses to choose delegates to local conventions. These delegates, in turn, choose those who will attend the state and national conventions. Other states use a combination of caucuses and primaries.

PRIMARIES—THE RUSH TO BE FIRST   Traditionally, states have held their primaries at various times over the first six months of a presidential election year. In an effort to make their primaries prominent in the media and influential in the political process, however, many states have moved the date of their primary to earlier in the year. This "front-loading" of the primaries started after the 1968 Democratic National Convention in Chicago, which appeared to be ruled by a few groups. In 1988, southern states created "Super Tuesday" by holding most of their primaries on the same day in early March. Then, many states in the Midwest, New England, and the Pacific West (including California) moved their primaries to an earlier date, too.

The practice of front-loading primaries has gained momentum over the last decade. The states with later primary dates found that most nominations were decided early in the season, leaving their voters "out of the action." As more states moved up their primary dates, however, the more

> **open primary** A primary in which voters can vote for a party's candidates regardless of whether they belong to the party.

important the early primaries became—and the more other states, to compete, also moved up their primaries.

This rush to be first was particularly notable in the year or so preceding the 2008 presidential primaries. By mid-2007, about half the states had moved, or planned to move, their primaries to earlier dates. Many of these states opted for February 5—or "Super-Super Tuesday," as some call it—as the date for their primaries.

Some Americans worry that with a shortened primary season, long-shot candidates will no longer be able to propel themselves into serious contention by doing well in small, early-voting states, such as New Hampshire or Iowa. Traditionally, for example, a candidate who had a successful showing in the New Hampshire primary had time to obtain enough financial backing to continue in the race. The candidate also had time to become known to the voters through political advertising, TV appearances, and speeches along the campaign trail. With the shortened primary season, the winners will be those candidates who can start their fund-raising early and load up on national TV spots. The fear is that an accelerated schedule of presidential primaries will likely favor the richest candidates. Indeed, in 2007 the media continually linked a candidate's potential for success to the amount of money the candidate was able to raise during each quarter of the year.

JOIN THE DEBATE

Should New Hampshire Hold the First Presidential Primary, No Matter What?

New Hampshire has a long-standing tradition of being the location of the first presidential primary every four years, usually in January or February. New Hampshire's current secretary of state, Bill Gardner, has a legal mandate from the state legislature to move the primary date as necessary to maintain New Hampshire's tradition of being first. Gardner has done so in the past, and he is willing to do so again, even if it means holding the New Hampshire primary in December!

Because New Hampshire holds its primary so early, presidential candidates of both parties start campaigning in the state long before the presidential elections.

Not only New Hampshire voters but also many voters in other states believe that New Hampshire should continue to hold the first primary. New Hampshire in general has a strong political culture. Its voters ask important questions of the candidates who campaign there in the freezing winter. According to Michael Whalley, a representative in the New Hampshire state legislature, "no other state—in a natural way, not an artificial way—can pay attention the way New Hampshire folks do." New Hampshire is one of the few places where there are actual face-to-face encounters between candidates and voters, often in people's homes. All eyes are on New Hampshire every four years. May the tradition continue.

Not all Americans agree that New Hampshire should forever have the first presidential primary. Nothing in the U.S. Constitution provides for it. Moreover, New Hampshire is certainly not a typical state—its voters tend to be mainly rural and white. Why should New Hampshire (and Iowa, which typically holds the first presidential caucuses) have such a disproportionate effect on who wins the nomination for president?

NATIONAL PARTY CONVENTIONS Born in the 1830s, the American national political convention is unique in Western democracies. Elsewhere, candidates for prime minister or chancellor are chosen within the confines of party councils. That is actually the way the framers wanted it done—the Constitution does not mention a nominating convention. Indeed, Thomas Jefferson

Library of Congress

This historical photo shows attendees at the 1952 Republican National Convention in Chicago. Notice that the vast majority of the delegates are white men.

Erik Freeland/Corbis

AP Photo/David J. Phillip

These photos of today's modern national conventions show the color and staging that make them appear to be more like infomercials than anything else. The reality is that the presidential and vice-presidential candidates have already been chosen and that voting at the national conventions is usually just a formality.

loathed the idea. He feared that if the presidential race became a popularity contest, it would develop into "mobocracy."

At one time, the conventions were indeed giant free-for-alls. It wasn't clear who the winning presidential and vice-presidential candidates would be until the delegates voted. As more states opted to hold primaries in which candidates ran and delegates were selected, the drama of national conventions diminished. Today, the conventions have been described as massive pep rallies. Nonetheless, each convention's task remains a serious one. In late summer, two to three thousand delegates gather at each convention to represent the wishes of the voters and political leaders of their home states. They adopt the official party platform and declare their support for the party's presidential and vice-presidential candidates.

On the first day of the convention, delegates hear the reports of the **Credentials Committee,** which inspects each prospective delegate's claim to be seated as a legitimate representative of her or his state. When the eligibility of delegates is in question, the committee decides who will be seated. In the evening, there is usually a keynote speaker to whip up enthusiasm among the delegates. The second day includes committee reports and debates on the party platform. The third day is devoted to nominations and voting. Balloting begins with

an alphabetical roll call in which states and territories announce their votes. By midnight, the convention's real work is over and the presidential candidate has been selected. The vice-presidential nomination and the acceptance speeches occupy the fourth day.

Many Americans complain that recent conventions have been little more than prolonged infomercials. Convention activities are highly staged events. Even so-called impromptu moments seem to have been well prepared. Furthermore, the major news networks have cut their convention

Credentials Committee
A committee of each national political party that evaluates the claims of national party convention delegates to be the legitimate representatives of their states.

THE REST OF THE WORLD

Real-World Politics in Second Life

Avatars discuss politics in Second Life's online fantasy world.

The three-dimensional online fantasy world Second Life, which now boasts more than five million registered participants, is increasingly being used to create cyberspace headquarters for various European political candidates. Candidates are finding that if they build virtual headquarters, real people come to see them in the form of *avatars*—the cartoon-like characters that represent people in the virtual world called Second Life. The French, in particular, appear to enjoy conducting real-world politics in the virtual world.

IT STARTED ON THE EXTREME RIGHT

During the latest French presidential elections, the National Front, an extreme right-wing, anti-immigration party, opened its virtual headquarters in Second Life. Mainstream French avatars responded immediately: they asked California-based Linden Lab, Second Life's creator, to prevent the National Front from having its headquarters in a virtual shopping mall. When the party stayed put, they picketed its virtual headquarters. When that did not work, virtual protesters fired fat pink pigs that exploded and splattered, causing the headquarters to collapse (virtually, of course).

THE MAINSTREAM CLIMBS ON THE BANDWAGON

French mainstream candidates from the center, the right, and the left soon followed the National Front in establishing headquarters in Second Life. During the presidential elections in France, all of the Second Life headquarters for the major candidates were highly active. This is not surprising because France is second only to the United States in the number of avatars. Several U.S. presidential candidates have also set up headquarters in Second Life, but so far they are seeing less activity than the French did.

Some politicians have found that their attempted forays into the virtual world are not appreciated. Italy's transportation minister, Antonio Di Petro, announced plans to set up his virtual office on a tropical island in Second Life. The virtual residents of that island staged a protest, claiming "We get enough politics there already!"

For Critical Analysis

Why would political candidates spend the time and effort to create headquarters in Second Life?

---

coverage dramatically since the 1980s. In view of these developments, some Americans question whether the conventions serve any purpose at all.

LO² THE MODERN POLITICAL CAMPAIGN

Once nominated, candidates focus on their campaigns. The term *campaign* originated in the military context. Generals mounted campaigns, using their scarce resources (soldiers and materials) to achieve military objectives. Using the term in a political context is apt. In a political campaign, candidates also use scarce resources (time and money) in an attempt to defeat their adversaries in the battle to win votes. (Today, campaign battles are often fought on the Web. For one example of such warfare, see this chapter's *The Rest of the World* feature.)

To run a successful campaign, the candidate's campaign staff must be able to raise funds for the effort, get media coverage, produce and pay for political ads, schedule the candidate's time effectively with constituent groups and potential supporters, convey the candidate's position on the issues, conduct research on the opposing candidate, and get the voters to go to the polls. When party identification was stronger and TV campaigning was still in its infancy, a strong party organization on the local, state, or national level could furnish most of the services and expertise that the candidate needed. Less effort was spent on advertising a single candidate's position and character because the party label communicated that information to many of the voters.

Today, party labels are no longer as important as they once were. In part, this is because fewer people identify with the major parties, as evidenced by the rising number of independent voters. Instead of relying so extensively on political parties, candidates now turn to professionals to manage their campaigns.

The Professional Campaign Organization

With the rise of candidate-centered campaigns in the past two decades, the role of the political party in managing campaigns has declined. Professional **political consultants** now manage nearly all aspects of a presidential candidate's campaign. Indeed, President George W. Bush said that his longtime political adviser Karl Rove was the "architect" of his reelection victory in 2004. Most candidates for governor, the House, and the Senate also rely on consultants. Political consultants generally specialize in a particular area of the campaign, such as researching the opposition, conducting polls, developing the candidate's advertising, or organizing "get out the vote" efforts. Nonetheless, most candidates have a campaign manager who coordinates and plans the **campaign strategy.** Figure 9–2 shows a typical presidential campaign organization. As this figure also indicates, the political party continues to play an important role in recruiting volunteers and getting out the vote.

political consultant
A professional political adviser who, for a large fee, works on an area of a candidate's campaign. Political consultants include campaign managers, pollsters, media advisers, and "get out the vote" organizers.

campaign strategy The comprehensive plan for winning an election developed by a candidate and his or her advisers. The strategy includes the candidate's position on issues, slogan, advertising plan, press events, personal appearances, and other aspects of the campaign.

FIGURE 9-2

A TYPICAL PRESIDENTIAL CAMPAIGN ORGANIZATION

Most aspects of a candidate's campaign are managed by professional political consultants, as this figure illustrates.

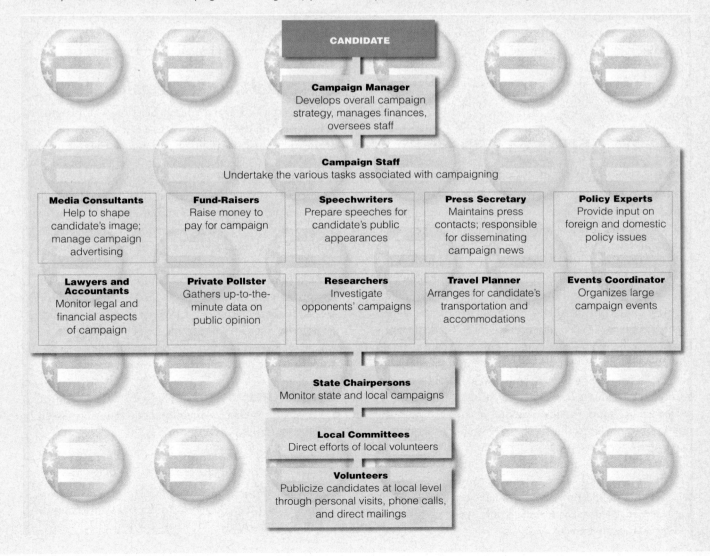

CANDIDATE

Campaign Manager
Develops overall campaign strategy, manages finances, oversees staff

Campaign Staff
Undertake the various tasks associated with campaigning

Media Consultants
Help to shape candidate's image; manage campaign advertising

Fund-Raisers
Raise money to pay for campaign

Speechwriters
Prepare speeches for candidate's public appearances

Press Secretary
Maintains press contacts; responsible for disseminating campaign news

Policy Experts
Provide input on foreign and domestic policy issues

Lawyers and Accountants
Monitor legal and financial aspects of campaign

Private Pollster
Gathers up-to-the-minute data on public opinion

Researchers
Investigate opponents' campaigns

Travel Planner
Arranges for candidate's transportation and accommodations

Events Coordinator
Organizes large campaign events

State Chairpersons
Monitor state and local campaigns

Local Committees
Direct efforts of local volunteers

Volunteers
Publicize candidates at local level through personal visits, phone calls, and direct mailings

A major development in contemporary American politics is the focus on reaching voters through effective use of the media, particularly television. Prior to the 2008 primaries, the candidates of each party participated in televised debates, letting viewers know their positions on various issues, such as health care. The major issue, of course, was what the candidate's position was with respect to the war in Iraq—the primary concern of voters at that time. (For a discussion of how the candidates of each party tackled the Iraq war issue, see this chapter's *The Politics of National Security* feature.)

At least half of the budget for a major political campaign is consumed by television advertising. The media consultant is therefore a pivotal member of the campaign staff. The nature of political advertising is discussed in more detail in Chapter 10. How candidates obtain the money needed to pay for advertising, consultants, and other campaign costs is discussed next.

> "IN CONSTANT PURSUIT OF **MONEY** TO FINANCE CAMPAIGNS, THE POLITICAL SYSTEM IS SIMPLY UNABLE TO FUNCTION. ITS DELIBERATIVE POWERS ARE **PARALYZED**."
>
> JOHN RAWLS,
> AMERICAN EDUCATOR
> 1921–2000

LO³ WHAT IT COSTS TO WIN

The modern political campaign is an expensive undertaking. Huge sums must be spent for professional campaign managers and consultants, television and radio ads, the printing of campaign literature, travel, office rent, equipment, and other necessities.

To get an idea of the cost of waging a campaign for Congress today, consider that candidates for the House of Representatives spent a total of more than $640 million on their campaigns in 2004, and candidates for the Senate spent a total of $490 million. Indeed, the South Dakota Senate race between Democratic incumbent Tom Daschle and Republican challenger John Thune cost $36 million alone. Thune emerged victorious over Daschle despite spending $5 million less than the former Senate minority leader.[4] Congressional candidates spent even more to obtain or retain seats during the 2006 midterm elections, particularly those running for the Senate. Total contributions to all Senate candidates from New York exceeded $50 million. Several other senatorial campaigns cost between $15 and $35 million. Candidates for the House of Representatives, as is typical, generally spent significantly less on their campaigns.

Presidential campaigns are even more costly. In 1992, Americans were stunned to learn that about $550 million had been spent in the presidential campaigns. In 1996, presidential campaign expenditures rose even higher, to about $600 million. In 2004, they climbed to nearly $830 million. In 2008, these costs are expected to exceed $1 billion, making the 2008 presidential campaigns the most expensive in history.

The connection between money and campaigns gives rise to some of the most difficult challenges in American politics. The biggest fear is that campaign contributors may be able to influence people running for office by giving large gifts or loans. Another possibility is that some special interest groups will try to buy favored treatment from those who are elected to office. In an attempt to prevent these abuses, the government regulates campaign financing.

The Federal Election Campaign Act

Congress passed the Federal Election Campaign Act (FECA) of 1971[5] in an effort to curb irregularities and abuses in the ways political campaigns were financed. The 1971 act placed no limit on overall spending but restricted the amount that could be spent on mass media advertising, including television. It limited the amount that candidates and their families could contribute to their own campaigns and required disclosure of all contributions and expenditures in excess of $100. In principle, the 1971 act limited the role of labor unions and corporations in political campaigns. Also in 1971, Congress passed a law that provided for a $1 checkoff on federal income tax returns for general campaign funds to be used by major-party presidential candidates. This law was first applied in the 1976 campaign. (Since then, the amount of the checkoff has been raised to $3.)

AMENDMENTS IN 1974 The 1971 act did not go far enough, however. Amendments to the act passed in 1974 essentially did the following:

■ *Created the Federal Election Commission (FEC) to administer and enforce the act's provisions.*

■ *Provided public financing for presidential primaries and general elections.* Presidential candidates who raise some money on their own in at least twenty

THE 2008 PRESIDENTIAL CAMPAIGNS AND THE WAR IN IRAQ

National security was not a very important issue in federal election campaigns during the 1990s. After all, the Soviet Union was no more, and the Cold War had ended. This changed with the terrorist attacks of September 11, 2001. Since then, national security has been one of the dominating factors in every campaign. During the 2008 presidential campaigns, every presidential hopeful had to come to grips with this issue.

U.S. troops in Iraq patrol a dangerous neighborhood.

THE REPUBLICANS WALKED A FINE LINE

In 2007, more than 70 percent of Americans opposed the war in Iraq. In contrast, some 62 percent of rank-and-file Republicans supported the war. The polls then showed that President Bush's approval rating had fallen below 30 percent. Not surprisingly, the numerous candidates for the 2008 Republican presidential nomination found themselves in a difficult position. On the one hand, they felt obligated to support Bush, at least in his initial decision to undertake the war in Iraq. On the other hand, given Bush's low approval ratings, they had to distinguish their policies from his in order to win the general election. Their solution was to support the war but stress that it had been mismanaged—and that they could do better. They also heartily endorsed a continuation of the global war on terrorism.

In any event, the concern over the war in Iraq crowded out many other important foreign policy issues from the presidential debates. There was relatively little talk about the Middle East peace process or about how to contain the nuclear ambitions of Iran and North Korea.

THE DEMOCRATIC CANDIDATES HAD A CLEAR SHOT—OR DID THEY?

About 70 percent of Americans were against the war, and most of them were Democrats or leaned toward the left of the political spectrum. Over two-thirds of Americans held Bush in low esteem, and most of them were Democrats or leaned in that direction. It seemed simple; the Democratic candidates would simply base their policy platforms on the failures of Bush's war in Iraq.

Well, not so fast. To be sure, all Democratic candidates for the presidential nomination had to strongly oppose the war to win the primaries and to become that party's chosen candidate. Nonetheless, some of the candidates had a hard time doing so because they voted to authorize the war in 2002—specifically, Hillary Clinton (D., N.Y.), John Edwards (formerly a Democratic senator from North Carolina), and Joseph Biden (D., Del.). One way out of that dilemma was to just state, as Hillary Clinton did, that had she known the facts she "certainly wouldn't have voted for the war." For some Democratic voters, though, this admission wasn't enough—they wanted her to apologize for making a mistake, which she refused to do.

The Democrats had another basic problem: they have a reputation for being the party that is not "tough" or "strong" on national security. A Democratic president who would take office in 2009 faced a "damned if you did, damned if you didn't" dilemma. She or he would be criticized if U.S. troops weren't withdrawn from Iraq but would also be blamed if they were withdrawn and a regional war ensued.

One thing was certain: whether a Democrat or a Republican was elected president in 2008, he or she would face criticism. If a Democrat won and tried to end the war in Iraq (or if a Republican won and tried to do the same), she or he would be attacked by hard-line conservatives for not being tough enough. If a Republican won and continued waging the war, he or she would likely come under criticism for "mismanaging" the nearly impossible situation in Iraq.

YOU BE THE JUDGE

Some have criticized the Republican candidates for approving Bush's decision to invade Iraq—even if they personally thought that going to war with Iraq was a bad idea—just to appeal to the Republican base. These critics contend that if political strategy is the final determinant in how candidates choose to stand on the issues, the chances of ending up with a president who can exercise genuine leadership are diminished. Others maintained that in order to win in the 2008 presidential primaries, the Republican candidates had to appeal to those rank-and-file Republicans who still supported Bush's war policy. Politically, they had no other choice if they wanted to be elected—and obtain the chance to exercise leadership. Where do you stand on this issue?

states can get funds from the U.S. Treasury to help pay for primary campaigns. For the general election campaign, presidential candidates receive federal funding for almost all of their expenses if they are willing to accept campaign-spending limits.

■ *Limited presidential campaign spending.* Any candidate accepting federal support must agree to limit expenditures to amounts set by federal law.

■ *Required disclosure.* Candidates must file periodic reports with the FEC that list the contributors to the campaign and indicate how the contributed money was spent.

■ *Limited contributions.* Individuals could contribute up to $1,000 to each candidate in each federal election or primary. The total limit for any individual in one year was $25,000. Groups could contribute a maximum of $5,000 to a candidate in any election.

JOIN THE DEBATE

Should Congressional Campaigns Be Publicly Financed?

Once elected, a member of Congress's first job is to be reelected. Veteran members of the House of Representatives advise newly elected members to "start raising money now . . . and have $1 million in the bank by the time the next race begins." For senators, $1 million is not nearly enough. In the last midterm elections, winning a Senate seat cost around $8 million, on average. Many members of Congress use their personal fortunes to finance their elections and reelections. It is not surprising that more than half of the senators are millionaires, as are more than one-third of House members. The fiftieth poorest member of Congress has a net worth of almost $5 million. Is wealth buying power? Is there a way to mitigate this problem? Some believe that there is.

Supporters of "Clean Elections" contend that candidates running for Congress should have public financing available, just as presidential candidates do. We need to level the playing field for congressional candidates so that personal wealth no longer matters. Today, seven states and two municipalities have so-called Clean

Elections laws providing for public financing for candidates. These laws allow qualified candidates to accept a public grant to run their campaigns, but if they do, they can no longer take private money. In some states, if they are running against a privately funded candidate who will outspend them, they qualify for additional public funding. Arizona and Maine have used this system to run their statewide and legislative races since 2000. More than half of the legislators in Arizona and 80 percent of those in Maine were elected using public funds. The results are sometimes startling. For example, in Maine a single mother who worked as a waitress became a state representative.

Those against public financing for congressional campaigns argue that the First Amendment guarantees freedom of expression, including political expression. If a wealthy person wants to express himself or herself by paying for extensive television advertising in order to win public office, no court or statute can prevent that person from doing so. Moreover, why should the public pay for the campaigns of third parties that often simply want to express a narrow view about a specific issue? States with Clean Elections laws cannot prevent third parties from obtaining public funding, even if the third party candidates have absolutely no chance of winning. This is a waste of taxpayers' dollars, not a benefit.

BUCKLEY v. VALEO   In a significant 1976 case, *Buckley v. Valeo,*[6] the United States Supreme Court declared unconstitutional the provision in the 1971 act that limited the amount each individual could spend on his or her own campaign. The Court held that a "candidate, no less than any other person, has a First Amendment right to engage in the discussion of public issues and vigorously and tirelessly to advocate his own election."

THE RISE OF PACS   The FECA allows corporations, labor unions, and special interest groups to set up *political action committees (PACs)* to raise money for candidates. For a PAC to be legitimate, the money must be raised from at least fifty volunteer donors and must be given to at least five candidates in the national elections. PACs can contribute up to $5,000 per candidate in each election, but there is no limit on the total amount of PAC contributions during an election cycle. As discussed in Chapter 6, the number of PACs has grown significantly since the 1970s, as have their campaign contributions. In the 2004 election cycle, about 36 percent of campaign funds spent on House races came from PACs.[7]

Skirting the Campaign-Financing Rules

The money spent on campaigns has been rising steadily for decades. Spending during the 2004 campaigns, though, marked a major leap—it was more than twice what it had been in 1996. Where does all this money come from? The answer is that individuals and corporations have found **loopholes**—legal ways of evading certain legal requirements—in the federal laws limiting campaign contributions.

SOFT MONEY The biggest loophole in the FECA and its amendments was that they did not prohibit individuals or corporations from contributing to political *parties*. Many contributors would make donations to the national parties to cover the costs of such activities as registering voters, printing brochures and fliers, advertising in the media (which often means running candidate-oriented ads), developing campaigns to "get out the vote," and holding fund-raising events. Contributions to political parties, instead of to particular candidates, are called **soft money** because, as one observer said, they are "so squishy." Even though soft money clearly was used to support the candidates, it was difficult to track exactly where the money was going.

Although this loophole had existed since the passage of a 1979 amendment to the federal election laws, it was little known or used until the 1990s. By 2000, though, the use of soft money had become standard operating procedure, and the parties raised nearly $463 million through soft money contributions. Soft dollars became the main source of campaign money in the presidential race, far outpacing PAC contributions and federal campaign funds. In both 1996 and 2000, the political parties and their interest group allies went to great lengths to skirt the laws that were put on the books in the 1970s.

INDEPENDENT EXPENDITURES Another major loophole in campaign-financing laws was that they did not prohibit corporations, labor unions, and special interest groups from making **independent expenditures** in an election campaign. Independent expenditures, as the term implies, are expenditures for activities that are independent from (not coordinated with) those of the candidate or a political party. In other words, interest groups can wage their own "issue" campaigns as long as they do not go so far as to say "Vote for Candidate X."

The problem is, where do you draw the line between advocating a position on a particular issue, such as abortion (which a group has a right to do under the First Amendment's guarantee of freedom of speech), and contributing to the campaign of a candidate who endorses that position? In addressing this thorny issue, the United States Supreme Court has developed two determinative tests. Under the first test, a group's speech is a campaign "expenditure" only if it explicitly calls for the election of a particular candidate. Using this test, the courts repeatedly have held that interest groups have the right to advocate their positions. For example, the Christian Coalition has the right to publish voter guides informing voters of candidates' positions. The second test applies when a group or organization has made expenditures explicitly for the purpose of endorsing a candidate. Such expenditures are permissible unless they were made in "coordination" with a campaign. According to the Supreme Court, an issue-oriented group has a First Amendment right to advocate the election of its preferred candidates as long as it acts independently.

In 1996, the Supreme Court held that these guidelines apply to expenditures by political parties as well. Parties may spend money on behalf of candidates if they do so independently—that is, if they do not let the candidates know how, when, or for what the money was spent.[8] As critics of this decision have pointed out, parties generally work closely with candidates, so establishing the "independence" of such expenditures is problematic.

> An **issue-oriented** group has a First Amendment right to advocate the election of its preferred candidates as long as it acts **independently.**

The Bipartisan Campaign Reform Act of 2002

Demand for further campaign-finance reform had been growing for several years, but in 2000 a Republican presidential candidate, John McCain,

loophole A legal way of evading a certain legal requirement.

soft money Campaign contributions not regulated by federal law, such as some contributions that are made to political parties instead of to particular candidates.

independent expenditure An expenditure for activities that are independent from (not coordinated with) those of a political candidate or a political party.

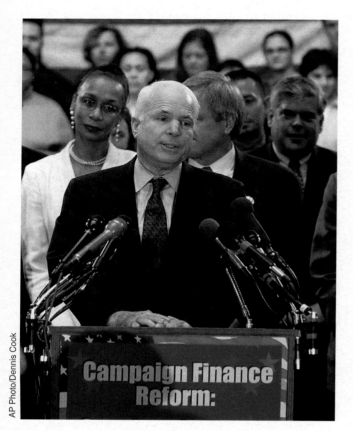

Senator John McCain (R., Ariz.) was a major sponsor of campaign-finance reform. He succeeded in passing the Bipartisan Campaign Reform Act of 2002.

made it one of the cornerstones of his campaign. McCain competed aggressively against George W. Bush in the Republican presidential primaries, and his continued popularity after he lost the Republican nomination forced Congress to address the issue in 2001. A series of corporate scandals, including the bankruptcies of Enron and WorldCom, both of which had been large campaign contributors, also kept campaign-finance reform in the public eye.

Forcing incumbent political leaders to address campaign-finance reform is one of the most difficult tasks in government. Most elected officials came to power under the existing laws. They recognize that setting tighter limits and closing loopholes could hurt their reelection bids in the future. Nonetheless, in 2002, Congress passed and the president signed the Bipartisan Campaign Reform Act.

CHANGES UNDER THE 2002 LAW The most significant change imposed by the 2002 law was to ban the large, unlimited contributions to national political parties known as soft money. The law also regulated the use of campaign ads paid for by interest groups. The 2002 act prohibited any such issue advocacy within thirty days of a primary election or sixty days of a general election.

The 2002 act increased the amount an individual can contribute to a federal candidate from $1,000 to $2,000. The amount that an individual can give to all federal candidates was raised from $25,000 per year to $95,000 over a two-year election cycle. Individuals can still contribute to state and local parties, so long as the contributions do not exceed $10,000 per year per individual. The new law went into effect on November 6, 2002.

As you read in Chapter 6, "issue advocacy" groups such as 527s have attempted to exploit soft money loopholes in the 2002 act. Because 527s technically do not endorse a particular candidate, they do not fall under the same campaign-financing restrictions as political parties and PACs. In the 2004 election cycle, 527s spent more than $550 million to "advocate positions" (see Figure 9–3).

CONSTITUTIONAL CHALLENGES TO THE 2002 LAW
Soon after the 2002 act was passed, several groups filed lawsuits challenging the constitutionality of its provisions. Supporters of the restrictions on campaign ads by special interest groups argued that the large amounts of funds spent on these ads create an appearance of corruption in the political process. In contrast, an attorney for the National Rifle Association (NRA), one of the plaintiffs claiming that the provision unconstitutionally restricts free speech, argued that because the NRA represents "millions of Americans speaking in unison . . . [it] is not a *corruption* of the democratic political process; it *is* the democratic political process."[9]

Those who drafted the law anticipated the constitutional challenges and included a provision in the law to expedite the legal process. The lawsuits went first to a three-judge panel of the U.S. District Court for the

FIGURE 9–3

EXPENDITURES BY 527s

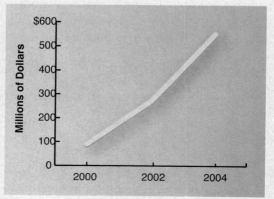

Source: Center for Public Integrity Analysis of Internal Revenue Service Reports.

District of Columbia and then directly to the United States Supreme Court. In December 2003, the Supreme Court upheld nearly all of the clauses of the act in *McConnell v. Federal Election Commission*.[10]

In 2007, however, the Supreme Court effectively invalidated a major part of the 2002 law and overruled a portion of the Supreme Court's 2003 decision upholding the act. In the four years since the earlier ruling, two new justices, both conservatives, were appointed to the Supreme Court, Chief Justice John Roberts, Jr., and Associate Justice Samuel Alito, Jr. In a close (five-to-four) decision, the conservative majority on the Court held that issue ads could not be prohibited in the time period preceding elections (thirty days before primary elections and sixty days before general elections) *unless* they were "susceptible of no reasonable interpretation other than as an appeal to vote for or against a specific candidate."[11] The Court concluded that restricting *all* television ads paid for by corporate or union treasuries in the weeks before an election amounted to censorship of political speech. "Where the First Amendment is implicated," said the Court, "the tie goes to the speaker, not the censor." The four justices who dissented from the ruling stated that the majority's decision stood the earlier Court ruling "on its head," and many critics of the decision agree.

Campaign Contributions and Policy Decisions

Considering the passion on both sides of the debate about campaign-finance reform, one might wonder how much campaign contributions actually influence policy decisions. Table 9–1 lists the top twenty industries and other groups contributing to both parties in the 2004 election cycle. These contributors must want something in return for their dollars, but what, exactly, does the money buy? Do these donations influence government policymaking?

Clearly, there is no reason to conclude that a member of Congress who received financial contributions from certain groups while campaigning for Congress will vote differently on policy issues than she or he would otherwise vote. After all, many groups make

TABLE 9–1

TOP INDUSTRIES AND OTHER GROUPS CONTRIBUTING FUNDS IN THE 2004 PRESIDENTIAL ELECTION CYCLE

Rank	Industry/Group	Amount	To Democrats	To Republicans
1	Retired People	$168,657,391	45%	55%
2	Lawyers/Law Firms	166,904,190	74	26
3	Real Estate	87,754,428	41	59
4	Securities/Investments	81,864,589	47	53
5	Health Professionals	67,463,548	37	62
6	Candidate Committees	64,776,591	61	39
7	Business Services	37,482,610	54	45
8	Insurance	34,312,720	32	68
9	Education	32,635,424	77	22
10	Leadership PACs	29,479,947	28	72
11	Commercial Banks	29,417,337	35	64
12	TV/Movies/Music	28,861,668	68	31
13	Computers/Internet	25,895,899	53	46
14	General Contractors	23,965,639	24	76
15	Lobbyists	23,833,436	48	52
16	Misc. Mfg./Distrib.	22,607,568	27	73
17	Oil & Gas	22,525,240	19	81
18	Automotive	18,545,416	22	78
19	Civil Servants	18,230,186	57	43
20	Pharm./Health Products	16,576,483	33	67

Source: Center for Responsive Politics, 2005.

contributions not so much to influence a candidate's views as to ensure that a candidate whose views the group supports will win the elections.

Many groups routinely donate to candidates from both parties so that, regardless of who wins, the groups will have access to the officeholder. Note that some of the groups listed in Table 9–1 contributed to both parties. Not surprisingly, campaign contributors find it much easier than other constituents to get in to see politicians or get them to return phone calls. Because politicians are more likely to be influenced by those with whom they have personal contacts, access is important for those who want to influence policymaking. The real question is whether money also buys votes.

LO⁴ HOW WE ELECT CANDIDATES

The drama surrounding both the 2000 and 2004 presidential elections probably caused Americans to learn more than they ever wanted to know about the election process in this country. The focus on the Florida vote in 2000 and the Ohio vote in 2004 taught citizens about the significance of balloting procedures, types of voting equipment, county election boards, state election laws, and state officials in the elective process. In 2000, even the courts became involved, and ultimately the United States Supreme Court cast the deciding "vote" on who would be our next president.

Types of Elections

The ultimate goal of the political campaign and the associated fundraising efforts is, of course, winning the election. The most familiar kind of election is the **general election,** which is a regularly scheduled election held in even-numbered years on the Tuesday after the first Monday in November. During general elections, the voters decide who will be the U.S. president, vice president, and senators and representatives in Congress. The president and vice president are elected every four years, senators every six years, and representatives every two years. General elections are also held to choose state and local government officials, often at the same time as those for national offices. A **special election** is held at the state or local level when the voters must decide an issue before the next general election or when vacancies occur by reason of death or resignation.

Types of Ballots

Since 1888, all states in the United States have used the **Australian ballot** —a secret ballot that is prepared, distributed, and counted by government officials at public expense. Two variations of the Australian ballot are used today. Most states use the **party-column ballot** (also called the Indiana ballot), which lists all of a party's candidates together in a single column under the party label. In some states, the party-column ballot allows voters to vote for all of a party's candidates for local, state, and national offices by registering a single vote. The major parties favor this ballot form because it encourages straight-ticket voting.

Other states use the **office-block ballot,** which lists together all of the candidates for each office. Politicians tend to dislike the office-block ballot because it places more emphasis on the office than on the party and thus encourages split-ticket voting.

Conducting Elections and Counting the Votes

Recall from Chapter 8 that local units of government, such as cities, are divided into smaller voting districts, or precincts. State laws usually restrict the size of precincts, and local officials set their boundaries. Within each precinct, voters cast their ballots at one polling place.

A precinct election board supervises the polling place and the voting process in each precinct. The board sets hours for the polls to be open according to the laws of the state and sees that ballots or voting machines are available. In most states, the board provides the list of registered voters and makes certain that only qualified voters cast ballots in that precinct. When the polls close, the board counts the votes and reports the results, usually to the county clerk or the board of elections. Representatives from each party, called **poll watchers,** are allowed at each polling place to make sure the election is run fairly and to avoid fraud.

Presidential Elections and the Electoral College

As you read in the *America at Odds* feature at the beginning of this chapter, when voters vote for president and vice president, they are not voting directly for the candidates. Instead, they are voting for **electors** who will cast their ballots in the **electoral college.** The electors are selected during each presidential election year by the states' political parties, subject to the laws of the state. Each state has as many electoral votes as it has U.S. senators and representatives (see Figure 9–4). In addition, there are three electors from the District of Columbia.

The electoral college system is a **winner-take-all system,** in which the candidate who receives the largest popular vote in a state is credited with all that state's electoral votes. The only exceptions are Maine and Nebraska.[12]

ELECTORAL COLLEGE VOTING   In December, after the general election, electors (either Democrats or Republicans, depending on which candidate won the state's popular vote) meet in their state capitals to cast their votes for president and vice president. When the Constitution was drafted, the framers intended that the electors would use their own discretion in deciding who would make the best president. Today, however, the electors usually vote for the candidates who won popular support in their states. The electoral college ballots are then sent to the Senate, which counts and certifies them before a joint session of Congress held early in January. The candidates who receive a majority of the electoral votes are officially declared president and vice president. To be elected, a candidate must receive more than half of the 538 electoral votes available. Thus, a candidate needs 270 votes to win. If no presidential candidate gets an electoral college majority (which has happened twice—in 1800 and 1824), the House of Representatives votes on the candidates, with each state delegation casting

AP Photo/Will Shilling

These electors have met to cast their votes for president and vice president. Normally, the candidates receiving the most popular votes also receive all of the votes of the electors in each state.

only a single vote. If no candidate for vice president gets a majority of electoral votes, the vice president is chosen by the Senate, with each senator casting one vote.

WERE THE 2000 ELECTIONS AN ANOMALY?   The events surrounding the 2000 presidential elections are still fresh in the minds of some Americans. It was the first time since 1888 that the electoral college system gave Americans a president who had not won the popular vote.[13] The events of the 2000 elections will undoubtedly be recounted in history books, but was the outcome an anomaly? Can we expect the winner of the popular vote also to win the electoral vote for the next 112 years? Or will presidential elections continue to be close in the near future, even as close as the 2000 elections?

In 2000, then vice president Al Gore won the popular vote by 540,000 votes. Nonetheless, on election night, the outcome in Florida, which

FIGURE 9-4

STATE ELECTORAL VOTES IN 2004 AND 2008

The map of the United States shown here is distorted to show the relative weights of the states in terms of the electoral votes in 2004 and 2008, following the changes required by the 2000 census. A candidate must win 270 electoral votes to be elected president.

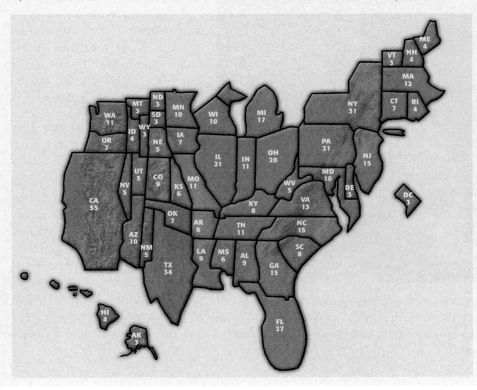

winner-take-all system
In most states, the system that awards all of the state's electoral votes to the candidate who receives the most popular votes in that state.

would have given Gore the winning votes in the electoral college, was deemed "too close to call." Initially, George W. Bush was leading Al Gore by only 1,700 votes, out of 6 million cast in that state. The first recount in Florida reduced Bush's lead to just over 300 votes. Controversy erupted over the types of ballots used, however, and some counties in Florida began recounting ballots by hand. This was the issue that ultimately came before the United States Supreme Court: Did manual recounts of some ballots but not others violate the Constitution's equal protection clause? On December 12, five weeks after the election, the Supreme Court ultimately ruled against the manual recounts. The final vote tally in Florida gave Bush a 537-vote lead, all of Florida's twenty-five electoral votes, and the presidency.[14]

Other recent presidential elections have been extremely close. In 1960, John F. Kennedy defeated Richard Nixon by fewer than 120,000 votes, out of 70 million cast, although Kennedy had a sizable victory in

"A POLITICIAN SHOULD HAVE THREE HATS: ONE FOR THROWING INTO THE RING, ONE FOR TALKING THROUGH, AND ONE FOR PULLING RABBITS OUT OF IF ELECTED."

CARL SANDBURG,
AMERICAN POET AND HISTORIAN
1878–1967

the electoral college. In 1968, a shift of only 60,000 votes to third-party candidate George C. Wallace would have thrown the race into the House of Representatives. Again in 1976, a shift of only a few thousand votes would have produced an electoral victory for Gerald Ford despite a popular vote win for Jimmy Carter.

THE 2004 ELECTIONS The 2004 presidential elections produced another close race, with President Bush edging Democratic challenger John Kerry by a mere thirty-five electors. Unlike in 2000, Bush won the popular vote in 2004, defeating Kerry by a 3 percentage point margin. Many commentators argued that the elections were decided by the closely contested vote in Ohio. A repeat of the 2000 fiasco in Florida was averted, however.

From early in the 2004 election cycle, Ohio had been viewed as a *battleground state*—a state where voters were not clearly leaning toward a particular candidate leading up to the elections. Some political analysts and news media outlets placed a great deal of emphasis on the so-called battleground states, arguing that these states could potentially decide the outcome with their electoral votes.

When a president wins by a wide margin in a so-called *landslide election*, what does that really mean? See this chapter's *Perception versus Reality* feature for an answer to that question.

FUTURE ELECTIONS ARE NOT EASY TO PREDICT Some scholars have suggested that we simply know too little about elections to make any predictions about the future. Polls are not as accurate as we hope. Voters are not as predictable as we think. Finally, variables such as third-party candidates and voter turnout will continue to affect future elections. Most political pundits, though, believed that the Democratic candidate

AP Photo/Victor R. Caivano

After claims of voting irregularities and improper voting procedures, many counties in Florida began manually recounting the votes cast for president in the 2000 elections. Here, these Florida officials attempted to establish the actual votes cast for the two candidates by holding up the voting punch cards to see if the "chads" had been clearly punched out or not.

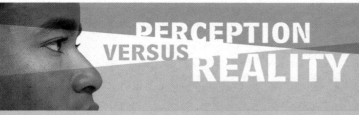

PERCEPTION VERSUS REALITY

Presidents and the "Popular Vote"

Every four years, American citizens go to the polls to cast their votes for the presidential candidate of their choice. Some presidential contests are very close, such as the 2000 race between Al Gore and George W. Bush and the 2004 race between John Kerry and Bush. Others are less so, such as the one between Lyndon Johnson and Barry Goldwater in 1964. When a presidential candidate wins the race by a wide margin, we may hear the result referred to as a *landslide election* or a *landslide victory* for the winning candidate.

The Perception

The traditional perception has been that, in general, our presidents are elected by a majority of eligible American voters. As the people's choice, the president is beholden to the wishes of the broad American electorate that voted him into office. A president who has been swept into office by a so-called landslide victory may claim to have received a "mandate from the people" to govern the nation. A president may assert that a certain policy or program he endorsed in campaign speeches is backed by popular support simply because he was elected to office by a majority of the voters.

The Reality

In reality, the "popular vote" is not all that popular, in the sense of representing the wishes of a majority of American citizens who are eligible to vote. In fact, the president of the United States has never received the votes of a majority of all adults of voting age. Lyndon Johnson, in 1964, came the closest of any president in history to gaining the votes of a majority of the voting-age public, and even he won the votes of less than 40 percent of those who were old enough to cast a ballot.

The hotly contested presidential elections of 2000 and 2004 were divisive, leaving the millions of Americans who had voted for the

losing candidates unhappy with the results. In neither 2000 nor 2004 did a candidate win a significant number of states by more than 20 percent of the vote. Indeed, in winning the elections of 2000 and 2004, Bush received the votes of a mere 24.5 percent and 27.6 percent of the voting-age population, respectively. Nonetheless, Bush claimed that his 2004 victory represented a "mandate" from the American people, saying: "I have earned capital in the campaign, political capital, and now I intend to spend it." Bush assumed that his reelection was a signal from the American people to push his controversial domestic ideas, such as Social Security reform, as well as an endorsement of his foreign policy and the war on terrorism. Yet 72.4 percent of the voting-age population did not vote for him.

It is useful to keep these figures in mind whenever a president claims to have received a mandate from the people. The truth is, no president has ever been elected with sufficient popular backing to make this a serious claim.

Cecil Stoughton/Corbis

President Lyndon Johnson, shown here campaigning in 1964, came closest to receiving the votes of the majority of the voting-age population.

BLOG ON

Dave Leip's Atlas of U.S. Presidential Elections hosts a major discussion site at **www.uselectionatlas.org** where hundreds of guests discuss election results. You can find detailed figures to back up your arguments elsewhere on Dave's site, along with an electoral college calculator that lets you figure out how many electoral votes a candidate will receive if he or she carries a particular share of the states.

for the presidency likely had a better chance than the Republican candidate in the 2008 presidential elections. This was because of the strong public opinion against the Republican administration and its policies at the time. If by some miracle the war in Iraq had been terminated before the 2008 presidential elections, the anti-Bush sentiment would have still remained significant. Consequently, the Democrats were guaranteed to go into those elections with a distinct advantage.

AMERICA AT ODDS:
Campaigns and Elections

The U.S. Constitution includes some provisions about elections, but it says nothing about how candidates will be selected or run for political office. In the very early years of the nation, many of the founders wondered how candidates would be nominated after George Washington left the presidency. Most envisioned that candidates would simply "stand" for election, rather than actively run for office. Instead of shaking hands and making speeches, candidates would stay on their farms and wait for the people's call, as Washington had done. Some of the framers believed that the electors of the electoral college would put forward candidates' names. Some observers believe that if the founders could see how presidential campaigns are conducted today, they would be shocked at how candidates "pander to the masses."

Whether they would be shocked at the costliness of modern campaigns is not as clear. After all, the founders themselves were an elitist, wealthy group, as are today's successful candidates for high political offices. In any event, Americans today are certainly shocked at how much money it takes to win political office. Seats in Congress and the presidency are increasingly held by millionaires. This means that someone without independent wealth or the ability to attract significant amounts of campaign contributions simply has no chance to compete, no matter how qualified that person may be. Campaign-finance reform laws have attempted to ease this problem by providing funds for presidential candidates. Yet to accept government funds, presidential candidates must forgo other financial backing. If a candidate has alternative sources of funds and wants to compete effectively in a presidential race, he or she is likely to refuse federal funding—as Hillary Clinton did during the 2008 presidential campaigns. Also, attempts to curb the influence of money in elections through campaign-finance reform may violate the constitutional right to free political expression—a value at the heart of our democracy. The old saying that "anyone can become president" in this country, if it was ever true, is certainly not a reality today. In fact, fewer and fewer Americans can even hope to win a seat in Congress.

Issues for Debate & Discussion

1. In democratically held elections in Palestine in 2006, the terrorist group known as Hamas won a majority of the legislative seats and thus majority control of the Palestinian government. Because of Hamas's terrorist activities and its stated desire to destroy the state of Israel, however, the Western powers have since refused to deal with Hamas as a legitimate governing force. Some Americans believe that any government elected by a majority of the people in a democratic election should be recognized as legitimate, regardless of that government's agenda, and that the decision of the United States not to recognize Hamas is contrary to the stated U.S. goal of supporting elections and spreading democracy to the Middle East. Others maintain that a terrorist group such as Hamas, regardless of how it came to power, should not be recognized as legitimate by other nations. What is your position on this issue?

2. Our Constitution states that the U.S. president should be elected by electors. We have come to call this system the electoral college. To abolish this electoral college requirement would thus require a constitutional amendment, and amending the Constitution, as you read in Chapter 2, is very difficult to do. Consider that over five hundred amendments to abolish the electoral college have been proposed, yet none has been adopted. Review the *Join the Debate* feature in Chapter 3 on page 55, which discusses a movement gaining momentum in some areas to skirt the Constitution's electoral college requirement by creating an interstate compact among the states to allow the president to be elected by popular vote. Do you agree that the president should be elected by popular vote? Why or why not? What is your position on this issue?

Take Action

As you have read in this chapter, many groups have worked toward reforming the way campaign funds are raised and spent in politics today. One nonprofit, nonpartisan, grassroots organization that lobbies for campaign-finance reform is Common Cause. In the photo below, a participant in Colorado Common Cause's effort to reform campaign financing holds up a mock-up of a TV remote control with a large mute button at a news conference. The group was asking voters to "mute" attack ads directed against a Colorado initiative to amend the state constitution to limit campaign financing and set contribution limits.

AP Photo/Ed Andrieski

- You can find out exactly what the letter of the law is with respect to campaign financing by accessing the Federal Election Commission's Web site. The commission has provided an online "Citizen's Guide" that spells out exactly what is and is not legal. You can also download actual data on campaign donations from the site. Go to **www.fec.gov**.

- To look at the data available from the Federal Election Commission in a more user-friendly way, you can access the following nonpartisan, independent site that allows you to type in an elected official's name and receive large amounts of information on contributions to that official. Go to **moneyline.cq.com/pml/home.do**.

- Another excellent source for information on campaign financing, including who's contributing what amounts to which candidates, is the Center for Responsive Politics. You can access its Web site at **www.opensecrets.org**.

- Common Cause offers similar information on its Web site at **www.commoncause.org**.

- Project Vote Smart offers information on campaign financing, as well as voting, on its Web site at **www.vote–smart.org**.

ONLINE RESOURCES FOR THIS CHAPTER

This text's Companion Web site, at **www.americaatodds. com,** offers links to numerous resources that you can utilize to learn more about the topics covered in this chapter.

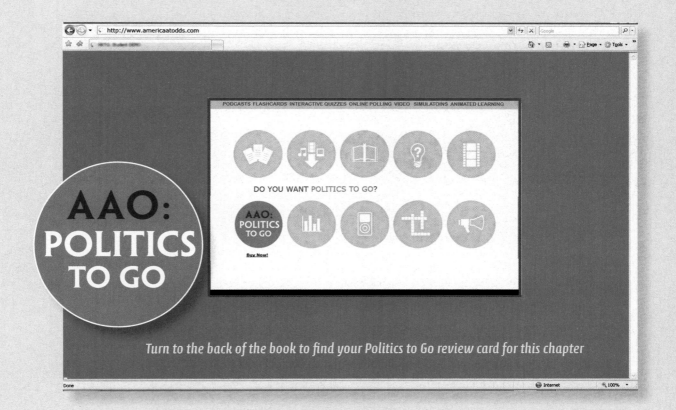

Turn to the back of the book to find your Politics to Go review card for this chapter

CHAPTER 10
POLITICS AND THE MEDIA

LEARNING OBJECTIVES

LO¹ Explain the role of a free press in a democracy.

LO² Summarize how television influences the conduct of political campaigns.

LO³ Explain why talk radio has been described as the "Wild West" of the media.

LO⁴ Describe types of media bias and explain how such bias affects the political process.

LO⁵ Indicate the extent to which the Internet is reshaping news and political campaigns.

AMERICA AT ODDS

ON PODCAST

Is the Web Creating a Dictatorship of the "Sort of" Informed?

Cyberspace is getting bigger every nanosecond of every day. In 1995, there were fewer than 20,000 Web sites. Today, there are more than 100 million. One blog tracker, Technorati, is tracking almost 90 million blogs, with nearly 200,000 being added daily. Bloggers update with new posts at a rate of eighteen per second, twenty-four hours a day. About 800 million adults log on to the Web during any given month. Popular social networking sites, such as MySpace, have close to 200 million personalized pages.

Gone are the days when you and your friends tromped to the library to research a paper. Why should you? You can go online and in a matter of seconds look up practically any subject through a search engine or through Wikipedia, the community-generated online collaborative encyclopedia. Of course, all major newspapers are online, as are transcripts of major television news programs. Increasingly, though, you may encounter a problem with accuracy. User-generated materials on such sites as YouTube, MySpace, and Wikipedia are notorious for being less than impartial and accurate. With so much information available from so many sources, is the Internet creating a mass of barely usable facts and opinions?

Web Information— Unreviewed and Unreliable

Some people warn that those doing research online should remember the saying "You get what you pay for." Most sources of information on the Internet are free. For example, nobody is paid to create the information or to edit it for Wikipedia. Although much of that information is quite good, some of it can be dead wrong. Just ask John Seigenthaler, Sr., an assistant to Attorney General Robert Kennedy in the early 1960s. For months, an article on Seigenthaler in Wikipedia stated that he was thought to have been "directly involved in the Kennedy assassinations of both John, and his brother Bobby." The article also stated that Seigenthaler had moved to the Soviet Union and lived there for thirteen years. The information was 100 percent wrong and was finally removed. Consider another aspect of Wikipedia. A creator of more than sixteen thousand Wikipedia entries identified himself as "a tenured professor of religion with a Ph.D. in theology." In reality, he was a twenty-four-year-old college dropout.

Today, we face a self-broadcasting culture, in which it is cheap or easy to create a blog, a Web site, or videos for YouTube. The distinction between trained experts and uninformed amateurs no longer seems to exist. Anonymous bloggers and videographers are not necessarily constrained by professional standards or editorial filters. Nonetheless, they can alter public debate and even manipulate public opinion. According to one writer on the subject, Andrew Keen, "Information on the Web involves a situation in which ignorance meets egotism meets bad taste meets mob rule."

LIGHTEN UP—THE CREAM WILL RISE TO THE TOP

Others think that such negative views of the Web are overblown. They point out that blogs were unknown a decade ago. So, too, was YouTube. It is only relatively recently that newspapers and television stations have created Web sites on which they post content. Times change, and perhaps they are changing too fast for some people, but ultimately that won't be a problem. We are not discussing an all-or-nothing situation. Information may seem to be drifting toward the "cult of the amateur," but, contrary to popular belief, the mainstream press and its methods of obtaining the news are not disappearing.

People who are serious about obtaining accurate, informed, and unbiased information don't go to social networking sites such as MySpace to obtain news. Moreover, serious college students doing research for term papers do not read just one source from somebody's blog. Instead, they access some of the approximately eighteen thousand academic databases. The *Chronicle of Higher Education* reports that an increasing number of colleges and universities have established new programs to teach undergraduates how to use the Internet and the online card catalogue to search for the best sources of information. Centuries ago, the printing press disrupted existing, tried-and-true sources of information. Today, the Internet is doing the same thing. New business models on the Web will create opportunities for information excellence to be rewarded. Ultimately, the American public will get the media that it deserves.

From its inception, the Web has always made both reliable and unreliable information available. Most users are aware of this problem and take steps to avoid it.

Where do you stand?

1. Because Wikipedia is anonymously generated for free, is there any way to check the reliability of its content? If not, what are the pitfalls of using it?
2. If it is difficult for businesses to sell news and information on the Internet because there are so many free competitors, what does that tell you about the value of for-fee information?

Explore this issue online

- One of the best ways to evaluate Wikipedia is to visit it yourself at **en.wikipedia.org**. For a sense of the articles, click on one of the links on the left, such as "Featured content" or "Random article." If you click on the "discussion" tab at the top of every article, you may see debates about how the article was written.
- For an online news source with a bent toward sensationalism, check out the Drudge Report at **www.drudgereport.com**. How is this site different from printed news sources?

"The press may not be successful much of the time in telling people **what** to think, but it is stunningly successful in telling its readers what to **think about.**"

BERNARD C. COHEN,
POLITICAL SCIENTIST
1926–PRESENT

INTRODUCTION

The debate over the reliability of information on the Web is just one aspect of an important topic that you will read about in this chapter: the role of the media in American politics. Strictly defined, the term *media* means communication channels. It is the plural form of *medium of communication*. In this strict sense, any method used by people to communicate—including the telephone—is a communication medium. In this chapter, though, we look at the **mass media**—channels through which people can communicate to mass audiences. These channels include the **print media** (newspapers and magazines) and the **electronic media** (radio, television, and, to an increasing extent, the Internet).

The media are a dominant presence in our lives largely because they provide entertainment. Americans today enjoy more leisure time than at any time in history, and we fill it up with books, movies, and television—a huge amount of television. But the media play a vital role in our political lives as well. The media have a wide-ranging influence on American politics, particularly during campaigns and elections. Politicians and political candidates have learned—often the hard way—that positive media exposure and news coverage are essential to winning votes.

As you read in Chapter 4, one of the

mass media Communication channels, such as newspapers and radio and television broadcasts, through which people can communicate to mass audiences.

print media Communication channels that consist of printed materials, such as newspapers and magazines.

electronic media Communication channels that involve electronic transmissions, such as radio, television, and, to an extent, the Internet.

most important civil liberties protected in the Bill of Rights is freedom of the press. Like free speech, a free press is considered a vital tool of the democratic process. If people are to cast informed votes, they must have access to a forum in which they can discuss public affairs fully and assess the conduct and competency of their officials. The media provide this forum. In contrast, government censorship of the press is common in many nations around the globe. These nations now include Russia, in which freedom of the press is rapidly disappearing—see this chapter's *The Rest of the World* feature for details.

LO¹ THE ROLE OF THE MEDIA IN A DEMOCRACY

The exact nature of the media's influence on the political process today is difficult to characterize. Clearly, what the media say and do has an impact on what Americans think about political issues. But just as clearly, the media also *reflect* what Americans think about politics. Some scholars argue that the media is the fourth "check" in our political system—checking and balancing the power of the president, the Congress, and the courts. The power of the media today is enormous, but how the media use their power is an issue about which Americans are often at odds.

JOIN THE DEBATE

Should the Media Be Prohibited from Publishing Secret Government Information?

According to an old saying about government secrets in wartime, "Loose lips sink ships." Revealing secret government information can harm any nation. After the terrorist attacks of September 11, 2001, the Bush administration implemented a number of secret programs as part of its war on terrorism. Over time, various administration officials who were concerned about the legality of these programs "leaked" information about them to members of the press. Not surprisingly, the pub-

Independent Media Have All but Disappeared in Russia

If you live in Russia and want to find out what is going on inside your country, you have to leave that country so that you can read the foreign press. This all started in 2000. Vladimir Putin, formerly an official in the KGB—the state security service in the former Soviet Union—became president and immediately tightened the government's grip on the Russian media. Putin sought to defuse any political dissent or criticism of the government, forcing media moguls with critical views to surrender their ownership of media outlets to the government. He described his media policies as an attempt to create a "manageable democracy."

THERE IS NO INDEPENDENT PRESS ANYMORE

In 2006, a Putin-connected businessperson, Alisher Usmanov, bought out the last remaining independent newspaper in Russia, *Kommersant.* Perhaps even more disturbing is the fact that since 2000, at least twenty-four Russian journalists have been killed. Among them was the editor of *Forbes Russia,* who was shot nine times outside his Moscow office.

This woman checks the news at an Internet café in Moscow.

AP Photo/Sergey Ponomarev

INDEPENDENT TV HAS LONG SINCE DISAPPEARED

Not only have the free print media disappeared, but there are no truly independent Russian TV stations anymore. All of the major television channels are state controlled. Even the smaller broadcasters, such as Ren-TV, no longer have any independence. Today, Russian television offers some of the blandest programming around, reminiscent of what it was like in Communist days.

THERE IS STILL THE INTERNET, THOUGH

As this book went to press, the Russian government had not yet cracked down on Internet use the way the Chinese government did. Internet news sites were still offering a variety of independent analyses of Russian politics. The problem is that only about 13 percent of Russians have access to the Internet. In any event, the Russian government started to talk openly about clamping down on the dissemination of Internet news. One high-placed government official, Valery Tishakov, said, "The Internet cannot exist without public monitoring; otherwise, it threatens to destroy the society."

For Critical Analysis

When there are no independent media, government leaders may not know what the public really thinks about important policy issues. Why might this problem matter to Russian government leaders in the long run?

---

lication of government secrets by the press led to several clashes and raised an important question: Should the government be allowed to prohibit the publication of secret information in the interest of national security? Or does the freedom of the press guaranteed by the First Amendment take priority in all such situations?

Many executive editors of the nation's most important news media outlets, such as the *New York Times,* argue that the founders believed that an aggressive, independent press was an important protective measure against the abuse of government power. Newspaper, magazine, and television news editors must assume that American citizens can be entrusted with compli-

cated and sometimes even unpleasant news about what their government is doing. We can't simply use the excuse that "we are at war" to quash sensitive information leaked to the press. When a government action is clearly wrong, the public outcry is and should be great. That is exactly what happened in 2005 when the press leaked that the National Security Agency had been wiretapping phone calls within the United States for years without a warrant.

Some government officials—and many average Americans—don't agree. Under the Espionage Act of 1917, it is a crime to "willfully communicate . . . to any person not entitled to receive it" any "information

Television images of death and suffering in Vietnam greatly influenced the U.S. public's desire to end that war in the early 1970s.

Here, terrorist Osama bin Laden, the presumptive head of al Qaeda, is shown in a video clip "lecturing" the world. Media coverage often influences not how we think, but what we think about.

related to the national defense which . . . the possessor has reason to believe could be used to the injury of the United States or to the advantage of any foreign nation." While the Espionage Act was intended to punish government employees and contractors for passing classified information to foreign agents, the act does not exempt any class of professionals, including reporters. When the U.S. government engages in a monitoring program to catch terrorists—by tracking international bank transfers, for example—the government needs its activities to remain secret. Once such programs are exposed, their usefulness either diminishes or disappears completely. The more terrorists know about how the United States is trying to thwart their actions, the worse off Americans are.

The Agenda-Setting Function of the Media

One of the criticisms often levied against the media is that they play too large a role in determining the issues, events, and personalities that are in the public eye. When people hear the evening's top news stories, they usually assume automatically that these stories concern the most important issues facing the nation. In actuality, the media decide the relative importance of issues by publicizing some issues and ignoring others, and by giving some stories high priority and others low priority. By helping to determine what people will talk and think about, the media set the *political agenda*—the issues that politicians will address. In other words, to borrow from Bernard Cohen's classic statement on the

media and public opinion, the press [media] may *not* be successful in telling people what to think, but it is "stunningly successful in telling its readers what to think about."[1]

For example, television played a significant role in shaping public opinion concerning the Vietnam War (1964–1975), which has been called the first "television war." Part of the public opposition to the war in the late 1960s came about as a result of the daily portrayal of the war's horrors on TV news programs. Film footage and narrative accounts of the destruction, death, and suffering in Vietnam—at the height of the war, some five hundred soldiers were being killed each week—brought the war into living rooms across the United States.

Current events in Iraq have also been the subject of constant news coverage. Some believe that the media played a crucial role in influencing public opinion at the outset of the war. Indeed, recently the media have been sharply criticized by media watchdog groups for failing to do more "fact checking" prior to the invasion of Iraq. Instead of investigating the Bush administration's assertions that Iraq had weapons of mass destruction and links to al Qaeda, the media just passed this information on to the public. If the media had done their job, claim these critics, there would have been little, if any, public support for going to war with Iraq.

The degree to which the media influence public opinion is not always all that clear, however. As you read in Chapter 8, some studies show that people filter the information they receive from the media through their own preconceived ideas about issues. Scholars who try to analyze the relationship between American politics and the media inevitably confront the chicken-and-egg conundrum: Do the media cause the public to hold certain views, or do the media merely reflect views that are formed independently of the media's influence?

The Medium Does Affect the Message

Of all the media, television has the greatest impact. Television reaches into almost every home in the United States. Virtually all homes have televisions. Even outside their homes, Americans can watch television—in airports, shopping malls, golf clubhouses, and medical offices. People can download TV programs to their iPods and view the programs whenever and wherever they want.

For some time, it was predicted that as more people used the Internet, fewer people would turn to television for news or entertainment. This prediction turned out to be off the mark. Today, Americans watch more television than ever, and it is the primary news source for more than 65 percent of Americans. Figure 10–1 shows the clear prominence of television when compared with other media.

As you will read shortly, politicians take maximum advantage of the power and influence of television. But does the television medium alter the presentation of political information in any way? If you compare the coverage given to an important political issue by the print media and by the TV networks, you will note some striking differences. For one thing, the print media (particularly leading newspapers such as the *Washington Post,* the *New York Times,* and the *Wall Street Journal*) treat an important issue in much more detail. In addition to news stories based on reporters' research, you will find editorials taking positions on the issue and arguments supporting those positions. Television news, in contrast, is often criticized as being too brief and too superficial.

> **sound bite** In televised news reporting, a brief comment, lasting for only a few seconds, that captures a thought or a perspective and has an immediate impact on the viewers.

TIME CONSTRAINTS The medium of television necessarily imposes constraints, particularly with respect to time, on how political issues are presented. News stories must be reported quickly, in only a few minutes or occasionally in only a **sound bite,** a brief comment lasting for just a few seconds that captures a thought or a perspective and has an immediate impact on the viewers.

A VISUAL MEDIUM Television reporting also relies extensively on visual elements, rather than words, to capture the viewers' attention. Inevitably, the photos or videos selected to depict a particular political event have exaggerated importance. The visual aspect of television contributes to its power, but it also creates a potential bias. Those watching the news presentation do not know what portions of a video being shown have been deleted, what other photos may have been taken, or whether other records of the event exist. This kind of "selection bias" will be discussed in more detail later in this chapter.

FIGURE 10-1

MEDIA USAGE BY CONSUMERS, 1988 TO PRESENT

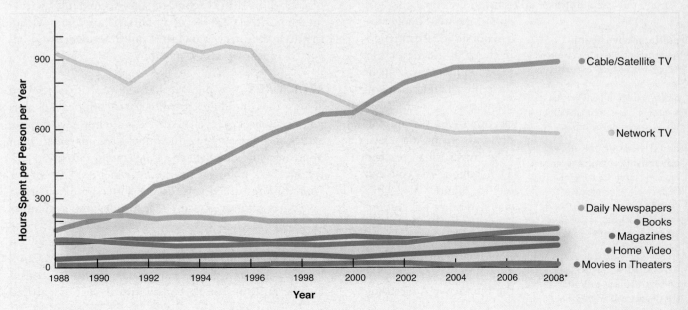

*Projected.
Source: U.S. Department of Commerce, *Statistical Abstract of the United States, 2007* (Washington, D.C.: U.S. Government Printing Office, 2007), p. 709.

TELEVISION IS "BIG BUSINESS" Today's TV networks compete aggressively with each other to air "breaking news" and to produce quality news programs. Competition in the television industry understandably has had an effect on how the news is presented. To make profits, or even stay in business, TV stations need viewers. And to attract viewers, the news industry has turned to "infotainment"—programs that inform and entertain at the same time. Slick sets, attractive reporters, and animated graphics that dance across the television screen are now commonplace on most news programs, particularly on the cable news channels.

TV networks also compete with each other for advertising income. Although the media in the United States are among the freest in the world, their programming nonetheless remains vulnerable to the influence of the political bias of their advertising sponsors.

LO² THE CANDIDATES AND TELEVISION

Given the TV-saturated environment in which we live, it should come as no surprise that candidates spend a great deal of time—and money—obtaining TV coverage through political ads, debates, and general news coverage. Candidates and their campaign managers realize that the time and money are well spent because television has an important impact on the way people see the candidates, understand the issues, and cast their votes.

Political Advertising

Today, televised **political advertising** consumes at least half of the total budget for a major political campaign. In the 2000 election cycle, $665 million was spent for political advertising on broadcast TV. In the 2004 election cycle, the amount of funds spent on television advertising reached $1.5 billion. As you can see in Figure 10–2, this was five times the amount spent in the 1992 election cycle. For the 2006 elections, this figure climbed to $1.6 billion. According to the Interactive Advertising

political advertising Advertising undertaken by or on behalf of a political candidate to familiarize voters with the candidate and his or her views on campaign issues; also advertising for or against policy issues.

negative political advertising Political advertising undertaken for the purpose of discrediting an opposing candidate in the eyes of the voters. Attack ads and issue ads are forms of negative political advertising.

attack ad A negative political advertisement that attacks the character of an opposing candidate.

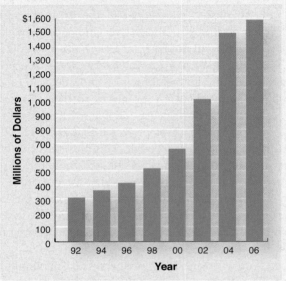

Sources: Television Bureau of Advertising, as presented in Lorraine Woellert and Tom Lowry, "A Political Nightmare: Not Enough Airtime," *BusinessWeek*, November 23, 2000, p. 111; and authors' updates.

FIGURE 10–2

POLITICAL AD SPENDING ON BROADCAST TELEVISION, 1992–2006

As you can see in this figure, spending for political advertising has increased steadily over the last eight elections.

Bureau, spending on political advertising could reach $10 billion in the 2008 election cycle.

Political advertising first appeared on television during the 1952 presidential campaign. At that time, there were only about 15 million television sets; today, there are well over 100 million. Initially, political TV commercials were more or less like any other type of advertising. Instead of focusing on the positive qualities of a product, thirty-second or sixty-second ads focused on the positive qualities of a political candidate. Within the decade, however, **negative political advertising** began to appear in the TV medium.

ATTACK ADS Despite the barrage of criticism levied against the candidates' use of negative political ads during recent election cycles, such ads are not new. Indeed, **attack ads**—advertising that attacks the character of an opposing candidate—have a long tradition in this country. In 1800, an article in the *Federalist Gazette of the United States* described Thomas Jefferson as having a "weakness of nerves, want of fortitude, and total imbecility of character." Two hundred and six years later, the candidates went even further, creating ads filled with allegations of moral bankruptcy and sexual perversion. For example, the Republican challenger for Wisconsin Democrat Ron Kind's congressional seat advertised that "Rep. Kind pays for sex!" Moreover, claimed the ads, the Democrat wanted to "let illegal aliens burn the American flag" and to "allow convicted child molesters to enter the country."

One news analyst claimed that the ads broadcast during the 2006 campaigns created "the most toxic campaign environment in memory."[2] Another reporter wrote that it was "kitchen-sink time: Desperate candidates are throwing everything."[3] Indeed, in the final weeks before the election, about 90 percent of the political advertising consisted of attack ads.

In his recent book, *Going Dirty: The Art of Negative Campaigning*,[4] David Mark notes that negative campaigning has increased sharply since the terrorist attacks of September 11, 2001. Since then, candidates have found that ads involving fear of terrorism resonate with voters, so they routinely accuse their opponents of lacking the ability to wage war on terrorism.

ISSUE ADS Candidates also use **issue ads**—ads that focus on flaws in the opponents' positions on issues. For example, in the 2004 presidential campaigns, rarely did the candidates attack each other personally. Rather, they leveled criticisms at each other's stated positions on various issues, such as the war in Iraq and Social Security, and previous actions with respect to those issues. Candidates also try to undermine their opponents' credibility by pointing to discrepancies between what the opponents say in their campaign speeches and their political records, such as voting records, which are available to the public and thus can easily be verified. As noted in Chapters 6 and 9, issue ads are also used by interest groups to gather support for candidates who endorse the groups' causes. As discussed in Chapter 9, Congress restricted the use of issue ads in the Bipartisan Campaign Reform Act of 2002. In 2007, however, the United States Supreme Court eased these restrictions considerably.[5]

Doyle, Dane, and Bernbach / Aretino Industries/ABC News

The "daisy" commercial (left) was used by President Lyndon B. Johnson in 1964. A remake (right) targeted Democratic candidate Al Gore in the 2000 elections. The ad contended that because the Clinton/Gore administration "sold" the nation's security "to Communist Red China in exchange for campaign contributions," China has "the ability to threaten our homes with long-range nuclear warheads." It then showed a girl, counting down as she plucked daisy petals. Her counting was then replaced by a countdown of a missile, which was followed by a nuclear bomb explosion. Then, the phrase, "Don't take a chance. Please vote Republican," appeared on the screen. The ad proved so controversial that it was pulled shortly after it began airing on television.

Issue ads can be even more devastating than personal attacks—as Barry Goldwater learned in 1964 when his opponent in the presidential race, President Lyndon Johnson, aired the "daisy girl" ad. This ad, which set new boundaries for political advertising, showed a little girl standing quietly in a field of daisies. She held a daisy and pulled off the petals, counting to herself. Suddenly, a deep voice was heard counting: "10, 9, 8, 7, 6 . . . ." When the countdown hit zero, the unmistakable mushroom cloud of an atomic bomb filled the screen. Then President Johnson's voice was heard saying, "These are the stakes: to make a world in which all of God's children can live, or to go into the dark. We must either love each other or we must die." A message on the screen then read: "Vote for President Johnson on November 3." The implication, of course, was that Goldwater would lead the country into a nuclear war.[6]

NEGATIVE ADVERTISING—IS IT GOOD OR BAD FOR OUR DEMOCRACY? The debate over the effect of negative advertising on our political system is ongoing. Some observers argue that negative ads can backfire. Extreme ads may create sympathy for the candidate being attacked rather than support for the attacker, particularly when the charges against

© The Cartoon Bank. Used with permission.

"The thing to do now, Senator, is to hit back with some negative advertising of our own."

issue ad A negative political advertisement that focuses on flaws in an opposing candidate's position on a particular issue.

The 1960 presidential debate between Republican Vice President Richard M. Nixon (left) and Senator John F. Kennedy, the Democratic presidential nominee (right), was viewed by many as helping Kennedy win at the polls.

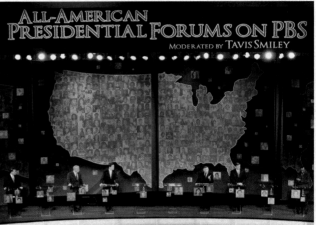

During 2007, many of the Democratic candidates for the presidential nomination (in the top photo) participated in numerous televised debates. The candidates seeking the Republican presidential nomination (in the bottom photo) did the same.

the candidate being attacked are not credible. Attack ads and "dirty tricks" used by both parties during a campaign may also alienate citizens from the political process itself and thus lower voter turnout in elections.

Yet candidates and their campaign managers typically assert that they use negative advertising simply because it works. Negative TV ads are more likely than positive ads to grab the viewers' attention and make an impression. Also, according to media expert Shanto Iyengar, "the more negative the ad, the more likely it is to get free media coverage. So there's a big incentive to go to extremes."[7] Others believe that negative advertising is a force for the good because it sharpens public debate, thereby enriching the democratic process. This is the position taken by Vanderbilt University political science professor John Geer. He contends that negative ads are likely to focus on substantive political issues instead of candidates' personal characteristics. Thus, negative ads do a better job of informing the voters about important campaign issues than positive ads do.[8]

Television Debates

Televised debates have been a feature of presidential campaigns since 1960, when presidential candidates Republican Richard M. Nixon and Democrat John F. Kennedy squared off in the first great TV debate. Television debates provide an opportunity for voters to find out how candidates differ on issues. They also allow candidates to capitalize on the power of television to improve their images or point out the failings of their opponents.

The presidential debates of 1992 included a third-party candidate, H. Ross Perot, along with the candidates from the two major parties, Republican George H. W.

Bush, the incumbent president, and Democrat Bill Clinton. In 1996, two third-party candidates, H. Ross Perot and John Hagelin, sought to participate in the TV debates but were prevented from doing so by the Commission for Presidential Debates.[9]

In 2000, the commission similarly excluded Ralph Nader and Pat Buchanan from the debates. That year, there were three presidential debates, each using a different format, between George W. Bush and Al Gore and one vice-presidential debate between their respective running mates, Dick Cheney and Joe Lieberman.

The 2004 debates followed the practice of excluding third-party candidates, once again denying independent Ralph Nader the opportunity to participate. Nevertheless, George W. Bush and John Kerry engaged in some spirited exchanges, filled with attacks on each other's viewpoints and stances. As in 2000, there were three presidential debates along with a vice-presidential debate between Dick Cheney and John Edwards. Much of the four debates' content focused on the war in Iraq, the threat of terrorism, health care, and the economy.

Senator John McCain (R., Ariz.) carried out a highly scripted trip to Iraq as part of his campaign to become the Republican presidential nominee in the 2008 presidential elections.

Jon Stewart, host of *The Daily Show with Jon Stewart*, presents a comical view of the news. A surprisingly high percentage of young people get their "news" from his show.

Many contend that the presidential debates offer a significant opportunity for voters to assess the personalities and issue positions of the candidates. Thus, the debates help to shape the outcome of the elections. Others doubt that these televised debates—or the "spins" put on them by political commentators immediately after they are over—have ever been taken very seriously by voters.

News Coverage

Whereas political ads are expensive, coverage by the news media is free. Accordingly, the candidates try to take advantage of the media's interest in campaigns to increase the quantity and quality of news coverage. This is not always easy. Generally, the media devote the lion's share of their coverage to polls showing who is ahead in the race.

In recent years, candidates' campaign managers and political consultants have shown increasing sophistication in creating newsworthy events for journalists and TV camera crews to cover, an effort commonly referred to as **managed news coverage.** For example, typically one of the jobs of the campaign manager is to create newsworthy events that demonstrate the candidate's strong points so that the media can capture this image of the candidate.[10]

Besides becoming aware of how camera angles and lighting affect a candidate's appearance, the political

> "FOR A **POLITICIAN** TO COMPLAIN ABOUT THE PRESS IS LIKE A SHIP'S CAPTAIN COMPLAINING ABOUT **THE SEA.**"
>
> ENOCH POWELL, BRITISH POLITICIAN 1912–1998

consultant plans political events to accommodate the press. The campaign staff attempts to make what the candidate is doing appear interesting. The staff also knows that journalists and political reporters compete for stories and that they can be manipulated by granting favors, such as an exclusive personal interview with the candidate. Each candidate's press advisers, often called **spin doctors,** also try to convince reporters to give the story or event a **spin,** or interpretation, that is favorable to the candidate.[11]

"Popular" Television

Although not normally regarded as a forum for political debate, television programs such as dramas, sitcoms, and late-night comedy shows often use political themes. For example, the popular courtroom drama *Law & Order* regularly broaches controversial topics such as the death penalty, the USA Patriot Act, and the rights of the accused. For years, the sitcom *Will and Grace* consistently brought to light issues regarding gay and lesbian rights. The dramatic

managed news coverage News coverage that is manipulated (managed) by a campaign manager or political consultant to gain media exposure for a political candidate.

spin doctor A political candidate's press adviser who tries to convince reporters to give a story or event concerning the candidate a particular "spin" (interpretation, or slant).

spin A reporter's slant on, or interpretation of, a particular event or action.

Talk radio is what many call the "Wild West" of the media. Howard Stern (on the left) has been considered the dean of over-the-top liberal talk show hosts. He is now heard only on Sirius Satellite Radio. Rush Limbaugh (center), in contrast, is considered the dean of conservative talk show hosts. Al Franken (on the right) is a liberal commentator who also said he would run for the U.S. Senate.

West Wing series gave viewers a glimpse into national politics as it told the story of a fictional presidential administration. Late-night shows and programs such as *The Daily Show with Jon Stewart* provide a forum for politicians to demonstrate their lighter sides.

LO³ TALK RADIO—THE WILD WEST OF THE MEDIA

Ever since Franklin D. Roosevelt held his first "fireside chats" on radio, politicians have realized the power of radio. Today, talk radio is a political force to be reckoned with. In 1988, there were 200 talk-show radio stations. Today, there are more than 1,200, and that number is growing. According to the most recent estimates, one in six Americans listens to talk radio regularly.

Talk radio is sometimes characterized as the Wild West of the media. Journalistic conventions do not exist. Political ranting and raving are common. Many popular talk shows do seem to have a conservative bent, but their supporters argue that talk radio has been a good way to counter the liberal bias in the print and TV media (we discuss bias in the media in the following section).

Some people are uneasy because talk shows empower fringe groups, perhaps magnifying their rage. Clearly, a talk show is not necessarily a democratic forum in which all views are aired. Talk-show hosts such as Rush Limbaugh do not attempt to hide their political biases; if anything, they exaggerate them for effect. Supporters of the sometimes outrageous, sometimes reactionary remarks broadcast during talk-radio shows reply that such shows are simply a response to consumer

demand. Furthermore, those who think that talk radio is good for the country argue that talk shows, taken together, provide a great populist forum for political debate. They maintain that in a sense, talk radio has become an equalizer because it is relatively inexpensive to start up a rival talk show.

Those who claim that talk-show hosts go too far in their rantings and ravings ultimately have to deal with the constitutional issue of free speech. After all, as First Amendment scholars point out, there is little the government can do about the forces that shape the media. The courts have always protected freedom of expression to the fullest extent possible, although, for many reasons, the government has been able to exercise some control over the electronic media—see the discussion of freedom of the press in Chapter 4.

LO⁴ THE QUESTION OF MEDIA BIAS

The question of media bias is important in any democracy. After all, for our political system to work, citizens must be well informed. And they can be well informed only if the news media, the source of much of their information, are fair and balanced. Today, however, relatively few Americans believe that the news media are unbiased in their reporting. Accompanying this perception is a notable decline in the public's confidence in the news media in recent years. In a 2007 Gallup poll measuring the public's confidence in various institutions, only 22 percent of the respondents stated that they had "a great deal" or "quite a lot" of confidence in newspa-

THE POLITICS OF NATIONAL SECURITY

COUNTERING ANTI-AMERICAN BIAS IN THE ARAB MEDIA

From the 1960s through the 1980s, there were numerous government-controlled radio stations throughout most Arab nations. The Arab public received censored news, and that was that. The same could be said for Arab television. In general, the Arab media were completely uncritical of their own governments but very critical of the United States.

Today, satellite television has brought dramatic changes to the media in the Middle East. There are more than three hundred satellite stations in that region. The most popular, boasting 70 million regular viewers, is Al Jazeera, based in Qatar. Since the war in Afghanistan, Al Jazeera has produced a lot of coverage of Osama bin Laden and his lieutenants. Although it is not accurate to say that Al Jazeera is 100 percent anti-American, its news coverage rarely, if ever, puts a positive slant on anything that America does, either domestically or internationally.

ENTER THE U.S. TAXPAYERS' EFFORT TO COUNTER ANTI-AMERICANISM

In 2004, the United States spent more than $100 million to create an all-Arabic news station called Al Hurra. Al Hurra was based on the concept of Radio Free America, which broadcast to people behind the so-called iron curtain between the end of World War II and the fall of communism in 1989. During its first few years, Al Hurra stood as the network that furthered freedom in the Middle East. Parliamentarians in Iraq saw it as an aid to creating a secular democracy there. Al Hurra broadcasts three separate feeds in Arabic—one to Arab nations, another to Europe, and one just for Iraq. Its mission statement calls for it to "showcase the American political process." For several years, it did that and more, highlighting human rights abuses and government corruption throughout the Middle East.

Today, critics of Al Hurra claim that it is "pandering to Arab sympathies," rather than countering anti-Americanism in the regional media. It even broadcast a live speech by radical Hezbollah leader Sheikh Hassan Nasrallah. It also broadcast an interview with an alleged al Qaeda operative, who on the air expressed joy that the terrorists of 9/11 "rubbed American noses in the dust."

REUTERS/Reuters TV courtesy of Al Hurra/Landov

EXCLUSIVE FOR ALHURRA

الحرة

YOU BE THE JUDGE

Some Americans point out that it is useless to try to fight anti-American bias in the Middle East through U.S.-sponsored news media. After all, anti-Americanism existed in some Arab countries even before the U.S. invasions of Afghanistan and Iraq, and American-sponsored media coverage of events is unlikely to change this. Others contend that the U.S. government should continue to create alternative sources of news information in Arabic in order to counter anti-Americanism, especially in the Middle East. Where do you stand on this issue?

pers, and just 23 percent responded the same for television news. These percentages are lower than they have been at any other time over the last two decades. Indeed, some analysts believe that the media are facing a crisis of confidence.

One of the problems the Bush administration faced in trying to "spread democracy" to the Middle East is the anti-American bias in the Arab media. This chapter's *The Politics of National Security* feature looks at that issue.

Partisan Bias

For years, conservatives have concluded that there is a liberal bias in the media, and liberals have complained that the media reflect a conservative bias. By and large, the majority of Americans think that the media reflect a liberal bias. According to a recent Gallup poll, 44 percent of the respondents believed that the news media were too liberal, whereas only 19 percent thought that the news media were too conservative. About 33 percent of those surveyed thought that the media covered the news "just about right."

Surveys and analyses of the attitudes and voting habits of reporters have confirmed that the wide majority of journalists do indeed hold liberal views. In a significant study conducted in the 1980s, the researchers found that the media producers, editors, and reporters (the "media elite") showed a notable liberal bias in their news coverage.[12] In 1992, Bill Clinton beat George H. W. Bush by 5 percent among the general public but, according to a Roper poll, by 82 percent among journalists. Polls taken over the past three decades have also consistently shown that national, Washington-based reporters are more likely to describe themselves as liberals than conservatives and that a majority of these reporters vote Democratic.

Nonetheless, a number of media scholars, including Kathleen Hall Jamieson, suggest that even if reporters hold liberal views, these views are not reflected in their reporting. Based on an extensive study of media coverage of presidential campaigns, Jamieson, director of the Annenberg Public Policy Center of the University of Pennsylvania, concludes that there is no systematic liberal or Democratic bias in news coverage.[13] Media analysts Debra and Hubert van Tuyll have similarly concluded that left-leaning reporters do not automatically equate to left-leaning news coverage. They point out that reporters are only the starting point for news stories. Before any story

"We are not afraid to **entrust** the American people with unpleasant facts, foreign ideas, . . . and competitive values. For a nation that is afraid to let its people judge the truth and falsehood in an **open market** is a nation that is afraid of its people."

JOHN F. KENNEDY,
THIRTY-FIFTH PRESIDENT OF THE UNITED STATES
1961–1963

goes to print or is aired on television, it has to go through a progression of editors and perhaps even the publisher. Because employees at the top of the corporate ladder in news organizations are more right leaning than left leaning, the end result of the editorial and oversight process is more balanced coverage.[14]

The Bias against Losers

Kathleen Hall Jamieson believes that media bias plays a significant role in shaping presidential campaigns and elections, but she argues that it is not a partisan bias. Rather, it is a bias against losers. A candidate who falls behind in the race is immediately labeled a "loser," making it even more difficult for the candidate to regain favor in the voters' eyes.[15]

Jamieson argues that the media use the winner-loser paradigm to describe events throughout the campaigns. Even a presidential debate is regarded as a "sporting

President George W. Bush holds a press conference in front of the White House press corps, a rather common event.

AP Photo/Charles Dharapak

Today, news organizations look for special niches around which to build their audiences. The photo above shows the broadcast newsroom for Fox News. On the top right, you see Bill O'Reilly (left) of the O'Reilly Factor, a Fox News cable program where O'Reilly covers various news stories and then provides commentary on them. On the bottom right is Keith Olbermann of Countdown, an MSNBC news program that highlights the day's top stories with interviews and commentary by Olbermann. Both shows often spark controversy for their commentaries and criticism of one another.

match" that results in a winner and a loser. Before the 2004 debates, reporters focused on what each candidate had to do to "win" the debate. When the debate was over, reporters immediately speculated about who had "won" as they waited for postdebate polls to answer that question. According to Jamieson, this approach "squanders the opportunity to reinforce learning." The debates are an important source of political information for the voters, and this fact is eclipsed by the media's win-lose focus.

"Selection Bias"

As mentioned earlier, television is big business, and maximizing profits from advertising is a major consideration in what television stations choose to air. After all, a station or network that incurs losses will eventually go bankrupt. The expansion of the media universe to include cable channels and the Internet has also increased the competition among news sources. As a result, news directors select programming they believe will attract the largest audiences and garner the highest advertising revenues.

Competition for viewers and readers has become even more challenging in the wake of a declining news audience. A recent survey and analysis of reporters' attitudes conducted by the Pew Research Center for the People and the Press, in conjunction with the Project for

Excellence in Journalism, found that every media sector except two is losing popularity. The two exceptions are the ethnic press, such as Latino newspapers and TV programs, and online sources—and even the online sector has stopped growing.[16]

SELECTION BIAS AND THE BOTTOM LINE   The Pew study also indicates that news organizations' struggles to stay afloat are having a notable effect on news coverage. The survey showed that a larger number of reporters (about 66 percent) than ever before agreed that "increased bottom-line pressure is seriously hurting the quality of news coverage." About one-third of the journalists—again, more than in previous surveys—stated that they have felt pressure from either advertisers or corporate owners concerning what to write or broadcast. In other words, these journalists believe that economic pressure—the need for revenues—is making significant inroads on independent editorial decision making. Generally, the study found that news reporters are not too confident about the future of journalism.

A CHANGING NEWS CULTURE   A number of studies, including the Pew study just cited, indicate that today's news culture is in the midst of change. News organizations are redefining their purpose and increasingly looking for special niches, or areas, around which to build their audiences. According to the Pew study, for some markets, the niche is *hyperlocalism*—that is, narrowing the focus of news

www.nytimes.com www.washingtonpost.com

Increasingly, Americans are receiving their news online. Virtually all print sources of news have online versions, such as the Washington Post and the New York Times shown here. Consequently, an increasing share of newspapers' revenues is coming from online advertising.

to the local area. For others, it is personal commentary, revolving around such TV figures as Bill O'Reilly, Larry King, or Keith Olbermann. In a sense, news organizations have begun to base their appeal less on *how* they cover the news and more on *what* they cover. Traditional journalism—fact-based reporting instead of opinion and punditry—is becoming a smaller part of this mix. Additionally, the emergence of "citizen journalism" on the Web by bloggers and others is having an impact on the popularity of traditional news.

LO⁵ POLITICAL NEWS AND CAMPAIGNS ON THE WEB

In a relatively brief span of time, the Internet has become a significant medium for the delivery of political news. Today, the great majority of Americans have Internet access, either in their homes or at school or at work. Worldwide, the number of Internet users has climbed to more than one billion. About two-thirds of Internet users now consider the Internet to be an important source of news. Certainly, news now abounds on the Web, and having an Internet strategy has become an integral part of political campaigning.

News Organizations Online

Almost every major news organization, both print and broadcast, currently delivers news via the Web. Indeed, an online presence is required to compete effectively with other traditional news companies for revenues. Studies of the media, including the study by the Pew Research Center and the Project for Excellence in Journalism (PEJ) mentioned earlier, note that the online share of newspaper company revenues has increased over the years. Today, for example, 14 percent of the *Washington Post*'s revenues are from online revenues. For the *New York Times*, this share is 8 percent.

Web sites for newspapers, such as the *Washington Post* and the *New York Times*, have a notable advantage over their printed counterparts. They can add breaking news to their sites, informing readers of events that occurred just minutes ago. Another advantage is that they can link the reader to more extensive reports on a particular topic. According to the Pew/PEJ study, though, many papers shy away from in-text linking, perhaps fearing that if readers leave the news organization's site, they may not return. Although some newspaper sites simply copy articles from their printed versions, the Web sites for major newspapers, including those for the *Washington Post* and the *New York Times*, offer a different array of coverage and options than their printed counterparts. Indeed, the Pew/PEJ study noted that the online versions of competing newspapers tend to be much more similar than their printed versions are.

A major problem facing these news organizations is that online news delivery, which has been a source of increasing revenues, is no longer a growing media sector. Also, readers or viewers of online newspapers and news programs are typically the same people who read the printed news editions and view news programs on TV. Web-only readers of a particular newspaper are a relatively small percentage of those going online for their news. Therefore, investing heavily in online news delivery may not be a solution for news companies seeking to increase readership and revenues.

Blogs and the Emergence of Citizen Journalism

As mentioned earlier, the news culture is changing, and at the heart of this change—and of most innovation in news delivery today—is the blogosphere. As you read in the chapter-opening *America at Odds* feature, there has been a virtual explosion of *blogs* (short for "Web logs") in recent years. According to the blog-tracking company Technorati, Inc., the number of blogs has been doubling every six months since 2003. To make their Web sites more competitive and appealing, and to counter the influence of blogs

citizen journalism The collection, analysis, and dissemination of information online by independent journalists, scholars, politicians, and the general citizenry.

run by private citizens and those not in the news business, the mainstream news organizations have themselves been adding blogs to their Web sites.

Blogs are offered by independent journalists, various scholars, political activists, and the citizenry at large. Anyone who wants to can create a blog and post news or information, including videos, to share with others. Many blogs are political in nature, both reporting political developments and affecting politics. Collectively, the collection, analysis, and dissemination of information online by the citizenry is referred to as **citizen journalism.** (Other terms that have been used to describe the news blogosphere include *people journalism* and *participatory journalism.* When blogs focus on news and developments in a specific community, the term *community journalism* is often applied.)

The increase in news blogs and do-it-yourself journalism on the Web clearly poses a threat to mainstream news sources. Compared to the operational costs faced by a major news organization, the cost of creating and maintaining blogs is trivial. How can major news sources adhere to their traditional standards and still compete with this new world of news generated by citizens?

www.npr.org/rss/podcast/podcast_directory.php
www.gop.com/Contribute

www.democrats.org/page/contribute/?source=NETA453
www.joinrudy2008.com/contribute

A growing number of Web sites present online news, without any print counterpart. Competition for "eyeballs" is intense.

JOIN THE DEBATE

Will Citizen Journalism Destroy Our News Culture?

Already, the blogosphere has created a fundamental change in our news culture. Simply put, traditional news organizations and professional journalists are no longer the gatekeepers of the news. In other words, they are no longer the determinative sources of what will or will not be "published." The agenda-setting function of the traditional media is also being threatened by the expansion of citizen journalism.

Some people believe that the growing popularity of citizen journalism may eventually destroy our news culture. For one thing, traditional news sources have long been guided by professional and ethical standards.

Among other things, these standards require journalists to make sure that the content of published news is accurate and verified. Such standards, however, need not apply to the blogosphere. Of course, some of the news offerings on blogs, such as a video of a political candidate describing an opponent in racially offensive terms, speak for themselves. Yet how will online readers know if a story told by a U.S. soldier about his or her experiences in the Iraq war is true—or even if that self-described soldier actually exists? Also, some blogs are written by bloggers who are secretly hired by companies to rave about their products or by political candidates to support their positions.

Other Americans contend that citizen journalism such as we're seeing today is important in a democracy because it provides more independent and wide-ranging information than mainstream news sources do.[17] Indeed, using cells phones or other digi-cams, citizens have often enriched coverage of major news events, such as Hurricane Katrina or a subway bombing. Moreover, a number of news blogs are now hiring professional journalists and establishing standards to govern their news reporting. In any event, claims this group, despite the credibility issues raised by news blogs, surveys have shown that the public has nearly as much confidence in citizen journalism as it does in mainstream news reporting.

Podcasting the News

Another nontraditional form of news distribution is **podcasting**—the distribution of audio or video files to a personal computer (PC) or a mobile device, such as an iPod.[18] Though still a relatively small portion of the overall news-delivery system, podcasts are becoming increasingly popular. Almost anyone can create a podcast and make it available for downloading onto PCs or mobile devices, and like blogs, podcasting is inexpensive. As you will read next, political candidates are using both blogging and podcasting as part of their Internet campaign strategy.

Cyberspace and Political Campaigns

Today's political parties and candidates realize the benefits of using the Internet to conduct online campaigns and raise funds. Voters also are increasingly using the Web to access information about parties and candidates, promote political goals, and obtain political news. Generally, the use of the Internet is an inexpensive way for candidates to contact, recruit, and mobilize supporters, as well as disseminate information on their positions on issues. In effect, the Internet can replace brochures, letters, and position papers. Individual voters or political party supporters can use the Internet to avoid having to go to special meetings or to a campaign site to do volunteer work or obtain information on a candidate's position.

That the Internet is now a viable medium for communicating political information and interacting with voters was made clear in the campaigns preceding the 2004 and 2006 elections. According to a Pew Research Center survey following the 2004 presidential elections, 29 percent of Americans said that they went online for election news, up from 4 percent who did so in the 1996 campaign. Nearly seven in ten of this group went online to seek information on the candidates' positions. Moreover, 43 percent of this group claimed that the information they found online affected their voting decisions.

podcasting The distribution of audio or video files to a personal computer or a mobile device, such as an iPod.

Podcasting has become an increasingly important news delivery vehicle. Many political candidates have created their own podcasts, as have sitting senators and representatives.

ONLINE FUND-RAISING   Today's political candidates are realizing that the Internet can be an effective—and inexpensive—way to raise campaign funds. The leading candidates in the 2004 presidential race all engaged in online fund-raising, as did the national committees of the Republican and Democratic parties.

Fund-raising on the Internet by presidential candidates became widespread after the Federal Election Commission decided, in June 1999, that the federal government could distribute matching funds for credit-card donations received by candidates via the Internet. In 2003, Democratic presidential hopeful Howard Dean showed the fund-raising power of the Internet by raising more than $20 million online. Political analysts marveled at Dean's success, especially in shifting the focus of campaign finance from a few large donors to countless small donors.

These important new Internet strategies were then adopted by the presidential campaigns of John Kerry and George W. Bush in 2004. The Democratic and Republican National Committees followed suit, as did candidates on the state and local levels. After witnessing Dean's success with online fund-raising, Kerry's campaign used similar strategies and raised nearly $82 million in online contributions. Bush's campaign, which used its Web site mainly to organize and communicate with supporters, collected only about $14 million online.

Prior to the 2006 midterm elections, both Republican and Democratic candidates increased the size of their campaign chests through online contributions. Often, Internet donations were small, such as $20 or $30, but they added up to a sizable amount. One of the most successful fund-raisers was MoveOn.org, which collected $28 million for Democratic campaigns. In the primary campaigns for the 2008 presidential elections, candidate Senator Barack Obama (D., Ill.) raised $32.5 million—more than any of the other presidential candidates—during just one three-month period in 2007. Of this amount, $10.3 million came from donations made over the Internet, half of which were in amounts of $25 or less. Obama declared that his fund-raising effort was "the largest grassroots campaign in history for this stage of a presidential race."

THE RISE OF THE INTERNET CAMPAIGN

An increasingly important part of political campaigning today is the Internet campaign. In addition to the overall campaign manager, candidates typically hire Web managers to manage their Internet campaigns. The job of the Web manager, or Web strategist, is to create a well-designed, informative, and user-friendly campaign Web site to attract viewers, hold their attention, manage their e-mail, and track their credit-card contributions. The Web manager also hires bloggers to promote the candidate's views, arranges for podcasting campaign information and updates to supporters, and hires staff to monitor the Web for news about the candidates and to track the online publications of *netroots groups*—online activists who support the candidate.

Controlling the "Netroots."

One of the challenges facing candidates today is trying to deliver a consistent campaign message to voters. Netroots—grassroots supporters of a candidate on the Internet—may publish online certain promotional ads or other materials that do not really represent the candidate's position. Similarly, an online group may attack the candidate's opponent in ways that the candidate does not approve. Yet no candidate wants to alienate these groups because they can raise significant sums of money and garner votes for the candidate. For example, as already mentioned, MoveOn.org raised $28 million for Democrats prior to the 2006 elections. Yet MoveOn.org is more left leaning on issues than a Democratic presidential candidate in 2008 would want to be—if that candidate hopes to gain the votes of more moderate voters.

"THE CITIZEN CAN BRING OUR POLITICAL AND GOVERNMENTAL INSTITUTIONS BACK TO LIFE, MAKE THEM RESPONSIVE AND ACCOUNTABLE, AND KEEP THEM HONEST. NO ONE ELSE CAN."

JOHN GARDNER,
AMERICAN NOVELIST
1933–1982

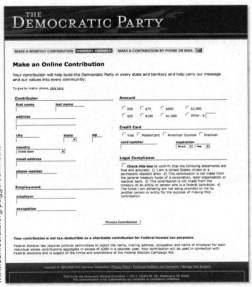

www.gop.com/Contribute

www.democrats.org/page/contribute

Both the Republican and Democratic parties have official Web sites. Today, these Web sites also serve as fund-raising vehicles and indeed are very successful.

The Candidates' 24/7 Exposure. Just as citizen journalism, discussed earlier, has altered the news culture, so have citizen videos changed the traditional campaign. For example, a candidate can never know when a comment that she or he makes may be caught on camera by someone with a cell phone or digital camera and published on the Internet for all to see. At times, such exposure can be devastating, as George Allen, the former Republican senator from Virginia, learned in the 2006 midterm elections. He was captured on video making a racial slur about one of his opponent's campaign workers. The video was posted on YouTube, and within a short time the major news organizations picked up the story. Many news commentators claimed that this video exposé gave Allen's Democratic opponent, Jim Webb, enough votes to win the race. A candidate's opponents may also

AP Photo/Alexa Welch Edlund/*Richmond Times-Dispatch*

During the 2006 senate elections, then Virginia Republican senator George Allen, shown here at a press conference, made an apparently disparaging comment about a person of Indian descent. It was captured on a digital camera and seen by millions on YouTube. He lost the election.

post on YouTube or some other site a compilation of video clips showing the candidate's comments over time on a specific topic, such as abortion or the Iraq war. The effect can be very damaging by making the candidate's "flip-flopping" on the issue so immediate.

This 24/7 exposure of the candidates also makes it difficult for the candidates to control their campaigns. Even videos on the lighter side, such as a video showing Hillary Clinton singing the "Star-Spangled Banner" when she didn't know that her lapel microphone was

on, can be embarrassing. The potential for citizen videos to destroy a candidate's chances is always there, creating a new type of uncertainty in political campaigning. By 2007, noted political commentator Andrew Sullivan had concluded that "one can safely predict that at some point in the wide-open race for the American presidency in 2008 at least one candidate will be destroyed by video-blogs and one may be handed a victory. Every gaffe will matter much more, and every triumph can echo for much longer."[19]

www.youtube.com

YouTube has become an unwitting political force. In 2007, millions of people heard Hillary Clinton (on the left) sing the national anthem off key. Republican presidential candidate Mitt Romney (center) saw his own inconsistencies on a YouTube video. Democratic presidential candidate Barack Obama (on the right) laid out his plans on YouTube for the 2008 presidential elections.

AMERICA AT ODDS:
Politics and the Media

The news business has been with us from the beginning of our republic. In the early years, the publication of ideas was largely through political pamphleteering. Yet the price of pamphlets often put them beyond the reach of most citizens. Even Senator William Maclay of Pennsylvania said that he could not afford to buy a copy of the *Federalist* and hoped that someone would lend him a copy. Nonetheless, by 1800 newspapers had begun to abound. In contrast to the 1720s, when there were fewer than a half-dozen newspapers in the colonies, by 1800 there were more than 230. By 1810, Americans were buying more than 22 million copies of 376 newspapers every year. Media bias has also always been with us. The first presidents and their political parties all had run-ins with the press, and

it was not too uncommon for a party to buy a newspaper operation and shut it down in an effort to control public opinion.

Today, as you have seen, the media continue to be accused of biased reporting. Conservatives accuse the news industry of reflecting a liberal bias, while liberals argue just the opposite. As one observer noted, though, if this is the case, then the news must be reflecting both liberal and conservative views. Generally, compared to other nations, Americans enjoy a news industry that is remarkably free from government interference. This is increasingly true in this new age of citizen journalism, in which any and all Americans, if they wish, can participate in the reporting and dissemination of news to the public.

Issues for Debate & Discussion

1. Some Americans, including many journalists, complain that the news media offer too much "shallow" coverage. For example, stories of Paris Hilton abound in the national media, while the deaths of thirty-two schoolchildren—mostly black, Hispanic, or poor—in Chicago during the past school year get scant attention. Others believe that the media are forced to focus on flashy events, including those involving celebrities, in order to survive in an increasingly competitive industry. On the whole, claims this group, given their constraints the media do a relatively good job of delivering the news to Americans. What is your position on this issue?
2. Review this chapter's *Join the Debate* feature on pages 218–220, which looks at the question of whether the media should be prohibited from publishing secret government information. What is your position on this issue?

Take Action

Today, the media are wide open for citizen involvement. You, too, can be a reporter of the news. You can create videos of events that you believe are newsworthy and post them online. You can podcast video or audio coverage of an event from your Web site. You can create a Web site for a blog of your own and invite others to participate. You, by yourself or with others, can set up a radio station to spread your views using the airwaves. For example, in the photo shown here, two citizens who supported a proposed Tennessee state tax reform set up their own radio station in Nashville to mock local radio personalities who were opposed to the reform. Lining the street nearby are other supporters of the tax reform.

AP Photo/John Russell

Local talk radio and news programs abound. They are often irreverent and operated by young people.

POLITICS ON THE WEB

- Literally thousands of news sources, including newspapers, news magazines, and television and radio stations, are now online. TotalNEWS offers a directory of more than a thousand news sources, including Fox News, MSNBC, CBS, ABC, and *USA Today*. To find TotalNEWS, go to **totalnews.com**.

- Newspapers.com features links to more than ten thousand newspapers nationwide. You can also search by categories such as business, college newspapers, and industry. Go to **www.newspapers.com**.

- The Claremont Institute is an interactive community that aims to bring Internet users together with public-policy organizations under "the broad umbrella of 'conservative' thoughts, ideas, and actions." It can be found at **www.townhall.com**.

- MoveOn.org, a liberal online group that promotes left-leaning values and Democratic candidates, is on the Web at **www.moveon.org**.

- The Polling Report Web site provides polling results on a number of issues, organized by topics. The site is easy to use and up to date. Go to **www.pollingreport.com**.

- A blog search engine with links to blogs in a variety of categories can be accessed at **www.blogsearchengine.com**.

ONLINE RESOURCES FOR THIS CHAPTER

This text's Companion Web site, at **www.americaatodds. com**, offers links to numerous resources that you can utilize to learn more about the topics covered in this chapter.

Turn to the back of the book to find your Politics to Go review card for this chapter

CHAPTER 11

CONGRESS

LEARNING OBJECTIVES

LO¹ Explain how seats in the House of Representatives are apportioned among the states.

LO² Describe the power of incumbency.

LO³ Identify the key leadership positions in Congress, describe the committee system, and indicate some important differences between the House of Representatives and the Senate.

LO⁴ Summarize the specific steps in the lawmaking process.

LO⁵ Indicate Congress's oversight functions and explain how Congress fulfills them.

LO⁶ Indicate what is involved in the congressional budgeting process.

AMERICA AT ODDS

Does Congress Have to Look Like America to Represent It?

The 110th Congress that began its term in January 2007 is, as Congress has always been, a predominantly white male institution. Of the 535 members of Congress (435 in the House and 100 in the Senate), 16.1 percent are women, 7.9 percent are African American, and 4.7 percent are Hispanic. In contrast, in the general population of the United States, 51 percent are women, 14.4 percent are Hispanic, and 12.1 percent are African American. Clearly, in terms of race and gender, Congress does not look like America. Does this matter?

In 1776, John Adams wrote of representative assemblies, "[They] should be in miniature an exact portrait of the people at large." James Wilson repeated the sentiment at the Constitutional Convention in 1787 when he said, "The legislature ought to be the most exact transcript of the whole society, . . . the faithful echo of the voices of the people." The theory of representation to which the founders subscribed dictates that the competing interests in society should be represented in Congress. Are race and gender among these "interests"? Can a man represent a woman's interests? Can a white person represent the interests of African Americans?

Demographic Balance Matters

Demographic balance in Congress matters because the experiences of different groups can lead to different perceptions, interests, and desires. Female legislators might be more interested in or sensitive to women's health issues or sexual harassment, for example. African Americans or Hispanics in Congress may be more concerned about the erosion of civil liberties than other members of Congress are. Can the interests of all Americans be adequately represented by white men?

Furthermore, about 35 percent of the members of Congress are millionaires, compared to only 1 percent of Americans. Many members of the House and Senate are lawyers. A large number also have significant investments in U.S. corporations. Several members take pay cuts when they come to Congress, where the annual salary is only $165,200. Of course, this is a very comfortable salary when compared to the median household income in the United States of about $47,000 per year.

The notion that our legislators should mirror their constituents in terms of race or gender, or even income or age, is called "descriptive representation" by political scientists. It has sometimes been dismissed by those outside academia as mere "political correctness" rather than genuine political reform. Still, proponents argue that descriptive representation is vital to overcoming the political marginalization of minorities and women in our society.

LEGISLATORS ARE THE TRUSTEES OF SOCIETY

No one disputes that a member of Congress has an obligation to his or her constituents. Less clear is the extent to which broad national interests should play a role in congressional representation. The "trustee" view of representation holds that legislators should act as the trustees of the broad interests of the entire society. If legislators believe that a national need outweighs the narrow interests of their constituents, they should vote their conscience. If legislators are trustees, then there is no reason why white males cannot represent the interests of women and minorities as well as any other group of legislators. For example, for decades, Ted Kennedy (D., Mass.), a white senator, has been well known for championing the cause of civil rights in Congress.

As you will read later in this chapter, one of the objections to racial *gerrymandering*—in which congressional districts are redrawn to maximize the number of minority group members within district boundaries—is that it assumes that people of a particular race, merely because of their race, think alike. Opponents of "descriptive representation" argue that there is no reason to assume that a black member of Congress can represent the interests of black people better than a white member of Congress. African Americans hold a broad range of views on the issues facing our nation, as do women, Hispanics, and Asians. As long as our views are represented, it does not matter whether our race or gender is represented.

Where do you stand?

1. Do you think that Congress needs to look like America to represent it?
2. Do you feel that your views and needs are adequately represented in Congress now?

Explore this issue online

- Women's Policy, Inc., provides information on the history, accomplishments, and current members of the Congressional Caucus for Women's Issues. You can access this site at **www.womenspolicy.org/caucus**.
- Ethnic Majority offers an interesting site that includes biographies of minority members of Congress, as well as demographic and civil rights information. Go to **www.ethnicmajority.com/congress.htm**.

INTRODUCTION

Congress is the lawmaking branch of government. When someone says, "There ought to be a law," at the federal level it is Congress that will make that law. The framers had a strong suspicion of a powerful executive authority. Consequently, they made Congress—not the executive branch (the presidency)—the central institution of American government. Yet, as noted in Chapter 2, the founders created a system of checks and balances to ensure that no branch of the federal government, including Congress, could exercise too much power.

Many Americans view Congress as a largely faceless, anonymous legislative body that is quite distant and removed from their everyday lives. Yet, as you read in the chapter-opening *America at Odds* feature, the people you elect to Congress represent and advocate your interests at the very highest level of power. Furthermore, the laws created by the men and women in the U.S. Congress affect the daily lives of every American in one way or another. Getting to know your congressional representatives and how they are voting in Congress on issues that concern you is an important step toward becoming an informed voter.

Because of the crucial importance of Congress in our system of government, a question that occurs to many is the following: What would happen if Congress were attacked by terrorists? This chapter's *The Politics of National Security* feature on the next page looks at what Congress has done (or not done) to date to prepare for such a crisis.

power and activity. The House was to represent the people as a whole, or the majority. The Senate was to represent the states and would protect the interests of small states by giving them the same number of senators (two per state) as the larger states.

Apportionment of House Seats

The Constitution provides for the **apportionment** (distribution) of House seats among the states on the basis of their respective populations. States with larger populations, such as California, have many more representatives than states with smaller populations, such as Wyoming. California, for example, currently has fifty-three representatives in the House; Wyoming has only one.

Every ten years, House seats are reapportioned based on the outcome of the decennial (ten-year) census conducted by the U.S. Census Bureau. Figure 11–1 on page 241 indicates the states that gained and lost seats based on population changes noted in the 2000 census. This redistribution of seats took effect with the 108th Congress, which was elected in 2002.

Each state is guaranteed at least one seat, no matter what its population. Today, seven states have only one representative.[1] The District of Columbia, American Samoa, Guam, and the U.S. Virgin Islands all send nonvoting delegates to the House. Puerto Rico, a self-governing possession of the United States, is represented by a nonvoting resident commissioner.

Every two years right after the congressional elections, there is a new "freshman" class in Washington, D.C. The one shown here is for the 110th Congress. This photo was taken one week after the elections in 2006.

LO¹ THE STRUCTURE AND MAKEUP OF CONGRESS

The framers agreed that the Congress should be the "first branch of the government," as James Madison said, but they did not agree on its organization. Ultimately, they decided on a *bicameral legislature*—a Congress consisting of two chambers. This was part of the Great Compromise, which you read about in Chapter 2. The framers favored a bicameral legislature so that the two chambers, the House and the Senate, might serve as checks on each other's

AP Photo/Dennis Cook

apportionment The distribution of House seats among the states on the basis of their respective populations.

THE POLITICS OF NATIONAL SECURITY

WHAT IF TERRORISTS ATTACKED CONGRESS?

We now know that the mastermind of the September 11, 2001, terrorist attacks wanted to make sure that the U.S. Congress would be in session on that day. We are not certain, but many believe that the fourth plane (United Flight 93), which crashed in a field in Pennsylvania on 9/11, was almost certainly headed for the Capitol. Had that airplane succeeded in crashing into the Capitol building, hundreds of members of Congress would have died, and others would have been unable to carry out their legislative functions. Given that the Constitution requires a quorum of a simple majority in each chamber in order to conduct official business, the House or the Senate, or possibly both, would have been, at least temporarily, out of business.

IN CASE OF ATTACK— A CONSTITUTIONAL AMENDMENT NEEDED

If a majority of the members of the House were killed or incapacitated, the House would be unable to meet until new members were elected because the Constitution does not allow members of the House to be appointed. In fact, soon after the 9/11 attacks, Representative Brian Baird (D., Wash.) drafted a constitutional amendment to provide for temporary appointments in the event of catastrophic attacks. Baird intended his proposed amendment to be a starting point for a debate on the issue. He wanted other members of Congress and their staffs, as well as those outside government, to come up with the details. One important detail was defining what constituted

incapacity. Other issues to be decided included who should make the appointments and for how long. Baird was unsuccessful in finding any support in Congress for such an amendment, however.

THE SENATE IS IN A DIFFERENT SITUATION

Let's not forget that soon after 9/11, several letters containing weapons-grade anthrax were sent to important leaders in the Senate. (Earlier, several people who had been exposed to the poison had died; others had become seriously ill.) What if this weapons-grade anthrax had been successfully introduced into the Senate ventilation system, killing or incapacitating more than fifty senators? According to the Seventeenth Amendment, executive apppointments can be made in the respective states to fill vacancies. A number of senators suffering from poor health have stayed in office for years, however, even though they have been unable to perform their duties. Thus, if more than fifty senators were incapacitated as a result of a terrorist attack, the Senate would be without a quorum. Again, a constitutional amendment—specifying that senators could be appointed to replace incapacitated (as opposed to deceased) senators—would need to be adopted to enable the Senate to function after such a catastrophe.

A SYMBOLIC CONGRESSIONAL RESPONSE

As the events of 9/11 began to fade, members of Congress lost interest in amending the Constitution. Instead, they opted for a poorly designed "expedited special-elections" bill that was added as an amendment to the legislative appropriations bill in 2005. Rather than address the problem of incapacitation, the new law simply changed the House rules on defining a quorum in the event of a catastrophe. Most constitutional scholars say that the new law is clearly unconstitutional.

YOU BE THE JUDGE

Some people believe that Congress has been remiss in its duties by not preparing for a catastrophe that could incapacitate so many members that Congress could not fulfill its legislative responsibilities. Others contend that the likelihood of such a catastrophe is so small that Congress's lack of substantive action in this regard is understandable, especially given that Congress has many other legislative priorities. Where do you stand on this issue?

Congressional Districts

Whereas senators are elected to represent all of the people in the state, representatives are elected by the voters of a particular area known as a **congressional district.** The Constitution makes no provisions for congressional districts, and in the early 1800s each state was given the right to decide whether to have districts at all. Most states set up single-member districts, in which voters in each district elected one of the state's representatives. In states that chose not to have districts, representatives were chosen at large, from the state as a whole. In 1842, however, Congress passed an act that required all states to send representatives to Congress from single-member districts, as you read in Chapter 7.

In the early 1900s, the number of House members increased as the population expanded. In 1929, however, a federal law fixed House membership at 435 members. Today, the 435 members of the House are chosen by the voters in 435 separate congressional districts across the country. If a state's population allows it to have only one representative, as is the situation in a few states, the entire state is one congressional district. In contrast, states with large populations have numerous districts. California, for example, because its population entitles it to send fifty-three representatives to the House, has fifty-three congressional districts.

The lines of the congressional districts are drawn by the authority of state legislatures. States must meet certain requirements, though, in drawing district boundaries. To ensure equal representation in the House, districts must contain, as nearly as possible, equal numbers of people. Additionally, each district must have contiguous boundaries and must be "geographically compact."

THE REQUIREMENT OF EQUAL REPRESENTATION   If congressional districts are not made up of equal populations, the value of people's votes is not the same. In the past, state legislatures often used this knowledge to their advantage. For example, traditionally, many state legislatures were controlled by rural areas. By drawing districts that were not equal in population, rural leaders attempted to curb the number of representatives from growing urban centers. At one point in the 1960s, in many states the largest district had twice the population of the smallest district. In effect, this meant that a person's vote in the largest district had only half the value of a person's vote in the smallest district.

For some time, the United States Supreme Court refused to address this problem. In 1962, however, in *Baker v. Carr,*[2] the Court ruled that the Tennessee state legislature's **malapportionment** was an issue that could be heard in the federal courts because it affected the constitutional requirement of equal protection under the law. Two years later, in *Wesberry v. Sanders,*[3] the Supreme Court held that congressional districts must have equal populations. This principle has come to be known as the **"one person, one vote" rule.** In other words, one person's vote has to count as much as another's vote.

FIGURE 11-1

REAPPORTIONMENT OF HOUSE SEATS FOLLOWING THE 2000 CENSUS

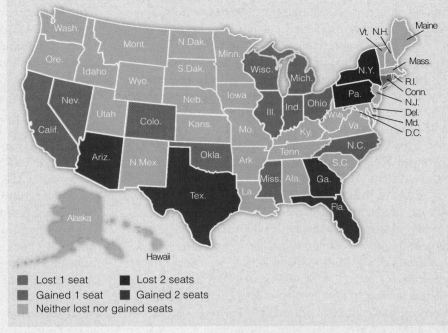

- ■ Lost 1 seat
- ■ Lost 2 seats
- ■ Gained 1 seat
- ■ Gained 2 seats
- ■ Neither lost nor gained seats

Source: U.S. Bureau of the Census.

congressional district The geographic area that is served by one member in the House of Representatives.

malapportionment A condition that results when, based on population and representation, the voting power of citizens in one district becomes more influential than the voting power of citizens in another district.

"one person, one vote" rule A rule, or principle, requiring that congressional districts have equal populations so that one person's vote counts as much as another's vote.

GERRYMANDERING   Although the Supreme Court, in the 1960s, ruled that congressional districts must be equal in population, it continued to be silent on the issue of gerrymandered districts. **Gerrymandering** occurs when a district's boundaries are drawn to maximize the influence of a certain group or political party. Where a party's voters are scarce, the boundaries can be drawn to include as many of the party's voters as possible. Where the party is strong, the lines are drawn so that the opponent's supporters are spread across two or more districts, thus diluting the opponent's strength. (The term *gerrymandering* was originally used in reference to the district lines drawn to favor the party of Governor Elbridge Gerry of Massachusetts prior to the 1812 election—see Figure 11–2.)

Although there have been constitutional challenges to political gerrymandering,[4] the practice continues. It was certainly evident following the 2000 census. Sophisticated computer programs can now analyze the partisan leanings of individual neighborhoods and city blocks. District lines are drawn to "pack" the opposing party's voters into the smallest number of districts or "crack" the opposing party's voters into several different districts. "Packing and cracking" makes congressional races less competitive. In 2003, for example, Texas adopted a controversial redistricting plan that was spearheaded by then House majority leader Tom DeLay (R., Tex.). DeLay and Texas Republicans used "pack and crack" tactics to redraw districts that had formerly leaned toward Democratic candidates. The plan effectively cost four Democratic representatives their seats in the 2004 elections.

Elbridge Gerry, governor of Massachusetts, 1810–1812.

Library of Congress

gerrymandering The drawing of a legislative district's boundaries in such a way as to maximize the influence of a certain group or political party.

minority–majority district A district whose boundaries are drawn so as to maximize the voting power of minority groups.

RACIAL GERRYMANDERING   Although political gerrymandering has a long history in this country, racial gerrymandering is a relatively new phenomenon. In the early 1990s, the U.S. Department of Justice instructed state legislatures to draw district lines to maximize the voting power of minority groups. As a result, several so-called **minority-majority districts** were created, many of which took on bizarre shapes. For example, North Carolina's newly drawn Twelfth Congressional District was 165 miles long—a narrow strip that, for the most part, followed Interstate 85. Georgia's new Eleventh District stretched from Atlanta to the Atlantic, splitting eight counties and five municipalities. The practice of racial gerrymandering has generated heated argument on both sides of the issue.

Some groups contend that minority-majority districts are necessary to ensure equal representation of minority groups, as mandated by the Voting Rights Act of 1965. They further contend that these districts have been instrumental in increasing the number of African Americans holding political office. Minority-majority districts in the South contain, on average, 45 percent nonblack voters, whereas before 1990, redistricting plans in the South created segregated, white-majority districts.[5]

FIGURE 11-2

THE FIRST "GERRYMANDER"

Prior to the 1812 elections, the Massachusetts legislature divided up Essex County in a way that favored Governor Elbridge Gerry's party; the result was a district that looked like a salamander. A newspaper editor of the time referred to it as a "gerrymander," and the name stuck.

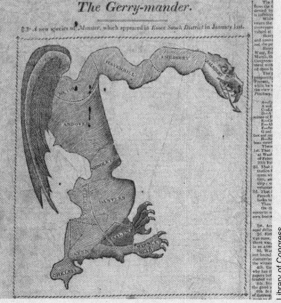

Library of Congress

Opponents of racial gerrymandering argue that such race-based districting is unconstitutional because it violates the equal protection clause. In a series of cases in the 1990s, the Supreme Court agreed and held that when race is the dominant factor in the drawing of congressional district lines, the districts are unconstitutional and must be redrawn.[6]

In 2001, however, the Supreme Court issued a ruling that seemed—at least to some observers—to be out of step with its earlier rulings. North Carolina's Twelfth District, which had been redrawn in 1997, was again challenged in court as unconstitutional, and a lower court agreed. When the case reached the Supreme Court, however, the justices concluded that there was insufficient evidence that race had been the dominant factor in redrawing the district's boundaries.[7]

"When a man assumes a **public trust,** he should consider himself a **public property.**"

THOMAS JEFFERSON,
THIRD PRESIDENT OF THE UNITED STATES
1801-1809

The Representation Function of Congress

Of the three branches of government, Congress has the closest ties to the American people. Members of Congress represent the interests and wishes of the constituents in their home states. At the same time, they must also consider larger national issues such as international trade and the environment. Oftentimes, legislators find that the interests of their constituents are at odds with the demands of national policy. For example, stricter regulations on air pollution would benefit the health of all Americans. Yet members of Congress who come from states where industry and mining are important might be afraid that new laws would hurt the local economy and cause companies to lay off workers. All members of Congress face difficult votes that set representational interests against lawmaking realities. There are several views on how legislators should fulfill their representation function.

THE TRUSTEE VIEW OF REPRESENTATION   Some believe that representatives should act as **trustees** of the broad interests of the entire society rather than serving only the narrow interests of their constituents. Under the trustee view, a legislator should act according to her or his conscience and perception of national needs. For example, a senator from North Carolina might support laws regulating the tobacco industry even though the state's economy could be negatively affected.

THE INSTRUCTED-DELEGATE VIEW OF REPRESENTATION
In contrast, others believe that members of Congress should behave as **instructed delegates.** The instructed-delegate view requires representatives to mirror the views of their constituents. Under this view, a senator from Nebraska would strive to obtain farm subsidies for corn growers, and a representative from the Detroit area would seek to protect the interests of the automobile industry.

THE PARTISAN VIEW OF REPRESENTATION Because the political parties often take different positions on legislative issues, there are times when members of Congress are most attentive to the wishes of the party leadership. Especially on matters that are controversial, the Republican members of Congress will be more likely to vote in favor of policies endorsed by a Republican president, while Democrats will be more likely to oppose them.

THE POLITICO STYLE   Typically, however, members of Congress combine these approaches in what is often called the "politico" style. Most representatives often find themselves in difficult positions that require them to weigh the broad interests of the entire society against the interests of their own constituents as well as their party. Legislators may take a trustee approach on some issues, adhere to the instructed-delegate view on other matters, and follow the party line on still others.

LO² CONGRESSIONAL ELECTIONS

The U.S. Constitution requires that representatives to Congress be elected every second year by popular vote. Senators are elected every six years, also (since the ratification of the Seventeenth Amendment) by popular vote. Under Article I, Section 4, of the Constitution, state legislatures control the "Times, Places and Manner of holding Elections for Senators and

trustee A view of the representation function that holds that representatives should serve the broad interests of the entire society, and not just the narrow interests of their constituents.

instructed delegate A view of the representation function that holds that representatives should mirror the views of the majority of their constituents.

Representatives." Congress, however, "may at any time by Law make or alter such Regulations." As you read in Chapter 9, control over the process of nominating congressional candidates has shifted from party conventions to direct primaries in which the party identifiers in the electorate select the candidates who will carry that party's endorsement into the actual election.

Who Can Be a Member of Congress?

The Constitution sets forth only a few qualifications that those running for Congress must meet. To be a member of the House, a person must be a citizen of the United States for at least seven years prior to his or her election, a legal resident of the state from which he or she is to be elected, and at least twenty-five years of age. To be elected to the Senate, a person must be a citizen for at least nine years, a legal resident of the state from which she or he is to be elected, and at least thirty years of age. The Supreme Court has ruled that neither the Congress nor the states can add to these three qualifications.[8]

Once elected to Congress, a senator or representative receives an annual salary from the government. He or she also enjoys certain perks and privileges. Additionally, if a member of Congress wants to run for reelection in the next congressional elections, that person's chances are greatly enhanced by the power that incumbency brings to a reelection campaign.

The Power of Incumbency

The power of incumbency has long been noted in American politics. Typically, incumbents win so often and by such large margins that some observers have claimed that our electoral system involves a kind of hereditary entitlement. As you can see in Table 11–1, most incumbents in Congress are reelected at election time.

Incumbent politicians enjoy several advantages over their opponents. A key advantage is their fund-raising ability. Most incumbent members of Congress have a much larger network of contacts, donors, and lobbyists than their opponents. Incumbents raise, on average, twice as much in campaign funds as their challengers. Other advantages that incumbents can put to work at election time include:

- *Congressional franking privileges*—members of Congress can mail newsletters and other correspondence to their constituents at the taxpayer's expense.

- *Professional staffs*—members have large administrative staffs both in Washington, D.C., and in their home districts.

- *Lawmaking power*—members of Congress can back legislation that will benefit their states or districts, and then campaign on that legislative record in the next election.

- *Access to the media*—because they are elected officials, members have many opportunities to stage events for the press and thereby obtain free publicity.

- *Name recognition*—incumbent members are far better known to the voters than challengers are.

Critics of the advantage enjoyed by incumbents argue that it reduces the competition necessary for a healthy democracy. It also suppresses voter turnout. Voters are less likely to turn out when an incumbent candidate is virtually guaranteed reelection. The solution often proposed to eliminate the power of incumbency is term limits. Persuading incumbent politicians to vote for term limits, however, is nearly impossible.

Female members of Congress still constitute only 16 percent of all members, whereas women make up more than 50 percent of the general population. In the Senate, female members of both parties often meet together as seen here in 2007.

Alex Wong/Getty Images

Congressional Terms and Term Limits

As you read earlier, members of the House of Representatives serve two-year terms, and senators serve six-year terms. This means that every two years, we hold congressional elections: the entire House of Representatives and a third of the Senate are up for election. In January of every odd-numbered year, a "new" Congress convenes (of course, two-thirds of the senators are not new, and most incumbents are reelected, so they are not new to Congress, either). Each Congress has been numbered consecutively, dating back to 1789. The Congress that convened in 2007 is the 110th.

Each congressional term is divided into two regular sessions, or meetings—one for each year. Until about 1940, Congress remained in session for only four or five months, but the complicated rush of legislation and increased demand for services from the public in recent years have forced Congress to remain in session through most of each year.[9] Both chambers, however, schedule short recesses, or breaks, for holidays and vacations. The president may call a *special session* during a recess, but because Congress now meets on nearly a year-round basis, such sessions are rare.

As you will read in Chapter 12, the president can serve for no more than two terms in office, thanks to the Twenty-second Amendment. There is no limit on the number of terms a senator or representative can serve, however. Indeed, Strom Thurmond (R., S.C.) served eight terms in the U.S. Senate, from 1955 until he retired, at the age of one hundred, in 2003. Efforts to pass a constitutional amendment that would impose term limits on members of Congress have had little success.

AP Photo/Ken Lambert

There is no limit to the number of terms a member of Congress can serve. Strom Thurmond (R., S.C.) served as a U.S. senator from 1955 until 2003, when he was one hundred years old.

LO[3] CONGRESSIONAL LEADERSHIP, THE COMMITTEE SYSTEM, AND BICAMERALISM

How each chamber of Congress is organized is largely a function of the two major political parties. The majority party in each chamber chooses the major officers of that chamber, controls

TABLE 11-1

THE POWER OF INCUMBENCY

House	Presidential-Year Elections							Midterm Elections							
	1980	1984	1988	1992	1996	2000	2004	1978	1982	1986	1990	1994	1998	2002	2006
Number of incumbent candidates	398	411	409	368	384	403	404	382	393	394	406	387	402	393	405
Reelected	361	392	402	325	361	394	397	358	354	385	390	349	395	383	382
Percentage of total	90.7	95.4	98.3	88.3	94.0	97.8	98.3	93.7	90.1	97.7	96.0	90.2	98.3	97.5	94.3
Defeated	37	19	7	43	23	9	7	24	39	9	16	38	7	10	23
Senate															
Number of incumbent candidates	29	29	27	28	21	29	26	25	30	28	32	26	29	28	29
Reelected	16	26	23	23	19	23	25	15	28	21	31	24	26	24	23
Percentage of total	55.2	89.6	85.2	82.1	90.5	79.3	96.2	60.0	93.3	75.0	96.9	92.3	89.7	85.7	79.3
Defeated	13	3	4	5	2	6	1	10	2	7	1	2	3	4	6

Sources: Norman Ornstein, Thomas E. Mann, and Michael J. Malbin, *Vital Statistics on Congress, 2001–2002* (Washington, D.C.: The AEI Press, 2002); and authors' updates.

When the Democrats took control of the House of Representatives after the 2006 midterm elections, they elected Nancy Pelosi (D., Calif.) as Speaker of the House and Steny H. Hoyer (D., Md.) as House majority leader. On the right, John Boehner (R., Ohio) was named House minority leader by the Republicans.

debate on the floor, selects all committee chairpersons, and has a majority on all committees.

House Leadership

Both the House and the Senate have systems of leadership. Before Congress begins work, members of each party in each chamber meet to choose their leaders. The Constitution provides for the presiding officers of the House and Senate; Congress may choose what other leaders it feels it needs.

SPEAKER OF THE HOUSE   Chief among the leaders in the House of Representatives is the **Speaker of the House.** This office is mandated by the Constitution and is filled by a vote taken at the beginning of each congressional term. The Speaker has traditionally been a longtime member of the majority party who has risen in rank and influence through years of service in the House. The candidate for Speaker is selected by the majority-party caucus; the House as a whole then approves the selection.

As the presiding officer of the House and the leader of the majority party, the Speaker has a great deal of power. In the nineteenth century, the Speaker had even more power and was known as the "king of the congressional mountain." Speakers known by such names as "Uncle Joe

Cannon" and "Czar Reed" ruled the House with almost exclusive power. A revolt in 1910 reduced the Speaker's powers and gave some of those powers to various committees. Today, the Speaker still has many important powers, including the following:

- The Speaker has substantial control over what bills get assigned to which committees.
- The Speaker presides over the sessions of the House, recognizing or ignoring members who wish to speak.
- The Speaker votes in the event of a tie, interprets and applies House rules, rules on points of order (questions about procedures asked by members), puts questions to a vote, and interprets the outcome of most of the votes taken.
- The Speaker plays a major role in making important committee assignments, which all members desire.
- The Speaker schedules bills for action.

The Speaker may choose whether to vote on any measure. If the Speaker chooses to vote, he or she appoints a temporary presiding officer (called a Speaker *pro tempore*), who then occupies the Speaker's chair. Under the House rules, the only time the Speaker *must* vote is to break a tie, because otherwise a tie automatically defeats a bill. The Speaker does not often vote, but by choosing to vote in some cases, the Speaker can actually cause a tie and defeat a proposal that is unpopular with the majority party.

MAJORITY LEADER   The **majority leader** of the House is elected by the caucus of party members to act as spokesperson for the party and to keep the party together. The

Speaker of the House The presiding officer in the House of Representatives. The Speaker has traditionally been a longtime member of the majority party and is often the most powerful and influential member of the House.

majority leader The party leader elected by the majority party in the House or in the Senate.

Within each party in the House of Representatives, there is a leadership position called the whip. *The main job of the party whips is to assist party leaders in getting members to vote along party lines. On the left is House majority whip James E. Clyburn from South Carolina. On the right is House Republican whip Roy Blunt from Missouri.*

majority leader's job is to help plan the party's legislative program, organize other party members to support legislation favored by the party, and make sure the chairpersons on the many committees finish work on bills that are important to the party. The House majority leader makes speeches on important bills, stating the majority party's position.

MINORITY LEADER The House **minority leader** is the leader of the minority party. Although not as powerful as the majority leader, the minority leader has similar respon-

After the Democrats took control of the U.S. Senate in the 2006 elections, Republican senator Mitch McConnell of Kentucky, left, was elected Senate minority leader for the 110th Congress. Democratic senator Harry Reid of Nevada, right, became the Senate majority leader.

sibilities. The primary duty of the minority leader is to maintain solidarity within the party. The minority leader persuades influential members of the party to follow its position and organizes fellow party members in criticism of the majority party's policies and programs.

WHIPS The leadership of each party includes assistants to the majority and minority leaders known as **whips.** Whips originated in the British House of Commons, where they were named after the "whipper in," the rider who keeps the hounds together in a fox hunt. The term was applied to assistant party leaders because of the pressure that they place on party members to follow the party's positions. Whips try to determine how each member is going to vote on certain issues and then advise the party leaders on the strength of party support. Whips also try to see that members are present when important votes are to be taken and that they vote with the party leadership. For example, if the Republican Party strongly supports a tax-cut bill, the Republican Party whip might meet with other Republican Party members in the House to try to persuade them to vote with the party.

Senate Leadership

The Constitution makes the vice president of the United States the president of the Senate. As presiding officer, the vice president may call on members to speak and put questions to a vote. The vice president is not an elected member of the Senate, however, and may not take part in Senate debates. The vice president may cast a vote in the Senate only in the event of a tie.

minority leader The party leader elected by the minority party in the House or in the Senate.

whip A member of Congress who assists the majority or minority leader in the House or in the Senate in managing the party's legislative preferences.

PRESIDENT PRO TEMPORE   Because vice presidents are rarely available to preside over the Senate, senators elect another presiding officer, the president pro tempore ("pro tem"), who serves in the absence of the vice president. The president pro tem is elected by the whole Senate and is ordinarily the member of the majority party with the longest continuous term of service in the Senate. In the absence of both the president pro tem and the vice president, a temporary presiding officer is selected from the ranks of the Senate, usually a junior member of the majority party.

PARTY LEADERS   The real power in the Senate is held by the majority leader, the minority leader, and their whips. The majority leader is the most powerful individual and chief spokesperson of the majority party. The majority leader directs the legislative program and party strategy. The minority leader commands the minority party's opposition to the policies of the majority party and directs the legislative strategy of the minority party.

Congressional Committees

Thousands of bills are introduced during every session of Congress, and no single member can possibly be adequately informed on all the issues that arise. The committee system is a way to provide for specialization, or a division of the legislative labor. Members of a committee can concentrate on just one area or topic—such as agriculture or transportation—and develop sufficient expertise to draft appropriate legislation when needed. The flow of legislation through both the House and the Senate is determined largely by the speed with which the members of these committees act on bills and resolutions. The permanent and most powerful committees of Congress are called **standing committees;** their names are listed in Table 11–2.

standing committee A permanent committee in Congress that deals with legislation concerning a particular area, such as agriculture or foreign relations.

subcommittee A division of a larger committee that deals with a particular part of the committee's policy area. Most of the standing committees in Congress have several subcommittees.

Before any bill can be considered by the entire House or Senate, it must be approved by a majority vote in the standing committee to which it was assigned. As mentioned, standing committees are controlled by the majority party in each chamber. Committee membership is generally divided between the parties according to the number of members in each chamber. In both the House and the Senate, committee *seniority*—the length of continuous service on a particular committee—typically plays a role in determining the committee chairpersons.

Most House and Senate committees are also divided into **subcommittees,** which have limited areas of jurisdiction. Today, there are more than two hundred subcommittees. There are also other types of committees in Congress. Special, or select, committees, which may be either permanent or temporary, are formed to study specific problems or issues. Joint committees are formed by the concurrent action of both chambers of Congress and consist of members from each chamber. Joint committees have dealt with the economy, taxation, and the Library of Congress. There are also conference committees, which include members from both the House and the Senate. They are formed for the purpose of achieving agreement between the House and the Senate on the exact wording of legislative acts when the

TABLE 11–2

STANDING COMMITTEES IN THE 110TH CONGRESS, 2007–2009

House Committees	Senate Committees
Agriculture	Agriculture, Nutrition, and Forestry
Appropriations	Appropriations
Armed Services	Armed Services
Budget	Banking, Housing, and Urban Affairs
Education and Labor	Budget
Energy and Commerce	Commerce, Science, and Transportation
Financial Services	Energy and Natural Resources
Foreign Affairs	Environment and Public Works
Homeland Security	Finance
House Administration	Foreign Relations
Judiciary	Health, Education, Labor, and Pensions
Natural Resources	Homeland Security and Governmental Affairs
Oversight and Government Reform	Judiciary
Rules	Rules and Administration
Science and Technology	Small Business and Entrepreneurship
Small Business	Veterans' Affairs
Standards of Official Conduct	
Transportation and Infrastructure	
Veterans' Affairs	
Ways and Means	

TABLE 11–3

MAJOR DIFFERENCES BETWEEN THE HOUSE AND THE SENATE

House*	Senate*
Members chosen from local districts	Members chosen from an entire state
Two-year term	Six-year term
Always elected by voters	Originally (until 1913) elected by state legislatures
May impeach (accuse, indict) federal officials	May convict federal officials of impeachable offenses
Larger (435 voting members)	Smaller (100 members)
More formal rules	Fewer rules and restrictions
Debate limited	Debate extended
Floor action controlled	Unanimous consent rules
Less prestige and less individual notice	More prestige and media attention
Originates bills for raising revenues	Power of "advice and consent" on presidential appointments and treaties
Local or narrow leadership	National leadership

*Some of these differences, such as term of office, are provided for in the Constitution, while others, such as debate rules, are not.

rules and more formal rules; otherwise no work would ever get done. The most obvious formal rules that are required have to do with debate on the floor.

The Senate normally permits extended debate on all issues that arise before it. In contrast, the House uses an elaborate system: the House **Rules Committee** normally proposes time limitations on debate for any bill, which are accepted or modified by the House. Despite its greater size, as a consequence of its stricter time limits on debate, the House is often able to act on legislation more quickly than the Senate.

two chambers pass legislative proposals in different forms. No bill can be sent to the White House to be signed into law unless it first passes both chambers in identical form.

Most of the actual work of legislating is performed by the committees and subcommittees (the "little legislatures"[10]) within Congress. In creating or amending laws, committee members work closely with relevant interest groups and administrative agency personnel. (For more details on the interaction among these groups, see the discussion of "iron triangles" in Chapter 13.)

The Differences between the House and the Senate

The major differences between the House and the Senate are listed in Table 11–3. To understand what goes on in the chambers of Congress, we need to look at the effects of bicameralism. Each chamber of Congress has developed certain distinct features. (For a discussion of the two chambers of the British Parliament and their respective functions, see this chapter's *The Rest of the World* feature on page 250.)

SIZE MATTERS Obviously, with 435 members, the House cannot operate the same way that the Senate can with only 100 members. (There are also nonvoting delegates from the District of Columbia, Guam, American Samoa, Puerto Rico, and the U.S. Virgin Islands in the House.) With its larger size, the House needs both more

IN THE SENATE, DEBATE CAN JUST KEEP GOING GOING At one time, both the House and the Senate allowed unlimited debates, but the House ended this practice in 1811. When unlimited debate in the Senate is used to obstruct legislation, it is called **filibustering.** The longest filibuster was waged by Senator Strom Thurmond of South Carolina, who held forth on the Senate floor for twenty-four hours and eighteen minutes in an attempt to thwart the passage of the 1957 Civil Rights Act.

Today, under Senate Rule 22, debate may be ended by invoking **cloture**—a method of closing debate and bringing the matter under consideration to a vote in the Senate. Sixteen senators must sign a petition requesting cloture, and then, after two days have elapsed, three-fifths of the entire membership must vote for cloture. Once cloture is invoked, each senator may speak on a bill for no more than one hour before a vote is taken. Additionally, a final vote must take place within one hundred hours after cloture has been invoked.

THE SENATE WINS THE PRESTIGE RACE, HANDS DOWN Because of the large number of representatives, few can garner the

Rules Committee A standing committee in the House of Representatives that provides special rules governing how particular bills will be considered and debated by the House. The Rules Committee normally proposes time limitations on debate for any bill, which are accepted or modified by the House.

filibustering The Senate tradition of unlimited debate, undertaken for the purpose of preventing action on a bill.

cloture A method of ending debate in the Senate and bringing the matter under consideration to a vote by the entire chamber.

How the British Parliament Differs from the U.S. Congress

The framers of the U.S. Constitution, for the most part, were used to the British form of government in which the central institution is the national legislature, known as Parliament. Like our own Congress, Parliament is a bicameral body: it is made up of the House of Commons and the House of Lords. Unlike Congress, however, the British Parliament (as in all parliamentary systems) is based on the *fusion* of powers rather than the *separation* of powers. It manages both the legislative and the executive powers of the nation. Parliament's legislative powers include passing and changing laws; its executive powers include choosing the prime minister, who is the leader of the majority party in the House of Commons, and the cabinet (the heads of executive agencies) that will serve the prime minister. Additionally, parliamentary leaders have the ability to prevent candidates for Parliament from running under their party label.

chamber. Unlike congressional committees, which specialize in areas such as agriculture or the armed forces, committees in the House of Commons are general committees that consider bills on a wide variety of subjects.

AP Photo/Rusell Boyce/Pool

While the House of Lords is called the upper chamber in the British Parliament, it has virtually no power today. Its members do engage in a lot of ceremony, however.

Press Association via AP Images

The House of Commons in the British Parliament is equivalent to the U.S. House of Representatives. Debate in "the Commons" is often acrimonious, filled with hooting, cheering, and nasty comments.

THE HOUSE OF COMMONS

The House of Commons is the legislative branch and currently consists of 646 elected officials. This lower house, known as "the Commons," is the more powerful of the two houses. Its members, known as Members of Parliament, or MPs, are popularly elected from geographic districts. Any MP is allowed to introduce legislation, but most measures are introduced by the government, which is made up of the prime minister and the cabinet collectively. The bill is then debated and sent to one of the eight standing committees that review bills and prepare them for final consideration by the full

THE HOUSE OF LORDS

The upper chamber of Parliament is known as the House of Lords. In the past, the House of Lords included 746 hereditary peers (members of the nobility who became so by birth) with such titles as *baron, viscount, earl,* and *duke.* Due to recent reforms, only 92 hereditary peers now sit in the House of Lords. The other members of the House of Lords include 544 persons who are appointed as peers for life by the queen and 26 bishops of the Church of England.

The House of Lords was once a powerful branch of the British government, but today it has little real authority over legislation. If the House of Lords defeats a bill passed in the Commons, the Commons need only pass it a second time in the next session to make the bill become law. The House of Lords may amend legislation, but any changes it makes can be canceled by the Commons.

For Critical Analysis

What is one of the key differences between the upper chamber of the British Parliament and the U.S. Senate?

prestige that a senator enjoys. Senators have relatively little difficulty in gaining access to the media. Members of the House, who run for reelection every two years, have to survive many reelection campaigns before they can obtain recognition for their activities. Usually, a representative has to become an important committee leader before she or he can enjoy the consistent attention of the national news media.

LO⁴ THE LEGISLATIVE PROCESS

Look at Figure 11–3 on the next page, which shows the basic elements of the process through which a bill becomes law at the national level. Not all of the complexities of the process are shown, to be sure. For example, the schematic does not indicate the extensive lobbying and media politics that are often involved in the legislative process. There is also no mention of the informal negotiations and "horse trading" that go on to get a bill passed.

The basic steps in the process are as follows:

1. **Introduction of legislation.** Most bills are proposed by the executive branch, although individual members of Congress or its staff can come up with ideas for new legislation; so, too, can private citizens or lobbying groups. Only a member of Congress can formally introduce legislation, however. In reality, an increasing number of bills are proposed, developed, and often written by the White House or an executive agency. Then a "friendly" senator or representative introduces the bill in Congress. Such bills are rarely ignored entirely, although they are often amended or defeated.

2. **Referral to committees.** As soon as a bill is introduced and assigned a number, it is sent to the appropriate standing committee. In the House, the Speaker assigns the bill to the appropriate committee. In the Senate, the presiding officer assigns bills to the proper committees. For example, a farm bill in the House would be sent to the Agriculture Committee; a gun control bill would be sent to the Judiciary Committee. A committee chairperson will typically send the bill on to

Any bill—even if the White House or an executive agency develops it—must be formally introduced by one or more members of Congress, as shown here.

Scott J. Ferrell/Congressional Quarterly/Getty Images

a subcommittee. For example, a Senate bill concerning additional involvement in NATO (North Atlantic Treaty Organization) in Europe would be sent to the Senate Foreign Relations Subcommittee on European Affairs. Alternatively, the chairperson may decide to put the bill aside and ignore it. Most bills that are pigeonholed in this manner receive no further action.

If a bill is not pigeonholed, committee staff members go to work researching the bill. The committee may hold public hearings during which people who support or oppose the bill may express their views. Committees also have the power to order witnesses to testify at public hearings. Witnesses may be executive agency officials, experts on the subject, or representatives of interest groups concerned about the bill.

The subcommittee must meet to approve the bill as it is, add new amendments, or draft a new bill. This meeting is known as the **markup session.** If members cannot agree on changes, a vote is taken. When a subcommittee completes its work, the bill goes to the full standing committee, which then meets for its own markup session. The committee may hold its own hearings, amend the subcommittee's version, or simply approve the subcommittee's recommendations.

> **markup session** A meeting held by a congressional committee or subcommittee to approve, amend, or redraft a bill.

3. **Reports on a bill.** Finally, the committee will report the bill back to the full chamber. It can report the bill favorably, report the bill with amendments, or report a newly written bill. It can also report a bill unfavorably, but usually such a bill will have been pigeonholed earlier instead. Along with the bill, the committee will send to the House or Senate a written report that explains the committee's actions, describes the bill, lists the major changes made by the committee, and gives opinions on the bill.

4. **The Rules Committee and scheduling.** Scheduling is an extremely important part of getting a bill enacted into law. A bill must be put on a calendar. Typically, the House Rules Committee plays a major role in the scheduling process. This committee, along with the House leaders, regulates

FIGURE 11-3

HOW A BILL BECOMES A LAW

This illustration shows the most typical way in which proposed legislation is enacted into law. The process is illustrated with two hypothetical bills, House bill No. 100 (HR 100) and Senate bill No. 200 (S 200). Bills must be passed by both chambers in identical form before they can be sent to the president. The path of HR 100 is traced by an orange line, and that of S 200 by a purple line. In practice, most bills begin as similar proposals in both chambers.

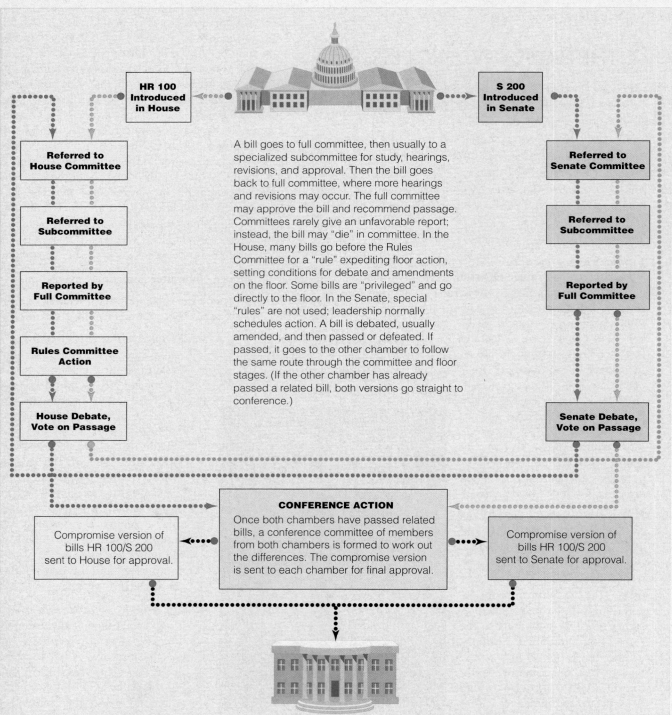

HR 100
Introduced
in House

S 200
Introduced
in Senate

Referred to
House Committee

Referred to
Subcommittee

Reported by
Full Committee

Rules Committee
Action

House Debate,
Vote on Passage

Referred to
Senate Committee

Referred to
Subcommittee

Reported by
Full Committee

Senate Debate,
Vote on Passage

A bill goes to full committee, then usually to a specialized subcommittee for study, hearings, revisions, and approval. Then the bill goes back to full committee, where more hearings and revisions may occur. The full committee may approve the bill and recommend passage. Committees rarely give an unfavorable report; instead, the bill may "die" in committee. In the House, many bills go before the Rules Committee for a "rule" expediting floor action, setting conditions for debate and amendments on the floor. Some bills are "privileged" and go directly to the floor. In the Senate, special "rules" are not used; leadership normally schedules action. A bill is debated, usually amended, and then passed or defeated. If passed, it goes to the other chamber to follow the same route through the committee and floor stages. (If the other chamber has already passed a related bill, both versions go straight to conference.)

Compromise version of
bills HR 100/S 200
sent to House for approval.

CONFERENCE ACTION
Once both chambers have passed related bills, a conference committee of members from both chambers is formed to work out the differences. The compromise version is sent to each chamber for final approval.

Compromise version of
bills HR 100/S 200
sent to Senate for approval.

A compromise bill approved by both chambers is sent to the president, who can sign it, veto it, or let it become law without the president's signature. Congress may override a veto by a two-thirds majority vote in each chamber.

the flow of the bills through the House. The Rules Committee will also specify the amount of time to be spent on debate and whether amendments can be made by a floor vote.

In the Senate, a few leading members control the flow of bills. The Senate brings a bill to the floor by "unanimous consent," a motion by which all members present on the floor set aside the formal Senate rules and consider a bill. In contrast to the procedure in the House, individual senators have the power to disrupt work on legislation.

> "YOU'VE GOT TO WORK THINGS OUT IN THE CLOAKROOM, AND WHEN YOU'VE GOT THEM WORKED OUT, YOU CAN DEBATE A LITTLE BEFORE YOU VOTE."
>
> LYNDON B. JOHNSON, THIRTY-SIXTH PRESIDENT OF THE UNITED STATES 1963–1969

5. *Floor debate.* Because of its large size, the House imposes severe limits on floor debate. The Speaker recognizes those who may speak and can force any member who does not "stick to the subject" to give up the floor. Normally, the chairperson of the standing committee reporting the bill will take charge of the session during which it is debated. You can often watch such debates on C-SPAN.

Only on rare occasions does a floor debate change anybody's mind. The written record of the floor debate completes the legislative history of the proposed bill in the event that the courts have to interpret it later on. Floor debates also give the full House or Senate the opportunity to consider amendments to the original version of the bill.

6. *Vote.* In both the House and the Senate, the members present generally vote for or against the bill. There

Most of the work in Congress is done in full committees and subcommittees. The provisions of various bills are debated, altered, and amended during these committee sessions.

Scott J. Ferrell/Congressional Quarterly/Getty Images

are several methods of voting, including voice votes, standing votes, and recorded votes (also called roll-call votes). Since 1973, the House has had electronic voting. The Senate does not have electronic voting, however.

7. *Conference committee.* To become a law, a bill must be passed in identical form by both chambers. When the two chambers pass separate versions of the same bill, the measure is turned over to a special committee called a **conference committee**—a temporary committee with members from the two chambers.

Most members of the committee are drawn from the standing committees that handled the bill in both chambers. In theory, the conference committee can consider only those points in a bill on which the two chambers disagree; no proposals are supposed to be added. In reality, however, the conference committee sometimes makes important changes in the bill or adds new provisions.

Once the conference committee members agree on the final compromise bill, a **conference report** is submitted to each house. The bill must be accepted or rejected by both houses as it was written by the committee, with no further amendments made. If the bill is approved by both chambers, it is ready for action by the president.

8. *Presidential action.* All bills passed by Congress have to be submitted to the president for approval. The president has ten days to decide whether to sign the bill or veto it. If the president does nothing, the bill goes into effect unless Congress has adjourned before the ten-day period expires. In that case, the bill dies in what is called a **pocket veto.**

9. *Overriding a veto.* If the president decides to veto a bill, Congress can still get the

conference committee A temporary committee that is formed when the two chambers of Congress pass separate versions of the same bill. The conference committee, which consists of members from both the House and the Senate, works out a compromise form of the bill.

conference report A report submitted by a congressional conference committee after it has drafted a single version of a bill.

pocket veto A special type of veto power used by the chief executive after the legislature has adjourned. Bills that are not signed by the president die after a specified period of time and must be reintroduced if Congress wishes to reconsider them.

bill enacted into law. With a two-thirds majority vote in both chambers, Congress can override the president's veto.

JOIN THE DEBATE

Should Congress Spend Time on "Symbolic Votes"?

In the summer of 2007, the Senate spent precious time debating a symbolic vote of no confidence against former attorney general Alberto Gonzales. Ultimately, the vote fell seven short of the sixty votes required to move the nonbinding resolution to a formal debate. Earlier in the year, Congress had spent time attempting to lift restrictions on federal funding for embryonic stem-cell research, even though it was clear that President George W. Bush would veto any such legislation (which he did do). Should Congress spend its time on such activities?

Many congressional observers believe that Congress does not even have enough time to debate important bills that may actually become law. We live under a government of laws, not under a government of symbolic actions undertaken by our nation's lawmakers. Any action by Congress that is nonbinding or that will certainly be vetoed by the president is equivalent to no action at all. Indeed, some people view it as a cowardly way to run the government. If Congress really wants to act, it has to pass actual legislation that has a chance of being signed by the president or use its "power of the purse" and refuse to fund programs that it would like to come to an end, such as the war in Iraq.

Supporters of symbolic votes argue that such actions are important because they send a message to the president and to the public. For example, in early 2007, the House passed a nonbinding resolution opposing the American troop buildup in Iraq, even though the members knew that the resolution would not have any effect on Bush's war policy. This vote, which was considered one of the Democratic Congress's first major acts of defiance, strongly indicated that the president was not going to have an easy time obtaining funding for the war in Iraq. As House Speaker Nancy Pelosi said, "The bipartisan resolution today is nonbinding, but it will send a strong message to the president: we are committed to supporting the troops and we disapprove of the escalation." Additionally, when

Mark Wilson/Getty Images

Soon after the Democrats took control of Congress in 2007, they staged several symbolic events protesting the continuation of the war in Iraq. Speaker of the House, Nancy Pelosi (far right), and Senate majority leader, Harry Reid (center), are shown here leaving one such event.

Congress is dissatisfied with a member of the president's cabinet, a nonbinding, no-confidence vote requires members of Congress to go on record for or against a particular presidential appointee. Such symbolic gestures do have value in making the president fully aware of who supports him or her and who doesn't.

LO⁵ INVESTIGATION AND OVERSIGHT

Steps 8 and 9 of the legislative process described on page 253 illustrate the integral role that both the executive and the legislative branches play in making laws. The relationship between Congress and the president is at the core of our system of government, although, to be sure, the judicial branch plays a vital role as well (see Chapter 14). One of the most important functions of Congress is its oversight of the executive branch and its many federal departments and agencies. The executive bureaucracy, which includes the president's cabinet departments, wields tremendous power, as you will read in Chapters 12 and 13. Congress can rein in that power by choosing not to provide the money necessary for the bureaucracy to function (the budgeting process will be discussed later in this chapter).

The House Judiciary Committee, shown here, approved three articles of impeachment against President Richard M. Nixon in late July 1974. The articles charged Nixon with obstruction of justice, abuse of power, and contempt of Congress. Nixon resigned on August 9, 1974, before the full House of Representatives voted on the articles. The Senate, therefore, was never able to try Nixon on any articles of impeachment.

The Investigative Function

Congress also has the authority to investigate the actions of the executive branch, the need for certain legislation, and even the actions of its own members. The Congressional Research Service and the Congressional Budget Office, for example, both provide members of Congress with vital information about policies and economic projections. The numerous congressional committees and subcommittees regularly hold hearings to investigate the actions of the executive branch. Congressional committees receive opinions, reports, and assessments on a broad range of issues.

Impeachment Power

Congress also has the power to impeach and remove from office the president, vice president, and other "civil officers," such as federal judges. To *impeach* means to accuse or charge a public official with improper conduct in office. The House of Representatives is vested with this power and has exercised it twice against the president; the House voted to impeach Andrew Johnson in 1868 and Bill Clinton in 1998. After a vote to impeach in the full House, the president is then tried in the Senate. If convicted by a two-thirds vote, the president is removed from office. Both Johnson and Clinton were acquitted by the Senate. A vote to impeach President Richard Nixon was pending before the full House of Representatives in 1974 when Nixon chose to resign. Nixon is the only president ever to resign from office.

Congress can also take action to remove other officials. The House of Representatives voted to impeach Judge Alcee Hastings in 1988, and the Senate removed him from the bench (he was later elected to the House in 1992). Only one United States Supreme Court justice has ever been impeached; the House impeached Samuel Chase in 1804, although he was later acquitted by the Senate.

Senate Confirmation

Article II, Section 2, of the Constitution states that the president may appoint ambassadors, justices of the Supreme Court, and other officers of the United States

The Senate has the power to confirm or reject a president's nominee for the United States Supreme Court, federal judgeships, and the president's cabinet. In 2005, the Senate questioned Supreme Court chief justice nominee, John Roberts (standing and facing the Senate committee). He was later confirmed.

"with the Advice and Consent of the Senate." The Constitution leaves the precise nature of how the Senate will give this "advice and consent" up to the lawmakers. In practice, the Senate confirms the president's nominees for the Supreme Court, other federal judgeships, and members of the president's cabinet. Nominees appear first before the appropriate Senate committee—the Judiciary Committee for federal judges, or the Foreign Relations Committee for the secretary of state, for example. If the individual committee approves of the nominee, the full Senate will vote on the nomination.

As you will read further in Chapters 12 and 14, Senate confirmation hearings have been very politicized at times. Judicial appointments often receive the most intense scrutiny by the Senate because the judges serve on the bench for life. The president has a somewhat freer hand with cabinet appointments because the heads of executive departments are expected to be loyal to the president. Nonetheless, Senate confirmation remains an important check on the president's power. We will discuss the relationship between Congress and the president in more detail in Chapter 12.

President George W. Bush speaks to reporters about the budget he submitted to Congress. Congress's power to control the "purse strings" of government is one of its most significant powers. Dirk Kempthorne, secretary of the interior, and Henry Paulson, Jr., secretary of the treasury, are seated to the right of the president.

Ron Sachs/Getty Images

LO⁶ THE BUDGETING PROCESS

authorization A part of the congressional budgeting process that involves the creation of the legal basis for government programs.

appropriation A part of the congressional budgeting process that involves determining how many dollars will be spent in a given year on a particular set of government activities.

entitlement program A government program (such as Social Security) that allows, or entitles, a certain class of people (such as the elderly) to receive special benefits. Entitlement programs operate under open-ended budget authorizations that, in effect, place no limits on how much can be spent.

The Constitution makes it very clear that Congress has the power of the purse. Only Congress can impose taxes, and only Congress can authorize expenditures. To be sure, the president submits a budget, but all final decisions are up to Congress.

The congressional budget is, of course, one of the most important determinants of what policies will or will not be implemented. For example, the president might order executive agencies under presidential control to undertake specific programs, but these orders are meaningless if there is no money to pay for their execution. It is Congress, after all, that has the power of the "purse strings," and this power is significant. Congress can therefore nullify a president's ambitious program by simply refusing to allocate the necessary money to executive agencies to implement it.

Thus, although the congressional budgeting process may seem abstract and unimportant to our everyday lives, it is in fact relevant. Also, tracking the various legislative acts and the amendments that are "tacked on" to various budget bills that are sure to pass can be an informative experience for any American concerned about how government policies are established and implemented.

Authorization and Appropriation

The budgeting process involves a two-part procedure. **Authorization** is the first part. It involves the creation of the legal basis for government programs. In this phase, Congress passes authorization bills outlining the rules governing the expenditure of funds. Limits may be placed on how much money can be spent and for what period of time.

Appropriation is the second part of the budgeting process. In this phase, Congress determines how many dollars will actually be spent in a given year on a particular set of government activities. Appropriations must never exceed the authorized amounts, but they can be less.

Many **entitlement programs** operate under open-ended authorizations that, in effect, place no limits on how much can be spent. The government is obligated to provide benefits, such as Social Security benefits, veterans' benefits, and the like, to persons who qualify under entitlement laws. The remaining federal programs are subject to discretionary spending and can be altered at will by Congress. National defense is the most important item in the discretionary-spending part of the budget.

JOIN THE DEBATE

Should "Earmarks" Be Banned?

In recent years, Congress has voted to fund a bridge to nowhere in Alaska, protection from blackbirds for sunflowers in North Dakota, a program to combat wild hogs in Missouri, and payment of storage fees for Georgia peanut farmers, among many other special projects. Every year, virtually every bill coming out of Congress includes "earmarked funds" for special interests or projects that are important to individual legislators. Much of this special interest spending consists of what is impolitely called *pork barrel* spending. The term *pork* comes from the idea that members of Congress "bring home the bacon" to their home states, usually in the form of additional federal spending that benefits local businesses and workers. In 2006 alone, there were 14,000 earmarks, costing taxpayers about $45 billion. In 2007, the estimate was more than $60 billion. Should earmarks be banned altogether?

Yes, argue most Americans, for it is time to end this unsightly "feeding frenzy" at every legislative session in

Earmarked spending, or pork-barrel legislation, often involves local construction projects, some of dubious value, such as a proposed bridge in Alaska to an island with only fifty inhabitants.

AP Photo/Hall Anderson/Ketchikan Daily News

Congress. Earmarks took off in Congress in the 1990s and have risen astronomically with members from both parties. The bridge to nowhere in Alaska mentioned earlier would have cost more than $200 million to link the small city of Ketchikan to Gravina Island—with a population of fifty. This would have been an obscene use of taxpayers' hard-earned dollars. If pork were banned, legislators would no longer be able to "bribe" other legislators by allowing them to include their pet projects in a bill if they agree to support certain legislation in return. In other words, so-called *logrolling* would be much more difficult without earmarks.

Those in favor of keeping earmarks point out that every member of Congress has constituents. Those constituents benefit from earmarked funds. Banning earmarks altogether would reduce the value of members of Congress to their own constituents and thereby weaken the ties between elected officials and their constituents. A less dramatic alternative involves simply more disclosure. Earmarks and their sponsors could be listed in the *Congressional Record* thirty days before the earmarks come up for final approval. In this way, everyone concerned will be able to protest the most abusive earmarks, such as the bridge to nowhere in Alaska, which ultimately was tabled as a result of the public furor. In any event, earmarks get a lot of press, but they represent only a trivial percentage of total federal spending.

The Actual Budgeting Process

Look at Figure 11–4 on the next page, which outlines the lengthy budgeting process. The process runs from January, when the president submits a proposed federal budget for the next **fiscal year,** to the start of that fiscal year on October 1. In actuality, about eighteen months prior to October 1, the executive agencies submit their requests to the Office of Management and Budget (OMB), and the OMB outlines a proposed budget. If the president approves it, the budget is officially submitted to Congress.

The legislative budgeting process begins eight to nine months before the start of the fiscal year. The **first budget resolution** is supposed to be passed in

fiscal year A twelve-month period that is established for bookkeeping or accounting purposes. The government's fiscal year runs from October 1 through September 30.

first budget resolution A budget resolution, which is supposed to be passed in May, that sets overall revenue goals and spending targets for the next fiscal year, which begins on October 1.

FIGURE 11-4

THE BUDGETING PROCESS

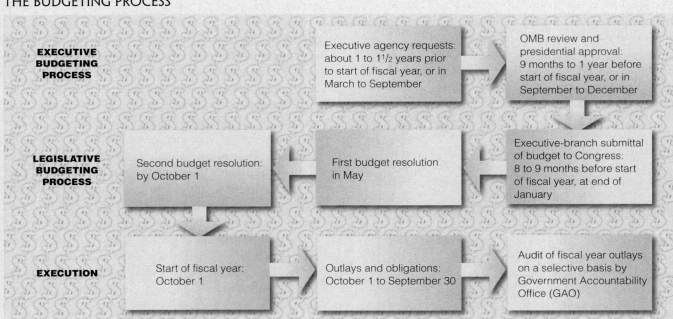

EXECUTIVE BUDGETING PROCESS

Executive agency requests: about 1 to 1½ years prior to start of fiscal year, or in March to September → OMB review and presidential approval: 9 months to 1 year before start of fiscal year, or in September to December

LEGISLATIVE BUDGETING PROCESS

Second budget resolution: by October 1 ← First budget resolution in May ← Executive-branch submittal of budget to Congress: 8 to 9 months before start of fiscal year, at end of January

EXECUTION

Start of fiscal year: October 1 → Outlays and obligations: October 1 to September 30 → Audit of fiscal year outlays on a selective basis by Government Accountability Office (GAO)

May. It sets overall revenue goals and spending targets and, by definition, the size of the federal budget deficit or surplus. The **second budget resolution,** which sets "binding" limits on taxes and spending, is supposed to be passed in September, prior to the beginning of the fiscal year on October 1. Whenever Congress is unable to pass a complete budget by October 1, it passes **continuing resolutions,** which enable the executive agencies to keep on doing whatever they were doing the previous year with the same amount of funding. Even continuing resolutions have not always been passed on time.

The budget process involves making predictions about the state of the U.S. economy for years to come. This process is necessarily very imprecise. Since 1996, both

> "WE THE PEOPLE ARE THE RIGHTFUL MASTERS OF BOTH CONGRESS AND THE COURTS."
>
> ABRAHAM LINCOLN, SIXTEENTH PRESIDENT OF THE UNITED STATES 1861-1865

Congress and the president have attempted to make ten-year projections for income (from taxes) and spending, but no one can know what the financial picture of the United States will look like in ten years. The workforce could grow or shrink, which would drastically alter government revenue from taxes. Any number of emergencies could arise that would require increased government spending—from going to war against terrorists to inoculating federal employees against smallpox. For a discussion of how congressional spending has affected the public debt, see this chapter's *Perception versus Reality* feature.

In any event, when you read about what the administration predicts the budget deficit (or surplus) will be in five or ten years, take such predictions with a grain of salt. There has never been such a long-term prediction that has come close to being accurate. Moreover, most times, the longest predictions made by administrations will come true or not when *another* administration is in office.

second budget resolution A budget resolution, which is supposed to be passed in September, that sets "binding" limits on taxes and spending for the next fiscal year.

continuing resolution A temporary resolution passed by Congress when an appropriations bill has not been passed by the beginning of the new fiscal year.

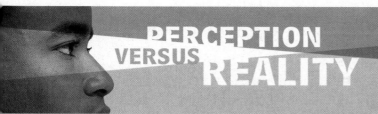

PERCEPTION VERSUS REALITY

IS OUR PUBLIC DEBT A PROBLEM?

As you have read in this chapter, Congress possesses the "power of the purse." After boasting a balanced budget between 1998 and 2001, Congress has overseen a significant increase in *deficit spending* in recent years. Each year that the government spends more than it collects in revenues, it runs a deficit. Any deficit spending is added to the *public debt,* which is often called the "national debt." Numerous economists have predicted that the United States could be headed toward an economic crisis if the public debt is not reduced.

The Perception

Many Americans believe that the public debt has grown to unprecedented amounts in recent years. The *gross,* or overall total, public debt is more than $9.5 trillion. This amount routinely increases by millions, and sometimes billions, of dollars on a daily basis. Foreigners —banks, corporations, individuals, and governments—hold a significant portion of the U.S. public debt, around 50 percent. Some fear that foreigners may "call in" their investments, causing a financial crisis in the United States as the government struggles to pay its debtors.

The Reality

In reality, the gross public debt is a misleading figure. The gross public debt includes government holdings of bonds issued by government agencies. These, of course, are simply reshufflings of IOUs within the U.S. government. For example, Congress has frequently authorized the use of money from the Social Security trust fund to pay for other government programs.

The more important figure when assessing the nation's financial liability is the *net* public debt, which is the gross public debt minus intragovernmental borrowing. The net public debt is the amount that the government owes to everyone else, and it is now almost

$5.3 trillion. Although this is still quite a large figure, it is much less daunting than the frequently cited $9.5 trillion.

Furthermore, the idea that the public debt has reached unprecedented levels is similarly misleading. The primary method of gauging the burden of the public debt is to view it in relation to the country's gross domestic product (GDP). GDP is the total market value of all *final* goods and services produced within the country's borders; it is a standard measure of economic well-being and strength. By the beginning of 2008, the net public debt was about 35 percent of the nation's GDP. This percentage is relatively low compared to the late 1940s, when the net public debt exceeded 100 percent of the nation's GDP (see Figure 11–5).

FIGURE 11–5

NET U.S. PUBLIC DEBT AS A PERCENTAGE OF GDP

During World War II (1939–1945), the net public debt grew dramatically. It fell until the 1970s, rose again until the early 1990s, and declined until the early 2000s.

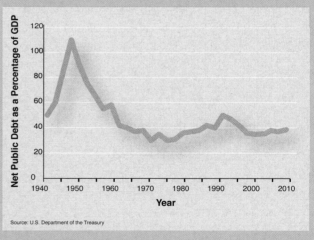

Source: U.S. Department of the Treasury

BLOG ON

Steve Conover, an ex-Fortune 500 executive, argues at **www.optimist123.com** that the national debt is widely misunderstood. In contrast, investment adviser Tim Iacono believes we are in a debt crisis that will end badly. His blogsite is at **www.themessthatgreenspanmade.blogspot.com**.

AMERICA AT ODDS:
Congress

When the founders drafted the Constitution, they envisioned that Congress would play the leading role in our national government. The founders, who were all too familiar with the treatment of the colonies by King George III of Britain, had a very real fear of tyranny and the arbitrary exercise of unchecked power by the executive. For the framers, the real governing was to be done by the legislative branch of government. For this reason, the powers of Congress are set forth in the first article of the U.S Constitution. The desire to prevent any one branch of government from becoming too powerful also caused the founders to include various checks and balances in the Constitution, as you read in Chapters 2 and 3.

Many Americans believe that the 109th Republican-led Congress, which stepped down in 2007 after the Democrats took control, largely failed in its oversight duties. Congress never made any serious attempt to check President George W. Bush's legislative agenda and administrative policymaking, even though legal scholars point out that several of his antiterrorism programs were clearly unconstitutional and others questionably so. The Democratic majority now in Congress has attempted to resume congressional oversight by investigating many of Bush's policies and programs, but because the Democrats have only a narrow majority in Congress, they have found it difficult to garner enough votes to bring proposed bills to the floor for a vote or to override threatened (or real) presidential vetoes. Clearly, today's Congress is not playing the strong and central role in the national government that was envisioned by the founders. Whether it can again resume such powers remains to be seen.

Issues for Debate & Discussion

1. For some time, Americans have debated whether something should be done to reform the redistricting process to reduce the electoral advantage enjoyed by congressional incumbents. Some groups have argued that the responsibility of redrawing congressional district lines after each census should be taken away from political partisans in state legislatures and given to a panel of nonpartisan retired judges instead. Others believe that there is nothing wrong with drawing district lines to ensure that a maximum number of people in a particular district will have views similar to those of their representative. What is your position on this issue?

2. Review this chapter's discussion of racial gerrymandering on pages 242–243. There, we stated that some Americans believe that minority-majority districts are necessary to ensure equal representation of minority groups, as mandated by the Voting Rights Act of 1965, and that these districts have helped to increase the number of African Americans holding political office. Others argue that race-based districting is unconstitutional because it violates the equal protection clause. What is your position on this issue?

Take Action

During each session of Congress, your senators and representative debate the pros and cons of proposed laws, some of which may affect your daily life or the lives of those you care about. If you want to let your voice be heard, you can do so simply by phoning or e-mailing your senators or your representative in the House. You can learn the names and contact information for the senators and representative from your area by going to the Web sites of the Senate and the House, which are given in this chapter's *Politics on the Web* feature. Your chances of influencing your members of Congress will be greater if you can convince others, including your friends and family members, to do likewise. Citizens often feel that such efforts are useless. Yet members of Congress *do* listen to their constituents and often *do* act in response to their constituents' wishes. Indeed, next to voting, contacting those who represent you in Congress is probably the most effective way to influence government decision making.

Kayte M. Deioma/PhotoEdit

Contacting U.S. representatives and senators is much easier today using the Internet. Next to voting, phoning, writing to, or e-mailing members of Congress is the most effective way to influence decision making in Washington, D.C.

- There is an abundance of online information relating to Congress and congressional activities. The THOMAS site (named for Thomas Jefferson), maintained by the Library of Congress, provides a record of all bills introduced into Congress, information about each member of Congress and how he or she voted on specific bills, and other data. Go to **thomas.loc.gov**.

- The U.S. Government Printing Office (GPO) Access on the Web offers information on Congress in session, bills pending and passed, and a history of the bills at **www.gpoaccess.gov**.

- To learn more about how a bill becomes a law, go to **www.vote-smart.org**.

  Click on "Political Resources" and scroll down to "Vote Smart Classroom." Select "An Introduction to the U.S. Government," and then choose "How a Bill Becomes Law."

- You can find e-mail addresses and home pages for members of the House of Representatives at **www.house.gov**.

- For e-mail addresses and home pages for members of the Senate, go to **www.senate.gov**.

- To have your local congressional representative's votes e-mailed to you every week, to post letters online and read what others are saying about elected officials, or to create and post a "soapbox action alert" to get others on your side of an issue, explore your options at **www.congress.org**.

ONLINE RESOURCES FOR THIS CHAPTER

This text's Companion Web site, at **www.americaatodds. com,** offers links to numerous resources that you can utilize to learn more about the topics covered in this chapter.

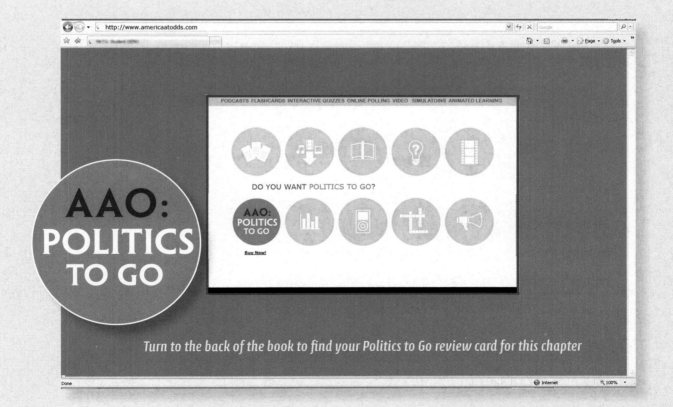

CHAPTER 12
THE PRESIDENCY

AMERICA AT ODDS

ON PODCAST

Will the Presidency of George W. Bush Be Classified as "One of the Worst"?

One of America's favorite pastimes is ranking presidents from "failure" to "great." Since 1948, historians Arthur M. Schlesinger, Sr., and his son, Arthur M. Schlesinger, Jr., have periodically asked more than fifty historians for their rankings of past presidents. Their latest ranking, in 1996, listed Lincoln, Washington, and Franklin D. Roosevelt as "great" presidents. The "failures" included Pierce, Grant, Hoover, Nixon, Andrew Johnson, Buchanan, and Harding. The latest ranking of presidents, undertaken by the Wall Street Journal and the Federalist Society in 2000, came up with about the same results.

Now scholars are debating how historians will rank George W. Bush. Everyone agrees (and he does, too) that he won't be listed as one of the "greats." But will he ultimately be listed as one of the "failures," perhaps the worst of all?

He May Not Rank as the Worst, but He Will Certainly Be Ranked as One of the Worst

Setting aside people's subjective views on President George W. Bush, many current historians believe that he will rank poorly in the list of presidents. Before the 2004 presidential elections, the History News Network conducted an informal survey of about four hundred historians. More than 81 percent of them considered the Bush administration a "failure." By 2007, a majority of voters in forty-three states disapproved of the way Bush was handling his job. The only other two-term president to hold this honor was Richard Nixon, and he reached that level only during the months preceding his resignation in 1974.

Historians claim that when enormous difficulties divide the nation, a president who governs erratically leaves the nation worse off. They contend that George W. Bush is indeed one of these presidents. They cite primarily his foreign policy blunders and military setbacks. Then they add unethical behavior within the executive branch, disastrous domestic policies, and numerous crises of public trust. He doesn't even have much support from the ardent conservative Republicans who elected him. After all, he has increased the size of the federal government more than any other president since Franklin D. Roosevelt (1933–1945).

PRESIDENTIAL RANKINGS MEAN NOTHING

Many people who do not agree with all of Bush's policies, particularly his foreign policy, certainly do not see him as our worst president. Let's assume that he has been a failure at foreign policy. His domestic policies are another story. Many of them have moved this country back on the right course. Don't forget that the economy was in the doldrums after the dot-com bust in 2000 and especially after the terrorist attacks in 2001. In contrast, by the fall of 2007, all of the stock market averages had risen considerably, and one of them had reached a historic high. At the same time, the unemployment rate was at an almost record low.

Besides, considering the liberal leanings of the current crop of history professors, surveys of historians hardly provide an objective view of where Bush will ultimately fit in the presidential rankings. In terms of domestic legislation, Bush has provided prescription drug insurance coverage for seniors, national standards for public education, and stricter air-pollution standards. In any event, time heals all. Don't forget that President Harry Truman (1945–1953) left office with an approval rating of barely 30 percent, yet historians now judge him much more positively and certainly don't categorize him as one of our worst presidents. Former president Jimmy Carter (1977–1981), a Democrat who was rated "average" by the Schlesinger poll in 1996, said that the Bush administration was "the worst in history." Given that Carter generally does not rank very high on historians' lists, this was equivalent to the pot calling the kettle black.

Where do you stand?

1. In making your judgment on whether a president is good or bad, what criteria do you use?
2. Why might the historical judgment on George W. Bush be different fifty years from now from what it is today?

Explore this issue online

- Charles Krauthammer is perhaps the most famous and influential neoconservative commentator, and he usually favors President George W. Bush. You can access his columns through the links at the end of his Wikipedia biography at **en.wikipedia.org/wiki/ Charles_Krauthammer**.
- In 2006, Sean Wilentz, a professor of history at Princeton, marshaled the case against President Bush at **www.rollingstone. com/news/coverstory/worst_president_in_history**. A simple Google search on "bush 'worst president'" also yields a vast collection of commentary.

INTRODUCTION

President Lyndon B. Johnson (1963–1969) stated in his autobiography[1] that "[o]f all the 1,886 nights I was President, there were not many when I got to sleep before 1 or 2 A.M., and there were few mornings when I didn't wake up by 6 or 6:30." President Harry Truman (1945–1953) once observed that no one can really understand what it is like to be president: there is no end to "the chain of responsibility that binds him," and he is "never allowed to forget that he is president." These responsibilities are, for the most part, unremitting. Unlike Congress, the president never adjourns.

Given the demands of the presidency, why would anyone seek the office? There are some very special perks associated with the presidency. The president enjoys, among other things, the use of the White House. The White House has 132 rooms located on 18.3 acres of land in the heart of the nation's capital. At the White House, the president in residence has a staff of more than eighty persons, including chefs, gardeners, maids, butlers, and a personal tailor. Amenities also include a tennis court, a swimming pool, bowling lanes, and a private movie theater. Additionally, the president has at his or her disposal a fleet of automobiles, helicopters, and jets (including *Air Force One*, which costs $58,600 an hour to run). For relaxation, the presidential family can go to Camp David, a resort hideaway in the Catoctin Mountains of Maryland. Other perks include free dental and medical care.

> **"No man** will ever bring out of the Presidency the reputation which carries him into it. To myself, personally, it brings nothing but increasing **drudgery** and daily loss of friends."
>
> THOMAS JEFFERSON,
> THIRD PRESIDENT OF THE UNITED STATES
> 1801–1809

These amenities are only a minor motivation for wanting to be president of the United States, however. A greater motivation is that the presidency is at the apex of the political ladder. It is the most powerful and influential political office that any one individual can hold. Presidents can help to shape not only domestic policy but also global developments. With the demise of the Soviet Union and its satellite Communist countries in the early 1990s, the president of the United States is regarded by some as the leader of the most powerful nation on earth. The president heads the greatest military force anywhere. It is not surprising, therefore, that many Americans aspire to attain this office. Beyond power, many presidential aspirants desire a place in history. Scholars and ordinary Americans alike have long debated presidential "greatness," as discussed in the chapter-opening *America at Odds* feature.

LO[1] WHO CAN BECOME PRESIDENT?

The notion that anybody can become president of this country has always been a part of the American dream. Certainly, the requirements for becoming president set forth in Article II, Section 1, of the Constitution are not difficult to meet:

President George W. Bush (right) speaks to his staff inside the private dining room at the White House before his address to the nation on September 11, 2001.

AP Photo/The White House/Paul Morse

No Person except a natural born Citizen, or a Citizen of the United States, at the time of the Adoption of this Constitution, shall be eligible to the Office of President; neither shall any Person be eligible to that Office who shall not have attained to the Age of thirty-five Years, and been fourteen Years a Resident within the United States.

It is true that modern presidents have included a haberdasher (Harry Truman), a peanut farmer (Jimmy Carter), and an actor (Ronald Reagan), although all of these men also had significant political experience before assuming the presidency. If you look at Appendix E, though, you will see that the most common previous occupation of U.S. presidents has been the legal profession. Out of forty-three presidents, twenty-six have been lawyers, and many presidents have been wealthy. Additionally, although the Constitution states that anyone who is thirty-five years of age or older can become president, the average age at inauguration has been fifty-four. The youngest person elected president was John F. Kennedy (1961–1963), who assumed the presidency at the age of forty-three (the youngest person to hold the office was Theodore Roosevelt, who was forty-two when he became president after the assassination of William McKinley); the oldest was Ronald Reagan (1981–1989), who was sixty-nine years old when he became president. Even the requirement that the president be a natural-born citizen has been questioned recently.

America is a nation of immigrants, so it strikes some as odd that a foreign-born person would be barred from aspiring to the presidency. Naturalized U.S. citizens are allowed to vote, to serve on juries, and to serve in the military. They are also allowed to serve as secretary of state and represent the nation in foreign affairs. Why can't they run for president? Critics of the Constitution's citizenship requirement think that the requirement should be abolished by a constitutional amendment. They point out that the clause was initially included in the Constitution to prevent European princes from attempting to force the young republic back under monarchical rule in the late 1700s. Clearly, the clause is now obsolete and should no longer apply.

Other Americans believe that the constitutional ban should remain. They argue that national security could be compromised by a foreign-born president. With the immense power that the president wields, especially in the realm of foreign policy, loyalty is of the utmost concern. The current war on terrorism only heightens the need to ensure that the president does not have divided loyalties. In addition, the Constitution is quite difficult to amend, requiring support from two-thirds of both chambers of Congress and ratification by three-fourths of the fifty states. The need for an amendment that would allow Schwarzenegger and other immigrants to run for president is hardly as pressing as the need for past antidiscrimination amendments such as those abolishing slavery and giving women the right to vote, opponents argue.

JOIN THE DEBATE

A Foreign-Born President?

As you just read, Article II of the Constitution states that "[n]o Person except a natural born Citizen . . . shall be eligible to the Office of President." This restriction has long been controversial, for it has kept many otherwise qualified Americans from running for president. These persons include California governor Arnold Schwarzenegger, who was born in Austria, and Michigan governor Jennifer M. Granholm, who was born in Canada, both of whom have been U.S. citizens for decades. John McCain's daughter Bridget, who was adopted from Bangladesh, is also among this excluded group—along with the other 13 million Americans born outside the United States.

To date, all U.S. presidents have been male, white, and (with the exception of John F. Kennedy, who was a Roman Catholic) from the Protestant tradition. Polls indicate, though, that many Americans expect to see a woman or an African American assume the office in the not-too-distant future. Recent polls indicate that between 89 and 94 percent of Americans would vote for a woman for president and about the same number would vote for an African American candidate.

LO² THE PRESIDENT'S MANY ROLES

As will be discussed shortly, the president has the authority to exercise a variety of powers; some of these are explicitly outlined in the Constitution, and some are simply required by the office—such as the power to persuade. In the course of exercising these powers, the president performs a variety of roles. For example, as commander in chief of the armed services, the president can exercise significant military powers. Which roles a president executes successfully usually depend on what is happening domestically and internationally, as well as on the president's personality. Some presidents, including Bill Clinton during his first term, have shown much more interest in domestic policy than in foreign policy. Others, such as George H. W. Bush (1989–1993), were more interested in foreign affairs than in domestic policies. Although George W. Bush might have desired to spend more time on his domestic agenda, since 2003 he has had to focus largely on the Iraq war, which has continued much longer than his administration anticipated.

Table 12–1 summarizes the major roles of the president. An important role is, of course, that of chief executive. Other roles include those of commander in chief, chief of state, chief diplomat, chief legislator, and political party leader.

Chief Executive

According to Article II of the Constitution,

The executive Power shall be vested in a President of the United States of America. . . . [H]e may require the Opin-

TABLE 12-1

ROLES OF THE PRESIDENT

Role	Description	Examples
Chief executive	Enforces laws and federal court decisions, along with treaties signed by the United States	• Can appoint, with Senate approval, and remove high-ranking officers of the federal government • Can grant reprieves, pardons, and amnesty • Can handle national emergencies during peacetime, such as riots or natural disasters
Commander in chief	Leads the nation's armed forces	• Can commit troops for up to ninety days in response to a military threat (War Powers Resolution) • Can make secret agreements with other countries • Can set up military governments in conquered lands • Can end fighting by calling a cease-fire (armistice)
Chief of state	Performs certain ceremonial roles as personal symbol of the nation	• Decorates war heroes • Dedicates parks and post offices • Throws out first pitch of baseball season • Lights national Christmas tree
Chief diplomat	Directs U.S. foreign policy and is the nation's most important representative in dealing with foreign countries	• Can negotiate and sign treaties with other nations, with Senate approval • Can make pacts (executive agreements) with other heads of state, without Senate approval • Can accept the legal existence of another country's government (power of recognition) • Receives foreign chiefs of state
Chief legislator	Informs Congress about the condition of the country and recommends legislative measures	• Proposes legislative program to Congress in traditional State of the Union address • Suggests budget to Congress and submits annual economic report • Can veto a bill passed by Congress • Can call special sessions of Congress
Political party leader	Heads political party	• Chooses a vice president • Makes several thousand top government appointments, often to party faithful (patronage) • Tries to execute the party's platform • May attend party fund-raisers • May help reelect party members running for office as mayors, governors, or members of Congress

ion, in writing, of the principal Officer in each of the executive Departments, upon any Subject relating to the Duties of their respective Offices . . . and he shall nominate, and by and with the Advice and Consent of the Senate, shall appoint . . . Officers of the United States . . . . [H]e shall take Care that the Laws be faithfully executed.

This constitutional provision makes the president of the United States the nation's **chief executive,** or the head of the executive branch of the federal government. When the framers created the office of the president, they created a uniquely American institution. Nowhere else in the world at that time was there a democratically elected chief executive. The executive branch is also unique among the branches of government because it is headed by a single individual—the president.

President Woodrow Wilson throwing out the first pitch on the opening day of the Major League Baseball season in 1916. This action is part of the president's role as chief of state.

Commander in Chief

The Constitution states that the president "shall be Commander in Chief of the Army and Navy of the United States, and of the Militia of the several States, when called into the actual Service of the United States." As **commander in chief** of the nation's armed forces, the president exercises tremendous power.

Under the Constitution, war powers are divided between Congress and the president. Congress was given the power to declare war and the power to raise and maintain the country's armed forces. The president, as commander in chief, was given the power to deploy the armed forces. The president's role as commander in chief has evolved over the last century. We will examine this shared power between the president and Congress in more detail later in this chapter.

Chief of State

Traditionally, a country's monarch has performed the function of chief of state—the country's representative to the rest of the world. The United States, of course, has no king or queen to act as **chief of state.** Thus, the president of the United States fulfills this role. The president engages in many symbolic or ceremonial activities, such as throwing out the first pitch to open the baseball sea-

son and turning on the lights of the national Christmas tree. The president also decorates war heroes, dedicates parks and post offices, receives visiting chiefs of state at the White House, and goes on official state visits to other countries. Some argue that presidents should not perform such ceremonial duties because they take time that the president should be spending on "real work." (See this chapter's *The Rest of the World* feature on the following page for more information on how other countries handle this issue.)

Chief Diplomat

A **diplomat** is a person who represents one country in dealing with representatives of another country. In the United States, the president is the nation's **chief diplomat.** The Constitution did not explicitly reserve this role to the president, but since the beginning of this nation, presidents have assumed the role based on their explicit constitutional powers to recognize foreign governments and, with the advice and consent of the Senate, to appoint ambassadors and

chief executive The head of the executive branch of government. In the United States, the president is the head of the executive branch of the federal government.

commander in chief The supreme commander of the military forces of the United States.

chief of state The person who serves as the ceremonial head of a country's government and represents that country to the rest of the world.

diplomat A person who represents one country in dealing with representatives of another country.

chief diplomat The role of the president in recognizing and interacting with foreign governments.

THE REST OF THE WORLD

Having a Separate Chief of State

In the seven Western European countries headed by royalty, the monarch is considered the chief of state and plays a ceremonial role. In the United Kingdom, for example, Queen Elizabeth II represents the state when she performs ceremonial duties, such as opening sessions of Parliament, christening ships, and holding receptions for foreign ambassadors.

In the monarchies of the Netherlands and Norway, the king or queen initiates the process of forming a government after national elections by determining which parties can combine to rule in a coalition. This process really depends on the results of the election and the desires of the political parties—yet the monarch must certify the results.

The majority of European states are not monarchies, but they nonetheless split the duties of government between a prime minister and a

Official Photograph by John Swannell

Queen Elizabeth II of the United Kingdom.

president. In Switzerland, for example, the president is elected indirectly by the legislature and assumes purely ceremonial duties.

Throughout Western Europe, the pattern is the same: presidents have ceremonial powers only. The single exception to this rule occurs in France, which has a presidential system in which the head of state has real political power, particularly in foreign affairs.

For Critical Analysis

What are the benefits of having a single person perform only chief-of-state activities? Are there any benefits to the American system, in which the functions of chief executive and chief of state are combined?

---

make treaties. As chief diplomat, the president directs the foreign policy of the United States and is its most important representative.

Chief Legislator

Nowhere in the Constitution do the words *chief legislator* appear. The Constitution, however, does require that the president "from time to time give to the Congress Information of the State of the Union, and recommend to their Consideration such Measures as he shall judge necessary and expedient." The president has, in fact, become a major player in shaping the congressional agenda—the set of measures that actually get discussed and acted on. This was not always the case. In the nineteenth century, some presidents preferred to let Congress lead the way in proposing and implementing policy. Since the administration of Theodore Roosevelt (1901–1909), however, presidents have taken an activist approach. Presidents are now expected to develop a legislative program and propose a

patronage The practice of giving government jobs to individuals belonging to the winning political party.

budget to Congress every year. This shared power often puts Congress and the president at odds—as you will read shortly.

Political Party Leader

The president of the United States is also the leader of his or her political party. The Constitution, of course, does not mention this role because, in the eyes of the founders, presidents (and other political representatives) were not to be influenced by "factional" (partisan) interests.

As party leader, the president exercises substantial powers. For example, the president chooses the chairperson of the party's national committee. The president can also exert political power within the party by using presidential appointment and removal powers. Naturally, presidents are beholden to the party members who put them in office, and usually they indulge in the practice of **patronage**—appointing individuals to government or public jobs—to reward those who helped them win the presidential contest. The president may also reward party members with fund-raising assistance (campaign financing was discussed in Chapter 9). The president is, in a sense, "fund-raiser in chief" for his or her party. Understandably, the use of patronage within the party system gives the president singular powers.

LO³ PRESIDENTIAL POWERS

The president exercises numerous powers. Some of these powers are set forth in the Constitution. Others, known as *inherent powers,* are those that are necessary to carry out the president's constitutional duties. We look next at these powers, as well as at the expansion of presidential powers over time.

The President's Constitutional Powers

As you have read, the constitutional source for the president's authority is found in Article II of the Constitution, which states, "The executive Power shall be vested in a President of the United States of America." The Constitution then sets forth the president's relatively limited constitutional responsibilities. Just how much power should be entrusted to the president was debated at length by the framers of the Constitution. On the one hand, they did not want a king. On the other hand, they believed that a strong executive was necessary if the republic was to survive. The result of their debates was an executive who was granted enough powers in the Constitution to balance those of Congress.

Article II grants the president broad but vaguely described powers. From the very beginning, there were different views as to what exactly the "executive Power" clause enabled the president to do. Nonetheless, Sections 2 and 3 of Article II list the following specific presidential powers:

- To serve as commander in chief of the armed forces and the state militias.

- To appoint, with the Senate's consent, the heads of the executive departments, ambassadors, justices of the Supreme Court, and other top officials.

- To grant reprieves and pardons, except in cases of impeachment.

- To make treaties, with the advice and consent of the Senate.

- To deliver the annual State of the Union address to Congress and to send other messages to Congress from time to time.

- To call either house or both houses of Congress into special sessions.

- To receive ambassadors and other representatives from foreign countries.

President George W. Bush announces that he will endorse a constitutional amendment that would ban gay marriage. The president often influences the legislative agenda in Congress.

Kevin Lamarque/Reuters/Landov

- To commission all officers of the United States.

- To ensure that the laws passed by Congress "be faithfully executed."

In addition, Article I, Section 7, gives the president the power to veto legislation. We discuss some of these powers in more detail below. As you will see, many of these powers are balanced by the powers of Congress. We address the complex relationship between the president and Congress in a later section of this chapter.

PROPOSAL AND RATIFICATION OF TREATIES A **treaty** is a formal agreement between two or more sovereign states. The president has the sole power to negotiate and sign treaties with other countries. The Senate, however, must approve the treaty by a two-thirds vote of the members present before it becomes effective. If the treaty is approved by the Senate and signed by the president, it becomes law.

Presidents have not always succeeded in winning the Senate's approval for treaties. Woodrow Wilson (1913–1921) lost his effort to persuade the Senate to approve the Treaty of Versailles,[2] the peace treaty that ended

treaty A formal agreement between the governments of two or more countries.

One of the significant powers of the president is the power to negotiate and sign treaties. Here, President Jimmy Carter (far left) and other officials watch as Panama's president, General Omar Torrijos, signs the Panama Canal Treaty on September 7, 1977.

World War I in 1918. Among other things, the treaty would have made the United States a member of the League of Nations. In contrast, Jimmy Carter (1977–1981) convinced the Senate to approve a treaty returning the Panama Canal to Panama by the year 2000 (over such objections as that of Senator S. I. Hayakawa, a Republican from California, who said, "We stole it fair and square"). The treaty was approved by a margin of a single vote.

THE POWER TO GRANT REPRIEVES AND PARDONS The president's power to grant a pardon serves as a check on judicial power. A *pardon* is a release from punishment or the legal consequences of a crime; it restores a person to the full rights and privileges of citizenship. In 1925, the United States Supreme Court upheld an expansive interpretation of the president's pardon power in a case involving an individual convicted for contempt of court. The Court held that the power covers all offenses "either before trial, during trial, or after trial, by individuals, or by classes, conditionally or absolutely, and this without modification or regulation by Congress."[3] The president can grant a pardon for any federal offense, except in cases of impeachment.

One of the most controversial pardons was that granted by President Gerald Ford (1974–1977) to former president Richard Nixon (1969–1974) after the Watergate affair, before any formal charges were brought in court. Sometimes pardons are granted to a class of individuals, as a general amnesty. For example, President Jimmy Carter (1977–1981) granted amnesty to approximately 10,000 people who had resisted the draft during the Vietnam War. Just before he left office in 2001, President Bill Clinton pardoned 140 individuals. Some of these pardons were controversial.

Even more controversial was President George W. Bush's decision, in 2007, to use his clemency powers to commute the prison sentence received by Lewis ("Scooter") Libby. Libby, who had served as Vice President Dick Cheney's chief of staff, was found guilty of several crimes, including perjury and obstruction of justice, in connection with the investigation of a leak made to the press. The leak exposed the identity of Central Intelligence Agency agent Valerie Plame. Plame's husband, Joseph Wilson, had earlier stated that key evidence cited by the Bush administration as a justification for invading Iraq did not, in fact, exist. Many Bush administration critics alleged that the exposure of Plame's identity was an attempt to "punish" Wilson for this action.

President Gerald Ford (right) reads a proclamation in the White House on September 9, 1974, granting former president Richard Nixon "a full, free and absolute pardon" for all "offenses against the United States" during the period of his presidency. Richard Nixon (left) had resigned as president just one month earlier.

THE PRESIDENT'S VETO POWER As noted in Chapter 11, the president can **veto** a bill passed by Congress. Congress can override the veto with a two-thirds vote by the members present in each chamber. The result of an overridden veto is that the bill becomes law against the wishes of the president. If the president does not send a bill back to Congress after ten congressional working days, the bill becomes law without the president's signature. If the president refuses to sign the bill and Congress adjourns within ten working days after the bill has been submitted to the president, the bill is killed for that session of Congress. As mentioned in Chapter 11, this is called a *pocket veto*.

Presidents used the veto power sparingly until the administration of Andrew Johnson (1865–1869). Johnson vetoed twenty-one bills, and his successor, Ulysses Grant (1869–1877), vetoed forty-five. Franklin D. Roosevelt (1933–1945) vetoed more bills by far than any of his predecessors or successors in the presidency. During his administration, there were 372 regular vetoes, 9 of which were overridden by Congress, and 263 pocket vetoes. By the end of his presidency in 2001, President Bill Clinton had vetoed thirty-seven bills. President George W. Bush, in contrast, used his veto power very sparingly. Indeed, during the first six years of his presidency, Bush vetoed only one bill—a proposal to expand the scope of stem-cell

When the president contemplates vetoing legislation, not all Americans are necessarily in agreement. In 2007, protesters—many of them children pulling wagons—gathered in front of the White House to ask President Bush not to veto legislation expanding a health insurance program for low-income children.

research. Bush vetoed so few bills, in large part, because the Republican-led Congress during those years strongly supported his agenda and undertook no actions to oppose it. In the first ten months after the Democrats took control of Congress in January 2007, however, Bush vetoed three bills and threatened to veto others.

Many presidents have complained that they cannot control "pork barrel" legislation—federal expenditures tacked onto bills to "bring home the bacon" to a particular congressional member's district. For example, expenditures on a specific sports stadium might be added to a bill involving crime. The reason is simple: without a line-item veto (the ability to veto just one item in a bill), to eliminate the "pork" in proposed legislation, the president would have to veto the entire bill—and that might not be feasible politically. Congress passed and President Clinton signed a line-item veto bill in 1996. The Supreme Court concluded in 1998 that it was unconstitutional, however.[4]

The President's Inherent Powers

In addition to the powers explicitly granted by the Constitution, the president also has *inherent powers*—powers that are necessary to carry out the specific responsibilities of the president as set forth in the

President Bill Clinton used line-item veto powers to eliminate nearly forty construction projects worth $287 million from a military construction bill during a ceremony in the Oval Office in 1997. The line-item veto legislation, passed in 1996, was ruled unconstitutional by the U.S. Supreme Court in 1998.

> **veto** A Latin word meaning "I forbid"; the refusal by an official, such as the president of the United States or a state governor, to sign a bill into law.

As commander in chief, George Washington used troops to put down a rebellion in Pennsylvania, and as chief diplomat, he made foreign policy without consulting Congress. This latter action laid the groundwork for the presidents' active role in the area of foreign policy.

By the time Abraham Lincoln gave his Inauguration Day speech, seven southern states had already seceded from the Union. Four more states seceded after he issued a summons to the militia. In 1863, during the Civil War, Lincoln issued the Emancipation Proclamation. Some scholars believe that his skillful and vigorous handling of the Civil War increased the power and prestige of the presidency.

When Franklin D. Roosevelt assumed the presidency in 1933, he launched his "Hundred Days" of legislation in an attempt to counter the effects of the Great Depression. Roosevelt's administration not only extended the role of the national government in regulating the nation's economic life but also further increased the power of the president.

Constitution. The presidency is, of course, an institution of government, but it is also an institution that consists, at any one moment in time, of one individual. That means that the lines between the presidential office and the person who holds that office often become blurred. Certain presidential powers that are today considered part of the rights of the office were simply assumed by strong presidents to be inherent powers of the presidency, and their successors then continued to exercise these powers.

President Woodrow Wilson clearly indicated this interplay between presidential personality and presidential powers in the following statement:

> The President is at liberty, both in law and conscience, to be as big a man as he can. His capacity will set the limit; and if Congress be overborne by him, it will be no fault of the makers of the Constitution—it will be from no lack of constitutional powers on his part, but only because the President has the nation behind him, and Congress has not.[5]

In other words, because the Constitution is vague as to the actual carrying out of presidential powers, presidents are left to define the limits of their authority—subject, of course, to the other branches of government.

As you will read in the following pages, Congress has sometimes allowed the president to exercise certain powers and has sometimes limited presidential powers.

Additionally, the Supreme Court, as the head of the judicial branch of the government and the final arbiter of the Constitution, can check the president's powers. The Court, through its power of judicial review, can determine whether the president, by taking a certain action, has exceeded the powers granted by the Constitution.

The Expansion of Presidential Powers

The Constitution defines presidential powers in very general language, and even the founders were uncertain just how the president would perform the various functions. Only experience would tell. Thus, over the past two centuries, the powers of the president have been defined and expanded by the personalities and policies of various White House occupants.

For example, George Washington (1789–1797) removed officials from office, interpreting the constitutional power to appoint officials as implying a power to remove them as well.[6] He established the practice of meeting regularly with the heads of the three departments that then existed and of turning to them for political advice. He set a precedent of the president acting as chief legislator by submitting proposed legislation to Congress. Abraham Lincoln (1861–1865), confronting the problems of the

Civil War during the 1860s, took several important actions while Congress was not in session. He suspended certain constitutional liberties, spent funds that Congress had not appropriated, blockaded southern ports, and banned "treasonable correspondence" from the U.S. mails. All of these actions were carried out in the name of his power as commander in chief and his constitutional responsibility to "take Care that the Laws be faithfully executed."

Other presidents, including Thomas Jefferson, Andrew Jackson, Woodrow Wilson, Franklin D. Roosevelt, and recently George W. Bush, have also greatly expanded the powers of the president. The power of the president continues to evolve, depending on the person holding the office, the relative power of Congress, and events at home and abroad.

THE EXPANSION OF THE PRESIDENT'S LEGISLATIVE POWERS

Congress has come to expect the president to develop a legislative program. From time to time the president submits special messages on certain subjects. These messages call on Congress to enact laws that the president thinks are necessary. The president also works closely with members of Congress to persuade them to support particular programs. The president writes, telephones, and meets with various congressional leaders to discuss pending bills. The president also sends aides to lobby on Capitol Hill. One study of the legislative process found that "no other single actor in the political system has quite the capability of the president to set agendas in given policy areas." As one lobbyist told a researcher, "Obviously, when a president sends up a bill [to Congress], it takes first place in the queue. All other bills take second place."

The Power to Persuade.
The president's political skills and ability to persuade others play a large role in determining the administration's success. According to Richard Neustadt, in his classic work entitled *Presidential Power*, "Presidential power is the power to persuade."[7] For all of the resources at the president's disposal, the president still must rely on the cooperation of others if the administration's goals are to be accomplished. After three years in office, President Harry Truman made this remark about the powers of the president:

> "All the president is, is a **glorified** public relations man who spends his time flattering, kissing, and kicking people to get them to do what they are **supposed** to do anyway."
>
> HARRY TRUMAN,
> THIRTY-THIRD PRESIDENT OF THE UNITED STATES
> 1945–1953

The president may have a great many powers given to him in the Constitution and may have certain powers under certain laws which are given to him by the Congress of the United States; but the principal power that the president has is to bring people in and try to persuade them to do what they ought to do without persuasion. That's what the powers of the president amount to.[8]

For example, President Bush embarked on an ambitious legislative agenda following his reelection in 2004. His ability to win congressional support for his plans depended largely on his persuasive power. (As you will read in this chapter's *Perception versus Reality* feature on page 274, however, President Bush did not rely solely on his persuasive powers to implement his agenda.) Persuasive powers are particularly important when divided government exists. If a president from one political party faces a Congress dominated by the other party, the president must overcome more opposition than usual to get legislation passed.

Going Public.
The president may also use a strategy known as "going public"[9]—that is, using press conferences, public appearances, and televised events to arouse public opinion in favor of certain legislative programs. The public may then pressure legislators to support the administration's programs. A president who has the support of the public can wield significant persuasive powers over Congress. Presidents who are voted into office through "landslide" elections have increased bargaining power because of their widespread popularity. Those with less popular support have less bargaining leverage.

JOIN THE DEBATE

The President and Moral Politics

Franklin D. Roosevelt once said, "The presidency is not merely an administrative office. That is the least of it. It is preeminently a place of moral leadership."[10]

PERCEPTION VERSUS REALITY

The President's Power to Persuade

President Theodore Roosevelt (1901–1909) once said that the American presidency was a "bully pulpit." He meant that the office of the presidency is a great place from which to pitch one's agenda to Congress, to the American public, and indeed to the rest of the world. Presidents indeed have the power to persuade.

The Perception

It is now a common assumption, particularly since the first appearance in 1960 of political scientist Richard Neustadt's book entitled *Presidential Power*, that the essence of presidential power is the power to persuade. Researchers point out the effectiveness of President Ronald Reagan (1981–1989) in pushing through significant tax-rate reductions in spite of a hostile Democratic Congress. They add as another example the ability of President Bill Clinton to mobilize the country and Congress in favor of welfare reform in the mid-1990s.

The Reality

Today, it is no longer necessary for presidents to persuade anybody to do anything, as long as they know how to use nonlegislative procedures to get what they want. As will be discussed shortly, the president has the ability to issue *executive orders*. Such orders explain how policies must be carried out in light of the laws that have been passed by Congress. These orders have the force of law. Presidents have issued thousands of such executive orders, and President George W. Bush has used them extensively. For example, Bush signed one to create military tribunals for trying "enemy combatants." In response to 9/11, he created the Office of Homeland Security by executive order. As you will read later in this chapter, President Bush also championed the idea of adding *signing statements* to legislation that he signed into law, giving himself the option to interpret if and how the law, or parts of it, were to be applied.

In other words, current presidents do not necessarily have to use their power of persuasion to get what they want. They can use other powers to simply circumvent the wishes of Congress and the public.[11]

BLOG ON

Like a number of other *Washington Post* columns, Dan Froomkin's "White House Watch" encourages reader feedback. It is listed, along with many others, at **www.washingtonpost.com/wp-srv/politics/politics_columnists.html**. Real Clear Politics, a conservative-leaning Web site, collects recent columns on the White House, many of which allow responses, at **www.realclearpolitics.com/topic/?topic=white_house**.

George W. Bush did not hesitate to apply his moral and religious values to his role as president. Many of his staunchest supporters were evangelical Christians who voted for him in the hope that he would champion what they considered to be moral causes, such as curtailing abortion rights, banning gay marriage, and endorsing "faith-based" services. During his presidency, Bush did not fail to "go public" on such issues, openly promoting his moral agenda to the American people.

In 2005, for example, Bush willingly supported emergency legislation passed by Congress to keep Terri Schiavo alive. Bush's moral leadership on this issue was applauded by many pro-life Americans and evangelical Christian supporters. Bush also held firmly to his belief that stem-cell research should be restricted. Indeed, as mentioned earlier, the only legislation that he vetoed during his first term in office was a bill to expand the scope of such research. He vetoed similar legislation again in

2007. The increasingly few Americans who continued to support Bush's position on stem-cell research, predominantly pro-life groups, admired his decision to hold firm to the view that, in his words, "Destroying human life in the hopes of saving human life is not ethical."[12]

Other Americans say that the president should not use the presidency as a pulpit for moral politics. They argue that the president should respect the constitutionally mandated separation of church and state and the right of Americans to believe as they will. Furthermore, they maintain that the federal government's involvement in the Schiavo matter blatantly violated the constitutionally established division of powers in our federal system. With respect to stem-cell research, President Bush was certainly entitled to his own personal opinions. But most Americans, including the Democratic majority and even several Republicans in Congress, supported expanded stem-cell research because of the medical benefits that result from it. Why should Bush, in defiance of public opinion and the majority in Congress, have acted as if he alone had the right to deny these benefits? Moral leadership is one thing. But moral leadership becomes an empty phrase when there are so few followers.

The Power to Influence the Economy.
Some of the greatest expansions of presidential power occurred during Franklin D. Roosevelt's administration. Roosevelt claimed the presidential power to regulate the economy during the Great Depression in the 1930s. Since that time, Americans have expected the president to be actively involved in economic matters and social programs. Today, Congress annually receives from the president a suggested budget and the *Economic Report of the President*. The budget message suggests what amounts of money the government will need for its programs. The *Economic Report of the President* presents the state of the nation's economy and recommends ways to improve it.

The Legislative Success of Various Presidents.
Look at Figure 12–1, which shows the success records of presidents in getting their legislation passed. Success is defined as how often the president won his way on roll-call votes on which he took a clear position. As you can see, typically a president's success record was very high when he first took office and then gradually declined. This is sometimes attributed to the president's "honeymoon period," when the Congress may be most likely to work with the president to achieve the president's legislative agenda. The media often put a great deal of emphasis on how successful a president is during the "first hundred days" in office. Ironically, this is also the period when the president is least experienced in the "ways" of the White House, particularly if the president was a Washington outsider, such as a state governor, before becoming president.

THE INCREASING USE OF EXECUTIVE ORDERS
As the nation's chief executive, the president is considered to have the inherent power to issue **executive orders,** which are presidential orders to carry out policies described in laws that have been passed by Congress. These orders have the force of law. Presidents have issued executive orders for a variety of purposes, including to establish procedures for appointing noncareer administrators, restructure the White House bureaucracy, ration consumer goods and administer wage and price controls under emergency conditions, classify government information as secret, implement affirmative action policies, and regulate the export of certain items. Presidents issue

executive order A presidential order to carry out a policy or policies described in a law passed by Congress.

FIGURE 12–1
PRESIDENTIAL SUCCESS RECORDS

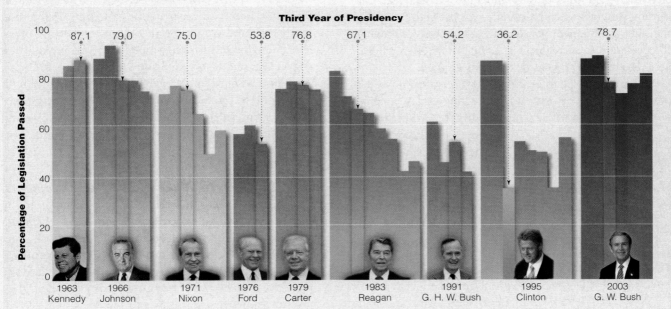

Source: *Congressional Quarterly Almanac.*

executive orders frequently, sometimes as many as one hundred a year. As mentioned earlier, President George W. Bush has made extensive use of executive orders to implement his policy decisions.

AN UNPRECEDENTED USE OF SIGNING STATEMENTS

As mentioned, President Bush made wide use of signing statements as a means to avoid being constrained by legislation. A **signing statement** is a written statement, appended to a bill at the time the president signs it into law, indicating how the president interprets that legislation. For example, in 2005 Congress passed a law that prohibited the military from using torture when trying to gain information from detainees designated as "enemy combatants." Bush signed the legislation, but he also added a signing statement that read, in part, "The executive branch shall construe [the law banning torture] in a manner consistent with the constitutional authority of the President to supervise the unitary executive branch and as Commander in Chief and consistent with the constitutional limitations on the judicial power." In other words, this statement says that Bush had the constitutional authority, as commander in chief, to order torture if he wanted to.

Signing statements have been used by presidents in the past but never to the extent that Bush used them. By the end of his first term, Bush had issued at least 435 such statements, almost as many as were issued by all of the previous presidents combined. In these statements, Bush challenged the constitutionality of 505 provisions of various bills that became law. By mid-2007, he had issued a total of more than 1,100 signing statements. According to a number of commentators, Bush used the signing statement as an alternative to the veto. In effect, the signing statement was like a line-item veto, allowing the president to disregard a specific provision in a bill if he chose to do so when the law was applied.

Recall from Chapter 2 that the Constitution vested the lawmaking authority solely in Congress. According to the founders, and the Constitution, the president can influence legislation only in a negative way—by exercising the veto power. According to a number of legal scholars, President Bush, by his use of signing statements, was effectively "making law" himself, thus skirting this constitutional requirement. Indeed, a task force of the American Bar

President George W. Bush is shown here approving a signing statement attached to a particular piece of legislation. By mid-2007, he had issued more than 1,100 such signing statements—more than all other previous presidents combined.

Association stated that Bush's use of signing statements to such a degree "raise[d] serious concerns crucial to the survival of our democracy." The task force called on Congress to exert more oversight and empower the courts to review presidential signing statements that essentially gave the president the right "to ignore or not enforce laws."[13]

EVOLVING PRESIDENTIAL POWER IN FOREIGN AFFAIRS

The precise extent of the president's power in foreign affairs is constantly evolving. The president is commander in chief and chief diplomat, but only Congress has the power to formally declare war, and the Senate must ratify any treaty that the president has negotiated with other nations. George Washington laid the groundwork for our long history of the president's active role in foreign policy. For example, when war broke out between Britain and France in 1793, Washington chose to disregard a treaty of alliance with France and to pursue a course of strict neutrality. Since that time, presidents have taken military actions and made foreign policy on many occasions without consulting Congress.

The Power to Make Executive Agreements.

Presidential power in foreign affairs is enhanced by the ability to make **executive agreements,** which are pacts between the president and other heads of state. Executive agreements do not require Senate approval (even though Congress may refuse to appropriate the necessary money to carry out the agreements), but they have the same legal status as treaties.

signing statement A written statement, appended to a bill at the time the president signs it into law, indicating how the president interprets that legislation.

executive agreement A binding international agreement, or pact, that is made between the president and another head of state and that does not require Senate approval.

Presidents form executive agreements for a wide range of purposes. Some involve routine matters, such as promises of trade or assistance to other countries. Others concern matters of great importance. In 1940, for example, President Franklin D. Roosevelt formed an important executive agreement with Prime Minister Winston Churchill of Great Britain. The agreement provided that the United States would lend American destroyers to Britain to help protect that nation and its shipping during World War II. In return, the British allowed the United States to use military and naval bases on British territories in the Western Hemisphere.

To prevent presidential abuse of the power to make executive agreements, Congress passed a law in 1972 that requires the president to inform Congress within sixty days of making any executive agreement. The law did not limit the president's power to make executive agreements, however, and they continue to be used far more than treaties in making foreign policy.

If one morning I walked on top of the water across the Potomac River, the headline that afternoon would read: 'President Can't Swim.'

LYNDON B. JOHNSON, THIRTY-SIXTH PRESIDENT OF THE UNITED STATES 1963–1969

Presidential Military Actions.
As you have read, the U.S. Constitution gives Congress the power to declare war. Consider, however, that although Congress has declared war in only five different conflicts during our nation's history,[14] the United States has engaged in more than two hundred activities involving the armed services. Before the United States entered World War II in 1941, Franklin D. Roosevelt ordered the Navy to "shoot on sight" any German submarine that appeared in the Western Hemisphere security zone. Without a congressional declaration of war, President Truman sent U.S. armed forces to Korea in 1950, thus involving American troops in the conflict between North and South Korea.

The United States also entered the Vietnam War (1964–1975) without a congressional declaration, and President Lyndon B. Johnson personally selected targets and ordered bombing missions during that war. President Nixon personally made the decision to invade Cambodia in 1970. President Reagan sent troops to Lebanon and Grenada in 1983 and ordered American fighter planes to attack Libya in 1986 in retaliation for terrorist attacks on American soldiers. No congressional vote was taken before President George H. W. Bush sent troops into Panama in 1989. Bush did, however, obtain congressional approval to use American troops to force Iraq to withdraw from Kuwait in 1991. President Clinton made the decision to send troops to Haiti in 1994 and to Bosnia in 1995, and to bomb Iraq in 1998. In 1999, he also decided to send U.S. forces, under the command of NATO (the North Atlantic Treaty Organization), to bomb Yugoslavia.

The War Powers Resolution.
As commander in chief, the president can respond quickly to a military threat without waiting for congressional action. This power to commit troops and to involve the nation in a war upset many members of Congress as the undeclared war in Vietnam dragged on for years into the 1970s. Criticism of the president's role in the Vietnam conflict led to the passage of the War

Franklin D. Roosevelt and Winston Churchill discuss matters relating to World War II aboard a British battleship in August 1941.

After the relatively quick and successful invasion of Iraq in 2003, the initial glow of victory started to fade. Many politicians and members of the public became increasingly skeptical of the United States' ability to actually "win" against the insurgents and different factions within Iraqi society. In September 2007, President Bush greeted U.S. Marines in a surprise visit to Iraq.

Harry Truman

Powers Resolution of 1973, which limits the president's war-making powers. The law, which was passed over Nixon's veto, requires the president to notify Congress within forty-eight hours of deploying troops. It also prevents the president from sending troops abroad for more than sixty days (or ninety days, if more time is needed for a successful withdrawal). If Congress does not authorize a longer period, the troops must be removed.

The War on Terrorism. President George W. Bush did not obtain a declaration of war from Congress for the war against terrorism that began on September 11, 2001. Instead, Congress invoked the War Powers Resolution and passed a joint resolution authorizing the president to use "all necessary and appropriate force against those nations, organizations, or persons he determines planned, authorized, committed, or aided the terrorist attacks that occurred on September 11, 2001." Also, in October 2002 Congress passed a joint resolution authorizing the use of U.S. armed forces against Iraq. The resolutions set no date for Bush to halt military operations, and, as a consequence, the president was able to invoke certain emergency wartime measures. For example, through executive order the president created military tribunals for trying terrorist suspects. The president also held American citizens as "enemy combatants," denying them access to their attorneys. In late 2007, because of the strong public opinion against continuing the Iraq war, the majority in Congress sought to repeal the 2002 authorization and pass legislation bringing the war to an end.

Nuclear Weapons. Since 1945, the president, as commander in chief, has been responsible for the most difficult of all military decisions—if and when to use nuclear weapons. In 1945, Harry Truman made the awesome decision to drop atomic bombs on the Japanese cities of Hiroshima and Nagasaki. "The final decision," he said, "on where and when to use the atomic bomb was up to me. Let there be no mistake about it." Today, the president travels at all times with the "football"—the briefcase containing the codes used to launch a nuclear attack.

LO⁴ CONGRESSIONAL AND PRESIDENTIAL RELATIONS

Despite the seemingly immense powers at the president's disposal, the president is limited in what he or she can accomplish, or even attempt. In our system of checks and balances, the president must share some powers with the legislative and judicial branches of government. And the president's power is checked not only by these institutions, but also by the media, public opinion, and the voters. The founders hoped that this system of shared power would lessen the chance of tyranny.

Some scholars believe the relationship between Congress and the president is the most important one in the American system of government. Congress traditionally has had the upper hand in relation to the president in some distinct areas, primarily in passing legislation. In some other areas, though, particularly in foreign affairs, the president can exert tremendous power that Congress is virtually unable to check.

Advantage: Congress

Congress has the advantage over the president in the areas of legislative authorization, the regulation of foreign and interstate commerce, and some budgetary matters. Of course, as you have already read, the president today proposes a legislative agenda and a budget to Congress every year. Nonetheless, only Congress has the power to pass the legislation and appropriate the money. The most the president can do constitutionally is veto an entire bill if it contains something that the president does not like. As noted, however, President Bush frequently used signing statements to avoid portions of bills that he did not approve.

As you have read, presidential popularity is considered to be a source of power for the president in relation to Congress. Presidents spend a great deal of time courting public opinion, eyeing the "presidential approval ratings," and meeting with the press. Much of this activity is for the purpose of gaining leverage with Congress. The president can put all of his or her persuasive powers to work in achieving a legislative agenda, but Congress retains the ultimate lawmaking authority.

DIVIDED GOVERNMENT When government is divided—with at least one house of Congress controlled by a different party than the White House—the president can have difficulty getting a legislative agenda to the floor for a vote. President Bill Clinton found this to be the case after the congressional elections of 1994 brought the Republicans to power in Congress. Clinton's success rate in implementing his legislative agenda dropped to 36.2 percent in 1995, after a high of 86.4 the previous year (see Figure 12–1 on page 275).

President Bush faced a similar problem in 2007, when the Democrats gained a majority in Congress. During his first six years as president, Bush had worked hand in hand with an extremely cooperative Republican-led Congress. After the Democrats became the majority, however, divided government existed once again.

DIFFERENT CONSTITUENCIES Congress and the president have different constituencies, and this fact influences their relationship. Members of Congress represent a state or a local district, and this gives them a particularly regional focus. As we discussed in Chapter 11, members of Congress like to have legislative successes of their own to bring home to their constituents—military bases that remain open, public-works projects that create

President George W. Bush addresses the U.S. Congress and the public in his State of the Union speech in January 2007.

AP Photo/Larry Downing/Pool

local jobs, or trade rules that benefit a big, local employer. Ideally, the president's focus should be on the nation as a whole: national defense, homeland security, the national economy. At times, this can put the president at odds even with members of his or her own party in Congress.

Furthermore, members of Congress and the president face different election cycles (every two years in the House, every six years in the Senate, and every four years for the president), and the president is limited to two terms in office. Consequently, the president and Congress sometimes feel a different sense of urgency about implementing legislation. For example, the president often senses the need to demonstrate legislative success during the first year in office, when the excitement over the elections is still fresh in the minds of politicians and the public.

"AS TO THE PRESIDENCY, THE TWO HAPPIEST DAYS OF MY LIFE WERE THOSE OF MY ENTRANCE UPON THE OFFICE AND MY SURRENDER OF IT."

MARTIN VAN BUREN, EIGHTH PRESIDENT OF THE UNITED STATES 1837–1841

Advantage: The President

The president has the advantage over Congress in dealing with a national crisis, in setting foreign policy, and in influencing public opinion. In times of crisis, the presidency is arguably the most crucial institution in government because, when necessary, the president can act quickly, speak with one voice, and represent the nation to the world. George W. Bush's presidency was unquestionably changed by the terrorist attacks of September 11, 2001. He represented the United States as it was under attack from foreign enemies and reeling from shock and horror. The president swiftly announced his resolve to respond to the terrorist attacks. No member of Congress could wield the kind of personal power that accrues to a president in a time of national crisis.

executive privilege An inherent executive power claimed by presidents to withhold information from, or to refuse to appear before, Congress or the courts. The president can also accord the privilege to other executive officials.

Watergate scandal A scandal involving an illegal break-in at the Democratic National Committee offices in 1972 by members of President Nixon's reelection campaign staff. Before Congress could vote to impeach Nixon for his participation in covering up the break-in, Nixon resigned from the presidency.

The framers of the Constitution recognized the need for individual leadership in foreign affairs. They gave the president the power to negotiate treaties and lead the armed forces. Some scholars have argued that recent presidents have abused the powers of the presidency by committing U.S. troops to undeclared or unpopular wars and by negotiating secret agreements without consulting Congress.

Others have argued that there is an unwritten "doctrine of necessity" under which presidential powers can and should be expanded during a crisis. When this has happened in the past, however, Congress has always retaken some control when the crisis was over, in a natural process of institutional give-and-take. One of the issues over which Americans were at odds was the Bush administration's claim that we were facing an unending crisis—the "war on terrorism." The dilemma facing Congress and the American people was how best to defend against the threat of terrorism while restoring normal government relations and procedures.

Executive Privilege

As you read in Chapter 11, Congress has the authority to investigate and oversee the activities of other branches of government. Nonetheless, both Congress and the public have accepted that a certain degree of secrecy by the executive branch is necessary to protect national security. Some presidents have claimed an inherent executive power to withhold information from, or to refuse to appear before, Congress or the courts. This is called **executive privilege**, and it has been invoked by presidents from George Washington to George W. Bush.

One of the problems with executive privilege is that it has been used for more purposes than simply to safeguard national security secrets. President Nixon invoked executive privilege in an attempt to avoid handing over taped White House conversations to Congress during the **Watergate scandal.** President Clinton invoked the privilege in an attempt to keep details of his sexual relationship with Monica Lewinsky a secret. President George W. Bush claimed executive privilege on numerous occasions. In his first term, he raised the privilege to prevent Tom Ridge, who was at the time

THE CASE OF THE DISAPPEARING DOCUMENTS

any commentators noted that secrecy pervaded the Bush administration; indeed, some claimed that Bush's government was the most secretive in U.S. history. One way to keep information secret from Congress and the public is, of course, to claim executive privilege when faced with a demand for documents. While the Bush administration claimed this privilege on occasion, it also used other methods to keep information secret.

PROGRAMS CARRIED OUT IN SECRET

As we have stressed throughout this text, in times of war, governments often engage in actions that would not be allowed during peacetime. Because the United States, at least in the Bush administration's eyes, was at war with terrorists, the administration undertook certain actions that it claimed were necessary for national security. Viewed from the perspective of a peacetime situation, however, those actions may have seemed excessive.

As mentioned before, Bush authorized the National Security Agency to carry out domestic surveillance, particularly via wiretapping, but the public only learned about it in 2005. The Federal Bureau of Investigation used so-called National Security Letters to obtain private telephone, banking, and other records, even though most such requests turned out to be unrelated to terrorism. The Bush administration also classified as "secret" literally millions of documents, most of which had nothing to do with national security.

MISSING DOCUMENTS

When documents cannot be found, then, of course, they cannot be turned over if Congress requests them. Additionally, lost documents cannot be made available to the public. Under the Freedom of Information Act (FOIA) of 1966, documents that are not classified as secret are supposed to be available to practically anyone who asks. Yet just try to exercise your rights under the FOIA. Your request may well be among the 76 percent of all FOIA requests that are met with the response that the documents being sought are missing or lost.

Bush White House e-mails seemingly went missing all the time. When Congress undertook an investigation of the Justice Department's firing of several U.S. attorneys for allegedly political reasons in 2007, the White House simply said that many of the relevant e-mails sought by Congress were missing or irretrievably lost. As another example of missing documents, after Hurricane Katrina devastated New Orleans in 2005, the American Society of Civil Engineers asked the Army Corps of Engineers for technical drawings of the failed levees. The Army Corps of Engineers said that it could not find them.

YOU BE THE JUDGE

Because the war on terrorism will never disappear, the American public is being asked to accept that government information will increasingly become less available, presumably in the name of national security. Many believe that the government should provide information on what it is doing, no matter what. Others argue that the government has the right to limit the public's access to its documents in order to secure the homeland. Where do you stand on this issue?

the president's homeland security adviser, from testifying before Congress. The Bush administration also refused to deliver information about Vice President Dick Cheney's meetings and other communications with certain industry representatives when Cheney was chairing a task force on energy policy.

After the Democrats took control of Congress in 2007 and began to investigate various actions undertaken by the Bush administration since 2001, they were frequently blocked in their attempts to obtain information by the claim of executive privilege. For example,

as you will read in Chapter 14, during Congress's investigation of the Justice Department's firing of several U.S. attorneys for allegedly political reasons, the Bush administration raised the claim of executive privilege to prevent several people from testifying or submitting requested documents to Congress.

After the war on terrorism began, the Bush administration maintained that it had been compelled—for our safety—to keep more information secret than ever before. Information about homeland security measures and protection of vital infrastructure, such as nuclear power facilities, was kept secret. In addition to claiming executive privilege, the Bush administration apparently used other techniques to avoid releasing certain documents, as you can read in this chapter's *The Politics of National Security* feature on page 281.

LO⁵ THE ORGANIZATION OF THE EXECUTIVE BRANCH

In the early days of this nation, presidents answered their own mail, as George Washington did. Only in 1857 did Congress authorize a private secretary for the president, to be paid by the federal government. Even Woodrow Wilson typed most of his correspondence, although by that time several secretaries were assigned to the president. When Franklin D. Roosevelt became president in 1933, the entire staff consisted of thirty-seven employees. Only after Roosevelt's New Deal and World War II did the presidential staff become a sizable organization.

The President's Cabinet

The Constitution does not specifically mention presidential assistants and advisers. The Constitution states only that the president "may require the Opinion, in writing, of the principal Officer in each of the executive Departments." Since the time of our first president, presidents have had an advisory group, or **cabinet,** to turn to for counsel. Originally, the cabinet consisted of only four officials—the secretar-

cabinet An advisory group selected by the president to assist with decision making. Traditionally, the cabinet has consisted of the heads of the executive departments and other officers whom the president may choose to appoint.

kitchen cabinet The name given to a president's unofficial advisers. The term was coined during Andrew Jackson's presidency.

ies of state, treasury, and war and the attorney general. Today, the cabinet includes fourteen secretaries and the attorney general (see Table 12–2 for the names of cabinet members as of 2007).

Because the Constitution does not require the president to consult with the cabinet, its use is purely discretionary. Some presidents have relied on the counsel of their cabinets. Other presidents solicited the opinions of their cabinets and then did what they wanted to do anyway. After a cabinet meeting in which a vote was seven nays against his one aye, President Lincoln supposedly said, "Seven nays and one aye, the ayes have it."[15] Still other presidents have sought counsel from so-called **kitchen cabinets.** A kitchen cabinet is a very informal group of persons, such as Ronald Reagan's trusted California coterie, to whom the president turns for advice. The term *kitchen cabinet* originated during the presidency of Andrew Jackson, who relied on the counsel of close friends who often met with him in the kitchen of the White House.

In general, few presidents have relied heavily on the advice of the formal cabinet, and often presidents meet with their cabinet heads only reluctantly. To a certain extent, the growth of other components of the executive branch has rendered the formal cabinet less significant as an advisory board to the president. Additionally, the

The word cabinet cannot be found in the U.S. Constitution. Rather, the Constitution refers to principal officers of each executive department. The formal cabinet today consists of fourteen secretaries and the attorney general. Some presidents rely very little on full cabinet meetings. The cabinet members of the Bush administration in the fall of 2007 are shown below.

AP Photo/Pablo Martinez Monsivais

TABLE 12-2

THE PRESIDENT'S CABINET AS OF 2007

AGRICULTURE Chuck Conner *Acting Secretary**	**HEALTH AND HUMAN SERVICES** Michael Leavitt	**LABOR** Elaine Chao
COMMERCE Carlos Gutierrez	**HOMELAND SECURITY** Michael Chertoff	**STATE** Condoleezza Rice
DEFENSE Robert Gates	**HOUSING AND URBAN DEVELOPMENT** Alphonso Jackson	**TRANSPORTATION** Mary Peters
EDUCATION Margaret Spellings	**INTERIOR** Dirk Kempthorne	**TREASURY** Henry Paulson, Jr.
ENERGY Samuel Bodman	**JUSTICE** Michael Mukasey	**VETERANS AFFAIRS** Gordon Mansfield *Acting Secretary**

*As of November, 2007, when this book went to press, no successor had yet been appointed.

department heads are at times more responsive to the wishes of their own staffs or to their own political ambitions than they are to the president. They may be more concerned with obtaining resources for their departments than with helping presidents achieve their goals. As a result, there is often a conflict of interest between presidents and their cabinet members. It is likely that formal cabinet meetings are held more out of respect for the cabinet tradition than for their problem-solving value.

The Executive Office of the President

In 1939, President Franklin D. Roosevelt set up the **Executive Office of the President (EOP)** to cope with the increased responsibilities brought on by the Great Depression. Since then, the EOP has grown significantly to accommodate the expansive role played by the national government, including the executive branch, in the nation's economic and social life.

The EOP is made up of the top advisers and assistants who help the president carry out major duties. The EOP also includes the staff of the First Lady. First Ladies have at times taken important, independent roles within the White House. For example, Eleanor Roosevelt wrote a newspaper column entitled "My Day" and advocated women's and civil rights. As First Lady, Hillary Clinton attempted to rally support for a national health-care system. She won a seat in the U.S. Senate following her husband's tenure in the White House, and in 2007, became a leading contender for the Democratic presidential nomination in 2008.

Over the years, the EOP has changed according to the needs and leadership style of each president. It has become an increasingly influential and important part

Executive Office of the President (EOP) A group of staff agencies that assist the president in carrying out major duties. Franklin D. Roosevelt established the EOP in 1939 to cope with the increased responsibilities brought on by the Great Depression.

TABLE 12-3

THE EXECUTIVE OFFICE OF THE PRESIDENT

Department	Year Established
White House Office	1939
Office of the Vice President	1939
Council of Economic Advisers	1946
National Security Council	1947
Office of the U.S. Trade Representative	1963
Council on Environmental Quality	1969
Office of Management and Budget	1970
Office of Science and Technology Policy	1976
Office of Administration	1977
Office of Policy Development	1977
—Domestic Policy Council	1993
—National Economic Council	1993
Office of National Drug Control Policy	1989

Source: *United States Government Manual, 2006–2007* (Washington, D.C.: U.S. Government Printing Office, 2006).

of the executive branch. Table 12–3 lists various offices within the EOP. We look at some of the key offices of the EOP in the following subsections.

THE WHITE HOUSE OFFICE   Of all of the executive staff agencies, the **White House Office** has the most direct contact with the president. The White House Office is headed by the **chief of staff,** who advises the president on important matters and directs the operations of the presidential staff. The chief of staff, who is often a close, personal friend of the president, has been one of the most influential presidential aides in recent years. A number of other top officials, assistants, and special assistants to the president also aid him or her in such areas as national security, the economy, and political affairs. The **press secretary** meets with reporters and makes public statements for the president. The counsel to the president serves as the White House lawyer and handles the president's legal matters. The White House staff also includes speechwriters, researchers, the president's physician, the director of the staff for the First Lady, and a correspondence secretary.

White House Office The personal office of the president. White House Office personnel handle the president's political needs and manage the media.

chief of staff The person who directs the operations of the White House Office and who advises the president on important matters.

press secretary A member of the White House staff who holds news conferences for reporters and makes public statements for the president.

Office of Management and Budget (OMB) An agency in the Executive Office of the President that assists the president in preparing and supervising the administration of the federal budget.

Altogether, the White House Office has more than four hundred employees.

The White House staff has several duties. First, the staff investigates and analyzes problems that require the president's attention. Staff members who are specialists in certain areas, such as diplomatic relations or foreign trade, gather information for the president and suggest solutions. White House staff members also screen the questions, issues, and problems that people present to the president, so matters that can be handled by other officials do not reach the president's desk. Additionally, the staff provides public relations support. For example, the press staff handles the president's relations with the White House press corps and schedules news conferences. Finally, the White House staff ensures that the president's initiatives are effectively transmitted to the relevant government personnel. Several staff members are usually assigned to work directly with members of Congress for this purpose.

THE OFFICE OF MANAGEMENT AND BUDGET   The **Office of Management and Budget (OMB)** was originally the Bureau of the Budget. Under recent presidents, the OMB has become an important and influential unit of the Executive Office of the President. The main function of the OMB is to assist the president in preparing the proposed annual budget, which the president must submit to Congress in January of each year (see Chapter 11 for details on preparing the annual budget). The federal budget lists the revenues and expenditures expected for the coming year. It indicates which programs the federal government will pay for and how much they will cost. Thus, the budget is an annual statement of the public policies of the United States translated into dollars and cents. Making changes in the budget is a key way for presidents to try to influence the direction and policies of the federal government.

The president appoints the director of the OMB with the consent of the Senate. The director of the OMB has become at least as important as the cabinet members and is often included in cabinet meetings. She or he oversees the OMB's work and argues the administration's position before Congress. The director also lobbies members of Congress to support the president's budget or to accept key features of it. Once the budget is approved by Congress, the OMB has the responsibility of putting it into practice. The OMB oversees the execution of the budget, checking the federal agencies to ensure that they use funds efficiently.

Beyond its budget duties, the OMB also reviews new bills prepared by the executive branch. It checks all legislative matters to be certain that they agree with the president's own position.

THE COUNCIL OF ECONOMIC ADVISERS The Employment Act of 1946 established the **Council of Economic Advisers (CEA)**, consisting of three members, to advise the president on economic matters. For the most part, the function of the CEA has been to prepare the annual economic report to Congress. Each of the three members is appointed by the president and can be removed at will.

THE NATIONAL SECURITY COUNCIL The **National Security Council (NSC)** was established in 1947 to manage the defense and foreign policy of the United States. Its members are the president, the vice president, and the secretaries of state and defense; it also has several informal advisers. The NSC is the president's link to his or her key foreign and military advisers. The president's special assistant for national security affairs heads the NSC staff.

Bill Pugliano/Getty Images

George W. Bush chose Dick Cheney (above) as his vice-presidential running mate. Cheney was seen as a person with extensive political experience, thereby countering the perception that Bush lacked national political experience when he was first elected. At times, Cheney was involved in headline-generating controversies.

The Vice Presidency and Presidential Succession

As a rule, presidential nominees choose running mates who balance the ticket or whose appointment rewards or appeases party factions. For example, a presidential candidate from the South may solicit a running mate from the West. President Clinton ignored this tradition when he selected Senator Al Gore of Tennessee as his running mate in 1992 and in 1996. Gore, close in age and ideology to Clinton, also came from the mid-South. Despite these similarities, Clinton gained two advantages by choosing Gore: Gore's appeal to environmentalists and Gore's compatibility with Clinton.

George W. Bush picked Dick Cheney, a well-known Republican with extensive political experience in Washington, D.C. Among other things, Cheney had held the post of secretary of defense in the administration of Bush's father (1989–1993). The appointment of Cheney helped Bush gather support from those who thought his lack of national political experience and familiarity with Washington politics would be a handicap.

THE ROLE OF VICE PRESIDENTS Vice presidents play a unique role in the American political system. On the one hand, they are usually regarded as appendages to the presidency and can wield little power on their own. For much of our history, the vice president has had almost no responsibilities. (In recent years, however, vice presidents, including Al Gore and Dick Cheney, have been important presidential advisers.) On the other hand, the vice

president is in a position to become the nation's chief executive should the president die, be impeached, or resign the presidential office. Eight vice presidents have become president because of the death of the president.

PRESIDENTIAL SUCCESSION One of the questions left unanswered by the Constitution was what the vice president should do if the president becomes incapable of carrying out necessary duties while in office. The Twenty-fifth Amendment to the Constitution, ratified in 1967, filled this gap. The amendment states that when the president believes that he or she is incapable of performing the duties of the office, he or she must inform Congress in writing of this fact. Then the vice president serves as acting president until the president can resume his or her normal duties. For example, President George W. Bush invoked the Twenty-fifth Amendment in 2007 before undergoing a minor surgical procedure.

When the president is unable to communicate, a majority of the cabinet, including the vice president, can declare that fact to Congress. Then the vice president serves as acting president until the president resumes normal duties. If a dispute arises over the return of the president's ability to discharge the normal functions of the presidential office, a two-thirds vote of

Council of Economic Advisers (CEA) A three-member council created in 1946 to advise the president on economic matters.

National Security Council (NSC) A council that advises the president on domestic and foreign matters concerning the safety and defense of the nation; established in 1947.

Congress is required to decide whether the vice president shall remain acting president or whether the president shall resume these duties.

The Twenty-fifth Amendment also addresses the question of how the president should fill a vacant vice presidency. Section 2 of the amendment states, "Whenever there is a vacancy in the office of the Vice President, the President shall nominate a Vice President who shall take office upon confirmation by a majority vote of both Houses of Congress."

In 1973, Gerald Ford became the first appointed vice president of the United States after Spiro Agnew was forced to resign. One year later, President Richard Nixon resigned, and Ford advanced to the office of president. President Ford named Nelson Rockefeller as his vice president. For the first time in U.S. history, neither the president nor the vice president was elected to his position.

What if both the president and the vice president die, resign, or are disabled? According to the Succession Act of 1947, then the Speaker of the House of Representatives will act as president on his or her resignation as Speaker and as representative. If the Speaker is unavailable, next in line is the president pro tem of the Senate, followed by members of the president's cabinet in the order of the creation of their departments (see Table 12–4).

In 1973, the vice president under President Richard Nixon resigned. Nixon appointed as his vice president Congressman Gerald Ford. In 1974 when Nixon resigned, Ford became president and appointed a vice president. For the first time in U.S. history, neither the president nor the vice president had been elected to those positions.

Four vice presidents succeeded to the presidency upon the assassination of the incumbent. Top row, left to right: Andrew Johnson for Abraham Lincoln in 1865, Chester Arthur for James Garfield in 1881, Theodore Roosevelt for William McKinley in 1901, and Lyndon Johnson for John Kennedy in 1963. Four vice presidents inherited the presidency after the natural death of the incumbent. Bottom row, left to right: John Tyler for William Henry Harrison in 1841, Millard Fillmore for Zachary Taylor in 1850, Calvin Coolidge for Warren Harding in 1923, and Harry Truman for Franklin Roosevelt in 1945.

TABLE 12–4

THE LINE OF SUCCESSION TO THE U.S. PRESIDENCY

1 Vice president
2 Speaker of the House of Representatives
3 President pro tem of the Senate
4 Secretary of the Department of State
5 Secretary of the Department of the Treasury
6 Secretary of the Department of Defense
7 Attorney general
8 Secretary of the Department of the Interior
9 Secretary of the Department of Agriculture
10 Secretary of the Department of Commerce
11 Secretary of the Department of Labor
12 Secretary of the Department of Health and Human Services
13 Secretary of the Department of Housing and Urban Development
14 Secretary of the Department of Transportation
15 Secretary of the Department of Energy
16 Secretary of the Department of Education
17 Secretary of the Department of Veterans Affairs
18 Secretary of the Department of Homeland Security

AMERICA AT ODDS:
The Presidency

Tenche Coxe, a prominent Philadelphian at the time the Constitution was written, once commented that the president's power regarding legislation "amounts to no more than a serious duty imposed upon him to request both houses to reconsider any matter on which he entertains doubts or feels apprehensions." This opinion was in keeping with the founders' views, which essentially gave the president only a "negative power" over legislation—that is, the veto power.

As you have read in this chapter, the powers of the presidency have expanded to the point at which the president engages in a significant amount of "lawmaking" through increasing use of executive orders and signing statements. Some political and legal scholars are deeply concerned about how President George W. Bush transformed the presidency. They claim that because Bush had a relatively free hand in determining and implementing national policy, without facing significant congressional or judicial checks on his asserted powers, he was able to set precedents that may be followed by subsequent presidential administrations. Clearly, many members of Congress believed that the legal justifications given by the Bush administration for many of its actions were invalid. Whether Congress has the will or the powers necessary to act on this belief—and whether the courts would support Congress in such an attempt—remains to be seen.

Issues for Debate & Discussion

1. As you read in this chapter, in 2007 President Bush commuted the sentence of Lewis ("Scooter") Libby, who was convicted of four felony counts, including perjury and obstruction of justice. Libby, who served as Vice President Dick Cheney's chief of staff, was unforthcoming at trial about whether the vice president or anyone in his office was responsible for leaking the identity of a CIA agent to the press. Many Americans concluded that Bush should not have shown such clemency to a member of his own administration. If nothing else, it was unethical, for it would lend credence to allegations that Libby had not implicated Cheney in the leak because Libby knew that he would eventually be granted clemency—if not fully pardoned, a possibility that President Bush had not ruled out. Others believe that the presidential power to grant clemency and pardons is not limited and that Bush did nothing unethical by showing clemency to Libby. What is your position on this issue?

2. Review the *Join the Debate* feature on pages 273–275, which discusses the debate over morality and political leadership. Do you believe that a U.S. president should be the "moral leader" of this country and base national policies—such as President Bush's faith-based initiatives—on religious beliefs? Or should the president avoid any intermingling of religious beliefs and policymaking? What is your position on this issue?

Take Action

President James Madison (1809–1817) once said, "The citizens of the United States are responsible for the greatest trust ever confided to a political society." Notice that Madison laid the responsibility for this trust on the "citizens," not the "government." Even though it may seem that one person can do little to affect government policymaking and procedures, this assumption has been proved wrong time and again. If you would like to influence the way that things are done in Washington, D.C., you can do so by helping to elect a president and members of Congress whose views you endorse and who you think would do a good job of running the country. Clearly, you will want to vote in the next elections. Before then, though, you could join others who share your political beliefs and work on behalf of one of the candidates. You could support a candidate in your home state or join others in "adopting" a candidate from another state who is facing a close race for a congressional seat. You can access that candidate's Web site and offer your services, such as calling voters of the candidate's party and urging them to go to the polls and vote for the candidate. You can also help raise funds for the candidate's campaign and, if you can afford it, even donate some money yourself.

AP Photo/Al Behrman

The campaign of Iraq War veteran Paul Hackett for the Senate during the 2006 elections generated national attention and raised anti-war awareness.

- The White House home page offers links to numerous sources of information on the presidency. You can access this site at **www.whitehouse.gov**.

- If you are interested in reading the inaugural addresses of American presidents from George Washington to George W. Bush, go to **www.bartleby.com/124**.

  In addition to the full text of the inaugural addresses, this site provides biographical information on the presidents.

- If you would like to research documents and academic resources concerning the presidency, a good Internet site to consult is that provided by the University of Virginia's Miller Center of Public Affairs at **www.americanpresident.org**.

- To access the various presidential libraries, visit the National Archives site at **www.archives.gov/presidential-libraries/index.html**.

ONLINE RESOURCES FOR THIS CHAPTER

This text's Companion Web site, at **www.americaatodds. com**, offers links to numerous resources that you can utilize to learn more about the topics covered in this chapter.

CHAPTER 13
THE BUREAUCRACY

LEARNING OBJECTIVES

LO¹ Describe the size and functions of the U.S. bureaucracy.

LO² Discuss the structure and basic components of the federal bureaucracy.

LO³ Indicate when the federal civil service was established and explain how bureaucrats get their jobs.

LO⁴ Explain how regulatory agencies make rules and how "iron triangles" affect policymaking in government.

LO⁵ Identify some of the ways in which the government has attempted to curb waste and improve efficiency in the bureaucracy.

AMERICA AT ODDS

Should the FDA Be More Vigilant?

The federal Food and Drug Administration (FDA) is the guardian of the safety of our prescription drugs. We expect the FDA to prevent unsafe prescription drugs from being released into the marketplace. In this area, however, the FDA has had a checkered history. It has approved some drugs that turned out to be overly dangerous, causing, for example, premature heart attacks in older Americans and muscle deterioration in those taking a cholesterol-lowering drug. One could say that the FDA has a thankless task because if it does not approve drugs that turn out to be useful or even life saving in other countries, the agency is accused of causing suffering and death in the United States. If the FDA approves drugs that end up creating unwanted and dangerous side effects, then its critics say that it isn't vigilant enough. As *New York Times* reporter Gardiner Harris once said, "Safety and speed are the Ying and Yang of drug regulations. Patients want immediate access to breakthrough medicines but also want to believe that the drugs are safe." These goals are typically incompatible.

Yes, the FDA Should Be More Vigilant and Take Longer to Approve Drugs

All we have to do is look at some recent scandals involving the FDA to know that it should be more vigilant. It should be less worried about speedy approvals and more concerned about the quality of its testing and documentation of prescription drug safety.

One of the latest FDA fiascoes involved the diabetes drug Avandia. Despite its staff members' misgivings, the FDA allowed this drug, which had potential cardiac side effects, to stay on the market without placing its strongest safety warnings on the drug's label. Only after several users of this drug died did the FDA react. The story was the same with the painkiller Vioxx. The agency ignored warnings from its staff about side effects, particularly with respect to heart attacks. Only after a number of long-term users of Vioxx suffered heart attacks did the agency request that Vioxx be pulled from the market.

There is no going back when someone suffers or dies from the side effects of a prescription drug. The FDA must institute stronger controls on new drugs.

MORE TESTING IS NOT NECESSARILY IN THE BEST INTERESTS OF AMERICANS

To be sure, the FDA could use more resources and force pharmaceutical companies to spend more money on testing to become aware of any adverse side effects of new drugs. In fact, if the FDA wants to make sure that there are no adverse side effects, it can simply state that no new drugs will ever be approved. But it would never take such an extreme position. In the meantime, if the FDA becomes even more vigilant over the safety of new drugs, countless American lives will be lost. After all, pharmaceutical companies' best interests are served by developing new drugs that help people stay alive, not kill them. Pharmaceutical companies have an incentive to seek approval of drugs that, *on net,* benefit American patients.

Consider Vioxx. Those who suffered heart problems had taken several doses of Vioxx every day for months on end. Generally, those who suffered heart complications had been taking the drug for more than a year and a half. In contrast, most of those who used Vioxx for short-term sports injuries found it to be a "miracle" drug. So, why not just place a warning on Vioxx stating that it is not for long-term use in heavy doses? That way, those who would benefit from the drug could still use it.

Consider also that the longer you keep new pharmaceuticals off the market, the more people suffer from the diseases those drugs were developed to cure. In the meantime, the people who die because a new drug was not available cannot raise their voices against the FDA's overvigilant regulation. They are the ones who truly lose from too much new drug testing.

Where do you stand?

1. Under what circumstances do you think that a new drug should *never* be allowed to come to market?
2. Assume that a patient has a seemingly incurable cancer and a new drug becomes available that has a 50 percent chance of extending the patient's life by at least three years but also a 50 percent chance of killing that person. Would you be in favor of allowing the patient to take the drug? Explain.

Explore this issue online

- Public Citizen's Health Research Group believes that the FDA is not strict enough in approving medicines and bowed to pressure from the George W. Bush administration on behalf of "Big Pharma." Visit their Web site at **www.citizen.org/hrg**.
- The Competitive Enterprise Institute believes that the FDA is much too slow to approve drugs and that demagoguery over problems with new medicines is widespread. See its arguments at **www.cei.org/sections/subsection.cfm?section=19**.

INTRODUCTION

Did you eat breakfast this morning? If you did, **bureaucrats**—individuals who work in the offices of government—had a lot to do with that breakfast. If you had bacon, the meat was inspected by federal agents. If you drank milk, the price was affected by rules and regulations of the Department of Agriculture. If you looked at a cereal box, you saw fine print about minerals and vitamins, which was the result of regulations made by several other federal agencies, including the Food and Drug Administration. If you ate leftover pizza for breakfast, bureaucrats made sure that the kitchen of the pizza house was sanitary and safe and that the employees who put together (and perhaps delivered) the pizza were protected against discrimination in the workplace.

Today, the word *bureaucracy* often evokes a negative reaction. For some, it conjures up visions of depersonalized automatons performing their chores without any sensitivity toward the needs of those they serve. For others, it is synonymous with government "red tape." A **bureaucracy,** however, is simply a large, complex administrative organization that is structured hierarchically in a pyramid-like fashion.[1] Government bureaucrats carry out the policies of elected govern-

These food inspectors are part of our federal bureaucracy that is responsible for the quality and safety of what we eat.

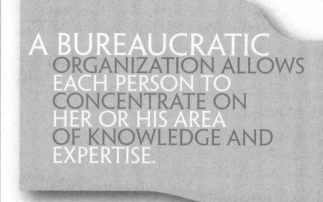

A BUREAUCRATIC ORGANIZATION ALLOWS EACH PERSON TO CONCENTRATE ON HER OR HIS AREA OF KNOWLEDGE AND EXPERTISE.

ment officials. Bureaucrats deliver our mail, clean our streets, teach in our public schools, run our national parks, and attempt to ensure the safety of our food and the prescription drugs that we take—as discussed in the chapter-opening *America at Odds* feature. Life as we know it would be impossible without government bureaucrats to keep our governments—federal, state, and local—in operation.

LO¹ THE NATURE AND SIZE OF THE BUREAUCRACY

The concept of a bureaucracy is not confined to the federal government. Any large organization has to have a bureaucracy. In each bureaucracy, everybody (except the head of the bureaucracy) reports to at least one other person. For the federal government, the head of the bureaucracy is the president of the United States, and the bureaucracy is part of the executive branch.[2]

A bureaucratic form of organization allows each person to concentrate on her or his area of knowledge and expertise. In your college or university, for example, you do not expect the basketball

Mike Mergen/Bloomberg News/Landov

bureaucrat An individual who works in a bureaucracy. As generally used, the term refers to a government employee.

bureaucracy A large, complex, hierarchically structured administrative organization that carries out specific functions.

FIGURE 13-1

GOVERNMENT EMPLOYMENT AT FEDERAL, STATE, AND LOCAL LEVELS

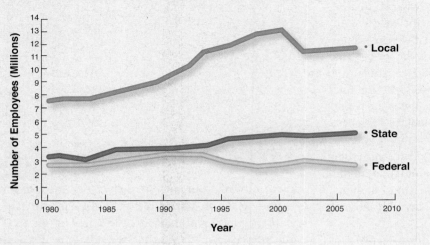

Source: U.S. Department of Commerce, Bureau of the Census.

of State (nine employees); (2) the Department of War (two employees); and (3) the Department of the Treasury (thirty-nine employees). By 1798, the federal bureaucracy was still quite small. The secretary of state had seven clerks. His total expenditures on stationery and printing amounted to $500, or about $8,438 in 2008 dollars. The Department of War spent, on average, a grand total of $1.4 million each year, or about $23.6 million in 2008 dollars.

Times have changed. Figure 13–1 shows the number of government employees since 1980. Most growth has been at the state and local levels. All in all, the three levels of government employ more than 16 percent of the civilian labor force. Today, more Americans are employed by government (at all three levels) than by the entire manufacturing sector of the U.S. economy.

During election campaigns, politicians throughout the nation claim they will "cut big government and red tape" and "get rid of overlapping and wasteful bureaucracies." For the last several decades, virtually every president has campaigned on a platform calling for a reduction in the size of the federal bureaucracy. Yet, at the same time, candidates promise to establish programs that require new employees—even if they are "consultants" who are not officially counted as part of the bureaucracy.

coach to solve the problems of the finance department. The reason the bureaucracy exists is that Congress, over time, has delegated certain tasks to specialists. For example, in 1914, Congress passed the Federal Trade Commission Act, which established the Federal Trade Commission to regulate deceptive and unfair trade practices. Those appointed to the commission were specialists in this area. Similarly, in 1972, Congress passed the Consumer Product Safety Act, which established the Consumer Product Safety Commission to investigate the safety of consumer products placed on the market. The commission is one of many federal administrative agencies.

Another key aspect of any bureaucracy is that the power to act resides in the *position* rather than in the *person*. In your college or university, the person who is president now has more or less the same authority as any previous president. Additionally, bureaucracies usually entail standard operating procedures—directives on what procedures should be followed in specific circumstances. Bureaucracies normally also have a merit system, meaning that people are hired and promoted on the basis of demonstrated skills and achievements.

The Growth of Bureaucracy

The federal government that existed in 1789 was small. It had three departments, each with only a few employees: (1) the Department

Every day, hundreds of thousands of government employees report to work at various federal buildings across the country. In spite of attempts to downsize the bureaucracy, the total number of people working for all levels of government has only leveled off in recent years.

Mark Richards/PhotoEdit

JOIN THE DEBATE

Is All the "Red Tape" Worth the Cost?

Everyone seems to hate "red tape" generated by the government. People complain that everything involving the government seems to entail a hassle. Businesses have to file apparently endless reports on compliance with workplace safety rules, environmental regulations, and requirements concerning corporate governance. Most so-called red tape results from regulations issued by administrative agencies. Congress has delegated to these agencies the nuts and bolts of implementing the laws passed by Congress and signed into law by the president. Scholars at the Mercatus Center at George Mason University and the Weidenbaum Center at Washington University claim that the U.S. government has been on a "regulatory rampage." In the last five years, the number of workers in regulatory agencies has risen by a third. Regulatory budgets are up by 50 percent after taking inflation into account. If all of the issues of the *Federal Register* (the published regulations of the federal government) from the Nixon presidency to the present were stacked on top of each other, the pile would be higher than the Washington Monument.

Many Americans view the estimated $1 trillion per year in lost output due to red tape as too high a cost to pay for the actual benefits of regulation. Each household implicitly pays $8,000 per year for these benefits, according to the Small Business Administration. The problem with administrative agencies is that they build on themselves. Only rarely has an agency been eliminated, even when its function has become outmoded. Administrative agencies' budgets hardly ever decline. Indeed, federal agencies thrive on creating red tape. Members of Congress

have no interest in reducing all this red tape. Why not? The reason is that constituents who need help figuring out or getting around red tape run to their member of Congress, who tries to set things straight. These constituents are then forever in their congressperson's debt.

Not so fast, say those in favor of increased regulation of the U.S. economy. Without regulations issued by administrative agencies, what would happen to food and drug safety, environmental protection, and workplace safety, among many other things? Red tape keeps growing because society is becoming more complex. Laws and regulations controlling pollution are necessary because clean air and water have such great societal benefits. Such laws address problems that only the government can solve. If the economy is left to the law of the jungle, it's always "the little guy" who suffers.

Creative Commons

The Washington Monument.

The Costs of Maintaining the Government

The costs of maintaining the government are high and growing. In 1929, government at all levels accounted for about 8.5 percent of the total national income in the United States. Today, that figure exceeds 30 percent. The average citizen pays a significant portion of his or her income to federal, state, and local governments. You do this by paying income taxes, sales taxes, property taxes, and many other types of taxes and fees. To fully understand the amount of money spent by federal, state, and local governments each year, consider that the same sum of money could be used to purchase all of the farmland in the United States plus all of the assets of the one hundred largest American corporations.

The government is costly, to be sure, but it also provides numerous services for Americans. Cutting back on the size of government inevitably means a reduction in those services.

FIGURE 13-2

THE ORGANIZATION OF THE FEDERAL GOVERNMENT

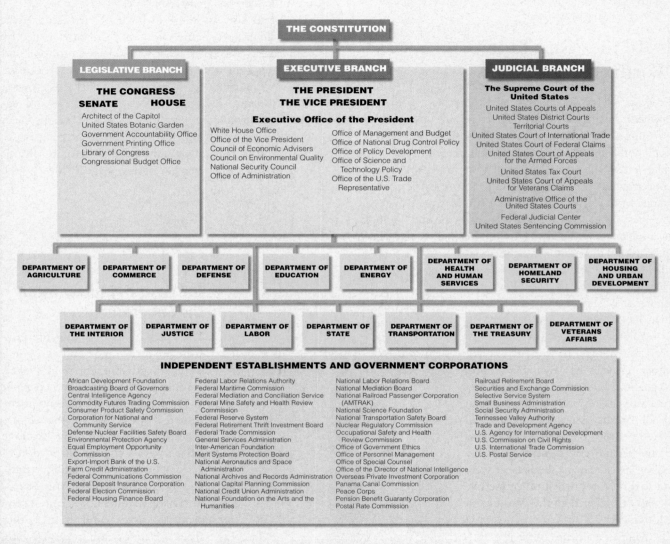

Source: *United States Government Manual, 2007/08* (Washington, D.C.: U.S. Government Printing Office, 2007).

LO² HOW THE FEDERAL BUREAUCRACY IS ORGANIZED

A complete organization chart of the federal government would cover an entire wall. A simplified version is provided in Figure 13–2. The executive branch consists of a number of bureaucracies that provide services to Congress, to the federal courts, and to the president directly. (For a comparison of the organization of the U.S. bureaucracy with that of other countries, see this chapter's *The Rest of the World* feature.)

The executive branch of the federal government includes four major types of structures:

- Executive departments.
- Independent executive agencies.
- Independent regulatory agencies.
- Government corporations.

Each type of structure has its own relationship to the president and its own internal workings.

THE REST OF THE WORLD

The U.S. Bureaucracy Really Is Special

Americans like to think that they are different, and with respect to the federal bureaucracy, they have a lot of facts to back them up.

CONTROL OVER THE BUREAUCRACY

Consider that in the United States, the federal bureaucracy is controlled by several institutions. The president and Congress can exercise control over any agency. If you ever get appointed to a senior position in the federal bureaucracy, you will have to deal with two masters: the one who appointed you (the executive branch) and the one who pays you (Congress). Several congressional committees or subcommittees may also be able to nose around in your affairs.

Not so in Great Britain. In that country and in most parliamentary systems, the prime minister controls the cabinet ministers (the equivalent of our "secretaries") who appoint the bureaucrats. Most British and French bureaucrats, for example, have little or nothing to do with Parliament. Rather, they take orders only from the ministers in charge of their departments.

FEDERAL VERSUS UNITARY SYSTEMS

Because the U.S. political system is federal, as opposed to unitary (see Chapter 3), most agencies in the federal bureaucracy have counterparts at the state or local level. The federal agencies often work together with state and local agencies in performing certain government functions. Consider the Department of Health and Human Services. It is involved with numerous state and local government agencies, and it often reimburses state and local governments for money spent on health care for lower-income people. The Department of Labor provides funds to state and local agencies to help pay for job-training programs.

In contrast, in any unitary system, by definition the number of subnational agencies is very limited. Local governments in France at the *départment* (a unit of government somewhat like our county) and municipal levels have limited control over housing, education, or health and employment programs. Those programs are all run by the central government.

IT COULD BE MUCH, MUCH DIFFERENT

Americans often complain about all of the bureaucratic "red tape" that they seem to face at every level of government. The British people also complain about their bureaucracy, but to a much greater extent than Americans do. When compared to some other countries, though, the U.S. bureaucracy really is special.

Suppose, for example, that you want to apply for a passport. In the United States, you would go to your local passport office, often located in a post office, and submit your application, plus the necessary identification papers and fees. Your passport and identification papers will be mailed to you within the time period specified. To be sure, sometimes problems arise, but normally the passport-application process involves only one step on your part.

Now suppose that you are an Iranian citizen and want to apply for a passport. You would need to find out how much and to whom you should make "grease payments" (customary payments to speed up the bureaucratic process). Then there is the difficulty of contacting the agency. The working day at the agency nearest you may end at 1:30 in the afternoon. The official in charge may be at lunch when you call or come by, or it may be one of many religious or other holidays. Once you have made the application, there may be delays for some other reason—perhaps the bar code machine is malfunctioning. "Call me tomorrow," the official may say day after day when you call to check on the status of your passport. Once you obtain your passport, it is customary to make the rounds and thank everyone you contacted, whether they actually helped you or not.

For Critical Analysis

Would a bureaucracy in a unitary system be more "efficient" than a bureaucracy in a federal system, such as the United States? Would a unitary or a federal system promote more responsiveness to citizens' needs?

The Executive Departments

You were introduced to the various executive departments in Chapter 12, when you read about how the president works with the cabinet and other close advisers. The fifteen executive departments, which are directly accountable to the president, are the major service organizations of the federal government. They are responsible for performing government functions, such as training troops (Department of Defense), printing money (Department of the Treasury), and enforcing federal laws setting minimum safety and health standards for workers (Department of Labor). Table 13–1 on the next two pages provides an overview of each of the departments within the executive branch.

TABLE 13-1

EXECUTIVE DEPARTMENTS

DEPARTMENT (Year Established)	PRINCIPAL DUTIES	SELECTED SUBAGENCIES
State (1789)	Negotiates treaties; develops our foreign policy; protects citizens abroad.	Passport Agency; Bureau of Diplomatic Security; Foreign Service; Bureau of Human Rights and Humanitarian Affairs; Bureau of Consular Affairs.
Treasury (1789)	Pays all federal bills; borrows money; collects federal taxes; mints coins and prints paper currency; supervises national banks.	Internal Revenue Service; U.S. Mint.
Interior (1849)	Supervises federally owned lands and parks; operates federal hydroelectric power facilities; supervises Native American affairs.	U.S. Fish and Wildlife Service; National Park Service; Bureau of Indian Affairs; Bureau of Land Management.
Justice (1870)	Furnishes legal advice to the president; enforces federal criminal laws; supervises the federal corrections system (prisons).	Federal Bureau of Investigation; Drug Enforcement Administration; Bureau of Prisons; U.S. Marshals Service.
Agriculture (1889)	Provides assistance to farmers and ranchers; conducts research to improve agricultural activity and to prevent plant disease; works to protect forests from fires and disease.	Soil Conservation Service; Agricultural Research Service; Food and Safety Inspection Service; Federal Crop Insurance Corporation; Farmers Home Administration.
Commerce (1903)	Grants patents and trademarks; conducts national census; monitors the weather; protects the interests of businesses.	Bureau of the Census; Bureau of Economic Analysis; Minority Business Development Agency; Patent and Trademark Office; National Oceanic and Atmospheric Administration.
Labor (1913)	Administers federal labor laws; promotes the interests of workers.	Occupational Safety and Health Administration; Bureau of Labor Statistics; Employment Standards Administration; Office of Labor-Management Standards.

TABLE 13-1

EXECUTIVE DEPARTMENTS (CONTINUED)

DEPARTMENT (Year Established)		PRINCIPAL DUTIES	SELECTED SUBAGENCIES
Defense (1949)*		Manages the armed forces (Army, Navy, Air Force, Marines); operates military bases.	National Security Agency; Joint Chiefs of Staff; Departments of the Air Force, Navy, Army.
Health and Human Services (1979)†		Promotes public health; enforces pure food and drug laws; is involved in health-related research.	Food and Drug Administration; Public Health Service, including the Centers for Disease Control and Prevention; Administration for Children and Families; Health Care Financing Administration.
Housing and Urban Development (1965)		Concerned with the nation's housing needs; develops and rehabilitates urban communities; promotes improvements in city streets and parks.	Office of Block Grant Assistance; Emergency Shelter Grants Program; Office of Urban Development Action Grants; Office of Fair Housing and Equal Opportunity.
Transportation (1967)		Finances improvements in mass transit; develops and administers programs for highways, railroads, and aviation.	Federal Aviation Administration; Federal Highway Administration; National Highway Traffic Safety Administration; Federal Transit Administration.
Energy (1977)		Involved in conservation of energy and resources; analyzes energy data; conducts research and development.	Office of Civilian Radioactive Waste Management; Office of Nuclear Energy; Energy Information Administration.
Education (1979)†		Coordinates federal programs and policies for education; administers aid to education; promotes educational research.	Office of Special Education and Rehabilitation Services; Office of Elementary and Secondary Education; Office of Postsecondary Education; Office of Vocational and Adult Education.
Veterans Affairs (1989)		Promotes the welfare of veterans of the U.S. armed forces.	Veterans Health Administration; Veterans Benefits Administration; National Cemetery System.
Homeland Security (2002)		Works to prevent terrorist attacks within the United States, reduce America's vulnerability to terrorism, and minimize the damage from potential attacks and natural disasters.	U.S. Customs and Border Protection; U.S. Citizenship and Immigration Services; U.S. Coast Guard; Secret Service; Federal Emergency Management Agency.

* Formed from the Department of War (1789) and the Department of the Navy (1798).
† Formed from the Department of Health, Education, and Welfare (1953).

Each department was created by Congress as the perceived need for it arose, and each department manages a specific policy area. In 2002, for example, Congress created the Department of Homeland Security to deal with the threat of terrorism. The head of each department is known as the secretary, except for the Department of Justice, which is headed by the attorney general. Each department head is appointed by the president and confirmed by the Senate.

A Typical Departmental Structure

Cabinet departments consist of the various heads of the department (the secretary of the department, deputy secretary, undersecretaries, and the like), plus a number of agencies. For example, the National Park Service is an agency within the Department of the Interior. The Drug Enforcement Administration is an agency within the Department of Justice.

Although there are organizational differences among the departments, each department generally follows a typi-cal bureaucratic structure. The Department of Agriculture provides a model for how an executive department is organized (see Figure 13–3).

One aspect of the secretary of agriculture's job is to carry out the president's agricultural policies. Another aspect, however, is to promote and protect the department. The secretary spends time ensuring that Congress allocates enough money for the department to work effectively. The secretary also makes sure that constituents, or the people the department serves—usually owners of major farming corporations—are happy. In general, the secretary tries to maintain or improve the status of the department with respect to all of the other departments and units of the federal bureaucracy.

The secretary of agriculture is assisted by a deputy secretary and several assistant secretaries and under-secretaries, all of whom are nominated by the president and put into office with Senate approval. The secretary and each assistant secretary have staff who help with all sorts of jobs, such as hiring new people and generating positive public relations for the Department of Agriculture.

FIGURE 13-3

THE ORGANIZATION OF THE DEPARTMENT OF AGRICULTURE

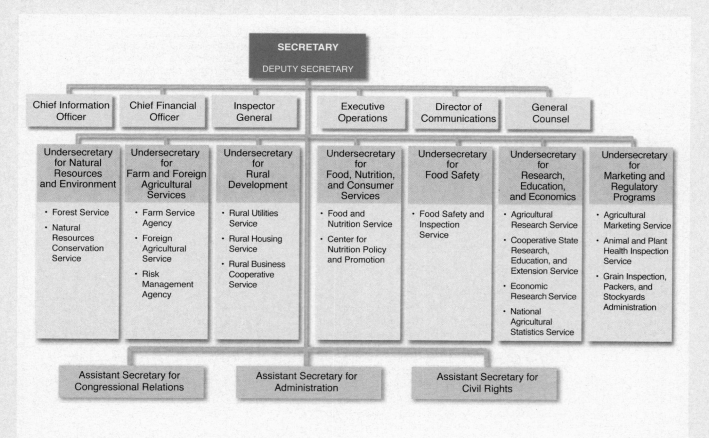

Source: *United States Government Manual, 2007/08* (Washington, D.C.: U.S. Government Printing Office, 2007).

Independent Executive Agencies

Independent executive agencies are federal bureaucratic organizations that have a single function. They are independent in the sense that they are not located within a department; rather, independent executive agency heads report directly to the president who has appointed them. A new federal independent executive agency can be created only through joint cooperation between the president and Congress.

Prior to the twentieth century, the federal government did almost all of its work through the executive departments. In the twentieth century, in contrast, presidents asked for certain executive agencies to be kept separate, or independent, from existing departments. Today, there are more than two hundred independent executive agencies.

Sometimes, agencies are kept independent because of the sensitive nature of their functions; at other times, Congress has created independent agencies to protect them from **partisan politics**—politics in support of a particular party. The Civil Rights Commission, which was created in 1957, is a case in point. Congress wanted to protect the work of the Civil Rights Commission from the influences not only of its own political interest groups but also of the president. The Central Intelligence Agency (CIA), which was formed in 1947, is another good example. Both Congress and the president know that the intelligence activities of the CIA could be abused if it were not independent. Finally, the General Services Administration (GSA) was created as an independent executive agency in 1949 to monitor federal government spending. To perform its function of overseeing congressional spending, it has to be an independent agency.

Among the more than two hundred independent executive agencies, a few stand out in importance either because

Independent executive agencies are part of the federal bureaucracy. One example is the Central Intelligence Agency (CIA). Former Air Force general Michael V. Hayden was confirmed as the CIA's director in May 2006.

Larry Downing/Reuters/Landov

of the mission they were established to accomplish or because of their large size. We list selected independent executive agencies in Table 13–2.

independent executive agency A federal agency that is not located within a cabinet department.

partisan politics Political actions or decisions that benefit a particular party.

TABLE 13-2

SELECTED INDEPENDENT EXECUTIVE AGENCIES

Name	Date Formed	Principal Duties
Central Intelligence Agency (CIA)	1947	Gathers and analyzes political and military information about foreign countries so that the United States can improve its own political and military status; conducts covert activities outside the United States.
General Services Administration (GSA)	1949	Purchases and manages all property of the federal government; acts as the business arm of the federal government, overseeing federal government spending projects; discovers overcharges in government programs.
National Science Foundation (NSF)	1950	Promotes scientific research; provides grants to all levels of schools for instructional programs in the sciences.
Small Business Administration (SBA)	1953	Promotes the interests of small businesses; provides low-cost loans and management information to small businesses.
National Aeronautics and Space Administration (NASA)	1958	Responsible for U.S. space program, including building, testing, and operating space vehicles.

TABLE 13-3

SELECTED INDEPENDENT REGULATORY AGENCIES

Name	Date Formed	Principal Duties
Federal Reserve System Board of Governors (Fed)	1913	Determines policy with respect to interest rates, credit availability, and the money supply.
Federal Trade Commission (FTC)	1914	Works to prevent businesses from engaging in unfair trade practices and to stop the formation of monopolies in the business sector; protects consumers' rights.
Securities and Exchange Commission (SEC)	1934	Regulates the nation's stock exchanges, where shares of stocks are bought and sold; requires full disclosure of the financial profiles of companies that wish to sell stocks and bonds to the public.
Federal Communications Commission (FCC)	1934	Regulates all communications by telegraph, cable, telephone, radio, and television.
National Labor Relations Board (NLRB)	1935	Protects employees' rights to join unions and to bargain collectively with employers; attempts to prevent unfair labor practices by both employers and unions.
Equal Employment Opportunity Commission (EEOC)	1964	Works to eliminate discrimination that is based on religion, gender, race, color, national origin, age, or disability; examines claims of discrimination.
Environmental Protection Agency (EPA)	1970	Undertakes programs aimed at reducing air and water pollution; works with state and local agencies to help fight environmental hazards.
Nuclear Regulatory Commission (NRC)	1974	Ensures that electricity-generating nuclear reactors in the United States are built and operated safely; regularly inspects operations of such reactors.

Independent Regulatory Agencies

Independent regulatory agencies are responsible for a specific type of public policy. Their function is to create and implement rules that regulate private activity and protect the public interest in a particular sector of the economy. They are sometimes called the "alphabet soup" of government because most such agencies are known in Washington by their initials.

One of the earliest independent regulatory agencies was the Interstate Commerce Commission (ICC), established in 1887. (This agency was abolished in 1995.) After the ICC was formed, other agencies were created to regulate aviation (the Civil Aeronautics Board, or CAB, which was abolished in 1985), communication (the Federal Communications Commission, or FCC), the stock market (the Securities and Exchange Commission, or SEC), and many other areas of business. Table 13–3 lists some major independent regulatory agencies.

independent regulatory agency A federal organization that is responsible for creating and implementing rules that regulate private activity and protect the public interest in a particular sector of the economy.

government corporation An agency of the government that is run as a business enterprise. Such agencies engage in primarily commercial activities, produce revenues, and require greater flexibility than that permitted in most government agencies.

Government Corporations

The newest form of federal bureaucratic organization is the **government corporation,** a business that is owned by the government. Government corporations are not exactly like corporations in which you buy stock, become a shareholder, and share in the profits by collecting dividends. The U.S. Postal Service is a government corporation, but it does not sell shares. If a government corporation loses money in the course of doing business, taxpayers, not shareholders, foot the bill.

Government corporations are like private corporations in that they provide a service that could be handled by the private sector. They are also like private corporations in that they charge for their services, though sometimes they charge less than what a consumer would pay for similar services provided by private-sector corporations. Table 13–4 lists selected government corporations.

LO³ HOW BUREAUCRATS GET THEIR JOBS

As already noted, federal bureaucrats holding top-level positions are appointed by the president and confirmed by the Senate. These bureaucrats include department and agency heads, their deputy and

TABLE 13-4

SELECTED GOVERNMENT CORPORATIONS

Name	Date Formed	Principal Duties
Tennessee Valley Authority (TVA)	1933	Operates a Tennessee River control system and generates power for a seven-state region and for U.S. aeronautics and space programs; promotes the economic development of the Tennessee Valley region; controls floods and promotes the navigability of the Tennessee River.
Federal Deposit Insurance Corporation (FDIC)	1933	Insures individuals' bank deposits up to $100,000; oversees the business activities of banks.
Export/Import Bank of the United States (Ex/Im Bank)	1933	Promotes American-made goods abroad; grants loans to foreign purchasers of American products.
National Railroad Passenger Corporation (AMTRAK)	1970	Provides a national and intercity rail passenger service network; controls more than 23,000 miles of track with about 505 stations.
U.S. Postal Service (formed from the old U.S. Post Office Department—the Post Office itself is older than the Constitution)	1971	Delivers mail throughout the United States and its territories; is the largest government corporation.

assistant secretaries, and so on. The list of positions that are filled by appointments is published after each presidential election in a document called *Policy and Supporting Positions*. The booklet is more commonly known as the "Plum Book," because the eight thousand jobs it summarizes are known as "political plums." Normally, these jobs go to those who supported the winning presidential candidate—in other words, the patronage system is alive and well but on a limited basis.

The rank-and-file bureaucrats—the rest of the federal bureaucracy—are part of the **civil service** (nonmilitary employment in government). They obtain their jobs through the Office of Personnel Management (OPM), an agency established by the Civil Service Reform Act of 1978. The OPM recruits, interviews, and tests potential government workers and determines who should be hired. The OPM makes recommendations to the individual agencies as to which persons meet the standards (typically, the top three applicants for a position), and the agencies generally decide whom to hire. The 1978 act also created the Merit Systems Protection Board (MSPB) to oversee promotions, employees' rights, and other employment matters. The MSPB evaluates charges of wrongdoing, hears employee appeals from agency decisions, and can order corrective action against agencies and employees.

The idea that the civil service should be based on a merit system dates back more than a century. The Civil Service Reform Act of 1883 established the principle of government employment on the basis

of merit through open, competitive examinations. Initially, only about 10 percent of federal employees were covered by the merit system. Today, more than 90 percent of the federal civil service is recruited on the basis of merit. Are public employees paid as well as workers in the private sector? For a discussion of this question, see this chapter's *Perception versus Reality* feature on the following page.

LO⁴ REGULATORY AGENCIES: ARE THEY THE FOURTH BRANCH OF GOVERNMENT?

In Chapter 2, we considered the system of checks and balances among the three branches of the U.S. government—executive, legislative, and judicial. Recent history, however, shows that it may be time to regard the regulatory agencies as a fourth branch of the government. Although the U.S. Constitution does not mention regulatory agencies, they can and do make **legislative rules** that are as legally binding as laws passed by Congress. With such powers, this administrative branch has an influence on

Lawrence Migdale/Stone/Getty

civil service Nonmilitary government employment.

legislative rule An administrative agency rule that carries the same weight as a statute enacted by a legislature.

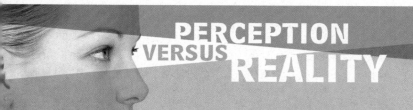

PERCEPTION VERSUS REALITY

Working for the Government at Low Pay

Most parents do not jump for joy at the thought of their children going to work for the government. Government work in general in the United States has never been considered the road to riches. Indeed, the general picture of government employment is quite negative.

The Perception

It is often assumed that only individuals working in the private sector can hope to receive large paychecks. Even a member of Congress makes far less than most operations officers in mid-level corporations. Although workers in the public sector receive paid-for medical insurance and a generous retirement program, the perception is that these benefits do not make up for the lower pay they earn.

The Reality

The Employee Benefit Research Institute has discovered that overall compensation costs for state and local governments are almost 50 percent higher than for private-sector employers. A typical hour's

work costs state and local governments more than $24 in wages and salaries, plus more than $11 in benefits. For that same hour of work, on average, a private-sector employer pays only about $17 in wages and salaries, plus about $7 in benefits.

Move now to the federal government. The U.S. Bureau of Economic Analysis estimates that federal civilian government workers earn $106,579 a year in total compensation (salaries, plus benefits), which is almost twice the $53,289 in compensation for the typical private-sector worker. It is therefore not surprising that Washington, D.C.—which is loaded with federal employees—is the fourth richest among this nation's 360 metropolitan areas. During the first half of this decade, wages and salaries for federal workers increased by 38 percent, compared to only a 15 percent increase for private-sector workers. Public-sector workers also enjoy pay bonuses amounting to 30 percent more than the bonuses received in the private sector. In addition, federal civil service rules bestow lifetime job security in the sense that it is extremely difficult to fire a federal employee.

BLOG ON

Arguments that government employees are overpaid are a constant theme of conservative blogs. Warren Meyer's Coyote Blog pays more attention to the topic than most. Visit it at **www.coyoteblog.com/coyote_blog/government**. YoungFeds.org bills itself as the place for young government professionals to meet, network, and advance. Its blog, at **www.youngfeds.org/blog**, is a place to get positive insights about government employees from the workers themselves.

---

the nation's businesses that rivals that of the president, Congress, and the courts. Indeed, most Americans do not realize how much of our "law" is created by regulatory agencies.

Regulatory agencies have been on the American political scene since the nineteenth century, but their golden age came during the regulatory explosion of the 1960s and 1970s. Congress itself could not have overseen the actual implementation of all of the laws that it was enacting at the time to control pollution and deal with other social problems. It therefore chose (and still chooses) to

enabling legislation
A law enacted by a legislature to establish an administrative agency. Enabling legislation normally specifies the name, purpose, composition, and powers of the agency being created.

delegate to administrative agencies the tasks involved in implementing its laws. By delegating some of its authority to an administrative agency, Congress may indirectly monitor a particular area in which it has passed legislation without becoming bogged down in the details relating to the enforcement of that legislation—details that are often best left to specialists. In recent years, the government has been hiring increasing numbers of specialists to oversee its regulatory work.

Agency Creation

To create an administrative agency, Congress passes **enabling legislation**, which specifies the name, purpose, composition, and powers of the agency being created.

Shawn Moore/OSHA

The Occupational Safety and Health Administration (OSHA) is responsible for workplace safety. These OSHA employees are inspecting a construction site for safety violations.

The Federal Trade Commission (FTC), for example, was created in 1914 by the Federal Trade Commission Act, as mentioned earlier. The act prohibits unfair and deceptive trade practices. The act also describes the procedures that the agency must follow to charge persons or organizations with violations of the act, and it provides for judicial review of agency orders.

Other portions of the act grant the agency powers to "make rules and regulations for the purpose of carrying out the Act," to conduct investigations of business practices, to obtain reports on business practices from interstate corporations, to investigate possible violations of federal antitrust statutes, to publish findings of its investigations, and to recommend new legislation. The act also empowers the FTC to hold trial-like hearings and to **adjudicate** (formally resolve) certain kinds of disputes that involve FTC regulations or federal antitrust laws. When adjudication takes place, within the FTC or any other regulatory agency, an administrative law judge (ALJ) conducts the hearing and, after weighing the evidence presented, issues an *order*. Unless it is overturned on appeal, the ALJ's order becomes final.

Enabling legislation makes the regulatory agency a potent organization. For example, the Securities and Exchange Commission (SEC) imposes rules regarding the disclosures a company must make to those who purchase its stock. Under its enforcement authority, the SEC also investigates and prosecutes alleged violations of these regulations. Finally, the SEC sits as judge and jury in deciding whether its rules have been violated and, if so, what punishment should be imposed on the

offender (although the judgment may be appealed to a federal court).

Rulemaking

A major function of a regulatory agency is **rulemaking**—the formulation of new regulations. The power that an agency has to make rules is conferred on it by Congress in the agency's enabling legislation. For example, the Occupational Safety and Health Administration (OSHA) was authorized by the Occupational Safety and Health Act of 1970 to develop and issue rules governing safety in the workplace. Under this authority, OSHA has issued various safety standards. For example, OSHA deemed it in the public interest to issue a rule regulating the health-care industry to prevent the spread of certain diseases, including acquired immune deficiency syndrome (AIDS). The rule specified various standards—on how contaminated instruments should be handled, for instance—with which employers in that industry must comply. Agencies cannot just make a rule whenever they wish, however. Rather, they must follow certain procedural requirements, particularly those set forth in the Administrative Procedure Act of 1946.

Agencies must also make sure that their rules are based on substantial evidence and are not "arbitrary and capricious." Therefore, before proposing a new rule, an agency may engage in extensive investigation (through research, on-site inspections of the affected industry, surveys, and the like) to obtain data on the problem to be addressed by the rule. Based on this information, the agency may undertake a cost-benefit analysis of a new rule to determine whether its benefits outweigh its costs. For example, when issuing new rules governing electrical equipment, OSHA predicted that they would cost business $21.7 billion annually but would save 60 lives and eliminate 1,600 worker injuries a year. The agency also estimated that its safety equipment regulations for manufacturing workers would

adjudicate To render a judicial decision. In regard to administrative law, the process in which an administrative law judge hears and decides issues that arise when an agency charges a person or firm with violating a law or regulation enforced by the agency.

rulemaking The process undertaken by an administrative agency when formally proposing, evaluating, and adopting a new regulation.

cost $52.4 billion, save 4 lives, and prevent 712,000 lost workdays because of injuries each year.

Don't get the idea that rulemaking is isolated from politics. Indeed, as you will read shortly, bureaucrats work closely with members of Congress as well as interest groups when making rules.

Policymaking and the Iron Triangle

Federal bureaucrats are expected to exhibit **neutral competency**, which means that they are supposed to apply their technical skills to their jobs without regard to political issues. In principle, they should not be swayed by the thought of personal or political gain. In reality, each independent agency and each executive department is interested in its own survival and expansion. Each is constantly battling the others for a larger share of the budget. All agencies and departments wish to retain or expand their functions and staffs; to do this, they must gain the goodwill of both the White House and Congress.

Although administrative agencies of the federal government are prohibited from directly lobbying Congress, departments and agencies have developed techniques to help them gain congressional support. Each organization maintains a congressional information office, which specializes in helping members of Congress by supplying any requested information and solving casework problems. For example, if a member of the House of Representatives receives a complaint from a constituent that his Social Security checks are not arriving on time, that member of Congress may go to the Social Security Administration and ask that something be done. Typically, requests from members of Congress receive immediate attention.

Analysts have determined that one way to understand the bureaucracy's role in policymaking is to examine the **iron triangle,** which is the three-way alliance among legislators (members of Congress), bureaucrats,

> ### GOVERNMENT
> # BUREAUCRACY:
> ## "A MARVELOUS LABOR-SAVING
> ## DEVICE WHICH ENABLES
> # TEN MEN TO DO
> ## THE WORK OF ONE."
>
> JOHN MAYNARD KEYNES,
> BRITISH ECONOMIST
> 1883–1946

and interest groups. (Iron triangles are also referred to as *subgovernments.*) Presumably, the laws that are passed and the policies that are established benefit the interests of all three sides of the iron triangle.

AGRICULTURE AS AN EXAMPLE Consider the bureaucracy within the Department of Agriculture. It consists of about 100,000 individuals working directly for the federal government and thousands of other individuals who work indirectly for the department as contractors, subcontractors, or consultants. Now consider that various interest groups or client groups are concerned with what certain bureaus or agencies in the Agriculture Department do for agribusinesses. Some of these groups are the American Farm Bureau Federation, the National Cattlemen's Beef Association, the National Milk Producers Federation, the National Corn Growers Association, and the various regional citrus growers associations.

Finally, take a close look at Congress and you will see that two major committees are concerned with agriculture: the House Committee on Agriculture and the Senate Committee on Agriculture, Nutrition, and Forestry. Each committee has several specialized subcommittees. The triangle is an alliance of bureaucrats, interest groups, and legislators who cooperate to create mutually beneficial regulations or legislation. Iron triangles, or policy communities, are well established in almost every part of the bureaucracy. Because of these connections between agricultural interest groups and policymakers within the government, the agricultural industry has benefited greatly over the years from significant farm subsidies.

CONGRESS'S ROLE The secretary of agriculture is nominated by the president (and confirmed by the Senate) and is the head of the Department of Agriculture. But that secretary cannot even buy a desk lamp if Congress does not approve the appropriations for the department's budget. Within Congress, the responsibility for considering the Department of Agriculture's request for funding belongs first to the House and Senate appropriations committees and then to the agriculture subcommittees under them. The members of those subcommittees, most of whom represent agricultural states, have been around a long time

neutral competency The application of technical skills to jobs without regard to political issues.

iron triangle A three-way alliance among legislators, bureaucrats, and interest groups to make or preserve policies that benefit their respective interests.

and have their own ideas about what is appropriate for the Agriculture Department's budget. They carefully scrutinize the ideas of the president and the secretary of agriculture.

THE INFLUENCE OF INTEREST GROUPS   Finally, the various interest groups—including producers of farm chemicals and farm machinery, agricultural cooperatives, grain dealers, and exporters—have vested interests in whatever the Department of Agriculture does and in whatever Congress lets the department do. Those interests are well represented by the lobbyists who crowd the halls of Congress. Many lobbyists have been working for agricultural interest groups for decades. They know the congressional committee members and Agriculture Department staff extremely well and routinely meet with them.

Issue Networks

The iron triangle relationship does not apply to all policy domains, however. When making policy decisions on environmental and welfare issues, for example, many members of Congress and agency officials rely heavily on "experts." Legislators and agency heads tend to depend on their staff members for specialized knowledge of rules, regulations, and legislation. These experts have frequently served variously as interest group lobbyists and as public-sector staff members during their careers, creating a revolving-door effect. They often have strong opinions and interests regarding the direction of policy and are thus able to exert a great deal of influence on legislators and bureaucratic agencies. The relationships among these experts, which are less structured than iron triangles, are often referred to as **issue networks.** Like iron triangles, issue networks are made up of people with similar policy concerns. Issue networks are less interdependent and unified than iron triangles, however, and often include more players, such as media outlets.[3] (See Figure 13–4.)

> **issue networks** Groups of individuals or organizations—which consist of legislators and legislative staff members, interest group leaders, bureaucrats, the media, scholars, and other experts—that support particular policy positions on a given issue.

LO⁵ CURBING WASTE AND IMPROVING EFFICIENCY

There is no doubt that our bureaucracy is costly. There is also little doubt that at times it can be wasteful and inefficient. Each year it is possible to cull through the budgets of the various federal agencies and discover quite outrageous examples of government waste. Here are some recent ones:

- More than $11 million paid to psychics by the Pentagon and the Central Intelligence Agency to discover whether the psychics would offer insights about foreign threats to the United States.

- Payments of more than $20 million a year to thousands of prison inmates through the Social Security Administration's Supplemental Income Program.

- A total of $10 million per year paid by the Department of Energy to its employees to encourage them to lose weight.

- More than $30 million paid over two years by the Internal Revenue Service to tax filers claiming nonexistent slavery tax credits.

- A total of $1.1 million spent for a program that informed tenants of public housing about the types of gemstones, incense, and clothing colors that would best improve their self-esteem.

The government has made several attempts to reduce waste, inefficiency, and wrongdoing. For example, over the years both the federal government and state governments have passed laws requiring more openness in government. Further attempts at bureaucratic reform have included, among other things, encouraging government employees to report to appropriate government officials any waste and wrongdoing that they observe.

FIGURE 13–4

ISSUE NETWORK: THE ENVIRONMENT

Executive Departments and Agencies
- Environmental Protection Agency
- Agriculture Department
- Energy Department
- Department of the Interior
- National Oceanic and Atmospheric Admin.
- Bureau of Land Management
- Army Corps of Engineers

Key Congressional Committees
- **Senate**
  Appropriations; Energy and Natural Resources; Environment and Public Works; Finance; Commerce, Science, and Transportation
- **House of Representatives**
  Agriculture; Appropriations; Natural Resources; Transportation and Infrastructure

Selected Interest Groups
- **Environmental Groups**
  Environmental Defense; Friends of the Earth; National Audubon Society; Clean Water Action; National Wildlife Federation; The Ocean Conservancy; American Forests
- **Industry Groups**
  Citizens for a Sound Economy; Edison Electric Institute; U.S. Chamber of Commerce; National Food Processors Association; International Wood Products Association; National Mining Association; American Resort Development Association

JOIN THE DEBATE

Should Federal Agencies Stop Spending So Much in July?

There is a saying within federal government agencies that Christmas comes in July. Why? The fourth quarter of the government's fiscal year begins in July, and the agencies go on a frantic spending spree. When it comes to budgets, government agencies know that the rule is "spend it or lose it." If an agency doesn't spend its allocated budget by the end of the fiscal year, it certainly is not going to get more the next year. Agency heads also know how to expand their power and prestige—by expanding their budgets.

It's time to stop this ridiculous Christmas-in-July spending game at the federal level. It's unseemly to see ads on the Internet for self-help guides that claim they can help you win your share of unprecedented federal spending "from now until September 30." The "now," of course, is July. There should be a rule that prohibits agencies from spending more in the fiscal fourth quarter than in any previous quarter. Heads of agencies may want to expand their power by spending more, but the American taxpayer doesn't want to pay for it. Typically, many agencies are allocated more funds than they know how to spend. At the end of fiscal year 2006, the Panama Canal Commission had $75 million that it could not figure out how to spend. At one point, the National Sheep Industry Improvement Center had $5 million more than it could spend.

Not everyone is so sure that changing the rate of federal agency spending throughout the fiscal year will change anything. Indeed, requiring that federal agencies spend no more in the last quarter than in any previous quarter might exacerbate the problem. After all, if you were running a federal agency and knew that you could not spend more in the fourth fiscal quarter than in the first, what would you do? You would make sure that you spent your approved money at a faster pace than you might have otherwise. Consequently, federal agencies might simply waste taxpayers' dollars throughout the fiscal year, rather than just in the fourth quarter. The key to

At the end of one fiscal year, the National Sheep Industry Improvement Center ended up with $5 million more than it could spend.

reducing government waste is not to prevent "Christmas in July" but to appropriate less money for the executive branch of the federal government.

Helping Out the Whistleblowers

The term **whistleblower,** as applied to the federal bureaucracy, has a special meaning: it is someone who blows the whistle, or reports, on gross governmental inefficiency, illegal action, or other wrongdoing. Federal employees are often reluctant to blow the whistle on their superiors, however, for fear of reprisals.

LEGISLATION PROTECTING WHISTLEBLOWERS To encourage federal employees to report government wrongdoing, Congress has passed laws to protect whistleblowers. The 1978 Civil Service Reform Act included some protection for whistleblowers by prohibiting reprisals against whistleblowers by their superiors. The act also set up the Merit Systems Protection Board as part of this protection. The Whistle-Blower Protection Act of 1989 provided further protection for whistleblowers. That act authorized the Office of Special Counsel (OSC), an independent agency, to investigate complaints of reprisals against whistleblowers. From time to time, Congress considers more whistleblower legislation to protect special groups, such as employees of government contractors and federal workers who blow the whistle on officials who intentionally alter or distort scientific data. Many federal agencies also have toll-free hot lines

whistleblower In the context of government employment, someone who "blows the whistle" (reports to authorities) on gross governmental inefficiency, illegal action, or other wrongdoing.

Creative Commons

that employees can use to anonymously report bureaucratic waste and inappropriate behavior.

WHISTLEBLOWERS CONTINUE TO FACE PROBLEMS

In spite of these laws, there is little evidence that whistleblowers are adequately protected against retaliation. According to a study conducted by the Government Accountability Office, 41 percent of the whistleblowers who turned to the OSC for protection during a recent three-year period reported that they were no longer employed by the agencies on which they blew the whistle. In 2006, the United States Supreme Court rendered a decision that will likely make it even more difficult for whistleblowers to obtain protection. The case involved an assistant district attorney who inquired in a written memo about whether a county sheriff's deputy had lied in an affidavit. As a result, the attorney was demoted and denied a promotion. The attorney then sued his employer for violating his right to free speech. The Supreme Court held, in a close (five-to-four) decision, that a public employee whose speech relates to official duties is not "speaking" as a citizen for First Amendment purposes.[4]

Many federal employees who have blown the whistle say that they would not do so again because it was so difficult to get help, and even when they did, the experience was a stressful ordeal. Creating more effective protection for whistleblowers remains an ongoing goal of the government. The basic problem, though, is that most organizations, including federal government agencies, do not like to have their wrongdoings and failings exposed, especially by insiders.

Improving Efficiency and Getting Results

The Government Performance and Results Act, which went into effect in 1997, has forced the federal government to change the way it does business. In pilot programs throughout the federal government, agencies have experienced a shakedown. Since 1997, virtually every agency (except the intelligence agencies) has had to describe its new goals and a method for evaluating how well those goals are met. A results-oriented goal of an agency could be as broad as lowering the number of highway traffic deaths or as narrow as trying to reduce the number of times an agency's phone rings before it is answered.

As one example, consider the National Oceanic and Atmospheric Adminstration (NOAA). It improved the effectiveness of its short-term forecasting services, particularly in issuing warnings of tornadoes. The warning time has increased from seven to nine minutes. This may seem insignificant, but it provides additional critical time for those in the path of a tornado.

President George W. Bush's "performance-based budgeting" further extends this idea of focusing on results. Performance-based budgeting is designed to increase overall agency performance and accountability by linking the funding of federal agencies to their actual performance. Numerous federal programs now have to meet specific performance criteria. If they do, they will receive more funds. If they do not, their funding will be reduced or removed entirely. To determine the extent to which performance criteria have been met, the Office of Management and Budget now "grades" each agency on how well it manages its operations, and these grades are considered during the budgeting process.

Another Approach—Pay-for-Performance Plans

For some time, the private sector has used pay-for-performance plans as a means to increase employee productivity and efficiency. About one-third of the major firms in this country use some kind of alternative pay system such as team-based

This photo shows the "guts" of the Space Weather Prediction Center (SWPC). This government agency operates around the clock. The number of staff varies with storm activity. On quiet days and nights, very few staff are present; when a dangerous weather pattern is developing, however, the staff doubles or triples.

NOAA's National Weather Service Collection

pay, skill-based pay, profit-sharing plans, or individual bonuses. In contrast, workers for the federal government traditionally have received fixed salaries; promotions and salary increases are given on the basis of seniority, not output.

The federal government has also been experimenting with pay-for-performance systems. For example, the U.S. Postal Service has implemented an Economic Value Added program, which ties bonuses to performance. As part of a five-year test of a new pay system, three thousand scientists working in Air Force laboratories received salaries based on actual results. Also, the Department of Veterans Affairs launched a skill-based pay project at its New York regional office.

Many hope that by offering such incentives, the government will be able to compete more effectively with the private sector for skilled and talented employees. Additionally, according to some, pay-for-performance plans will go a long way toward countering the entitlement mentality that has traditionally characterized employment within the bureaucracy.

Privatization

Another alternative for reforming the federal bureaucracy is **privatization,** which means turning over certain types of government work to the private sector. Privatization can take place by contracting out (outsourcing) work to the private sector or by "managed competition" in which the task of providing public services is opened up to competition. In managed competition, both the relevant government agency and private firms can compete for the work. Vouchers are another way in which certain services traditionally provided by government, such as education, can be provided on the open market. The government pays for the vouchers, but the services are provided by the private sector.

State and local governments have been experimenting with privatization for some time. Virtually all of the states have privatized at least a few of their services, and some states, including California, Colorado, and Florida, have privatized more than one hundred activities formerly undertaken by government. In Scottsdale, Arizona, the city contracts for fire protection. In Baltimore, Maryland, nine of the city's schools are outsourced to private entities. In other cities, services ranging from janitorial work to managing recreational facilities are handled by the private sector.

The Bush administration attempted to follow the states' lead and privatize work undertaken by some 850,000 federal workers. Whether airport traffic control, military support services, and a host of other federal services should also be privatized was debated in think tanks and, to some extent, by policymakers. One issue that was of foremost concern to Americans was whether Social Security should be partially privatized. Another controversial issue concerned the extent to which the Bush administration outsourced jobs related to the Iraq war to private contractors—see this chapter's *The Politics of National Security* feature for a discussion of this topic.

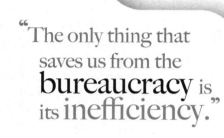

"The only thing that saves us from the **bureaucracy** is its inefficiency."

EUGENE J. MCCARTHY,
U.S. SENATOR FROM MINNESOTA
1959–1971

Is It Possible to Reform the Bureaucracy?

Some claim that the bureaucracy is so massive, unwieldy, and self-perpetuating that it is impossible to reform. Attempts at reform, including those just discussed, can, at most, barely touch the surface of the problem.

BUREAUCRATIC INERTIA In large part, this is because the positions over which the president has direct or indirect control, through the appointment process, amount to fewer than 1 percent of the 2.7 million civilian employees who work for the executive branch. The bureaucracy is also deeply entrenched and is often characterized by inertia and by slow-moving responses to demands for change. As Laurence J. Peter, of "Peter Principle" fame, once said, a "bureaucracy defends the status quo long past the time when the quo has lost its status." It should come as no surprise, then, that virtually every president in modern times has found it difficult to exercise much control over the bureaucracy.

Complicating the problem is the fact that political appointees often know little about the work of the agency to which they are appointed and are rarely trained specifically in the areas that they supervise. Typically, they must look for assistance to the rank-and-file staff, whose jobs do not come and go with each administration. Furthermore, federal employees have significant

privatization The transfer of the task of providing services traditionally provided by government to the private sector.

THE POLITICS OF NATIONAL SECURITY

OUTSOURCING WAR-RELATED WORK—GOOD OR BAD?

When many Americans think of "outsourcing," they tend to worry about Americans losing call-center and other jobs to those living in countries such as India. Not too many people are aware of how much outsourcing the United States did to further the war effort in Iraq.

THE BUSH ADMINISTRATION'S UNPRECEDENTED USE OF OUTSOURCING

Outsourcing has been a favorite federal government activity since the Clinton administration reduced the federal workforce to its lowest level in decades. After waging the wars in Afghanistan and Iraq, the Bush administration pushed the level of outsourcing to the $450-billion-a-year mark.

In 2007, for example, the U.S. government employed private contracting firms to provide truck drivers, translators, and construction personnel in Iraq. A little-known fact was that the number of private contractors killed in Iraq started to match the number of U.S. soldiers killed there, at least on a quarterly basis.

OUTSOURCING AN ARMY

Americans may see nothing wrong with outsourcing the operations of driving trucks and building roads. But would they have been so unconcerned if they had known that the outsourcing also involved the buildup of a virtual private army in Iraq? Yet that was exactly what was happening in Iraq. The private warriors were not called soldiers, but rather security personnel. The U.S. military used 20,000 to 30,000 private security personnel to offset troop shortages. These armed contractors served as personal security guards for important commanding officers. They protected convoys and guarded weapons and ammunition dumps. Some of these private contractors were Americans, but many were foreigners. For example, one retired special operations officer commanded five hundred private Kurdish guards who protected an immense warehouse filled with weapons and ammunitions on the outskirts of Baghdad.

Each of these private security personnel cost the U.S. government about $1,500 per day. That may seem high, but it was much less than the cost of sending one additional U.S. soldier to Iraq because

of all of the backup personnel necessary for each member of the U.S. military stationed there. The U.S. military claimed that such private contractors were used only for defensive operations. Nevertheless, being limited to defensive operations did not prevent a significant number of these private "soldiers" from dying. According to a former British special forces officer, about 1,500 British and U.S. private security personnel had lost their lives in Iraq as of mid-2007.

The federal government has increasingly used outsourcing for military-related activities. The person in this photo works for a private contractor assigned to protect important people living in or visiting Iraq. In the fall of 2007, security personnel from one such private firm mistakenly killed innocent Iraqi civilians and raised new questions about the appropriateness of such private-contractor outsourcing.

AP Photo/Jacob Silberberg

YOU BE THE JUDGE

Some argued that the government's outsourcing of war-related jobs, even routine jobs, to private contractors was more efficient and cost-effective than providing additional soldiers on the ground in Iraq. Others believed that the outsourcing of tasks traditionally handled by soldiers masked the actual number of fighting personnel in Iraq and the number of casualties there. Where do you stand on this issue? Do you agree with either of these positions? If so, why?

rights. Once a federal worker is hired, firing him or her is extremely difficult, regardless of job performance. Similarly, once a federal agency is created, it takes on a life of its own and tends to become permanent. Indeed, President Ronald Reagan (1981–1989) once commented that "a government bureau is the nearest thing to eternal life we'll ever see on this earth."[5]

CHANGES DURING THE BUSH ADMINISTRATION

President George W. Bush attempted to overcome some of the problems just mentioned by issuing an executive order establishing a Regulatory Policy Office (RPO) within each federal agency. The order called for each RPO to be headed by a political appointee with the authority to review and approve agency guidelines. In the regulatory process, such guidelines are important because they set forth the agency's directions on how certain laws that it administers will be interpreted and implemented. Bush's stated goal in establishing these RPOs was to promote consistent policymaking and rulemaking throughout the executive branch of government.

Bush's order establishing the RPOs was very controversial. Critics of the Bush administration saw the order as simply an attempt to politicize the bureaucracy to an extent hitherto unknown. Indeed, some former bureaucrats complained that the requirement of loyalty to President Bush and his policies often interfered with their work.

One of the strongest criticisms of the Bush administration with respect to the bureaucracy concerned the extent to which loyalty to the president and to the Republican Party—rather than to qualifications and expertise—was required of appointees within the Department of Justice. You will read about the controversy over this issue in Chapter 14's opening *America at Odds* feature on page 314.

> "**Bureaucracy** defends the status quo long past the time when the quo has lost its **status**."
>
> LAURENCE J. PETER,
> AMERICAN EDUCATOR
> 1919–1990

Government in the Sunshine

The past four decades saw a trend toward more openness in government. The theory was that because Americans pay for the government, they own it—and they have a right to know what the government is doing with the taxpayers' dollars.

In response to pressure for more government openness and disclosure, Congress passed the Freedom of Information Act in 1966. This act required federal agencies to disclose any information in agency files, with some exceptions, to any persons requesting it. Since the 1970s, "sunshine laws," which require government meetings to be open to the public, have been enacted at all levels of American government. During the Clinton administration (1993–2001), Americans gained even greater access to government information as federal and state agencies went online.

The trend toward greater openness in government came to an abrupt halt on September 11, 2001. In the wake of the terrorist attacks on the World Trade Center and the Pentagon, the government began tightening its grip on information. In the months following the attacks, hundreds of thousands of documents were removed from government Web sites. No longer can the public access plans of nuclear power plants, descriptions of airline security violations, or maps of pipeline routes. Agencies were instructed to be more cautious about releasing information in their files and were given new guidelines on what should be considered public information. State and local agencies followed the federal government's lead. Some states barred access to such information as emergency preparedness evacuation plans. Others established commissions or panels whose activities are exempt from state sunshine laws. As you read in Chapter 12, the Bush administration made it much more difficult to obtain information about the government than it was under previous administrations.

AMERICA AT ODDS:
The Bureaucracy

The bureaucracy is sometimes called the "fourth branch of government." It is not, of course, a part of the government established by the founders of this nation, and certainly the framers of the Constitution could not have anticipated the massive size of today's bureaucracy or the power that it wields over the life of the nation. Although the story is often told about the red tape and wasteful spending generated by our bureaucracy, all in all, as you read in this chapter's *The Rest of the World* feature on page 295, the U.S. bureaucracy compares favorably to bureaucracies in other countries.

Presidential administrations have been challenged time and again by bureaucrats who resist reform measures in order to maintain or expand their "turf"—their jobs and responsibilities within the government. Laws governing federal workers make it extremely difficult to replace inefficient employees. Inadequate "whistleblower" protections make it difficult for bureaucrats who are aware of waste or wrongdoing to inform the relevant government office of such problems. Political appointments to offices within an administration may be based on loyalty to the president rather than on the appointees' expertise or qualifications in the relevant area. Almost inevitably, the U.S. government faces the same problems—sluggishness, inefficiency, and a certain degree of incompetence—with its bureaucracy that many large businesses and organizations throughout the country also face. The only major difference is the size and scope of the U.S. bureaucracy—and the effect that its actions can have on the daily lives of all Americans. Some attempts to reform the bureaucracy over the years have resulted in less waste and more efficiency; others have been less successful. One thing is certain: the need to reform the bureaucracy will be with us for a long time to come.

Issues for Debate & Discussion

1. Former surgeon general Richard H. Carmona testified to a congressional panel in 2007 that the Bush administration would not allow him to speak or issue reports about certain topics, including stem-cell research, emergency contraception, sex education, and mental and global health issues. Carmona said that he was also ordered to mention President Bush three times on every page of his speeches, to make speeches to support Republican political candidates, and to attend political briefings.[6] Some Americans believe that the Bush administration went too far in politicizing federal agencies and their activities. Others claim that if a president is to succeed in implementing a policy agenda, such control over agency leadership is essential. What is your position on this issue?

2. As you know, the Constitution authorized only Congress to make laws at the federal level. Congress, however, after enacting a statute, typically leaves it up to an administrative agency to interpret and apply the law. Consequently, through their rule-making functions, regulatory agencies staffed by bureaucrats, not Congress, make much of the "law" in the United States. For example, much of the body of environmental law consists of regulations issued by the Environmental Protection Agency. Some believe that Congress should not delegate so much lawmaking authority to federal administrative agencies. After all, bureaucrats are not elected, as members of Congress are, so they should not, in fact, be "making the law." Others contend that if Congress did not delegate such work to agencies, it would get little done. Moreover, members of Congress normally do not have as much expertise in a given area, such as environmental science, as agency officials do. What is your position on this issue?

Take Action

Although this chapter's focus is on the federal bureaucracy, realize that all levels of government require bureaucracies to implement their goals. In virtually every community, however, there are needs that government agencies cannot meet. Often, agencies simply lack the funds to hire more personnel or to provide assistance to those in need. To help address these needs, many Americans do volunteer work. If you want to take action in this way, check with your local government offices and find out which agencies or offices have volunteer programs. Volunteer opportunities on the local level can range from helping the homeless and mentoring children in a local school to joining a local environmental clean-up effort. Decide where your interests lie, and consider volunteering your time in a local bureaucracy.

Volunteers answer "hot lines" that teenagers can call when they need help. Many volunteers at such "hot line" services have found this type of work especially rewarding.

AP Photo/Lennox McLendon

- For information on the government, including the Web sites for federal agencies, go to the federal government's "gateway" Web site at **www.usa.gov**.

- The Web site of the Office of Management and Budget offers information ranging from new developments in administrative policy, to the costs of the bureaucracy, to paperwork-reduction efforts. You can access the OMB directly at **www.omb.gov**.

- To learn more about the mission of the General Services Administration (GSA) and its role in managing the federal bureaucracy, go to **www.gsa.gov**.

- Federal World is a government site that contains links to numerous federal agencies and government information. You can find this site at **www.fedworld.gov**.

- If you want to get an idea of what federal agencies are putting on the Web, you can go to the Department of Commerce's Web site at **www.commerce.gov**.

- The *Federal Register* is the official publication for executive-branch documents. This publication, which includes the orders, notices, and rules of all federal administrative agencies, is online at **www.access.gpo.gov**.

From this home page, click on "A-Z Resource List," which is listed in the "GPO Access" section. Scroll down until you see *Federal Register*.

- The *United States Government Manual* contains information on the functions, organization, and administrators of every federal department. You can now access the most recent edition of the manual online at **www.access.gpo.gov**.

From this home page, click on "A-Z Resource List," which is listed in the "GPO Access" section. Scroll down until you see *U.S. Government Manual*.

ONLINE RESOURCES FOR THIS CHAPTER

This text's Companion Web site, at **www.americaatodds. com**, offers links to numerous resources that you can utilize to learn more about the topics covered in this chapter.

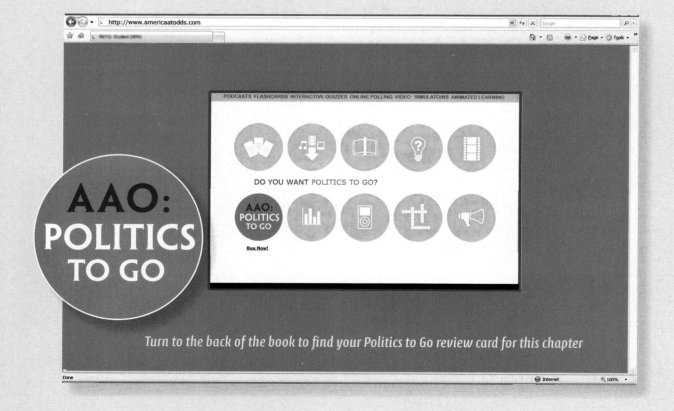

Turn to the back of the book to find your Politics to Go review card for this chapter

CHAPTER 14
THE JUDICIARY

LEARNING OBJECTIVES

LO¹ Summarize the origins of the American legal system and the basic sources of American law.

LO² Delineate the structure of the federal court system.

LO³ Indicate how federal judges are appointed.

LO⁴ Explain how the federal courts make policy.

LO⁵ Describe the role of ideology and judicial philosophies in judicial decision making.

LO⁶ Identify some of the criticisms of the federal courts and some of the checks on the power of the courts.

AMERICA AT ODDS

Justice for All–Or Just Party Loyalists?

You can't miss it in the press. Each time a new administration takes office, the president appoints a new cabinet, including the person who heads the Department of Justice. When George W. Bush became president, he appointed Alberto Gonzales, first as White House counsel and then, in 2004, as attorney general to head the Justice Department. Among the Justice Department's many divisions and agencies are the ninety-three U.S. attorney offices located throughout the United States. The U.S. attorneys prosecute a variety of federal crimes, including public corruption and terrorism. U.S. attorneys have the power to wiretap people's homes, seize property, and put people in prison. The appointment of the attorney general must be confirmed by the Senate. So, too, must the appointments of the U.S. attorneys.

Clearly, the appointments of the attorney general and the U.S. attorneys are partisan affairs. Democratic presidents normally appoint Democrats, and Republicans normally appoint Republicans, to these offices. Nonetheless, the Justice Department is expected to be above politics. Once the appointments have been confirmed, those who work in the Justice Department are supposed to act as nonpartisan, neutral decision makers in performing the duties of their offices. They are supposed to be insulated from outside pressures, including pressures from the president and his or her staff and from members of Congress.

In 2006, the public learned that the Justice Department had fired eight U.S. attorneys for allegedly political reasons. Congress investigated the allegations, and the testimony presented at congressional hearings confirmed that the allegations were probably true. Americans are at odds over whether such clearly political actions by the Justice Department are proper or even legal.

What Happened at the Justice Department Was Clearly Wrong

Of course, politics play a role in policy implementation in every administration. The Bush administration, though, went further than any previous presidential administration in politicizing the executive branch of government. Loyalty to Bush and his policies appeared to have been the only criterion for deciding who should be nominated to various posts in the administration. Even though the attorney general and the U.S. attorneys are ordinarily nominated based on their partisanship, once in office they are supposed to act as neutral dispensers of justice, not as a support team for the Republican Party.

The eight U.S. attorneys dismissed by the Justice Department were obviously fired for political reasons. In one instance, President Bush personally took action in response to a complaint about a U.S. attorney made by a senator from New Mexico. It was also claimed that an attorney was fired for pursuing corruption charges against a former Republican congressman and that another was fired for failing to bring voter fraud cases after a Republican candidate was narrowly defeated in the 2004 governor's race in the state of Washington. Indeed, a former aide to then attorney general Alberto Gonzales, Monica Goodling, admitted under oath that she investigated the party affiliations and even the campaign contributions of applicants for U.S. attorney and other nonpolitical jobs in the department.

THE JUSTICE DEPARTMENT IS STILL BUSINESS AS USUAL

Some commentators believe that there is nothing new about the supposed politicization of the Justice Department. U.S. attorneys are appointed by the president and confirmed by the Senate. Usually, only lawyers who share the president's party affiliation are considered, and it is customary for U.S. attorneys to submit their resignations when the opposition party wins the presidency. During presidential campaigns, candidates promise to pursue certain policies if they are elected. Once in office, a president owes it to the voters to carry out those policies. What better way to do so than to appoint party loyalists everywhere, including the Justice Department? When then attorney general Gonzales (he resigned in August 2007) fired the U.S. attorneys before their terms had expired, he was not doing anything illegal. Indeed, because of a provision added to the USA Patriot Act when it was reauthorized in 2006, the Justice Department had the ability to appoint new U.S. attorneys without Senate approval. Gonzales was just following the law at the time (since then that law has been changed).

Where do you stand?

1. Should the adage "To the victor belong the spoils" apply to the Justice Department after a party wins an election? Why or why not?
2. While all ninety-three U.S. attorneys were let go when Bill Clinton became president, there were no congressional investigations. In contrast, when Bush fired eight U.S. attorneys, Congress immediately began to investigate into the matter. Why do you think Congress reacted differently in these two situations?

Explore this issue online

- Wikipedia contains a surprising amount of up-to-date information on major controversies, including this one. See what Wikipedia had to say at **en.wikipedia.org/wiki/Dismissal_of U.S._attorneys_controversy** and at **en.wikipedia.org/wiki/Alberto_Gonzales**. Some conservatives claim that Wikipedia has an anti-conservative bias, and these articles are a good place to begin investigating whether that is so.

INTRODUCTION

As you read in this chapter's opening *America at Odds* feature, the possibility of having justice dispensed with a partisan bias has elicited a great deal of controversy. Also controversial is the policymaking function of the United States Supreme Court. After all, when the Court renders an opinion on how the Constitution is to be interpreted, it is, necessarily, making policy on a national level. To understand the nature of this controversy, you first need to understand how the **judiciary** (the courts) functions in this country. We begin by looking at the origins and sources of American law. We then examine the federal (national) court system, at the apex of which is the United States Supreme Court.

LO¹ THE ORIGINS AND SOURCES OF AMERICAN LAW

The American colonists brought with them the legal system that had developed in England over hundreds of years. Thus, to understand how the American legal system operates, we need to go back in time to the early English courts and the traditions they established.

The Common Law Tradition

After the Normans conquered England in 1066, William the Conqueror and his successors began the process of unifying the country under their rule. One of the

means they used to this end was the establishment of the "king's courts," or *curiae regis*. Before the Norman Conquest, disputes had been settled according to the local legal customs and traditions in various regions of the country. The law developed in the king's courts applied to the country as a whole. What evolved in these courts was the beginning of the **common law**—a body of general rules prescribing social conduct that was applied throughout the entire English realm.

THE RULE OF PRECEDENT The early English courts developed the common law rules from the principles underlying judges' decisions in actual legal controversies. Judges attempted to be consistent, and whenever possible, they based their decisions on the principles applied in earlier cases. They sought to decide similar cases in a similar way and considered new cases with care, because they knew that their decisions would make new law. Each interpretation became part of the law on the subject and served as a legal **precedent**—that is, a decision that furnished an example or authority for deciding subsequent cases involving similar legal principles or facts.

The practice of deciding new cases with reference to former decisions, or precedents, eventually became a cornerstone of the English and American judicial systems. The practice forms a doctrine called *stare decisis*¹ ("to stand on decided cases"). Under this doctrine, judges are obligated to follow the precedents established in their jurisdictions. For example, if the Supreme Court of Georgia holds that a state law requiring political candidates to pass drug tests is unconstitutional, that decision will control the outcome of future cases on that issue brought before the

U.S. attorneys (below) are appointed by the president with the advice and consent of the Senate. They serve under the direction of the attorney general.

AP Photo/Dennis Cook

judiciary The courts; one of the three branches of the federal government in the United States.

common law The body of law developed from judicial decisions in English and U.S. courts, not attributable to a legislature.

precedent A court decision that furnishes an example or authority for deciding subsequent cases involving identical or similar facts and legal issues.

stare decisis A common law doctrine under which judges normally are obligated to follow the precedents established by prior court decisions.

state courts in Georgia. Similarly, a decision on a given issue by the United States Supreme Court (the nation's highest court) is binding on all inferior (lower) courts. For example, if the Georgia case on drug testing is appealed to the United States Supreme Court and the Court agrees that the Georgia law is unconstitutional, the high court's ruling will be binding on *all* courts in the United States. In other words, similar drug-testing laws in other states would be invalid and unenforceable.

DEPARTURES FROM PRECEDENT Sometimes a court will depart from the rule of precedent if it decides that a precedent is simply incorrect or that technological or social changes have rendered the precedent inapplicable. Cases that overturn precedent often receive a great deal of publicity. For example, in 1954, in *Brown v. Board of Education of Topeka*,[2] the United States Supreme Court expressly overturned precedent when it concluded that separate educational facilities for African Americans, which had been upheld as constitutional in numerous prior cases under the "separate-but-equal" doctrine[3] (see Chapter 5), were inherently unequal and violated the equal protection clause. The Supreme Court's departure from precedent in *Brown* received a tremendous amount of publicity as people began to realize the political and social ramifications of this change in the law.

More recently, the Supreme Court departed from precedent when it held in a 2003 case, *Lawrence v. Texas*,[4] that a Texas sodomy law (see Chapter 5) violated the U.S. Constitution. In that case, the Court concluded that consensual sexual conduct, including homosexual conduct, was part of the liberty protected by the due process clause of the Constitution. This decision overturned the Court's established precedent on such laws— specifically, its ruling in *Bowers v. Hardwick*,[5] a 1986 case in which the Court upheld a Georgia sodomy statute.

Sources of American Law

In any governmental system, the primary function of the courts is to interpret and apply the law. In the United States, the courts interpret and apply

AP Photo

The 1954 landmark decision in *Brown v. Board of Education* declared racial segregation in public schools unconstitutional. For more than a decade afterward, billboards like the one in the photo were erected along many highways by the John Birch Society, protesting Chief Justice Earl Warren's support of civil rights.

numerous sources of law when deciding cases. We look here only at the **primary sources of law**—that is, sources that *establish* the law—and the relative priority of these sources when particular laws come into conflict.

CONSTITUTIONAL LAW The U.S. government and each of the fifty states have separate written constitutions that set forth the general organization, powers, and limits of their respective governments. **Constitutional law** consists of the rights and duties set forth in these constitutions.

The U.S. Constitution is the supreme law of the land. As such, it is the basis of all law in the United States. Any law that violates the Constitution is invalid and unenforceable. Because of its paramount importance in the American legal system, the complete text of the U.S. Constitution is found in Appendix B.

The Tenth Amendment to the U.S. Constitution reserves to the states and to the people all powers not granted to the federal government. Each state in the union has its own constitution. Unless they conflict with the U.S. Constitution or a federal law, state constitutions are supreme within the borders of their respective states.

STATUTORY LAW Statutes enacted by legislative bodies at any level of government make up another source of law, which is generally referred to as **statutory law.** Federal statutes—laws enacted by the U.S. Congress— apply to all of the states. State statutes—laws enacted by state legislatures—apply only within the state that enacted the law. Any state statute that conflicts with

---

primary source of law
A source of law that establishes the law. Primary sources of law include constitutions, statutes, administrative agency rules and regulations, and decisions rendered by the courts.

constitutional law Law based on the U.S. Constitution and the constitutions of the various states.

statutory law The body of law enacted by legislatures (as opposed to constitutional law, administrative law, or case law).

the U.S. Constitution, with federal laws enacted by Congress, or with the state's constitution will be deemed invalid, if challenged in court, and will not be enforced. Statutory law also includes the ordinances (such as local zoning or housing-construction laws) passed by cities and counties, none of which can violate the U.S. Constitution, the relevant state constitution, or any existing federal or state laws.

"IT IS BETTER, SO THE FOURTH AMENDMENT TEACHES, THAT THE GUILTY SOMETIMES GO FREE THAN THAT CITIZENS BE SUBJECT TO EASY ARREST."

WILLIAM O. DOUGLAS,
ASSOCIATE JUSTICE OF THE U.S. SUPREME COURT
1939-1975

ADMINISTRATIVE LAW Another important source of American law consists of **administrative law**—the rules, orders, and decisions of administrative agencies. As you read in Chapter 13, at the federal level, Congress creates executive agencies, such as the Food and Drug Administration and the Environmental Protection Agency, to perform specific functions. Typically, when Congress establishes an agency, it authorizes the agency to create rules that have the force of law and to enforce those rules by bringing legal actions against violators. Rules issued by various government agencies now affect virtually every aspect of our economy. For example, almost all of a business's operations, including the firm's capital structure and financing, its hiring and firing procedures, its relations with employees and unions, and the way it manufactures and markets its products, are subject to government regulation.

Government agencies exist at the state and local levels as well. States commonly create agencies that parallel federal agencies. Just as federal statutes take precedence over conflicting state statutes, federal agency regulations take precedence over conflicting state regulations.

CASE LAW As is evident from the discussion of the common law tradition, another basic source of American law consists of the rules of law announced in court decisions, or **case law.** These rules of law include interpretations of constitutional provisions, of statutes enacted by legislatures, and of regulations issued by administrative agencies. Thus, even though a legislature passes a law to govern a certain area, how that law is interpreted and applied depends on the courts. The importance of case law, or judge-made law, is one of the distinguishing characteristics of the common law tradition.

Civil Law and Criminal Law

All of the sources of law just discussed can be classified in other ways as well. One of the most significant classification systems divides all law into two categories: civil law and criminal law. **Civil law** spells out the duties that individuals in society owe to other persons or to their governments, excluding the duty not to commit crimes. Typically, in a civil case, a private party sues another private party (although the government can also sue a party for a civil law violation). The object of a civil lawsuit is to make the defendant—the person being sued—comply with a legal duty (such as a contractual promise) or pay money damages for failing to comply with that duty.

Criminal law, in contrast, has to do with wrongs committed against the public as a whole. Criminal acts are prohibited by local, state, or federal government statutes. Thus, criminal defendants are prosecuted by public officials, such as a district attorney (D.A.), on behalf of the government, not by their victims or other private parties. In a criminal case, the government seeks to impose a penalty (a fine and/or imprisonment) on a person who has violated a criminal law. When someone robs a convenience store, that person has committed a crime and, if caught and proved guilty, will normally be in prison for some period of time.

Basic Judicial Requirements

A court cannot decide just any issue at any time. Before any court can hear and decide a case, specific requirements must be met. To a certain extent, these

administrative law The body of law created by administrative agencies (in the form of rules, regulations, orders, and decisions) in order to carry out their duties and responsibilities.

case law The rules of law announced in court decisions. Case law includes the aggregate of reported cases that interpret judicial precedents, statutes, regulations, and constitutional provisions.

civil law The branch of law that spells out the duties that individuals in society owe to other persons or to their governments, excluding the duty not to commit crimes.

criminal law The branch of law that defines and governs actions that constitute crimes. Generally, criminal law has to do with wrongful actions committed against society for which society demands redress.

"**OUR CONSTITUTION IS**
COLORBLIND,
AND NEITHER KNOWS NOR
TOLERATES CLASSES
AMONG CITIZENS."

JOHN MARSHALL HARLAN,
ASSOCIATE JUSTICE OF THE U.S. SUPREME COURT
1877–1911

Most cases start in some type of trial court, where testimony is taken and other evidence evaluated. Trial courts exist in all fifty state court systems. In the federal court system, trial courts are called district courts.

John Neubauer/PhotoEdit

requirements act as restraints on the judiciary because they limit the types of cases that courts can hear and decide. Courts also have procedural requirements that frame the judicial process.

JURISDICTION   In Latin, *juris* means "law," and *diction* means "to speak." Therefore, **jurisdiction** literally refers to the power "to speak the law." Jurisdiction applies either to the geographic area in which a court has the right and power to decide cases, or to the right and power of a court to decide matters concerning certain persons, property, or subject matter. Before any court can hear a case, it must have jurisdiction over the person against whom the suit is brought, the property involved in the suit, and the subject matter.

A state trial court (a **trial court** is, as the term implies, a court in which a trial is held and testimony taken), for example, usually has jurisdictional authority over the residents of a particular area of the state, such as a county or district. A state's highest court (often called the state supreme court)[6] has jurisdictional authority over all residents within the state. In some cases, if an individual has committed an offense such as injuring someone in an automobile accident or selling defective goods within the state, the court can exercise jurisdiction even if the individual

is a resident of another state. State courts can also exercise jurisdiction over people who do business within the state. A New York company that distributes its products in California, for example, can be sued by a California resident in a California state court.

Because the federal (national) government is a government of limited powers, the jurisdiction of the federal courts is limited. Article III, Section 2, of the Constitution states that the federal courts can exercise jurisdiction over all cases "arising under this Constitution, the Laws of the United States, and Treaties made, or which shall be made, under their Authority." Whenever a case involves a claim based, at least in part, on the U.S. Constitution, a treaty, or a federal law, a federal question arises. Any lawsuit involving a **federal question** can originate in a federal court.

Federal courts can also exercise jurisdiction over cases involving **diversity of citizenship.** Such cases may arise when the parties in a lawsuit live in different states or when one of the parties is a foreign government or a foreign citizen. Before a federal court can take jurisdiction in a diversity case, the amount in controversy must be more than $75,000.

STANDING TO SUE   To bring a lawsuit before a court, a person must have **standing to sue,** or a sufficient "stake" in the matter to justify bringing a suit. Thus, the party bringing the suit must have suffered a harm or been threatened with a harm by the action at issue,

jurisdiction The authority of a court to hear and decide a particular case.

trial court A court in which trials are held and testimony taken.

federal question A question that pertains to the U.S. Constitution, acts of Congress, or treaties. A federal question provides a basis for federal court jurisdiction.

diversity of citizenship A basis for federal court jurisdiction over a lawsuit that arises when (1) the parties in the lawsuit live in different states or when one of the parties is a foreign government or a foreign citizen, and (2) the amount in controversy is more than $75,000.

and the issue must be justiciable. A **justiciable**[7] **controversy** is one that is real and substantial, as opposed to hypothetical or academic.

The requirement of standing clearly limits the issues that can be decided by the courts. For example, suppose that an environmental interest group sues a company for polluting a local stream in violation of federal law. Even if the company is, in fact, violating federal law, the group cannot sue the firm unless it can produce evidence that its members have actually been harmed, or are about to be harmed, by the polluting activity.

Federal laws often include provisions specifying when an individual or group will have standing to sue for violations of the law. Federal laws may also be enacted for the purpose of denying standing to sue in certain situations. For example, Valerie Plame's civil suit against Vice President Dick Cheney, former White House aide Lewis (Scooter) Libby, and other Bush administration officials, for allegedly leaking her identity as a Central Intelligence Agency agent to the press,[8] was dismissed by a federal court for lack of standing. The court noted that a federal law prohibits lawsuits against federal officials for actions taken in their official capacity.

Former CIA agent Valerie Plame's lawsuit against Vice President Dick Cheney and other Bush administration officials for leaking her identity as a secret agent to the media was dismissed for lack of standing to sue.

COURT PROCEDURES   Both the federal and the state courts have established procedural rules that apply in all cases. These procedures are designed to protect the rights and interests of the parties, ensure that the litigation proceeds in a fair and orderly manner, and identify the issues that must be decided by the court—thus saving court time and costs. Different procedural rules apply in criminal and civil cases. Generally, criminal procedural rules attempt to ensure that defendants are not deprived of their constitutional rights.

Parties involved in civil or criminal cases must comply with court procedural rules or risk being held in contempt of court. A party who is held in contempt of court can be fined, taken into custody, or both. A court must take care to ensure that the parties—and the court itself—comply with procedural requirements. Procedural errors often serve as grounds for a mistrial or for appealing the court's decision to a higher tribunal.

LO² THE FEDERAL COURT SYSTEM

The federal court system is a three-tiered model consisting of U.S. district courts (trial courts), U.S. courts of appeals, and the United States Supreme Court. Figure 14–1 on the next page shows the organization of the federal court system.

Bear in mind that the federal courts constitute only one of the fifty-two court systems in the United States. Each of the fifty states has its own court system, as does the District of Columbia. No two state court systems are exactly the same, but generally each state has different levels, or tiers, of courts, just as the federal system does. Generally, state courts deal with questions of state law, and the decisions of a state's highest court on matters of state law are normally final. If a federal question is involved, however, a decision of a state supreme court may be appealed to the United States Supreme Court.

We discuss the federal court system in the pages that follow. In addition, we will look at the role of the federal courts in the war on terrorism.

U.S. District Courts

On the lowest tier of the federal court system are the U.S. district courts, or federal trial courts. These are the courts in which cases involving federal laws begin, and the cases are decided by a judge or a jury (if it is a jury trial). There is at least one federal district court in every state, and there is one in the District of Columbia. The number of judicial districts varies over time, primarily owing to population changes and corresponding caseloads. Currently, there are ninety-four judicial districts; Figure 14–2 on page 321 shows their geographic boundaries. The federal

standing to sue The requirement that an individual must have a sufficient stake in a controversy before he or she can bring a lawsuit. The party bringing the suit must demonstrate that he or she has either been harmed or been threatened with a harm.

justiciable controversy A controversy that is not hypothetical or academic but real and substantial; a requirement that must be satisfied before a court will hear a case.

system also includes other trial courts, such as the Court of International Trade and others shown in Figure 14–1. These courts have limited, or specialized, subject-matter jurisdiction; that is, they can exercise authority only over certain subjects.

U.S. Courts of Appeals

On the middle tier of the federal court system are the U.S. courts of appeals. Courts of appeals, or **appellate courts,** do not hear evidence or testimony. Rather, an appellate court reviews the transcript of the trial court's proceedings, other records relating to the case, and the attorneys' respective arguments as to why the trial court's decision should or should not stand. In contrast to a trial court, where normally a single judge presides, an appellate court consists of a panel of three or more judges. The task of the appellate court is to determine whether the trial court erred in applying the law to the facts and issues involved in a particular case.

There are thirteen U.S. courts of appeals in the United States. The courts of appeals for twelve of the circuits, including the Court of Appeals for the D.C. Circuit, hear appeals from the U.S. district courts located within their respective judicial circuits (see Figure 14–2). Appeals from decisions made by federal administrative agencies, such as the Federal Trade Commission, may also be made to the U.S. courts of appeals. The Court of Appeals for the Federal Circuit has national jurisdiction over certain types of cases, such as those concerning patent law and some claims against the national government.

The decisions of the federal appellate courts may be appealed to the United States Supreme Court. If a decision is not appealed, or if the high court declines to review the case, the appellate court's decision is final.

The United States Supreme Court

The highest level of the three-tiered model of the federal court system is the United States Supreme Court. According to Article III of the U.S. Constitution, there is only one national Supreme Court. Congress is empowered to create additional ("inferior") courts as it deems necessary. The inferior courts that Congress has created include the second tier in our model—the U.S. courts of appeals—as well as the district courts and any other courts of limited, or specialized, jurisdiction.

The United States Supreme Court consists of nine justices—a chief justice and eight associate justices—although that number is not mandated by the Constitution. The Supreme Court has original, or trial, jurisdiction only in rare instances (set forth in Article III, Section 2). In other words, only rarely does a case originate at the Supreme Court level. Most of the Court's work is as an appellate court. The Supreme Court has appellate authority over cases decided by the U.S. courts of appeals, as well as over some cases decided in the state courts when federal questions are at issue.

THE WRIT OF CERTIORARI   To bring a case before the Supreme Court, a party may request that the Court issue a **writ of *certiorari*,**[9] popularly called "cert.," which is an order that the Supreme Court issues to a lower court requesting the latter to send it the record of the case in question. Parties can petition the Supreme Court to issue a writ of *certiorari,* but whether the Court will do so is entirely within its discretion. The Court will

appellate court A court having appellate jurisdiction that normally does not hear evidence or testimony but reviews the transcript of the trial court's proceedings, other records relating to the case, and the attorneys' respective arguments as to why the trial court's decision should or should not stand.

writ of *certiorari* An order from a higher court asking a lower court for the record of a case.

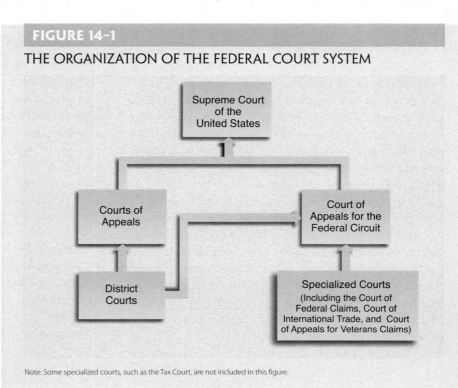

FIGURE 14-1

THE ORGANIZATION OF THE FEDERAL COURT SYSTEM

Supreme Court of the United States

Courts of Appeals

Court of Appeals for the Federal Circuit

District Courts

Specialized Courts (Including the Court of Federal Claims, Court of International Trade, and Court of Appeals for Veterans Claims)

Note: Some specialized courts, such as the Tax Court, are not included in this figure.

not issue a writ unless at least four of the nine justices approve. In no instance is the Court required to issue a writ of *certiorari*.[10]

Most petitions for writs of *certiorari* are denied. A denial is not a decision on the merits of a case, nor does it indicate that the Court agrees with a lower court's opinion. Furthermore, the denial of a writ has no value as a precedent. A denial simply means that the decision of the lower court remains the law within that court's jurisdiction.

WHICH CASES REACH THE SUPREME COURT?

There is no absolute right to appeal to the United States Supreme Court. Although thousands of cases are filed with the Supreme Court each year, on average the Court hears fewer than one hundred. As Figure 14–3 on the following page shows, the number of cases heard by the Court each year has declined significantly since the 1980s. In large part, this has occurred because the Court has raised its standards for accepting cases in recent years.

Typically, the Court grants petitions for cases that raise important policy issues that need to be addressed. In its most recent term, for example, the Court heard cases involving such pressing issues as:

- Whether local school districts' racial-integration policies violate the Constitution's equal protection clause.
- Whether a federal law banning partial-birth abortions should be upheld.
- Whether a state can pass a law that allows people the right to die by physician-assisted suicide.

If the lower courts have rendered conflicting opinions on an important issue, the Supreme Court may review a case involving that issue to define the law on the matter. For example, in 2002 the Court agreed to review two cases raising the issue of whether affirmative action programs (see Chapter 5) violate the equal protection clause of the Constitution. Different federal

FIGURE 14-2

U.S. COURTS OF APPEALS AND U.S. DISTRICT COURTS

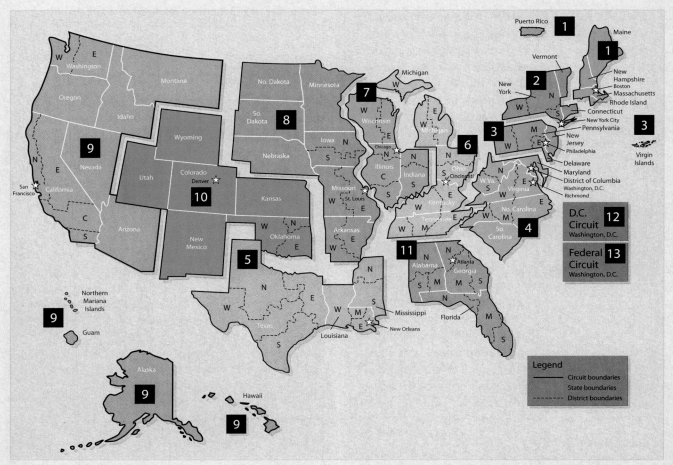

Source: Administrative Office of the United States Courts.

FIGURE 14-3

THE NUMBER OF SUPREME COURT OPINIONS

The number of Supreme Court opinions peaked at 151 in the 1982 term and more or less has been declining steadily ever since. During the 2006 term (ending in June 2007), the Court issued 75 opinions.

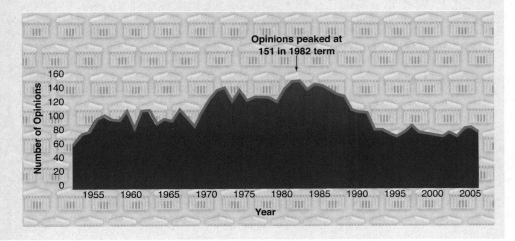

appellate courts had reached conflicting opinions on this issue.

SUPREME COURT OPINIONS Like all appellate courts, the United States Supreme Court normally does not hear any evidence. The Court's decision in a particular case is based on the written record of the case and the written arguments (legal briefs) that the attorneys submit. The attorneys also present **oral arguments**—arguments presented in person rather than on paper—to the Court, after which the justices discuss the case in **conference.** The conference is strictly private—only the justices are allowed in the room.

When the Court has reached a decision, the chief justice, if in the majority, assigns the task of writing the Court's **opinion** to one of the justices. When the chief justice is not in the majority, the most senior justice voting with the majority assigns the writing of the Court's opinion. The

oral argument An argument presented to a judge in person by an attorney on behalf of her or his client.

conference In regard to the Supreme Court, a private meeting of the justices in which they present their arguments with respect to a case under consideration.

opinion A written statement by a court expressing the reasons for its decision in a case.

concurring opinion A statement written by a judge or justice who agrees (concurs) with the court's decision, but for reasons different from those in the majority opinion.

dissenting opinion A statement written by a judge or justice who disagrees with the majority opinion.

opinion outlines the reasons for the Court's decision, the rules of law that apply, and the judgment.

Often, one or more justices who agree with the Court's decision may do so for different reasons than those outlined in the majority opinion. These justices may write **concurring opinions,** setting forth their own legal reasoning on the issue. Frequently, one or more justices disagree with the Court's conclusion. These justices may write **dissenting opinions,** outlining the reasons they feel the majority erred in arriving at its decision. Although a dissenting opinion does not affect the outcome of the case before the Court, it may be important later. In a subsequent case concerning the same issue, a jurist or attorney may use the legal reasoning in the dissenting opinion as the basis for an argument to reverse the previous decision and establish a new precedent.

The Courts and the War on Terrorism

After the beginning of the Bush administration's so-called war on terrorism, the administration held hundreds of suspected terrorists at the U.S. Naval Base at

The United States Supreme Court chamber. In 1935, the Court moved from its quarters in the Capitol building to its own building, constructed with white Vermont marble.

Guantánamo Bay, Cuba. Many of those detained in the Guantánamo prison were foreign fighters captured during the war in Afghanistan, which was waged shortly after the September 11, 2001, terrorist attacks. Other suspected terrorists were also sent to the prison. The prisoners, designated as *enemy combatants,* were not allowed to exercise any of the rights available to American citizens or even to prisoners of war under international law.

From the outset, the Bush administration and the federal courts engaged in a legal tug-of-war over the rights of these prisoners. In 2004, the United States Supreme Court held that the Bush administration's treatment of the detainees at Guantánamo violated the U.S. Constitution.[11] The Republican-led 109th Congress then passed legislation in an attempt to overcome the Court's objections. The legislation called for the establishment of special military tribunals to hear the prisoners' cases. In 2006, the Supreme Court held that the tribunals did not meet the requirements of due process, including the right to *habeas corpus*.[12] As you will read shortly, the right to *habeas corpus* (Latin for "you have the body") enables a person being detained by the government to question the legality of the detention before a court. In response to the Court's 2006 decision, Congress passed (and President Bush signed) the Military Commissions Act (MCA) of 2006.

"As nightfall does not come at once, neither does **oppression.** In both instances, . . . we must be aware of change in the air, however slight, lest we become unwitting victims of the darkness."

WILLIAM O. DOUGLAS,
ASSOCIATE JUSTICE OF THE U.S. SUPREME COURT
1939–1975

Many civil liberties organizations were vehemently opposed to this legislation. For example, the American Civil Liberties Union's executive director Anthony Romero said, "With his signature, President Bush enacts a law that is both unconstitutional and un-American. This president will be remembered as the one who undercut the hallmark of *habeas corpus* in the name of the war on terror. Nothing separates America more from our enemies than our commitment to fairness and the rule of law, but the bill signed today is an historic break because it turns Guantánamo Bay and other U.S. facilities into legal no-man's lands."

The MCA established special military commissions that would hear prisoners' *habeas corpus* challenges. Only after a military commission had rendered its decision could a prisoner appeal the case to a federal court. When the MCA was challenged as unconstitutional, a federal appellate court ruled in favor of the Bush administration.[13] The Supreme Court refused to hear that case, meaning that the appellate court's decision was allowed to stand. A short time later, however, the Court agreed to review, during its 2007–2008 term, another case involving the rights of prisoners at Guantánamo.

Senator Patrick Leahy (D., Vt.) holds up a copy of the U.S. Constitution during a U.S. Senate Judiciary Committee oversight hearing on the Justice Department, on Capitol Hill in 2002. The committee questioned then attorney general John Ashcroft on possible loss of citizens' privacy in the fight against terrorism.

Reuters/Hyungwon Kang

JOIN THE DEBATE

Is the Right to *Habeas Corpus* All That Important?

The right to *habeas corpus* dates back to medieval England. This right can be traced to the Magna Carta, or "Great Charter" of 1215. Later, the English Parliament passed the *Habeas Corpus* Act of 1679. When the U.S. Constitution was drafted, the framers, in Article I, Section 9, included the following words: "The Privilege of the Writ of Habeas Corpus shall not be suspended, unless when in Cases of Rebellion or Invasion the public Safety may require it." The suspension of the right to *habeas corpus* for the hundreds of detainees in Guantánamo Bay Naval Base in Cuba created much controversy.

Some Americans are not concerned about the supposed lack of the right to *habeas corpus* for the enemy combatants detained at Guantánamo. After all, the Military Commissions Act of 2006 gives them an opportunity to contest their status before a Combatant Status Review Tribunal. If they do not like the tribunal's conclusions, then they can exercise their right to *habeas corpus* and contest the legality of their detention before a federal court. Our government has not acted arbitrarily and capriciously. U.S. officials are holding enemy combatants in Guantánamo because they were fighting against the United States during the war in Afghanistan or were otherwise detained as persons with suspected links to terrorism. These individuals typically have

Guantánamo Bay detainees were handcuffed and blindfolded when they first arrived at the military base in Cuba.

AP Photo/Shane T. McCoy/U.S. Navy

"Freedom of the person under the protection of *habeas corpus* [is] one of the essential principles of our government."

THOMAS JEFFERSON,
THIRD PRESIDENT OF THE UNITED STATES
1801–1809

vowed to destroy the United States. None of us wants another September 11; our government is doing all that it can to prevent another catastrophe. If that means that one of our civil liberties—*habeas corpus*—is suspended for a few individuals, that is a sacrifice worth making.

Other Americans are aghast at what has happened to the detainees at Guantánamo. The right to *habeas corpus* underlies all of our civil liberties. None of the rights set forth in the Bill of Rights would have any value if someone could be thrown into prison without recourse to a court. That is essentially what has happened to the so-called enemy combatants. They have access to a court only *after* the Combatant Status Review Tribunal has reviewed their status, and that could take years. And some prisoners at Guantánamo are finding it difficult, if not impossible, to obtain a review by the tribunal. Thus, the detainees have virtually no right to *habeas corpus*. Although *habeas corpus* was suspended during the Civil War, that was an entirely different situation. We are not technically at war now, and there is no rebellion or invasion.

LO³ FEDERAL JUDICIAL APPOINTMENTS

Unlike state court judges, who are often elected, all federal judges are appointed. Article II, Section 2, of the Constitution authorizes the president to appoint the justices of the Supreme Court with the advice and consent of the Senate. Laws enacted by Congress provide that the same procedure is to be used for appointing judges to the lower federal courts as well.

Federal judges receive lifetime appointments (because under Article III of the Constitution they "hold their Offices during good Behaviour"). Federal judges may be removed from office through the impeachment process, but such proceedings are extremely rare and are usually undertaken only if a judge engages in blatantly illegal conduct, such as bribery. In the history of this nation, only thirteen federal judges have been impeached, seven of whom were removed from office. Normally, federal judges serve until they resign, retire, or die.

Although the Constitution sets no specific qualifications for those who serve on the Supreme Court, all who have done so share one characteristic: all have been attorneys. The backgrounds of the Supreme Court justices have been far from typical of the characteristics of the American public as a whole. Table 14–1 summarizes the backgrounds of all of the 110 United States Supreme Court justices to 2008.

The Nomination Process

The president receives suggestions and recommendations as to potential nominees for Supreme Court positions from various sources, including the Justice Department, senators, other judges, the candidates themselves, state political leaders, bar associations, and other interest groups. After selecting a nominee, the president submits her or his name to the Senate for approval. The Senate Judiciary Committee then holds hearings and makes its recommendation to the Senate, where it takes a majority vote to confirm the nomination.

When judges are nominated to the district courts (and, to a lesser extent, the U.S. courts of appeals), a senator of the president's political party from the state where there is a vacancy traditionally has been allowed to veto the president's choice. This practice is known as **senatorial courtesy.** At one time, senatorial courtesy sometimes even permitted senators from the opposing party to veto presidential choices. Because of senatorial courtesy, home-state senators of the president's party may also be able to influence the choice of the nominee.

It should come as no surprise that partisanship plays a significant role in the president's selection of nominees to the federal bench, particularly to the Supreme Court, the crown jewel of the federal judiciary. Traditionally, presidents have attempted to strengthen their legacies by appointing federal judges with similar political and philosophical views. (For a further discussion of judicial appointments and presidential legacies, see this chapter's *Perception versus Reality* feature on the next page.) In the history of the Supreme Court, fewer than 13 percent of

the justices nominated by a president have been from an opposing political party.

Appointments to the U.S. courts of appeals can also have a lasting impact. Recall that these

TABLE 14–1

BACKGROUNDS OF UNITED STATES SUPREME COURT JUSTICES TO 2008

	Number of Justices (110 = Total)
Occupational Position before Appointment	
Private legal practice	25
State judgeship	21
Federal judgeship	30
U.S. attorney general	7
Deputy or assistant U.S. attorney general	2
U.S. solicitor general	2
U.S. senator	6
U.S. representative	2
State governor	3
Federal executive post	9
Other	3
Religious Affiliation	
Protestant	83
Roman Catholic	13
Jewish	6
Unitarian	7
No religious affiliation	1
Age on Appointment	
Under 40	5
41–50	32
51–60	59
61–70	14
Political Party Affiliation	
Federalist (to 1835)	13
Jeffersonian Republican (to 1828)	7
Whig (to 1861)	1
Democrat	44
Republican	44
Independent	1
Education	
College graduate	94
Not a college graduate	16
Gender	
Male	108
Female	2
Race	
Caucasian	108
African American	2

Sources: *Congressional Quarterly, Congressional Quarterly's Guide to the U.S. Supreme Court* (Washington, D.C.: Congressional Quarterly Press, 1997); and authors' update.

senatorial courtesy
A practice that allows a senator of the president's party to veto the president's nominee to a federal court judgeship within the senator's state.

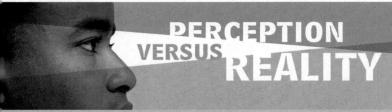

PERCEPTION VERSUS REALITY

Judicial Appointments and Presidential Legacies

It is not unusual for a U.S. president to want to create a legacy—a long-lasting imprint on American politics. In principle, a sitting president can make a mark on the future by appointing (always with the consent of the Senate) federal court judges who share the president's political philosophy. Every year, there are numerous vacancies within the federal judiciary, and occasionally a vacancy occurs on the United States Supreme Court.

The Perception

It is commonly perceived that a president will naturally nominate federal judges who share the president's political and philosophical views. Certainly, this was a widely held assumption when Bill Clinton became president in 1992. Prior to his election, Clinton campaigned in favor of what are generally considered liberal causes—abortion rights, gay rights, and more aggressive enforcement of environmental laws. He also promised to appoint more minorities and women to federal court benches. Consequently, the public's initial perception of Clinton was that he was going to appoint liberal-leaning individuals to the federal judiciary.

The Reality

In reality, presidential appointments do not always fulfill the expectations of the president's party. Certainly, this was true with respect to Clinton's appointments. To be sure, during his first years in office, Clinton appointed

AP Photo/Charles Dharapak

more women and minorities to the federal bench than his predecessors had. Nonetheless, Clinton spurned activists and ideologues in his court appointments, choosing instead cautious moderates, such as respected state jurists and partners in large law firms. Prospective nominees were never asked their views on abortion, and even some pro-lifers were appointed. His Supreme Court nominees—Ruth Bader Ginsburg and Stephen Breyer—were clear moderates who were easily confirmed. Indeed, the moderation and compromise that marked the Clinton administration's judicial appointments caused some Democrats to view the Clinton years as a lost opportunity to pursue a liberal policy agenda.

Keep in mind that often an important consideration in nominating a particular judicial candidate to a federal court bench is whether the candidate is likely to be confirmed by the Senate. Although the Democrats controlled the Senate, Clinton demonstrated an interest in avoiding confirmation battles by choosing nominees who were less liberal than some he could have named. President George W. Bush, however, seemed less concerned with Senate confirmation politics and appointed strong conservatives to the Supreme Court. Because of his appointments of Chief Justice John Roberts , Jr., and Associate Justice Samuel Alito, Jr., Bush's presidency will no doubt leave a lasting imprint on the ideological position of the Supreme Court. Many Court watchers have commented that a rightward shift of the Court has already become evident.

Justice Samuel Alito, Jr.

BLOG ON

Few better perches exist from which to view the workings of the nation's highest court than SCOTUSblog, the United States Supreme Court's blog, at **www.scotusblog.com**. Sponsored by the law firm of Akin, Gump, Strauss, Hauer, and Feld, SCOTUSblog provides expert commentary that will let you decide whether President George W. Bush left a conservative legacy by appointing Justice Samuel Alito, Jr., to replace retired Justice Sandra Day O'Connor.

courts occupy the level just below the Supreme Court in the federal court system. Also recall that the decisions rendered by these courts—about 60,000 per year—are final unless overturned by the Supreme Court. Given that the Supreme Court renders opinions in fewer than one hundred cases a year, the decisions of the federal appellate courts have a wide-reaching impact on American society. For example, a decision interpreting the federal Constitution by the U.S. Court of Appeals

for the Ninth Circuit, if not overruled by the Supreme Court, establishes a precedent that will be followed in the states of Alaska, Arizona, California, Hawaii, Idaho, Montana, Nevada, Oregon, and Washington.

Confirmation or Rejection by the Senate

The president's nominations are not always confirmed. In fact, almost 20 percent of presidential nominations for the Supreme Court have been either rejected or not acted on by the Senate. The process of nominating and confirming federal judges, especially Supreme Court justices, often involves political debate and controversy. Many bitter battles over Supreme Court appointments have ensued when the Senate and the president have disagreed on political issues.

From 1893 until 1968, the Senate rejected only three Court nominees. From 1968 through 1986, however, two presidential nominees to the highest court were rejected, and two more nominations, both by President Ronald Reagan, failed in 1987. First, the Senate rejected Robert Bork, who faced sometimes hostile questioning about his views on the Constitution during the confirmation hearings. Next, Reagan nominated Douglas Ginsburg, who ultimately withdrew his nomination when the press leaked information about his alleged use of marijuana during the 1970s. Finally, the Senate approved Reagan's third choice, Anthony Kennedy. Although both of President George H. W. Bush's nominees to the Supreme Court— David Souter and Clarence Thomas—were confirmed by the Senate, Thomas's nomination aroused considerable controversy. Thomas's confirmation hearings were extremely volatile and received widespread publicity on national television. The nation watched as Anita Hill, a former aide, leveled charges of sexual harassment at Thomas.

In 1993, President Bill Clinton had little trouble gaining approval for his nominee to fill the seat left vacant by Justice Byron White. Ruth Bader Ginsburg became the second female Supreme Court justice, the first being Sandra Day O'Connor, who was appointed by President Reagan in 1981. When Justice Harry Blackmun retired in 1994, Clinton nominated Stephen Breyer to fill Blackmun's seat. Breyer was confirmed without significant opposition.

Judicial Appointments and the Bush Administration

Prior to both the 2000 and 2004 presidential elections, there was much conjecture about how the election outcomes might affect the federal judiciary—particularly, the makeup of the United States Supreme Court. No justice retired from the Supreme Court during George W. Bush's first term as president. During his second term, however, the death of Chief Justice William Rehnquist and the retirement of Justice Sandra Day O'Connor allowed Bush

The Senate has the ultimate say over who becomes a justice of the United States Supreme Court. Here, Ruth Bader Ginsburg faces questioning by members of the Senate Judiciary Committee. On August 10, 1993, she became the 107th justice of the Supreme Court—and one of only two women ever to be appointed to that tribunal.

to appoint two new justices to the Court. Bush nominated John G. Roberts, Jr., as chief justice to replace Chief Justice Rehnquist; and Samuel A. Alito, Jr., as associate justice to replace Justice O'Connor. Both nominees were confirmed by the Senate with relatively little difficulty.

As president, Bush also filled numerous vacancies on the lower courts, including vacancies on the benches of the U.S. courts of appeals. By mid-2007, Republican appointees made up about 60 percent of the federal judiciary.

JOIN THE DEBATE

Does Partisan Ideology Matter in Supreme Court Appointments?

During President Bush's first term, he had no chance to appoint any new justices to the United States Supreme Court. During his second term, however, he appointed not only a new chief justice, John Roberts, Jr., but also a new associate justice, Samuel Alito, Jr. Many believe that the obvious conservative leanings of these two latest Supreme Court appointments will matter in both

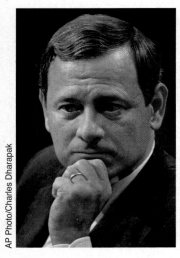

Chief Justice John Roberts.

the short and the long run. Others are not so sure.

The previous Rehnquist Court was already considered conservative, but its decisions were not necessarily consistent. Now consider that during the Roberts Court's first term (2005–2006), Roberts usually voted with the Court's most conservative justices, Clarence Thomas and Antonin Scalia. Roberts, for example, joined Scalia's opinion for the Court holding that evidence could be used in court in a criminal case even if the evidence had been obtained after the police forcibly entered a home without first knocking on the door and announcing their presence (that is, without following the previously established "knock and announce rule"). During its second term (2006–2007), the Roberts Court continued to issue conservative rulings. For example, Roberts voted with Kennedy, Scalia, Thomas, and Alito to uphold the 2003 federal law banning partial-birth abortion. Clearly, partisan ideology does matter when it comes to Supreme Court appointments.

Not everyone believes that the partisan views of Supreme Court appointees are that important. After all, presidents may nominate Supreme Court justices, but the Senate has to approve them. Moreover, in the past, some seemingly conservative nominees have not turned out to be conservative justices once on the bench. A good example is David Souter, who was appointed to the Court by Republican President George H. W. Bush (1989–1993). Bush thought that Souter would take a conservative approach when analyzing cases before the Court. In fact, Souter has become a leading counterforce to the Court's conservatives.

Justice David Souter.

Future Justice Sandra Day O'Connor swearing-in at her Senate confirmation hearings in 1981. Sandra Day O'Connor became the first woman to serve as a United States Supreme Court justice.

Consider also Sandra Day O'Connor, the first female justice, who was considered a conservative when she was appointed but gradually became less conservative as a justice. She became a pragmatic voice on the high court bench, even joining forces with the liberals on the Court on a number of issues, including abortion. Thus, the degree to which partisan ideology matters in Supreme Court appointments is greatly overrated.

LO⁴ THE COURTS AS POLICYMAKERS

In a common law system, such as that of the United States, judges and justices play a major role in government. In part, this is because of the doctrine of *stare decisis*, which theoretically obligates judges to follow precedents. Additionally, unlike judges in some other countries, U.S. judges have the power to decide on the constitutionality of laws or actions undertaken by the other branches of government.

Clearly, the function of the courts is to interpret and apply the law, not to make law—that is the function of the legislative branch of government. Yet judges can and do "make law"; indeed, they cannot avoid making law in some cases because the law does not always provide clear answers to questions that come before the courts. The text of the U.S. Constitution, for example, is set forth in broad terms. When a court interprets a constitutional provision and applies that interpretation to a specific set of circumstances, the court is essentially "making the law" on that issue. Examples of how the courts, and especially the United States Supreme Court, make law abound. Consider privacy rights, which we discussed in Chapter 4. Nothing in the Constitution or its amendments specifically states that we have a right to privacy. Yet the Supreme Court, through various decisions, has established such a right by deciding that it is implied by several constitutional amendments. The Court has also held that this right to privacy includes a number of specific rights, such as the right to have an abortion.

Statutory provisions and other legal rules also tend to be expressed in general terms, and the courts must decide how those general provisions and rules apply to specific cases. Consider the Americans with Disabilities Act of 1990. The act requires employers to reasonably accommodate the needs of employees with disabilities. But the act does not say exactly what employers must do to "reasonably accommodate" such persons. Thus, the courts must decide, on a case-by-case basis, what this phrase means. Additionally, in some cases there is no relevant law or precedent to follow. In recent years, for example, courts have been struggling with new kinds of legal issues stemming from new communications technology, including the Internet. Until legislative bodies enact laws governing these issues, it is up to the courts to fashion the law that will apply—and thus make policy.

The Impact of Court Decisions

As already mentioned, how the courts interpret particular laws can have a widespread impact on society. For example, in 1996, in *Hopwood v. Texas*,[14] the U.S. Court of Appeals for the Fifth Circuit held that an affirmative action program implemented by the University of Texas School of Law in Austin was unconstitutional. The program allowed admissions officials to take race and other factors into consideration when determining which students would be admitted. The court stated that the program violated the equal protection clause because it discriminated in favor of minority applicants. The court further held that the use of race even as a means to achieve diversity on college campuses violated the Constitution's equal protection mandate. The court's decision in *Hopwood* set a precedent for all federal courts within the Fifth Circuit's jurisdiction (which covers Louisiana, Mississippi, and Texas). Thus, whenever similar affirmative action programs in those states were challenged, the federal courts hearing the cases had to apply the law as interpreted by the Court of Appeals for the Fifth Circuit.

Decisions rendered by the United States Supreme Court, of course, have an even broader impact on American society, because all courts in the nation are obligated to follow precedents set by the high court. For example, in 2003 the Supreme Court issued a ruling on affirmative action programs at the University of Michigan. Unlike the appeals court in the *Hopwood* case, the Supreme Court held that diversity on college campuses is a legitimate goal and that affirmative action programs that take race into consideration as part of an examination of each applicant's background do not necessarily violate the equal protection clause of the Constitution. This decision rendered any contrary ruling, including the ruling by the court in the *Hopwood* case, invalid.[15]

Thus, when the Supreme Court interprets laws, it establishes national policy. If the Court deems that a law passed by Congress or a state legislature violates the Constitution, for example, that law will be void and unenforceable in any court within the United States.

These University of Michigan students show their support for their campus's affirmative action program. The United States Supreme Court has ruled that diversity on college campuses is a legitimate goal and that limited affirmative action programs can be used to achieve this goal.

AP Photo/John F. Martin

Judicial Review in Other Nations

The concept of judicial review was pioneered by the United States. Some maintain that one of the reasons the doctrine was readily accepted in this country was that it fit well with the checks and balances designed by the founders. Today, all established constitutional democracies have some form of judicial review—the power to rule on the constitutionality of laws—but its form varies from country to country.

For example, Canada's Supreme Court can exercise judicial review but is barred from doing so if a law includes a provision explicitly prohibiting such review. In France, the Constitutional Council rules on the constitutionality of laws *before* the laws take effect. Laws can be referred to the council for *prior* review by the president, the prime minister, and the heads of the two chambers of parliament. Prior review is also an option in Germany and Italy, if requested by the national or a regional government. In contrast, the United States Supreme Court does not give advisory opinions; the Supreme Court will render a decision only when there is an actual dispute concerning an issue.

For Critical Analysis

Why do you think that the United States Supreme Court never gives advisory opinions?

The Power of Judicial Review

Recall from Chapter 2 that the U.S. Constitution divides government powers among the executive, legislative, and judicial branches. This division of powers is part of our checks and balances system. Essentially, the founders gave each branch of government the constitutional authority to check the other two branches. The federal judiciary can exercise a check on the actions of either of the other branches through its power of **judicial review.**

The Constitution does not actually mention judicial review. Rather, the Supreme Court claimed the power for itself in *Marbury v. Madison*.[16] In that case, which was decided by the Court in 1803, Chief Justice John Marshall held that a provision of a 1789 law affecting the Supreme Court's jurisdiction violated the Constitution and was thus void. Marshall declared, "It is emphatically the province and duty of the judicial department [the courts] to say what the law is. . . . If two laws conflict with each other, the courts must decide on the operation of each. . . . So if a law be in opposition to the constitution . . . the court must determine which of these conflicting rules governs the case. This is the very essence of judicial duty."

Although the Constitution did not explicitly provide for judicial review, most constitutional scholars believe that the framers intended that the federal courts should have this power. In *Federalist Paper* No. 78, Alexander Hamilton clearly espoused the doctrine of judicial review. Hamilton stressed the importance of the "complete independence" of federal judges and their special duty to "invalidate all acts contrary to the manifest tenor of the Constitution." Without judicial review by impartial courts, there would be nothing to ensure that the other branches of government stayed within constitutional limits when exercising their powers, and "all the reservations of particular rights or privileges would amount to nothing." Chief Justice Marshall shared Hamilton's views and adopted Hamilton's reasoning in *Marbury v. Madison*. (For a discussion of judicial review in other nations, see this chapter's *The Rest of the World* feature.)

Judicial Activism versus Judicial Restraint

As already noted, making policy is not the primary function of the federal courts. Yet it is unavoidable that courts do, in fact, influence or even establish policy when they interpret and apply the law. Further, the power of judicial review gives the courts, and particularly the Supreme Court, an important policymaking tool. When the Supreme Court upholds or invalidates a state or federal statute, the consequences for the nation can be profound.

judicial review The power of the courts to decide on the constitutionality of legislative enactments and of actions taken by the executive branch.

One issue that is often debated is how the federal courts should wield their policymaking power, particularly the power of judicial review. Often, this debate is couched in terms of judicial activism versus judicial restraint.

ACTIVIST VERSUS RESTRAINTIST JUSTICES Although the terms *judicial activism* and *judicial restraint* do not have precise meanings, generally an activist judge or justice believes that the courts should actively use their powers to check the actions of the legislative and executive branches to ensure that they do not exceed their authority. A restraintist judge or justice, in contrast, generally assumes that the courts should defer to the decisions of the legislative and executive branches, because members of Congress and the president are elected by the people whereas federal court judges are not. In other words, the courts should not thwart the implementation of legislative acts unless they are clearly unconstitutional.

POLITICAL IDEOLOGY AND JUDICIAL ACTIVISM/ RESTRAINT One of the Supreme Court's most activist eras occurred during the period from 1953 to 1969 under the leadership of Chief Justice Earl Warren. The Warren Court propelled the civil rights movement

Chief Justice Earl Warren (1897-1974) presided over the United States Supreme Court from 1953 to 1969. The Warren Court played a significant role in furthering the civil rights of African Americans and other minorities.

Library of Congress

"EVERYTHING I DID IN MY LIFE THAT WAS WORTHWHILE I CAUGHT HELL FOR."
EARL WARREN, CHIEF JUSTICE OF THE U.S. SUPREME COURT 1953-1969

forward by holding, among other things, that laws permitting racial segregation violated the equal protection clause (see Chapter 5).

Because of the activism of the Warren Court, the term *judicial activism* has often been linked with liberalism. Indeed, many liberals are in favor of an activist federal judiciary because they believe that the judiciary can "right" the "wrongs" that result from unfair laws or from "antiquated" legislation at the state and local levels. Neither judicial activism nor judicial restraint is necessarily linked to a particular political ideology, however. In fact, many observers now claim that the Supreme Court is actively pursuing a conservative agenda.

LO⁵ IDEOLOGY AND THE COURTS

The policymaking role of the courts gives rise to an important question: To what extent do ideology and personal policy preferences affect judicial decision making? Numerous scholars have attempted to answer this question, especially with respect to Supreme Court justices.

Ideology and Supreme Court Decisions

In one study, conducted while William Rehnquist headed the Supreme Court, judicial scholars Jeffrey Segal and Harold Spaeth concluded that "the Supreme Court decides disputes in light of the facts of the case vis-à-vis the ideological attitudes and values of the justices. Simply put, Rehnquist votes the way he does because he is extremely conservative."[17] The authors maintained that Supreme Court justices base their decisions on policy preferences simply because they are free to do so—they are not accountable to the electorate because they are not elected to their positions. The desire to attain higher office is also not a factor in the Court's decision making

The Roberts Court is shown here as of late 2007. The majority of the Court is considered to be politically conservative, and indeed, the Court's more recent decisions seem to reflect this conservatism.

because the justices are at the apex of the judicial career ladder.

Few doubt that ideology affects judicial decision making, although, of course, other factors play a role as well. Different courts (such as a trial court and an appellate court) can look at the same case and draw different conclusions as to what law is applicable and how it should be applied. Certainly, there are numerous examples of ideology affecting Supreme Court decisions. As new justices replace old ones and new ideological alignments are formed, the Court's decisions are affected. Yet many scholars argue that there is no real evidence indicating that personal preferences influence Supreme Court decisions to an *unacceptable* extent.

Keep in mind that judicial decision making, particularly at the Supreme Court level, can be very complex. When deciding cases, the Supreme Court often must consider any number of sources, including constitutions, statutes, and administrative agency regulations—as well as cases interpreting relevant portions of those sources. At times, the Court may also take demographic data, public opinion, foreign laws, and other factors into account when deciding an issue. How much weight is given to each of these sources or factors will vary from justice to justice. After all, reasoning of any kind, including judicial reasoning, does not take place in a vacuum. It is only natural that a justice's life experiences, personal biases, and intellectual abilities and predispositions will touch on the reasoning process.

Nevertheless, when reviewing a case, a Supreme Court justice does not start out with a conclusion (such as "I don't like this particular law that Congress passed") and then look for legal sources to support that conclusion.

In contrast to the liberal Supreme Court under Earl Warren (1953–1969) and to a lesser extent under Warren Burger (1969–1986), today's Court is generally conservative. The Court began its rightward shift after President Ronald Reagan (1981–1989) appointed conservative William Rehnquist as chief justice in 1986, and the Court moved further to the right as other conservative appointments to the bench were made by Reagan and George H. W. Bush (1989–1993).

The Supreme Court justices pose with President Ronald Reagan (sitting fourth from left) in 1981. The only justice from that era still on the Court today is Justice John Paul Stevens (standing in the back row, on the far left).

Ideology and the Roberts Court

Many Supreme Court scholars believe that the appointments of John Roberts (as chief justice) and Samuel Alito (as associate justice) have caused the Court to drift even further to the right.[18] Certainly, the five conservative justices now on the bench voted together and cast the deciding votes in numerous cases during the Roberts Court's first two terms.[19] The remaining justices hold liberal-to-moderate views and often form an opposing bloc.

A notable change in the Court occurred when Alito replaced retiring justice Sandra Day O'Connor. O'Connor had often been the "swing" vote on the Court, sometimes voting with the liberal bloc and at other times siding with the conservatives. Although O'Connor was a conservative, she was also a pragmatist—and her decisions often were determined by practical considerations. On the Roberts Court, to the extent that there is a swing voter, it is Justice Anthony Kennedy, who is generally more conservative in his views than O'Connor was. In many significant rulings of the Court's 2005 and 2006 terms, Kennedy voted with the conservative right.

Certainly, today's Court is strongly divided ideologically. In the Court term ending in June 2007, one-third of the decisions rendered by the Court were reached by five-to-four votes—the highest portion of such votes in more than a decade. Some commentators have noted also that the ideological division on the Court has widened—that is, the distance between the views of the liberal-to-moderate justices and those on the Court's right is greater than it has been in the past.

Approaches to Legal Interpretation

It would be a mistake to look at the judicial philosophy of today's Supreme Court solely in terms of the political ideologies of liberalism and conservatism, however. In fact, some Supreme Court scholars have suggested that other factors are as important as, or even more important than, the justices' political philosophies in determining why they decide as they do. These

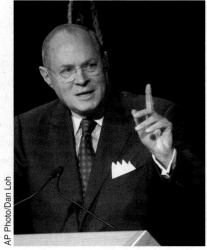

Justice Anthony Kennedy has often held the "swing" vote in the closely divided Roberts Court.

Justice John Paul Stevens is now the most senior member of the Court and is a voice of moderation in the increasingly conservative court.

factors include the justices' attitudes toward legal interpretation and their perceptions of the Supreme Court's role in the federal judiciary.

STRICT VERSUS BROAD CONSTRUCTION Legal scholars have often used the terms *strict* and *broad* construction to describe how judges and justices interpret the law. Generally, strict constructionists look to the letter of the law as written when trying to decipher its meaning, whereas broad constructionists look more to the purpose and context of the law. Strict constructionists believe that the letter of the law should guide the courts' decisions. Broad constructionists believe that the law is an evolving set of standards and is not fixed in concrete. Generally, broad constructionists are more willing to "read between the lines" of a law to serve what they perceive to be the law's intent and purpose.

Strict construction of the law is often linked with conservative views, and broad construction with liberal views. The conservative justices on today's Supreme Court are often labeled strict constructionists because they give great weight to the text of the law.

THE ROLE OF THE SUPREME COURT How justices view the role of the Supreme Court in the federal judiciary also affects their decision making. Two of the Court's justices—Antonin Scalia and Stephen Breyer—have made public their different visions of the Court's role. For Justice Scalia, a conservative voice on the Court, the Court should establish clear rules for the lower courts to follow when they apply the law. For Justice Breyer, who holds moderate-to-liberal views, the Court's role should be to establish flexible standards for the lower courts to apply on a case-by-case basis. This rules-versus-standards debate is reflected in the justices' opinions.

In one case, for example, Breyer, who wrote the majority opinion, concluded that a seniority system in the workplace should "ordinarily" take priority over a disabled worker's right to "reasonable accommodation" under

AP Photo/Lawrence Jackson

AP Photo/Mark Duncan

Justice Stephen Breyer.   *Justice Antonin Scalia.*

the Americans with Disabilities Act (ADA) of 1990—see Chapter 5. Yet, stated Breyer, there might be special circumstances that would make a disabled worker's reassignment to another position "reasonable" even though an employee with more seniority also had a right to the position. In other words, Breyer left the door open for the lower courts to deal with the question on a case-by-case basis, in light of the surrounding circumstances. Justice Scalia, in his dissent, concluded that a seniority system should always prevail. Saying that it should "ordinarily" prevail did not give any clear guidance to the lower courts and turned the "reasonable accommodation" provision in the ADA into a "standardless grab bag."[20]

These two positions reflect totally different concepts of the Court's role. For Scalia, it would be irresponsible to leave the law in such an indeterminate state. Therefore, the justices must provide strong guidance for the lower courts. For Breyer, an absolutist approach is unworkable. In a "participatory democracy," claims Breyer, the Court should not stand in the way of a new understanding of the law that "bubbles up from below."[21] Justice Clarence Thomas often agrees with Scalia on this issue, preferring that the Court give definite guidance to the lower courts when a case presents an opportunity to do so. The decisions of Chief Justice Roberts tend to reflect reasoning closer to Breyer's on this point. Yet Roberts's decisions also reflect a cautious and carefully reasoned approach to legal interpretation and a tendency to prefer only "incremental" changes in existing case law. Critics of the Court's 2007 decision on partial-birth abortion (see Chapter 4), for example, contend that although the Court did not overrule the *Roe v. Wade* decision outright, the decision on partial-birth abortion is part of a process of "chipping away" at rights previously upheld by the Supreme Court.

Constitutional Interpretation: Original Intent versus Modernism

The terms *strict construction* and *broad construction* describe different approaches to interpreting the law generally. These approaches may be used when determining the meaning of any law, whether it be a statutory provision, a specific regulation, or a constitutional clause. When discussing *constitutional* interpretation, however, the terms *original intent* and *modernism* are often used to describe the differences in Supreme Court justices' reasoning.

ORIGINAL INTENT   Some of the justices believe that to determine the meaning of a particular constitutional phrase, the Court should look to the intentions of the founders. What did the framers of the Constitution themselves intend when they included the phrase in the document? In other words, what was the "original intent" of the phrase? To discern the intent of the founders, the justices should look to sources that shed light on the founders' views. These sources include contemporary writings by the founders, newspaper articles, the *Federalist Papers,* and notes taken during the Constitutional Convention. Justice Antonin Scalia, one of the Court's most conservative justices, gives some insight into this approach to constitutional interpretation in his book, *A Matter of Interpretation.*[22] In response to those who maintain that the Constitution is a "living Constitution" and should be interpreted in light of society's needs and practices today, Scalia contends that constitutional principles are fixed, not evolving: "The Constitution that I interpret and apply is not living, but dead."

Justice Clarence Thomas.

AP Photo/Charles Dharapak

MODERNISM   Other justices, sometimes referred to as "modernists," believe that the Constitution is indeed a "living" document that evolves to meet changing times and new social needs. Otherwise, how could the Constitution even be relevant to today's society? How could the opinions of

Justice Ruth Bader Ginsburg.

a small group of white men who drafted the document more than two hundred years ago possibly apply to today's large and diverse population? Moreover, the founders themselves often disagreed on what the Constitution should specify. Additionally, if original intent is the goal, what about the intentions of those who ratified the Constitution? Shouldn't they be taken into consideration also? The modernist approach to constitutional interpretation thus looks at the Constitution in the context of today's society and considers how today's life affects the words in the document. Modernists also defend their approach by stating that the founders intentionally left many constitutional provisions vague so that future generations could interpret the document in a manner that would meet the needs of a growing nation.

LO⁶ ASSESSING THE ROLE OF THE FEDERAL COURTS

The federal courts have often come under attack, particularly in the last decade or so, for many reasons. This should come as no surprise in view of the policymaking power of the courts. Because of our common law tradition, the federal judiciary in the United States has always played a far more significant role in politics and government than do the judiciaries in countries that do not have a common law system. After all, just one Supreme Court decision can establish what national policy will be on such issues as abortion, racial segregation, or online pornography.

Criticisms of the Federal Courts

Certainly, policymaking by unelected judges and justices in the federal courts has serious implications in a democracy. Some Americans, including a number of socially conservative members of the House of Representatives, contend that making policy from the bench has upset the balance of powers envisioned by the framers of the

> "I shall not at any time **surrender** my belief that the [Constitution] itself should be our guide, not our own concept of what is fair, *decent*, and right."
>
> HUGO L. BLACK,
> ASSOCIATE JUSTICE OF THE U.S. SUPREME COURT
> 1937–1971

Constitution. They cite Thomas Jefferson, who once said, "To consider the judges as the ultimate arbiters of all constitutional questions [is] a very dangerous doctrine indeed, and one which would place us under the despotism of an oligarchy."[23] This group believes that we should rein in the power of the federal courts, and particularly judicial activism. Indeed, from the the mid-1990s until 2007, when the Republicans controlled Congress, a number of bills to restrain the power of the federal judiciary were introduced in Congress. Among other things, it was proposed that Congress, not the Supreme Court, have the ultimate say in determining the meaning of the Constitution; that judges who ignore the will of Congress or follow foreign laws be impeached; that federal courts not be allowed to decide certain types of cases, such as those involving abortion or the place of religion in public life; and that Congress should be empowered to use its control over the judiciary to punish judges who overstep their authority.

The Case for the Courts

On the other side of the debate over the courts are those who claim that a strong case can be made for leaving the courts alone. Several federal court judges have sharply criticized congressional efforts to interfere with their authority. They claim that such efforts violate the Constitution's separation of powers. Other critics of Congress's attacks on the federal judiciary include James M. Jeffords, a former independent senator from Vermont, who likened the federal court system to a referee: "The first lesson we teach children when they enter competitive sports is to respect the referee, even if we think he [or she] might have made the wrong call. If our children can understand this, why can't our political leaders?"[24]

Others argue that there are already sufficient checks on the courts, some of which we look at next. Additionally, Americans traditionally have held the federal courts, and particularly the Supreme Court, in high regard.

JUDICIAL TRADITIONS AND DOCTRINES One check on the courts is judicial restraint. Supreme Court justices traditionally have exercised a great deal of self-restraint. Justices sometimes admit to making decisions that fly in the face of their personal values and policy preferences, simply because they feel obligated to do so in view of existing law. Self-restraint is also mandated by various judicially established traditions and doctrines, including the doctrine of *stare decisis,* which theoretically obligates the Supreme Court to follow its own precedents. Furthermore, the Supreme Court will not hear a meritless appeal just so it can rule on the issue. Finally, more often than not, the justices narrow their rulings to focus on just one aspect of an issue, even though there may be nothing to stop them from broadening their focus and thus widening the impact of their decisions.

OTHER CHECKS The judiciary is subject to other checks as well. Courts may make rulings, but they cannot force federal and state legislatures to appropriate the funds necessary to carry out those rulings. For example, if the Supreme Court decides that prison conditions must be improved, a legislature has to find the funds to carry out the ruling. Additionally, legislatures can rewrite (amend) old laws or pass new ones in an at-

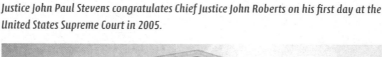

"IT IS CONFIDENCE IN THE MEN AND WOMEN WHO ADMINISTER THE JUDICIAL SYSTEM THAT IS THE TRUE BACKBONE OF THE RULE OF LAW."

JOHN PAUL STEVENS,
ASSOCIATE JUSTICE OF THE U.S. SUPREME COURT
1975–PRESENT

tempt to negate courts' rulings. This may happen when a court interprets a statute in a way that Congress had not intended. Congress may also propose amendments to the Constitution to reverse Supreme Court rulings, and Congress has the authority to limit or otherwise alter the jurisdiction of the lower federal courts. Finally, although it is most unlikely, Congress could even change the number of justices on the Supreme Court, in an attempt to change the ideological balance on the Court.

THE PUBLIC'S REGARD FOR THE SUPREME COURT
As mentioned, some have proposed that Congress, not the Supreme Court, be the final arbiter of the Constitution. In debates on this topic, one factor is often overlooked: the American public's high regard for the Supreme Court and the federal courts generally. The Court continues to be respected as a fair arbiter of conflicting interests and the protector of constitutional rights and liberties. Even when the Court issued its decision to halt the manual recount of votes in Florida following the 2000 elections, which effectively handed the presidency to George W. Bush, Americans respected the Court's decision-making authority—even though many disagreed with the Court's decision. Polls continue to show that Americans have more trust and confidence in the Supreme Court than they do in Congress. In the eyes of many Americans, the Supreme Court stands in sharp contrast to a Congress that seems incapable of rising above the partisan bickering of Washington politics.

Justice John Paul Stevens congratulates Chief Justice John Roberts on his first day at the United States Supreme Court in 2005.

AP Photo/Manuel Balce Ceneta

AMERICA AT ODDS: The Judiciary

"The Judicial Department comes home in its effect to every man's fireside: it passes on his property, his reputation, his life, his all." So stated John Marshall, chief justice of the United States Supreme Court from 1801 to 1835. If you reflect a moment on these words, you will realize their truth. A single Supreme Court decision can affect the lives of millions of Americans. For example, the Court's decision in *Brown v. Board of Education of Topeka* signaled a movement toward racial integration not only in the schools but in all of American society. In 1973, the Supreme Court, in *Roe v. Wade,* held that the constitutional right to privacy included the right to have an abortion. This decision has also affected the lives of millions of Americans.

The influence wielded by the Supreme Court today and the public's high regard for the Court are a far cry from the place that the Supreme Court held in public esteem at the beginning of this nation. Indeed, the Court's first chief justice, John Jay, thought that the Court had little stature and would never play an important role in American society. After resigning as chief justice and serving as governor of New York, Jay refused to return to the Court, even though President John Adams had appointed him for a second time. The third chief justice, Oliver Ellsworth, decided not to return to the bench after being sent as an envoy to France. When the nation's capital was moved to Washington, the Supreme Court was not even included in the plans for the new government buildings. Because of this oversight, the Court had to sit in various rooms of the Capitol building until it finally moved into its own building in 1935. Over time, however, the Court established its reputation as a branch of government capable of dispensing justice in a fair and reasonable manner. Although today's conservative Court may not have the admiration of more liberally inclined individuals (just as a more liberal-leaning Court led by Chief Justice Earl Warren frustrated conservatives in the mid-1900s), by and large the Court continues to balance the scales of justice in a way acceptable to most Americans.

Issues for Debate & Discussion

1. On a few occasions in the last several years, the Supreme Court has looked to the decisions of foreign courts and international human rights laws when deciding cases. Some of these cases involved gay rights, affirmative action, and juveniles and the death penalty. Some jurists, politicians, and other Americans believe that it is inappropriate for our nation's highest court to look to any laws other than U.S. laws for guidance. This group also asserts that measuring the constitutionality of U.S. policies against the yardstick of foreign practices poses a threat to our national sovereignty. Others argue that we should not ignore the opinions and laws of the rest of our world and that it is vitally important to try to attain a deeper understanding of human rights on a worldwide level. What is your position on this issue?

2. Some Americans believe that partisanship should never be a factor in selecting Supreme Court justices because their decisions have such a far-reaching effect on our society. Rather, Supreme Court nominees should be confirmed by a special Senate committee consisting of senators from both parties. Others claim that this is unnecessary because the ideology of Supreme Court justices is not that important—once on the high court bench, partisan ideology does not factor into the justices' decision making. What is your position on this issue?

Take Action

In this chapter, you have learned about the role played by the judiciary in our system of government. If you feel strongly about a particular judicial nominee, contact the U.S. senators from your state and voice your opinion. To get a better understanding of court procedures, consider visiting your local county court when a trial is in session (check with the clerk of the court before entering the trial room, though). If you have an opportunity to participate in a mock trial at your school, consider doing so. In the photo below, a College of William and Mary law student stands at the podium, left, and makes opening remarks to a jury during a mock trial of a terrorist. The mock trial relied heavily on computer technology and the Internet to bring together the witnesses, lawyers, judge, and jury.

AP Photo/Gary C. Knapp

- An excellent Web site for information on the justices of the United States Supreme Court is **www.oyez.org**.

  This site offers biographies of the justices, links to opinions they have written, and, for justices who have served after 1920, video and audio materials. Oral arguments before the Supreme Court are also posted on this site.

- Another helpful Web site is **www.law.cornell.edu/supct/index.html**.

  This is the index of the United States Supreme Court. It has recent Court decisions by year and name of party, and it also has selected historic decisions rendered by the Court.

- The Supreme Court makes its opinions available online at its official Web site. Go to **www.supremecourtus.gov**.

- FindLaw offers a free searchable database of Supreme Court decisions since 1907 at **www.findlaw.com**.

- Increasingly, decisions of the state courts are also becoming available online. You can search through the texts of state cases that are on the Internet, as well as federal cases and state and federal laws, by accessing WashLaw at **www.washlaw.edu**.

- To learn more about the federal court system, go to **www.uscourts.gov**.

  This is the home page for the federal courts. Among other things, you can follow the "path" a case takes as it moves through the federal court system.

ONLINE RESOURCES FOR THIS CHAPTER

This text's Companion Web site, at **www.americaatodds.com**, offers links to numerous resources that you can utilize to learn more about the topics covered in this chapter.

Turn to the back of the book to find your Politics to Go review card for this chapter

In Congress, July 4, 1776

A Declaration by the Representatives of the United States of America, in General Congress assembled. When in the Course of human Events, it becomes necessary for one People to dissolve the Political Bands which have connected them with another, and to assume among the Powers of the Earth, the separate and equal Station to which the Laws of Nature and of Nature's God entitle them, a decent Respect to the Opinions of Mankind requires that they should declare the causes which impel them to the Separation.

We hold these Truths to be self-evident, that all Men are created equal, that they are endowed by their Creator with certain unalienable Rights, that among these are Life, Liberty, and the Pursuit of Happiness—That to secure these Rights, Governments are instituted among Men, deriving their just Powers from the Consent of the Governed, that whenever any Form of Government becomes destructive of these Ends, it is the Right of the People to alter or to abolish it, and to institute new Government, laying its Foundation on such Principles, and organizing its Powers in such Forms, as to them shall seem most likely to effect their Safety and Happiness. Prudence, indeed, will dictate that Governments long established should not be changed for light and transient Causes; and accordingly all Experience hath shewn, that Mankind are more disposed to suffer, while Evils are sufferable, than to right themselves by abolishing the Forms to which they are accustomed. But when a long Train of Abuses and Usurpations, pursuing invariably the same Object, evinces a Design to reduce them under absolute Despotism, it is their Right, it is their Duty, to throw off such Government, and to provide new Guards for their future Security. Such has been the patient Sufferance of these Colonies; and such is now the Necessity which constrains them to alter their former Systems of Government. The History of the present King of Great-Britain is a History of repeated Injuries and Usurpations, all having in direct Object the Establishment of an absolute Tyranny over these States. To prove this, let Facts be submitted to a candid World.

He has refused his Assent to Laws, the most wholesome and necessary for the public Good.

He has forbidden his Governors to pass Laws of immediate and pressing Importance, unless suspended in their Operation till his Assent should be obtained; and when so suspended, he has utterly neglected to attend to them.

He has refused to pass other Laws for the Accommodation of large Districts of People, unless those People would relinquish the Right of Representation in the Legislature, a Right inestimable to them, and formidable to Tyrants only.

He has called together Legislative Bodies at Places unusual, uncomfortable, and distant from the Depository of their Public Records, for the sole Purpose of fatiguing them into Compliance with his Measures.

He has dissolved Representative Houses repeatedly, for opposing with manly Firmness his Invasions on the Rights of the People.

He has refused for a long Time, after such Dissolutions, to cause others to be elected; whereby the Legislative Powers, incapable of Annihilation, have returned to the People at large for their exercise; the State remaining in the mean time exposed to all the Dangers of Invasion from without, and Convulsions within.

He has endeavoured to prevent the Population of these States; for that Purpose obstructing the Laws for Naturalization of Foreigners; refusing to pass others to encourage their Migrations hither, and raising the Conditions of new Appropriations of Lands.

He has obstructed the Administration of Justice, by refusing his Assent to Laws for establishing Judiciary Powers.

He has made Judges dependent on his Will alone, for the Tenure of their offices, and the Amount and payment of their Salaries.

He has erected a Multitude of new Offices, and sent hither Swarms of Officers to harrass our People, and eat out their Substance.

He has kept among us, in Times of Peace, Standing Armies, without the consent of our Legislatures.

He has affected to render the Military independent of, and superior to the Civil Power.

He has combined with others to subject us to a Jurisdiction foreign to our Constitution, and unacknowledged by our Laws; giving his Assent to their Acts of pretended Legislation:

For quartering large Bodies of Armed Troops among us:

For protecting them, by a mock Trial, from Punishment for any Murders which they should commit on the Inhabitants of these States:

For cutting off our Trade with all Parts of the World:

For imposing Taxes on us without our Consent:

For depriving us, in many cases, of the Benefits of Trial by Jury:

For transporting us beyond Seas to be tried for pretended Offences:

For abolishing the free System of English Laws in a neighbouring Province, establishing therein an arbitrary Government, and enlarging its Boundaries, so as to render it at once an Example and fit Instrument for introducing the same absolute Rule into these Colonies:

For taking away our Charters, abolishing our most valuable Laws, and altering fundamentally the Forms of our Governments:

For suspending our own Legislatures, and declaring themselves invested with Power to legislate for us in all Cases whatsoever.

He has abdicated Government here, by declaring us out of his Protection and waging War against us.

He has plundered our Seas, ravaged our Coasts, burnt our towns, and destroyed the Lives of our People.

He is, at this Time, transporting large Armies of foreign Mercenaries to compleat the works of Death, Desolation, and Tyranny, already begun with circumstances of Cruelty and Perfidy, scarcely paralleled in the most barbarous Ages, and totally unworthy the Head of a civilized Nation.

He has constrained our fellow Citizens taken Captive on the high Seas to bear Arms against their Country, to become the Executioners of their Friends and Brethren, or to fall themselves by their Hands.

He has excited domestic Insurrections amongst us, and has endeavoured to bring on the Inhabitants of our Frontiers, the merciless Indian Savages, whose known Rule of Warfare, is an undistinguished Destruction, of all Ages, Sexes and Conditions.

In every state of these Oppressions we have Petitioned for Redress in the most humble Terms: Our repeated Petitions have been answered only by repeated Injury. A Prince, whose Character is thus marked by every act which may define a Tyrant, is unfit to be the Ruler of a free People.

Nor have we been wanting in Attentions to our British Brethren. We have warned them from Time to Time of Attempts by their Legislature to extend an unwarrantable Jurisdiction over us. We have reminded them of the Circumstances of our Emigration and Settlement here. We have appealed to their native Justice and Magnanimity, and we have conjured them by the Ties of our common Kindred to disavow these Usurpations, which, would inevitably interrupt our Connections and Correspondence. They too have been deaf to the Voice of Justice and of Consanguinity. We must, therefore, acquiesce in the Necessity, which denounces our Separation, and hold them, as we hold the rest of Mankind, Enemies in War, in Peace, Friends.

We, therefore, the Representatives of the UNITED STATES OF AMERICA, in General Congress Assembled, appealing to the Supreme Judge of the World for the Rectitude of our Intentions, do, in the Name, and by the Authority of the good People of these Colonies, solemnly Publish and Declare, That these United Colonies are, and of Right ought to be, Free and Independent States; that they are absolved from all Allegiance to the British Crown, and that all political Connection between them and the State of Great-Britain, is and ought to be totally dissolved; and that as Free and Independent States, they have full Power to levy War, conclude Peace, contract Alliances, establish Commerce, and to do all other Acts and Things which Independent States may of right do. And for the support of this declaration, with a firm Reliance on the Protection of divine Providence, we mutually pledge to each other our lives, our Fortunes, and our sacred Honor.

Preamble

We the People of the United States, in Order to form a more perfect Union, establish Justice, insure domestic Tranquility, provide for the common defence, promote the general Welfare, and secure the Blessings of Liberty to ourselves and our Posterity, do ordain and establish this Constitution for the United States of America.

Article I

SECTION 1.   All legislative Powers herein granted shall be vested in a Congress of the United States, which shall consist of a Senate and House of Representatives.

SECTION 2.   The House of Representatives shall be composed of Members chosen every second Year by the People of the several States, and the Electors in each State shall have the Qualifications requisite for Electors of the most numerous Branch of the State Legislature.

No Person shall be a Representative who shall not have attained to the Age of twenty five Years, and been seven Years a Citizen of the United States, and who shall not, when elected, be an Inhabitant of that State in which he shall be chosen.

Representatives and direct Taxes shall be apportioned among the several States which may be included within this Union, according to their respective Numbers, which shall be determined by adding to the whole Number of free Persons, including those bound to Service for a Term of Years, and excluding Indians not taxed, three fifths of all other Persons. The actual Enumeration shall be made within three Years after the first Meeting of the Congress of the United States, and within every subsequent Term of ten Years, in such Manner as they shall by Law direct. The Number of Representatives shall not exceed one for every thirty Thousand, but each State shall have at Least one Representative; and until such enumeration shall be made, the State of New Hampshire shall be entitled to chuse three, Massachusetts eight, Rhode Island and Providence Plantations one, Connecticut five, New York six, New Jersey four, Pennsylvania eight, Delaware one, Maryland six, Virginia ten, North Carolina five, South Carolina five, and Georgia three.

When vacancies happen in the Representation from any State, the Executive Authority thereof shall issue Writs of Election to fill such Vacancies.

The House of Representatives shall chuse their Speaker and other Officers; and shall have the sole Power of Impeachment.

SECTION 3.   The Senate of the United States shall be composed of two Senators from each State, chosen by the Legislature thereof, for six Years; and each Senator shall have one Vote.

Immediately after they shall be assembled in Consequence of the first Election, they shall be divided as equally as may be into three Classes. The Seats of the Senators of the first Class shall be vacated at the Expiration of the second Year, of the second Class at the Expiration of the fourth Year, and of the third Class at the Expiration of the sixth Year, so that one third may be chosen every second Year; and if Vacancies happen by Resignation, or otherwise, during the Recess of the Legislature of any State, the Executive thereof may make temporary Appointments until the next Meeting of the Legislature, which shall then fill such Vacancies.

No Person shall be a Senator who shall not have attained to the Age of thirty Years, and been nine Years a Citizen of the United States, and who shall not, when elected, be an Inhabitant of that State for which he shall be chosen.

The Vice President of the United States shall be President of the Senate, but shall have no Vote, unless they be equally divided.

The Senate shall chuse their other Officers, and also a President pro tempore, in the Absence of the Vice President, or when he shall exercise the Office of President of the United States.

The Senate shall have the sole Power to try all Impeachments. When sitting for that Purpose, they shall be on Oath or Affirmation. When the President of the United States is tried, the Chief Justice shall preside: And no Person shall be convicted without the Concurrence of two thirds of the Members present.

Judgment in Cases of Impeachment shall not extend further than to removal from Office, and disqualification to hold and enjoy any Office of honor, Trust, or Profit under the United States: but the Party convicted shall nevertheless be liable and subject to Indictment, Trial, Judgment, and Punishment, according to Law.

SECTION 4. The Times, Places and Manner of holding Elections for Senators and Representatives, shall be prescribed in each State by the Legislature thereof; but the Congress may at any time by Law make or alter such Regulations, except as to the Places of chusing Senators.

The Congress shall assemble at least once in every Year, and such Meeting shall be on the first Monday in December, unless they shall by Law appoint a different Day.

SECTION 5. Each House shall be the Judge of the Elections, Returns, and Qualifications of its own Members, and a Majority of each shall constitute a Quorum to do Business; but a smaller Number may adjourn from day to day, and may be authorized to compel the Attendance of absent Members, in such Manner, and under such Penalties as each House may provide.

Each House may determine the Rules of its Proceedings, punish its Members for disorderly Behavior, and, with the Concurrence of two thirds, expel a Member.

Each House shall keep a Journal of its Proceedings, and from time to time publish the same, excepting such Parts as may in their Judgment require Secrecy; and the Yeas and Nays of the Members of either House on any question shall, at the Desire of one fifth of those Present, be entered on the Journal.

Neither House, during the Session of Congress, shall, without the Consent of the other, adjourn for more than three days, nor to any other Place than that in which the two Houses shall be sitting.

SECTION 6. The Senators and Representatives shall receive a Compensation for their Services, to be ascertained by Law, and paid out of the Treasury of the United States. They shall in all Cases, except Treason, Felony and Breach of the Peace, be privileged from Arrest during their Attendance at the Session of their respective Houses, and in going to and returning from the same; and for any Speech or Debate in either House, they shall not be questioned in any other Place.

No Senator or Representative shall, during the Time for which he was elected, be appointed to any civil Office under the Authority of the United States, which shall have been created, or the Emoluments whereof shall have been increased during such time; and no Person holding any Office under the United States, shall be a Member of either House during his Continuance in Office.

SECTION 7. All Bills for raising Revenue shall originate in the House of Representatives; but the Senate may propose or concur with Amendments as on other Bills.

Every Bill which shall have passed the House of Representatives and the Senate, shall, before it become a Law, be presented to the President of the United States; If he approve he shall sign it, but if not he shall return it, with his Objections to the House in which it shall have originated, who shall enter the Objections at large on their Journal, and proceed to reconsider it. If after such Reconsideration two thirds of that House shall agree to pass the Bill, it shall be sent together with the Objections, to the other House, by which it shall likewise be reconsidered, and if approved by two thirds of that House, it shall become a Law. But in all such Cases the Votes of both Houses shall be determined by Yeas and Nays, and the Names of the Persons voting for and against the Bill shall be entered on the Journal of each House respectively. If any Bill shall not be returned by the President within ten Days (Sundays excepted) after it shall have been presented to him, the Same shall be a Law, in like Manner as if he had signed it, unless the Congress by their Adjournment prevent its Return in which Case it shall not be a Law.

Every Order, Resolution, or Vote, to which the Concurrence of the Senate and House of Representatives may be necessary (except on a question of Adjournment) shall be presented to the President of the United States; and before the Same shall take Effect, shall be approved by him, or being disapproved by him, shall be repassed by two thirds of the Senate and House of Representatives, according to the Rules and Limitations prescribed in the Case of a Bill.

SECTION 8. The Congress shall have Power To lay and collect Taxes, Duties, Imposts and Excises, to pay the Debts and provide for the common Defence and general Welfare of the United States; but all Duties, Imposts and Excises shall be uniform throughout the United States;

To borrow Money on the credit of the United States;

To regulate Commerce with foreign Nations, and among the several States, and with the Indian Tribes;

To establish an uniform Rule of Naturalization, and uniform Laws on the subject of Bankruptcies throughout the United States;

To coin Money, regulate the Value thereof, and of foreign Coin, and fix the Standard of Weights and Measures;

To provide for the Punishment of counterfeiting the Securities and current Coin of the United States;

To establish Post Offices and post Roads;

To promote the Progress of Science and useful Arts, by securing for limited Times to Authors and Inventors the exclusive Right to their respective Writings and Discoveries;

To constitute Tribunals inferior to the supreme Court;

To define and punish Piracies and Felonies committed on the high Seas, and Offenses against the Law of Nations;

To declare War, grant Letters of Marque and Reprisal, and make Rules concerning Captures on Land and Water;

To raise and support Armies, but no Appropriation of Money to that Use shall be for a longer Term than two Years;

To provide and maintain a Navy;

To make Rules for the Government and Regulation of the land and naval Forces;

To provide for calling forth the Militia to execute the Laws of the Union, suppress Insurrections and repel Invasions;

To provide for organizing, arming, and disciplining, the Militia, and for governing such Part of them as may be employed in the Service of the United States, reserving to the States respectively, the Appointment of the Officers, and the Authority of training the Militia according to the discipline prescribed by Congress;

To exercise exclusive Legislation in all Cases whatsoever, over such District (not exceeding ten Miles square) as may, by Cession of particular States, and the Acceptance of Congress, become the Seat of the Government of the United States, and to exercise like Authority over all Places purchased by the Consent of the Legislature of the State in which the Same shall be, for the Erection of Forts, Magazines, Arsenals, dock-Yards, and other needful Buildings;—And

To make all Laws which shall be necessary and proper for carrying into Execution the foregoing Powers, and all other Powers vested by this Constitution in the Government of the United States, or in any Department or Officer thereof.

SECTION 9. The Migration or Importation of such Persons as any of the States now existing shall think proper to admit, shall not be prohibited by the Congress prior to the Year one thousand eight hundred and eight, but a Tax or duty may be imposed on such Importation, not exceeding ten dollars for each Person.

The privilege of the Writ of Habeas Corpus shall not be suspended, unless when in Cases of Rebellion or Invasion the public Safety may require it.

No Bill of Attainder or ex post facto Law shall be passed.

No Capitation, or other direct, Tax shall be laid, unless in Proportion to the Census or Enumeration herein before directed to be taken.

No Tax or Duty shall be laid on Articles exported from any State.

No Preference shall be given by any Regulation of Commerce or Revenue to the Ports of one State over those of another: nor shall Vessels bound to, or from, one State be obliged to enter, clear, or pay Duties in another.

No Money shall be drawn from the Treasury, but in Consequence of Appropriations made by Law; and a regular Statement and Account of the Receipts and Expenditures of all public Money shall be published from time to time.

No Title of Nobility shall be granted by the United States: And no Person holding any Office of Profit or Trust under them, shall, without the Consent of the Congress, accept of any present, Emolument, Office, or Title, of any kind whatever, from any King, Prince, or foreign State.

SECTION 10. No State shall enter into any Treaty, Alliance, or Confederation; grant Letters of Marque and Reprisal; coin Money; emit Bills of Credit; make any Thing but gold and silver Coin a Tender in Payment of Debts; pass any Bill of Attainder, ex post facto Law, or Law impairing the Obligation of Contracts, or grant any Title of Nobility.

No State shall, without the Consent of the Congress, lay any Imposts or Duties on Imports or Exports, except what may be absolutely necessary for executing its inspection Laws: and the net Produce of all Duties and Imposts, laid by any State on Imports or Exports, shall be for the Use of the Treasury of the United States; and all such Laws shall be subject to the Revision and Controul of the Congress.

No State shall, without the Consent of Congress, lay any Duty of Tonnage, keep Troops, or Ships of War in time of Peace, enter into any Agreement or Compact with another State, or with a foreign Power, or engage in War, unless actually invaded, or in such imminent Danger as will not admit of delay.

Article II

SECTION 1.   The executive Power shall be vested in a President of the United States of America. He shall hold his Office during the Term of four Years, and, together with the Vice President, chosen for the same Term, be elected, as follows:

Each State shall appoint, in such Manner as the Legislature thereof may direct, a Number of Electors, equal to the whole Number of Senators and Representatives to which the State may be entitled in the Congress; but no Senator or Representative, or Person holding an Office of Trust or Profit under the United States, shall be appointed an Elector.

The Electors shall meet in their respective States, and vote by Ballot for two Persons, of whom one at least shall not be an Inhabitant of the same State with themselves. And they shall make a List of all the Persons voted for, and of the Number of Votes for each; which List they shall sign and certify, and transmit sealed to the Seat of the Government of the United States, directed to the President of the Senate. The President of the Senate shall, in the Presence of the Senate and House of Representatives, open all the Certificates, and the Votes shall then be counted. The Person having the greatest Number of Votes shall be the President, if such Number be a Majority of the whole Number of Electors appointed; and if there be more than one who have such Majority, and have an equal Number of Votes, then the House of Representatives shall immediately chuse by Ballot one of them for President; and if no Person have a Majority, then from the five highest on the List the said House shall in like Manner chuse the President. But in chusing the President, the Votes shall be taken by States, the Representation from each State having one Vote; A quorum for this Purpose shall consist of a Member or Members from two thirds of the States, and a Majority of all the States shall be necessary to a Choice. In every Case, after the Choice of the President, the Person having the greater Number of Votes of the Electors shall be the Vice President. But if there should remain two or more who have equal Votes, the Senate shall chuse from them by Ballot the Vice President.

The Congress may determine the Time of chusing the Electors, and the Day on which they shall give their Votes; which Day shall be the same throughout the United States.

No person except a natural born Citizen, or a Citizen of the United States, at the time of the Adoption of this Constitution, shall be eligible to the Office of President; neither shall any Person be eligible to that Office who shall not have attained to the Age of thirty five Years, and been fourteen Years a Resident within the United States.

In Case of the Removal of the President from Office, or of his Death, Resignation or Inability to discharge the Powers and Duties of the said Office, the same shall devolve on the Vice President, and the Congress may by Law provide for the Case of Removal, Death, Resignation or Inability, both of the President and Vice President, declaring what Officer shall then act as President, and such Officer shall act accordingly, until the Disability be removed, or a President shall be elected.

The President shall, at stated Times, receive for his Services, a Compensation, which shall neither be increased nor diminished during the Period for which he shall have been elected, and he shall not receive within that Period any other Emolument from the United States, or any of them.

Before he enter on the Execution of his Office, he shall take the following Oath or Affirmation: "I do solemnly swear (or affirm) that I will faithfully execute the Office of President of the United States, and will to the best of my Ability, preserve, protect and defend the Constitution of the United States."

SECTION 2.   The President shall be Commander in Chief of the Army and Navy of the United States, and of the Militia of the several States, when called into the actual Service of the United States; he may require the Opinion, in writing, of the principal Officer in each of the executive Departments, upon any Subject relating to the Duties of their respective Offices, and he shall have Power to grant Reprieves and Pardons for Offenses against the United States, except in Cases of Impeachment.

He shall have Power, by and with the Advice and Consent of the Senate to make Treaties, provided two thirds of the Senators present concur; and he shall nominate, and by and with the Advice and Consent of the Senate, shall appoint Ambassadors, other public Ministers and Consuls, Judges of the supreme Court, and all other Officers of the United States, whose Appointments are not herein otherwise provided for, and which shall be established by Law; but the Congress may by Law vest the Appointment of such inferior Officers, as they think proper, in the President alone, in the Courts of Law, or in the Heads of Departments.

The President shall have Power to fill up all Vacancies that may happen during the Recess of the Senate, by granting Commissions which shall expire at the End of their next Session.

SECTION 3. He shall from time to time give to the Congress Information of the State of the Union, and recommend to their Consideration such Measures as he shall judge necessary and expedient; he may, on extraordinary Occasions, convene both Houses, or either of them, and in Case of Disagreement between them, with Respect to the Time of Adjournment, he may adjourn them to such Time as he shall think proper; he shall receive Ambassadors and other public Ministers; he shall take Care that the Laws be faithfully executed, and shall Commission all the Officers of the United States.

SECTION 4. The President, Vice President and all civil Officers of the United States, shall be removed from Office on Impeachment for, and Conviction of, Treason, Bribery, or other high Crimes and Misdemeanors.

Article III

SECTION 1. The judicial Power of the United States, shall be vested in one supreme Court, and in such inferior Courts as the Congress may from time to time ordain and establish. The Judges, both of the supreme and inferior Courts, shall hold their Offices during good Behaviour, and shall, at stated Times, receive for their Services a Compensation, which shall not be diminished during their Continuance in Office.

SECTION 2. The judicial Power shall extend to all Cases, in Law and Equity, arising under this Constitution, the Laws of the United States, and Treaties made, or which shall be made, under their Authority;—to all Cases affecting Ambassadors, other public Ministers and Consuls;—to all Cases of admiralty and maritime Jurisdiction;—to Controversies to which the United States shall be a Party;—to Controversies between two or more States;—between a State and Citizens of another State;—between Citizens of different States;—between Citizens of the same State claiming Lands under Grants of different States, and between a State, or the Citizens thereof, and foreign States, Citizens or Subjects.

In all Cases affecting Ambassadors, other public Ministers and Consuls, and those in which a State shall be a Party, the supreme Court shall have original Jurisdiction. In all the other Cases before mentioned, the supreme Court shall have appellate Jurisdiction, both as to Law and Fact, with such Exceptions, and under such Regulations as the Congress shall make.

The Trial of all Crimes, except in Cases of Impeachment, shall be by Jury; and such Trial shall be held in the State where the said Crimes shall have been committed; but when not committed within any State, the Trial shall be at such Place or Places as the Congress may by Law have directed.

SECTION 3. Treason against the United States, shall consist only in levying War against them, or, in adhering to their Enemies, giving them Aid and Comfort. No Person shall be convicted of Treason unless on the Testimony of two Witnesses to the same overt Act, or on Confession in open Court.

The Congress shall have Power to declare the Punishment of Treason, but no Attainder of Treason shall work Corruption of Blood, or Forfeiture except during the Life of the Person attainted.

Article IV

SECTION 1. Full Faith and Credit shall be given in each State to the public Acts, Records, and judicial Proceedings of every other State. And the Congress may by general Laws prescribe the Manner in which such Acts, Records and Proceedings shall be proved, and the Effect thereof.

SECTION 2. The Citizens of each State shall be entitled to all Privileges and Immunities of Citizens in the several States.

A Person charged in any State with Treason, Felony, or other Crime, who shall flee from Justice, and be found in another State, shall on Demand of the executive Authority of the State from which he fled, be delivered up, to be removed to the State having Jurisdiction of the Crime.

No Person held to Service or Labour in one State, under the Laws thereof, escaping into another, shall, in Consequence of any Law or Regulation therein, be discharged from such Service or Labour, but shall be delivered up on Claim of the Party to whom such Service or Labour may be due.

SECTION 3. New States may be admitted by the Congress into this Union; but no new State shall be formed or erected within the Jurisdiction of any other State; nor any State be formed by the Junction of two or more States, or Parts of States, without the Consent of the Legislatures of the States concerned as well as of the Congress.

The Congress shall have Power to dispose of and make all needful Rules and Regulations respecting the Territory or other Property belonging to the United

States; and nothing in this Constitution shall be so construed as to Prejudice any Claims of the United States, or of any particular State.

SECTION 4.   The United States shall guarantee to every State in this Union a Republican Form of Government, and shall protect each of them against Invasion; and on Application of the Legislature, or of the Executive (when the Legislature cannot be convened) against domestic Violence.

Article V

The Congress, whenever two thirds of both Houses shall deem it necessary, shall propose Amendments to this Constitution, or, on the Application of the Legislatures of two thirds of the several States, shall call a Convention for proposing Amendments, which, in either Case, shall be valid to all Intents and Purposes, as part of this Constitution, when ratified by the Legislatures of three fourths of the several States, or by Conventions in three fourths thereof, as the one or the other Mode of Ratification may be proposed by the Congress; Provided that no Amendment which may be made prior to the Year One thousand eight hundred and eight shall in any Manner affect the first and fourth Clauses in the Ninth Section of the first Article; and that no State, without its Consent, shall be deprived of its equal Suffrage in the Senate.

Article VI

All Debts contracted and Engagements entered into, before the Adoption of this Constitution shall be as valid against the United States under this Constitution, as under the Confederation.

This Constitution, and the Laws of the United States which shall be made in Pursuance thereof; and all Treaties made, or which shall be made, under the Authority of the United States, shall be the supreme Law of the Land; and the Judges in every State shall be bound thereby, any Thing in the Constitution or Laws of any State to the Contrary notwithstanding.

The Senators and Representatives before mentioned, and the Members of the several State Legislatures, and all executive and judicial Officers, both of the United States and of the several States, shall be bound by Oath or Affirmation, to support this Constitution; but no religious Test shall ever be required as a Qualification to any Office or public Trust under the United States.

Article VII

The Ratification of the Conventions of nine States shall be sufficient for the Establishment of this Constitution between the States so ratifying the Same.

Amendment I [1791]

Congress shall make no law respecting an establishment of religion, or prohibiting the free exercise thereof; or abridging the freedom of speech, or of the press; or the right of the people peaceably to assemble, and to petition the Government for a redress of grievances.

Amendment II [1791]

A well regulated Militia, being necessary to the security of a free State, the right of the people to keep and bear Arms, shall not be infringed.

Amendment III [1791]

No Soldier shall, in time of peace be quartered in any house, without the consent of the Owner, nor in time of war, but in a manner to be prescribed by law.

Amendment IV [1791]

The right of the people to be secure in their persons, houses, papers, and effects, against unreasonable searches and seizures, shall not be violated, and no Warrants shall issue, but upon probable cause, supported by Oath or affirmation, and particularly describing the place to be searched, and the persons or things to be seized.

Amendment V [1791]

No person shall be held to answer for a capital, or otherwise infamous crime, unless on a presentment or indictment of a Grand Jury, except in cases arising in the land or naval forces, or in the Militia, when in actual service in time of War or public danger; nor shall any person be subject for the same offense to be twice put in jeopardy of life or limb; nor shall be compelled in any criminal case to be a witness against himself, nor be deprived of life, liberty, or property, without due process of law; nor shall private property be taken for public use, without just compensation.

Amendment VI [1791]

In all criminal prosecutions, the accused shall enjoy the right to a speedy and public trial, by an impartial jury of the State and district wherein the crime shall have been committed, which district shall have been previously ascertained by law, and to be informed of the nature and cause of the accusation; to be confronted with the witnesses against him; to have compulsory process for obtaining witnesses in his favor, and to have the Assistance of Counsel for his defence.

Amendment VII [1791]

In Suits at common law, where the value in controversy shall exceed twenty dollars, the right of trial by jury shall be preserved, and no fact tried by a jury, shall be otherwise re-examined in any Court of the United States, than according to the rules of the common law.

Amendment VIII [1791]

Excessive bail shall not be required, nor excessive fines imposed, nor cruel and unusual punishments inflicted.

Amendment IX [1791]

The enumeration in the Constitution, of certain rights, shall not be construed to deny or disparage others retained by the people.

Amendment X [1791]

The powers not delegated to the United States by the Constitution, nor prohibited by it to the States, are reserved to the States respectively, or to the people.

Amendment XI [1798]

The Judicial power of the United States shall not be construed to extend to any suit in law or equity, commenced or prosecuted against one of the United States by Citizens of another State, or by Citizens or Subjects of any Foreign State.

Amendment XII [1804]

The Electors shall meet in their respective states, and vote by ballot for President and Vice-President, one of whom, at least, shall not be an inhabitant of the same state with themselves; they shall name in their ballots the person voted for as President, and in distinct ballots the person voted for as Vice-President, and they shall make distinct lists of all persons voted for as President, and of all persons voted for as Vice-President, and of the number of votes for each, which lists they shall sign and certify, and transmit sealed to the seat of the government of the United States, directed to the President of the Senate;—The President of the Senate shall, in the presence of the Senate and House of Representatives, open all the certificates and the votes shall then be counted;—The person having the greatest number of votes for President, shall be the President, if such number be a majority of the whole number of Electors appointed; and if no person have such majority, then from the persons having the highest numbers not exceeding three on the list of those voted for as President, the House of Representatives shall choose immediately, by ballot, the President. But in choosing the President, the votes shall be taken by states, the representation from each state having one vote; a quorum for this purpose shall consist of a member or members from two-thirds of the states, and a majority of all states shall be necessary to a choice. And if the House of Representatives shall not choose a President whenever the right of choice shall devolve upon them, before the fourth day of March next following, then the Vice-President shall act as President, as in the case of the death or other constitutional disability of the President.—The person having the greatest number of votes as Vice-President, shall be the Vice-President, if such number be a majority of the whole number of Electors appointed, and if no person have a majority, then from the two highest numbers on the list, the Senate shall choose the Vice-President; a quorum for the purpose shall consist of two-thirds of the whole number of Senators, and a majority of the whole number shall be necessary to a choice. But no person constitutionally ineligible to the office of President shall be eligible to that of Vice-President of the United States.

Amendment XIII [1865]

SECTION 1.   Neither slavery nor involuntary servitude, except as a punishment for crime whereof the party shall have been duly convicted, shall exist within the United States, or any place subject to their jurisdiction.

SECTION 2.   Congress shall have power to enforce this article by appropriate legislation.

Amendment XIV [1868]

SECTION 1. All persons born or naturalized in the United States, and subject to the jurisdiction thereof, are citizens of the United States and of the State wherein they reside. No State shall make or enforce any law which shall abridge the privileges or immunities of citizens of the United States; nor shall any State deprive any person of life, liberty, or property, without due process of law; nor deny to any person within its jurisdiction the equal protection of the laws.

SECTION 2. Representatives shall be apportioned among the several States according to their respective numbers, counting the whole number of persons in each State, excluding Indians not taxed. But when the right to vote at any election for the choice of electors for President and Vice President of the United States, Representatives in Congress, the Executive and Judicial officers of a State, or the members of the Legislature thereof, is denied to any of the male inhabitants of such State, being twenty-one years of age, and citizens of the United States, or in any way abridged, except for participation in rebellion, or other crime, the basis of representation therein shall be reduced in the proportion which the number of such male citizens shall bear to the whole number of male citizens twenty-one years of age in such State.

SECTION 3. No person shall be a Senator or Representative in Congress, or elector of President and Vice President, or hold any office, civil or military, under the United States, or under any State, who having previously taken an oath, as a member of Congress, or as an officer of the United States, or as a member of any State legislature, or as an executive or judicial officer of any State, to support the Constitution of the United States, shall have engaged in insurrection or rebellion against the same, or given aid or comfort to the enemies thereof. But Congress may by a vote of two-thirds of each House, remove such disability.

SECTION 4. The validity of the public debt of the United States, authorized by law, including debts incurred for payment of pensions and bounties for services in suppressing insurrection or rebellion, shall not be questioned. But neither the United States nor any State shall assume or pay any debt or obligation incurred in aid of insurrection or rebellion against the United States, or any claim for the loss or emancipation of any slave; but all such debts, obligations and claims shall be held illegal and void.

SECTION 5. The Congress shall have power to enforce, by appropriate legislation, the provisions of this article.

Amendment XV [1870]

SECTION 1. The right of citizens of the United States to vote shall not be denied or abridged by the United States or by any State on account of race, color, or previous condition of servitude.

SECTION 2. The Congress shall have power to enforce this article by appropriate legislation.

Amendment XVI [1913]

The Congress shall have power to lay and collect taxes on incomes, from whatever source derived, without apportionment among the several States, and without regard to any census or enumeration.

Amendment XVII [1913]

SECTION 1. The Senate of the United States shall be composed of two Senators from each State, elected by the people thereof, for six years; and each Senator shall have one vote. The electors in each State shall have the qualifications requisite for electors of the most numerous branch of the State legislatures.

SECTION 2. When vacancies happen in the representation of any State in the Senate, the executive authority of such State shall issue writs of election to fill such vacancies: Provided, That the legislature of any State may empower the executive thereof to make temporary appointments until the people fill the vacancies by election as the legislature may direct.

SECTION 3. This amendment shall not be so construed as to affect the election or term of any Senator chosen before it becomes valid as part of the Constitution.

Amendment XVIII [1919]

SECTION 1. After one year from the ratification of this article the manufacture, sale, or transportation of intoxicating liquors within, the importation thereof into, or the exportation thereof from the United States and all territory subject to the jurisdiction thereof for beverage purposes is hereby prohibited.

SECTION 2. The Congress and the several States shall have concurrent power to enforce this article by appropriate legislation.

SECTION 3. This article shall be inoperative unless it shall have been ratified as an amendment to the Constitution by the legislatures of the several States, as provided in the Constitution, within seven years from the date of the submission hereof to the States by the Congress.

Amendment XIX [1920]

SECTION 1. The right of citizens of the United States to vote shall not be denied or abridged by the United States or by any State on account of sex.

SECTION 2. Congress shall have power to enforce this article by appropriate legislation.

Amendment XX [1933]

SECTION 1. The terms of the President and Vice President shall end at noon on the 20th day of January, and the terms of Senators and Representatives at noon on the 3d day of January, of the years in which such terms would have ended if this article had not been ratified; and the terms of their successors shall then begin.

SECTION 2. The Congress shall assemble at least once in every year, and such meeting shall begin at noon on the 3d day of January, unless they shall by law appoint a different day.

SECTION 3. If, at the time fixed for the beginning of the term of the President, the President elect shall have died, the Vice President elect shall become President. If the President shall not have been chosen before the time fixed for the beginning of his term, or if the President elect shall have failed to qualify, then the Vice President elect shall act as President until a President shall have qualified; and the Congress may by law provide for the case wherein neither a President elect nor a Vice President elect shall have qualified, declaring who shall then act as President, or the manner in which one who is to act shall be selected, and such person shall act accordingly until a President or Vice President shall have qualified.

SECTION 4. The Congress may by law provide for the case of the death of any of the persons from whom the House of Representatives may choose a President whenever the right of choice shall have devolved upon them, and for the case of the death of any of the persons from whom the Senate may choose a Vice President whenever the right of choice shall have devolved upon them.

SECTION 5. Sections 1 and 2 shall take effect on the 15th day of October following the ratification of this article.

SECTION 6. This article shall be inoperative unless it shall have been ratified as an amendment to the Constitution by the legislatures of three-fourths of the several States within seven years from the date of its submission.

Amendment XXI [1933]

SECTION 1. The eighteenth article of amendment to the Constitution of the United States is hereby repealed.

SECTION 2. The transportation or importation into any State, Territory, or possession of the United States for delivery or use therein of intoxicating liquors, in violation of the laws thereof, is hereby prohibited.

SECTION 3. This article shall be inoperative unless it shall have been ratified as an amendment to the Constitution by conventions in the several States, as provided in the Constitution, within seven years from the date of the submission hereof to the States by the Congress.

Amendment XXII [1951]

SECTION 1. No person shall be elected to the office of the President more than twice, and no person who has held the office of President, or acted as President, for more than two years of a term to which some other person was elected President shall be elected to the office of President more than once. But this Article shall not apply to any person holding the office of President when this Article was proposed by the Congress, and shall not prevent any person who may be holding the office of President, or acting as President, during the term within which this Article becomes operative from holding the office of President or acting as President during the remainder of such term.

SECTION 2. This article shall be inoperative unless it shall have been ratified as an amendment to the Constitution by the legislatures of three-fourths of the several States within seven years from the date of its submission to the States by the Congress.

Amendment XXIII [1961]

SECTION 1.   The District constituting the seat of Government of the United States shall appoint in such manner as the Congress may direct:

A number of electors of President and Vice President equal to the whole number of Senators and Representatives in Congress to which the District would be entitled if it were a State, but in no event more than the least populous state; they shall be in addition to those appointed by the states, but they shall be considered, for the purposes of the election of President and Vice President, to be electors appointed by a state; and they shall meet in the District and perform such duties as provided by the twelfth article of amendment.

SECTION 2.   The Congress shall have power to enforce this article by appropriate legislation.

Amendment XXIV [1964]

SECTION 1.   The right of citizens of the United States to vote in any primary or other election for President or Vice President, for electors for President or Vice President, or for Senator or Representative in Congress, shall not be denied or abridged by the United States, or any State by reason of failure to pay any poll tax or other tax.

SECTION 2.   The Congress shall have power to enforce this article by appropriate legislation.

Amendment XXV [1967]

SECTION 1.   In case of the removal of the President from office or of his death or resignation, the Vice President shall become President.

SECTION 2.   Whenever there is a vacancy in the office of the Vice President, the President shall nominate a Vice President who shall take office upon confirmation by a majority vote of both Houses of Congress.

SECTION 3.   Whenever the President transmits to the President pro tempore of the Senate and the Speaker of the House of Representatives his written declaration that he is unable to discharge the powers and duties of his office, and until he transmits to them a written declaration to the contrary, such powers and duties shall be discharged by the Vice President as Acting President.

SECTION 4.   Whenever the Vice President and a majority of either the principal officers of the executive departments or of such other body as Congress may by law provide, transmit to the President pro tempore of the Senate and the Speaker of the House of Representatives their written declaration that the President is unable to discharge the powers and duties of his office, the Vice President shall immediately assume the powers and duties of the office as Acting President.

Thereafter, when the President transmits to the President pro tempore of the Senate and the Speaker of the House of Representatives his written declaration that no inability exists, he shall resume the powers and duties of his office unless the Vice President and a majority of either the principal officers of the executive department or of such other body as Congress may by law provide, transmit within four days to the President pro tempore of the Senate and the Speaker of the House of Representatives their written declaration that the President is unable to discharge the powers and duties of his office. Thereupon Congress shall decide the issue, assembling within forty-eight hours for that purpose if not in session. If the Congress, within twenty-one days after receipt of the latter written declaration, or, if Congress is not in session, within twenty-one days after Congress is required to assemble, determines by two-thirds vote of both Houses that the President is unable to discharge the powers and duties of his office, the Vice President shall continue to discharge the same as Acting President; otherwise, the President shall resume the powers and duties of his office.

Amendment XXVI [1971]

SECTION 1.   The right of citizens of the United States, who are eighteen years of age or older, to vote shall not be denied or abridged by the United States or by any State on account of age.

SECTION 2.   The Congress shall have power to enforce this article by appropriate legislation.

Amendment XXVII [1992]

No law, varying the compensation for the services of the Senators and Representatives, shall take effect, until an election of Representatives shall have intervened.

Appendix C

Supreme Court Justices since 1900

CHIEF JUSTICES

Name	Years of Service	State App'd from	Appointing President	Age App'd	Political Affiliation	Educational Background*
Fuller, Melville Weston	1888–1910	Illinois	Cleveland	55	Democrat	Bowdoin College; studied at Harvard Law School
White, Edward Douglass	1910–1921	Louisiana	Taft	65	Democrat	Mount St. Mary's College; Georgetown College (now University)
Taft, William Howard	1921–1930	Connecticut	Harding	64	Republican	Yale; Cincinnati Law School
Hughes, Charles Evans	1930–1941	New York	Hoover	68	Republican	Colgate University; Brown; Columbia Law School
Stone, Harlan Fiske	1941–1946	New York	Roosevelt, F.	69	Republican	Amherst College; Columbia
Vinson, Frederick Moore	1946–1953	Kentucky	Truman	56	Democrat	Centre College
Warren, Earl	1953–1969	California	Eisenhower	62	Republican	University of California, Berkeley
Burger, Warren Earl	1969–1986	Virginia	Nixon	62	Republican	University of Minnesota; St. Paul College of Law (Mitchell College)
Rehnquist, William Hubbs	1986–2005	Virginia	Reagan	62	Republican	Stanford; Harvard; Stanford University Law School
Roberts, John G., Jr.	2005–present	District of Columbia	G. W. Bush	50	Republican	Harvard; Harvard Law School

*Source: Educational background information derived from Elder Witt, *Guide to the U.S. Supreme Court,* 2d ed. (Washington, D.C.: Congressional Quarterly Press, Inc., 1990). Reprinted with the permission of the publisher.

ASSOCIATE JUSTICES

Name	Years of Service	State App'd from	Appointing President	Age App'd	Political Affiliation	Educational Background*
Harlan, John Marshall	1877–1911	Kentucky	Hayes	61	Republican	Centre College; studied law at Transylvania University
Gray, Horace	1882–1902	Massachusetts	Arthur	54	Republican	Harvard College; Harvard Law School
Brewer, David Josiah	1890–1910	Kansas	Harrison	53	Republican	Wesleyan University; Yale; Albany Law School
Brown, Henry Billings	1891–1906	Michigan	Harrison	55	Republican	Yale; studied at Yale Law School and Harvard Law School
Shiras, George, Jr.	1892–1903	Pennsylvania	Harrison	61	Republican	Ohio University; Yale; studied law at Yale and privately
White, Edward Douglass	1894–1910	Louisiana	Cleveland	49	Democrat	Mount St. Mary's College; Georgetown College (now University)
Peckham, Rufus Wheeler	1896–1909	New York	Cleveland	58	Democrat	Read law in father's firm

ASSOCIATE JUSTICES (CONTINUED)

Name	Years of Service	State App'd from	Appointing President	Age App'd	Political Affiliation	Educational Background*
McKenna, Joseph	1898–1925	California	McKinley	55	Republican	Benicia Collegiate Institute, Law Dept.
Holmes, Oliver Wendell, Jr.	1902–1932	Massachusetts	Roosevelt, T.	61	Republican	Harvard College; studied law at Harvard Law School
Day, William Rufus	1903–1922	Ohio	Roosevelt, T.	54	Republican	University of Michigan; University of Michigan Law School
Moody, William Henry	1906–1910	Massachusetts	Roosevelt, T.	53	Republican	Harvard; Harvard Law School
Lurton, Horace Harmon	1910–1914	Tennessee	Taft	66	Democrat	University of Chicago; Cumberland Law School
Hughes, Charles Evans	1910–1916	New York	Taft	48	Republican	Colgate University; Brown University; Columbia Law School
Van Devanter, Willis	1911–1937	Wyoming	Taft	52	Republican	Indiana Asbury University; University of Cincinnati Law School
Lamar, Joseph Rucker	1911–1916	Georgia	Taft	54	Democrat	University of Georgia; Bethany College; Washington and Lee University
Pitney, Mahlon	1912–1922	New Jersey	Taft	54	Republican	College of New Jersey (Princeton); read law under father
McReynolds, James Clark	1914–1941	Tennessee	Wilson	52	Democrat	Vanderbilt University; University of Virginia
Brandeis, Louis Dembitz	1916–1939	Massachusetts	Wilson	60	Democrat	Harvard Law School
Clarke, John Hessin	1916–1922	Ohio	Wilson	59	Democrat	Western Reserve University; read law under father
Sutherland, George	1922–1938	Utah	Harding	60	Republican	Brigham Young Academy; one year at University of Michigan Law School
Butler, Pierce	1923–1939	Minnesota	Harding	57	Democrat	Carleton College
Sanford, Edward Terry	1923–1930	Tennessee	Harding	58	Republican	University of Tennessee; Harvard; Harvard Law School
Stone, Harlan Fiske	1925–1941	New York	Coolidge	53	Republican	Amherst College; Columbia University Law School
Roberts, Owen Josephus	1930–1945	Pennsylvania	Hoover	55	Republican	University of Pennsylvania; University of Pennsylvania Law School
Cardozo, Benjamin Nathan	1932–1938	New York	Hoover	62	Democrat	Columbia University; two years at Columbia Law School
Black, Hugo Lafayette	1937–1971	Alabama	Roosevelt, F.	51	Democrat	Birmingham Medical College; University of Alabama Law School
Reed, Stanley Forman	1938–1957	Kentucky	Roosevelt, F.	54	Democrat	Kentucky Wesleyan University; Foreman Yale; studied law at University of Virginia and Columbia University; University of Paris
Frankfurter, Felix	1939–1962	Massachusetts	Roosevelt, F.	57	Independent	College of the City of New York; Harvard Law School
Douglas, William Orville	1939–1975	Connecticut	Roosevelt, F.	41	Democrat	Whitman College; Columbia University Law School

ASSOCIATE JUSTICES (CONTINUED)

Name	Years of Service	State App'd from	Appointing President	Age App'd	Political Affiliation	Educational Background*
Murphy, Frank	1940–1949	Michigan	Roosevelt, F.	50	Democrat	University of Michigan; Lincoln's Inn, London; Trinity College
Byrnes, James Francis	1941–1942	South Carolina	Roosevelt, F.	62	Democrat	Read law privately
Jackson, Robert Houghwout	1941–1954	New York	Roosevelt, F.	49	Democrat	Albany Law School
Rutledge, Wiley Blount	1943–1949	Iowa	Roosevelt, F.	49	Democrat	University of Wisconsin; University of Colorado
Burton, Harold Hitz	1945–1958	Ohio	Truman	57	Republican	Bowdoin College; Harvard University Law School
Clark, Thomas Campbell	1949–1967	Texas	Truman	50	Democrat	University of Texas
Minton, Sherman	1949–1956	Indiana	Truman	59	Democrat	Indiana University College of Law; Yale Law School
Harlan, John Marshall	1955–1971	New York	Eisenhower	56	Republican	Princeton; Oxford University; New York Law School
Brennan, William J., Jr.	1956–1990	New Jersey	Eisenhower	50	Democrat	University of Pennsylvania; Harvard Law School
Whittaker, Charles Evans	1957–1962	Missouri	Eisenhower	56	Republican	University of Kansas City Law School
Stewart, Potter	1958–1981	Ohio	Eisenhower	43	Republican	Yale; Yale Law School
White, Byron Raymond	1962–1993	Colorado	Kennedy	45	Democrat	University of Colorado; Oxford University; Yale Law School
Goldberg, Arthur Joseph	1962–1965	Illinois	Kennedy	54	Democrat	Northwestern University
Fortas, Abe	1965–1969	Tennessee	Johnson, L.	55	Democrat	Southwestern College; Yale Law School
Marshall, Thurgood	1967–1991	New York	Johnson, L.	59	Democrat	Lincoln University; Howard University Law School
Blackmun, Harry A.	1970–1994	Minnesota	Nixon	62	Republican	Harvard; Harvard Law School
Powell, Lewis F., Jr.	1972–1987	Virginia	Nixon	65	Democrat	Washington and Lee University; Washington and Lee University Law School; Harvard Law School
Rehnquist, William H.	1972–1986	Arizona	Nixon	48	Republican	Stanford; Harvard; Stanford University Law School
Stevens, John Paul	1975–present	Illinois	Ford	55	Republican	University of Colorado; Northwestern University Law School
O'Connor, Sandra Day	1981–2006	Arizona	Reagan	51	Republican	Stanford; Stanford University Law School
Scalia, Antonin	1986–present	Virginia	Reagan	50	Republican	Georgetown University; Harvard Law School
Kennedy, Anthony M.	1988–present	California	Reagan	52	Republican	Stanford; London School of Economics; Harvard Law School
Souter, David Hackett	1990–present	New Hampshire	Bush, G. H. W.	51	Republican	Harvard; Oxford University
Thomas, Clarence	1991–present	District of	Bush, G. H. W.	43	Republican	Holy Cross College; Yale Law Columbia School
Ginsburg, Ruth Bader	1993–present	District of Columbia	Clinton	60	Democrat	Cornell University; Columbia Law School
Breyer, Stephen G.	1994–present	Massachusetts	Clinton	55	Democrat	Stanford; Oxford University; Harvard Law School
Alito, Samuel Anthony, Jr.	2006–present	New Jersey	G. W. Bush	55	Republican	Princeton University; Yale Law School

Appendix D

Party Control of Congress since 1900

Congress	Years	President	Majority Party in House	Majority Party in Senate
57th	1901–1903	T. Roosevelt	Republican	Republican
58th	1903–1905	T. Roosevelt	Republican	Republican
59th	1905–1907	T. Roosevelt	Republican	Republican
60th	1907–1909	T. Roosevelt	Republican	Republican
61st	1909–1911	Taft	Republican	Republican
62d	1911–1913	Taft	Democratic	Republican
63d	1913–1915	Wilson	Democratic	Democratic
64th	1915–1917	Wilson	Democratic	Democratic
65th	1917–1919	Wilson	Democratic	Democratic
66th	1919–1921	Wilson	Republican	Republican
67th	1921–1923	Harding	Republican	Republican
68th	1923–1925	Coolidge	Republican	Republican
69th	1925–1927	Coolidge	Republican	Republican
70th	1927–1929	Coolidge	Republican	Republican
71st	1929–1931	Hoover	Republican	Republican
72d	1931–1933	Hoover	Democratic	Republican
73d	1933–1935	F. Roosevelt	Democratic	Democratic
74th	1935–1937	F. Roosevelt	Democratic	Democratic
75th	1937–1939	F. Roosevelt	Democratic	Democratic
76th	1939–1941	F. Roosevelt	Democratic	Democratic
77th	1941–1943	F. Roosevelt	Democratic	Democratic
78th	1943–1945	F. Roosevelt	Democratic	Democratic
79th	1945–1947	Truman	Democratic	Democratic
80th	1947–1949	Truman	Republican	Democratic
81st	1949–1951	Truman	Democratic	Democratic
82d	1951–1953	Truman	Democratic	Democratic
83d	1953–1955	Eisenhower	Republican	Republican
84th	1955–1957	Eisenhower	Democratic	Democratic
85th	1957–1959	Eisenhower	Democratic	Democratic
86th	1959–1961	Eisenhower	Democratic	Democratic
87th	1961–1963	Kennedy	Democratic	Democratic
88th	1963–1965	Kennedy/Johnson	Democratic	Democratic
89th	1965–1967	Johnson	Democratic	Democratic
90th	1967–1969	Johnson	Democratic	Democratic
91st	1969–1971	Nixon	Democratic	Democratic
92d	1971–1973	Nixon	Democratic	Democratic
93d	1973–1975	Nixon/Ford	Democratic	Democratic
94th	1975–1977	Ford	Democratic	Democratic
95th	1977–1979	Carter	Democratic	Democratic
96th	1979–1981	Carter	Democratic	Democratic
97th	1981–1983	Reagan	Democratic	Republican
98th	1983–1985	Reagan	Democratic	Republican
99th	1985–1987	Reagan	Democratic	Republican
100th	1987–1989	Reagan	Democratic	Democratic
101st	1989–1991	G. H. W. Bush	Democratic	Democratic
102d	1991–1993	G. H. W. Bush	Democratic	Democratic
103d	1993–1995	Clinton	Democratic	Democratic
104th	1995–1997	Clinton	Republican	Republican
105th	1997–1999	Clinton	Republican	Republican
106th	1999–2001	Clinton	Republican	Republican
107th	2001–2003	G. W. Bush	Republican	Democratic
108th	2003–2005	G. W. Bush	Republican	Republican
109th	2005–2007	G. W. Bush	Republican	Republican
110th	2007–2009	G. W. Bush	Democratic	Democratic

Appendix E

Information on U.S. Presidents

	Term of Service	Age at Inauguration	Party Affiliation	College or University	Occupation or Profession
1. George Washington.........	1789–1797	57	None		Planter
2. John Adams................	1797–1801	61	Federalist	Harvard	Lawyer
3. Thomas Jefferson...........	1801–1809	57	Democratic-Republican	William and Mary	Planter, Lawyer
4. James Madison.............	1809–1817	57	Democratic-Republican	Princeton	Lawyer
5. James Monroe	1817–1825	58	Democratic-Republican	William and Mary	Lawyer
6. John Quincy Adams........	1825–1829	57	Democratic-Republican	Harvard	Lawyer
7. Andrew Jackson	1829–1837	61	Democrat		Lawyer
8. Martin Van Buren..........	1837–1841	54	Democrat		Lawyer
9. William H. Harrison	1841	68	Whig	Hampden-Sydney	Soldier
10. John Tyler	1841–1845	51	Whig	William and Mary	Lawyer
11. James K. Polk..............	1845–1849	49	Democrat	U. of N. Carolina	Lawyer
12. Zachary Taylor	1849–1850	64	Whig		Soldier
13. Millard Fillmore	1850–1853	50	Whig		Lawyer
14. Franklin Pierce	1853–1857	48	Democrat	Bowdoin	Lawyer
15. James Buchanan	1857–1861	65	Democrat	Dickinson	Lawyer
16. Abraham Lincoln	1861–1865	52	Republican		Lawyer
17. Andrew Johnson...........	1865–1869	56	National Union†		Tailor
18. Ulysses S. Grant	1869–1877	46	Republican	U.S. Mil. Academy	Soldier
19. Rutherford B. Hayes........	1877–1881	54	Republican	Kenyon	Lawyer
20. James A. Garfield	1881	49	Republican	Williams	Lawyer
21. Chester A. Arthur	1881–1885	51	Republican	Union	Lawyer
22. Grover Cleveland	1885–1889	47	Democrat		Lawyer
23. Benjamin Harrison..........	1889–1893	55	Republican	Miami	Lawyer
24. Grover Cleveland	1893–1897	55	Democrat		Lawyer
25. William McKinley...........	1897–1901	54	Republican	Allegheny College	Lawyer
26. Theodore Roosevelt........	1901–1909	42	Republican	Harvard	Author
27. William H. Taft	1909–1913	51	Republican	Yale	Lawyer
28. Woodrow Wilson	1913–1921	56	Democrat	Princeton	Educator
29. Warren G. Harding.........	1921–1923	55	Republican		Editor
30. Calvin Coolidge............	1923–1929	51	Republican	Amherst	Lawyer
31. Herbert C. Hoover..........	1929–1933	54	Republican	Stanford	Engineer
32. Franklin D. Roosevelt.......	1933–1945	51	Democrat	Harvard	Lawyer
33. Harry S Truman............	1945–1953	60	Democrat		Businessman
34. Dwight D. Eisenhower.......	1953–1961	62	Republican	U.S. Mil. Academy	Soldier
35. John F. Kennedy	1961–1963	43	Democrat	Harvard	Author
36. Lyndon B. Johnson..........	1963–1969	55	Democrat	Southwest Texas State	Teacher
37. Richard M. Nixon	1969–1974	56	Republican	Whittier	Lawyer
38. Gerald R. Ford‡	1974–1977	61	Republican	Michigan	Lawyer
39. James E. Carter, Jr.	1977–1981	52	Democrat	U.S. Naval Academy	Businessman
40. Ronald W. Reagan	1981–1989	69	Republican	Eureka College	Actor
41. George H. W. Bush..........	1989–1993	64	Republican	Yale	Businessman
42. William J. Clinton...........	1993–2001	46	Democrat	Georgetown	Lawyer
43. George W. Bush	2001–2009	54	Republican	Yale	Businessman

*Church preference; never joined any church.
†The National Union Party consisted of Republicans and War Democrats. Johnson was a Democrat.
**Inaugurated Dec. 6, 1973, to replace Agnew, who resigned Oct. 10, 1973.
‡Inaugurated Aug. 9, 1974, to replace Nixon, who resigned that same day.
§Inaugurated Dec. 19, 1974, to replace Ford, who became president Aug. 9, 1974.

	Religion	Born	Died	Age at Death	Vice President	
1.	Episcopalian	Feb. 22, 1732	Dec. 14, 1799	67	John Adams	(1789–1797)
2.	Unitarian	Oct. 30, 1735	July 4, 1826	90	Thomas Jefferson	(1797–1801)
3.	Unitarian*	Apr. 13, 1743	July 4, 1826	83	Aaron Burr	(1801–1805)
					George Clinton	(1805–1809)
4.	Episcopalian	Mar. 16, 1751	June 28, 1836	85	George Clinton	(1809–1812)
					Elbridge Gerry	(1813–1814)
5.	Episcopalian	Apr. 28, 1758	July 4, 1831	73	Daniel D. Tompkins	(1817–1825)
6.	Unitarian	July 11, 1767	Feb. 23, 1848	80	John C. Calhoun	(1825–1829)
7.	Presbyterian	Mar. 15, 1767	June 8, 1845	78	John C. Calhoun	(1829–1832)
					Martin Van Buren	(1833–1837)
8.	Dutch Reformed	Dec. 5, 1782	July 24, 1862	79	Richard M. Johnson	(1837–1841)
9.	Episcopalian	Feb. 9, 1773	Apr. 4, 1841	68	John Tyler	(1841)
10.	Episcopalian	Mar. 29, 1790	Jan. 18, 1862	71		
11.	Methodist	Nov. 2, 1795	June 15, 1849	53	George M. Dallas	(1845–1849)
12.	Episcopalian	Nov. 24, 1784	July 9, 1850	65	Millard Fillmore	(1849–1850)
13.	Unitarian	Jan. 7, 1800	Mar. 8, 1874	74		
14.	Episcopalian	Nov. 23, 1804	Oct. 8, 1869	64	William R. King	(1853)
15.	Presbyterian	Apr. 23, 1791	June 1, 1868	77	John C. Breckinridge	(1857–1861)
16.	Presbyterian*	Feb. 12, 1809	Apr. 15, 1865	56	Hannibal Hamlin	(1861–1865)
					Andrew Johnson	(1865)
17.	Methodist*	Dec. 29, 1808	July 31, 1875	66		
18.	Methodist	Apr. 27, 1822	July 23, 1885	63	Schuyler Colfax	(1869–1873)
					Henry Wilson	(1873–1875)
19.	Methodist*	Oct. 4, 1822	Jan. 17, 1893	70	William A. Wheeler	(1877–1881)
20.	Disciples of Christ	Nov. 19, 1831	Sept. 19, 1881	49	Chester A. Arthur	(1881)
21.	Episcopalian	Oct. 5, 1829	Nov. 18, 1886	57		
22.	Presbyterian	Mar. 18, 1837	June 24, 1908	71	Thomas A. Hendricks	(1885)
23.	Presbyterian	Aug. 20, 1833	Mar. 13, 1901	67	Levi P. Morton	(1889–1893)
24.	Presbyterian	Mar. 18, 1837	June 24, 1908	71	Adlai E. Stevenson	(1893–1897)
25.	Methodist	Jan. 29, 1843	Sept. 14, 1901	58	Garret A. Hobart	(1897–1899)
					Theodore Roosevelt	(1901)
26.	Dutch Reformed	Oct. 27, 1858	Jan. 6, 1919	60	Charles W. Fairbanks	(1905–1909)
27.	Unitarian	Sept. 15, 1857	Mar. 8, 1930	72	James S. Sherman	(1909–1912)
28.	Presbyterian	Dec. 29, 1856	Feb. 3, 1924	67	Thomas R. Marshall	(1913–1921)
29.	Baptist	Nov. 2, 1865	Aug. 2, 1923	57	Calvin Coolidge	(1921–1923)
30.	Congregationalist	July 4, 1872	Jan. 5, 1933	60	Charles G. Dawes	(1925–1929)
31.	Friend (Quaker)	Aug. 10, 1874	Oct. 20, 1964	90	Charles Curtis	(1929–1933)
32.	Episcopalian	Jan. 30, 1882	Apr. 12, 1945	63	John N. Garner	(1933–1941)
					Henry A. Wallace	(1941–1945)
					Harry S Truman	(1945)
33.	Baptist	May 8, 1884	Dec. 26, 1972	88	Alben W. Barkley	(1949–1953)
34.	Presbyterian	Oct. 14, 1890	Mar. 28, 1969	78	Richard M. Nixon	(1953–1961)
35.	Roman Catholic	May 29, 1917	Nov. 22, 1963	46	Lyndon B. Johnson	(1961–1963)
36.	Disciples of Christ	Aug. 27, 1908	Jan. 22, 1973	64	Hubert H. Humphrey	(1965–1969)
37.	Friend (Quaker)	Jan. 9, 1913	Apr. 22, 1994	81	Spiro T. Agnew	(1969–1973)
					Gerald R. Ford**	(1973–1974)
38.	Episcopalian	July 14, 1913	Dec. 26, 2006	93	Nelson A. Rockefeller§	(1974–1977)
39.	Baptist	Oct. 1, 1924			Walter F. Mondale	(1977–1981)
40.	Disciples of Christ	Feb. 6, 1911	June 5, 2004	93	George H. W. Bush	(1981–1989)
41.	Episcopalian	June 12, 1924			J. Danforth Quayle	(1989–1993)
42.	Baptist	Aug. 19, 1946			Albert A. Gore	(1993–2001)
43.	Methodist	July 6, 1946			Dick Cheney	(2001–2009)

The founders completed drafting the U.S. Constitution in 1787. It was then submitted to the thirteen states for ratification, and a major debate ensued. As you read in Chapter 2, on the one side of this debate were the Federalists, who urged that the new Constitution be adopted. On the other side of the debate were the Anti-Federalists, who argued against ratification.

During the course of this debate, three men well known for their Federalist views—Alexander Hamilton, James Madison, and John Jay—wrote a series of essays in which they argued for immediate ratifcation of the Constitution. The essays appeared in the New York City Independent Journal *in October 1787, just a little over a month after the Constitutional Convention adjourned. Later, Hamilton arranged to have the essays collected and published in book form. The articles filled two volumes, both of which were published by May 1788. The essays are often referred to collectively as the* Federalist Papers.

Scholars disagree as to whether the Federalist Papers *had a significant impact on the decision of the states to ratify the Constitution. Nonetheless, many of the essays are masterpieces of political reasoning and have left a lasting imprint on American politics and government. Above all, the* Federalist Papers *shed an important light on what the founders intended when they drafted various constitutional provisions.*

Here we present just two of these essays, Federalist Paper No. 10 *and* Federalist Paper No. 51. *Each essay was written by James Madison, who referred to himself as "Publius." We have annotated each document to clarify the meaning of particular passages. The annotations are set in italics to distinguish them from the original text of the documents.*

#10

Federalist Paper No. 10 is a classic document that is often referred to by teachers of American government. Authored by James Madison, it sets forth Madison's views on factions in politics. The essay was written, in large part, to counter the arguments put forth by the Anti-Federalists that small factions might take control of the government, thus destroying the representative nature of the republican form of government established by the Constitution. The essay opens with a discussion of the "dangerous vice" of factions and the importance of devising a form of government in which this vice will be controlled.

Among the numerous advantages promised by a well-constructed Union, none deserves to be more accurately developed than its tendency to break and control the violence of faction. The friend of popular governments never finds himself so much alarmed for their character and fate as when he contemplates their propensity to this dangerous vice. He will not fail, therefore, to set a due value on any plan which, without violating the principles to which he is attached, provides a proper cure for it. The instability, injustice, and confusion introduced into the public councils have, in truth, been the mortal diseases under which popular governments have everywhere perished, as they continue to be the favorite and fruitful topics from which the adversaries to liberty derive their most specious declamations. The valuable improvements made by the American constitutions on the popular models, both ancient and modern, cannot certainly be too much admired; but it would be an unwarrantable partiality to contend that they have as effectually obviated the danger on this side, as was wished and expected. Complaints are everywhere heard from our most considerate and virtuous citizens, equally the friends of public and private faith and of public and personal liberty, that our governments are too unstable, that the public good is disregarded in the conflicts of rival parties, and that measures are too often decided, not according to the rules of justice and the rights of the minor party, but by the superior force of an interested and overbearing majority. However anxiously we may wish that these complaints had no foundation, the evidence of known facts will not permit us to deny that they are in some degree true. It will be found, indeed, on a candid review of our situation, that some of the distresses under which we labor have been erroneously charged on the operation of our governments; but it will be found, at the same time, that other causes will not alone account for many of our heaviest misfortunes; and, particularly, for that prevailing and increasing distrust of public engagements and alarm for private rights which are echoed from one end of the continent to the other. These must be chiefly, if not wholly, effects of the unsteadiness and injustice with which a factious spirit has tainted our public administration.

In the following paragraph, Madison clarifies for his readers his understanding of what the term faction *means.*

By a faction I understand a number of citizens, whether amounting to a majority or minority of the whole, who are united and actuated by some common impulse of passion, or of interest, adverse to the rights of other citizens, or the permanent and aggregate interests of the community.

In the following passages, Madison looks at the two methods of curing the "mischiefs of factions." One of these methods is removing the causes of faction. The other is to control the effects of factions.

There are two methods of curing the mischiefs of faction: the one, by removing its causes; the other, by controlling its effects.

There are again two methods of removing the causes of faction: the one, by destroying the liberty which is essential to its existence; the other, by giving to every citizen the same opinions, the same passions, and the same interests.

It could never be more truly said than of the first remedy that it was worse than the disease. Liberty is to faction what air is to fire, an aliment without which it instantly expires. But it could not be a less folly to abolish liberty, which is essential to political life, because it nourishes faction than it would be to wish the annihilation of air, which is essential to animal life, because it imparts to fire its destructive agency.

The second expedient is as impracticable as the first would be unwise. As long as the reason of man continues fallible, and his is at liberty to exercise it, different opinions will be formed. As long as the connection subsists between his reason and his self-love, his opinions and his passions will have a reciprocal influence on each other; and the former will be objects to which the latter will attach themselves. The diversity in the faculties of men, from which the rights of property originate, is not less an insuperable obstacle to a uniformity of interests. The protection of these faculties is the first object of government. From the protection of different and unequal faculties of acquiring property, the possession of different degrees and kinds of property immediately results; and from the influence of these on the sentiments and views of the respective proprietors ensues a division of the society into different interests and parties.

The latent causes of faction are thus sown in the nature of man; and we see them everywhere brought into different degrees of activity, according to the different circumstances of civil society. A zeal for different opinions concerning religion, concerning government, and many other points, as well of speculation as of practice; an attachment to different leaders ambitiously contending for pre-eminence and power; or to persons of other descriptions whose fortunes have been interesting to the human passions, have, in turn, divided mankind into parties, inflamed them with mutual animosity, and rendered them much more disposed to vex and oppress each other than to co-operate for their common good. So strong is this propensity of mankind to fall into mutual animosities that where no substantial occasion presents itself the most frivolous and fanciful distinctions have been sufficient to kindle their unfriendly passions and excite their most violent conflicts. But the most common and durable source of factions has been the various and unequal distribution of property. Those who hold and those who are without property have ever formed distinct interests in society. Those who are creditors, and those who are debtors, fall under a like discrimination. A landed interest, a manufacturing interest, a mercantile interest, a moneyed interest, with many lesser interests, grow up of necessity in civilized nations, and divide them into different classes, actuated by different sentiments and views. The regulation of these various and interfering interests forms the principal task of modern legislation and involves the spirit of party and faction in the necessary and ordinary operations of government.

No man is allowed to be a judge in his own cause, because his interest would certainly bias his judgment, and, not improbably, corrupt his integrity. With equal, nay with greater reason, a body of men are unfit to be both judges and parties at the same time; yet what are many of the most important acts of legislation but so many judicial determinations, not indeed concerning the rights of single persons, but concerning the rights of large bodies of citizens? And what are the different classes of legislators but advocates and parties to the causes which they determine? Is a law proposed concerning private debts? It is a question to which the creditors are parties on one side and the debtors on the other. Justice ought to hold the balance between them. Yet the parties are, and must be, themselves the judges; and the most numerous party, or in other words, the most powerful faction must be expected to prevail. Shall domestic manufacturers be encouraged, and in what degree, by restrictions on foreign manufacturers?

Are questions which would be differently decided by the landed and the manufacturing classes, and probably by neither with a sole regard to justice and the public good. The apportionment of taxes on the various descriptions of property is an act which seems to require the most exact impartiality; yet there is, perhaps, no legislative act in which greater opportunity and temptation are given to a predominant party to trample on the rules of justice. Every shilling with which they overburden the inferior number is a shilling saved to their own pockets.

It is in vain to say that enlightened statesmen will be able to adjust these clashing interests and render them all subservient to the public good. Enlightened statesmen will not always be at the helm. Nor, in many cases, can such an adjustment be made at all without taking into view indirect and remote considerations, which will rarely prevail over the immediate interest which one party may find in disregarding the rights of another or the good of the whole.

The inference to which we are brought is that the causes of faction cannot be removed and that relief is only to be sought in the means of controlling its effects.

In the preceding passages, Madison has explored the causes of factions and has concluded that they cannot "be removed" without removing liberty itself, which is one of the causes, or altering human nature. He now turns to a discussion of how the effects of factions might be controlled.

If a faction consists of less than a majority, relief is supplied by the republican principle, which enables the majority to defeat its sinister views by regular vote. It may clog the administration, it may convulse the society; but it will be unable to execute and mask its violence under the forms of the Constitution. When a majority is included in a faction, the form of popular government, on the other hand, enables it to sacrifice to its ruling passion or interest both the public good and the rights of other citizens. To secure the public good and private rights against the danger of such a faction, and at the same time to preserve the spirit and the form of popular government, is then the great object to which our inquiries are directed. Let me add that it is the great desideratum by which alone this form of government can be rescued from the opprobrium under which it has so long labored and be recommended to the esteem and adoption of mankind.

According to Madison, one way of controlling the effects of factions is to make sure that the majority is not able to act in "concert," or jointly, to "carry into effect schemes of oppression."

By what means is this object attainable? Evidently by one of two only. Either the existence of the same passion or interest in a majority at the same time must be prevented, or the majority, having such coexistent passion or interest, must be rendered, by their number and local situation, unable to concert and carry into effect schemes of oppression. If the impulse and the opportunity be suffered to coincide, we well know that neither moral nor religious motives can be relied on as an adequate control. They are not found to be such on the injustice and violence of individuals, and lose their efficacy in proportion to the number combined together, that is, in proportion as their efficacy becomes needful.

From this view of the subject it may be concluded that a pure democracy, by which I mean a society consisting of a small number of citizens, who assemble and administer the government in person, can admit of no cure for the mischiefs of faction. A common passion or interest will, in almost every case, be felt by a majority of the whole; a communication and concert results from the form of government itself; and there is nothing to check the inducements to sacrifice the weaker party or an obnoxious individual. Hence it is that such democracies have ever been spectacles of turbulence and contention; have ever been found incompatible with personal security or the rights of property; and have in general been as short in their lives as they have been violent in their deaths. Theoretic politicians, who have patronized this species of government, have erroneously supposed that by reducing mankind to a perfect equality in their political rights, they would at the same time be perfectly equalized and assimilated in their possessions, their opinions, and their passions.

In the following six paragraphs, Madison sets forth some of the reasons why a republican form of government promises a "cure" for the mischiefs of factions. He begins by clarifying the difference between a republic and a democracy. He then describes how in a large republic, the elected representatives of the people will be large enough in number to guard against factions— the "cabals," or concerted actions, of "a few." On the one hand, representatives will not be so removed from their local districts as to be unacquainted with their constituents' needs. On the other hand, they will not be "unduly attached" to local interests and unfit to understand "great and national objects." Madison concludes that the Constitution "forms a happy combination in this respect."

A republic, by which I mean a government in which the scheme of representation takes place, opens a different prospect and promises the cure for which we are seeking. Let us examine the points in which it varies from pure democracy, and we shall comprehend both the nature of the cure and the efficacy which it must derive from the Union.

The two great points of difference between a democracy and a republic are: first, the delegation of the government, in the latter, to a small number of citizens elected by the rest; secondly, the greater number of citizens and greater sphere of country over which the latter may be extended.

The effect of the first difference is, on the one hand, to refine and enlarge the public views by passing them through the medium of a chosen body of citizens, whose wisdom may best discern the true interest of their country and whose patriotism and love of justice will be least likely to sacrifice it to temporary or partial considerations. Under such a regulation it may well happen that the public voice, pronounced by the representatives of the people, will be more consonant to the public good than if pronounced by the people themselves, convened for the purpose. On the other hand, the effect may be inverted. Men of factious tempers, of local prejudices, or of sinister designs, may, by intrigue, by corruption, or by other means, first obtain the suffrages, and then betray the interests of the people. The question resulting is, whether small or extensive republics are most favorable to the election of proper guardians of the public weal; and it is clearly decided in favor of the latter by two obvious considerations.

In the first place it is to be remarked that however small the republic may be the representatives must be raised to a certain number in order to guard against the cabals of a few; and that however large it may be they must be limited to a certain number in order to guard against the confusion of a multitude. Hence, the number of representatives in the two cases not being in proportion to that of the constituents, and being proportionally greatest in the small republic, it follows that if the proportion of fit characters be not less in the large than in the small republic, the former will present a greater option, and consequently a greater probability of a fit choice.

In the next place, as each representative will be chosen by a greater number of citizens in the large than in the small republic, it will be more difficult for unworthy candidates to practice with success the vicious arts by which elections are too often carried; and the suffrages of the people being more free, will be more likely to center on men who possess the most attractive merit and the most diffusive and established characters.

It must be confessed that in this, as in most other cases, there is a mean, on both sides of which inconveniencies will be found to lie. By enlarging too much the number of electors, you render the representative too little acquainted with all their local circumstances and lesser interests; as by reducing it too much, you render him unduly attached to these, and too little fit to comprehend and pursue great and national objects. The federal Constitution forms a happy combination in this respect; the great and aggregate interests being referred to the national, the local and particular to the State legislatures.

In the remaining passages of this essay, Madison looks at another "point of difference" between a republic and a democracy. Specifically, a republic can encompass a larger territory and a greater number of citizens than a democracy can. This fact, too, argues Madison, will help to control the influence of factions because the interests that draw people together to act in concert are typically at the local level and would be unlikely to affect or dominate the national government. As Madison states, "The influence of factious leaders may kindle a flame within their particular States but will be unable to spread a general conflagration through the other States." Generally, in a large republic, there will be numerous factions, and no particular faction will be able to "pervade the whole body of the Union."

The other point of difference is the greater number of citizens and extent of territory which may be brought within the compass of republican than of democratic government; and it is this circumstance principally which renders factious combinations less to be dreaded in the former than in the latter. The smaller the society, the fewer probably will be the distinct parties and interests composing it; the fewer the distinct parties and interests, the more frequently will a majority be found of the same party; and the smaller the number of individuals composing a majority, and the smaller the compass within which they are placed, the more easily will they concert and execute their plans of oppression. Extend the sphere and you take in a greater variety of parties and interests; you make it less probable that a majority of the whole will have a common motive to invade the rights of other citizens; or if such a common motive exists, it will be more difficult for all who feel it to discover their own strength and to act in unison with each other. Besides other impediments, it may be remarked that, where there is a consciousness of unjust or dishonorable purposes, communication is always checked by distrust in proportion to the number whose concurrence is necessary.

Hence, it clearly appears that the same advantage which a republic has over a democracy in controlling the effects of faction is enjoyed by a large over a small republic—is enjoyed by the Union over the States composing it. Does this advantage consist in the substitution of representatives whose enlightened views and virtuous sentiments render them superior to local prejudices and to schemes of injustice? It will not be denied that the representation of the Union will be most likely to possess these requisite endowments. Does it consist in the greater security afforded by a greater variety of parties, against the event of any one party being able to outnumber and oppress the rest? In an equal degree does the increased variety of parties comprised within the Union increase this security. Does it, in fine, consist in the greater obstacles opposed to the concert and accomplishment of the secret wishes of an unjust and interested majority? Here again the extent of the Union gives it the most palpable advantage.

The influence of factious leaders may kindle a flame within their particular States but will be unable to spread a general conflagration through the other States. A religious sect may degenerate into a political faction in a part of the Confederacy; but the variety of sects dispersed over the entire face of it must secure the national councils against any danger from that source. A rage for paper money, for an abolition of debts, for an equal division of property, or for any other improper or wicked project, will be less apt to pervade the whole body of the Union than a particular member of it, in the same proportion as such a malady is more likely to taint a particular county or district than an entire State.

In the extent and proper structure of the Union, therefore, we behold a republican remedy for the diseases most incident to republican government. And according to the degree of pleasure and pride we feel in being republicans ought to be our zeal in cherishing the spirit and supporting the character of federalists.

Publius
(James Madison)

#51

Federalist Paper *No. 51, which was also authored by James Madison, is one of the classics in American political theory. Recall from Chapter 2 that a major concern of the founders was to create a relatively strong national government but one that would not be capable of tyrannizing over the populace. In the following essay, Madison sets forth the theory of "checks and balances." He explains that the new Constitution, by dividing the national government into three branches (executive, legislative, and judicial), offers protection against tyranny.*

To what expedient, then, shall we finally resort, for maintaining in practice the necessary partition of power among the several departments as laid down in the Constitution? The only answer that can be given is that as all these exterior provisions are found to be inadequate the defect must be supplied, by so contriving the interior structure of the government as that its several constituent parts may, by their mutual relations, be the means of keeping each other in their proper places. Without presuming to undertake a full development of this important idea I will hazard a few general observations which may perhaps place it in a clearer light, and enable us to form a more correct judgment of the principles and structure of the government planned by the convention.

In the following two paragraphs, Madison explains that to ensure that the powers of government are genuinely separated, it is important that each of the three branches of government (executive, legislative, and judicial) should have a "will of its own." Among other things, this means that persons in one branch should not depend on persons in another branch for the "emoluments annexed to their offices" (pay, perks, and privileges). If they did, then the branches would not be truly independent of one another.

In order to lay a due foundation for that separate and distinct exercise of the different powers of government, which to a certain extent is admitted on all hands to be essential to the preservation of liberty, it is evident that each department should have a will of its own; and consequently should be so constituted that the members of each should have as little agency as possible in the appointment of the members of the others. Were this principle rigorously adhered to, it would require that all the appointments for the supreme executive, legislative, and judiciary magistracies should be drawn from the same fountain of authority, the people, through channels having no communication whatever with one another. Perhaps such a plan of constructing the several departments would be less difficult in practice than it may in contemplation appear. Some difficulties, however, and some additional expense would attend the execution of it. Some deviations, therefore, from the principle must be admitted. In the constitution of the judiciary department in particular, it might be inexpedient to insist rigorously on the principle: first, because peculiar qualifications being essential in the members, the primary consideration ought to be to select that mode of choice which best secures these qualifications; second, because the permanent tenure by which the appointments are held in that department must soon destroy all sense of dependence on the authority conferring them.

It is equally evident that the members of each department should be as little dependent as possible on those of the others for the emoluments annexed to their offices. Were the executive magistrate, or the judges, not independent of the legislature in this particular, their independence in every other would be merely nominal.

One of the striking qualities of the theory of checks and balances as posited by Madison is that it assumes that persons are not angels but driven by personal interests and motives. In the following two paragraphs, which are among the most widely quoted of Madison's writings, he stresses that the division of the government into three branches helps to check personal ambitions. Personal ambitions will naturally arise, but they will be linked to the constitutional powers of each branch. In effect, they will help to keep the three branches separate and thus serve the public interest.

But the great security against a gradual concentration of the several powers in the same department consists in giving to those who administer each department the necessary constitutional means and personal motives to resist encroachments of the others. The provision for defense must in this, as in all other cases, be made commensurate to the danger of attack. Ambition must be made to counteract ambition. The interest of the man must be connected with the constitutional rights of the place. It may be a reflection on human nature that such devices should be necessary to control the abuses of government. But what is government itself but the greatest of all reflections on human nature? If men were angels, no government would be necessary. If angels were to govern men, neither external nor internal controls on government would be necessary. In framing a government which is to be administered by men over men, the great difficulty lies in this: you must first enable the government to control the governed; and in the next place oblige it to control itself. A dependence on the people is, no doubt, the primary control on the government; but experience has taught mankind the necessity of auxiliary precautions.

This policy of supplying, by opposite and rival interests, the defect of better motives, might be traced through the whole system of human affairs, private as well as public. We see it particularly displayed in all the subordinate distributions of power, where the constant aim is to divide and arrange the several offices in such a manner as that each may be a check on the other—that the private interest of every individual may be a sentinel over the public rights. These inventions of prudence cannot be less requisite in the distribution of the supreme powers of the State.

In the next two paragraphs, Madison first points out that the "legislative authority necessarily predominates" in a republican form of government. The "remedy" for this lack of balance with the other branches of government is to divide the legislative branch into two chambers with "different modes of election and different principles of action."

But it is not possible to give to each department an equal power of self-defense. In republican government, the legislative authority necessarily predominates. The remedy for this inconveniency is to divide the legislature into different branches; and to render them, by different modes of election and different principles of action, as little connected with each other as the nature of their common functions and their common dependence on the society will admit. It may even be necessary to guard against dangerous encroachments by still further precautions. As the weight of the legislative authority requires that it should be thus divided, the weakness of the executive may require, on the other hand, that it should be fortified. An absolute negative on the legislature appears, at first view, to be the natural defense with which the executive magistrate should be armed. But perhaps it would be neither altogether safe nor alone sufficient. On ordinary occasions it might not be exerted with the requisite firmness, and on extraordinary occasions it might be perfidiously abused. May not this defect of an absolute negative be supplied by some qualified connection between this weaker department and the weaker branch of the stronger department, by which the latter may be led to support the constitutional rights of the former, without being too much detached from the rights of its own department?

If the principles on which these observations are founded be just, as I persuade myself they are, and they be applied as a criterion to the several State constitutions, and to the federal Constitution, it will be found that if the latter does not perfectly correspond with them, the former are infinitely less able to bear such a test.

In the remaining passages of this essay, Madison discusses the importance of the division of government powers between the states and the national government. This division of powers, by providing additional checks and balances, offers a "double security" against tyranny.

There are, moreover, two considerations particularly applicable to the federal system of America, which place that system in a very interesting point of view.

First. In a single republic, all the power surrendered by the people is submitted to the administration of a single government; and the usurpations are guarded against by a division of the government into distinct and separate departments. In the compound republic of America, the power surrendered by the people is first divided between two distinct governments, and then the portion allotted to each subdivided among distinct and separate departments. Hence a double security arises to the rights of the people. The different governments will control each other, at the same time that each will be controlled by itself.

Second. It is of great importance in a republic not only to guard the society against the oppression of its rulers, but to guard one part of the society against the injustice of the other part. Different interests necessarily exist in different classes of citizens. If a majority be united by a common interest, the rights of the minority will be insecure. There are but two methods of providing against this evil: the one by creating a will in the community independent of the majority—that is, of the society itself; the other, by comprehending in the society so many separate descriptions of citizens as will render an unjust combination of a majority of the whole very improbable, if not impracticable. The first method prevails in all governments possessing an hereditary or self-appointed authority. This, at best, is but a precarious security; because a power independent of the society may as well espouse the unjust views of the major as the rightful interests of the minor party, and may possibly be turned against both parties. The second method will be exemplified in the federal republic of the United States. Whilst all authority in it will be derived from and dependent on the society, the society itself will be broken into so many parts, interests and classes of citizens, that the rights of individuals, or of the minority, will be in little danger from interested combinations of the majority. In a free government the security for civil rights must be the same as that for religious rights. It consists in the one case in the multiplicity of interests, and in the other in the multiplicity of sects. The degree of security in both cases will depend on the number of interests and sects; and this may be presumed to depend on the extent of country and number of people comprehended under the same government. This view of the subject must particularly recommend a proper federal system to all the sincere and considerate friends of republican government, since it shows that in exact proportion as the territory of the Union may be formed into more circumscribed Confederacies, or States, oppressive combinations of a majority will be facilitated;

the best security, under the republican forms, for the rights of every class of citizen, will be diminished; and consequently the stability and independence of some member of the government, the only other security, must be proportionally increased. Justice is the end of government. It is the end of civil society. It ever has been and ever will be pursued until it be obtained, or until liberty be lost in the pursuit. In a society under the forms of which the stronger faction can readily unite and oppress the weaker, anarchy may as truly be said to reign as in a state of nature, where the weaker individual is not secured against the violence of the stronger; and as, in the latter state, even the stronger individuals are prompted, by the uncertainty of their condition, to submit to a government which may protect the weak as well as themselves; so, in the former state, will the more powerful factions or parties be gradually induced, by a like motive, to wish for a government which will protect all parties, the weaker as well as the more powerful. It can be little doubted that if the State of Rhode Island was separated from the Confederacy and left to itself, the insecurity of rights under the popular form of government within such narrow limits would be displayed by such reiterated oppressions of factious majorities that some power altogether independent of the people would soon be called for by the voice of the very factions whose misrule had proved the necessity of it. In the extended republic of the United States, and among the great variety of interests, parties, and sects which it embraces, a coalition of a majority of the whole society could seldom take place on any other principles than those of justice and the general good; whilst there being thus less danger to a minor from the will of a major party, there must be less pretext, also, to provide for the security of the former, by introducing into the government a will not dependent on the latter, or, in other words, a will independent of the society itself. It is no less certain than it is important, notwithstanding the contrary opinions which have been entertained, that the larger the society, provided it lie within a practicable sphere, the more duly capable it will be of self-government. And happily for the *republican cause,* the practicable sphere may be carried to a very great extent by a judicious modification and mixture of the *federal principle.*

Publius
(James Madison)

Appendix G

How to Read Case Citations and Find Court Decisions

Many important court cases are discussed in references in endnotes throughout this book. Court decisions are recorded and published. When a court case is mentioned, the notation that is used to refer to, or to cite, the case denotes where the published decision can be found.

State courts of appeals decisions are usually published in two places, the state reports of that particular state and the more widely used *National Reporter System* published by West Group. Some states no longer publish their own reports. The *National Reporter System* divides the states into the following geographic areas: Atlantic (A. or A.2d, where *2d* refers to *Second Series*), South Eastern (S.E. or S.E.2d), South Western (S.W., S.W.2d, or S.W.3d), North Western (N.W. or N.W.2d), North Eastern (N.E. or N.E.2d), Southern (So. or So.2d), and Pacific (P., P.2d, or P.3d).

Federal trial court decisions are published unofficially in West's *Federal Supplement* (F.Supp. or F.Supp.2d), and opinions from the circuit courts of appeals are reported unofficially in West's *Federal Reporter* (F., F.2d, or F.3d). Opinions from the United States Supreme Court are reported in the *United States Reports* (U.S.), the *Lawyers' Edition of the Supreme Court Reports* (L.Ed.), West's *Supreme Court Reporter* (S.Ct.), and other publications. The *United States Reports* is the official publication of United States Supreme Court decisions. It is published by the federal government. Many early decisions are missing from these volumes. The citations of the early volumes of the *U.S. Reports* include the names of the actual reporters, such as Dallas, Cranch, or Wheaton. *McCulloch v. Maryland,* for example, is cited as 17 U.S. (4 Wheat.) 316. Only after 1874 did the present citation system, in which cases are cited based solely on their volume and page numbers in the *United States Reports,* come into being. The *Lawyers' Edition of the Supreme Court Reports* is an unofficial and more complete edition of Supreme Court decisions. West's *Supreme Court Reporter* is an unofficial edition of decisions dating from October 1882. These volumes contain headnotes and numerous brief editorial statements of the law involved in the case.

State courts of appeals decisions are cited by giving the name of the case; the volume, name, and page number of the state's official report (if the state publishes its own reports); the volume, unit, and page number of the *National Reporter;* and the volume, name, and page number of any other selected reporter. Federal court citations are also listed by giving the name of the case and the volume, name, and page number of the reports. In addition to the citation, this textbook lists the year of the decision in parentheses. Consider, for example, the case *United States v. Curtiss-Wright Export Co.,* 299 U.S. 304 (1936). The Supreme Court's decision of this case may be found in volume 299 of the *United States Reports* on page 304. The case was decided in 1936.

Today, many courts, including the United States Supreme Court, publish their opinions online. This makes it much easier for students to find and read cases, or summaries of cases, that have significant consequences for American government and politics. To access cases via the Internet, use the URLs given in the *Politics on the Web* section at the end of Chapter 14.

Notes

CHAPTER 1
1. Harold Lasswell, *Politics: Who Gets What, When, and How* (New York: McGraw-Hill, 1936).
2. Charles Lewis, *The Buying of Congress* (New York: Avon Books, 1998), p. 346.
3. As quoted in Paul M. Angle and Earl Schenck Miers, *The Living Lincoln* (New York: Barnes & Noble, 1992), p. 155.
4. Martin J. Wade and William F. Russell, *The Short Constitution* (Iowa City: American Citizen Publishing Co., 1920), p. 38.
5. John W. Dean, *Conservatives without Conscience* (New York: Penguin, 2007), p. 11.

CHAPTER 2
1. See David Cole, *Less Safe, Less Free: The Failure of Preemption in the War on Terror* (New York: The New Press, 2007).
2. The first *European* settlement in North America was St. Augustine, Florida (a city that still exists), which was founded on September 8, 1565, by the Spaniard Pedro Menéndez de Ávilés.
3. Archaeologists have recently discovered the remains of a colony at Popham Beach, on the southern coast of what is now Maine, that was established at the same time as the colony at Jamestown. The Popham colony disbanded after thirteen months, however, when the leader, after learning that he had inherited property back home, returned—with the other colonists—to England.
4. John Camp, *Out of the Wilderness: The Emergence of an American Identity in Colonial New England* (Middleton, Conn.: Wesleyan University Press, 1990).
5. Jon Butler, *Becoming America: The Revolution before 1776* (Cambridge, Mass.: Harvard University Press, 2000).
6. Paul S. Boyer et al., *The Enduring Vision: A History of the American People* (Lexington, Mass.: D. C. Heath, 1996).
7. Corsets are close-fitting undergarments that were worn at the time by both men and women to give the appearance of having a smaller waist. Whalebone was inserted in the corsets to make them stiff, and lacing was used to tighten them around the body.
8. Much of the colonists' fury over British policies was directed personally at King George III, who had ascended the British throne in 1760 at the age of twenty-two, rather than at Britain or British rule *per se*. If you look at the Declaration of Independence in Appendix A, you will note that much of that document focuses on what "He" (George III) has or has not done. George III's lack of political experience, his personality, and his temperament all combined to lend instability to the British government at this crucial point in history.
9. *The Political Writings of Thomas Paine*, Vol. 1 (Boston: J. P. Mendum Investigator Office, 1870), p. 46.
10. The equivalent in today's publishing world would be a book that sells between nine million and eleven million copies in its first year of publication.
11. As quoted in Winthrop D. Jordan et al., *The United States*, 6th ed. (Englewood Cliffs, N.J.: Prentice Hall, 1987).
12. Some scholars feel that Locke's influence on the colonists, including Thomas Jefferson, has been exaggerated. For example, Jay Fliegelman states that Jefferson's fascination with the ideas of Homer, Ossian, and Patrick Henry "is of greater significance than his indebtedness to Locke." Jay Fliegelman, *Declaring Independence: Jefferson, Natural Language, and the Culture of Performance* (Stanford, Calif.: Stanford University Press, 1993).
13. Well before the Articles were ratified, many of them had, in fact, already been implemented. The Second Continental Congress and the thirteen states conducted American military, economic, and political affairs according to the standards and form specified later in the Articles of Confederation. See Robert W. Hoffert, *A Politics of Tensions: The Articles of Confederation and American Political Ideas* (Niwot, Colo.: University Press of Colorado, 1992).
14. Contrary to the standard argument that patriotism and civic duty encouraged state cooperation, some scholars have claimed that material gain and local interests held the union together under the Articles of Confederation. Keith L. Dougherty, *Collective Action under the Articles of Confederation* (New York: Cambridge University Press, 2001).
15. Shays' Rebellion was not merely a small group of poor farmers. The participants and their supporters represented whole communities, including some of the wealthiest and most influential families of Massachusetts. Leonard L. Richards, *Shays' Rebellion: The American Revolution's Final Battle* (Philadelphia: University of Pennsylvania Press, 2003).
16. Madison was much more "republican" in his views than Hamilton. See Lance Banning, *The Sacred Fire of Liberty: James Madison and the Founding of the Federal Republic* (Ithaca, N.Y.: Cornell University Press, 1995).
17. The State House was later named Independence Hall. This was the same room in which the Declaration of Independence had been signed eleven years earlier.
18. Charles A. Beard, *An Economic Interpretation of the Constitution of the United States* (New York: Macmillan, 1913; New York: Free Press, 1986).
19. Morris was partly of French descent, which is why his first name may seem unusual. Note that naming one's child *Gouverneur* was not common at the time in any language, even French.
20. Quoted in J. J. Spengler, "Malthusianism in Late Eighteenth-Century America," *American Economic Review*, Vol. 25 (1935), p. 705.
21. For further detail on Wood's depiction of the founders' views, see Gordon S. Wood, *Revolutionary Characters: What Made the Founders Different* (New York: Penguin Press, 2006).
22. Some scholarship suggests that the *Federalist Papers* did not play a significant role in bringing about the ratification of the Constitution. Nonetheless, the papers have lasting value as an authoritative explanation of the Constitution.
23. The papers written by the Anti-Federalists are now online (see the *Politics on the Web* section at the end of Chapter 2 for the Web URL). For essays on the positions, arranged in topical order, of both the Federalists and the Anti-Federalists in the ratification debate, see John P. Kaminski and Richard Leffler, *Federalists and Antifederalists: The Debate over the Ratification of the Constitution,* 2d ed. (Madison, Wis.: Madison House, 1998).
24. The concept of the separation of powers generally is credited to the French political philosopher Montesquieu (1689–1755), who included it in his monumental two-volume work entitled *The Spirit of Laws,* published in 1748.
25. The Constitution does not explicitly mention the power of judicial review, but the delegates at the Constitutional Convention probably assumed that the courts would have this power. Indeed, Alexander Hamilton, in *Federalist Paper* No. 78, explicitly outlined the concept of judicial review. In any event, whether the founders intended for the courts to exercise this power is a moot point, because in an 1803 decision, *Marbury v. Madison,* the Supreme Court claimed this power for the courts—see Chapter 14.
26. Eventually, Supreme Court decisions led to legislative reforms relating to apportionment. The amendment concerning compensation of members of Congress became the Twenty-seventh Amendment to the Constitution when it was ratified 203 years later, in 1992.

CHAPTER 3
1. The federal models used by the German and Canadian governments provide interesting comparisons with the U.S. system. See Arthur B. Gunlicks, *Laender and German Federalism* (Manchester, England: Manchester University Press, 2003); and Jennifer Smith, *Federalism* (Vancouver: University of British Columbia Press, 2004).
2. Text of an address by the president to the National Conference of State Legislatures, Atlanta, Georgia (Washington, D.C.: The White House, Office of the Press Secretary, July 30, 1981).
3. An excellent illustration of this principle was President Dwight Eisenhower's disciplining of Arkansas governor Orval Faubus when he refused to allow a Little Rock high school to be desegregated in 1957. Eisenhower federalized the National Guard to enforce the court-ordered desegregation of the school.
4. 5 U.S. 137 (1803).
5. 4 Wheaton 316 (1819).
6. 9 Wheaton 1 (1824).
7. *Hammer v. Dagenhart,* 247 U.S. 251 (1918). This decision was overruled in *United States v. Darby,* 312 U.S. 100 (1941).
8. *Wickard v. Filburn,* 317 U.S. 111 (1942).
9. *McLain v. Real Estate Board of New Orleans, Inc.,* 444 U.S. 232 (1980).
10. 514 U.S. 549 (1995).
11. *Printz v. United States,* 521 U.S. 898 (1997).
12. *United States v. Morrison,* 529 U.S. 598 (2000).
13. 127 S.Ct. 1438 (2007).
14. National Governors Association statement on "Federalism, Preemption, and Regulatory Reform," December 2, 2002.
15. Although Louisiana prohibited minors from purchasing alcohol, it did not prohibit bars and alcohol retailers from selling alcohol to minors. Not until 1996, when President Bill Clinton threatened to withhold federal highway funds from Louisiana, did that state fully comply with the drinking-age requirement.

CHAPTER 4
1. 7 Peters 243 (1833).
2. We look further at this denial of *habeas corpus* to the prisoners held at Guantánamo in Chapter 14.
3. 330 U.S. 1 (1947).
4. 370 U.S. 421 (1962).
5. 449 U.S. 39 (1980).
6. *Wallace v. Jaffree,* 472 U.S. 38 (1985).
7. See, for example, *Brown v. Gwinnett County School District,* 112 F.3d 1464 (1997).

8. *Santa Fe Independent School District v. Doe,* 530 U.S. 290 (2000).
9. 393 U.S. 97 (1968).
10. *Edwards v. Aguillard,* 482 U.S. 578 (1987).
11. 403 U.S. 602 (1971).
12. *Mitchell v. Helms,* 530 U.S. 793 (2000).
13. *Zelman v. Simmons-Harris,* 536 U.S. 639 (2002).
14. *Holmes v. Bush* (Fla.Cir.Ct. 2002). For details about this case, see David Royse, "Judge Rules School Voucher Law Violates Florida Constitution," *USA Today,* August 6, 2002, p. 7D.
15. 98 U.S. 145 (1878).
16. For more information on this case, see Bill Miller, "Firefighters Win Ruling in D.C. Grooming Dispute," *The Washington Post,* June 23, 2001, p. B01.
17. *Schenck v. United States,* 249 U.S. 47 (1919).
18. 341 U.S. 494 (1951).
19. *Brandenburg v. Ohio,* 395 U.S. 444 (1969).
20. *Liquormart v. Rhode Island,* 517 U.S. 484 (1996).
21. For more information on this case, see Samuel Maull, "Judges Rule against 2 Accused of Praising Sept. 11 Attacks," *The Washington Post,* March 31, 2002, p. A6.
22. 413 U.S. 15 (1973).
23. *Reno v. American Civil Liberties Union,* 521 U.S. 844 (1997).
24. *Ashcroft v. American Civil Liberties Union,* 542 U.S. 656 (2004). In March 2007, a federal district court judge in Philadelphia ruled that the act was unconstitutional. The case will likely reach the Supreme Court at some point in the future.
25. *United States v. American Library Association,* 539 U.S. 194 (2003).
26. *Ashcroft v. Free Speech Coalition,* 535 U.S. 234 (2002).
27. *Davis v. Monroe County Board of Education,* 526 U.S. 629 (1999).
28. *Morse v. Frederick,* 127 S.Ct. 2618 (2007).
29. See, for example, *Doe v. University of Michigan,* 721 F.Supp. 852 (1989).
30. "Meeting Minutes of the Wesleyan Student Assembly Meeting, 2002–2003," October 2, 2002, p. 10.
31. 249 U.S. 47 (1919).
32. 268 U.S. 652 (1925).
33. 484 U.S. 260 (1988).
34. *Smith v. Collin,* 439 U.S. 916 (1978).
35. *City of Chicago v. Morales,* 527 U.S. 41 (1999).
36. *Gallo v. Acuna,* 14 Cal.4th 1090 (1997).
37. Brandeis made this statement in a dissenting opinion in *Olmstead v. United States,* 277 U.S. 438 (1928).
38. 381 U.S. 479 (1965).
39. The state of South Carolina challenged the constitutionality of this act, claiming that the law violated states' rights under the Tenth Amendment. The Supreme Court, however, held that Congress had the authority, under its commerce power, to pass the act because drivers' personal information had become articles of interstate commerce. *Reno v. Condon,* 528 U.S. 141 (2000).
40. 410 U.S. 113 (1973). Jane Roe was not the real name of the woman in this case. It is a common legal pseudonym used to protect a party's privacy.
41. See, for example, the Supreme Court's decision in *Lambert v. Wicklund,* 520 U.S. 1169 (1997). The Court held that a Montana law requiring a minor to notify one of her parents before getting an abortion was constitutional.
42. *Schenck v. ProChoice Network,* 519 U.S. 357 (1997); and *Hill v. Colorado,* 530 U.S. 703 (2000).
43. *Stenberg v. Carhart,* 530 U.S. 914 (2000).
44. *Gonzales v. Carhart,* 127 S.Ct. 1610 (2007).
45. *Washington v. Glucksberg,* 521 U.S. 702 (1997).
46. *Gonzales v. Oregon,* 546 U.S. 243 (2006).
47. 372 U.S. 335 (1963).
48. *Mapp v. Ohio,* 367 U.S. 643 (1961).
49. 384 U.S. 436 (1966). In 1968, Congress passed legislation including a provision that reinstated the previous rule that statements made by defendants can be used against them as long as the statements were made voluntarily. This provision was never enforced, however, and only in 1999 did a court try to enforce it. The case ultimately came before the Supreme Court, which held that the *Miranda* rights were based on the Constitution and thus could not be overruled by legislative act. See *Dickerson v. United States,* 530 U.S. 428 (2000).
50. *Moran v. Burbine,* 475 U.S. 412 (1986).
51. *Arizona v. Fulminante,* 499 U.S. 279 (1991).
52. *Davis v. United States,* 512 U.S. 452 (1994).
53. Thomas P. Sullivan, *Police Experiences with Recording Custodial Interrogations* (Chicago: Northwestern University School of Law Center on Wrongful Convictions, Summer 2004), p. 4.
54. This example is drawn from Brenda Koehler, "Respond Locally to National Issues," in *50 Ways to Love Your Country* (Maui, Hawaii: Inner Ocean Publishing, 2004), pp. 110–111.

CHAPTER 5

1. *Michael M. v. Superior Court,* 450 U.S. 464 (1981).
2. See, for example, *Craig v. Boren,* 429 U.S. 190 (1976).
3. *Orr v. Orr,* 440 U.S. 268 (1979).
4. *Mississippi University for Women v. Hogan,* 458 U.S. 718 (1982).
5. 518 U.S. 515 (1996).
6. 163 U.S. 537 (1896).
7. 347 U.S. 483 (1954).
8. 349 U.S. 294 (1955).
9. *Swann v. Charlotte-Mecklenburg Board of Education,* 402 U.S. 1 (1971).
10. *Keyes v. School District No. 1,* 413 U.S. 189 (1973).
11. *Milliken v. Bradley,* 418 U.S. 717 (1974).

12. *Riddick v. School Board of City of Norfolk,* 627 F.Supp. 814 (E.D.Va. 1984).
13. 515 U.S. 70 (1995).
14. As cited in Tamar Lewin and David M. Herszenhorn, "Money, Not Race, Fuels New Push to Buoy Schools," *The New York Times,* June 30, 2007.
15. *Ledbetter v. Goodyear Tire & Rubber Co.,* 127 S.Ct. 2162 (2007).
16. See *Meritor Savings Bank, FSB v. Vinson,* 477 U.S. 57 (1986); and *Harris v. Forklift Systems, Inc.,* 510 U.S. 17 (1993).
17. *Oncale v. Sundowner Offshore Services,* 523 U.S. 75 (1998).
18. *Faragher v. City of Boca Raton,* 524 U.S. 775 (1998).
19. The Supreme Court upheld these actions in *Hirabayashi v. United States,* 320 U.S. 81 (1943); and *Korematsu v. United States,* 323 U.S. 214 (1944).
20. This siege was the subject of Dee Brown's best-selling book, *Bury My Heart at Wounded Knee* (New York: Holt, Rinehart & Winston, 1971).
21. *County of Oneida, New York v. Oneida Indian Nation,* 470 U.S. 226 (1985).
22. *Kimel v. Florida Board of Regents,* 528 U.S. 62 (2000).
23. *Board of Trustees of the University of Alabama v. Garrett,* 531 U.S. 356 (2001).
24. 539 U.S. 558 (2003).
25. 517 U.S. 620 (1996).
26. 438 U.S. 265 (1978).
27. 515 U.S. 200 (1995).
28. 84 F.3d 720 (5th Cir. 1996).
29. 539 U.S. 244 (2003).
30. 539 U.S. 306 (2003).
31. 127 S.Ct. 2738 (2007).

CHAPTER 6

1. *Democracy in America,* Vol. 1, ed. by Phillip Bradley (New York: Knopf, 1980), p. 191.
2. Pronounced ah-*mee*-kus *kure*-ee-eye.
3. Fred McChesney, *Money for Nothing: Politicians, Rent Extraction and Political Extortion* (Cambridge, Mass.: Harvard University Press, 1997).
4. The Agricultural Adjustment Act of 1933 (declared unconstitutional) was replaced by the 1937 Agricultural Adjustment Act, which later was changed and amended several times.
5. 545 U.S. 913 (2005).
6. *United States v. Harriss,* 347 U.S. 612 (1954).

CHAPTER 7

1. Letter to Francis Hopkinson written from Paris while Jefferson was minister to France, as cited in John P. Foley, ed., *The Jeffersonian Cyclopedia* (New York: Russell & Russell, 1967), p. 677.
2. From the names of the twins in Lewis Carroll's *Through the Looking Glass and What Alice Found There,* first published in London in 1862–1863.
3. The term *third party,* although inaccurate (because sometimes there have been fourth parties, fifth parties, and even more), is commonly used to refer to a minor party.
4. Today, twelve states have multimember districts for their state houses, and a handful also have multimember districts for their state senates.
5. In most states, a person must declare a preference for a particular party before voting in that state's primary election (discussed in Chapter 9). This declaration is usually part of the voter-registration process.
6. For an interesting discussion of the pros and cons of patronage from a constitutional perspective, see the majority opinion versus the dissent in the Supreme Court case *Board of County Commissioners v. Umbehr,* 518 U.S. 668 (1996).
7. Kathleen Hall Jamieson, *Everything You Think You Know about Politics . . . and Why You're Wrong* (New York: Basic Books, 2000).

CHAPTER 8

1. Doris A. Graber, *Mass Media and American Politics,* 7th ed. (Washington, D.C.: CQ Press, 2005).
2. John M. Benson, "When Is an Opinion Really an Opinion?" *Public Perspective,* September/October 2001, pp. 40–41.
3. As quoted in Karl G. Feld, "When Push Comes to Shove: A Polling Industry Call to Arms," *Public Perspective,* September/October 2001, p. 38.
4. Pew Research Center for the People and the Press, survey conducted September 21–October 4, 2006, and reported in "Who Votes, Who Doesn't, and Why," released October 28, 2006.
5. *Smith v. Allwright,* 321 U.S. 649 (1944).
6. As quoted in Owen Ullman, "Why Voter Apathy Will Make a Strong Showing," *Business Week,* November 4, 1996.
7. Gordon S. Wood, *Revolutionary Characters: What Made the Founders Different* (New York: Penguin Press, 2006), p. 248.
8. *Ibid.,* p. 271.
9. Thomas E. Mann and Norman J. Ornstein, *The Broken Branch: How Congress Is Failing America and How to Get It Back on Track* (New York: Oxford University Press, 2006), p. 277.

CHAPTER 9

1. Today, there are one hundred senators in the Senate and 435 members of the House of Representatives. In addition, the District of Columbia has three electoral votes.
2. This group includes those who support the National Popular Vote movement, a proposed interstate compact. This movement was discussed in Chapter 3, in the *Join the Debate* feature on page 55.

3. The word *caucus* apparently was first used in the name of a men's club, the Caucus Club of colonial Boston, sometime between 1755 and 1765. (Many early political and government meetings took place in pubs.) The origin of the word is unknown, but some scholars have concluded it is of Algonquin origin.
4. Center for Responsive Politics, 2005.
5. This act is sometimes referred to as the Federal Election Campaign Act of 1972 because it became effective in that year. The official date of the act, however, is 1971.
6. 424 U.S. 1 (1976).
7. Center for Responsive Politics, 2005.
8. *Colorado Republican Federal Campaign Committee v. Federal Election Commission*, 518 U.S. 604 (1996).
9. Quoted in George Will, "The First Amendment on Trial," *The Washington Post*, December 1, 2002, p. B07.
10. 540 U.S. 93 (2003).
11. *Federal Election Commission v. Wisconsin Right to Life, Inc.*, 127 S.Ct. 2652 (2007).
12. These states award one electoral vote to the candidate who wins the popular vote in a congressional district and an additional two electoral votes to the winner of the statewide popular vote. Other states have considered similar plans.
13. In 1824, no candidate received a majority of electoral votes; John Quincy Adams was elected president by the House of Representatives. Rutherford B. Hayes lost the popular vote in 1876, but after the resolution of an electoral dispute, he ultimately won a majority of electoral votes. In 1888, Benjamin Harrison lost the popular vote, but won a majority of electoral votes.
14. For a more detailed account of the 2000 presidential elections, see *36 Days: The Complete Chronicle of the 2000 Presidential Election Crisis* (New York: Times Books, 2001), by correspondents of *The New York Times*.

CHAPTER 10

1. Bernard Cohen, *The Press and Foreign Policy* (Princeton, N.J.: Princeton University Press, 1963), p. 81.
2. Adam Nagourney, "Campaigns Unified by Toxic Theme," *International Herald Tribune*, September 28, 2006, p. 4.
3. Michael Grunwald, "The Year of Playing Dirtier," *The Washington Post*, October 27, 2006, p. A1.
4. David Mark, *Going Dirty: The Art of Negative Campaigning* (Lanham, Md.: Rowman & Littlefield, 2007).
5. *Federal Election Commission v. Wisconsin Right to Life, Inc.*, 127 S.Ct. 2652 (2007).
6. Interestingly, in the 2000 campaigns, a Texas group supporting George W. Bush's candidacy paid for a remake of the "daisy" commercial, but the target in the new ad was Al Gore.
7. As quoted in Grunwald, "The Year of Playing Dirtier," p. A1.
8. John G. Geer, *In Defense of Negativity: Attack Ads in Presidential Campaigns* (Chicago: University of Chicago Press, 2006).
9. The commission's action was upheld by a federal court. See *Perot v. Federal Election Commission*, 97 F.3d 553 (D.C.Cir. 1996).
10. For more details on how political candidates manage news coverage, see Doris A. Graber, *Mass Media and American Politics*, 7th ed. (Washington, D.C.: CQ Press, 2005).
11. For suggestions on how to dissect "spin" and detect when language is steering one toward a conclusion, see Brooks Jackson and Kathleen Hall Jamieson, *unSpun: Finding Facts in a World of Disinformation* (New York: Random House, 2007).
12. S. Robert Lichter, Stanley Rothman, and Linda S. Lichter, *The Media Elite* (New York: Adler & Adler, 1986).
13. Kathleen Hall Jamieson, *Everything You Think You Know about Politics . . . and Why You're Wrong* (New York: Basic Books, 2000), pp. 187–195.
14. Debra Reddin van Tuyll and Hubert P. van Tuyll, "Political Partisanship," in Wm. David Sloan and Jenn Burleson Mackay, eds. *Media Bias: Finding It, Fixing It* (Jefferson, N.C.: McFarland, 2007), pp. 35–49.
15. Jamieson, *Everything You Think You Know about Politics*, pp. xiii–xiv.
16. *The State of the News Media 2007: An Annual Report on American Journalism*, by the Pew Research Center for the People and the Press and the Project for Excellence in Journalism, 2007.
17. See, for example, Shayne Bowman and Chris Willis, *We Media: How Audiences Are Shaping the Future of News and Information* (Reston, Va.: American Press Institute Media Center, 2003), p. 9.
18. The term *podcasting* is used for this type of information delivery because initially podcasts were downloaded onto Apple's iPods.
19. Andrew Sullivan, "Video Power: The Potent New Political Force," *The Sunday Times*, February 4, 2007.

CHAPTER 11

1. These states are Alaska, Delaware, Montana, North Dakota, South Dakota, Vermont, and Wyoming.
2. 369 U.S. 186 (1962).
3. 376 U.S. 1 (1964).
4. See, for example, *Davis v. Bandemer*, 478 U.S. 109 (1986).
5. *Amicus curiae* brief filed by the American Civil Liberties Union (ACLU) in support of the appellants in *Easley v. Cromartie*, 532 U.S. 234 (2001).
6. See, for example, *Shaw v. Reno*, 509 U.S. 630 (1993); *Miller v. Johnson*, 515 U.S. 900 (1995); *Shaw v. Hunt*, 517 U.S. 899 (1996); and *Bush v. Vera*, 517 U.S. 952 (1996).
7. *Easley v. Cromartie*, 532 U.S. 234 (2001).

8. *Powell v. McCormack*, 395 U.S. 486 (1969).
9. Some observers maintain that another reason Congress *can* stay in session longer is the invention of air-conditioning. Until the advent of air-conditioning, no member of Congress wanted to stay in session during the hot and sticky late spring, summer, and early fall months.
10. A term used by Woodrow Wilson in *Congressional Government* (New York: Meridian Books, 1956 [first published in 1885]).

CHAPTER 12

1. Lyndon B. Johnson, *The Vantage Point: Perspectives of the Presidency, 1963–1969* (New York: Henry Holt & Co., 1971).
2. Versailles, located about twenty miles from Paris, is the name of the palace built by King Louis XIV of France. It served as the royal palace until 1793 and was then converted into a national historical museum, which it remains today. The preliminary treaty ending the American Revolution was signed by the United States and Great Britain at Versailles in 1783.
3. *Ex parte Grossman*, 267 U.S. 87 (1925).
4. *Clinton v. City of New York*, 524 U.S. 417 (1998).
5. As cited in Lewis D. Eigen and Jonathan P. Siegel, *The Macmillan Dictionary of Political Quotations* (New York: Macmillan, 1993), p. 565.
6. The Constitution does not grant the president explicit power to remove from office officials who are not performing satisfactorily or who do not agree with the president. In 1926, however, the Supreme Court prevented Congress from interfering with the president's ability to fire those executive-branch officials whom he had appointed with Senate approval. See *Myers v. United States*, 272 U.S. 52 (1926).
7. Richard E. Neustadt, *Presidential Power: The Politics of Leadership* (New York: John Wiley, 1960), p. 10.
8. As quoted in Richard M. Pious, *The American Presidency* (New York: Basic Books, 1979), pp. 51–52.
9. A phrase coined by Samuel Kernell in *Going Public: New Strategies of Presidential Leadership*, 2d ed. (Washington, D.C.: Congressional Quarterly Press, 1992).
10. Franklin D. Roosevelt, as quoted in *The New York Times*, November 13, 1932.
11. For further discussion of this view of presidential powers, see Kenneth R. Mayer, *With the Stroke of a Pen: Executive Orders and Presidential Power* (Princeton, N.J.: Princeton University Press, 2002); and William G. Howell, *Power without Persuasion: The Politics of Direct Presidential Action* (Princeton, N.J.: Princeton University Press, 2001).
12. As quoted in Sheryl Gay Stolberg, "Bush Vetoes Measure on Stem Cell Research," *The New York Times*, June 21, 2007.
13. As quoted in Mark Silva, "ABA Task Force Warns of President's Signing Statements," *Chicago Tribune*, July 23, 2006.
14. Congress used its power to declare war in the War of 1812, the Mexican War (1846–1848), the Spanish-American War (1898), and World War I (U.S. involvement lasted from 1916 until 1918) and on six different occasions during World War II (U.S. involvement lasted from 1941 until 1945).
15. As quoted in Thomas E. Cronin, *The State of the Presidency*, 2d ed. (Boston: Little, Brown, 1980), p. 11.

CHAPTER 13

1. This definition follows the classical model of bureaucracy put forth by German sociologist Max Weber. See Max Weber, *Theory of Social and Economic Organization*, Talcott Parsons, ed. (New York: Oxford University Press, 1974).
2. It should be noted that although the president is technically the head of the bureaucracy, the president cannot always control the bureaucracy—as you will read later in this chapter.
3. For an insightful analysis of the policymaking process in Washington, D.C., and the role played by various groups in the process, see Morton H. Halperin and Priscilla A. Clapp, with Arnold Kanter, *Bureaucratic Politics and Foreign Policy*, 2d ed. (Washington, D.C.: The Brookings Institution, 2006). Although the focus of the book is on foreign policy, the analysis applies in many ways to the general policymaking process.
4. *Garcetti v. Ceballos*, 126 S.Ct. 1951 (2006).
5. As quoted in George Melloan, "Bush's Toughest Struggle Is with His Own Bureaucracy," *The Wall Street Journal*, June 25, 2002, p. A13.
6. Gardiner Harris, "Surgeon General Sees Four-Year Term as Compromised," *The New York Times*, July 11, 2007.

CHAPTER 14

1. Pronounced *ster*-ay dih-*si*-sis.
2. 347 U.S. 483 (1954).
3. See *Plessy v. Ferguson*, 163 U.S. 537 (1896).
4. 539 U.S. 558 (2003).
5. 478 U.S. 186 (1986).
6. Although a state's highest court is often referred to as the state supreme court, there are exceptions. In the New York court system, for example, the supreme court is a trial court, and the highest court is called the New York Court of Appeals.
7. Pronounced jus-*tish*-a-bul.
8. As discussed in Chapter 12, in a criminal case brought against Libby by a government prosecutor in connection with this leak to the press, Libby was convicted of perjury and obstruction of justice, among other things. President Bush commuted Libby's prison sentence, so he served no time in prison.
9. Pronounced sur-shee-uh-*rah*-ree.

10. Between 1790 and 1891, Congress allowed the Supreme Court almost no discretion over which cases to decide. After 1925, in almost 95 percent of appealed cases the Court could choose whether to hear arguments and issue an opinion. Beginning with the term in October 1988, mandatory review was virtually eliminated.

11. *Hamdi v. Rumsfeld*, 542 U.S. 507 (2004).

12. *Hamdan v. Rumsfeld*, 126 S.Ct. 2749 (2006).

13. *Boumediene v. Bush*, 476 F.3d 981 (D.C.Cir. 2007).

14. 84 F.3d 720 (5th Cir. 1996).

15. *Grutter v. Bollinger*, 539 U.S. 306 (2003).

16. 5 U.S. (1 Cranch) 137 (1803). The Supreme Court had considered the constitutionality of an act of Congress in *Hylton v. United States,* 3 U.S. 171 (1796), in which Congress's power to levy certain taxes was challenged. That particular act was ruled constitutional, rather than unconstitutional, however, so this first federal exercise of judicial review was not clearly recognized as such. Also, during the decade before the adoption of the federal Constitution, courts in at least eight states had exercised the power of judicial review.

17. Jeffrey A. Segal and Harold J. Spaeth, *The Supreme Court and the Attitudinal Model* (New York: Cambridge University Press, 1993), p. 65.

18. For an analysis of the Roberts Court's first term by a Georgetown University law professor, see Jonathan Turley, "The Roberts Court: Seeing Is Believing," *USA Today,* July 6, 2006, p. 11A.

19. For summaries of the major cases decided during the Roberts Court's second term (ending in June 2007) by a Pulitzer Prize winner and longtime Court watcher, see Linda Greenhouse, "In Steps Big and Small, Supreme Court Moved Right," *The New York Times,* July 1, 2007.

20. *U.S. Airways v. Barnett,* 535 U.S. 391 (2002).

21. As quoted in Linda Greenhouse, "The Competing Visions of the Role of the Court," *The New York Times,* July 7, 2002, p. 3.

22. Antonin Scalia, *A Matter of Interpretation* (Ewing, N.J.: Princeton University Press, 1997).

23. Letter by Thomas Jefferson to William C. Jarvis, 1820, in Andrew A. Lipscomb and Albert Ellery Bergh, *The Writings of Thomas Jefferson,* Memorial Edition (Washington, D.C.: Thomas Jefferson Memorial Association of the United States, 1904).

24. As quoted in Carl Hulse and David D. Kirkpatrick, "DeLay Says Federal Judiciary Has 'Run Amok,' Adding Congress Is Partly to Blame," *The New York Times,* April 8, 2005, p. 5.

Glossary

adjudicate To render a judicial decision. In regard to administrative law, the process in which an administrative law judge hears and decides issues that arise when an agency charges a person or firm with violating a law or regulation enforced by the agency.

administrative law The body of law created by administrative agencies (in the form of rules, regulations, orders, and decisions) in order to carry out their duties and responsibilities.

affirmative action A policy calling for the establishment of programs that give special consideration, in jobs and college admissions, to members of groups that have been discriminated against in the past.

agents of political socialization People and institutions that influence the political views of others.

Anti-Federalists A political group that opposed the adoption of the Constitution because of the document's centralist tendencies and because it did not include a bill of rights.

appellate court A court having appellate jurisdiction that normally does not hear evidence or testimony but reviews the transcript of the trial court's proceedings, other records relating to the case, and the attorneys' respective arguments as to why the trial court's decision should or should not stand.

apportionment The distribution of House seats among the states on the basis of their respective populations.

appropriation A part of the congressional budgeting process that involves determining how many dollars will be spent in a given year on a particular set of government activities.

Articles of Confederation The nation's first national constitution, which established a national form of government following the American Revolution. The Articles provided for a confederal form of government in which the central government had few powers.

attack ad A negative political advertisement that attacks the character of an opposing candidate.

Australian ballot A secret ballot that is prepared, distributed, and counted by government officials at public expense; used by all states in the United States since 1888.

authority The ability to exercise power, such as the power to make and enforce laws, legitimately.

authorization A part of the congressional budgeting process that involves the creation of the legal basis for government programs.

autocracy A form of government in which the power and authority of the government are in the hands of a single person.

biased sample A poll sample that does not accurately represent the population.

bicameral legislature A legislature made up of two chambers, or parts. The United States has a bicameral legislature, composed of the House of Representatives and the Senate.

bill of attainder A legislative act that inflicts punishment on particular persons or groups without granting them the right to a trial.

Bill of Rights The first ten amendments to the U.S. Constitution. They list the freedoms—such as the freedoms of speech, press, and religion—that a citizen enjoys and that cannot be infringed on by the government.

block grant A federal grant given to a state for a broad area, such as criminal justice or mental-health programs.

bureaucracy A large, complex, hierarchically structured administrative organization that carries out specific functions.

bureaucrat An individual who works in a bureaucracy. As generally used, the term refers to a government employee.

busing The transportation of public school students by bus to schools physically outside their neighborhoods to eliminate school segregation based on residential patterns.

cabinet An advisory group selected by the president to assist with decision making. Traditionally, the cabinet has consisted of the heads of the executive departments and other officers whom the president may choose to appoint.

campaign strategy The comprehensive plan for winning an election developed by a candidate and his or her advisers. The strategy includes the candidate's position on issues, slogan, advertising plan, press events, personal appearances, and other aspects of the campaign.

case law The rules of law announced in court decisions. Case law includes the aggregate of reported cases that interpret judicial precedents, statutes, regulations, and constitutional provisions.

categorical grant A federal grant targeted for a specific purpose as defined by federal law.

caucus A meeting held by party leaders to choose political candidates. The caucus system of nominating candidates was eventually replaced by nominating conventions and, later, by direct primaries.

checks and balances A major principle of American government in which each of the three branches is given the means to check (to restrain or balance) the actions of the others.

chief diplomat The role of the president in recognizing and interacting with foreign governments.

chief executive The head of the executive branch of government. In the United States, the president is the head of the executive branch of the federal government.

chief of staff The person who directs the operations of the White House Office and who advises the president on important matters.

chief of state The person who serves as the ceremonial head of a country's government and represents that country to the rest of the world.

citizen journalism The collection, analysis, and dissemination of information online by independent journalists, scholars, politicians, and the general citizenry.

civil disobedience The deliberate and public act of refusing to obey laws thought to be unjust.

civil law The branch of law that spells out the duties that individuals in society owe to other persons or to their governments, excluding the duty not to commit crimes.

civil liberties Individual rights protected by the Constitution against the powers of the government.

civil rights The rights of all Americans to equal treatment under the law, as provided for by the Fourteenth Amendment to the Constitution.

civil rights movement The movement in the 1950s and 1960s, by minorities and concerned whites, to end racial segregation.

civil service Nonmilitary government employment.

closed primary A primary in which only party members can vote to choose that party's candidates.

cloture A method of ending debate in the Senate and bringing the matter under consideration to a vote by the entire chamber.

commander in chief The supreme commander of the military forces of the United States.

commerce clause The clause in Article I, Section 8, of the Constitution that gives Congress the power to regulate interstate commerce (commerce involving more than one state).

commercial speech Advertising statements that describe products. Commercial speech receives less protection under the First Amendment than ordinary speech.

common law The body of law developed from judicial decisions in English and U.S. courts, not attributable to a legislature.

competitive federalism A model of federalism devised by Thomas R. Dye in which state and local governments compete for businesses and citizens, who in effect "vote with their feet" by moving to jurisdictions that offer a competitive advantage.

concurrent powers Powers held by both the federal and the state governments in a federal system.

concurring opinion A statement written by a judge or justice who agrees (concurs) with the court's decision, but for reasons different from those in the majority opinion.

confederal system A league of independent sovereign states, joined together by a central government that has only limited powers over them.

confederation A league of independent states that are united only for the purpose of achieving common goals.

conference In regard to the Supreme Court, a private meeting of the justices in which they present their arguments with respect to a case under consideration.

conference committee A temporary committee that is formed when the two chambers of Congress pass separate versions of the same bill. The conference committee, which consists of members from both the House and the Senate, works out a compromise form of the bill.

conference report A report submitted by a congressional conference committee after it has drafted a single version of a bill.

congressional district The geographic area that is served by one member in the House of Representatives.

conservatism A set of beliefs that includes a limited role for the national government in helping individuals and in the economic affairs of the nation, support for traditional values and lifestyles, and a cautious response to change.

Constitutional Convention The convention (meeting) of delegates from the states that was held in Philadelphia in 1787 for the purpose of amending the Articles of Confederation. In fact, the delegates wrote a new constitution (the U.S. Constitution) that established a federal form of government to replace the governmental system that had been created by the Articles of Confederation.

constitutional law Law based on the U.S. Constitution and the constitutions of the various states.

continuing resolution A temporary resolution passed by Congress when an appropriations bill has not been passed by the beginning of the new fiscal year.

cooperative federalism The theory that the states and the federal government should cooperate in solving problems.

Council of Economic Advisers (CEA) A three-member council created in 1946 to advise the president on economic matters.

Credentials Committee A committee of each national political party that evaluates the claims of national party convention delegates to be the legitimate representatives of their states.

criminal law The branch of law that defines and governs actions that constitute crimes. Generally, criminal law has to do with wrongful actions committed against society for which society demands redress.

D

***de facto* segregation** Racial segregation that occurs not as a result of deliberate intentions but because of past social and economic conditions and residential patterns.

***de jure* segregation** Racial segregation that is legally sanctioned—that is, segregation that occurs because of laws or decisions by government agencies.

delegate A person selected to represent the people of one geographic area at a party convention.

democracy A system of government in which the people have ultimate political authority. The word is derived from the Greek *demos* (people) and kratia (rule).

devolution The surrender or transfer of powers to local authorities by a central government.

dictatorship A form of government in which absolute power is exercised by a single person who usually has obtained his or her power by the use of force.

diplomat A person who represents one country in dealing with representatives of another country.

direct democracy A system of government in which political decisions are made by the people themselves rather than by elected representatives. This form of government was practiced in some areas of ancient Greece.

direct primary An election held within each of the two major parties—Democratic and Republican—to choose the party's candidates for the general election.

direct technique Any method used by an interest group to interact with government officials directly to further the group's goals.

dissenting opinion A statement written by a judge or justice who disagrees with the majority opinion.

diversity of citizenship A basis for federal court jurisdiction over a lawsuit that arises when (1) the parties in the lawsuit live in different states or when one of the parties is a foreign government or a foreign citizen, and (2) the amount in controversy is more than $75,000.

divine right theory A theory that the right to rule by a king or queen was derived directly from God rather than from the consent of the people.

division of powers A basic principle of federalism established by the U.S. Constitution. In a federal system, powers are divided between units of government (such as the federal and state governments).

double jeopardy To prosecute a person twice for the same criminal offense; prohibited by the Fifth Amendment in all but a few circumstances.

dual federalism A system of government in which both the federal and the state governments maintain diverse but sovereign powers.

due process clause The constitutional guarantee, set out in the Fifth and Fourteenth Amendments, that the government will not illegally or arbitrarily deprive a person of life, liberty, or property.

due process of law The requirement that the government use fair, reasonable, and standard procedures whenever it takes any legal action against an individual; required by the Fifth and Fourteenth Amendments.

E

elector A member of the electoral college.

electoral college The group of electors who are selected by the voters in each state to elect officially the president and vice president. The number of electors in each state is equal to the number of that state's representatives in both chambers of Congress.

electorate All of the citizens eligible to vote in a given election.

electronic media Communication channels that involve electronic transmissions, such as radio, television, and, to an extent, the Internet.

enabling legislation A law enacted by a legislature to establish an administrative agency. Enabling legislation normally specifies the name, purpose, composition, and powers of the agency being created.

entitlement program A government program (such as Social Security) that allows, or entitles, a certain class of people (such as the elderly) to receive special benefits. Entitlement programs operate under open-ended budget authorizations that, in effect, place no limits on how much can be spent.

equal employment opportunity A goal of the 1964 Civil Rights Act to end employment discrimination based on race, color, religion, gender, or national origin and to promote equal job opportunities for all individuals.

equal protection clause Section 1 of the Fourteenth Amendment, which states that no state shall "deny to any person within its jurisdiction the equal protection of the laws."

equality A concept that holds, at a minimum, that all people are entitled to equal protection under the law.

espionage The practice of spying on behalf of a foreign power to obtain information about government plans and activities.

establishment clause The section of the First Amendment that prohibits Congress from passing laws "respecting an establishment of religion." Issues concerning the establishment clause often center on prayer in public schools, the teaching of fundamentalist theories of creation, and government aid to parochial schools.

ex post facto **law** A criminal law that punishes individuals for committing an act that was legal when the act was committed but that has since become a crime.

exclusionary rule A criminal procedural rule requiring that any illegally obtained evidence not be admissible in court.

executive agreement A binding international agreement, or pact, that is made between the president and another head of state and that does not require Senate approval.

Executive Office of the President (EOP) A group of staff agencies that assist the president in carrying out major duties. Franklin D. Roosevelt established the EOP in 1939 to cope with the increased responsibilities brought on by the Great Depression.

executive order A presidential order to carry out a policy or policies described in a law passed by Congress.

executive privilege An inherent executive power claimed by presidents to withhold information from, or to refuse to appear before, Congress or the courts. The president can also accord the privilege to other executive officials.

expressed powers Constitutional or statutory powers that are expressly provided for by the Constitution or by congressional laws.

F

faction A group of persons forming a cohesive minority.

federal mandate A requirement in federal legislation that forces states and municipalities to comply with certain rules. If the federal government does not provide funds to the states to cover the costs of compliance, the mandate is referred to as an *unfunded* mandate.

federal question A question that pertains to the U.S. Constitution, acts of Congress, or treaties. A federal question provides a basis for federal court jurisdiction.

federal system A form of government that provides for a division of powers between a central government and several regional governments. In the United States, the division of powers between the national government and the fifty states is established by the Constitution.

federalism A system of shared sovereignty between two levels of government—one national and one subnational—occupying the same geographic region.

Federalists A political group, led by Alexander Hamilton and John Adams, that supported the adoption of the Constitution and the creation of a federal form of government.

"fighting words" Words that, when uttered by a public speaker, are so inflammatory that they could provoke the average listener to violence.

filibustering The Senate tradition of unlimited debate, undertaken for the purpose of preventing action on a bill.

first budget resolution A budget resolution, which is supposed to be passed in May, that sets overall revenue goals and spending targets for the next fiscal year, which begins on October 1.

First Continental Congress The first gathering of delegates from twelve of the thirteen colonies, held in 1774.

fiscal federalism The power of the national government to influence state policies through grants.

fiscal year A twelve-month period that is established for bookkeeping or accounting purposes. The government's fiscal year runs from October 1 through September 30.

free exercise clause The provision of the First Amendment stating that the government cannot pass laws "prohibiting the free exercise" of religion. Free exercise issues often concern religious practices that conflict with established laws.

free rider problem The difficulty faced by interest groups that lobby for a public good. Individuals can enjoy the outcome of the group's efforts without having to contribute, such as by becoming members of the group.

fundamental right A basic right of all Americans, such as all First Amendment rights. Any law or action that prevents some group of persons from exercising a fundamental right will be subject to the "strict-scrutiny" standard, under which the law or action must be necessary to promote a compelling state interest and must be narrowly tailored to meet that interest.

G

gender gap A term used to describe the difference between the percentage of votes cast for a particular candidate by women and the percentage of votes cast for the same candidate by men.

general election A regularly scheduled election to elect the U.S. president, vice president, and representatives and senators in Congress. General elections are held in even-numbered years on the Tuesday after the first Monday in November.

gerrymandering The drawing of a legislative district's boundaries in such a way as to maximize the influence of a certain group or political party.

glass ceiling The often subtle obstacles to advancement faced by professional women in the workplace.

government The individuals and institutions that make society's rules and that also possess the power and authority to enforce those rules.

government corporation An agency of the government that is run as a business enterprise. Such agencies engage in primarily commercial activities, produce revenues, and require greater flexibility than that permitted in most government agencies.

grandfather clause A clause in a state law that restricted the franchise (voting rights) to those whose grandfathers had voted; one of the techniques used in the South to prevent African Americans from exercising their right to vote.

Great Compromise A plan for a bicameral legislature in which one chamber would be based on population and the other chamber would represent each state equally. The plan, also known as the Connecticut Compromise, resolved the small-state/large-state controversy.

I

ideologue An individual who holds very strong political opinions.

ideology Generally, a system of political ideas that are rooted in religious or philosophical beliefs concerning human nature, society, and government.

implied powers The powers of the federal government that are implied by the expressed powers in the Constitution, particularly in Article I, Section 8.

independent executive agency A federal agency that is not located within a cabinet department.

independent expenditure An expenditure for activities that are independent from (not coordinated with) those of a political candidate or a political party.

independent regulatory agency A federal organization that is responsible for creating and implementing rules that regulate private activity and protect the public interest in a particular sector of the economy.

indirect technique Any method used by interest groups to influence government officials through third parties, such as voters.

inherent powers The powers of the national government that, although not always expressly granted by the Constitution, are necessary to ensure the nation's integrity and survival as a political unit. Inherent powers include the power to make treaties and the power to wage war or make peace.

institution An ongoing organization that performs certain functions for society.

instructed delegate A view of the representation function that holds that representatives should mirror the views of the majority of their constituents.

interest group An organized group of individuals sharing common objectives who actively attempt to influence policymakers in all three branches of the government and at all levels.

interstate commerce Trade that involves more than one state.

iron triangle A three-way alliance among legislators, bureaucrats, and interest groups to make or preserve policies that benefit their respective interests.

issue ad A negative political advertisement that focuses on flaws in an opposing candidate's position on a particular issue.

issue networks Groups of individuals or organizations—which consist of legislators and legislative staff members, interest group leaders, bureaucrats, the media, scholars, and other experts—that support particular policy positions on a given issue.

J

judicial review The power of the courts to decide on the constitutionality of legislative enactments and of actions taken by the executive branch.

judiciary The courts; one of the three branches of the federal government in the United States.

jurisdiction The authority of a court to hear and decide a particular case.

justiciable controversy A controversy that is not hypothetical or academic but real and substantial; a requirement that must be satisfied before a court will hear a case.

K

kitchen cabinet The name given to a president's unofficial advisers. The term was coined during Andrew Jackson's presidency.

L

labor force All of the people over the age of sixteen who are working or actively looking for jobs.

legislative rule An administrative agency rule that carries the same weight as a statute enacted by a legislature.

***Lemon* test** A three-part test enunciated by the Supreme Court in the 1971 case of *Lemon v. Kurtzman* to determine whether government aid to parochial schools is constitutional. To be constitutional, the aid must (1) be for a clearly secular purpose; (2) in its primary effect, neither advance nor inhibit religion; and (3) avoid an "excessive government entanglement with religion." The *Lemon* test has also been used in other types of cases involving the establishment clause.

libel A published report of a falsehood that tends to injure a person's reputation or character.

liberalism A set of political beliefs that includes the advocacy of active government, including government intervention to improve the welfare of individuals and to protect civil rights.

liberty The freedom of individuals to believe, act, and express themselves freely so long as doing so does not infringe on the rights of other individuals in the society.

limited government A form of government based on the principle that the powers of government should be clearly limited either through a written document or through wide public understanding; characterized by institutional checks to ensure that government serves public rather than private interests.

literacy test A test given to voters to ensure that they could read and write and thus evaluate political information; a technique used in many southern states to restrict African American participation in elections.

lobbying All of the attempts by organizations or by individuals to influence the passage, defeat, or contents of legislation or to influence the administrative decisions of government.

lobbyist An individual who handles a particular interest group's lobbying efforts.

loophole A legal way of evading a certain legal requirement.

M

Madisonian Model The model of government devised by James Madison in which the powers of the government are separated into three branches: executive, legislative, and judicial.

majority leader The party leader elected by the majority party in the House or in the Senate.

majority party The political party that has more members in the legislature than the opposing party.

malapportionment A condition that results when, based on population and representation, the voting power of citizens in one district becomes more influential than the voting power of citizens in another district.

managed news coverage News coverage that is manipulated (managed) by a campaign manager or political consultant to gain media exposure for a political candidate.

markup session A meeting held by a congressional committee or subcommittee to approve, amend, or redraft a bill.

mass media Communication channels, such as newspapers and radio and television broadcasts, through which people can communicate to mass audiences.

Mayflower Compact A document drawn up by Pilgrim leaders in 1620 on the ship *Mayflower.* The document stated that laws were to be made for the general good of the people.

media Newspapers, magazines, television, radio, the Internet, and any other printed or electronic means of communication.

minority leader The party leader elected by the minority party in the House or in the Senate.

minority party The political party that has fewer members in the legislature than the opposing party.

minority-majority district A district whose boundaries are drawn so as to maximize the voting power of minority groups.

***Miranda* warnings** A series of statements informing criminal suspects, on their arrest, of their constitutional rights, such as the right to remain silent and the right to counsel; required by the Supreme Court's 1966 decision in *Miranda* v. *Arizona.*

moderate A person whose views fall in the middle of the political spectrum.

monarchy A form of autocracy in which a king, queen, emperor, empress, tsar, or tsarina is the highest authority in the government; monarchs usually obtain their power through inheritance.

N

national convention The meeting held by each major party every four years to select presidential and vice-presidential candidates, write a party platform, and conduct other party business.

national party chairperson An individual who serves as a political party's administrative head at the national level and directs the work of the party's national committee.

national party committee The political party leaders who direct party business during the four years between the national party conventions, organize the next national convention, and plan how to obtain a party victory in the next presidential elections.

National Security Council (NSC) A council that advises the president on domestic and foreign matters concerning the safety and defense of the nation; established in 1947.

natural rights Rights that are not bestowed by governments but are inherent within every man, woman, and child by virtue of the fact that he or she is a human being.

necessary and proper clause Article I, Section 8, Clause 18, of the Constitution, which gives Congress the power to make all laws "necessary and proper" for the federal government to carry out its responsibilities; also called the *elastic clause.*

negative political advertising Political advertising undertaken for the purpose of discrediting an opposing candidate in the eyes of the voters. Attack ads and issue ads are forms of negative political advertising.

neutral competency The application of technical skills to jobs without regard to political issues.

New Deal A program ushered in by the Roosevelt administration in 1933 to bring the United States out of the Great Depression. The New Deal included many government spending and public-assistance programs, in addition to thousands of regulations governing economic activity.

new federalism A plan to limit the federal government's role in regulating state governments and to give the states increased power to decide how they should spend government revenues.

nominating convention An official meeting of a political party to choose its candidates. Nominating conventions at the state and local levels also select delegates to represent the citizens of their geographic areas at a higher-level party convention.

O

obscenity Indecency or offensiveness in speech, expression, behavior, or appearance. Whether specific expressions or acts constitute obscenity normally is determined by community standards.

Office of Management and Budget (OMB) An agency in the Executive Office of the President that assists the president in preparing and supervising the administration of the federal budget.

office-block ballot A ballot that lists together all of the candidates for each office.

"one person, one vote" rule A rule, or principle, requiring that congressional districts have equal populations so that one person's vote counts as much as another's vote.

open primary A primary in which voters can vote for a party's candidates regardless of whether they belong to the party.

opinion A written statement by a court expressing the reasons for its decision in a case.

oral argument An argument presented to a judge in person by an attorney on behalf of her or his client.

P

parliament The name of the national legislative body in countries governed by a parliamentary system, as in Great Britain and Canada.

partisan politics Political actions or decisions that benefit a particular party.

party elite A loose-knit group of party activists who organize and oversee party functions and planning during and between campaigns.

party identifier A person who identifies himself or herself as being a member of a particular political party.

party platform The document drawn up by each party at its national convention that outlines the policies and positions of the party.

party ticket A list of a political party's candidates for various offices.

party-column ballot A ballot (also called the Indiana ballot) that lists all of a party's candidates under the party label. Voters can vote for all of a party's candidates for local, state, and national offices by making a single "X" or pulling a single lever.

patron An individual or organization that provides financial backing to an interest group.

patronage The practice of giving government jobs to individuals belonging to the winning political party.

peer group Associates, often those close in age to oneself; may include friends, classmates, co-workers, club members, or religious group members. Peer group influence is a significant factor in the political socialization process.

picket-fence federalism A model of federalism in which specific policies and programs are administered by all levels of government—national, state, and local.

pluralist theory A theory that views politics as a contest among various interest groups—at all levels of government—to gain benefits for their members.

pocket veto A special type of veto power used by the chief executive after the legislature has adjourned. Bills that are not signed by the president die after a specified period of time and must be reintroduced if Congress wishes to reconsider them.

podcasting The distribution of audio or video files to a personal computer or a mobile device, such as an iPod.

police powers The powers of a government body that enable it to create laws for the protection of the health, morals, safety, and welfare of the people. In the United States, most police powers are reserved to the states.

political action committee (PAC) A committee that is established by a corporation, labor union, or special interest group to raise funds and make contributions on the establishing organization's behalf.

political advertising Advertising undertaken by or on behalf of a political candidate to familiarize voters with the candidate and his or her views on campaign issues; also advertising for or against policy issues.

political consultant A professional political adviser who, for a large fee, works on an area of a candidate's campaign. Political consultants include campaign managers, pollsters, media advisers, and "get out the vote" organizers.

political culture The set of ideas, values, and attitudes about government and the political process held by a community or a nation.

political party A group of individuals who organize to win elections, operate the government, and determine policy.

political socialization A learning process through which most people acquire their political attitudes, opinions, beliefs, and knowledge.

politics The process of resolving conflicts over how society should use its scarce resources and who should receive various benefits, such as public health care and public higher education. According to Harold Lasswell, politics is the process of determining "who gets what, when, and how" in a society.

poll tax A fee of several dollars that had to be paid before a person could vote; a device used in some southern states to prevent African Americans from voting.

poll watcher A representative from one of the two major political parties who is allowed to monitor a polling place to make sure that the election is run fairly and to avoid fraud.

power The ability to influence the behavior of others, usually through the use of force, persuasion, or rewards.

precedent A court decision that furnishes an example or authority for deciding subsequent cases involving identical or similar facts and legal issues.

precinct A political district within a city (such as a block or a neighborhood) or a portion of a rural county; the smallest voting district at the local level.

preemption A doctrine rooted in the supremacy clause of the Constitution that provides that national laws or regulations governing a certain area take precedence over conflicting state laws or regulations governing that same area.

press secretary A member of the White House staff who holds news conferences for reporters and makes public statements for the president.

primary A preliminary election held for the purpose of choosing a party's final candidate.

primary source of law A source of law that establishes the law. Primary sources of law include constitutions, statutes, administrative agency rules and regulations, and decisions rendered by the courts.

print media Communication channels that consist of printed materials, such as newspapers and magazines.

privatization The transfer of the task of providing services traditionally provided by government to the private sector.

probable cause Cause for believing that there is a substantial likelihood that a person has committed or is about to commit a crime.

public opinion poll A numerical survey of the public's opinion on a particular topic at a particular moment.

public opinion The views of the citizenry about politics, public issues, and public policies; a complex collection of opinions held by many people on issues in the public arena.

public services Essential services that individuals cannot provide for themselves, such as building and maintaining roads, providing welfare programs, operating public schools, and preserving national parks.

public-interest group An interest group formed for the purpose of working for the "public good." Examples of public-interest groups are the American Civil Liberties Union and Common Cause.

push poll A campaign tactic used to feed false or misleading information to potential voters, under the guise of taking an opinion poll, with the intent to "push" voters away from one candidate and toward another.

Q

quota system A policy under which a specific number of jobs, promotions, or other types of placements, such as university admissions, must be given to members of selected groups.

R

racial profiling A form of discrimination in which law enforcement assumes that people of a certain race are more likely to commit crimes. Racial profiling has been linked to more frequent traffic stops of African Americans by police and increased security checks of Arab Americans in airports.

radical left Persons on the extreme left side of the political spectrum who would like to significantly change the political order, usually to promote egalitarianism (human equality).

radical right Persons on the extreme right side of the political spectrum. The radical right includes reactionaries (who would like to return to the values and social systems of some previous era) and libertarians (who believe in no regulation of the economy or individual behavior, except for defense and law enforcement).

random sample In the context of opinion polling, a sample in which each person within the entire population being polled has an equal chance of being chosen.

rating system A system by which a particular interest group evaluates (rates) the performance of legislators based on how often the legislators have voted with the group's position on particular issues.

rational basis test A test (also known as the "ordinary-scrutiny" standard) used by the Supreme Court to decide whether a discriminatory law violates the equal protection clause of the Constitution. Few laws evaluated under this test are found invalid.

realigning election An election in which the popular support for and relative strength of the parties shift as the parties are reestablished with different coalitions of supporters.

representative democracy A form of democracy in which the will of the majority is expressed through smaller groups of individuals elected by the people to act as their representatives.

republic Essentially, a term referring to a representative democracy—in which there is no king or queen and the people are sovereign. The people elect smaller groups of individuals to act as the people's representatives.

reverse discrimination The assertion that affirmative action programs that require special consideration for minorities discriminate against those who have no minority status.

rule of law A basic principle of government that requires both those who govern and those who are governed to act in accordance with established law.

rulemaking The process undertaken by an administrative agency when formally proposing, evaluating, and adopting a new regulation.

Rules Committee A standing committee in the House of Representatives that provides special rules governing how particular bills will be considered and debated by the House. The Rules Committee normally proposes time limitations on debate for any bill, which are accepted or modified by the House.

S

sabotage A destructive act intended to hinder a nation's defense efforts.

sample In the context of opinion polling, a group of people selected to represent the population being studied.

sampling error In the context of opinion polling, the difference between what the sample results show and what the true results would have been had everybody in the relevant population been interviewed.

school voucher An educational certificate, provided by the government, that allows a student to use public funds to pay for a private or a public school chosen by the student or his or her parents.

secession The act of formally withdrawing from membership in an alliance; the withdrawal of a state from the federal Union.

second budget resolution A budget resolution, which is supposed to be passed in September, that sets "binding" limits on taxes and spending for the next fiscal year.

Second Continental Congress The congress of the colonies that met in 1775 to assume the powers of a central government and to establish an army.

seditious speech Speech that urges resistance to lawful authority or that advocates the overthrowing of a government.

self-incrimination Providing damaging information or testimony against oneself in court.

senatorial courtesy A practice that allows a senator of the president's party to veto the president's nominee to a federal court judgeship within the senator's state.

separate-but-equal doctrine A United States Supreme Court doctrine holding that the equal protection clause of the Fourteenth Amendment did not forbid racial segregation as long as the facilities for blacks were equal to those provided for whites. The doctrine was overturned in the *Brown v. Board of Education of Topeka* decision of 1954.

separation of powers The principle of dividing governmental powers among the executive, the legislative, and the judicial branches of government.

sexual harassment Unwanted physical contact, verbal conduct, or abuse of a sexual nature that interferes with a recipient's job performance, creates a hostile environment, or carries with it an implicit or explicit threat of adverse employment consequences.

Shays' Rebellion A rebellion of angry farmers in western Massachusetts in 1786, led by former Revolutionary War captain Daniel Shays. This rebellion and other similar uprisings in the New England states emphasized the need for a true national government.

signing statement A written statement, appended to a bill at the time the president signs it into law, indicating how the president interprets that legislation.

sit-in A tactic of nonviolent civil disobedience. Demonstrators enter a business, college building, or other public place and remain seated until they are forcibly removed or until their demands are met. The tactic was used successfully in the civil rights movement and in other protest movements in the United States.

slander The public utterance (speaking) of a statement that holds a person up for contempt, ridicule, or hatred.

social conflict Disagreements among people in a society over what the society's priorities should be with respect to the use of scarce resources.

social contract A voluntary agreement among individuals to create a government and to give that government adequate power to secure the mutual protection and welfare of all individuals.

soft money Campaign contributions not regulated by federal law, such as some contributions that are made to political parties instead of to particular candidates.

Solid South A term used to describe the tendency of the southern states to vote Democratic after the Civil War.

solidarity Mutual agreement with others in a particular group.

sound bite In televised news reporting, a brief comment, lasting for only a few seconds, that captures a thought or a perspective and has an immediate impact on the viewers.

Speaker of the House The presiding officer in the House of Representatives. The Speaker has traditionally been a longtime member of the majority party and is often the most powerful and influential member of the House.

special election An election that is held at the state or local level when the voters must decide an issue before the next general election or when vacancies occur by reason of death or resignation.

spin A reporter's slant on, or interpretation of, a particular event or action.

spin doctor A political candidate's press adviser who tries to convince reporters to give a story or event concerning the candidate a particular "spin" (interpretation, or slant).

standing committee A permanent committee in Congress that deals with legislation concerning a particular area, such as agriculture or foreign relations.

standing to sue The requirement that an individual must have a sufficient stake in a controversy before he or she can bring a lawsuit. The party bringing the suit must demonstrate that he or she has either been harmed or been threatened with a harm.

stare decisis A common law doctrine under which judges normally are obligated to follow the precedents established by prior court decisions.

statutory law The body of law enacted by legislatures (as opposed to constitutional law, administrative law, or case law).

straw poll A nonscientific poll; a poll in which there is no way to ensure that the opinions expressed are representative of the larger population.

subcommittee A division of a larger committee that deals with a particular part of the committee's policy area. Most of the standing committees in Congress have several subcommittees.

supremacy clause Article VI, Clause 2, of the Constitution, which makes the Constitution and federal laws superior to all conflicting state and local laws.

suspect classification A classification, such as race, that provides the basis for a discriminatory law. Any law based on a suspect classification is subject to strict scrutiny by the courts—meaning that the law must be justified by a compelling state interest.

symbolic speech The expression of beliefs, opinions, or ideas through forms other than speech or print; speech involving actions and other nonverbal expressions.

T

third party In the United States, any party other than one of the two major parties (Republican and Democratic).

three-fifths compromise A compromise reached during the Constitutional Convention by which it was agreed that three-fifths of all slaves were to be counted for purposes of representation in the House of Representatives.

trade organization An association formed by members of a particular industry, such as the oil industry or the trucking industry, to develop common standards and goals for the industry. Trade organizations, as interest groups, lobby government for legislation or regulations that specifically benefit their groups.

treason As enunciated in Article III, Section 3, of the Constitution, the act of levying war against the United States or adhering (remaining loyal) to its enemies.

treaty A formal agreement between the governments of two or more countries.

trial court A court in which trials are held and testimony taken.

trustee A view of the representation function that holds that representatives should serve the broad interests of the entire society, and not just the narrow interests of their constituents.

two-party system A political system in which two strong and established parties compete for political offices.

tyranny The arbitrary or unrestrained exercise of power by an oppressive individual or government.

U

unicameral legislature A legislature with only one chamber.

unitary system A centralized governmental system in which local or subdivisional governments exercise only those powers given to them by the central government.

V

veto A Latin word meaning "I forbid"; the refusal by an official, such as the president of the United States or a state governor, to sign a bill into law.

veto power A constitutional power that enables the chief executive (president or governor) to reject legislation and return it to the legislature with reasons for the rejection. This prevents or at least delays the bill from becoming law.

vital center The center of the political spectrum, or those who hold moderate political views. The center is vital because without it, it may be difficult, if not impossible, to reach the compromises that are necessary to a political system's continuity.

W

ward A local unit of a political party's organization, consisting of a division or district within a city.

Watergate scandal A scandal involving an illegal break-in at the Democratic National Committee offices in 1972 by members of President Nixon's reelection campaign staff. Before Congress could vote to impeach Nixon for his participation in covering up the break-in, Nixon resigned from the presidency.

whip A member of Congress who assists the majority or minority leader in the House or in the Senate in managing the party's legislative preferences.

whistleblower In the context of government employment, someone who "blows the whistle" (reports to authorities) on gross governmental inefficiency, illegal action, or other wrongdoing.

White House Office The personal office of the president. White House Office personnel handle the president's political needs and manage the media.

white primary A primary election in which African Americans were prohibited from voting. The practice was banned by the Supreme Court in 1944.

winner-take-all system In most states, the system that awards all of the state's electoral votes to the candidate who receives the most popular votes in that state.

writ of *certiorari* An order from a higher court asking a lower court for the record of a case.

writ of *habeas corpus* An order that requires an official to bring a specified prisoner into court and explain to the judge why the person is being held in prison.

Index

unitary system of government in, 50, 51
World War II and, 112, 162, 278
Japanese Americans
income and education of, 112
internment of, during World War II, 95, 112
Jarrah, Ziad, 48
Jay, John, 35, 36, 337
Jazz, 14
Jefferson, Thomas, 32, 54, 76, 83, 200–201,
264, 273, 324, 335
Declaration of Independence and, 28–29,
35
election of 1796 and, 150
election of 1800 and, 150
on political parties, 149
as victim of negative political media, 222
Jeffersonian Republicans (Democratic Republi-
cans), 149, 150, 197
Jeffords, James M., 335
Jim Crow laws, 101
Job Corps, 59
John (king of England), 10
John Birch Society, 316
John Warner National Defense Authorization
Act (2007), 65
Johnson, Andrew, 255, 263, 271, 286
Johnson, Lyndon B., 104, 118, 253, 264, 277,
286
"daisy girl" ad and, 223
election of 1964 and, 213, 223
Great Society programs and, 59–60, 66
Vietnam War and, 277
Joyce, James, 84
Judd, Walter H., 9
Judge(s)
administrative law (ALJ), 303
federal. *See also* United States Supreme
Court, justice(s) of
impeachment and, 40, 325
lifetime appointments of, 40, 324–325
law made by, 317
Judicial activism, 330–331
Judicial restraint, 330–331
Judicial review, 39, 57, 272, 330, 331
Judiciary, 314–338. *See also* Court(s)
checks and balances and. *See* Checks and
balances
federal. *See* Federal court system
judicial activism versus judicial restraint
and, 330–331
power of judicial review and, 39, 57, 272,
330, 331
Jurisdiction
defined, 318
of Supreme Court, 320
Justice Department. *See* United States Department of Justice
Justiciable controversy, 319

K

Kavenoki, Gene, 105
Keen, Andrew, 217
Kempthorne, Dirk, 283
Kennedy, Anthony, 327, 328, 333
Kennedy, John Fitzgerald, 126, 156, 217, 228,
265, 286
election of 1960 and, 152, 212
Kennedy, Robert, 217
Kennedy, Ted, 238
Kerry, John, 139, 159, 168, 180, 182, 189, 190,
191, 212, 213, 224, 232
Keynes, John Maynard, 304
Kim Jong Il, 8
Kind, Ron, 222–223
King, Angus, 166
King, Larry, 230
King, Martin Luther, Jr., 37, 103, 104, 105,

114, 185
King's courts *(curiae regis)*, 315
Kitchen cabinet, 282
Kommersant, 219
Koran (Qur'an), 9
"Koreagate" scandal, 142
Korean War, 134, 277. *See also* North Korea;
South Korea
National Guard in, 65
Kosovo, U.S. military intervention in, 65
Ku Klux Klan, 89
Kurdistan Alliance, 154
Kuwait
invaded by Iraq, 277. *See also* First Gulf
War
plane with coffins photographed in, 88
U.S. military intervention in, 65, 277

L

Labor, interest groups representing, 132–133
Labor force, 133
Land-grant colleges, 66
Landon, Alfred, 179
Landslide election, 179, 212, 213, 273
Lantos, Tom, 13
Lasswell, Harold, 4
Latin America
Hispanics in U.S. from, 110
immigrants from, 112
Latinos. *See* Hispanics
Law(s). *See also* Legislation
administrative, 317. *See also* Rulemaking
American
origins of, 315–319
sources of, 316–317
primary, 316
"antiloitering," 88–89
based upon suspect classification, 100
case, 317
civil, 317
Clean Elections, 206
common. *See* Common law
constitutional, 316, 317. *See also* United
States Constitution
criminal, 317
due process of, 74–75, 92–93, 116, 316
election, two-party system favored by, 153
equal protection of, 11, 12, 72, 99–100,
100, 101, 117, 120, 121, 123, 212, 243,
316, 329
ex post facto, 73
gun control, 126, 137, 140
how a bill becomes, illustrated, 252
interpretation of, approaches to, 333–334
Jim Crow, 101
judge-made, 317
made by regulatory agencies, 301–302
rule of, 38–39, 336
sodomy, 116
source of, primary, 316
statutory, 316–317
"sunshine," 310
Law & Order, 225
Lawrence, D. H., 84
Lawrence v. Texas, 116, 117, 316
Lawsuit
basic judicial requirements for, 317–319
by interest groups, 130, 140
standing to bring, 318–319
League of Nations, 269–270
League of Women Voters of the United States
(LWVUS)
budget of, 128
profile of, 129
Leahy, Patrick J., 48, 323
Leavitt, Michael, 283
Lebanon, 277

Ledbetter, Lilly, 109
Lee, Richard Henry, 28
Legislation. *See also* Law(s)
enabling, 302–303
"pork-barrel," 257, 271
presidential signing statements and, 40–41,
274, 276, 279
Legislator, chief, 268
Legislature(s)
bicameral, 10, 33, 239, 249, 250
colonial, 24–25
"little," 249
state. *See* State legislature(s)
unicameral, 29
in United States. *See* Congress
Legitimate power, 4
Lemon test, 80
Lemon v. Kurtzman, 80
Lenin, Vladimir, 6
Lewinsky, Monica, 280
Libby, Lewis "Scooter," 270, 319
Libel, 83–84
Liberal, 15. *See also* Liberalism
Liberalism
"big government" and, 15
defined, 15
Democratic Party and, 16, 17, 192
Libertarian Party, 157, 163, 192
Libertarians, 16
Liberty(ies)
civil. *See* Civil liberties
defined, 12
as natural right, 12, 13
Library of Congress, 248
Libya, attacked by American fighter planes,
277
Lieberman, Joe, 224
Life events, major, political socialization and,
176–178
Limbaugh, Rush, 226
Limited government, 10, 12, 29, 38–39
Lincoln, Abraham, 5–6, 9, 58, 258, 286
cabinet and, 282
civil liberties suspended by, 273
Civil War and, 272–273
election of 1860 and, 148, 150, 151, 152
Emancipation Proclamation and, 272
ranked as "great" president, 263
signing statements and, 40
Linden Lab, 202
Line-item veto, 271, 276
Literacy test, 185
Literary Digest, 179
Litigation. *See* Lawsuit
"Little legislatures," 249
"Little Rock Nine," 102
Livingston, Philip, 28
Livingston, Robert, 57
Lobbying, 130. *See also* Interest group(s);
Lobbyist(s)
defined, 136
effectiveness of, 137
by governments, 136
rating systems and, 138
reforms and, 143, 144
regulation of, 142
scandals involving, in early 2000s, 143–144
at state level, 136–137
today's lobbying establishment and,
140–142
Lobbying Disclosure Act (1995), 142–143
Lobbyist(s). *See also* Interest group(s);
Lobbying
defined, 136, 143
former members of Congress as, 141
professional, 141
Local government(s). *See also* Government(s)
employment by, 292